Think you've heard of everything?
How about:

THE HIGH-TECH TOILET: With a heated seat, automatic lid lifter and air freshener, this Japanese-designed unit sells for $699! [p. 294]

THE FOUR-MINUTE OPERA: Performed in Wales in 1993, *The Sands of Time* ran 4 minutes 9 seconds. For a British performance it was trimmed to 3 minutes 34 seconds! [p. 216]

THE SLOWEST ESCAPED PET: Chester the tortoise made a break for it from his home in Lyde, England, in 1960. He was found by a neighbor 35 years later, only 2,250 yards away! [p. 173]

THE FEET WITH SHOE SIZE 29½ [p. 261]
THE 1.1-TON CHOCOLATE BAR [p. 95]
BILL GATES'S $55 MILLION
"INTELLIGENT" HOUSE [p. 108]
THE 100 MPH ROLLER COASTER [p. 223]

PLUS!
THE WORLD'S MOST DANGEROUS
ROADS [p. 318]
THE BIGGEST MASS BUNGEE JUMP [p. 351]
THE MOST VALUABLE GUITAR [p. 163]
THE WORLD'S WORST
ART COLLECTION [p. 240]

ALL THIS AND MUCH, MUCH MORE!

P9-DWK-216

Abbreviations and Measurements

Guinness World Records uses both metric and imperial measurements (imperial in brackets). The only exception to this rule is for some scientific data, where metric measurements only are universally accepted, and for some sports data.

"GDR" (the German Democratic Republic) refers to the East German state which unified with West Germany in 1990. The abbreviation is used for sporting records broken before 1990.

The Union of Soviet Socialist Republics split into a number of parts in 1991, the largest of these being Russia. The Commonwealth of Independent States replaced it, and the abbreviation "CIS" is used mainly for sporting records broken at the 1992 Olympic Games.

Accreditation

Guinness World Records Ltd. has a very thorough accreditation system for records verification. However, while every effort is made to ensure accuracy, Guinness World Records Ltd. cannot be held responsible for any errors contained in this work. Feedback from our readers on any points of accuracy is always welcomed.

General Warning

Attempting to break records or set new records can be dangerous. Appropriate advice should be taken first, and all record attempts are undertaken entirely at the participant's risk. In no circumstances will Guinness World Records Ltd. have any liability for death or injury suffered in any record attempts. Guinness World Records Ltd. has complete discretion over whether or not to include any particular records in the book.

GUINNESS
WORLD
RECORDS

2000

MILLENNIUM EDITION

GUINNESS PUBLISHING LTD.

BANTAM BOOKS
NEW YORK • TORONTO • LONDON • SYDNEY • AUCKLAND

This edition contains the complete text of the original hardcover edition.
NOT ONE WORD HAS BEEN OMITTED.

GUINNESS WORLD RECORDS 2000
*A Bantam Book / Published by arrangement with
Guinness Publishing Ltd.*

Bantam edition / May 2000

*Guinness World Records, The Guinness Book of Records, Guinness, and
the Star Figure logo are trademarks of Guinness World Records Limited,
London, used under license by Bantam Books, a division of Random House, Inc.*

ISBN 0-553-58268-2

Published simultaneously in the United States and Canada

*Bantam Books are published by Bantam Books, a division of Random House, Inc. Its
trademark, consisting of the words "Bantam Books" and the portrayal of a rooster, is
Registered in U.S. Patent and Trademark Office and in other countries. Marca Registrada.
Bantam Books, 1540 Broadway, New York, New York 10036.*

PRINTED IN THE UNITED STATES OF AMERICA

OPM 10 9 8 7 6 5 4 3 2 1

INTRODUCTION

The theme of our Year 2000 *Guinness Book of Records* is celebration.

It has been an extraordinary year for record breakers worldwide and an amazing year for us, too. We decided to celebrate with our silver memento cover, a brand-new design, and new records that define the limits of human achievement as we head into the new millennium.

Which records spring to mind? One of the last great aviation journeys—the circumnavigation of the globe by balloon—was finally made by Bertrand Piccard and Brian Jones. Maurice Greene smashed the world 100-meter record by 0.05 seconds, the biggest margin to be taken off this record since electronic timing began in the 1960s. In music, Lauryn Hill won a record-breaking five Grammys. In sports, Pete Sampras won his 12th Grand Slam tournament at Wimbledon, equaling Roy Emerson's record set in 1967. And at the cinema, Mike Myers' *Austin Powers* sequel became the highest-grossing film comedy in the United States during its first weekend of release.

We broke records, too. *The Guinness Book of Records* remains the world's biggest-selling copyright book, and this year we achieved the highest print-run record for a color hardback title. Millions are also watching our new TV shows on both sides of the Atlantic, so the fascinating world of records is reaching a bigger audience than ever.

We are sure you will enjoy what we believe is the most significant *Guinness Book of Records* ever.

GUINNESS WORLD RECORDS 2000

MANAGING EDITOR
Nic Kynaston

EDITORIAL MANAGER
Rhonda Carrier

PICTURE EDITOR
Gregory King

GUINNESS MEDIA INC., USA

CEO/PUBLISHER
Mark C. Young

RESEARCH MANAGER
John W. Hansen

GUINNESS WORLD RECORDS, LONDON

RESEARCH MANAGER
Geoff Trotter

RESEARCH COORDINATOR
Shelley Flacks

PUBLISHING DIRECTOR
Ian Castello-Cortes

MANAGING DIRECTOR
Christopher Irwin

TABLE OF CONTENTS

COURAGE

SPACE HEROES

Fastest Speeds Attained   The record for the greatest speed at which a human being has ever traveled is 24,791 mph, achieved by the crew of the command module of *Apollo 10* (Col. Thomas Stafford, CDR. Eugene Cernan, and CDR. John Young, all US) on the craft's trans-Earth return flight in May 1969.

GREATEST ALTITUDE ATTAINED   The crew of *Apollo 13* (from left to right: Jack Swigert, Jim Lovell, and Fred Haise, all US) were a record distance of 158 miles from the moon's surface and 248,655 miles from Earth's surface on April 15, 1970. The mission was dramatized in the movie *Apollo 13* (1995), which starred Tom Hanks as Lovell.

Greatest Altitude Attained by a Woman   Kathryn Thornton (US) attained an altitude of 375 miles after an orbital engine burn on December 10, 1993, during the *STS 61 Endeavour* mission.

Most Isolated Human Being   The greatest distance that a person has ever been from a fellow human being is 2,234 miles 1,330 yd. This was experienced by command module pilot Alfred Worden during the US *Apollo 15* lunar mission, which lasted from July 30 to August 1, 1971. Fellow astronauts David Scott and James Irwin were at Hadley Base exploring the moon's surface.

Most Experienced Space Traveler   Russian doctor Valeriy Poliyakov clocked up 678 days 16 hr. 33 min. 16 sec. during two space missions.

MOST SPACE JOURNEYS Story Musgrave (US) made a record six space shuttle missions between 1983 and 1996, giving him a total of 53 days' flight experience. He is pictured at right alongside the space shuttle *Columbia*, in which he flew his last mission. On that occasion, from November 19 to December 7, 1996, the shuttle made a record 278 Earth orbits and traveled over 7 million miles in 17 days 15 hr. 53 min. Capt. John Young (US) was the first person to make a total of six spaceflights, from 1965 to 1983. In doing so, he acquired 34 days' flight experience. The only other astronaut to have made six space flights is Franklin Chang-Diaz (Costa Rica), who flew on six missions between 1986 and 1998 and has logged 52 days in space.

Most People in Space at Once On March 14, 1995, a record 13 people were in space at the same time: seven Americans aboard the US *STS 67 Endeavour*, three CIS cosmonauts aboard the Russian *Mir* space station, and two CIS cosmonauts and a US astronaut aboard the CIS *Soyuz TM21*.

Most Nationalities in Space Five countries had astronauts or cosmonauts in space on July 31, 1992: four Russian cosmonauts and one Frenchman were aboard *Mir*, and one Swiss, one Italian, and five US astronauts were on *STS 46 Atlantis*.

On February 22, 1996, there were four US, one Swiss, and two Italian astronauts on *STS 75 Columbia* and one German and four Russian cosmonauts aboard the *Mir* space station.

Biggest Shuttle Crew Two shuttles have had a crew of eight: *STS 61A Challenger*, which was launched on October 30, 1995, and *STS 71 Atlantis*, which docked with the Mir space station on July 7, 1995.

Most People Aboard a Spacecraft In June 1995, a record 10 people (four Russians and six Americans) were aboard the *Mir* station.

Longest Lunar Mission The crew of *Apollo 17* (Capt. Eugene Cernan and Dr. Harrison Hagen Schmitt, both US) were on the surface of the moon for a record 74 hr. 59 min. during a lunar mission lasting 12 days 13 hr. 51 min. (December 7 to 19, 1972).

Longest Shuttle Flight *Columbia*'s 21st mission, *STS 80*, began on November 19, 1996, and lasted for 17 days 15 hr. 53 min. 26 sec. (to main gear shutdown), beating its own previous record. Bad weather at the Kennedy Space Center in Florida meant that the landing had to be postponed for two days.

Longest Manned Spaceflight Valeriy Poliyakov was launched to the Russian *Mir* space station aboard *Soyuz TM18* on January 8, 1994, and landed aboard *Soyuz TM20* on March 22, 1995, after a spaceflight lasting 437 days 17 hr. 58 min. 16 sec.

Most Trips Around Earth by a Space Station   By March 2, 1999, *Mir* had completed more than 75,000 trips around Earth. By the time of its scheduled landing, the station will have been in orbit for 13 years.

Biggest Space Funeral   The ashes of 24 space pioneers and enthusiasts, including *Star Trek* creator Gene Roddenberry and counterculture guru Dr. Timothy Leary, were sent into orbit in April 1997 on Spain's *Pegasus* rocket, at a cost of $5,000 each. They will stay in orbit for $3\frac{1}{2}$ to 10 years.

Farthest Final Resting Place   In January 1998, 1 oz. of the ashes of the celebrated geologist Dr. Eugene Shoemaker (US) was launched aboard NASA's *Lunar Prospector* as it set out on a one-year mapping mission above the moon's surface. When its power fails, the craft will crash to the moon's surface, carrying Shoemaker's remains with it. He once said that never having been to the moon was his greatest disappointment.

Largest Audience for a Space Event   The broadcast of the first moon walk by the *Apollo 11* astronauts (Neil Armstrong and Edwin "Buzz" Aldrin) in July 1969 was watched by an estimated 600 million people worldwide (about one-fifth of the world's population at that time).

LONGEST SPACEFLIGHT BY A WOMAN   The longest spaceflight by a woman lasted 188 days 4 hr. 14 sec., when Shannon Lucid (US) was launched to the *Mir* space station aboard the US space shuttle *STS 76 Atlantis* on March 22, 1996, and landed aboard *STS 79 Atlantis* on September 26 of that year. Her stay is also the longest by any US astronaut. Upon returning to Earth, she was awarded the Congressional Space Medal of Honor by President Clinton.

SHORTEST SPACEFLIGHT   The shortest manned spaceflight ever was made on the first of the *Mercury* missions by CDR. Alan Shepard (US) aboard *Freedom 7* on May 5, 1961. The suborbital mission lasted 15 min. 28 sec. and made Shepard the second person to fly into space— Yuri Gagarin (USSR) was the first, on April 12, 1961. Shepard is pictured here (back row, left) with the six other astronauts on the *Mercury* team.

Oldest Astronaut   The oldest astronaut is John Glenn Jr., who was 77 years 103 days old when he was launched into space as part of the crew of *Discovery STS-95* on October 29, 1998. The mission lasted 11 days, landing on November 7, 1998.

Astronaut Responsible for Most Laptop Computers   Spanish astronaut Pedro Duque had to look after a total of 19 laptop computers aboard *Discovery* in October 1998.

EPIC ADVENTURERS

Biggest Ancient Civilization Discovery   In the late 1820s, deserting soldier Charles Masson discovered the ruins of the world's biggest ancient civilization—the Indus Valley civilization at Harappa, India (now Pakistan). Extensive excavations carried out at the site by Rai Bahadur Daya Ram Sahni in 1920 indicated that the civilization dated back to 3300 B.C. The discovery of a second site at Mohenjo-daro showed that the Harappans used the same sized bricks and standard weights for 1,000 miles and that the civilization supported a population of 50,000 at certain periods. More recent

MOST GENERATIONS OF ADVENTURERS IN ONE FAMILY Jacques Piccard (left of picture) is seen saying good-bye to his son Bertrand before the latter set off on his successful attempt to circumnavigate the world in a balloon in January 1999. Jacques and Bertrand represent the second and third generations of a well-known family of adventurers. Jacques' father, August Piccard, made the first successful balloon flight into the stratosphere when he ascended to 51,790 ft. above Augsburg, Germany, in May 1931. He subsequently made a second successful ascent and went on to build a bathyscaphe, a revolutionary type of submarine that is capable of descending to the bottom of the ocean. In January 1960, Jacques realized his father's dream by manning the bathyscaphe to a record depth of 35,797 ft.

excavations have shown that it extended even farther than had been thought, stretching along and beyond the banks of the ancient Ghaggar-Hakra (Saraswati) River and covering an area of 220,000 miles^2 from Baluchistan, Pakistan, in the west to Uttar Pradesh, India, in the east and Bombay (Mumbai), India, in the south. The majority of the civilization's cities have still to be excavated, and its script has not yet been deciphered.

Biggest Inca Discovery   The Yale University Peruvian Expeditions of 1911–12 and 1914–15, both led by US historian Hiram Bingham, resulted in the discovery of the "lost" Inca cities of Machu Picchu and Vitcos—two of the most important archaeological finds in the Americas.

Fastest Desert Crossing   In 1998, Moroccan adventurer Mohammed Ahansal completed the Marathon des Sables in a record time of 16 hr. 22 min. 29 sec. The marathon, which has been held every year since 1986, is a six-day event in which runners must cross 137 miles of the Sahara Desert, where temperatures regularly reach 120°F. The runners carry food, clothes, a sleeping bag, and a first-aid kit with them and have to prepare their own meals. The youngest person to have competed in the marathon is a 16-year-old boy, and the oldest is a 76-year-old man. In April 1999, 584 people from 27 countries took part in the marathon.

Longest Journey in a Leather Boat In 1976, British adventurer Tim Severin set out to prove that the voyage allegedly made by St. Brendan to the New World could have been accomplished. Following instructions given in medieval writings, he built a boat by tanning ox hides with oak bark, stretching them across a wooden frame, and then sewing them in place with leather thread. The resulting vessel, similar to the curraghs still made in Ireland, took him and his crew from Tralee Bay in Kerry, Republic of Ireland, to the coast of Newfoundland, Canada, after 13 months, 4,500 miles, and stopovers in the Hebrides, the Faeroe Islands, and Iceland.

Fastest Solo Row Across the Atlantic (East to West) From December 1969 to July 1970, Sidney Genders (UK) rowed from Las Palmas, Canary Islands, to Antigua, West Indies—a distance of 3,800 miles—in 73 days 8 hours.

First People to Reach the North Pole The American Arctic explorer Robert Peary is widely regarded as the first person to have reached the North

GREATEST DISTANCE TRAVELED ON A MODERN-DAY ABORIGINAL RAFT In 1947, Norwegian explorer and archaeologist Thor Heyerdahl set out to convince the scientific community that ancient mariners regularly crossed the world's great oceans. He was particularly keen to show that migrants to Polynesia had come not from the east, as was generally believed, but from the west, with the Pacific's currents. To this end, Heyerdahl built a replica of an aboriginal balsa-wood raft, which he named *Kon-Tiki,* and, together with five companions, crossed the 4,970 miles from Callio, Peru, to Raroia Atoll, Polynesia, in 101 days. The success of the voyage proved that Polynesia's settlers could indeed have been Peruvians. Heyerdahl is pictured here with a model of *Kon-Tiki*.

FASTEST SOLAR-POWERED TRANSPACIFIC CROSSING In 1996, Kenichi Horie (Japan) made the fastest crossing of the Pacific ever in a solar-powered boat when he traveled 10,000 miles from Salinas, Ecuador, to Tokyo, Japan, in 148 days. His cigar-shaped vessel *Malt's Mermaid* (seen left with Horie) was 9½ yd. long, weighed 813 lb., and was powered by 130 ft.² of solar panels. It was partly made from a quantity of recycled aluminum equivalent to more than 20,000 drink cans.

Pole. Peary set off on his expedition from Cape Columbia, Ellesmere Island, Canada, on March 1, 1909, with his associate Matt Henson, seven other Americans, 17 Eskimo, 19 sledges, and 133 dogs. The expedition reached a latitude of 88° N at the end of March, and the final supporting party turned back, leaving Peary, Henson, four Eskimo, and 40 dogs to make the final dash for 90° N—the location of the pole. On April 6, Peary made observations indicating that he had reached his destination. Although Frederick Cook (also US) challenged his claim and asserted that he had reached the pole first earlier that month, the US Congress acknowledged Peary's achievement in 1911.

First People to Reach the South Pole On December 14, 1911, a party of five Norwegians led by Capt. Roald Amundsen reached the South Pole after a 53-day march with dog sledges from the Bay of Whales, Antarctica. They narrowly beat the five-man team of explorers led by British explorer Capt. Robert Falcon Scott.

Longest Trek in Antartica The longest unsupported trek ever made in Antarctica is 1,348 miles, by Sir Ranulph Fiennes (team leader) and Dr. Michael Stroud. The pair set out from Gould Bay on November 9, 1992, reached the South Pole on January 16, 1993, and finally abandoned their walk on the Ross Ice Shelf on February 11 of the same year.

Youngest Person to Walk to the Magnetic North Pole On May 7, 1997, Giles Kershaw (UK) reached the magnetic North Pole after walking a distance of at least 360 miles. He was only 22 years 351 days old.

First Solo Transatlantic Flight The first person to fly solo across the Atlantic was Capt. (later Brig. Gen.) Charles Lindbergh of Minnesota. Lindbergh set out from Roosevelt Field in Long Island, New York, at 12:52 pm GMT on May 20, 1927, and landed at Le Bourget airfield, Paris, France, at 10:21 pm GMT on May 21, 1927. The 3,610-mile journey therefore took him a total of 33 hr. 29 min. Lindbergh flew in the 220-hp Ryan monoplane *Spirit of St. Louis*.

First Solo Transatlantic Flight by a Woman On May 20, 1932, Amelia Earhart of Kansas became the first woman and second person to

FIRST PERSON TO COMPLETE THE ADVENTURER'S GRAND SLAM British adventurer David Hempleman-Adams (pictured right) is the first person to have completed the Adventurer's Grand Slam, a grueling challenge that involves climbing the highest peak on every continent and visiting all four poles. Hempleman-Adams began his quest in 1980 by climbing Mt. McKinley in Alaska. He completed it 18 years later when he and fellow adventurer Rune Gjeldnes walked to the North Pole from March to May 1998.

make a solo transatlantic flight when she piloted a single-engine Lockheed Vega from Harbour Grace, Newfoundland, Canada, to Londonderry, Republic of Ireland, in 13 hr. 30 min. Earhart later became the first person to fly solo across the Pacific from Honolulu, Hawaii, to Oakland, California. She then went on to make two unsuccessful attempts to circumnavigate the world. On July 2, 1937, after completing 22,000 miles of her second attempt, Earhart set off with her navigator from Lae, Papua New Guinea, for Howland Island in the Pacific. Neither was ever seen again.

CIRCUMNAVIGATORS

Longest Nonstop Around-the-World Flight   The duration record is 64 days 22 hr. 19 min. 5 sec., by Robert Timm and John Cook in a Cessna 172 Hacienda. They took off from McCarran Airfield in Las Vegas, Nevada, just before 3:53 pm local time on December 4, 1958, and landed at the same airfield just before 2:12 pm on February 7, 1959. They covered a distance equivalent to six times around the world and refueled without making any landings.

Fastest Around-the-World Flight   The fastest flight under FAI (Fédération Aéronautique Internationale) rules, which define circumnavigations as flights that exceed the length of the tropics of Cancer or Capricorn (22,858.8 miles), was 31 hr. 27 min. 49 sec., by an Air France Concorde

FASTEST AROUND-THE-WORLD DRIVE (CURRENT RULES) Between October 1 and December 11, 1997, Garry Sowerby, Colin Bryant, and Graham McGaw (UK) circumnavigated the globe in a Vauxhall Frontera in 21 days 2 hr. 14 min., following current *Guinness® Book of Records* regulations. They traveled 18,344 miles, starting and finishing their journey in Greenwich, London, England.

(Capts. Michel Dupont and Claude Hetru) from JFK Airport in New York, eastbound via Toulouse, Dubai, Bangkok, Guam, Honolulu, and Acapulco from August 15 to 16, 1995. There were 80 passengers and 18 crew on board.

Fastest Around-the-World Journeys by Scheduled Flight The fastest around-the-world journey taking in antipodal points was by David Sole (UK), who traveled 25,917 miles in 64 hr. 2 min. from May 2 to 5, 1995.

Brother Michael Bartlett of Sandy, England, flew around the world on scheduled flights in a time of 58 hr. 44 min. in 1995, taking in the airports closest to antipodal points and covering 25,816 miles.

The world's fastest circumnavigation using scheduled flights under FAI regulations was 44 hr. 6 min., by David J. Springbett (UK). He traveled a distance of 23,068 miles from January 8 to 10, 1980.

Oldest Person to Complete an Around-the-World Flight Fred Lasby (b. 1912) made a solo around-the-world flight at the age of 82 in his single-engine Piper Comanche. He left Fort Myers, Florida, on June 30, 1994, and flew 23,218 miles westward with 21 stops, arriving back at Fort Myers on August 20, 1994.

Fastest Helicopter Circumnavigation In 1996, Ron Bower and John Williams (both US) flew around the world in a Bell helicopter in 17 days 6 hr. 14 min. 25 sec. Bower also holds the eastbound record of 24 days 4 hr. 36 min., which he set in a Bell JetRanger III in 1994.

Fastest Ultralight Circumnavigation Brian Milton (UK) landed at Brooklands Airfield in Surrey, England, on July 21, 1998, after circumnavigating the globe in an ultralight aircraft. During his trip, which covered 24,000 miles in 120 days, he was held for 27 days by the Russian authorities and made seven emergency landings in Saudi Arabia.

Fastest Marine Circumnavigations   The fastest marine circumnavigation was 74 days 22 hr. 17 min., by the 92-ft.-long catamaran *Enza*, sailed by Peter Blake (NZ) and Robin Knox-Johnston (UK) from Ushant, France, between January 16 and April 1, 1994.

The record for the world's fastest solo nonstop marine circumnavigation is 109 days 8 hr. 48 min., by the 60-ft.-long monohull *Ecureuil d'Aquitaine II,* sailed by Titouan Lamazou (France) from Les Sables d'Olonne, France, between November 1989 and March 1990.

Youngest Solo Marine Circumnavigator   The youngest person to sail solo around the world was David Dicks (Australia), who was 18 years 41 days old when he arrived back in Fremantle, Western Australia, after 264 days 16 hr. 49 min. on November 16, 1996.

Fastest Circumnavigation in a Power Vessel   On July 3, 1998, the *Cable & Wireless Adventurer* circumnavigated the world in 74 days 20 hr. 58 min. The 115-ft.-long boat traveled more than 26,000 miles, breaking the 38-year-old record set by USS *Triton*, a submarine that circumnavigated the globe in 83 days 9 hr. 54 min.

FASTEST HELICOPTER CIRCUMNAVIGATION BY A WOMAN   **The record for the first and fastest helicopter circumnavigation by a woman is held by 57-year-old British grandmother Jennifer Murray, who, with copilot Quentin Smith, flew a Robinson R44 35,698 miles in 97 days in 1997. They crossed 26 countries, made 80 refueling stops, and took time to visit the Monaco Grand Prix and the ceremonies marking the handover of Hong Kong to China. They also flew over one of the world's highest ice caps, at an altitude of 9,600 ft., in a temperature of 8.6°F. The journey raised $162,500 for the Save the Children Fund. Upon the pair's return to the starting point of Denham, England, they were greeted by friends including the Duchess of York.**

LONGEST NONSTOP BALLOON JOURNEY On March 20, 1999, the *Breitling Orbiter 3,* piloted by Bertrand Piccard of Switzerland (left of picture) and Brian Jones of the UK (right of picture), reached Mauritania, having traveled a distance of 26,600 miles. It thus became the first balloon to circumnavigate the globe nonstop. The journey, which began in Château d'Oex, Switzerland, lasted 19 days 1 hr. 49 min.

Fastest Motorcycle Circumnavigation Nick Sanders (UK) made a 19,930-mile circumnavigation in a record riding time of 31 days 20 hr. from April 18 to June 9, 1997, starting and finishing in Calais, France.

Longest Cycle Journeys Jay Aldous and Matt DeWaal (US) cycled 14,290 miles in a time of 106 days on an around-the-world trip in 1984, starting and finishing in Salt Lake City, Utah.

Tal Burt (Israel) circumnavigated the world from Place du Trocadéro in Paris, France, in 77 days 14 hr. in 1992. He covered 13,253 miles.

Phil and Louise Shambrook (UK) traveled 23,701 miles around the world on a tandem from December 17, 1994 to October 1, 1997.

Fastest Circumnavigation by Car The record for the first and fastest circumnavigation of the world by car, under the rules applicable in 1989 and 1991, embracing more than an equator's length of driving (24,901.41 road miles), is held by Mohammed Salahuddin Choudhury and his wife, Neena, of Calcutta, India. The first circumnavigation took 69 days 19 hr. 5 min. from September 9 to November 17, 1989. Starting and finishing in Delhi, India, the Choudhurys drove a 1989 Hindustan Contessa Classic car.

MOUNTAINEERS

First Person to Climb Mt. Everest The summit of Mt. Everest (29,029 ft. in altitude) was first reached in May 1953 by Edmund Hillary (New Zealand), shortly followed by Sherpa Tenzing Norgay (Nepal), in an expedition led by John Hunt (UK).

First Woman to Climb Mt. Everest Solo In May 1994, 33-year-old Alison Hargreaves (UK) became the first woman to reach the summit of Mt. Everest alone and without oxygen supplies. Hargreaves was one of seven climbers who died during a descent from the summit of K2 in August 1995.

Youngest Person to Climb Mt. Everest Shambu Tamang (Nepal) was the youngest person ever to ascend Mt. Everest, reaching the summit at the age of 17 years 6 months 15 days on May 5, 1973.

Oldest Person to Climb Mt. Everest Ler Sarkisor (Armenia, resident in Georgia) became the oldest person to reach the summit of Mt. Everest on May 12, 1999, at the age of 60 years 161 days.

Most Ascents of Mt. Everest Sherpa Ang Rita (Nepal) has scaled Mt. Everest a record 10 times (in 1983, 1984, 1985, 1987, 1988, 1990, 1992, 1993, 1995, and 1996), each time without the use of bottled oxygen.

Most People on the Summit of Mt. Everest in One Day On May 10, 1993, 40 climbers (32 men and eight women) from nine expeditions and 10 countries reached the summit of Mt. Everest.

Most People from One Expedition to Climb Mt. Everest The Mount Everest International Peace Climb, a team of US, Soviet, and Chinese climbers led by James Whittaker (US), succeeded in putting a record 10 people on the summit of Mt. Everest from May 7 to 10, 1990.

HIGHEST CLIMB BY AN AMPUTEE On May 27, 1998, Tom Whittaker (UK; pictured above) became the first amputee ever to climb to the summit of Mt. Everest. Whittaker, who lost a leg after a road accident in 1979, wears an artificial limb below the knee. Currently working as an outdoor-activities instructor in Arizona, he is soon to begin training as an astronaut with NASA and if chosen for a flight will become the first amputee in space.

FASTEST ASCENT OF MT. EVEREST FROM BASE CAMP TO SUMMIT
Kaji Sherpa (Nepal) became the fastest person to climb from base
camp, which is located at an altitude of 17,552 ft., to the summit of
Mt. Everest when he made the ascent in 20 hr. 24 min. on October 17,
1998. Climbing on the Nepalese side to the South Col, he took 2 hr. 5
min. off the record set by Marc Batard (France) on September 25 to 26,
1988. Kaji Sherpa used oxygen on the descent; Batard went without
oxygen on ascent and descent.

Fastest Ski Down Mt. Everest   In September 1992, Pierre Tardivel
(France) skied 10,500 ft. from the south summit of Mt. Everest to base
camp in three hours of jump turns. Tardivel has notched up more than 60
first descents of mountains, mostly in the Alps.

Oldest Person to Climb Mt. Kilimanjaro   William Masheu (Tanza-
nia) was born in 1929 and began working as a mountain guide at Mt. Kilimanjaro in 1953. He was still climbing the mountain regularly in 1999.

First Person to Climb the Seven Summits   The first person to scale
the highest peak on every continent (counting Puncak Jayakesuma on Irian
Jaya, Indonesia, as the highest peak in Oceania) was Patrick Morrow
(Canada), who completed his conquest on May 7, 1986.

Fastest Ascent of the Seven Summits   In 1990, New Zealanders
Gary Ball, Peter Hillary (son of Sir Edmund Hillary), and Andy Hall completed an ascent of the seven summits in a record time of seven months.

First People to Climb the Trango Towers   The main summit of the
Trango Towers was first climbed by Glenn Rowell, John Roskelly, Kim
Schmitz, and Dennis Henner (all US) in 1977. The Trango Towers, which
are next to the Baltoro Glacier on the approach to K2, the Gasherbrums,

MOST SUCCESSFUL MOUNTAINEER   Italian climber Reinhold Messner (above) has scaled 14 of the world's mountains over 26,250 ft. in altitude without oxygen. In 1982, he successfully ascended Kanchenjunga, which made him the first person ever to climb the world's three highest mountains—the others being Mt. Everest and K2. In August 1980, Messner was also the first person to make the entire climb of Mt. Everest solo.

and Broad Peak in Kashmir, are home to the largest vertical faces in the world. Their three summits are all over 19,685 ft. high, with the main summit standing at 20,625 ft.

Most European Summits Climbed   British climber Eamon Fullen has climbed the highest mountains in 45 European countries—more than any other person. He began with Mt. Elbrus in Russia, Europe's highest point, in August 1992, and by the end of May 1999, he only had the highest peaks in Georgia and Turkey to go.

First Ascent of Mt. Drohmo   Doug Scott and Roger Mear (both UK) made the first ascent of Mt. Drohmo, which is at an altitude of 22,490 ft., on October 8, 1998. Mt. Drohmo, in eastern Nepal, was first attempted by a Swiss expedition in 1949.

First Ascent of Cross Peak   Cross Peak, a 20,800-ft. mountain southwest of Mt. Drohmo, was first climbed by Misako Miyazawa (Japan) and Pemba Lama, Gumba Sherpa, and Kancha Sunwar (all Nepal) on October 8, 1998. The mountain is not currently on the Nepalese Tourism Ministry's list of peaks open to climbers and had only been attempted once before, by a Japanese expedition in 1963.

Most Difficult Free Climb   Aktion Direkt, in the Frankenjura, Germany, was first climbed by Wolfgang Gullich (Germany) in 1994. It has a 9A difficulty rating because of its overhang and small holds.

Highest Bivouac   Mark Whetu (New Zealand) and Michael Rheinberger (Australia) reached the summit of Mt. Everest on May 26, 1994, and bivouacked 66 ft. below the summit. Rheinberger died the next day during the descent.

Highest Unclimbed Peak   At 27,600 ft., Lhotse Middle Peak is the highest peak yet to be climbed. It is the intermediate summit of Mt. Lhotse, the world's fourth-highest mountain, on the border of China and Nepal.

HEROES OF THE DEEP

Greatest Ocean Descents   In January 1960, the Swiss-built US Navy bathyscaphe *Trieste*, which was manned by Dr. Jacques Piccard (Switzerland) and Lt. Donald Walsh (US), reached a record depth of 35,797 ft. in the Challenger Deep of the Mariana Trench in the Pacific Ocean—the lowest point of Earth's surface.

On August 11, 1989, the *Shinkai 6500* reached a depth of 21,414 ft. in the Japan Trench off Sanriku, Japan—the greatest descent by a manned vessel currently in commission. The vessel is capable of surveying about 96% of Japan's 200-mile exclusion zone and about 98% of the oceans around the world.

Longest Deep Dive   Richard Presley (US) spent a record 69 days 19 min. in an underwater module in a lagoon in Key Largo, Florida, from May 6 to July 14, 1992. The test was carried out as part of Project Atlantis, which aimed to explore the human factors of life in an underwater environment.

Longest Simulated Saturation Deep Dive   Arnaud Denechaud de Feral (France) performed a simulated saturation dive of 73 days, from

MOST IMPORTANT DIVING INVENTION French explorer and filmmaker Jacques Cousteau is pictured with an Aqua Lung. He invented the device, which provides a self-contained supply of compressed air, in collaboration with French engineer Emile Gagnan in 1943, freeing divers from the need to stay connected to their ships through air tubes. Cousteau, who ran his expeditions from the ship *Calypso*, introduced millions to life under the sea with films such as *The Silent World* (France, 1952).

October 9 to December 21, 1989, in a hyperbaric chamber, simulating a depth of 985 ft., as part of the HYDRA 9 operation carried out by COMEX S.A. at Marseilles, France. He was breathing "hydrox," a mixture of hydrogen and oxygen.

Longest Simulated Deep Dive On November 20, 1992, during a 43-day dive, Théo Mavrostomos (France) dived to a depth of 2,300 ft. of seawater in a hyperbaric chamber as part of the COMEX S.A. HYDRA 10

GREATEST WRECK FINDER Robert Ballard (US) gained international fame in 1985 when he located the remains of the *Titanic*, which had been on the Atlantic seabed since being sunk by an iceberg in 1912. This photograph shows him with a model of the ill-fated vessel. He was also responsible for finding the German battleship *Bismarck*, which was sunk by the Royal Navy in 1942, the British ocean liner *Lusitania*, torpedoed by a German submarine in 1915, the *Andrea Doria*, and the *Britannica*. In July 1997, he pinpointed the biggest concentration of Roman ships ever found in the deep sea. The eight vessels, some 2,000 years old, lay 2,500 ft. beneath the waves on an ancient Mediterranean trade route off the coast of Tunisia.

MOST PIRATE SHIPS DISCOVERED Barry Clifford (US) has discovered three authenticated wrecks of pirate vessels: in July 1998, he found the 18th-century *Whydah* off Cape Cod, Massachusetts, and in November of the same year, he discovered two 17th-century vessels off the coast of Venezuela. He is pictured holding a cannonball from one of the latter ships.

operation in Marseilles, France. He was breathing "hydreliox" (a mixture of hydrogen, oxygen, and helium).

Deepest Scuba Dive The record for the deepest dive made with scuba (self-contained underwater breathing apparatus) gear is held by Jim Bowden of the United States. In April 1994, Bowden dived to a depth of 1,000 ft. in the freshwater Zacatón Cave in Mexico.

Deepest Salvage Operations The greatest depth at which salvage has been successfully carried out is 17,251 ft. A helicopter had crashed into the Pacific Ocean in August 1991, with the loss of four lives. Crew of the USS *Salvor* and personnel from Eastport International managed to raise the wreckage to the surface on February 27, 1992, so that authorities could try to determine the cause of the accident.

The deepest salvage operation ever achieved with divers was on the wreck of HM cruiser *Edinburgh*, which sank on May 2, 1942, in the Barents Sea off northern Norway in 803 ft. of water. Over 31 days from September 7 to October 7, 1981, 12 divers worked on the wreck in pairs. A total of 460 gold ingots were recovered, making it the only totally successful marine salvage to date.

Most Valuable Shipwreck The late Mel Fisher (US), one of the most famous 20th-century treasure hunters, found the *Nuestra Señora de Atocha* off the Key West coast in Florida in 1985. The ship carried 36 tons of gold and silver and some 70 lb. of emeralds when it went down in a hurricane in September 1622.

Biggest Cargo of Gold Found in a Submarine Wreck   In May 1995, Paul R. Tidwell (US) discovered 2 tons of gold, 207 tons of tin, 49 tons of raw rubber, and 3 tons of quinine in a 357-ft.-long Japanese submarine. The sub, which had also carried 109 men, had been destroyed by a 500-lb. US bomb on June 23, 1944. Tidwell is now working to recover the vessel, which is submerged at a depth of 17,000 ft., 1,200 miles west of Cape Verde in the Atlantic Ocean.

Biggest Discovery of Porcelain   In 1994, treasure hunter Dorian Ball and his company, Malaysia Historic Salvors (MHS), unearthed a record $5 million worth of Chinese Qing porcelain from the British trading ship *Diana*, which had sunk off the Straits of Melaka in 1817.

SPEED STARS

Highest Speed Reached in a Rocket Car   The record for the highest speed ever attained in a rocket-engined car is 631.367 mph over the first kilometer (1,094 yd.) by *The Blue Flame* driven by Gary Gabelich on the Bonneville Salt Flats, Utah, on October 23, 1970. Gary Gabelich's car was powered by a rocket engine that had the capacity to develop thrust up to 22,000 pounds.

Highest Speed Reached in a Wheel-Driven Car   The highest speed ever reached in a wheel-driven car is 432.692 mph by Al Teague (US) in a car titled *Speed-O-Motive/Spirit of '76* over the final 132 ft. of a one-mile run at Bonneville Salt Flats, Utah, on August 21, 1991. Teague averaged a speed of 425.230 mph for the entire mile.

Fastest Woman on Land   The world's fastest woman on land is Kitty Hambleton, who reached a speed of 524.016 mph in the rocket-powered *SM1 Motivator* in the Alvard Desert, Oregon, on December 6, 1976.

FASTEST "TOP FUEL" DRAG RACER   Seen here, Jim Butler driving a drag racer owned by Dennis Lanham. The record for the fastest "top fuel" drag racer is held by Gary Scelzi (US), the 1998 National Hot Rod Association (NHRA) Winston Champion, who achieved a speed of 326.44 mph from a standing start over 440 yd. during a meet in Houston, Texas, in November 1998.

FASTEST LAND SPEED   The one-mile land speed record is 763.035 mph by Andy Green (UK) in *Thrust SSC* in the Black Rock Desert, Nevada, in October 1997. The car, designed by Richard Noble, is powered by two Rolls-Royce jet engines, which generate 20.57 tons of thrust. It is the first car to have exceeded the speed of sound.

Fastest "Funny Car" Drag Racer   John Force (US) reached a speed of 323.89 mph from a standing start over 440 yd. in his '98 Ford Mustang "funny car" during a drag meet in Englishtown, New Jersey, in May 1998.

Highest Speed Reached in a Steam Car   On August 19, 1985, Robert Barber broke the 79-year-old speed record for a steam car when *Streamin' Demon* reached 145.6 mph at Bonneville Salt Flats, Utah.

Fastest Hearse Driver   Rock Griffith (US) covered 440 yd. in 16.058 seconds, reaching a speed of 85.47 mph in a 1964 Pontiac hearse at Pomona, California, on October 25, 1998.

Fastest Reverse Driver   The highest average speed attained in any nonstop reverse drive exceeding 500 miles is 36.3 mph by John Smith (US). He drove a 1983 Chevrolet Caprice Classic 501 miles in 13 hr. 48 min. at the I-94 Speedway, Fergus Falls, Minnesota, on August 11, 1996.

Fastest Side-Wheel Driver   Göran Eliason (Sweden) set the world record for driving on two side wheels of a car when he attained a speed of 112.62 mph over a 328-ft. flying start in a Volvo 850 Turbo at Såtenäs, Sweden, on April 19, 1997.

Fastest Gravity Formula One Driver   Alternative International Sports, the sanctioning body for Gravity Formula One racing, recognizes

FASTEST CYCLIST ON A GLACIER
The fastest speed ever attained cycling down a glacier is 132 mph by downhill mountain bike racer Christian Taillefer of France (pictured here) on a Peugeot Cycle at the Speed Ski Slope in Vars, France, in March 1998.

Dwight Garland (US) as the fastest driver after he attained a speed of 64.02 mph on September 26, 1998. A Gravity Formula One car has a tubular steel chassis and runs on pneumatic racing slicks. The rider is protected by a roll cage and roll bar and is held in place by a five-point racing harness.

Fastest Person on Ice   The record for the highest speed achieved on ice (without rails) is 247.93 mph set by Sammy Miller in the rocket-powered sled *Oxygen* on Lake George, New York, on February 15, 1981.

Fastest Motorcyclist   On July 14, 1990, US rider Dave Campos set the world speed record on the 23-ft.-long streamline *Easyrider*, powered by two 1,491 cc Ruxton Harley-Davidson engines, at Bonneville Salt Flats, Utah. Campos' overall average speed was 322.15 mph, and he completed the faster run at an even higher average speed of 322.87 mph.

Fastest Wheelie   Jarrod Frost holds the record for the fastest wheelie when he reached a speed of 172.6 mph on the back wheel of his Spondon Turbo Suzuki 1200 at Jurby Airfield, Isle of Man, on July 5, 1997.

Fastest Cyclist   The highest speed ever achieved on a pedaled bicycle is 166.944 mph by Fred Rompelberg (Netherlands) at Bonneville Salt Flats, Utah, on October 3, 1995. His world record attempt was greatly assisted by the slipstream created from his lead vehicle.

Fastest People in the Air   Captain Eldon Joersz and Major George Morgan Jr. attained a record speed of 2,193.17 mph in a Lockheed SR-71A Blackbird over a 15-mile-941-yd. course near Beale Air Force Base, California, on July 28, 1976.

Fastest Transatlantic Flights   Major James Sullivan and Major Noel Widdifield flew a Lockheed SR-71A Blackbird from New York City to London, England, in 1 hr. 54 min. 56.4 sec. in 1974. The average speed for the 3,461.53-mile journey was 1,806.96 mph. Their time would have been even faster if they had not needed to refuel in midair in the middle of their journey.

The fastest time in which a solo pilot has crossed the Atlantic is 8 hr. 47 min. 32 sec. at an average speed of 265.1 mph—a record set by Captain John Smith in a Rockwell Commander 685 twin turboprop in 1978. He flew from Gander, Newfoundland, Canada, to Gatwick Airport, England.

Fastest Helicopter Pilots   The fastest average speed attained in a helicopter (under FAI rules) is 249.09 mph by John Eggington and Derek

Clews on August 11, 1986, in a Westland Lynx demonstrator over Glastonbury, England.

Fastest Autogiro Pilot   Wing Commander Kenneth Wallis flew his WA-116/F/S autogiro, with a 45kW 60-hp Franklin aero engine, at a speed of 120.3 mph over a 1-mile 1,521-yd. course at Marham, England, on September 18, 1986.

Fastest Person on Water   The official water speed record is 275.8 knots (317.6 mph) by Ken Warby (Australia) on Blowering Dam Lake, Australia, in his hydroplane, *Spirit of Australia*, on October 8, 1978. Warby had reached an estimated 300 knots (345 mph) in the same craft and on the same lake on November 20, 1977, but that speed had not been officially confirmed.

STUNT HEROES

Most Stunts by a Living Actor   Jackie Chan, the Hong Kong actor, director, producer, stunt coordinator, and writer, has appeared in more than 65 films, including *The Big Brawl* (1980) and *Rumble in the Bronx* (1996). He made his debut in *Big and Little Wong Tin Bar* (Hong Kong, 1962) at the age of eight. No insurance company will underwrite Chan's productions, in which he performs all his own stunts. After a number of stuntmen were injured during the making of *Police Story* (Hong Kong, 1985), the star formed the Jackie Chan Stuntmen Association, training stuntmen personally and paying their medical bills out of his own pocket.

Most Prolific Movie Stuntmen   Vic Armstrong (UK) has doubled for every actor playing James Bond, and in a career spanning three decades, has performed stunts in more than 200 films, including *Raiders of the Lost Ark* (1981). He has coordinated stunts for movies such as *Tomorrow Never Dies* (UK/US, 1997) and is married to stuntwoman Wendy Leech, whom he met when they doubled for the stars of *Superman* (1978).

Yakima Canutt (US) performed stunts in more than 150 films in his 15-year career. In 1941, he broke his ankles, and thereafter, he devoted his time to creating stunts and handling the action scenes in Hollywood movies, including the chariot race in *Ben Hur* (1959). In 1966, he was awarded an Oscar for his stunt work.

Most Expensive Aerial Stunt   Simon Carne performed one of the most dangerous aerial stunts ever when he moved between two jets at an altitude of 2 miles 1,480 yd. for *Cliffhanger* (1993). The stunt, performed only once because it was so risky, cost a record $1 million. Sylvester Stallone, the film's star, is said to have offered to reduce his fee by the same amount to ensure that the stunt was made.

Biggest Film Stunt Budget   More than $3 million of the $200-million budget for *Titanic* (1997) went toward the movie's stunts. In the most complex scene, 100 stuntpeople leaped, fell, and slid 70 ft. as the ship broke in

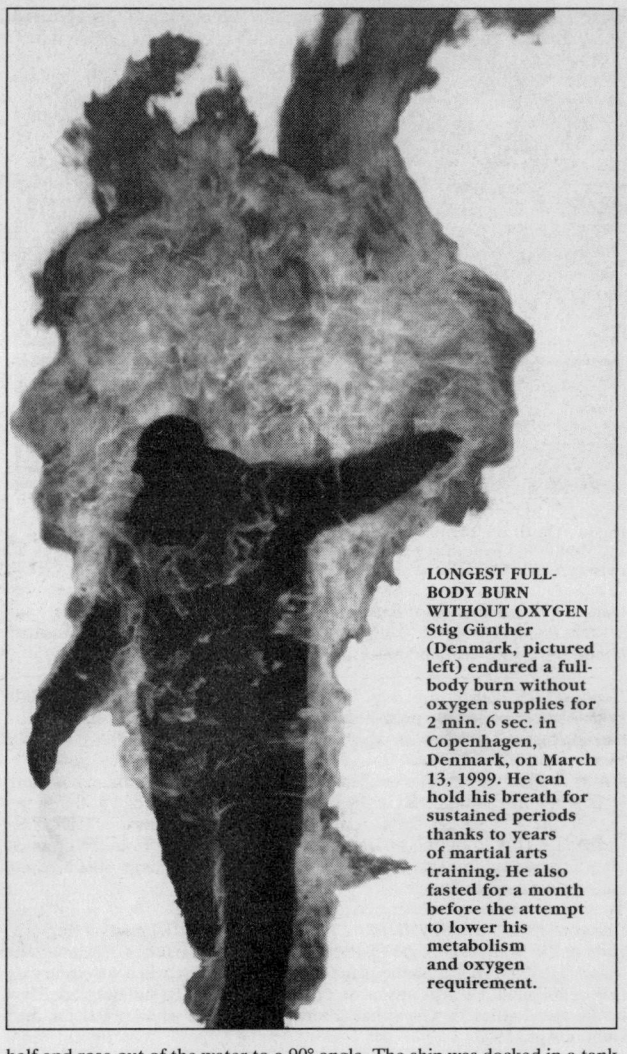

LONGEST FULL-BODY BURN WITHOUT OXYGEN Stig Günther (Denmark, pictured left) endured a full-body burn without oxygen supplies for 2 min. 6 sec. in Copenhagen, Denmark, on March 13, 1999. He can hold his breath for sustained periods thanks to years of martial arts training. He also fasted for a month before the attempt to lower his metabolism and oxygen requirement.

half and rose out of the water to a 90° angle. The ship was docked in a tank filled with 17 million gallons of water.

Biggest Coordinator of Film Aerial Stunts Flying Pictures of Surrey, England, has planned and coordinated air stunts for more than 200

LONGEST BLINDFOLD SKYWALK Jay Cochrane (US) walked between the towers of the Flamingo Hilton in Las Vegas, Nevada, on November 11, 1998. Cochrane was blindfolded and traversed 600 ft. of tightrope between the two towers.

feature films, including *Cliffhanger* (1993), *GoldenEye* (UK/US, 1995), and *Mission Impossible* (1996). They have also coordinated the aerial stunts for hundreds of TV shows and advertisements.

Highest Dive into an Air Bag   Stig Günther (Denmark) jumped from a height of 343 ft. into a 39-ft.-4 $^1/_2$-in. x 49-ft.-2 $^1/_2$-in. x 14-ft.-9-in. air bag on August 7, 1998.

Highest Free Fall   The greatest height from which a stuntman has ever leaped in a free fall is 1,100 ft., by Dar Robinson from a ledge at the summit of the CN Tower in Toronto, Canada, for the movie *Highpoint* (Canada, 1979). Robinson's parachute opened just 300 ft. from the ground after a six-second free fall. He was paid $150,000 for the jump—the highest fee ever for a single stunt.

Longest Free Fall Sky Glide   Adrian Nicholas (UK) made a free-fall glide in the horizontal plane of 10 miles over Yolo County, California, on March 12, 1999. He exited the plane at 33,850 ft. and reached speeds in excess of 100 mph. His feat was made possible with a flying suit developed by his mentor Patrick de Gayardon (France), who died while practicing the stunt in April 1998.

Longest Ramp Jump in a Car   The longest ramp jump made in a car, with the car landing on its wheels and driving on afterward, is 237 ft., by Ray Baumann (Australia) at Ravenswood International Raceway in Perth, Western Australia, on August 23, 1998.

Longest Leap in a Monster Truck   Dan Runte (US) jumped 141 ft. 10 in. in *Bigfoot 14* on March 8, 1998. The 4.6-ton truck, topped by a 1998 Ford F-150 fiberglass body and producing 1,500 hp, set the record at the Williams Gateway Airport in Mesa, Arizona. The previous record—141 ft. 1 in.—was set by Fred Shafer (US) in *Bearfoot* in November 1996.

Longest Backward Motorcycle Jump   Roger "Mr. Backward" Riddell (US) jumped seven cars—a distance of 60 ft.—riding backward on a 650 cc Honda motorcycle in Franklin, Indiana, in May 1987.

Highest Building-to-Building Motorcycle Jump   On August 1, 1998, Joe Reed (US) jumped from one 145-ft. building to another on a 250 cc dirt bike in Los Angeles, California. The gap between the buildings was 65 ft., and Reed had a run-up of 116 ft.

Most Blown-Up Person   Allison Bly (US) has blown herself up more than 1,100 times inside a box she calls "The Coffin," using explosives that make the equivalent sound of two sticks of dynamite. The 1,100th detonation was shown on December 8, 1998, on the TV show *Guinness® World Records: Primetime*.

GREATEST HEIGHT RANGE PLAYED BY A STUNTMAN   Stuntman **Riky Ash** from Nottingham, England, is pictured with a 3-ft.-6-in.-tall boy for whom he doubled during the filming of the BBC TV show *Out Of The Blue* in February 1995. He also doubled for a 6-ft.-4-in. adult in the ITV series *Heartbeat* in March 1998. Riky, who stands 5 ft. 3 in. tall and is 31 years old, has been a stuntman for six years. He has doubled for over 150 children and for characters spanning an age range of 6 to 70 years.

LIFESAVERS

Oldest Lifesaving Organization   The Royal National Lifeboat Institution (RNLI), a British lifesaving society, was formed by royal edict in March 1824 and celebrated its 175th anniversary in 1999. By April 1999, the organization had saved 132,500 lives. The RNLI currently has 223 lifeboat stations around the coasts of the UK and Ireland, with a total of 4,200 volunteer crew members.

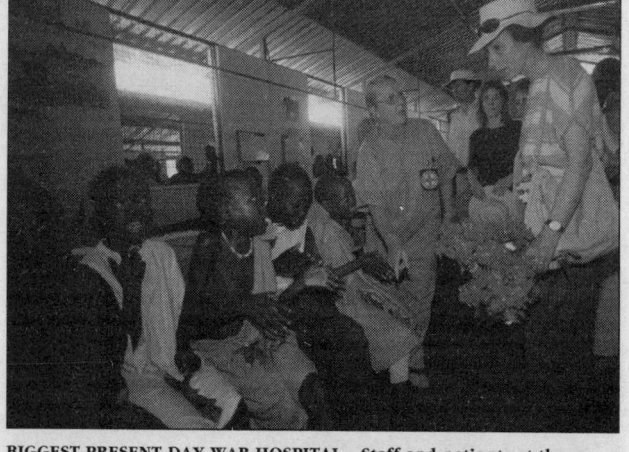

BIGGEST PRESENT-DAY WAR HOSPITAL   Staff and patients at the International Committee of the Red Cross (ICRC) Hospital in Lopiding, Kenya, are seen with the Princess Royal, Princess Anne. Founded in 1987 with just 40 beds, it is now the world's largest war hospital, with a capacity of 560 beds. It has treated approximately 17,000 victims of the long-running civil war in neighboring Sudan since its establishment, fitting 1,500 with artificial limbs. About 70% of the admitted patients have gunshot wounds, and the vast majority are civilians.

Most Lifesaving Awards   The greatest number of awards won by a member of the British Royal Life Saving Society is 234, by Eric Deakin of Hightown, England, since 1960.

Youngest Recipients of Lifesaving Awards   Ryan Woods of Kent, England, became the youngest person ever to receive a bravery award when he was presented with the Royal Humane Society's "Testimonial on Parchment" at the age of 4 years 52 days. The award was made in recognition of his actions during an accident in Portugal in July 1997. Ryan had saved his grandmother's life by climbing for help when the car they were traveling in plunged down a steep cliff.

Kristina Stragauskaite of Skirmantiskis, Lithuania, was awarded a medal for "Courage in Fire" when she was just 4 years 252 days old, making her the youngest female ever to earn such an honor. She had saved the lives of her younger brother and sister when a fire started in the family's home on April 7, 1989, while her parents were out. The award was decreed by the presidium of the then Lithuanian Soviet Socialist Republic.

The youngest person to receive an official gallantry award is Julius Rosenberg of Winnipeg, Canada, who was given the Canadian Medal of Bravery in March 1994 for foiling the efforts of a black bear that had attacked his three-year-old sister in September 1992. Julius, who was five years old at the time of the incident, had managed to save his sister by growling at the bear.

MOST ARTISTS SAVED Varian Fry (pictured left), "The Artists' Schindler," journeyed from the US to France in 1940 with a list of 200 prominent artists and intellectuals known to be in parts of Nazi-occupied Europe. He subsequently helped to save about 4,000 people from the Gestapo, among them some of the most famous cultural figures of our age, including Max Ernst, Marc Chagall, André Breton, and Nobel Prize-winning chemist Otto Meyerhof. Fry was arrested and deported in 1942. In 1997, the Israeli Yad Vashem Memorial Museum awarded the late hero its highest accolade, naming him one of the Righteous Among the Nations. He was the first US citizen to receive the tribute.

Biggest Rescue Without Loss of Life All 2,689 people aboard the *Susan B. Anthony* survived when the ship sank off the coast of Normandy, France, on June 7, 1944.

Oldest Lifeguard Lee Wee Wong (Singapore) was born in 1929 and has been a volunteer lifeguard since 1966 and a professional since 1973. Although he reached the age of 70 in 1999, he still beats many younger guards in the annual fitness test required to renew his license.

Longest Hiatus Before Bravery Award On May 19, 1997, Murphy, an Australian army donkey, was posthumously awarded the RSPCA Australia Purple Cross, an award for animal bravery, on behalf of all the donkeys that had served in the Gallipoli campaign in 1915–16. During the abortive offensive in the Dardanelles, Turkey, Murphy carried wounded servicemen from the front down rocky, exposed gullies to field hospitals.

Most Successful Flying Doctor Service The Australian Royal Flying Doctor Service was set up in 1928. In 1998, the service's 53 doctors, 103

BIGGEST VOLUNTEER AMBULANCE ORGANIZATION Abdul Sattar Edhi (Pakistan, pictured above) began his ambulance service in 1948 by ferrying injured people to the hospital and has since developed a service that attracts funds of $5 million per year, with no government assistance. His radio-linked network includes 500 ambulances throughout Pakistan, and he has also set up 300 relief centers, three air ambulances, 24 hospitals, three drug-rehabilitation centers, women's centers, free dispensaries, adoption programs, and soup kitchens that feed 100,000 people a month. He has paid for and supervised the training of 17,000 nurses. The ambulance service even picks up corpses, and the organization arranges Muslim burials. Edhi has not taken a vacation in 45 years.

nurses, and 95 pilots treated 181,621 patients, performed 21,604 aerial evacuations, and flew a total of 8.3 million miles. The area covered by the Royal Flying Doctor Service measures 2.76 million miles^2.

Most Lives Saved by a Seat-Belt Innovation The three-point safety belt, invented by Swedish engineer Nils Bohlin, was patented in 1959 by Volvo. Inertia-roll technology was developed by the same company in 1968. The US National Highway and Traffic Safety Administration estimates that seat belts have prevented 55,600 deaths and 1.3 million injuries in the last decade in the US alone, saving $105 billion in medical costs.

Most People Rescued by One Dog The most famous canine rescuer of all time is Barry, a St. Bernard who saved more than 40 people during his 12-year career in the Swiss Alps. His best-known rescue was that of a boy who lay half frozen under an avalanche in which his mother had died. Barry spread himself across the boy's body to warm him up and licked the child's face to wake him, before carrying him to the nearest house.

Lowest Midair Rescue by a Parachutist On October 16, 1988, Eddie Turner saved the life of fellow parachutist Frank Farnan, who was unconscious after being injured in a collision while jumping out of an aircraft at 13,000 ft. Turner pulled Farnan's rip cord at 1,800 ft. over Clewiston, Florida, less than 10 seconds from impact.

Biggest CPR Training Session On May 19, 1997, the American Heart Association, Dutchess Region, trained 1,320 people in cardiopulmonary resuscitation and early defibrillation awareness at the Casperkill Conference Center in Dutchess County, New York.

Biggest Blood Donation The Valle de Cauca, Colombia, branch of the Red Cross organized the world's biggest blood donor session in Cali, Colombia, on December 13, 1997. A total of 3,295 units of blood were taken from 3,403 donors in 12 hours.

Most Blood Platelet Donations Robert J. Watson of Sudbury, Massachusetts, has been a platelet pheresis donor on a weekly basis at Children's Hospital in Boston, Massachusetts, since November 1986. He made his 500th platelet donation on June 8, 1999.

SURVIVORS

Greatest Age Reached by a Titanic ***Survivor*** Edith Haisman, who died in a nursing home in Southampton, England, at the age of 100 in January 1997, was 15 years old when *Titanic* struck an iceberg and sank on the night of April 14, 1912. She could remember sitting in one of the ship's lifeboats watching her father, Thomas Brown, standing on deck holding a glass of brandy and a cigar and saying "I'll see you in New York!" He was taking his family from South Africa to Seattle, Washington, where they intended to start a hotel business. Edith appeared in public in 1993 to accept her father's gold watch, which had been recovered from the wreckage.

Longest Period Survived Without Food and Water Andreas Mihavecz of Bregenz, Austria, lived for 18 days without food and water after police in Höchst, Austria, put him into a holding cell in a local government building and then forgot about him. The 18-year-old, who had been a passenger in a crashed car, was discovered close to death.

Longest Fall Survived by an Infant In November 1997, an 18-month-old baby named Alejandro fell 65 ft. 7 in. from the seventh-floor kitchen window of his parents' apartment in Murcia, Spain. Although no one witnessed the fall, the baby's bruises and a damaged clothesline below indicated that he hit the clothesline before landing on a street-level sky-

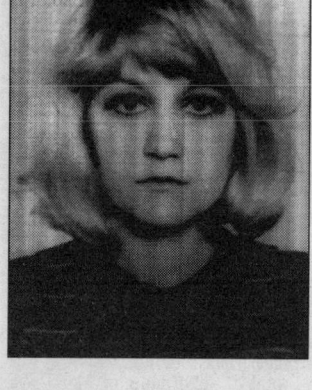

LONGEST FALL SURVIVED WITHOUT A PARACHUTE On January 26, 1972, Vesna Vulovic (pictured left), a flight attendant from Yugoslavia, survived a fall from an altitude of 33,330 ft. when the DC-9 airplane in which she was traveling blew up over Srbskà Kamenice, Czechoslovakia (now Czech Republic). The other 27 passengers on board the plane were killed.

light. Doctors at the nearby Virgen de Arrixaca hospital confirmed that the only damage suffered by Alejandro, besides the bruises, was a broken tooth and a split lip.

Most Lightning Strikes Survived   Roy Sullivan, a park ranger from Virginia, was struck by lightning a record seven times in the course of his life: in 1942, when he lost a big toenail; in 1969, when he lost his eyebrows; in 1970, when his left shoulder was seared; in 1972, when his hair caught fire; in 1973, when his hair caught fire and his legs were seared; in 1976, when his ankle was injured; and in 1977, when he received chest and stomach burns. Sullivan committed suicide in September 1983, reportedly after being rejected in love.

Longest Period Survived in an Underground Cavern   Speleologist George Du Prisne was exploring caves in Wisconsin in 1983 when he fell into an underground river and was sucked down a water siphon into a cavern. Rescuers abandoned their search after four days, but Du Prisne was alive, surviving on fish and algae scraped from the cavern's walls. Determined to escape, he unraveled orange yarn from his shirt and tied it to the legs of a dozen bats. Residents of a nearby town saw the bats and he was saved 13 days later.

Longest Periods Survived on Rafts   Poon Lim of the British Merchant Navy survived on a raft for a record 133 days after his ship, the *SS Ben Lomond*, was torpedoed in the Atlantic 565 miles west of St. Paul's Rocks on November 23, 1942. He was picked up by a fishing boat off Salinópolis, Brazil, on April 5, 1943, and was able to walk ashore.

The longest period two people on a raft have survived is 177 days. Tabwai Mikaie and Arenta Tebeitabu from the island of Nikunau in Kiribati, together with a fellow fisherman, were caught in a cyclone shortly after setting out on a trip in their 13-ft.-long open dinghy on November 17, 1991. The three were found washed ashore 1,100 miles away in Western Samoa (now Samoa) on May 11, 1992. The third man had died a few days previously.

Longest Time Survived Adrift in a Fishing Boat   On January 4, 1999, a drifting Nicaraguan fishing boat with a crew of seven was found by Norwegian oil tanker *Joelm* 497 miles southwest of the Nicaraguan port San Juan del Sur. The fishermen had been lost at sea for a record 35 days

YOUNGEST *TITANIC* SURVIVOR   Millvina Dean was just eight weeks old when she traveled third-class on *Titanic* with her parents and 18-month-old brother. She, her mother, and her brother all survived when the ship sank, but her father, Bert, was among the 1,517 passengers who were never seen again. Millvina is pictured here with CDR. P.H. Nargeolet, who was with her on the M. V. *Royal Majesty* when it sailed to the site where *Titanic* sank and watched research vessels try to raise part of the ship's hull. The attempt was unsuccessful.

after the engine of their vessel ceased working. They had survived by eating turtle flesh and drinking turtle blood.

Deepest Underwater Escapes   The greatest depth from which anyone has been rescued is 1,575 ft. On August 29, 1973, Roger Chapman and Roger Mallinson became trapped in the mini-submarine *Pisces III* for 76 hours after it sank 150 miles southeast of Cork, Republic of Ireland. The vessel was hauled to the surface on September 1 by the cable ship *John Cabot* after work by *Pisces V, Pisces II,* and the remote-control recovery vessel *Curv*.

The greatest depth from which an escape has been made without any equipment is 225 ft. Richard Slater escaped from the rammed submersible *Nekton Beta* off Catalina Island, California, on September 28, 1970.

Longest Periods Survived Underwater Without Equipment   In 1991, Michael Proudfoot was investigating a sunken naval cruiser around Baja California, Mexico, when he smashed his scuba regulator and lost all his air. Unable to make it back to the ship's hull, Proudfoot found a big bubble of air trapped in the galley and a tea urn almost full of freshwater. By rationing the water, breathing shallowly, and eating sea urchins, he managed to stay alive for two days before being rescued.

In 1986, two-year-old Michelle Funk from Salt Lake City, Utah, made a full recovery after spending 1 hr. 6 min. underwater. She had fallen into a creek.

LONGEST TIME SPENT TRAPPED FOLLOWING A MINING ACCIDENT
In July 1998, miner Georg Hainzl (pictured here) was found alive after
spending 10 days at a depth of 207 ft. in a collapsed mine in the village
of Lassing, Austria. Ten miners sent to rescue him died after being
trapped in mud slides.

Highest Parachute Escape   Flight Lieutenant J. de Salis and Flying
Officer P. Lowe (both UK) escaped at an altitude of 56,000 ft. over Derby,
England, on April 9, 1958.

Lowest Parachute Escape   Squadron Leader Terence Spencer (UK)
made the lowest parachute escape ever, at 30 to 40 ft. over Wismar Bay in
the Baltic Sea on April 19, 1945.

Most Labor Camp Escapes   Tatyana Mikhailovna Russanova, a former Soviet citizen who now lives in Haifa, Israel, escaped from Stalinist labor camps in the former Soviet Union a total of 15 times between 1943 and
1954. She was recaptured and sentenced 14 times. All of her escapes have
been judicially recognized by independent Russian lawyers, but only nine
of them were recognized by Soviet Supreme Court officials.

Youngest Person to Survive a Car Crash   On February 25, 1999, Virginia Rivero from Misiones, Argentina, went into labor at her home and
walked to a nearby road to hitchhike to the hospital. Offered a lift by two
men, she then gave birth to a baby girl in the backseat of their car. When she
told them she was about to have a second baby, the driver overtook the car
in front, only to collide with a vehicle. Virginia and her newborn daughter
were ejected through the back door of the car and suffered minor injuries,
but Virginia was able to stand up and flag down another car, which took
them to the hospital. Once there, she gave birth to a baby boy.

KNOWLEDGE

SCIENCE 1

Newest and Heaviest Element   In January 1999, a team of scientists based at the Lawrence Livermore National Laboratory in California and the Joint Institute for Nuclear Research in Dubna, Russia, announced the creation of what may be the world's newest and heaviest element, element 114. It contains 114 protons, is claimed to be much more stable than other superheavy atoms, and resulted from the bombardment of a neutron-enriched plutonium isotope by a calcium isotope.

Strongest Acid Solution   Solutions of strong acids and alkalis tend toward pH values of 0 and 14, respectively, but this scale is inadequate for describing the "superacids"—the strongest of which is an 80% solution of antimony pentafluoride in hydrofluoric acid (fluoro-antimonic acid $HF:SbF_5$). The $H\emptyset$ acidity function of this solution has not been measured, but even a weaker 50% solution is 1,018 times stronger than concentrated sulfuric acid.

Most Lethal Artificial Chemical   The compound 2, 3, 7, 8-tetra-chlorodibenzo-*p*-dioxin, or TCDD, is the most deadly of the 75 known dioxins. It is 150,000 times more lethal than cyanide.

MOST POWERFUL NERVE GAS   Ethyl S-2-diisopropylaminoethylmethyl phosphonothiolate, known as VX, which was developed at the Chemical Defence Experimental Establishment in Porton Down, England, in 1952, is 300 times more powerful than the phosgene ($COCl_2$) used in World War I. A lethal dosage of VX is $1/93$ oz./ft.^{3} airborne or $1/675,000$ oz. administered orally.

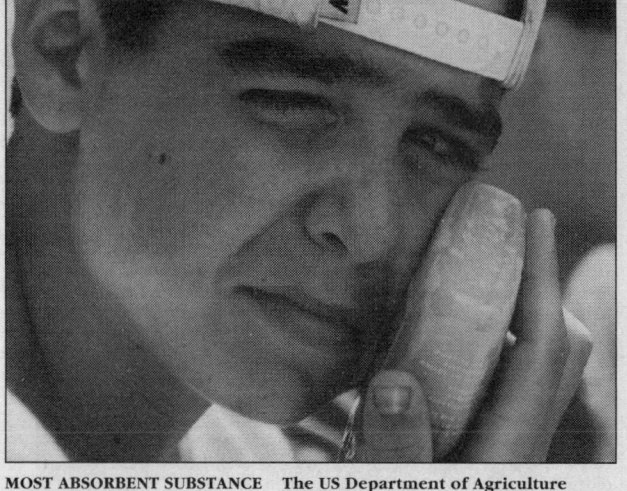

MOST ABSORBENT SUBSTANCE The US Department of Agriculture Research Service announced on August 18, 1974, that "H-span" or Super Slurper, composed of 50% starch derivative and 25% each of acrylamide and acrylic acid, can, when treated with iron, hold 1,300 times its own weight in water. Its ability to maintain a constant temperature for a long time makes it ideal for reusable ice packs, as demonstrated by this 14-year-old baseball fan cooling off at a Detroit Tigers game.

Most Magnetic Substance Neodymium iron boride $Nd_2Fe_{14}B$ has a maximum energy product (defined as the greatest amount of energy that a magnet can supply when operating at a particular operating point) of up to 280 $kJ/m.^3$.

Bitterest Substance The bitterest-tasting substances are based on the denatonium cation and produced commercially as benzoate and saccharide. Taste detection levels can be as low as one part in 500 million, and a dilution of one part in 100 million will leave a lingering taste.

Sweetest Substances Talin, which is obtained from arils (appendages found on certain seeds) of the katemfe plant (*Thaumatococcus daniellii*), is 6,150 times as sweet as sucrose (table sugar). The plant is found in parts of west Africa.

Densest Element The densest substance on Earth is the metal osmium (Os—element 76), at $13^9/_{50}$ oz./in.^{3}.

The singularities at the centers of black holes are calculated to have infinite density.

Least Dense Solid The solid substances with the lowest density are silica aerogels, in which tiny spheres of bonded silicon and oxygen atoms are joined into long strands separated by pockets of air. The lightest of these aerogels, with a density of only 5 oz./ft.^{3}, was produced at the Lawrence Livermore National Laboratory in California. It will be used mainly in space to collect micrometeoroids and the debris present in comets' tails.

SMALLEST AMOUNT OF SUBSTANCE In 1997, the chemistry of Seaborgium (Sg — element 106) was deduced from the production of only seven atoms. It was named in honor of Dr. Glenn Seaborg (pictured), the late Nobel Prize-winning physicist who discovered plutonium.

Highest Temperature The highest temperature created by humans is 950 million°F—30 times hotter than the center of the sun—on May 27, 1994, at the Tokamak Fusion Test Reactor at the Princeton Plasma Physics Laboratory in New Jersey, using a deuterium-tritium plasma mix.

Highest Superconducting Temperature In April 1993, at the Laboratorium für Festkörperphysik in Zurich, Switzerland, bulk superconductivity with a maximum transition temperature of −221.3°F was achieved in a mixture of oxides of mercury, barium, calcium, and copper, $HgBa_2Ca_{23}Cu_3O_1+x$, and $HgBa_2CaCu_2O_6+x$. Claims to higher temperatures are unsubstantiated.

Hottest Flame   The hottest flame is produced by carbon subnitride (C_4N_2), which, at 1 atmosphere pressure, can generate a flame of 9,010°F.

Lowest Temperature   The absolute zero of temperature—zero K on the Kelvin scale—corresponds to −459.67°F, a point when all atomic and molecular thermal motion ceases. The lowest temperature reached is 280 picoKelvin (280 trillionths of a degree), in a nuclear demagnetization device at the Low Temperature Laboratory of the Helsinki University of Technology in Finland and announced in February 1993.

Most Elusive Protein   Biochemists at Harvard School of Medicine in Boston, Massachusetts, made a major discovery relating to protein behavior in 1990. It had been believed that blocks of proteins, made up of amino acids, could only be split and rejoined by other proteins called enzymes. The Harvard team monitored a type of tiny protein, known as an intein, separating from a longer protein chain and then rejoining the chain's two cut ends, removing any indication of its former presence within the chain. It is hoped that the unique capabilities of inteins may help in the fight against diseases such as TB and leprosy.

Biggest Galaxy   The central galaxy of the Abell 2029 galaxy cluster, 1,070 million light-years from Earth, has a major diameter of 5.6 million light-years—80 times the diameter of the Milky Way.

Brightest Galaxy   The brightest galaxy appears to be AMP 08279+5255, a remote galaxy with a red shift (a measure of lengthening wavelengths of light) of 3.87 and a luminosity 5×10^{15} times that of the sun.

Remotest Object   The remotest known object is an unnamed galaxy of red shift 6.68, discovered by Hsiao Wen-chen, Kenneth Lanzetta, and Sebastian Pascarelle (all US) in 1998. The view that this gives us is of the universe when it was only 10% of its present age—the most distant view of prehistory ever obtained.

Biggest Star   The M-class supergiant Betelgeuse has a diameter of 610 million miles, making it 700 times bigger than the sun.

Biggest Satellite   The biggest satellite of any planet in our solar system is Ganymede, in the orbit of Jupiter, with a diameter of 3,273 miles and a mass of 1.48^{20} tons—2.017 times that of the moon.

Best-Hidden Stars   In February 1999, Dr. Rabindra Mohaptra of the University of Maryland announced that clumps of matter known as MACHOs (Massive Compact Halo Objects), at the edge of the Milky Way, may be stars from a "mirror sector" of the galaxy. Invisible to us but detectable because of their gravity's bending of light from background stars, they may have mirror planets orbiting them, populated by life-forms that can see their mirror stellar systems but are blind to ours in just the same manner as we are to theirs.

SCIENCE 2

Smallest Artifact   The tips of probes on scanning tunneling microscopes (STMs) have been shaped to end in a single atom—the last three layers form the world's smallest human-made pyramid, of seven, three, and one atoms. In January 1990, it was announced that scientists at the IBM Almaden Research Center in San Jose, California, had used an STM to move and reposition single atoms of xenon on a nickel surface in order to spell out the initials "IBM." Other laboratories have used similar techniques on single atoms of other elements.

Most Heat-Resistant Substance   The existence of a complex material known as NFAAR, or Ultra Hightech Starlite, was announced in April 1993. Invented by Maurice Ward (UK), it can temporarily resist plasma temperatures (18,032°F).

Most Powerful Light Source   Of continuously burning light sources, the most powerful is a 313-kW high-pressure argon arc lamp of 1.2 million candles, completed by Vortek Industries Ltd. of Vancouver, British Columbia, Canada, in March 1984.

Most Powerful Electric Current   The largest electric current was achieved by scientists at Oak Ridge National Laboratory in the US in April 1996. They sent a current of 2 million amperes/cm.^{3} down a superconducting wire. Household wires carry a current of less than 1,000 amperes/cm.^{3}.

LONGEST ECLIPSES   The longest possible solar eclipse (when the moon passes between the sun and Earth) is 7 min. 31 sec. The longest in recent times lasted 7 min. 8 sec., west of the Philippines in 1955, and a 7-min. 29-sec. eclipse is predicted to occur in the mid-Atlantic in 2186. A mother and child are pictured in Bangkok, Thailand, on October 24, 1995, during an eclipse that was total in some areas of the country. The longest possible lunar eclipse (when the moon passes into Earth's shadow) is 1 hr. 47 min. — this will be visible on the west coast of North America on July 16, 2000.

Biggest Solar Power Plant   In terms of nomi-

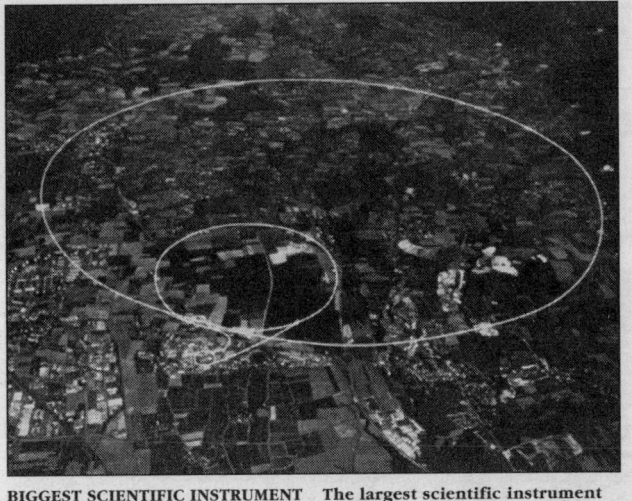

BIGGEST SCIENTIFIC INSTRUMENT The largest scientific instrument is the Large Electron Positron (LEP) storage ring at CERN in Geneva, Switzerland, which is 17 miles in circumference. The ring itself has a diameter of 12 ft. 6 in. Over 66,152 tons of technical equipment have been installed in the tunnel and its eight working zones.

nal capacity, the largest solar electric power facility in the world is the Harper Lake Site (LSP 8 & 9) in the Mojave Desert, California, operated by UC Operating Services. These two solar electric generating stations (SEGS) have a nominal capacity of 160 MW (80 MW each). The station site covers 1,280 acres.

Biggest DC Generator The largest DC generator, with an overall capacity of 51,300 kW, was developed by Mitsubishi Electric for use in nuclear fusion experiments. Installed in the Japan Atomic Energy Research Institute in May 1995, it is 54 ft. long and weighs 389 tons.

Fastest Centrifuge The highest artificial rotary speed ever achieved by a centrifuge is 4,500 mph, by a tapered 6-in. carbon fiber rod rotating in a vacuum at Birmingham University in England in 1975. Ultracentrifuges were invented by the Swedish chemist Theodor Svedberg in 1923 and are used to separate mixtures of organic substances. To allow them to go faster, friction is reduced by supporting the spinning rotor by a magnetic field and enclosing it in a vacuum.

Finest Balance The Sartorius Microbalance Model 4108, manufactured in Göttingen, Germany, can weigh objects of up to $^{18}/_{1,000}$ oz. to an accuracy of 3.5×10^{-10} oz., which is equivalent to a little more than one-sixtieth of the weight of the ink on this period.

Finest Cut The Large Optics Diamond Turning Machine at the Lawrence Livermore National Laboratory in California was reported in

June 1983 to be able to sever a human hair lengthwise a total of 3,000 times.

Fastest Signal   In 1996, a team of physicists at Cologne University in Germany announced that they had accomplished what Einstein's special theory of relativity had considered impossible—they had sent a signal at a speed exceeding that of light. The signal was a portion of Mozart's 40th Symphony, sent to confirm the findings of an earlier experiment in which microwaves were split in two, one part being sent through a special filter and the other through air. Both should have been traveling at the speed of light, but the microwaves sent through the filter were found to be traveling 4.7 times faster than those sent through the air.

Longest Scientific Index   The 12th collective *Index of Chemical Abstracts*, completed in December 1992, contains 35,137,626 entries in 215,880 pages and 115 volumes and weighs 544 lb. It provides references to 3,052,700 published documents in the field of chemistry.

Most Complete Sequencing of a Multicellular Animal's Genome The first multicellular animal whose entire genome (genetic code) has been sequenced is *Caenorhabditis elegans*, a $3/100$-in.-long soil-dwelling nematode worm. Although its entire adult body consists of only 959 cells (humans have trillions), it has 100 million genetic bases comprising at least

LONGEST-STANDING MATH PUZZLE   Andrew Wiles (UK), currently at Princeton University in New Jersey, is pictured in front of Fermat's last theorem. In 1998, Wiles was awarded the $200,000 King Faisal International Prize for proving the conjecture of the 17th-century French mathematician Pierre de Fermat. The problem had left the world's greatest mathematicians baffled for 350 years.

18,000 genes, and more than 50% of known human genes correspond with versions possessed by *C. elegans*. The task of mapping the worm's entire genome was the brainchild of Dr. Sydney Brenner, who initiated the project in the 1960s at the Medical Research Council's Laboratory of Molecular Biology in the UK and began the actual sequencing in 1990.

Earliest Machine to Levitate a Living Creature Dr. Andre Geim and colleagues at Nijmegen University in Amsterdam, Netherlands, used a superconducting magnet to enable a live frog to float in midair in 1997. They also performed the experiment with fish and grasshoppers.

Earliest Teleportation Researchers led by Anton Zeilinger at Innsbruck University in Austria have teleported a single photon (a particle of light). Physical properties of the photon were transferred instantly to another photon without any connection or communication between them. The experiment requires three photons—the original and a pair of "entangled" photons, whose quantum properties (or spin) are complementary. When the spin of the original photon and one of the other two is measured, the third takes on the spin of the first. Popular interest in the principle of teleportation was first kindled in the 1960s by the popular television sci-fi series *Star Trek*.

INVENTORS

Most Patents Held by One Inventor The US inventor Thomas Alva Edison registered the most patents of any inventor in history: he held a total of 1,093, some jointly with other inventors. They included the carbon transmitter (which was used as a microphone in the production of Alexander Graham Bell's telephone), the motion-picture projector, and the incandescent electric lamp.

Earliest Recorded US Patent The first patent issued in the US was to Samuel Hopkins for potash, a substance used in fertilizer, on July 31, 1790. The patent was countersigned by President George Washington.

Youngest US Patent Holder Sydney Dittman of Houston, Texas, was two years old when she submitted an application to the US Patent Office. Her patent for an "Aid for Grasping Round Doorknobs" was granted when she was four years old, on August 3, 1993.

Biggest Damages in a Patent Case On August 31, 1993, Litton Industries Inc. of Los Angeles, California, was awarded a record $1.2 billion in damages from Honeywell Inc. in a case involving a patent for airline navigation systems. Litton had filed a suit in March 1990, which was followed by a counterclaim from Honeywell nine months later.

Earliest Cash Dispenser One of the biggest developments in personal finance in the 20th century, the world's first cash dispenser was installed at Barclays Bank in Enfield, England, on June 27, 1967. Invented by

MOST SUCCESSFUL CLOCK RADIO British inventor Trevor Bayliss devised the BayGen free-play/free-power clock radio in 1993, and his Baygen factory in Cape Town, South Africa, currently produces 20,000 units a month. The radio is popular in Africa and other regions where electricity sources can be scarce.

John Shepherd-Barron and developed by De La Rue, the machine operated on a voucher system. The maximum amount that could be withdrawn at one time was $28.

Earliest Air Conditioner US inventor Willis Haviland Carrier, later dubbed the "Father of Cool," designed and built the first air-conditioning system in 1902. It was devised for a printer in New York City, who had found that temperature fluctuations were causing his paper to warp, resulting in the misalignment of the colored inks. Carrier's patent was granted in 1906.

Earliest Ballpoint Pen The Hungarian journalist László Biro created the first ballpoint pen in collaboration with his brother Georg in 1938. Biro took his inspiration from watching newspaper ink dry quickly, leaving the paper smudge-free. This thicker ink would not flow from a conventional nib, so he designed the ballpoint and in doing so revolutionized pen design. One of the first organizations to exploit Biro's idea was the British Royal Air Force, whose pilots needed a pen that would not leak at high altitudes, as the fountain pen did. The biro's success with the RAF brought it into the limelight.

Most Widespread Contact Lens Design Czech researcher Otto Wichterle invented the soft contact lens in 1956. The development gave rise to a huge industry, with over 100 million people wearing soft lenses worldwide.

Earliest Floppy Disk   In 1971, a team of IBM engineers led by Alan Shugart (US) invented the floppy disk. The 8-in.² plastic disk was nick-named "floppy" because of its flexibility. Shugart went on to refine the design for Wang Computers, producing a 5¼-in. flexible disk and disk drive in 1976. In 1981, Sony was the first to introduce the 3½-in.² drives and diskettes that are standard in modern personal-computer systems.

Most Successful Instant Camera   Edwin Land (US), founder of the Polaroid Corporation in 1937, created a system of one-step photography that used the principle of diffusion transfer to reproduce the image recorded by the camera lens directly onto a photosensitive surface, which functioned as both film and photo. Land first demonstrated the Polaroid camera at a meeting of the Optical Society of America in February 1947. Color Polaroids followed in 1963. In 1998, the Polaroid Corporation generated $1.86 billion in revenue.

Most Successful Portable Music System   The Sony Corporation developed the Walkman in 1979, the first model on the market being the TPS-L2. By April 1999, Cassette Walkman sales totaled 195 million units, the CD Discman had sold 54 million, and the MiniDisc Walkman had sold 6.9 million.

Most Widespread Video Recording System   Charles Ginsburg of San Francisco, California, led the research team at Ampex Corporation in de-

MOST "USELESS" INVENTIONS   Kenji Kawakami has popularized the concept of *chindogu*, which he defines as "inventions that seem like they're going to make life a lot easier, but don't." The Japanese journalist is the founder of the 10,000-member International *Chindogu* Society and has published two books on the subject, *101 Unuseless Japanese Inventions* and *99 More Unuseless Inventions: The Art Of Chindogu*. Examples of these inventions include: tiny dusters that slip onto a cat's paws and clean surfaces as it walks over them; a fish face cover, to spare the cook that traumatic stare into the dead fish's eyes; a back-scratching T-shirt; and a chin-operated light switch. The books include membership forms for the *Chindogu* Society and rules for creating prototypes.

veloping the first practical videotape recorder (VTR). The system used a rapidly rotating recording head to apply high-frequency signals onto a reel of magnetic tape. The VTR revolutionized television broadcasting, as recorded programs that could be edited replaced most live broadcasts. In 1956, CBS became the first network to employ VTR technology.

The VHS system was invented by JVC in 1976. By 1997, the market for blank VHS tapes alone had reached a total of $2.2 billion.

Most Widespread Helicopter Design Igor Sikorsky, originally from Ukraine, designed the world's first successful multi-motor airplane and the world's first true production helicopter. Educated in Russia and Paris, Sikorsky emigrated to the US after the Russian Revolution, establishing himself as an aircraft designer. Sikorsky's US Patent 1,994,488, filed on June 27, 1931, marked the crucial breakthrough in helicopter technology. In late 1938, the management of United Aircraft (now United Technologies) approved his experimental helicopter, and on September 14, 1939, the VS-300 made its first flight. His single-rotor design, a major breakthrough in helicopter technology, remains the dominant configuration today.

Most Widespread Fastening Device In 1893, Whitcomb Judson (US) patented a "Clasp Locker," the precursor to the modern zipper. Working with businessman Col. Lewis Walker, Judson launched the Universal Fastener Company to promote the device. Gideon Sundback (Sweden) rose to the position of head designer at Universal, and after years of work, he came up with the zipper in December 1913, registering a patent in 1917. The name "zipper" comes from the B.F. Goodrich company, which renamed the device when it was added to their rubber-boot range.

Most Successful Soft Drink Pharmacist Dr. John Stith Pemberton introduced Coca-Cola in Atlanta, Georgia, in May 1886. For 5 cents, consumers could enjoy a glass of Coca-Cola at the soda fountain at Jacobs' Pharmacy, and sales averaged nine drinks per day. In 1998, the world's most popular soft drink had sales of more than 683 million drinks per day. The total sales for the company in 1998 were over $18.8 billion, and the worldwide market share was 51%.

Most Lives Saved by Air-Bag Technology　　William R. Carey, a project engineer with the US firm Eaton, Yale, and Town, was the first to develop the air bag for installation into automobiles and make it a practical safety feature. He registered his patent in 1969. As of May 1999, air bags, which deploy at 200 mph, were credited with saving more than 4,230 lives in the US alone.

ARCHITECTS & MASTERBUILDERS

Tallest Structure　　The world's tallest structure is a stayed television transmitting tower 2,064 ft. high, near Fargo, North Dakota. It was built for KTHI-TV between October 2 and November 1, 1963, by Hamilton Erection, Inc. of York, South Carolina. A mast constructed at Konstantynow, Poland, took the record in July 1974, with a height of 2,117 ft. 4½ in., but following its collapse in August 1991, the record reverted to the KTHI tower.

Tallest Building　　The CN Tower in Toronto, Canada, is the world's tallest self-supporting building. It is 1,815 ft. 5 in. in height and was built between 1973 and 1975 at a cost of $63 million. The tower was designed by architects John Andrews, Webb Zerafa, Menkes Housden, and E.R. Baldwin.

BIGGEST HINDU TEMPLE OUTSIDE INDIA　　The Shri Swaminarayan Temple in Neasden, London, England, is the largest Hindu temple outside India. It was built by His Holiness Pramukh Swami Maharaj (pictured), a 79-year-old Indian sadhu (holy man), and is made of 2,565 tons of Bulgarian limestone and 1,814 tons of Italian marble, which was first shipped to India to be carved by a team of 1,526 sculptors. The temple cost $19.2 million to build.

Tallest Apartment Buildings   The John Hancock Center in Chicago, Illinois, is 1,127 ft. tall and has 100 stories, of which only floors 44 to 92 are residential. The remaining floors are used for offices. Engineer Fazlur Kahn worked with architect Bruce Graham to devise a "braced tube" system that carries the load of the building downward so efficiently that the building requires one-third less steel per square foot than conventional buildings.

The tallest purely residential apartment building is the 70-story Lake Point Tower in Chicago, Illinois, which is 640 ft. high and has 879 apartments.

Biggest Block of Apartments   The largest aggregation of residential blocks is the Barbican Estate in the City of London, England, which was designed in 1959 by architects Chamberlin, Powell, & Bond. The site occupies a total of 40 acres and includes 2,014 apartments and 1,710 parking spaces.

Biggest Urban Complex   Pudong New Area, which faces the Chinese city of Shanghai across the Huangpu River, covers an area of 201 square miles and had a population of 1.4 million in 1995. The New Area comprises the Lujiazui export-processing zone, the Waigaoqiao free-trade zone, and the Zhangjiang hi-tech zone. Construction began in April 1990, and by February 1999, a total of 5,548 projects had found foreign investors. More than 80 structures are currently being built in the finance and trade zone, including what will eventually become the world's tallest office building, the Universal Financial Center.

Biggest Rentable Office Complex   The World Trade Center in New York City has a total of 12 million ft.^{2} of rentable space available in its seven buildings, including 4.37 million ft.^{2} in each of the twin towers. About 50,000 people work in some 500 companies and organizations located in the complex, and another 70,000 tourists and businesspeople visit it every day.

Biggest Administrative Building   The Pentagon in Arlington, Virginia, designed by George Bergstrom, covers the largest ground area of any office building. Built to house the US Defense Department's offices, it was completed on January 15, 1943, and cost an estimated $83 million. Its five stories enclose a floor area of 149.2 acres.

Biggest Single Construction Project   The Three Gorges Dam in China, which is due for completion in 2009, will span 1.44 miles, stand nearly 600 ft. high, and boast 26 supersized turbines and generators. It will create a reservoir with a surface area equivalent to Singapore. It has been estimated that the project will cost $24.5 billion.

Most Expensive Stadium   The $466-million Stade de France in the Paris suburb of Saint-Denis, France, was built for the 1998 soccer World Cup and was the venue for the home team's 3-0 victory over Brazil in the final. The stadium, which is able to seat 80,000 spectators, has a massive roof with little visible means of support, although it contains steelwork weighing as much as the Eiffel Tower. It was designed by architects Michel Macary, Aymeric Zublena, Michel Regembal, and Claude Constantini in association with three leading French construction companies—Bouygues, GTM, and SGE.

Biggest Museum Gallery   The biggest gallery in the Guggenheim Museum in Bilbao, Spain, is 450 ft. long and 98 ft. wide. The $100-million art

museum was designed by American architect Frank Gehry and opened to the public on October 10, 1997.

Biggest Igloo With a total floor area of 53,821 ft.^{2} and the capacity to sleep up to 150 guests per night, the Ice Hotel in Jukkasjarvi, Sweden, is the world's biggest igloo. Rebuilt every December for the past five years, the igloo increases in size every year. It currently features ice sculptures, a movie theater, saunas, an ice bar, and the world's only ice chapel.

Longest Bridge The Second Lake Pontchartrain Causeway, which joins Mandeville and Metrairie, Louisiana, is 23 miles 1,538 yd. long. The bridge was completed in 1969.

Longest Cable Suspension Bridge The Akashi-Kaikyo road bridge in Japan has a main span of 6,532 ft. It took eight years to build, and when it was finished in 1997, it also broke records for the highest bridge towers, at 974 ft. 5 in., and the largest supporting cable diameter, at 3 ft. 8 in.

Architects & Masterbuilders ● 47

RECORD-BREAKING ARCHITECT   British architect Lord Foster is pictured outside the Reichstag in Berlin, Germany. He redesigned the old parliament building for the relocation of the government back to Berlin from Bonn. He is also the designer of the world's largest airport, Chep Lap Kok, in Hong Kong, China, and Europe's tallest building, the Commerzbank, in Frankfurt, Germany.

Longest Undersea Tunnel   The $17-billion Channel Tunnel, which runs underneath the English Channel between Folkestone, England, and Calais, France, was constructed between December 1987 and December 1990. It was officially opened by Queen Elizabeth II of the United Kingdom and President François Mitterrand of France on May 6, 1994. Each of the twin rail tunnels is 31 miles 53 yd. long and has a diameter of 24 ft. 11 in. Plans for a tunnel under the English Channel were first proposed during the Napoleonic Wars at the beginning of the 19th century.

Longest Road Tunnel   The two-lane St. Gottard road tunnel from Göschenen to Airlo, Switzerland, is 10 miles 246 yd. long and was opened to traffic in September 1980. Construction began in 1969 and cost $420 million. During the tunnel's construction, 19 workers lost their lives.

Biggest Railroad Station   Grand Central Terminal in New York City was designed by two firms of US architects—Warren and Whetmore and Reed & Stem at the beginning of the 20th century with money provided by the millionaire William Vanderbilt. The station covers a record 48 acres on two levels, with 41 tracks on the upper level and 26 on the lower. On average, more than 550 trains and 210,000 commuters use it every day.

MEDICAL HEROES

Longest Time a Patient Has Been Kept Alive Without a Pulse
In August 1998, Julie Mills, a student teacher, was kept alive without a pulse for six days by the AB180 Left Ventricular Assist Device. This gave her heart a chance to repair itself following a bout of viral myocarditis. The device, which was implanted by cardiac specialist Stephen Westaby at the John Radcliffe Hospital in Oxford, England, circulated blood around Ms. Mills' body in a continuous flow instead of mimicking the pumping action of the heart—hence the absence of a pulse. She was the fourth person to have the device implanted since its development in the US and the first to survive the procedure.

Longest Time after Which a Surgeon Has Restored Speech   In January 1998, 40-year-old Tim Heilder received a donor voice box and windpipe in an operation performed by Dr. Marshall Strome at the Cleveland Clinic in Ohio. Heilder had lost his voice following a motorcycle accident at the age of 21, when doctors removed his voice box to save his life. Three days after the transplant, Heilder said his first words in 19 years.

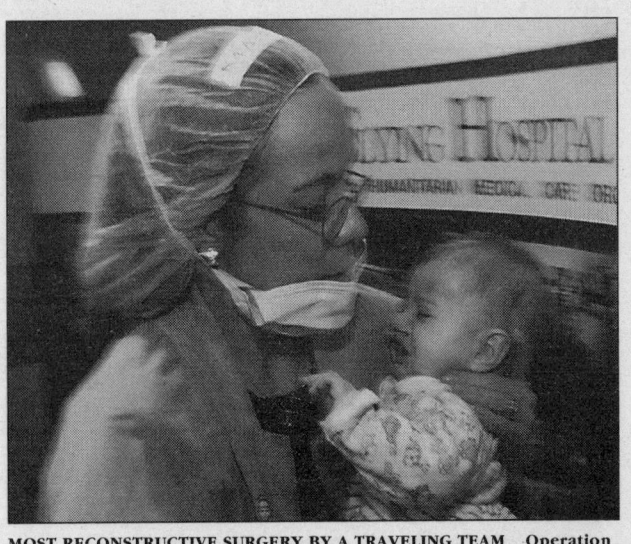

MOST RECONSTRUCTIVE SURGERY BY A TRAVELING TEAM   Operation Smile's "World Journey of Hope '99" lasted from February 5 to April 14, 1999, during which time a team of volunteer doctors visited 18 countries and treated 5,139 patients. They repaired cleft lips and cleft palates and performed surgery on facial tumors, burns, and facial injuries. Operation Smile was founded in 1982 by Bill Magee, a plastic surgeon, and his wife, Kathy, a nurse, in Norfolk, Virginia.

Most Organs Transplanted in a Single Operation   Dr. Andreas Tzakis transplanted seven organs—a liver, pancreas, stomach, large and small intestines, and two kidneys—into a 10-month-old Italian girl during 16 hours of surgery at Jackson Children's Hospital in Miami, Florida, on March 23, 1997. The girl suffered from megacystismicrocolon syndrome, a rare congenital defect that interferes with the body's ability to absorb nutrients.

Youngest Patient to Undergo a Transplant   On November 8, 1996, one-hour-old Cheyenne Pyle became the youngest patient ever to undergo a transplant when she received a donor heart at Jackson Children's Hospital in Miami, Florida. The six-hour operation, performed by Dr. Richard Perryman, involved draining Cheyenne's blood and cooling her body to 62.6°F, the temperature at which organs cease to function. Dr. Perryman then had to complete the transplant within an hour to prevent damage to her other organs. Cheyenne's new heart was the size of a Ping-Pong ball.

Youngest Patient to Undergo a Liver Transplant   The youngest patient to undergo a liver transplant was Baebhen Schuttke, who was just five days old when she received part of a 10-year-old child's liver in August 1997. Baebhen suffered liver failure 24 hours after her birth. She was flown to King's College Hospital in London, England, where surgeon Mohammed Rela led the delicate seven-hour operation to transplant a single

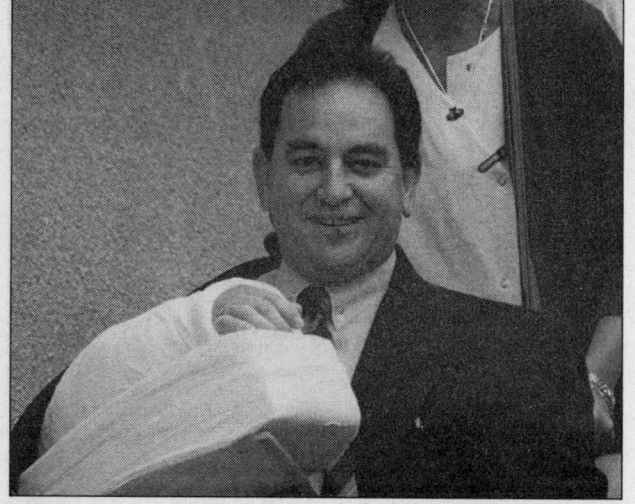

EARLIEST HAND TRANSPLANT   On September 24, 1998, an international team of eight surgeons in Lyon, France, performed the world's first hand transplant ever when they stitched the hand of a dead man to the wrist of 48-year-old Australian Clint Hallam (pictured above). Hallam had lost his hand in a chain saw accident nine years earlier. It takes about 12 months to establish whether or not such a transplant is successful.

GREATEST DISTANCE BETWEEN DOCTOR AND PATIENT Dr. Daniel Carlin of Boston, Massachusetts, is pictured with a photograph of Russian yachtsman Victor Yazykov, whose life he saved with the help of the Internet. Yazykov was taking part in a solo around-the-world yacht race in November 1998 when he developed an abscess under the skin of his elbow. Fearing that the abscess could burst and eventually kill him, Carlin sent him an E-mail telling him how to cut and drain it. Yazykov performed the operation successfully, but the bleeding continued. Carlin discovered that Yazykov was taking aspirin, which acts as an anticoagulant. When Yazykov stopped taking it, the wound stopped bleeding. A few days later, he sailed into Cape Town, South Africa, 9,906 miles from Boston.

lobe from the donor liver into her body. For two weeks, the surgical wound was left open, covered by a dressing, until the liver had shrunk to the correct size. She has now fully recovered.

Least Blood Transfused During a Transplant Operation In June 1996, a transplant team led by surgeon Stephen Pollard from St. James' University Hospital in Leeds, England, performed a liver transplant on 47-year-old housewife Linda Pearson without any blood being transfused. Such an operation usually requires 4–6 pints of blood, but Pearson is a Jehovah's Witness and therefore cannot receive any blood that is not her own. The surgeons operated slowly, keeping incisions small to minimize blood loss. In addition, Pearson had been prepared for the operation by having daily injections of the hormone erythropoietin, which allowed her to sustain a greater blood loss than normal by stimulating the production of her red blood cells. The surgeons had agreed with a Jehovah's Witness liaison team that, even if the patient's life was under threat during the operation, no blood would be given to her.

Youngest Recipient of Two Donor Hearts In 1992, Sophie Parker, then two years old, underwent a seven-hour operation at Harefield Hospital in London, England, to give her a donor heart to complement her weak natural heart. The operation was performed by Dr. Ashgar Khaghani, who arranged the two hearts in a piggyback fashion. In March 1998, it became evident that Sophie's natural heart was no longer functioning properly, so it was replaced with a second donor heart in another operation at Harefield. Sophie thus became the youngest transplant patient to receive two donor hearts.

Earliest Brain Cell Transplant   The first brain cell transplant ever was performed by a team of doctors from the University of Pittsburgh Medical Center in Pennsylvania, on June 23, 1998. The aim of the operation was to reverse the damage caused by a stroke to 62-year-old Alma Cerasini, who had suffered paralysis of her right arm and leg and the loss of most of her speech. The team has subsequently performed 11 more operations of this type.

Earliest Artificial Heart Transplant   From December 1 to 2, 1982, Dr. William DeVries performed the first artificial heart transplant ever, on Dr. Barney Clark at the Utah Medical Center in Salt Lake City, Utah. The new "heart" was a Jarvik 7, designed by Dr. Robert Jarvik. Clark survived until March 23, 1983.

Most Successful Bionic Arm   In 1993, bioengineers at the Margaret Rose Hospital in Edinburgh, Scotland, created a new arm for hotel owner Campbell Aird, who had had his right arm amputated in 1982 after he developed muscular cancer. Called the Edinburgh Modular Arm System, the limb is packed with microchips, position control circuits, miniature motors, gears, and pulleys. It rotates at the shoulder and wrist, bends at the elbow, and can grip using artificial fingers. When Aird wants to move the arm, an array of microsensors inside a special cap allow him to do so by picking up electrical pulses sent by his brain.

Earliest Cyberclinic   In March 1997, clinical psychologist Dr. Kimberley Young (US) established the Virtual Clinic, the world's first psychiatric cybercenter for Internet addicts and those with related mental health problems. Dr. Young aims, via the Internet, to provide help for people experiencing such things as addiction to the Web, troublesome E-mail affairs, and Star Trek addiction, as well as more conventional mental health problems like depression and anxiety. Dr. Young's clinic can be found at www.netaddiction.com/clinic.htm/.

ZOOLOGY 1

Biggest Animal   The blue whale (*Balaenoptera musculus*) weighs 3 tons at birth and reaches an average weight of 26 tons by the age of 12 months. A record-breaking 209-ton, 90-ft.-6-in.-long female blue whale was caught in 1947.

Tallest Mammal   Male giraffes (*Giraffa camelopardis*) grow to a height of about 18 ft. The tallest specimen on record was a 19-ft.-tall Masai bull (*Giraffa camelopardis tippelskirchi*) named George, who died in Chester Zoo in England in 1969.

Smallest Mammal   The smallest specimens of the bumblebee, or Kitti's hog-nosed, bat (*Craesonycteris thonglongyai*), found in limestone caves on the Kwae Noi River in Kanchanaburi Province, Thailand, have a head–body length of $1^7/_{50}$ in. and a wingspan of about $5^1/_{10}$ in. They weigh $^3/_{50}$ oz.

SLOWEST MAMMAL The three-toed sloth (*Bradypus tridactylus*) of tropical South America has an average ground speed of between 6 and 8 ft. per minute, or $^7/_{100}$–$^1/_{10}$ mph. In the trees, it can accelerate to 15 ft. per minute, or $^{17}/_{100}$ mph.

Biggest Primate The biggest primates are the male eastern lowland gorillas (*Gorilla gorilla graueri*) found in the eastern Congo (formerly Zaire). They have a bipedal standing height of 5 ft. 9 in. and weigh 360 lb.

Smallest Primate The smallest true primate (excluding tree shrews, which are normally classified separately) is the pygmy mouse lemur (*Microcebus myoxinus*), which has recently been rediscovered in the deciduous forests of western Madagascar. It has a head–body length of about $2^2/_5$ in., a tail length of $5^2/_5$ in., and an average weight of $1^1/_{10}$ oz.

Longest-Lived Primate The greatest age recorded for a nonhuman primate is 59 years 5 months, for a chimpanzee (*Pan troglodytes*) named Gamma, who died at the Yerkes Primate Research Center in Atlanta, Georgia, on February 19, 1992. Gamma was born at the Florida branch of the Yerkes Center in September 1932.

Longest-Lived Monkey The world's oldest monkey, a male white-throated capuchin (*Cebus capucinus*) named Bobo, died on July 10, 1988, at age 53 years.

Biggest Rodent The capybara (*Hydrochaerus hydrochaeris*) of northern South America has a head-and-body length of 3 ft. 3 in.–4 ft. 3 in. and can weigh up to 174 lb. One cage-fat specimen weighed 250 lb.

Smallest Rodent Several species compete for the title of smallest rodent in the world. The northern pygmy mouse (*Baiomys taylori*) of Mexico and of Arizona and Texas and the Baluchistan pygmy jerboa (*Salpingotulus michaelis*) of Pakistan both have a head–body length of as little as 1²/₅ in. and a tail length of 2⁴/₅ in.

Longest-Lived Rodent   The greatest age reported for a rodent is 27 years 3 months, for a Sumatran crested porcupine (*Hystrix brachyura*) that died in Washington, DC, on January 12, 1965.

Longest Hibernation by a Rodent   Arctic ground squirrels (*Spermophilus parryi*) living in northern Canada and Alaska hibernate for nine months of the year.

Biggest Pinniped   The largest of the 34 known species of pinniped is the southern elephant seal (*Mirounga leonina*) of the subantarctic islands. Bulls average 16 ft. 6 in. in length from the tip of the inflated snout to the tips of the outstretched tail flippers, have a maximum girth of 12 ft., and weigh about 2–3.5 tons. The largest accurately measured specimen of the elephant seal was a bull that weighed at least 4 tons and measured 21 ft. 4 in. after flensing (stripping of the blubber or skin). Its original length was estimated to be about 22 ft. 6 in. It was killed at Possession Bay, South Georgia, on February 28, 1913.

MOST EXPENSIVE RETURN TO THE WILD   The return of the orca whale Keiko to a near-natural environment has cost the Free Willy Keiko Foundation over $22 million. The star of the film *Free Willy* (1993) was captured off the coast of Iceland in the late 1970s and kept in a cramped tank in Mexico until 1996, when he was taken to a $7.3-million saltwater tank with a giant-screen color television in Newport, Oregon—an operation that cost $10 million overall. In September 1998, he was returned to a $12-million soccer-field-sized pen off the Westmann Islands, Iceland, with mesh sides to allow fish in and a clear plastic bottom.

MOST ENDANGERED FELINE
The most endangered feline is the Sumatran tiger (*Panthera tigris*), of which there are only about 20 specimens in the wild. The species is expected to become extinct in the near future, following the Caspian tiger, which died out in the 1970s, and the Bali tiger, which disappeared in the 1940s. As with most endangered mammals, the main threats to tigers' survival are hunting and loss of natural habitat.

Smallest Pinniped   The smallest pinniped is the Galapagos fur seal (*Arctocephalus galapagoensis*). Adult females average 3 ft. 11 in. in length and weigh about 60 lb. Males are usually considerably larger, averaging 4 ft. 11 in. in length and weighing about 141 lb.

Biggest Bird   The largest living bird is the ostrich (*Struthio camelus*). Male examples of this flightless subspecies can be up to 9 ft. tall and weigh 345 lb.

Smallest Bird   The smallest bird is the bee hummingbird (*Mellisuga helenae*) of Cuba and the Isle of Pines, South Carolina. Males measure 2¼ in. in total length—half of which is taken up by the bill and tail—and weigh ⁷/₁₂₅ oz. Females are slightly larger.

Rarest Bird   In the wild, Spix's macaw (*Cyanopsitta*

MOST EXPERT TOOL USER
Chimpanzees (*Pan troglodytes*) can make and use tools with greater expertise than any other mammal except humans: they use straw and twigs to extract termites; branches to investigate out-of-reach objects; stones to hammer open hard-shelled nuts; pointed sticks to pry pieces of nut from shells; and leaves as cloths to remove dirt from their bodies and as sponges to obtain water.

spixii) is as rare as it is possible to be without actually becoming extinct. Ornithologists searching for the bird in 1990 managed to locate only one survivor, believed to be a male, living in a remote corner of northeastern Brazil. The only hope for its survival now lies in one of the 31 or so individuals known to be in captivity.

Longest Feathers   The longest feathers grown by any bird are those of the Phoenix fowl, or Yokohama chicken (a strain of the red jungle fowl *Gallus gallus*), which has been bred in southwestern Japan for ornamental purposes since the mid-17th century. In 1972, a tail covert measuring 34 ft. 9½ in. was reported for a rooster owned by Masasha Kubota of Kochi, Shikoku, Japan.

ZOOLOGY 2

Heaviest Insect   The heaviest insects are the Goliath beetles (family Scarabaeidae) of equatorial Africa. The largest are *Goliathus regius, G. meleagris, G. goliathus* (=*G. giganteus*), and *G. druryi*. In measurements of one series of males (females are smaller), the lengths from the tips of the small frontal horns to the end of the abdomen were 4⅓ in., with weights of 2½–3½ oz.

BIGGEST SPIDER   The largest known spider is the goliath bird-eating spider (*Theraphosa leblondi*), mainly found in the coastal rain forests of northeast South America. Two specimens with leg spans of 11 in. have been reported: one found in Rio Cavro, Venezuela, in April 1965; and one bred by Robert Bustard of Alyth, Scotland, that was measured in February 1998.

MOST DESTRUCTIVE INSECT The most destructive insect is the desert locust (*Schistocerca gregaria*) of Africa and western Asia. Certain weather conditions can induce swarms that devour almost all vegetation in their path. In one day, 50 million locusts can eat food that would sustain 500 people for a year. Moroccan villagers are pictured with a day's catch of dead insects.

Longest Insect The longest recorded insect in the world is *Pharnacia kirbyi*, a stick insect from the rain forests of Borneo. The longest known specimen is in the Natural History Museum in London, England. It has a body length of 1 ft. 9/10 in. and a total length, including the legs, of 1 ft. 9½ in. In the wild, this species is often found with some legs missing, because they are so long and easily trapped when the insect sheds its skin.

Oldest Insects The longest-lived insects are the splendor beetles (family Buprestidae). A specimen of *Buprestis aurulenta* appeared in 1983 in a house in Prittlewell, Essex, England, after at least 51 years as a larva.

Fastest Flying Insect The highest maintainable airspeed of any insect, including deer botflies (*Cephenemyia pratti*), hawkmoths (*Sphingidae*), horseflies (*Tabanus bovinus*), and some tropical butterflies (*Hesperiidae*), is 24 mph. The fastest flying insect is the Australian dragonfly (*Austrophlebia costalis*), which can reach 36 mph in short bursts.

Fastest Land Insect The fastest insects on land are large tropical cockroaches of the family Dictyoptera. The record is 3.36 mph, or 50 body lengths per second, registered by *Periplaneta americana* at the University of California at Berkeley in 1991.

Loudest Insect The African cicada (*Brevisana brevis*) produces a calling song with a mean sound pressure level of 106.7 decibels at a distance of 1 ft. 7½ in. These songs play a vital role in cicada communication and reproduction.

Biggest Butterfly The largest butterfly is the Queen Alexandra's birdwing (*Ornithoptera alexandrae*) of Papua New Guinea. Females can have a wingspan exceeding 11 in. and weigh over 9/10 oz.

BIGGEST LIZARD Male Komodo dragons (*Varanus komodoensis*) average 7 ft. 5 in. in length and weigh about 130 lb. A Komodo on display in St. Louis, Missouri, in 1937 was a record 10 ft. 2 in. long and weighed 365 lb. The species is found on the Indonesian islands of Komodo, Rintja, Padar, and Flores. A specimen is pictured with naturalist Terry Fredering (US).

Biggest Fish The largest fish is the rare plankton-feeding whale shark (*Rhincodon typus*), found in the Atlantic, Pacific, and Indian Oceans. The largest recorded example was 41 ft. 6 in. long, measured 23 ft. around the thickest part of the body, and weighed an estimated 15–21 tons. It was captured off Baba Island, near Karachi, Pakistan, on November 11, 1949.

Shortest Fish The shortest recorded marine fish—and the shortest vertebrate—is the dwarf goby (*Trimmatom nanus*) of the Indo-Pacific. Average lengths recorded during a 1978/79 expedition were $1/3$ in. for males and $7/20$ in. for females.

Fastest Fish The cosmopolitan sailfish (*Istiophorus platypterus*) is considered the fastest species of fish over short distances, although practical difficulties make measurements extremely difficult to secure. In a series of speed trials at the Long Key Fishing Camp in Florida, one sailfish took out 300 ft. of fishing line in three seconds, which is equivalent to a velocity of 68 mph.

Biggest Starfish The largest of the 1,600 known species of starfish is the very fragile brisingid *Midgardia xandaros*. A specimen collected by a team from Texas A&M University in the Gulf of Mexico in 1968 measured 4 ft. 6 in. from tip to tip, but its disc was only 1 in. in diameter.

Smallest Starfish The smallest known starfish is the asterinid sea star *Patiriella parvivipara* discovered by Wolfgang Zeidler on the west coast of the Eyre peninsula in South Australia in 1975. It has a diameter of less than $7/20$ in.

Biggest Amphibians The largest amphibians are the giant salamanders (family Cryptobranchidae), of which there are three species. The record holder is the Chinese giant salamander (*Andrias davidianus*), which lives in mountain streams in northeastern, central, and southern China. One record-breaking specimen collected in Hunan Province measured 5 ft. 11 in. in length and weighed 143 lb.

Biggest Chelonian   The largest chelonian is the leatherback turtle (*Dermochelys coriacea*), which averages 6–7 ft. from the tip of the beak to the end of the tail (carapace 5–5 ft. 6 in.) and about 7 ft. across the front flippers and weighs up to 1,000 lb. The largest leatherback ever recorded is a male found dead on a beach in Gwynedd, Wales, on September 23, 1988. It measured 9 ft. 5½ in. over the carapace and 9 ft. across the front flippers and weighed 2,120 lb.

Biggest Marine Crustacean   The largest crustacean is the *taka-ashi-gani*, or giant spider crab (*Macrocheira kaempferi*). The biggest specimen had a record claw span of 12 ft. 1½ in. and weighed 40 lb.

Biggest Freshwater Crustacean   The largest freshwater crustacean is the crayfish, or crawfish (*Astacopsis gouldi*), found in Tasmania, Australia. Specimens of up to 2 ft. in length have been measured, possibly weighing as much as 9 lb.

Biggest Jellyfish   An Arctic giant (*Cyanea capillata arctica*) of the northwestern Atlantic that washed up in Massachusetts Bay in 1870 had a bell diameter of 7 ft. 6 in. and tentacles stretching 120 ft.

Biggest Land Gastropod   The largest known land gastropod is the African giant snail (*Achatina achatina*), the largest recorded specimen of which measured 15½ in. from snout to tail when fully extended (shell length 10¾ in.) in December 1978 and weighed 2 lb. It was collected in Sierra Leone in June 1976 and was named Gee Geronimo by its owner, Christopher Hudson (UK).

ACHIEVEMENT

STRENGTH

Great Displays of Human Strength   On June 20, 1997, Otto Acron stopped two Cessna 300-hp airplanes from taking off in opposite directions for more than 15 seconds at Hervey Bay, Queensland, Australia.

David Huxley single-handedly pulled a 170-ton Qantas Boeing 747-400 a distance of 298 ft. 6 in. across the tarmac at Sydney Airport, Australia, in October 1997.

Grant Edwards of Sydney, Australia, single-handedly pulled a 182-ton train a distance of 120 ft. 9 in. along a railroad track at the NSW Rail Transport Museum, Thirlmere, Australia, on April 4, 1996.

Juraj Barbaric single-handedly pulled a 327-ton train a record distance of 25 ft. 3 in. along a railroad track at Kosice, Slovakia, on May 25, 1996.

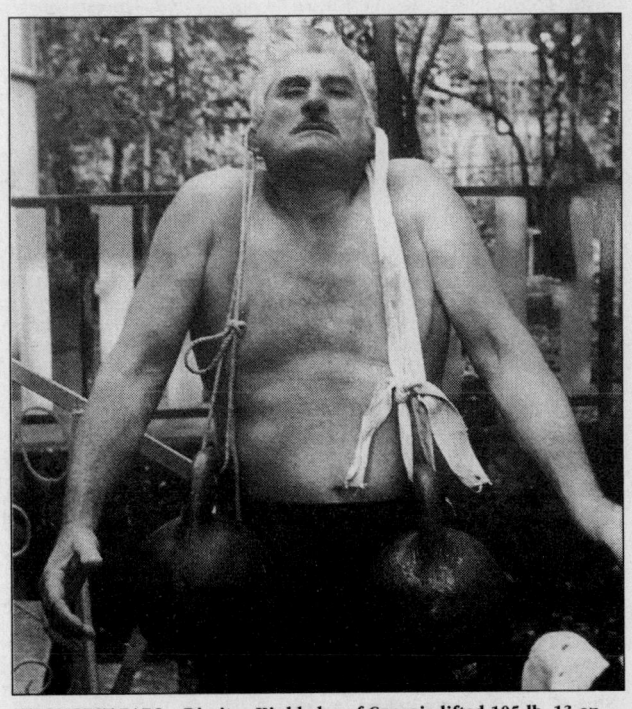

STRONGEST EARS   Dimitry Kinkladze of Georgia lifted 105 lb. 13 oz. with his ears—a 70-lb.-9-oz. weight hung from the left ear and a 35-lb.-4-oz. weight from the right ear—for 10 minutes at Batumi, Georgia, on November 2, 1997.

Maurice Catarcio (US) became the oldest person to pull a passenger vessel on September 12, 1998, at the age of 69 years 6 months. Catarcio pulled the *Silver Bullet* (40 tons dwt) with a total of 125 people on board a distance of 300 ft., using only his feet for propulsion, in Sunset Lake, New Jersey.

Yuri Scherbina, a power juggler from Ukraine, threw a 35-lb.-4$^1/_2$-oz. weight ball from hand to hand 100 times on Mount Elbrus at an altitude of 13,800 ft. in July 1995.

Khalil Oghaby (Iran) lifted an elephant weighing about 2 tons off the ground using a harness and platform at Gerry Cottle's Circus, United Kingdom, in 1975.

Greatest Lift Using Teeth   Walter Arfeuille of Ieper-Vlamertinge, Belgium, lifted weights totaling 620 lb. 10 oz. a record 6¾ in. off the ground with his teeth in Paris, France, on March 31, 1990.

Greatest Pull Using Teeth   Robert Galstyan of Masis, Armenia, pulled two railroad cars a distance of 23 ft. along a railroad track with his teeth at Shcherbinka, Moscow, Russia, on July 21, 1992. The cars weighed a total of 199 tons.

Fastest Beer Keg Lifter   Tom Gaskin lifted a 137-lb.-8-oz. keg of beer above his head 902 times in six hours at Liska House, Newry, Northern Ireland, on October 26, 1996.

Greatest Distance Covered While Carrying Beer Steins   Duane Osborn covered a record distance of 49 ft. 2½ in. while holding five full steins of beer in each hand in a time of 3.65 seconds. He was participating in a contest held on July 10, 1992, at Cadillac, Michigan.

Greatest Distance Covered While Carrying a Brick   The greatest distance over which a brick weighing 10 lb. has been carried in a designated ungloved hand in an uncradled downward pincers grip is 77 miles 880 yd., by Paddy Doyle (UK), who traveled from Birmingham to Lower Shuckburgh, England, and back, from February 11 to 12, 1998.

Greatest Weight of Bricks Lifted   The record for the greatest weight of bricks lifted belongs to Fred Burton of Cheadle, England, who held 20 bricks weighing a record total of 226 lb. 7 oz. for two seconds on June 5, 1998.

Most Bricks Lifted   In 1992, Russell Bradley of Worcester, England, lifted a record 31 bricks—laid side by side—from a table and held them at chest height for two seconds.

Most Bricks Balanced on Head   John Evans (UK) balanced 101 bricks weighing 416 lb. on his head for 10 seconds on the National Lottery program on December 24, 1997.

Most Milk Crates Balanced on Head   In 1997, John Evans (UK) balanced 95 crates, each weighing 3 lb., on his head for 10 seconds at Kerr Street Green, Northern Ireland.

Strongest Hod Carrier   On November 20, 1993, Russell Bradley from Worcester, England, carried bricks with a combined weight of 582 lb. in a

GREATEST WEIGHT BENCH-PRESSED James Henderson (US) holds the world powerlifting record for the bench-press in the 125+ kg class, lifting 322.5 kg in 1997. Pictured is Anthony Clarke, the 1994 record-holder, who is also able to push a 3-ton elephant around in a wheelbarrow and lift cars off their back wheels with ease.

hod (trough for carrying bricks) weighing 105 lb. 13 oz. for 16 ft. 5 in. before climbing to a height of 8 ft. 2 in. This made a total weight of 687 lb. 13 oz.

Most Milk Crates Balanced on Chin Terry Cole (UK) balanced 29 milk crates on his chin for a specified minimum time of 10 seconds on May 16, 1994.

Fastest Coal-Carrying Marathon Brian Newton of Leicester, England, covered 26 miles 385 yd. carrying a 112-lb. open bag of household coal in 8 hr. 26 min. on May 27, 1983.

Greatest Field Gun Pull Three teams of eight men from the British Army's 72 Ordnance Company (V) RAOC pulled a 25-lb. field gun 110 miles 1,041 yd. in 24 hours at Donnington, England, from April 2 to 3, 1993. The field gun pull is a traditional military test of strength, discipline, and teamwork.

Heaviest Wheelbarrow Pushed The heaviest loaded one-wheeled wheelbarrow pushed for a minimum distance of 200 ft. weighed 3.75 tons

HEAVIEST CAR BALANCED ON HEAD   John Evans (UK) is pictured here balancing a Nissan on his head at the Great World City Shopping Center in Singapore. Evans is the current holder of the record for balancing a car on one's head, having balanced a Chevrolet weighing 350 lb. for 12 seconds at the Master Locksmith pub in Derby, England, on November 4, 1997. Evans is the holder of many strength-related Guinness records and makes regular appearances on *Guinness® World Records* TV shows. He claims to have the strongest neck in the world and has offered $3,315 to anybody who breaks one of his records.

gross. It was pushed 243 ft. by John Sarich at London, Ontario, Canada, on February 19, 1987.

Most Tires Supported   Gary Windebank of Romsey, England, supported 96 car tires weighing 1,440 lb. in February 1984.

Greatest Display of Lung Power   In 1994, Nicholas Mason of Manchester, England, inflated a balloon weighing 2 lb. 3 oz. to a diameter of 8 ft. in 45 min. 2.5 sec.

Heaviest Harrijasoketa Lift   Mieltxo Saralegi took 18 seconds to lift a rectangular stone weighing 721 lb. at Anoeta sports arena, San Sebastián (Donostia), Spain, on February 7, 1998. Harrijasoketa is an ancient Basque sport.

SKILL

Most Boomerangs Caught   Lawrence West from Basingstoke, England, threw and caught a boomerang 20 times in one minute at the Indoor Boomerang Throwing Competition held on BBC TV's *Tomorrow's World* on March 20, 1998.

Longest Non-Stop Sepak Takraw Ball Juggling   Ahmad Tajuddin from Malaysia juggled a sepak takraw ball (a ball made of cane) for three hours non-stop in September 1996. He juggled the ball 10,000 times with his right foot without letting it touch the ground.

Most Flaming Torches Juggled   Anthony Gatto (US) juggled seven flaming torches at the International Jugglers Association Festival in Baltimore, Maryland, in July 1989.

Fastest Pool Table Clearance   The fastest time for potting all 15 standard pool balls on a standard table is 26.5 seconds, by Dave Pearson (UK). He performed the feat at Pepper's Bar & Grill, Windsor, Ontario, Canada, on April 4, 1997.

Tallest Tower of Plates   On February 9, 1999, during *La Fiesta Magistral Ultra* at Mar del Plata, Buenos Aires, Argentina, a 195-ft. 10-in. high tower of plates was constructed. It consisted of 10,038 plates and also holds the record for the most plates washed up at one time. Just one pint bottle of dishwashing liquid was used to clean all the plates.

Most Dominoes Stacked   Ralf Laue of Leipzig, Germany, successfully stacked 529 dominoes on a single supporting domino on June 26, 1997, at the Ramada Hotel, Linz, Austria.

MOST SWORDS SWALLOWED   **Bradley Byers of Idaho swallowed nine 27-in. swords on the TV show *Guinness® World Records: Primetime* on October 16, 1998. The women's record is held by Amy Saunders (UK), who swallowed five swords between 14 in. and 20 in. in length on the British show *Guinness® World Records* on April 28, 1999.**

GREATEST WEIGHT BALANCED ON TEETH On April 28, 1999, Frank Simon from Key West, Florida, balanced a motorbike weighing 135 lb. on his teeth for 14.5 seconds on the British TV show *Guinness® World Records*. He balanced the bike on its kickstand and did not use a special mouth guard—his only concession to protecting his mouth was a piece of cloth covering his teeth. In doing so, he broke his own record, set on *Guinness® World Records: Primetime* on November 20, 1998, when he balanced a motorbike weighing 129 lb. for 15.25 seconds. He also balanced a number of other objects on his teeth during the show, including a stove and a refrigerator.

Most Eggs Balanced The most eggs balanced on end simultaneously on a flat surface by one person is 210, by Kenneth Epperson of Monroe, Georgia, on September 23, 1990.

The most eggs simultaneously balanced by a group is 467 by a class at Bayfield School, Colorado, on March 20, 1986.

Longest Egg Throw Johnny Dell Foley threw a fresh hen's egg a distance of 323 ft. 2 in. without breaking it on November 12, 1978, at Jewett, Texas. The egg was caught by Keith Thomas.

Longest Flying Disc Throws The World Flying Disc (frisbee) Federation distance record for men is 693 ft. 4 in., achieved by Scott Stokely (US) on April 5, 1998, in Kingston, New Mexico.

The official flying disc distance record for women is 447 ft. 3 in., by Anni Kreml (US) at Fort Collins, Colorado, on August 21, 1994.

Longest Cowpat Throw The greatest distance that a cowpat has ever been thrown under the "non-sphericalization and 100% organic" rule is 266 ft., by Steve Urner at the Mountain Festival, Tehachapi, California, on August 14, 1981.

Longest Gum Boot Throws A size 8½ Challenger Dunlop boot was thrown a record distance of 209 ft. 9 in. by Teppo Luoma in Hämeenlinna, Finland, on October 12, 1996.

The women's record for the longest gum boot throw is 134 ft. 1 in., by Sari Tirkkonen at Turku, Finland, on April 19, 1996.

Longest Spear Throw   The farthest that a spear has been thrown using an atlatl, a handheld device that fits onto it, is 848 ft. 6½ in., by David Engvall at Aurora, Colorado, on July 15, 1995.

Youngest Cider-Pouring Champion   Jorge Alberto Ramos became the youngest-ever champion *escanciador* (cider pourer) at the age of 19 in 1998 when he won the annual Concurso de Escanciadores in Nava, Asturias, Spain. Each participant has to pour the contents of a cider bottle (23.7 fl. oz.) into five glasses, each of which has to contain 4.4 fl. oz. of cider. The competitor has to leave a maximum of 1.7 fl. oz. of cider in the bottle after pouring.

Longest Bubble   Alan McKay of Wellington, New Zealand, created a 105-ft.-long bubble on August 9, 1996. He used a bubble wand, dishwashing liquid, glycerine, and water.

Largest Bubble Wall   Fan-Yang of Mississauga, Ontario, Canada, created a 156-ft. bubble wall with an area of about 4,000 ft.² at the Kingdome Pavilion, Seattle, Washington, on August 11, 1997. The bubble stayed up continuously for between 5 and 10 seconds.

Biggest Bubble Gum Bubble
The greatest reported diameter of a bubble gum bubble is 23 in. It was blown by Susan Montgomery Williams of Fresno, California, at the ABC-TV studios in New York City on July 19, 1994.

Fastest Straight-Razor Shaver
The record for the most people shaved with a straight razor in 60 minutes is 278, by Tom Rodden of Chatham, England on November 10, 1993, for BBC TV's *Record Breakers* show. Averaging 12.9 seconds per face, he drew blood seven times.

Fastest Safety-Razor Shaver
The fastest barber using a retractable safety razor to shave is Denny Rowe (UK), who shaved

GREATEST WEIGHT BALANCED ON A KNIFE   Ali Bandbaz balanced his brother Massoud on two 14½-in. daggers with a tip width of only ³/₈ in. on *Guinness® World Records: Primetime* on November 20, 1998. The brothers, from Tehran, Iran, placed the daggers in their mouths, and Massoud, who weighs 150 lb., was balanced unaided for 29 seconds. The feat had never been attempted before.

1,994 men in 60 minutes at Herne Bay, England, on June 19, 1988. He took an average of 1.8 seconds to shave each person and drew blood just four times.

Greatest Grape Catch   The greatest-ever distance at which a grape thrown from level ground has been caught in the mouth is 327 ft. 6 in. by Paul Tavilla at East Boston, Massachusetts, on May 27, 1991. The grape was thrown by James Deady.

Longest Spits   The greatest recorded distance that a cherry pit has been spit is 95 ft. 1 in., by Horst Ortmann at Langenthal, Germany, on August 27, 1994.

David O'Dell of Apple Valley, California, spit a wad of tobacco a record distance of 53 ft. 3 in. at the 22nd World Tobacco Spitting Championships at Calico Ghost Town, California, in March 1997.

The greatest distance that a watermelon seed has been spit is 75 ft. 2 in., by Jason Schayot at De Leon, Texas, on August 12, 1995.

Fastest Talkers   Sean Shannon (Canada) recited Hamlet's "To Be or Not to Be" soliloquy (260 words) in a time of 23.8 seconds (equivalent to 655 words per minute) in Edinburgh, Scotland, on August 30, 1995.

Steve Briers (UK) recited the lyrics of Queen's album *A Night at the Opera* backward at Tenby, Wales, in 9 min. 58.44 sec. on February 6, 1990.

Most Beer Coasters Flipped   Dean Gould (UK) flipped a pile of 111 beer coasters (consisting of 0.04-in.-thick wood-pulp board) through an angle of 180° and caught them at Edinburgh, Scotland, on January 13, 1993.

Most Playing Cards Identified   Jim Karol successfully identified 15 playing cards randomly selected by 15 different people from one deck of cards in one minute on December 10, 1998. A line of students took turns to select a card from Karol, which he then identified without them showing him the card. Karol, of Clinton, New York, set the record at Springfield College, Massachusetts.

ENDURANCE

Longest Backward Unicycle   Ashrita Furman (US) rode a unicycle backward for a distance of 53 miles 299 yd. at Forest Park, New York, on September 16, 1994.

Longest Barrel Roll   A team of 10 people from Tecza sports club, Lódz, Poland, rolled a 140-lb. barrel a distance of 124 miles 598 yd. in 24 hours from September 1 to 2, 1995.

Greatest Distance Covered on a Pogo Stick   Ashrita Furman (US) set a distance record of 23 miles 182 yd. in 12 hr. 27 min. at Queensborough Community College Track, New York, on June 22, 1997.

MOST "BLINDFOLD" CHESS WINS
In January 1947, in São Paulo, Brazil, Miguel Najdorf (Argentina) played 45 simultaneous chess games over 23 hr. 25 min. against some of the best players in Brazil. He sat in a separate room from his opponents and never saw the boards, speaking his moves into a microphone. He won 39, drew four, and lost only two. Najdorf was at a chess tournament in Argentina when the Germans invaded his native Poland in 1939, and he soon became an Argentinian citizen. He died in July 1997 at the age of 87.

Longest Bathtub Push The greatest distance covered in 24 hours pushing a wheeled bathtub with a passenger is 318 miles 1,689 yd. by a team of 25 from Tea Tree Gully Baptist Church, Westfield Shoppingtown Plaza, Australia, from March 11 to 12, 1995.

Longest Crawl The longest continuous voluntary crawl was 31 miles 778 yd. by Peter McKinlay and John Murrie, who crawled a total of 115

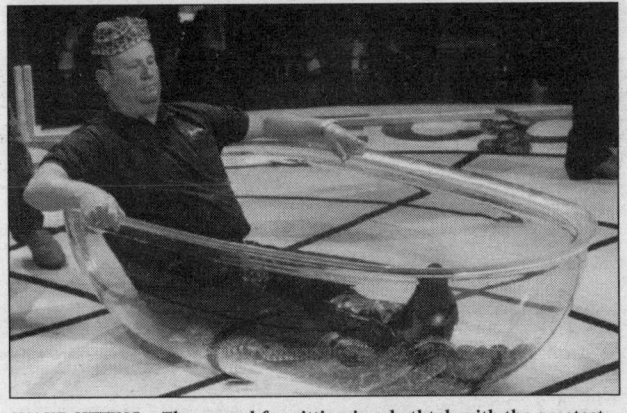

SNAKE SITTING The record for sitting in a bathtub with the greatest number of poisonous snakes is currently held by Jackie Bibby of Fort Worth, Texas, who sat with a total of 35 rattlesnakes on June 17, 1998. The record was broadcast on the television series *Guinness® World Records: Primetime* (above). Bibby has competed at the American National Rattlesnake Sacking Championships, which are held every spring at the Taylor Chamber of Commerce, Texas. He has received numerous awards for his proficiency with snakes, including the Riled Rattlesnake Round-Up Safety Award.

LONGEST RADIO DJ MARATHON The world's longest radio DJ marathon under *The Guinness ® Book of Records* guidelines was achieved by Simon Mayo of BBC Radio 1 in London, England, for the charity Comic Relief. He played records for 37 hours, from 9 am on March 11 to 10 pm on March 12, 1999, with visits from comedians Dawn French and Jennifer Saunders (top left), fellow Radio 1 DJ Zoë Ball (top right), and TV star Terry Wogan (middle left).

laps on an athletics track at Falkirk, Scotland, from March 28 to 29, 1992. *The Guinness ® Book of Records* guidelines state that in a crawling record attempt, either knee must keep unbroken contact with the ground.

Over 15 months ending on March 9, 1985, Jagdish Chander (India) crawled 870 miles from Aligarh to Jammu, India, in order to appease the Hindu goddess Mata.

Longest Kiss Mark and Roberta Griswold from Allen Park, Michigan, kissed continuously for a record 29 hours at the "Breath Savers Longest Kiss Challenge" in New York from March 24 to 25, 1998. The couple remained standing without any rest breaks throughout the attempt to capture the record.

Most People Kissed Alfred Wolfram of Minnesota kissed 11,030 people in eight hours at the Minnesota Renaissance Festival on September 12, 1998—about one every 2.6 seconds.

LONGEST HAND RAISING Amar Bharti of India claims to have kept his right hand raised for 26 years as a gesture of devotion to the Hindu god Shiva. In 1973, he decided to raise his right arm 90° in the air. His fingers have withered into the palm of his hand, his knuckles are white with rot, and his nails have grown long and twisted.

Longest Dance Marathon
The most taxing marathon dance staged as a public spectacle was performed by Mike Ritof and Edith Boudreaux, who logged 5,148 hr. 28 min. 30 sec. to win $2,000 at the Merry Garden Ballroom, Chicago, Illinois, from August 29, 1930, to April 1, 1931. Rest periods were progressively cut from 20 to 10 to five minutes per hour to none. They were permitted to shut their eyes for a maximum of 15 seconds at a time.

Most Step-Ups Terry Heidt completed 3,967 step-ups in an hour at Penticton High School, British Columbia, Canada, on April 18, 1997, using a 15-in.-high exercise bench.

Longest Cardiopulmonary Resuscitation Brent Shelton and John Ash completed a cardiopulmonary resuscitation (CPR) marathon (15 compressions alternating with two breaths) lasting 130 hours from October 28 to November 2, 1991, at Regina, Saskatchewan, Canada.

Longest Clapping Session The record for continuous clapping (defined as sustaining an average 160 claps per minute, audible at 360 ft.) is 58 hr. 9 min. set by V. Jeyaraman of Tamil Nadu, India, from February 12 to 15, 1988.

Most Yo-Yo Loops "Fast" Eddy McDonald of Toronto, Canada, completed 21,663 loops with a yo-yo in three hours on October 14, 1990, in Boston, Massachusetts, having previously set a one-hour speed record of 8,437 loops at Cavendish, Prince Edward Island, Canada, on July 14, 1990.

Longest Time Spent Balancing on One Foot Arulanantham
Suresh Joachim (Sri Lanka) balanced on one foot for a record 76 hr. 40
min. at Uihara Maha Devi Park Open Air Stadium, Sri Lanka, from May
22 to 25, 1997.

Longest Static Wall Sit Rajkumar Chakraborty (India) stayed in an
unsupported sitting position against a wall for 11 hr. 5 min. at Panposh
Sports Hostel, Rourkela, India, on April 22, 1994.

Longest Time Spent Motionless Radhey Shyam Prajapati (India)
stood motionless for 18 hr. 5 min. 50 sec. at Gandhi Bhawan, Bhopal,
India, from January 25 to 26, 1996.

TEAMWORK

Loudest Scream by a Crowd A scream registering 126.3 dB was measured at the Party in the Park pop concert featuring Robbie Williams, Boyzone and All Saints in Hyde Park, London, England, by Trevor Lewis of
CEL Instruments on July 5, 1998.

Biggest Piano Orchestra A total of 96 pianists on 96 pianos performed together at the Old Castle, Koldinghus, Kolding, Denmark, on
May 2, 1996. They were conducted by José Ribera.

LONGEST PAPERCLIP CHAIN A chain of 60,000 paperclips measuring
10 miles 303 yd. was put together by a team of 60 volunteers at
Lympsham First School, Somerset, England, between May 2 and 3, 1998.

BIGGEST SAND CASTLES AND SAND SCULPTURES The world's tallest sand castle (above) was made at Duquoin State Fairground, Illinois, from August 26 to September 2, 1998, by the Totally In Sand team. It was 24 feet tall. Under *The Guinness Book of Records* rules, sand sculptures can be built with mechanical assistance, but builders of sand castles are restricted to using hands, buckets, and spades. The longest ever sand castle was made by staff and pupils of Ellon Academy, Aberdeenshire, Scotland, on March 24, 1988. It was 5 miles 352 yd. long. The world's longest sand sculpture was the GTE Directories Ultimate Sandcastle, built at Myrtle Beach, South Carolina, on May 31, 1991. It stretched 16 miles 686 yd.

Biggest Drum Band On March 15, 1998, a total of 1,700 musicians in Huesca, Spain, formed the largest-ever drum band. The event was organized by the Certamen de Bandas de Huesca.

Biggest Drum Ensemble On August 9, 1998, 1,850 people played the tune "Yamabiko" on 1,845 Japanese drums for 25 minutes at Ire Stadium, Muroran City, Japan.

Longest Human Chain On August 23, 1989, an estimated 1 million people joined hands to form a chain 370 miles long across Estonia, Latvia, and Lithuania. It marked the 50th anniversary of the Russo-German pact that led to the Baltic States' annexation.

Biggest Breakfast   On April 17, 1998, 13,797 people ate a breakfast of Kellogg's cereals at Dubai Creekside Park, United Arab Emirates.

Biggest Coffee Morning   On October 4, 1996, a total of 513,659 people attended 14,652 coffee mornings (a traditional UK gathering) held simultaneously throughout the United Kingdom as part of the Macmillan Cancer Fund Appeal, raising a total of $2.34 million.

Biggest Children's Party   The International Year of the Child party held in Hyde Park, London, England, on May 30–31, 1979, was attended by a record 160,000 children.

Most Kissing Couples   The greatest number of couples to have kissed in the same place at the same time was 1,543 at the Sarnia Sports and Entertainment Center, Ontario, Canada, on February 13, 1999.

Biggest Human Conveyor Belt   On September 7, 1998, 1,000 students formed a human conveyor belt and carried a surfboard over the top at the University of Guelph, Ontario, Canada.

Biggest Dance   An estimated 72,000 people took part in a Chicken Dance during the Canfield Fair in Ohio on September 1, 1996.

Longest Conga   On March 13, 1988, the Miami Super Conga, held in conjunction with Calle Ocho—a Cuban-American celebration of life held in Miami, Florida—consisted of a total of 119,986 people.

Biggest Tap Dance   A record-breaking 6,776 people tap-danced outside Macy's department store in New York City on August 17, 1997.

Biggest Line Dance   On January 25, 1997, in Tamworth, Australia, 5,502 people country line danced to Brooks and Dunn's extended-play version of "Bootscootin' Boogie," which lasts for 6 min. 28 sec.

Biggest "YMCA" Dance   On November 1, 1997, 6,907 students from Southwest Missouri State University danced to the song "YMCA" for five minutes while it was performed live by the group Village People at the University's Plaster Stadium.

Biggest Human Mobile   On August 6, 1998, the Circus of Horrors broke its own record when it created a human mobile out of 20 people in Edinburgh, Scotland.

Most Objects Juggled   On August 7, 1998, a total of 1,508 people juggled 4,524 objects at the European Juggling Convention in Edinburgh, Scotland.

Most Dominoes Toppled   Sixty students at Expo Centrum FEC, Leeuwarden, Netherlands, set up 2.3 million dominoes over a seven-week period. Of these, 1,605,757 fell with one push on August 28, 1998.

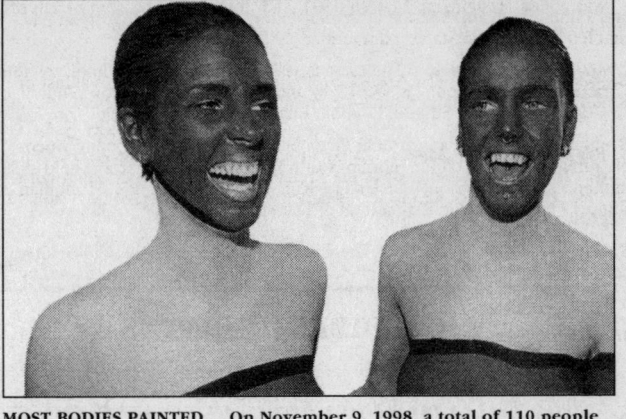

MOST BODIES PAINTED On November 9, 1998, a total of 110 people had their bodies painted for the Living Bridges celebrations held in Rotterdam, Netherlands.

Biggest Game of Pass the Parcel On February 28, 1998, a record 3,918 people (mainly high school students and students from Nanyang Technology University, Singapore) unwrapped 2,200 layers of a parcel that initially measured 4 ft. 11 in. x 4 ft. 11 in. x 1 ft. 7½ in. The entire process took two and a half hours. The prize in the middle of the parcel was a gift certificate for a mobile telephone.

Biggest Game of Musical Chairs The biggest known game of musical chairs started with 8,238 participants and was held at the Anglo-Chinese School, Singapore, on August 5, 1989. Xu Chong Wei sat on the final chair.

Longest Bucket Chain On August 5, 1997, a total of 6,569 boys representing the Boy Scouts of America made a fire-service bucket chain that stretched for a record length of 2 miles 59 yd. as part of the National Scout Jamboree held in Fort A.P. Hills, Virginia. The scouts started with 140 gallons of water and managed to spill only 14 gallons, finishing with 126 gallons.

Longest Daisy Chain The longest-ever daisy chain measured 6,980 ft. 7 in. and was made in seven hours by villagers of Good Easter, Chelmsford, England, on May 27, 1985. The teams are limited to 16 members.

Longest Dancing Dragon On December 21, 1997, a Chinese dancing dragon measuring a record 1 mile 936 yd. was brought to life by 3,760 people at Happy Valley Racecourse, Hong Kong.

Longest Human Centipede On September 2, 1996, 1,665 college students from the University of Guelph, Ontario, Canada, moved 98 ft. 5 in. with their ankles tied together. They all remained upright.

Longest Leapfrog The greatest distance covered by leapfroggers was 996 miles 292 yd. by 14 students from Stanford University, California, who started leapfrogging on May 16, 1991, and stopped 244 hr. 43 min. later on May 26.

Most Shoes Shined   The most shoes ever shined "on the hoof" by four people in eight hours is 14,975 by members of the London Church of Christ at Leicester Square, London, England, on June 15, 1996.

Biggest Origami Model   A paper crane with a wingspan of 207 ft. 9 in. was folded by residents of Atika Prefecture, Odate, Japan, on August 1, 1998. Consisting of 45,156 ft.^{2} of paper, it took 200 people seven hours to create.

INCREDIBLE JOURNEYS

Longest Walk in the Western Hemisphere   George Meegan from Rainham, England, walked 19,019 miles from Ushuaia, the southern tip of South America, to Prudhoe Bay in northern Alaska, in 2,426 days from January 26, 1977, to September 18, 1983. He thus completed the first traverse of the Americas and the Western Hemisphere.

Longest Backward Walk   Plennie Wingo of Abilene, Texas, made an 8,000-mile transcontinental walk from Santa Monica, California, to Istanbul, Turkey, from April 15, 1931, to October 24, 1932.

Longest Backward Run   Arvind Pandya of India ran backward from Los Angeles to New York City in 107 days between August 18 and December 3, 1984, covering more than 3,100 miles. He also ran backward from John O'Groat's, Scotland, to Land's End, England, in a time of 26 days 7 hr. from April 6 to May 2, 1990, covering a total distance of 940 miles.

LONGEST "WALK ON WATER" Rémy Bricka of Paris, France, holds the record for the longest "walk on water" after covering 3,502 miles from Tenerife, Canary Islands, to Trinidad in the Caribbean from April 2 to May 31, 1988. He "walks" with 13-ft.-9-in.-long ski floats attached to his feet, moving in the same way as cross-country skiers do but using a double-headed paddle instead of ski poles.

LONGEST ROLLING JOURNEY Lotan Baba (right), an Indian sadhu (holy man), rolled his body 2,485 miles 973 yd. from Ratlam to Jammu, India, over eight months in 1994. He rolled an average of 6–7 miles and covered a maximum distance of 13 miles per day. The purpose of the rolling journey was to pay homage to the goddess Vaishno Devi to achieve peace and unity for India. During the rolls, Baba did not eat and only took sips of water and smoked the occasional cigarette. His body was covered with blisters after completing the journey to the Vaishno Devi temple on the 5,000-ft. mountain in Katra.

Longest Horse-Drawn Journey The Grant family from the United Kingdom covered a distance of more than 17,200 miles during an around-the-world trip in a horse-drawn caravan. They began their journey at Vierhouten, Netherlands, on October 25, 1990, and returned to the UK early in 1998 after traveling through Belgium, France, Italy, Austria, northern Yugoslavia (which became Slovenia while they were there), Hungary, Russia, the Ukraine, Kazakhstan, Mongolia, China, Japan, the US, and Canada. They sold their house to finance the trip, which cost them $96,000 over seven years.

Longest Unicycle Ride Akira Matsushima from Japan unicycled a record 3,261 miles across the US from Newport, Oregon, to Washington, DC, between July 10 and August 22, 1992.

Longest One-Way Tandem Ride Laura Geoghean and Mark Tong traveled 20,155 miles on a tandem bike from London, England, to Sydney, Australia, from May 21, 1994, to November 11, 1995.

Longest Stilts Walks The greatest distance ever covered on stilts is 3,008 miles, by Joe Bowen from Los Angeles, California, to Bowen, Kentucky, from February 20 to July 26, 1980.

In 1891, Sylvain Dornon walked from Paris, France, to Moscow, Russia, on stilts in either 50 or 58 stages, covering a distance of 1,830 miles at a much greater speed than Bowen's.

Longest Walk on Hands The record for the greatest distance ever covered by a person walking on their hands is 870 miles, by Johann Hurlinger (Austria) in 1900. He walked from Vienna, Austria, to Paris, France, in a total of 55 daily 10-hour stints, averaging a speed of 1.58 mph.

Longest Land Row Rob Bryant of Fort Worth, Texas, covered a total distance of 3,280 miles on a land-rowing machine. Bryant left Los Angeles, California, on April 2, 1990, and reached Washington, DC, on July 30.

Longest Pizza Delivery Route Eagle Boys Dial-a-Pizza in Christchurch, New Zealand, regularly delivers pizzas to Scott Base, Antarctica, for the New Zealand Antarctic Program. The pizzas are cooked, packed, and shipped to a military airfield, where they are then loaded onto a C.130 Hercules. They arrive at the base nine hours later, complete with reheating instructions.

Most Countries Traveled Through in 24 Hours The most countries traveled through entirely by train in 24 hours is 11, by Alison Bailey, Ian Bailey, John English, and David Kellie from May 1 to 2, 1993. They started their journey in Hungary and continued through Slovakia, the Czech Republic, Austria, Germany, Liechtenstein, Switzerland, France, Luxembourg, and Belgium and arrived in the Netherlands 22 hr. 10 min. after setting off.

Longest Journey by Car Since October 16, 1984, Emil and Liliana Schmidt from Switzerland have traveled 300,000 miles through 125 countries in a Toyota Landcruiser.

Longest Taxi Ride The longest taxi ride on record covered a distance of 21,691 miles from London, England, to Cape Town, South Africa, and back, at a cost of $62,908. It was made by Jeremy Levine, Mark Aylett, and Carlos Arrese from June 3 to October 17, 1994.

Longest Journey in a 2CV Between October 9, 1958, and November 12, 1959, Jacques Seguela and Jean-Claude Baudot (both of France) drove 62,139 miles in a Citroën 2CV (AZ), now housed in the Le Mans Motor Museum, France. They drove through 50 countries and crossed five continents. Seguela and Baudot spent 2,247 hours at the wheel and used up 1,321 gallons of gas, achieving an average fuel consumption of 46 mpg.

Longest Journey by Amphibious Car The longest journey in an amphibious car was undertaken by Ben Carlin (Australia) in the amphibious jeep *Half-Safe*. He completed the last leg of the Atlantic crossing (the English Channel) on August 24,1951. He arrived back in Montreal, Canada, on May 8, 1958, having completed 39,000 miles over land and 9,600 miles by sea and river. Carlin was accompanied on the transatlantic stage of the journey by his ex-wife Elinore.

Longest Moped Journey Adam Paul rode a record 48,000 miles from Cape Horn, Chile, to the Cape of Good Hope, South Africa, on a 90cc Honda moped between April 10, 1996, and March 15, 1998.

LONGEST WALK The greatest distance that has ever been walked is 33,151 miles, by Arthur Blessitt of North Fort Myers, Florida. He began his journey on December 25, 1969, and has visited 277 nations. He has carried a large wooden cross with him on his entire journey and has been accompanied by his wife, Denise, to 224 of the countries he has visited.

Longest Paddle-Boat Journey Kenichi Horie of Kobe, Japan, set a paddle-boating distance record of 4,660 miles. He left Honolulu, Hawaii, on October 30, 1992, and arrived at Naha, Okinawa, Japan, on February 17, 1993.

Fastest Transatlantic Row New Zealanders Phil Stubbs and Robert Hamill rowed across the Atlantic Ocean in a record time of 41 days between October 12 and November 22, 1997, starting their journey from Tenerife, Canary Islands, and finishing at Port St. Charles, Barbados. The previous record for rowing across the Atlantic was 73 days, by Britons Sean Crowley and Mike Nestor in 1986.

Longest Lawn-Mower Ride In the summer of 1997, 12-year-old Ryan Tripp made a 3,366-mile journey by lawn mower across the US, raising $10,400 for a sick

baby in his hometown. Beginning in Salt Lake City, Utah, Ryan rode the Walker 25-hp mower along secondary roads approved by police, following a lead car driven by friends and family. Ryan's father, Todd, followed in a pickup truck with an equipment trailer. The mower was fitted with road tires and had extra springs and seat padding to make the trip comfortable for Ryan. Nineteen states and 42 days later, he arrived at the Capitol in Washington, DC, where he was welcomed by Utah senator Orrin Hatch.

Fastest Trans-America Crossing on a Skateboard   Jack Smith (US) skateboarded across the US in 1976 and 1984. The first trip took 32 days to complete with two companions, and the second trip, which he made with three team members, took just 26 days.

RACING

Fastest Tree Climber   The world record for climbing up and down a 100-ft. fir spar pole is 24.82 seconds by Guy German of Sitka, Alaska, on July 3, 1988. His climb was part of the World Championship Timber Carnival held in Albany, Oregon.

Fastest Coconut Tree Climber   The fastest time in which a 29-ft.-6-in.-tall coconut tree has been climbed barefoot is 4.88 seconds by Fuatai Solo of Western Samoa (now Samoa) at the Coconut Tree Climbing Competition (held annually at Sukana Park, Fiji) on August 22, 1980. After being declared the winner for the third time running, Fuatai climbed the tree again, this time clutching the prize money of $100 in his mouth.

Fastest Wool-Sack Racer   Paul Elliot achieved the fastest-ever individual time in the World Woolsack Championships held annually at

BIGGEST PLASTIC DUCK RACE   On May 26, 1997, a record 100,000 yellow plastic ducks raced down a 1,094-yd. stretch of the river Avon, Bath, England. Organizers loaded all the ducks into a container and, at a signal from a cannon at precisely 2 pm, tipped them all into the river. It took 2 hr. 15 min. for duck no. 24,359, owned by Chris Green from Dauntsey, England, to win. With almost half the ducks sponsored at $1.64 each, the event raised nearly $81,910 for the charity Water Aid.

Tetbury, England, with a record 53.05 seconds in 1994. Competitors have to race up and down a steep hill carrying a 60-lb. bag of wool on their shoulders.

Fastest Bog Snorkeler Steve Madeline has won the annual World Bog Snorkeling Championship at Llanwrtyd Wells, Wales, on a record two occasions in 1989 and 1994. Contestants swim two lengths of a 196-ft.-10-in.-long bog filled with weeds, leeches, and newts.

Fastest Wheelbarrow Racers The fastest time taken to complete a 1-mile wheelbarrow race is 4 min. 48.51 sec. by Piet Pitzer and Jaco Erasmus at Transvalia High School, Vanderbijlpark, South Africa, on October 3, 1987.

Fastest Bed Racers The fastest time in the 2-mile 56-yd. Knaresborough Bed Race, Yorkshire, England, is 12 min. 9 sec. by the Vibroplant team in June 1990.

Fastest Bathtub Racer The record time for a 36-mile bathtub race over water is 1 hr. 22 min. 27 sec. by Greg Mutton at the Grafton Jacaranda Festival, Australia, on November 8, 1987.

Fastest Pancake Racer The fastest time ever achieved in the annual 420-yd. pancake race held in Melbourne, Australia, is 59.5 seconds set by Jan Stickland on February 19, 1985.

Fastest Stilt Walker
The fastest stilt walker is Roy Luiking, who cov-

FASTEST STAMP LICKER Diane Sheer of London, England, licked and affixed 225 stamps onto envelopes in a time of five minutes on August 3, 1997. According to *The Guinness® Book of Records* guidelines, one stamp must be gummed securely to the top right-hand corner of each envelope. Stamps are counted if they are placed at an angle but disqualified if they are upside down.

FASTEST SPEED IN A HUMAN-POWERED SUBMARINE   The fastest
speed ever attained by a human-powered propeller submarine is
6.696±0.06 knots by *Substandard*, designed and crewed by William
Nicoloff (US), using a two-blade-propeller propulsion system on
March 30, 1996. The fastest speed recorded for a human-powered non-
propeller submarine is 2.9±0.1 knots by *Subdude*, designed by the
Scripps Institute of Oceanography, University of California, San Diego,
using a horizontal oscillating-foil propulsion system on August 21,
1992. The submarine was crewed by Kimball Millikan and Ed Trevino
with team leader Kevin Hardy.

ered 328 ft. on 1-ft.-high stilts in a record 13.01 seconds at Didam,
Netherlands, on May 28, 1992.

Fastest Speed Marcher   Paddy Doyle marched 1 mile while carrying a
rucksack weighing 40 lb. on his back in a record time of 5 min. 35 sec. at
Ballycotton, Republic of Ireland, on March 7, 1993.

Fastest Bed Maker   The shortest time in which one person has made a
bed is 28.2 seconds by Wendy Wall of Hebersham, Sydney, Australia, on
November 30, 1978.

Fastest Coal Carrier   David Jones carried a 110-lb. bag over the 3,321-
ft. course at Gawthorpe, England, in a record 4 min. 6 sec. in April 1991.

Fastest Coal Shoveler   The record for the fastest time in which a
1,120-lb. hopper has been filled with coal is 26.59 seconds by Wayne Miller
at Wonthaggi, Australia, on April 17, 1995.

Fastest Wife-Carrier   Jouni Jussila carried his wife, Tiina, over the World
Wife-Carrying Championship course—a 771-ft.-long obstacle course that includes chest-high water and two wooden stiles—in a record time of 1 min. 5 sec.
in 1997. It was Jussila's fifth success in the annual contest, which is held in Sonka-
järvi, Finland. The winner takes home gallons of beer equivalent to the weight of
his partner, who need not be his wife but must be over the age of 17 and wear a
crash helmet.

FASTEST BIRD RACES
Ostriches are the fastest birds on land and can run at speeds of up to 45 mph for 30 minutes without rest. Making the most of the birds' speed and size, the annual Rocky Mountain Ostrich Festival, held in Colorado, features ostrich racing as one of its highlights.

Fastest Sack Racer Ashrita Furman of Jamaica, New York, completed a 6-mile-376-yd. sack race in a record time of 1 hr. 25 min. 10 sec. at Mount Rushmore National Park, South Dakota, on August 6, 1998.

Fastest Window Cleaner On March 29, 1999, Terry Burrows of South Ockenden, England, cleaned three standard 45-in.^{2} office windows with 2 gallons of water and a 11¾-in.-long squeegee in only 15.59 seconds on the BBC TV program *Blue Peter*.

Fastest Drummer Rory Blackwell of Starcross, England, played 400 separate drums in a record time of 16.2 seconds on May 29, 1995.

Fastest Inverted Sprinter On February 19, 1994, Mark Kenny of Norwood, Massachusetts, sprinted 164 ft. on his hands in a time of 16.93 seconds.

Fastest Typists Stella Pajunas (now Garnand) typed 216 words in one minute on an IBM machine in Chicago, Illinois.

Gregory Arakelian of Herndon, Virginia, set a speed record of 158 wpm (with two errors) on a PC in the Key Tronic World Invitational Type-Off on September 24, 1991.

Michael Shestov set a numerical record by typing spaced numbers from 1 to 801 (without any errors) in five minutes on a PC in New York City on April 2, 1996.

Fastest Stair Climbers Dennis W. Martz set the record for ascending 100 stories in June 1978, when he climbed the stairs of the Detroit Plaza Hotel in Michigan in a time of 11 min. 23.8 sec.

The fastest time in which the 1,760 steps of the CN Tower in Toronto, Canada—the world's tallest freestanding structure—have been climbed is 7 min. 52 sec. by Brendan Keenoy on October 29, 1989.

Fastest Racing Snail The record holder at the annual World Snail Racing Championships in Congham, England, is Archie, trained by Carl Banham. His best time over the 13-in. course was 2 min. 20 sec.

GOLDEN OLDIES

Oldest People The oldest living person whose date of birth can be verified is Sarah Clark Knauss, who was born on September 24, 1880. Older than the Eiffel Tower, she is from Hollywood, Pennsylvania, and now lives in Allentown, Pennsylvania. She was married in 1901 and has a daughter in her nineties, a grandson, three great-granddaughters, five great-great-grandchildren, and one great-great-great-grandson.

The oldest person for whom there is irrefutable evidence was Jeanne

OLDEST BARTENDER Angelo Cammarata is seen taking a break behind his bar in Pittsburgh, Pennsylvania. The 85-year-old, who is known as "Camm" to his customers and neighbors, is the world's oldest bartender. He first stepped behind a bar just minutes after the end of Prohibition in 1933, when his father decided to start serving alcohol in the family's grocery store and ice cream parlor. The grocery and ice cream businesses later folded. Today, Camm's bar, Cammarata's, is run with the help of his two sons, John and Frank.

OLDEST PEOPLE TO FLY Retired Wing Commander Kenneth Wallis of Norfolk, England, is pictured flying the gyroplane *Little Nellie*. Wallis is the oldest pilot to set an aviation world record, having made the fastest-ever climb to 9,842 ft. in a gyroplane on March 19, 1998, at the age of 81 years 336 days. The oldest person ever to qualify as a pilot is Burnet Patten of Victoria, Australia, who obtained his flying license on May 2, 1997, at the age of 80. Clarence Cornish of Indianapolis, Indiana, piloted aircraft until the age of 97. He died 18 days after his last flight on December 4, 1995. The oldest person to fly as a passenger was Charlotte Hughes of Redcar, England, who was given a flight on Concorde from London, England, to New York City as a 110th birthday present in 1987. She flew again in 1992 at age 115.

Calment of France. She was born on February 21, 1875, and died on August 4, 1997, aged 122.

The world's oldest man was Shigechiyo Izumi of Japan, who lived for an authenticated 120 years 237 days. Born on June 29, 1865, he was recorded as a six-year-old in Japan's first-ever census, in 1871. He worked until he was 105, drank *shochu* (liquor distilled from barley), and took up smoking when he was 70. Izumi attributed his long life to "God, Buddha, and the Sun." He died on February 21, 1986, after developing pneumonia.

Oldest Groom Harry Stevens was 103 years old when he married 84-year-old Thelma Lucas at the Caravilla Retirement Home in Wisconsin on December 3, 1984.

Oldest Bride   Minnie Munro became the world's oldest known bride when she married Dudley Reid at the age of 102 in Point Clare, Australia, on May 31, 1991. The groom was 83.

Longest Marriages   Cousins Sir Temulji Bhicaji Nariman and Lady Nariman from India were married when they were both five years old in 1853. Their marriage lasted 86 years until Sir Temulji's death at age 91 years 11 months in 1940.

   Records show that Lazarus Rowe and Molly Webber, who were both born in 1725, married in 1743. Molly died in June 1829 at Limington, Maine after 86 years of marriage.

Longest Engagement   Octavio Guillén and Adriana Martínez from Mexico finally married in June 1969 after a 67-year engagement. Both were 82 years old when they wed.

Oldest Divorcing Couple   The divorcing couple with the highest combined age were Simon and Ida Stern of Milwaukee, Wisconsin. When they divorced in February 1984, he was 97, and she was 91.

Oldest Dwarf   Hungarian-born Susanna Bokonyi, alias "Princess Susanna," of New Jersey was the world's oldest-ever dwarf when she died aged 105 on August 24, 1984. She was 3 ft. 4 in. tall.

Oldest Chorus Line Performer   Irus Guarino (b. 1909) of Boston, Massachusetts, has been dancing in the chorus line of the Ziegfeld Girls of Florida since 1986. She first performed in a show at the age of 18 and was the center girl with the Ritz Brothers in New York City.

Oldest Person to Have a No. 1 Hit   "What a Wonderful World" gave jazz trumpeter and singer Louis Armstrong a No. 1 hit in the UK in 1968. It reached No. 1 in several other countries as late as 1970, when he was 69. Armstrong was almost 63 when he had his first US No. 1 hit, "Hello Dolly!" in 1964. He initially became popular in the 1920s as a result of his recordings with the Hot Five and the Hot Seven.

Oldest Person to Visit Both Poles   Major Will Lacy (UK) visited the North Pole on April 9, 1990, at the age of 82 and the South Pole on December 20, 1991, at 84 years old. On both trips, he landed and left by light aircraft.

Oldest Drivers   Layne Hall of Silver Creek, New York, was issued a license on June 15, 1989, when, according to the license, he was 109 years old. He died on November 20, 1990, but according to his death certificate, he was then only 105.

   Mrs. Maude Tull of Inglewood, California, began driving at the age of 91 after her husband died. She was issued a replacement license on February 5, 1976, when she was 104.

Oldest Motorcyclist   Arthur Cook (b. June 13, 1895) of Exeter, England, still rides his Suzuki 125 GS Special motorcycle every day.

Oldest Professional Drag Racer   Eddie Hill (US), who is now 63 years old, is still regularly racing at speeds in excess of 300 mph.

OLDEST ATHLETE   Baba Joginder Singh throws a discus at the 1998 Indian National Athletics Meet for Veterans, held in Thane, Bombay (Mumbai). Singh, who won the gold medal in the event, is believed to be 105 years old and was the only competitor aged over 100. As a teenager, he represented India in a 1910 World Championship event held in Berlin, Germany.

Oldest Cresta Run Rider   Prince Constantin of Liechtenstein rode the Cresta Run toboggan course at the record-breaking age of 86 years 49 days on February 10, 1998.

Oldest Windsurfer   Charles Ruijter of the Netherlands took up windsurfing in 1978 at the age of 63. Now 84, he still sails in the lakes around Eindhoven, Netherlands.

Oldest Olympic Medalist   Oscar Swahn from Sweden was in the winning Running Deer shooting team at the age of 64 in 1912 and was a silver medalist in the same event in 1920 at the age of 72.

Oldest Hot-Air Balloonist   Florence Laine of New Zealand flew in a balloon at the age of 102 at Cust, New Zealand, on September 26, 1996.

Oldest Tightrope Walker   William Ivy Baldwin became the world's oldest-ever tightrope walker when he crossed South Boulder Canyon, Colorado, on his 82nd birthday on July 31, 1948. The wire he walked across was 320 ft. long, and the drop was 125 ft.

Oldest Parachutists Hildegarde Ferrera became the oldest parachutist ever when she made a tandem parachute jump at the age of 99 at Mokuleia, Hawaii, in 1996.

The oldest male parachutist is George Salyer, who made a tandem jump from 12,000 ft. aged 97 years 9 days at Harvey Airfield, Snohomish, Washington, on June 27, 1998.

Sylvia Brett became the oldest female solo parachutist at the age of 80 years 166 days. She jumped at Cranfield, England, on August 23, 1986.

EATING & DRINKING

Most Expensive Meal per Head In September 1997, three diners at the restaurant Le Gavroche in London, England, spent $20,945.92 on just one meal. Only $345.92 went on food: cigars and spirits accounted for $1,352, and the remaining $19,248 went on six bottles of wine. The most expensive bottle, a 1985 Romanée-Conti costing $7,920, proved "a bit young," so they gave it to the restaurant staff.

BIGGEST FOOD FIGHT In 1998, about 30,000 people spent one hour throwing around 90 tons of tomatoes at each other in the town of Buñol near Valencia, Spain, which holds its annual "Tomatina" Festival on the last Wednesday of August. The origins of the festival are unclear—some villagers maintain it began by chance when a truck accidentally discharged its load of tomatoes. Others say it started after the Spanish Civil War at a rally opposing General Franco's dictatorship. Today, attendants dump the ripe fruit onto the streets from the backs of trucks for people to scoop up and throw.

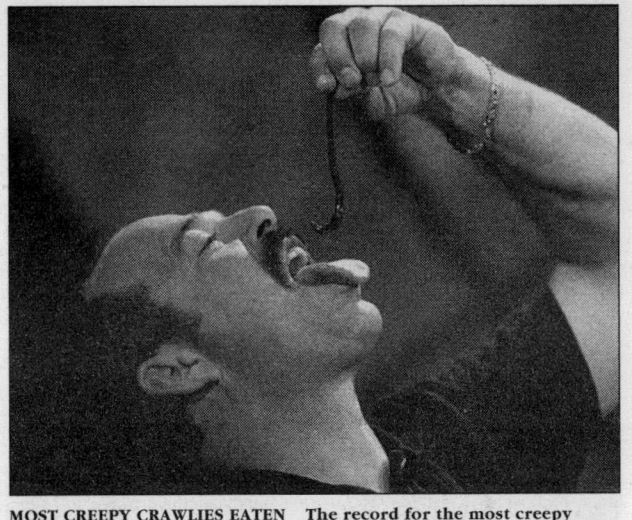

MOST CREEPY CRAWLIES EATEN The record for the most creepy crawlies eaten is held by Mark Hogg of Louisville, Kentucky, who consumed 62 night crawlers in 30 seconds on November 19, 1998, on the TV show *Guinness® World Records: Primetime*. Mark discovered he had a talent for eating the animals when he was put through army survival training in the jungles of Panama, where he had to survive for six weeks with minimum supplies. He supplemented his rations by eating vegetation, worms, and grubs. This need not be as unhealthy as it sounds, since worms contain more protein by weight than chicken and tuna. Mark eats the live worms by tilting his head back and swallowing them whole. He refuses to eat sushi, because he thinks eating raw fish is disgusting.

Most Expensive Steak Wagyu cattle, which have been bred around the Japanese city of Kobe for centuries, provide the world's most expensive steak. The herds have a remarkable genetic purity, and the cows are treated like royalty, regularly rubbed down with saké, and fed huge amounts of beer. Their stress-free life is said to explain the quality of their flesh. On the rare occasions when Kobe beef is available in the West, it costs about $160/lb.

Most Expensive Spices Prices for wild ginseng (the root of *Panax quinquefolium*) from China's Chan Pak mountain area peaked at $18,678,624/oz. in Hong Kong in November 1979. Total annual shipments of the spice—thought by many to be an aphrodisiac—from Jilin Province do not exceed 8 lb. 13 oz.

The most expensive widely used spice is saffron, made from the dried stigmas of *Crocus sotivus*. Saffron costs $4 for ¹⁄₅₀₀ oz.

Hottest Spice A mere ³⁄₁₀₀ oz. of Red "Savina" Habanero (1994 special), developed by GNS Spices of Walnut, California, can produce detectable "heat" in 1,272 lb. of bland sauce.

Most Expensive Caviar Almas caviar, consisting of the yellow eggs from albino beluga sturgeons, sells for $1,000 for 1¾ oz.

Most Expensive Shellfish The Percebes barnacle, known as the "truffle of the seas," costs a record $176/lb. The barnacles need large amounts of oxygen to survive and so have to attach themselves to rocks where the waves are at their most violent and the water is very aerated. Fishermen risk their lives to catch them in the uninhabited Sisargas Islands off Spain. These mollusks are so highly prized that a festival, the Fiesta de Los Percebes, is held in their honor.

Biggest Feast A feast held by Atul Dalpatlal Shah to celebrate his inauguration as a monk was attended by a record 150,000 guests. It took place in Ahmadabad, India, on June 2, 1991.

Most Expensive Chili Con Carne The most expensive chili con carne is served by Chasen's of West Hollywood and costs $16.75 per ½ lb. Film legend Elizabeth Taylor had some flown to her when she was busy filming *Cleopatra* (1963).

Most Expensive Fruit In 1977, restaurant manager Leslie Cooke paid $906 for 1 lb. of strawberries at an auction in Dublin, Republic of Ireland.

Most Expensive Truffle The world's most expensive truffle is *Tuber magmatum pico*, a rare white truffle found in Alba, Italy, which sells for $8,820/lb. Scientists have been unable to cultivate the fungus, which can only be found by trained pigs or dogs.

Most Expensive Coffee The Indonesian coffee Kopi Luwak sells for $75 per ¼ lb., partly because of its rarity but also because of the way it is processed. The beans from which it is made are ingested by a small tree-dwelling animal called the *Paradoxurus* before being extracted from the excreta of the animals and made into Kopi Luwak.

Most Restaurants Visited Fred Magel of Chicago, Illinois, dined out a record 46,000 times in 60 countries over a period of 50 years as a restaurant grader.

Highest-Altitude Dinner Party The greatest altitude at which a formal meal has been eaten is 22,205 ft., by nine members of the Ansett Social Climbers of Sydney, Australia, who scaled Mt. Huascarán, Peru, with a dining table, chairs, wine and a three-course meal on June 28, 1989. At the summit, the men dressed up in top hats and thermal black ties and the women in gowns.

Most Metal Eaten Michel Lotito, also known as Monsieur Mangetout, of Grenoble, France, has been eating metal and glass since 1959. He cuts up objects such as bicycles and grocery carts with an electric power saw to make small pieces, which he then swallows like a pill—something that would normally prove fatal and should never be attempted. By October 1997, the 47-year-old had eaten nearly eight tons of metal in his 22-year career.

Strongest Alcohol The Estonian Liquor Monopoly marketed 98% (196° proof) alcohol distilled from potatoes when the country was inde-

MOST EXPENSIVE FISH In January 1992, a 715-lb. bluefin tuna sold for $83,500—almost $117/lb.—in Tokyo, Japan. The tuna was reduced to 2,400 servings of sushi for wealthy diners at $75 per serving. The estimated takings from this one fish were $180,000.

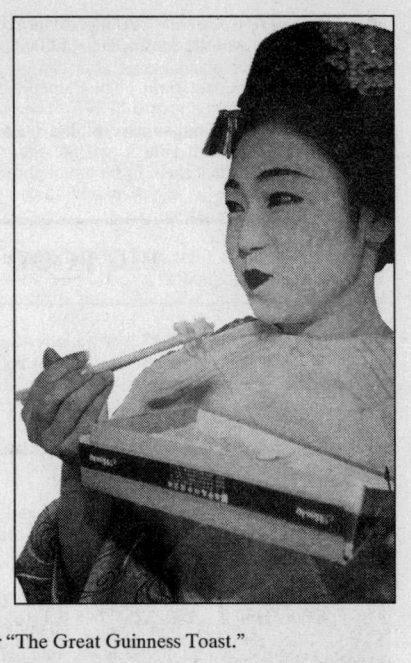

pendent between the two World Wars.

Baz's Super Brew, brewed by Barrie Parish at the Parish Brewery, Somerby, England, has an alcohol volume of 23%, making it the world's strongest beer.

Biggest Toast On February 26, 1999, a record 197,648 people gathered simultaneously in pubs, restaurants, and bars in 74 metropolitan areas of the US at 11 pm (EST) for "The Great Guinness Toast."

Biggest Wine Tasting On November 22, 1986, about 4,000 people consumed a total of 9,360 bottles of wine at a tasting sponsored by the TV station KQED in San Francisco, California.

Biggest Wine Sale Andrew Lloyd Webber's 18,000-bottle wine collection sold for $6 million at Sotheby's in London, England, on May 21, 1997. It was described at the time as the greatest single-owner wine collection ever offered at auction. The total price exceeded the estimate of $3.3–4.4 million.

Most Valuable Bottle of Wine In December 1985, $136,248 was paid for a bottle of 1787 Château Lafite at Christie's in London, England. It was engraved with the initials of Thomas Jefferson, the third US president. In 1986, its cork slipped, spoiling the wine.

Most Expensive Glass of Wine A record $1,453 was paid for the first glass of Beaujolais Nouveau 1993 produced by Maison Jaffelin, Beaune, France. It was bought by Robert Denby at Pickwick's, a British pub in Beaune.

Most Expensive Liquor The most expensive liquor on sale is Springbank 1919 Malt Whisky, a bottle of which costs $10,800 at Fortnum & Mason in London, England.

Most Valuable Liquor The highest price paid for liquor at auction was $79,552 for a bottle of 50-year-old Glenfiddich whisky. It sold to an anonymous Italian businessman at a charity auction in Milan, Italy, in 1992.

Biggest Pub The Mathäser in Munich, Germany seats 5,500 people and sells 84,470 pints of beer daily.

BIG FOOD

Biggest Curry On May 17, 1998, a curry weighing more than 2.65 tons was made by a team from the Raj restaurant in Maldon, England. This record-breaking curry, which was made in a specially designed pot 7 ft. 6 in. in diameter and 4 ft. deep, contained 1 ton of vegetables, 176 lb. 8 oz. of coconut powder, 44 lb. 2 oz. of tamarind, 22 lb. of tandoori paste, 88 lb. 3 oz. of food coloring, and 6 lb. 10 oz. of garam masala. It was divided into 13,500 portions.

Longest Sushi Roll Six hundred members of the Nikopoka Festa committee made a sushi roll (*kappamaki*) that was 3,279 ft. long at Yoshii, Japan, on October 12, 1997.

BIGGEST ONION BHAJI Chefs at the Jinnah Restaurant, Flaxton, England, created the world's biggest onion bhaji on November 10, 1998. It weighed 6 lb. 4 oz. and measured 1 ft. 8 in. in diameter.

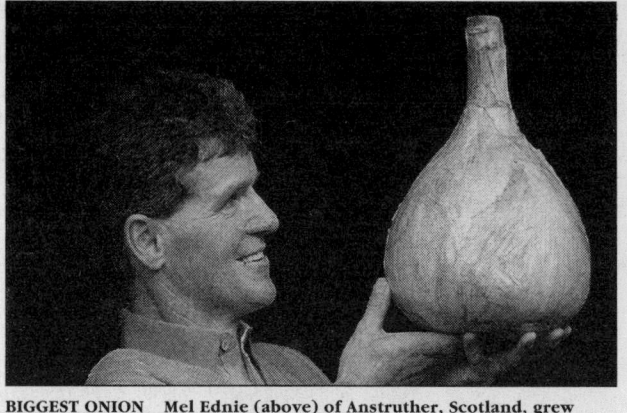

BIGGEST ONION Mel Ednie (above) of Anstruther, Scotland, grew the world's largest onion, weighing a record 15 lb. 5 oz., in 1997. Currently, the most successful cultivator of giant vegetables is Bernard Lavery of Rhondda, Wales, who holds the world records for the heaviest cabbage (124 lb.), carrot (15 lb. 11 oz.), and zucchini (64 lb.) and for the longest corncob (3 ft.).

Biggest Chinese Dumpling The Hong Kong Union of Chinese Food and Culture Ltd. and the Southern District Committee made a 1,058-lb. 3-oz. Chinese dumpling on July 5, 1997, to celebrate the return of Hong Kong to China.

Most Mussels Cooked On September 5, 1998, 12 people cooked over 1.5 tons of mussels in one pan during a five-hour period at Oostduinkerke-Bad, Flanders, Belgium.

Longest Satay On June 20, 1998, a satay 90 yd. in length was made at the Thomson Community Club in Singapore.

Biggest Bowl of Spaghetti On August 16, 1998, a bowl of spaghetti weighing 605 lb. was cooked by Consolidated Communications in London, England, on behalf of Walt Disney Home Video to celebrate the rerelease of *Lady and the Tramp* (1955).

Biggest Restaurant Steak A 12-lb. 8-oz. rump steak (precooked weight) is available from the Kestrel Inn, Hatton, England. It takes about 40 minutes to cook (to a medium/well-done state) and costs $128. If a customer finishes the steak, the management will make a donation to charity.

Biggest Gyro A gyro weighing a record 1.03 tons and measuring 3 ft. 11 in. in width and 5 ft. 3 in. in height was created by Kadir Cetinkaya at the Zürich Summer Festival in Switzerland in July 1998.

Biggest Hamburger The biggest hamburger ever weighed 2.5 tons and was made at the Outagamie County Fairgrounds in Seymour, Wisconsin, on August 5, 1989.

Biggest Shortcake A 827-ft², 3,628-ton strawberry shortcake was made by the Greater Plant City Chamber of Commerce in Plant City, Florida, on February 19, 1999. It was topped with 1,360 lb. of whipping cream and 3,995 lb. of strawberries.

Longest Strudel A 1-mile 70-yd.-long apple strudel was made in Karlsruhe, Baden-Württemberg, Germany, on May 26, 1994.

Longest Banana Split A 4-mile 965-yd. banana split was made by residents of Selinsgrove, Pennsylvania, on April 30, 1988.

Biggest Ice Cream Sundae On July 24, 1988, the biggest ice cream sundae ever, weighing 22.59 tons, was put together by Palm Dairies Ltd. of Edmonton, Alberta, Canada. The finished concoction included 18.38 tons of ice cream, 3.98 tons of syrup, and 537 lb. 3 oz. of topping.

Biggest Ice Cream Soda Float On April 3, 1998, Denny's and Coca-Cola concocted a 2,505-gallon ice cream float at North Druid Hill in Atlanta, Georgia. It contained 1,750 gallons of Coca-Cola and 750 lb. of ice cream.

BIGGEST SAUSAGES The longest continuous sausage on record extended a distance of 28 miles 1,354 yd. It was made by M & M Meat Shops and J.M. Schneider Inc. at Kitchener, Ontario, Canada, in April 1995. Pictured here are children from Srednja Backa, Yugoslavia, during their attempt to beat the record. The biggest salami weighed 1,492 lb. 5 oz. and was 68 ft. 9 in. long. It was made by staff of A/S Svindlands Pølsefabrikk at Flekkefjord, Norway in July 1992. The biggest ever bratwurst, which measured 1 mile 1,630 yd. in length, was made at Jena, Germany, on September 18, 1994.

Biggest Ice Lollipop Between August 1 and 30, 1997, Iglo-Ola Produktie B.V. of Hellendoorn, Netherlands, manufactured a Rocket Ice weighing 8.236 tons. It was 21 ft. 4 in. long and 7 ft. 5 in. wide and averaged 3 ft. 7 in. in thickness.

Biggest Doughnut A jelly doughnut weighing 1.5 tons and measuring 16 ft. in diameter was baked by representatives of Hemstrought's Bakeries, Donato's Bakery, and the radio station WKLL-FM at Utica, New York, on January 21, 1993.

BIGGEST PUMPKIN Soji Shirai from Ashibetsu City, Japan, stands next to a pumpkin he grew weighing 970 lb. An average pumpkin (*Cucurbita peto*) weighs between 2 lb. 2 oz. and 4 lb. 4 oz. The world's largest-ever pumpkin was grown by Gary Burke of Simcoe, Ontario, Canada. It weighed 1,092 lb. on October 3, 1998.

Biggest Gelatin Dessert A 9,246-gal. watermelon-flavored pink gelatin dessert was made by Paul Squires and Geoff Ross at Roma Street Forum, Brisbane, Australia, on February 5, 1981.

Biggest Chocolate Candy Bar An 8-ft.-11-in.-long, 3-ft.-11-in.-wide, 1-ft.-deep Cadbury's Dairy Milk bar weighing 1.1 tons was made in Birmingham, England, on October 5, 1998.

Tallest Chocolate Model In November 1997, the Richemont Club built a 49-ft.-1-in.-long, 15-ft.-5-in.-wide, 24-ft.-6-in.-high chocolate model dinosaur in the Zuid shopping center, Ghent, Belgium.

Biggest Christmas Log On December 25, 1997, a 2.3-ton Christmas log was made, displayed, and eaten at the Mercure Hotel in Bangkok, Thailand. This largest-ever Christmas log, which was 27 ft. 6 in. long and 2 ft. wide, was made by 10 staff members and took 360 hours to prepare. The ingredients included 462 lb. 15 oz. of flour, 661 lb. 6 oz. of sugar, 264 lb. 9 oz. of butter, 264 lb. 9 oz. of evaporated milk, and 594 eggs. The log was sliced into 19,212 portions.

Biggest Pineapple   The world's biggest pineapple was grown by E. Kamuk of Ais Village, Papua New Guinea, in 1994. It weighed 17 lb. 12 oz.

Biggest Apple   The record for the heaviest apple is 3 lb. 11 oz., grown by Alan Smith of Linton, England.

Biggest Broccoli   A head of broccoli weighing 35 lb. was grown by John and Mary Evans of Palmer, Alaska, in 1993.

Biggest Garlic   The biggest head of garlic ever, weighing 2 lb. 10 oz., was grown by Robert Kirkpatrick of Eureka, California, in 1985.

Biggest Squash   The biggest squash ever recorded was grown by John Handbury of Chesterfield, England, in 1998. It weighed 135 lb.

COLLECTORS

Biggest Jet Fighter Collection   Michel Pont, a French wine maker, has a personal collection of 100 jet fighter planes, ranging from British *Vampires* to Russian *MiGs* to a rare French Dassault *Mirage 4*. Pont started collecting jet fighters in 1986, having collected motorbikes since 1958 and cars since 1970. By January 1998, the 66-year-old had accumulated 70 different types of jet fighter, 500 motorcycles, and a series of crimson Abarth racing cars.

Biggest Model Aircraft Collection   Bader Yousif Murad of Bahrain has been collecting model aircraft since his 10th birthday in 1978 after he was given a secondhand model of a KLM B747-200. He now owns 1,105 model aircraft, representing more than 440 airlines. Over the last 20 years, his collection, which grows by about 10 models a month, has cost him $30,000.

Biggest Passport Collection   Guy Van Keer of Brussels, Belgium, owns 4,260 passports and other travel documents used in lieu of passports. They represent 130 different countries and were issued between 1615 and the present day.

Biggest Scratch Card Collection   Darren Haake of Bateau Bay, Australia, has amassed a record total of 277,820 scratch cards since he began collecting in 1993.

Biggest Bus Ticket Collection   Yacov Yosipovv of Tel Aviv, Israel, has collected more than 14,000 used bus tickets, each one different in some way.

Biggest Marble Collection   Over the past 46 years, printer Sam McCarthy-Fox from Worthing, England, has built up a collection of 40,000 marbles. These include antique marbles and fiber-optic examples made from semiprecious stones.

Biggest Whiskey Collections Edoardo Giaccone of Brescia, Italy, owned 5,502 unduplicated and unopened full-sized whiskey bottles, including bourbons and Irish whiskeys. He died in 1997, leaving his collection to Guiseppe Begnoni of Bologna, Italy.

Claive Vidiz, president of the Brazilian Association of Whiskey Collectors, owns 2,571 original—and full—bottles of Scotch whiskey. The bottles are kept in a museum that was specially built for the collection in São Paulo, Brazil.

Biggest Beer Can Collection William Christensen of Madison, New Jersey, has collected more than 75,000 different beer cans from about 125 countries and territories.

Biggest Collection of Airplane Sick Bags Nick Vermeulen (Netherlands) has built up a record-breaking collection of 2,112 different airplane sick bags. The bags come from a total of 470 different airlines.

Biggest Lawn Mower Collection The Hall and Duck Trust Collection of Vintage Lawn Mowers belonging to Andrew Hall and Michael Duck of Windsor, England, contains more than 680 different lawn mowers.

LARGEST BALLPOINT PEN COLLECTION Angelica Unverhau of Dinslaken, Germany, has collected 168,700 ballpoint pens. This figure excludes duplicates and includes examples from 137 countries. She began collecting pens nine years ago after becoming fascinated by the many forms and varieties available. The most expensive pen in the collection is one made out of gold and white gold worth over $500.

BIGGEST GARFIELD COLLECTION Mike Drysdale and Gayle Brennan of Los Angeles, California, have collected about 3,000 items related to their favorite comic strip character, Garfield. The couple has turned their home into a gigantic shrine to the famous cat. Every corner is crammed with cuddly toys, videos, bedding, crockery, radios, windup toys, and other Garfield-related items. The collection was started in 1994, when Gayle bought a Garfield bed for the couple's cats. The characters of the lasagna-loving pet, his canine companion, Odie, and their long-suffering owner, Jon, were created by US cartoonist Jim Davis in 1978. The comic strip now has a daily worldwide circulation of 220 million. Ironically, Davis doesn't own a cat, as his wife is allergic to them.

Biggest Movie Camera Collection Retired postman Dimitrios Pistiola of Athens, Greece, has collected 440 movie cameras dating from 1901 to the present day.

Biggest Colored Vinyl Record Collection Alessandro Benedetti of Monsummano Terme, Italy, has collected 780 records made from colored vinyl.

Biggest Barbie Doll Collection Tony Mattia of Brighton, England, has 1,125 Barbie dolls in his collection—about half the designs produced since Mattel launched the doll in the US in 1959. He changes the dolls' costumes once a month and regularly brushes their hair.

Biggest Bandage Collection Brian Viner of London, England, has collected about 3,750 unused sticking bandages of many different colors, styles, shapes, and sizes.

Biggest Handcuff Collection Locksmith Chris Gower of Dorset, England, has amassed 412 pairs of handcuffs since he began collecting them in 1968. His interest in handcuffs is from a fascination with escapology.

Biggest Collection of Swatch Watches Fiorenzo Barindelli of Lombardy, Italy, has amassed 3,524 Swatch watches. He owns an example of

BIGGEST *STAR WARS* COLLECTION Jason Joiner of Ealing, London, England, a special-effects expert who has worked on the *Star Wars* prequels, has a collection of more than 20,000 *Star Wars* toys. His collection also includes one of the original C3PO robots, an original R2D2, and an original Darth Vader costume, all used in one of the first three *Star Wars* films released.

every watch documented in every Swatch catalog since 1983, as well as some prototypes and special-edition pieces, and plans to open a Swatch museum in the year 2000.

Biggest Collection of Chamber Pots Manfred Klauda of Germany has collected 9,400 different chamber pots, some dating back to the 16th century.

Biggest Piggy Bank Collection Ove Nordström of Spånga, Sweden, has amassed a collection of 4,175 different money holders shaped like pigs.

WEALTH

SUPER RICH

Richest Women   The world's richest women are the widow and daughter of Sam Walton, founder of Wal-Mart. *Forbes* estimates that his wife Helen and daughter Alice are each worth $16 billion.

Lilliane Bettencourt, who is the heiress to the L'Oréal and Nestlé empire, has a fortune that has been estimated at $13.9 billion.

Richest Royal in Europe   The richest royal in Europe is Queen Beatrix of Holland, with a net worth of $5.2 billion. Queen Beatrix ascended the throne when her mother, Queen Juliana, abdicated on April 20, 1980.

Biggest Bequests   In 1991, the US publishing tycoon Walter Annenberg announced his intention to leave his $1-billion collection of artwork to the Metropolitan Museum of Art in New York City.

In 1997, media tycoon Ted Turner pledged a total of $1 billion to United Nations causes, which include anti-land mine and refugee-aid programs.

GREATEST PHILANTHROPISTS   Doris Bryant (above), the sister of the world's richest investor, Warren Buffett, is known as the "Sunshine Lady." She appoints "sunbeams" who assist her to "spread a kindly light on the world," and her foundation has awarded $3 million to good causes in her home state of North Carolina. The greatest philanthropist of all time was steel and manufacturing magnate Andrew Carnegie, who distributed almost all his fortune to public-library construction and the setting up of a number of educational and research institutions. His wealth was estimated at $250 million in 1901.

RICHEST ROYAL The world's richest royal is Hassanal Bolkiah, the Sultan of Brunei, with a fortune estimated at $30 billion earned from oil and gas. He is also Asia's richest man, the richest oil tycoon in the world, and the owner of the world's biggest residential palace (*see Homes & Hotels*). As well as ruling Brunei, the Sultan is prime minister, defense minister, and finance minister and provides free education and health care for the citizens of his country.

Most Expensive Houses In 1997, Wong Yuk Kwan, the chairman of Pearl Oriental Holdings, purchased two properties in the Skyhigh development in Hong Kong, China—one for $70.2 million and one for $48.9 million.

Most Expensive Islands The 40,000-acre island of Niihau, Hawaii, is the largest privately owned island in the US. It has been valued at $100 million.

The most expensive island currently on the market is D'Arros in the Seychelles. The atoll, which covers an area of 600 acres and has a private lagoon, an airstrip, and three homes, can be bought for $21 million.

BIGGEST DIVORCE SETTLEMENT The world's largest publicly declared divorce settlement ever amounted to $874 million plus property. It was secured in 1982 by the lawyers of Soraya Khashoggi (on the left of the picture) from her husband, Adnan (right), a Saudi entrepreneur and property owner.

Most Luxurious Liner The 1000-ft.-long *The World of ResidenSea*, which is being built by a German shipyard, is expected to cost $529.7 million and will be the most luxurious liner ever built. It will have a staff of 500, seven restaurants, a movie theater, a casino, a nightclub, bars, a Roman spa, a house of worship, a library, museums, a business service center, a licensed stock and bond broker, shops, a swimming pool, a retractable marina for water sports, a golf academy, a tennis court, and a helicopter pad. Due to be launched in the year 2000, it has 250 oceangoing apartments that are on the market for $1.3 to 5.8 million each. The most expensive apartments are the 2,152-ft.^{2} three-bedroom, three-bathroom penthouses.

Most Luxurious Private Jet The most luxurious private jet in the world is the $35-million *Gulfstream V*. The jet is able to cruise at 52,000 ft., making it the highest-flying passenger aircraft after Concorde. It is also the fastest long-range executive jet, with a maximum speed of nearly 600 mph and a range of 7,485 miles—meaning that it can fly to any destination in the world with only one stop for refueling. If fitted with customized extras, the cost of the *Gulfstream V* rises to $40 million.

YOUNGEST MULTIBILLIONAIRE Athina Onassis Roussel, the granddaughter of shipping magnate Aristotle Onassis, inherited an estimated $5-billion empire and the Greek island of Skorpios in 1988, at the age of three. She will have control of the fortune in 2003, when she is 18.

Biggest Private Rolls-Royce Fleet Sultan Hassanal Bolkiah of Brunei, who was the world's richest man until Microsoft boss Bill Gates (*see Tycoons & High Earners*) exceeded him in wealth, is believed to have the biggest private collection of Rolls-Royce cars. The fleet has been estimated to consist of 150 vehicles. Together with his brother Prince Jefri, the Sultan is reported to own another 1,998 luxury cars.

Most Expensive Watch Collection Prince Jefri, the younger brother of the Sultan of Brunei, is reported to have paid $5.2 million for 10 gem-studded watches.

Most Raised by a Private Art Collection at Auction   A collection belonging to Victor and Sally Ganz, including works by Pablo Picasso and Jasper Johns, raised a total of $207.4 million at Christie's in New York City in November 1997.

Largest Stable   The Godolphin stable, owned by the ruling Maktoum family of Dubai, headed by Sheikh Mohammed al Maktoum, consists of 850 horses in training, 70 brood mares, 18 stallions, 12 studs, and 25 trainers. Maintenance costs total $408.98 million a year.

Biggest Rock Heiress   Lisa Marie Presley, Elvis' daughter, inherited $130 million from her father. She received an installment of $38 million on her 30th birthday, in 1997. When Elvis died, his estate faced liquidation, but it has since been turned into one of the world's most successful merchandising enterprises.

TYCOONS & HIGH EARNERS

Richest Person of all Time   John D. Rockefeller's wealth was estimated at about $900 million in 1913, equivalent to $189.6 billion in today's terms, making him the richest person of all time. Having made a fortune in the oil business, Rockefeller retired in 1897. By 1922, he had given away $1 billion to his family and to charity, keeping just $20 million for himself.

Richest Businessman   According to *Forbes* magazine, Bill Gates, the founder, chairman, and chief executive officer of Microsoft Corporation, is the richest man in the world today. His fortune is estimated at $90 billion.

Richest Businesswoman   Doris Fisher, half of the hus-

RICHEST BUSINESS FAMILY IN EUROPE   Paul Sacher (left) was Europe's richest man, worth an estimated $13.1 billion when he died in May 1999. His family has an inherited fortune of $17 billion from Swiss pharmaceuticals giant Roche, but no longer control the company. The richest pharmaceuticals tycoon is Novartis chief Pierre Landolt (Switzerland), who has a family fortune of $6.4 billion.

band-and-wife team that opened its first Gap outlet in 1969, is worth an estimated $4.3 billion. Often described as the self-made "king and queen of khaki," Donald and Doris Fisher averaged $9 billion in sales in 1999, with more than 2,500 stores around the world, including Gap-Kids, Old Navy, and Banana Republic. Their three sons control shares worth $5.6 billion.

Richest Business Family The Walton family, the children and widow of Wal-Mart founder Sam Walton, are the richest business family in the world, according to *Forbes* magazine, with an estimated combined fortune of $79.8 billion. Sam Walton opened his first "small town discount store" in Arkansas in 1962. Today, Wal-Mart is the largest retailer in the US, with sales of $118 billion and 2,399 stores, 451 member-only warehouse clubs, and 625 international branches. S. Robson Walton, the current chairman, is estimated to be worth $15.8 billion.

RICHEST MAN IN RUSSIA Vladimir Potanin, the richest man in Russia, according to *Forbes*, is the founder and president of Oneximbank. Worth $1.6 billion in 1998, which he earned through oil, metals, and telecommunications, as well as banking, 38-year-old Potanin was also the first-ever deputy prime minister of the Russian Federation, in 1996.

Richest Businessman in Asia Alwaleed Bin Talal Bin Abdulaziz Alsaud is the richest businessman in Asia, with an estimated fortune of $15 billion. Building on an inheritance (a small fraction of his present wealth), Alwaleed has made a fortune in the business world by shrewd investment in companies such as Citicorp.

Richest Businessmen in Europe Theo and Karl Albrecht from Germany and their family have a combined fortune of $13.6 billion, which was amassed from their 10% share in Europe's most successful discount food retailer, Aldi. The Aldi Group has 4,000 stores in Europe and 509 stores in the US.

Richest Businessman in Latin America Carlos Slim Helu, the head of the Mexican conglomerate Grupo Carso, is the richest businessman in Latin America. His three sons run Carso and its financial arm, Inbursa; their combined family fortune runs to $8 billion.

RICHEST AUTOMOBILE TYCOON Ferdinand Piech (above), Volkswagen's chairman, is the richest automobile tycoon. His family, which has a fortune of $5 billion, owns 76% of Porsche AG.

Richest Businessman in Africa Nicky Oppenheimer, chairman of the South African diamond and mining empire De Beers, has a family fortune that is estimated at $2.2 billion.

Richest Media Tycoon Kenneth Thomson (Canada), head of Thomson Corp., has a fortune of $11.9 billion. Thomson publishes about 70 local and national newspapers in North America, including Toronto's *Globe and Mail*, but the company is now focusing more on electronic information.

Richest Candy Tycoon The three Mars siblings have a fortune amounting to $12 billion from candy company giant Mars Inc. and from pet food and prepared-food empires.

Richest Cosmetics Tycoons Leonard A. and Ronald S. Lauder and their family have a combined fortune of $8.8 billion. Leonard runs Estée Lauder, the cosmetics company that was founded by his mother.

Richest Jeans Tycoon The richest jeans tycoon is Robert D. Haas, the great-great-grandnephew of the founder of jeans manufacturer Levi Strauss Co., who has a fortune of $8.2 billion together with his family.

Highest-Earning Chief Executive Officer Michael Eisner, chairman and chief executive officer of Disney, earned $589.1 million in the financial year 1998/99—a figure that includes salary, bonus, and stock gains. Eisner's total earnings over the five-year period 1995–99 were $631.02 million.

Highest-Earning Internet CEO Stephen Case, the founder of America Online, is the highest-paid internet CEO. He earned $159.2 million in 1998/99, of which $158.06 million was stock gains.

Highest-Earning CEO in the Computer Industry   Craig Barrett, chief executive officer of Intel, makers of the Pentium processor, earned $116.8 million in 1999, including $114.2 million in stock gains.

Highest-Earning Chief Executive Officer in Financial Services In 1998/99, Philip J. Purcell, the CEO of investment bank Morgan Stanley, earned $49 million, making him the highest-paid financial services CEO in the world. Over the four-year period 1995-99, Purcell earned a total of $108.1 million.

Richest Investor   Warren Buffett, the head of Berkshire Hathaway, is the world's richest investor, estimated to be worth $36 billion. His fortune is second only to that of Microsoft founder and chairman Bill Gates.

Youngest "Super-Rich" Tycoon   Jerry Yang, the 30-year-old co-founder of internet search engine Yahoo! Inc., is worth an estimated $4 billion according to *Forbes* magazine. Yahoo!'s recent acquisition of GeoCities extended the company's reach into personal web pages, while its acquisition of broadcast.com has broadened its profile in the web-based audio and video arena. Yang owns about 11% of the company.

Greatest Personal Financial Recovery   In 1989, Donald Trump owned two casinos, an airline, buildings in New York City, and a 280-ft. yacht, as well as other property worth an estimated $1.7 billion. The onset of the recession and the slumping property market of the late 1980s pushed his businesses into $8.8 billion of debt. His assets have now, according to *Forbes* magazine, crept up to $1.5 billion, although Trump himself claims to be worth $5 billion. In 1998, Trump bought the GM Building in New York City and, thanks to the strength of the property market, now has few vacancies in his eponymously named buildings.

HOMES & HOTELS

Biggest Non-Palatial Residence   The largest non-palatial residence in the world is St. Emmeram Castle in Regensburg, Germany, which has 517 rooms and a total floor area of 231,000 ft.^{2}. It was owned by Prince Johannes von Thurn und Taxis, whose family used only 95 of the rooms. The castle is valued at more than $202 million.

Biggest Residential Palace   Owned by the Sultan of Brunei, Istana Nurul Iman in Bandar Seri Begawan, Brunei, was completed in 1984 at a reported cost of $422 million. It has 1,788 rooms, 257 toilets, and an underground garage.

Biggest Hollywood Home   The Manor on Mapleton Drive, Hollywood, California, was built for Aaron Spelling. It occupies 36,500 ft.^{2} on a 65,000-ft.^{2} plot of land. The estate includes a doll museum, four bars, three kitchens, a gymnasium, a theater, eight two-car garages, an Olympic-size

swimming pool, a bowling alley, a skating rink, six formal gardens, 12 fountains, and a room in which to wrap gifts. Spelling is the producer of a number of TV series, including *Beverly Hills 90210*.

Biggest Modern Underground House

Underhill in Holme, England, has an internal area of 3,500 ft.². The home of architect Arthur Quarmby since 1976, it cannot be seen from the surrounding moorland.

Most "Intelligent" House

Bill Gates' house, which was estimated by King County assessors to have cost $55 million to build over seven years, uses state-of-the-art information technology to tailor itself to the preferences of guests. Everyone who enters is given an electronic pin that can be detected by sensors in each room, enabling the house to set the services and entertainments to their requirements. The sensors also control lights and appliances, turning them off automatically when someone leaves a room. Gates' hi-tech home is situated on the eastern shore of Lake Washington, Washington.

Most Energy-Efficient House

The Autonomous House in Southwell, England, produces more energy

BIGGEST HOTEL Workers are pictured putting the finishing touches on the 45-ton lion which stands at the entrance to the MGM Grand Hotel and Casino in Las Vegas, Nevada. The hotel, which has four 30-story towers and covers an area of 112 acres, is the biggest in the world. It has 5,005 rooms (including 751 suites), 10 restaurants, three lounges, four tennis courts, a 15,222-seat arena, and a 32.8-acre outdoor theme park. Its 170,000-ft.² casino, which has four separate themed areas, contains thousands of slot machines. When they are not gambling or spending their money in the hotel's numerous specialty shops, guests can relax in the swimming pool area, which is the biggest in Nevada and features a 40-seater spa tub, two waterfalls, and a giant fountain.

HIGHEST HOTEL The Grand Hyatt Shanghai in Pudon, China, is the highest hotel in the world. It occupies the top 35 floors of the 88-story Jin Mao Tower (pictured right), the tallest building in China and the third tallest in the world. The hotel, which opened for business on March 18, 1999, offers spectacular views over the Bund and the adjacent Huang Pu River.

than it uses. Photovoltaic panels provide electricity, and the 1,450 kWh produced by the house annually is sold back to the UK National Grid.

Biggest Hotel Lobby The lobby at the Hyatt Regency, San Francisco, California is 350 ft. long and 160 ft. wide. With its 170-ft. high ceiling, the lobby is as tall as a 17-story building.

Longest Hotel on Wheels The longest of the Orient Express luxury trains, which travel between Paris, France, and Istanbul, Turkey, is 1,644 ft. long. All its cars are originals from the 1920s and 1930s.

Highest-Altitude Hotel The Hotel Everest View above Namche, Nepal—the village closest to Everest base camp—is at a record height of 13,000 ft.

Northern-Most Hotel The world's most northern full-service hotel is the Svalbard Polar Hotel Longyearbyen, Svalbard, Norway. Svalbard consists of several islands, from Bjornoya in the south to Rossoya in the north, Europe's northern-most point. About 60% of the archipelago is covered by ice.

Most Expensive Hotel Room The 10-room Bridge Suite at the Royal Towers of Atlantis in the Bahamas can be rented for $25,000 per night. The price includes two entertainment centers, a bar lounge, a baby grand piano, and a dining room containing a 22-carat-gold chandelier.

Longest Hotel Swimming Pool The Hyatt Regency Cerromar Beach Resort in Puerto Rico has a 1,755-ft.-long swimming pool that covers 4 1/2 acres and consists of five connected pools with water slides, a subterranean Jacuzzi, tropical landscaping, and 14 waterfalls. It takes 15 minutes to float from one end of the pool to the other.

Most Fountains in a Hotel There are more than 1,000 fountains on the 12-acre artificial lake at the Bellagio, Las Vegas, Nevada. The foun-

MOST "INTELLIGENT" TOWN Construction workers are pictured posing outside a house in Celebration, Florida. Located south of Orlando, Celebration is a futuristic town designed by Disney. Each of the town's 8,000 homes has a high-speed ISDN link, with cable TV, multimedia resources, video on demand, and an internet connection. Despite its high-tech amenities, Celebration has been designed to look like an old-fashioned American town, with grid-pattern streets, white picket fences, and a traditional downtown area. Cycling and walking paths link every part of the community. Celebration has been under construction since 1996 and has a current population of approximately 1,000, which is expected to reach 20,000 by 2015.

tains shoot water 244 ft. into the air, accompanied by surround-sound music and a light display featuring 4,000 programmed lights.

Biggest Mural in a Hotel The biggest hotel mural in the world is *The Great Motherland of China* at the Island Shangri-La Hotel in Hong Kong, China. The world's largest Chinese landscape painting, it measures 167 ft. x 50 ft. and is 16 stories high. It can be viewed from a glass elevator between the 41st and the 56th floors.

Biggest Hotel Rolls-Royce Fleet The Peninsula Group has purchased a total of 50 Rolls-Royces since its first order of seven Brewster Green Silver Shadows in 1970. The most recent order was for nine Silver Spurs. The Peninsula Hong Kong in China has a fleet of 14 Rolls-Royces (13 Silver Spurs and a 1934 Phantom II), while the Palace Hotel Beijing, China, the Peninsula Bangkok, Thailand, and the Peninsula Beverly Hills, California, have two Rolls-Royce limousines each.

Highest Density of Hotel Rooms Las Vegas, Nevada, which is known for its casino-hotels, has a total of 109,365 hotel rooms. Ten of the largest hotels in the world are in Las Vegas.

Highest Concentration of Theme Hotels   There are more than 16 theme hotels on the Strip in Las Vegas, with themes ranging from Treasure Island to Venetian. The Luxor has a sphinx, a black pyramid, and an obelisk; New York New York features, a one-third scale New York skyline; and Paris has a half-scale Eiffel Tower.

CULT OBJECTS

Most Expensive Barbie Dolls Sold at Auction   The highest price paid for a non-mass-produced Barbie doll was $26,500, at the 95th Harley-Davidson Anniversary Benefit for the Muscular Dystrophy Association in Milwaukee, Wisconsin, on June 13, 1998. The doll was dressed in a genuine leather replica of Harley-Davidson-approved clothing and was seated on top of a licensed Harley-Davidson bike replica, which was actually a telephone.

The most valuable mass-produced Barbie Dolls are #1 Brunettes that have never been removed from their boxes and 1967 Japanese side-part Brunettes, with rare pink skin, non-twist waists, and bendable legs. Both fetch about $9,500 each.

Most Valuable GI Joe   On August 19, 1994, at an auction at Christie's in New York City to commemorate the 30th anniversary of GI Joe, a unique GI Joe fighter pilot action figure sold for $5,750.

MOST VALUABLE RUBIK'S CUBE
To commemorate the 15th anniversary of Rubik's Cube in 1995, Diamond Cutters International produced the Masterpiece Cube, the only limited edition Rubik's Cube. The actual-size, fully functional replica features 22.5 karats of amethyst, 34 karats of rubies, and 34 karats of emeralds, all set in 18-karat gold. It has been valued at about $1.5 million. Professor Erno Rubik of Hungary, who invented the original cube, is pictured with an example of his brainchild.

Most Valuable Pair of Jeans In March 1997, Levi Strauss & Co. paid a vintage denim dealer in New York City $25,000 for a pair of their Levi's 501 jeans believed to have been made between 1886 and 1902.

Most Valuable Spice Girls Costume The Union Jack costume worn by former Spice Girl Geri Halliwell at the 1997 Brit Awards ceremony sold for $66,112 at an auction at Sotheby's in London, England, on September 16, 1998.

Most Valuable Pez Dispensers A one-piece shiny Gold Elephant, a Mickey Mouse softhead, and a headless dispenser embossed with the words "PEZ-HAAS" were sold for $6,000 each, a total of $18,000, by David Welch, an author and Pez dealer. The dispensers were made in the late 1940s to early 1950s to dispense Pez candy, invented in 1927 as an alternative to smoking.

Most Expensive Pinball Machine A unique pinball machine produced in February 1992 is reported to have been sold for $120,000 in Los Angeles, California. It was named *Aaron Spelling* after the American TV producer.

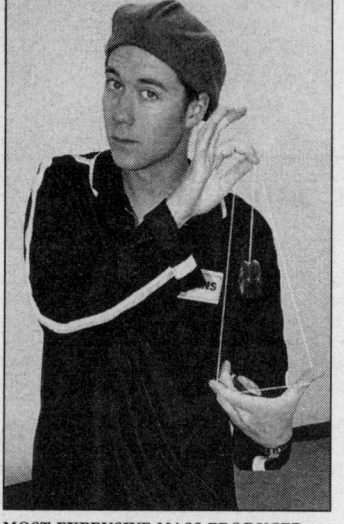

MOST EXPENSIVE MASS-PRODUCED YO-YO Cold Fusion and Cold Fusion GT yo-yos, manufactured by Playmaxx Inc., retail between $150 and $250 and are the most expensive mass-produced yo-yos in the world. There is also a special version called Gold Fusion, which is plated with 24-k gold and sells for between $200 and $300. In 1998, Playmaxx Inc. generated approximately $96 million in retail sales and was given the "Craze Of The Year" Award by the British Toy Association. Yo-yo champion Yo-Hans is pictured publicizing his 1998 single "Walk ... (The Dog) Like An Egyptian."

Most Valuable Zippo Lighter An original 1933 Zippo lighter was sold for $10,000 by Ira Pilossof on July 12, 1998. The lighter was an early 1933 model without any slash marks on the two corners—all later models had these corner marks. This is the first Zippo model ever produced (formerly referred to as a 1932) and is the most sought after and highly prized among Zippo collectors.

Most Valuable Bubble Car In March 1997, the British entrepreneur Peter de Savary paid $38,640 for a three-wheeled German-built 1962 Messerschmitt KR 200 "Bubble Top"—a record for any Messerschmitt car. The 191cc two-seater had been expected to sell for $12,800. De Savary also paid record prices for a 1962 Trojan 200 and a 1959 Goggomobil T400, the world's smallest limousine. They were put up for auction at Christie's in London, England, by Canadian bubble-gum magnate Bruce Weiner.

MOST VALUABLE JUKEBOX The 1933 Wurlitzer Debutante Model (pictured), the world's first jukebox, was sold in Cumming, Georgia, for a record $45,903 on June 27, 1997. The Wurlitzer company was founded in 1856 and also makes electric organs and pianos. The most famous Wurlitzer jukebox is the 1100, designed by Paul Fuller in 1948.

Most Expensive Mini Car The one-of-a-kind Mini Limo, commissioned by Rover Group and built by John Cooper Garages, cost $80,000 when it was delivered in September 1997. The two-door Mini boasted a $12,836 Alpine Mini-Disc sound system and seats costing $9,627.

Most Valuable Swiss Army Knife An 18-karat gold Swiss army knife, produced by Swiss jeweler Luzius Elmer, has a current retail price of $4,299.

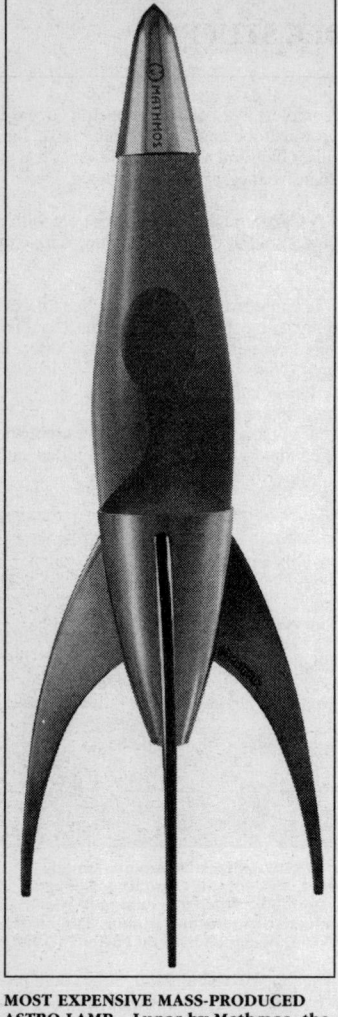

MOST EXPENSIVE MASS-PRODUCED ASTRO LAMP Lunar by Mathmos, the company that has manufactured the original Astro lamp since 1963, retails at $488. The lamp, which comes in two different color combinations, is 2 ft. 7½ in. tall with a polished aluminum base and cap.

Most Valuable Swatch Watch A limited edition Swatch—one of only 120 made—designed in 1985 by French artist Christian Chapiron (known as Kiki Picasso) sold at auction at Sotheby's in Milan, Italy, in 1989 for $45,000. When they were first released, the watches were given away for free.

Least Profitable Photograph On March 5, 1960, Alberto Diaz Gutiérrez (known as Alberto Korda) took a photograph of the Argentinian revolutionary Ernesto "Che" Guevara at a memorial ceremony in Havana, Cuba. In 1967, the year Guevara was killed while attempting to foment a revolution in Bolivia, Korda gave the picture to the Italian publisher Feltrinelli but did not charge him because he considered him "a friend of the Revolution." Feltrinelli exploited Guevara's iconic status in the 1960s counterculture and sold 2 million posters in six months. Korda never received a penny in royalties or copyright.

Most Valuable Warhol Picture Andy Warhol's screen print *Orange Marilyn* sold for $17.3 million at Sotheby's in New York City in May 1998. Warhol was one of the leading figures in the pop-art movement, which began in the 1950s and also included Roy Lichtenstein, Claes Oldenburg, and Peter Blake. Popular images such as Coca-Cola bottles, Campbell's soup cans, and Marilyn Monroe's face were elevated to cult status through Warhol's use of repetition and garish coloring. Warhol, who also made films such as *Flesh* (1968) and *Andy Warhol's Dracula* (1974), died in 1987.

VALUABLE STUFF 1

Most Valuable Luggage A complete set of Louis Vuitton luggage, which includes an armoire trunk, a wardrobe trunk, a steamer trunk, four matching suitcases, a hat box, a cruiser bag, and a jewelry case, costs a total of $601,340, making it the most expensive luggage set in the world.

Most Valuable Vanity Case A Cartier jeweled vanity case set with a fragment of ancient Egyptian steel was sold at Christie's in New York City for the record sum of $189,000 in November 1993.

Most Valuable Shoes In 1977, Emperor Field Marshal Jean Bédel Bokassa of the Central African Empire (now the Central African Republic) commissioned a pair of pearl-studded shoes from the House of Berluti in Paris, France, for his self-coronation. Costing $85,000, they are the most expensive pair of shoes ever made.

The most expensive shoes on the market cost $28,800 and are made by the design company Gina of London, England. The size 5 sandals are made out of alligator skin, lined with kid leather, and have buckles studded with diamonds. They were designed by Aydin Kurdash.

Most Valuable Cuff Links Gianni Vivé Sulman of Marylebone, London, England, has produced 73 pairs of cuff links costing a record $39,750 each. They are made from 18-karat gold set with diamonds.

Most Valuable Cigars On November 16, 1997, an Asian buyer

MOST VALUABLE BARBIE DOLL
The Mattel toy company celebrated the 40th anniversary of the introduction of its Barbie doll in March 1999 by creating a one-of-a-kind customized Barbie worth $82,870. Produced in association with the diamond company De Beers, the doll was unveiled at David Morris Jewelers in London, England, and contains 160 diamonds weighing nearly 20 karats set in 18-karat white gold. The train is secured by a diamond bow centering around the letter B. The bow itself can be removed and worn as a brooch. A headdress, drop earrings, and dress ring, all made of diamonds set in 18-karat white gold, complete the aquamarine silk outfit.

MOST VALUABLE GEM MODEL CAR The Gem Prowler, which has been valued at $210,000, was cut from the world's largest amethyst—a rough amethyst from Bolivia that started out at 15,000 karats and finished at 9,600 karats. Its other components include 1 lb. of white gold and 18 karats of white and canary diamonds. The windshield is carved out of rock crystal. It was created by US firm Diamond Cutters International for Chrysler Plymouth to inaugurate the launch of the latter's new Roadster in 1997.

paid a record $16,560 each for 25 Trinidad cigars made by the Cuban National Factory. The sale took place at Christie's, London, England.

Most Valuable Slice of Cake In February 1998, a piece of cake left over from the wedding of the Duke of Windsor and Wallis Simpson more than 60 years earlier sold at Sotheby's in New York City for the record sum of $29,900 to California entrepreneur Benjamin Yim and his wife, Amanda. The cake, which formed part of the Windsor collection auction, had been expected to fetch a maximum of $1,000 at the sale.

Most Valuable Ice Hockey Puck The Million Dollar Puck, created by Diamond Cutters International of Houston, Texas, is made of platinum, diamonds, and emeralds. The puck, which is actual-size, is covered in 733 stones, including 171 karats in diamonds and four karats in emeralds. It was created for the Houston Aeros Hockey Team in 1996 and is valued at more than $1 million.

Most Valuable Jigsaw Puzzle Custom-made Stave "Dollhouse Village" puzzles, which have 2,640 pieces, were created by Steve Richardson of Norwich, Vermont, and cost $14,500 each in June 1999, making them the world's most expensive jigsaw puzzles.

Most Valuable Board Game The most expensive commercially available board game is the deluxe version of Outrage!, which is produced by Imperial Games of Southport, England. The game, in which participants have to steal the Crown Jewels from the Tower of London, retails at $6,621.

Most Valuable Monopoly Set   An exclusive $2-million Monopoly set was created by the jeweler Sidney Mobell of San Francisco in 1988. The board is made from 23-karat gold, and the dice have 42 full cut diamonds for spots.

Most Valuable Dinky Toy   On October 14, 1994, a collector paid $20,312 for a 1937 Dinky Bentalls store delivery van at Christie's, London, England.

MOST VALUABLE WEDDING DRESS   Sabrina Battaglia (Italy) poses in a wedding dress costing $6 million, made for her marriage on December 7, 1998. The most expensive wedding outfit ever was created by Hélène Gainville, with jewels by Alexander Reza, and was valued at $7.3 million. The dress was unveiled in Paris, France, on March 23, 1989.

MOST VALUABLE DECKED CHRISTMAS TREE On December 5, 1996, the world's most expensive decorated Christmas tree ever was erected in the Place du Rhône, Geneva, Switzerland. It was decorated with ornaments donated by Piaget International SA; their total value was $8,885,588, excluding tax. Each contained a total of 31 watches and 11 pieces of jewelry.

Most Valuable World Cup Replica A soccer World Cup "decoy" trophy sold for the sum of $407,200—12 times the estimated price—at Sotheby's, London, England, in July 1997. The gold-painted trophy, a replica of the one that was won by England in 1966, was ordered by the Football Association after the real cup was stolen in 1966. The original was later discovered by a dog named Pickles, but for two years the replica was passed off as the genuine Jules Rimet trophy and was protected by security guards to keep up the pretense for the public.

Most Valuable Fragments of Other Planets A piece of Martian meteorite fetched $7,333—more than 1,000 times its weight in gold—at Phillips in New York City in May 1998. The rock, which measures $^7/_{100} \times ^7/_{100} \times ^3/_{20}$ in. and weighs $^9/_{1,000}$ oz., was found in Brazil in 1958 and was expected to sell for $1,600–$3,200.

Sotheby's in New York City sold $^1/_{100}$ oz. (or less than two karats) of rock from the moon for $442,500 in 1993. A total of 800 lb. of lunar rock exists on Earth, compared with 90 lb. of Martian rock.

VALUABLE STUFF 2

Most Valuable Sacred Object The 15th-century gold Buddha in Wat Trimitr Temple in Bangkok, Thailand, has the highest intrinsic value of any sacred object in the world—$38.3 million at the June 1999 price of $259 per troy ounce. It is 10 feet tall and weighs an estimated $5^1/_2$ tons. The gold under the plaster exterior was only discovered in 1954.

Most Valuable Missing Art Treasure The Amber Room, presented to Catherine the Great of Russia by Frederick William l of Prussia in 1716, was installed in the Catherine Palace near St. Petersburg, Russia. It consisted of intricately carved amber panels and decorated chairs, tables, and amber ornaments. In 1941, invading Germans dismantled the room and took it back to Germany, where it was reassembled in the castle at Königsberg, East Prussia (now Kaliningrad, Russia). The Amber Room was

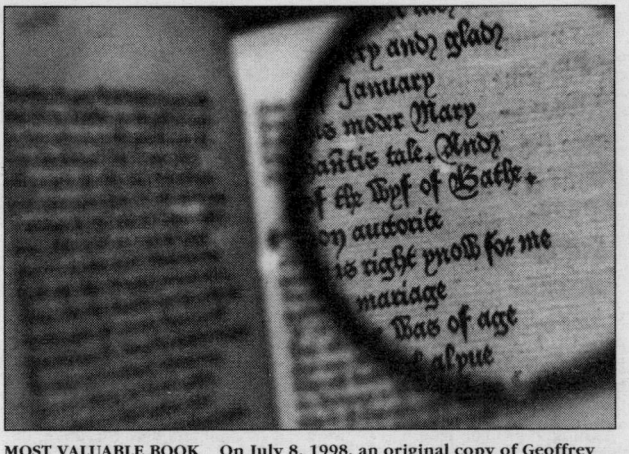

MOST VALUABLE BOOK   On July 8, 1998, an original copy of Geoffrey Chaucer's *Canterbury Tales* sold at Christie's in London, England, for a record $7,394,400—more than nine times the expected price. The book was the first major work printed in England by William Caxton, in 1477.

crated up and put into storage in 1945 and subsequently disappeared. A single panel resurfaced in Germany in 1997.

Most Valuable Diary   A dog-eared diary reportedly telling the story of Davy Crockett's last moments at the Alamo but often dismissed as a forgery was sold at auction for $350,000 in Los Angeles in November 1998. The diary, said to have been written by a Mexican officer called José Enrique de la Pena, seems to refute the legend that Crockett met a heroic end in battle, instead stating that he was taken prisoner and executed by the Mexican forces who took the fortress from its Texan defenders in 1836. Sold to an unnamed bidder, the diary consists of two handwritten sheaves bound with ragged ribbons.

Most Valuable Illustrated Manuscript   The *Codex Leicester*, an illustrated manuscript in which Leonardo da Vinci predicted the invention of the submarine and the steam engine, sold at auction for $30.8 million at Christie's in New York City on November 11, 1994. Bought by Microsoft chief Bill Gates, the world's wealthiest man, it is the only Leonardo manuscript in private hands.

Most Valuable Letters   The highest price paid for a signed letter is $748,000 for a letter written by Abraham Lincoln on January 8, 1863. It was sold to Profiles in History of Beverly Hills, California, at Christie's in New York City on December 5, 1991.

The highest price paid for a letter signed by a living person is $12,500 for a letter from President Ronald Reagan praising Frank Sinatra. It was sold at the Hamilton Galleries on January 22, 1981.

Most Valuable Music Manuscripts   The highest amount paid for a musical manuscript is $4.136 million by London dealer James Kirkman at

Sotheby's in London, England, on May 22, 1987, for a 508-page bound volume of nine complete symphonies in the hand of their composer, Wolfgang Amadeus Mozart.

The highest price paid for a single musical manuscript is $2,008,380 for the autographed copy of the Piano Sonata in E Minor, Opus 90, by Ludwig van Beethoven, at Sotheby's in London, England, on December 6, 1991.

Most Valuable Flag　A white ensign found by the British explorer Captain Robert Falcon Scott on a beach in Antarctica in 1902 sold for $45,868 at Christie's in London, England, in October 1997. It had been expected to fetch $8,151.

Most Valuable Banknotes　The highest price achieved at auction for a single lot of banknotes is a record $424,578, paid by Richard Lobel on behalf of a consortium at Phillips in London, England, on February 14, 1991. The lot consisted of a cache of more than 17 million British military notes found in a vault in Berlin, Germany.

Most Valuable Coin　An 1804 silver dollar—one of only 15 left and valued at $500,000—fetched $1.815 million at auction in New York City on April 8, 1997. The coin had been owned by banker Louis Eliasberg, the only person known to have ever owned a complete collection of US coins.

Most Valuable Stamp　The most valuable stamp is the Swedish treskilling, which was sold for $2.3 million in November 1996.

Most Valuable Set of Stamps　A set of 48 twopenny blue stamps in mint condition was discovered in a rolled-up leather writing case in Dalkeith Palace, Midlothian, Scotland, by Alexander Martin when he was compiling an inventory of the palace's contents. The set has been valued at $4.56 million, based on a single mint-condition stamp selling for $8,287. The stamps, which have been owned by three different collectors since their discovery in 1945, are now to be sold on the open market.

Most Valuable Carpet　The Spring carpet of Khusraw, which was made for the audience hall of the Sassanian palace at Ctesiphon, Iraq, was the most valuable carpet ever made. It consisted of about

MOST VALUABLE *SS TITANIC* ITEMS　Pictured here is a cast-iron nameplate and a White Star Line flag retrieved from a lifeboat after the sinking of the *SS Titanic* in April 1912. They were auctioned for $79,500 at Christie's in New York City on June 9, 1998. The demand for items connected to the ill-fated liner has increased massively since the release of director James Cameron's film *Titanic* (1997).

MOST VALUABLE VIOLIN The Kreutzer, a violin created by Antonio Stradivari in 1727, was sold for $1,516,000 at Christie's in London, England, on April 1, 1998.

7,000 ft.^{2} of silk and gold thread encrusted with emeralds. The carpet was cut up as booty by looters in A.D. 635. Had it remained intact it would now be worth approximately $1.66 million.

Most Valuable Fountain Pen The biggest sum ever paid for a fountain pen was $218,007 for the "Anémone" fountain pen, made by French company Réden, in February 1988. Bought by a Japanese collector, the pen was encrusted with a total of 600 precious stones, including emeralds, amethysts, rubies, sapphires, and onyx, and took a team of skilled craftsmen more than a year to complete.

Most Valuable Surgical Instrument The highest price ever paid for a surgical instrument is $34,848 for a 19th-century German medical chain-

MOST VALUABLE EGG Fabergé, the Russian jewelers, created about 56 Imperial Eggs between 1885 and 1917. The most valuable is embellished with more than 3,000 diamonds. In November 1994, it sold at Christie's in Geneva, Switzerland, for $5,587,308.

saw sold at Christie's in London, England, on August 19, 1993.

Most Valuable Piano
The highest price ever paid for a piano is $1.2 million for a Steinway created under the direction of Sir Lawrence Alma-Tadema, which sold at auction at Christie's in London, England, on November 7, 1997. It was purchased by the Sterling and Francine Clark Art Institute in Williamstown, Massachusetts.

Most Valuable Magic Lantern The highest price ever paid for a magic-lantern slide projector is $51,536 for a *c.* 1880 Newton & Co. Triunial lantern sold at Christie's in London, England, on January 17, 1996.

Most Valuable Camera The highest price ever paid for a camera is $59,459 at Christie's in London, England, on November 25, 1993. The camera had been customized for Sultan Abdel Aziz of Morocco in 1901, when each of its metal components was replaced with gold parts by the manufacturer for a costly sum of $9,820 paid by the sultan.

SHOPPING

Biggest Credit Card Transaction In 1995, Eli Broad of Los Angeles, California, purchased Roy Lichtenstein's painting *I… I'm Sorry* (1965-66) for the sum of $2.5 million, paying with his American Express card. The highest credit card transaction to date, it earned Broad a total of 2.5 million air miles.

Most Credit Cards Walter Cavanagh from Santa Clara, California, has a total of 1,397 different credit cards, which together are worth more than $1.65 million in credit. He keeps his collection in the world's longest wallet, which is 250 ft. in length and weighs 38 lb. 8 oz.

Biggest Shopping Center The West Edmonton Mall in Alberta, Canada, was opened in 1981 and completed four years later. The mall is the size of 110 soccer fields, covers an area of 5.2 million ft.^{2} on a 121-acre site, and houses more than 800 stores and services, as well as 11 major department stores. It serves approximately 20 million customers annually and provides parking for 20,000 vehicles. A water park, golf course, ice rink, and chapel can all be found inside.

Biggest Shopping Center in Europe Bluewater in Kent, England, opened in March 1999 and covers an area of 1.675 million ft.^{2}, of which 1.5 million ft.^{2} is retail space. It currently contains 201 shops, three department stores, three malls, and three leisure villages. It has parking for more than 13,000 cars and is surrounded by a landscaped park and a lake.

Biggest Open-Air Shopping Center Ala Moana Center in Honolulu, Hawaii, has more than 200 shops over a 50-acre site, making it the world's largest open-air shopping center. The center is visited by more than 56 million shoppers every year.

MOST EXPENSIVE SHOPPING STREET Shoppers wait outside the jewelry store Tiffany & Co. on Fifth Avenue in New York City. Fifth Avenue is the most expensive street in the world in which to rent store space, at $580/ft.^{2}. Other retailers with outlets there include the department store Saks Fifth Avenue and the toy store FAO Schwarz. It is followed in cost by 57th Street, also in New York City ($500/ft.^{2}) and Oxford Street in London, England ($400/ft.^{2}).

MOST MALLS IN ONE COUNTRY   Shoppers are seen streaming through the Forum Shops in Caesar's Palace, a gigantic hotel and casino complex in Las Vegas, Nevada. The Forum Shops, which are set in a replica of an ancient Roman street, attract approximately 20 million visitors per year and feature everything from upmarket fashion boutiques such as Gucci, Versace, and Bernini to smaller specialty stores and a number of restaurants. The US has more shopping malls (defined as enclosed, climate-controlled environments typically anchored by at least one major department store with an area of more than 400,000 ft.^{2}) than any other country, with a total of 1,897 to date. If they are added to the number of grocery-, drug-, or discount-anchored centers (which are generally of open-air design), the total number of shopping centers is 42,048.

Biggest Departement Store   At 2.15 million ft.^{2}, the world's largest department store by area is Macy's, an 11-story building occupying an entire block in Herald Square, New York City. The company has a chain of department stores across the US and was one of the first major retailers to place such stores in shopping centers.

Longest Mall   The longest shopping mall in the world is located inside the $64 million shopping center in Milton Keynes, England. The mall is a total of 2,360 ft. in length.

Biggest Underground Shopping Complex   The biggest underground shopping complex is the PATH Walkway in Toronto, Canada, which has 16 miles 1,368 yd. of shopping arcades with 4 million ft.^{2} of retail space.

Biggest Open-Air Market   The San José flea market sits on 120 acres of land in the heart of Silicon Valley, California. The market was officially opened in 1960 on an abandoned cattle feedlot and had 20 vendors and about 100 customers. Today, it averages more than 6,000 vendors and 80,000 visitors each week and has a management staff of 150.

Biggest Duty-Free Center   Heathrow Airport, London, England, currently has the biggest turnover of any duty-free center in the world, with

$396 million in 1997. Following Heathrow, Honolulu Airport in Hawaii is second, with a turnover of $360 million. The third-biggest duty-free center is Schiphol Airport in Amsterdam, Netherlands, with a turnover of $335.3 million.

Most Stores Owned by One Company On January 28, 1996, the Woolworth Corporation of New York had 8,178 retail stores worldwide—the most that any company has ever had. The company's founder, Frank Winfield Woolworth, opened his first store, The Great Five Cent Store, in Utica, New York, in 1879. Woolworth no longer trades in the US.

Biggest Electronics Retailer Best Buy Co. Inc. is the biggest retailer of consumer electronics, home-office products, audio-video equipment, entertainment software, and domestic appliances, with 1998 sales topping $8.3 billion. It is ranked 199th in the *Fortune 500* list.

Most Electronics Retail Outlets Radio Shack has more than 6,900 stores and franchises selling electronics and computers across the United States.

Biggest Toy Store Chain Toys 'R' Us, based in Paramus, New Jersey, has a total of 1,000 stores and 43 million ft.^{2} of retail space worldwide. The largest single Toys 'R' Us store is the branch in Birmingham, England, at 65,000 ft.^{2}.

BIGGEST FASHION RETAIL CHAIN Gap Inc. has almost 2,400 stores selling its casual clothing in Canada, France, Germany, Japan, the UK, and the US. The company, which was founded in San Francisco, California, in 1969, had sales of $6,507.8 million in 1998. It is currently rated No. 174 in the *Fortune 500* list. Its profile has risen in recent years thanks to its innovative advertising, featuring stars such as Aerosmith and Iggy Pop.

Greatest Sales per Unit Area   The record for the greatest sales figures in relation to area of selling space is held by Richer Sounds plc, a British hi-fi retail chain. Sales at its branch in London Bridge Walk, England, reached a peak of $27,830/ft.^{2} for the year ending December 31, 1994.

Most Shoppers at One Department Store   The most visitors to a single department store in one day is an estimated 1.07 million to the Nextage Shanghai in China on December 20, 1995.

Biggest Garage Sale   The record for the greatest amount of money raised at a one-day garage sale is $214,085.99, at the 62nd one-day garage sale organized by the Winnetka Congregational Church, Illinois, in May 1994.

The White Elephant Sale at the Cleveland Convention Center, Ohio, raised $427,935.21 over two days from October 18 to 19, 1983.

Biggest Wholesale Mart   The world's biggest wholesale merchandise mart is the Dallas Market Center, Texas, which has a total floor area of approximately 6.9 million ft.^{2}. It houses a total of 2,580 permanent showrooms displaying the merchandise of more than 50,000 manufacturers.

GAMBLING

Biggest Casino   Foxwoods Resort in Connecticut houses the biggest casino in the world, with a gaming area that covers 192,670 ft.^{2} Its facilities include a total of 3,854 slot machines, 234 gaming tables, and seats for 3,500 bingo players.

Biggest Lottery   In the 1997/98 financial year, the UK National Lottery, operated by Camelot plc, was ranked the world's single largest lottery in sales terms by an independent survey in *La Fleur's Lottery World* magazine. Total ticket sales for the lottery came to $9,256.5 million for the year.

Most Millionaires Created by a Single Lottery Draw   Millions 2000, which culminates on January 1, 2000, aims to award a top prize of $48 million and to make 2,000 other people millionaires. Tickets for this millennium lottery cost $9.60 and give entry to monthly draws. The lottery pays out a monthly jackpot of $96,000 in cash, as well as awarding prizes such as cars and vacations. Four billion tickets will have to be sold to meet the anticipated jackpots. It has been set up by the International Lottery in Liechtenstein Foundation in order to raise more than $1.5 billion for various humanitarian causes around the world.

Most Efficient Lottery   The UK National Lottery returns more money to good causes and the government, both in terms of cash and as a percentage of sales revenue, than any other lottery in the world, according to an independent survey in *La Fleur's Lottery World* magazine. Camelot, the lottery organizer, returned $4,105.1 million—44.3% of its total sales—in 1997/98.

BIGGEST POKER PRIZE Huck Seed (above right) of Las Vegas, Nevada, won a pot of $2.3 million from Dr. Bruce Van Horn (above left) of Ada, Oklahoma, en route to winning the 27th Annual World Series Poker Championship on May 16, 1996. Seed's first-place finish in the $10,000 Buy-In No-Limit Texas Holdem competition also earned him a prize of $1 million. Van Horn won a $585,000 runner-up prize. An engineering student, Seed took a leave of absence from college in 1989, began making money as a professional poker player, and never returned to his studies.

Highest Spending per Capita in a Lottery The Massachusetts Lottery is the top lottery in the world in terms of ticket sales per person—$525 per capita was spent on tickets in 1998.

Fastest-Selling Lottery Tickets Powerball lottery tickets in Wisconsin were selling at a rate of 380,000 an hour when the jackpot reached a lump-sum payment of $137 million, or $10 million every year for the next 25 years.

Biggest Slot Machine Jackpot The biggest-ever slot machine jackpot was $27,582,539 won by an anonymous Las Vegas woman on a Megabucks machine at the Palace Station Hotel and Casino, Las Vegas, Nevada, on November 15, 1998. The winner, a former flight attendant in her mid-60s, had won over $680,000 on another slot machine (the Wheel Of Fortune MegaJackpot) less than a month before.

Biggest Video Poker Jackpot In April 1998, a grandmother from San Antonio, Texas, hit a jackpot of $839,306.92—the world's biggest-ever video poker jackpot—on the Five Duck Frenzy™ machine at the Las Vegas Club, Las Vegas, Nevada.

Earliest Full House "Full House" calls were made on the 15th number by Norman A. Wilson at Guide Post Working Men's Club, Bedlington, England, on June 22, 1978; Anne Wintle of Bryncethin, Wales, in Bath, England, on August 17, 1982; and Shirley Lord at Kahibah Bowling Club, Australia, on October 24, 1983.

Latest Full House "House" was not called until the 86th number at the Hillsborough Working Men's Club, Sheffield, England, on January 11, 1982. There were 32 winners.

BIGGEST INDIVIDUAL LOTTERY WIN Maria Grasso, a babysitter from Boston, Massachusetts, won the $197-million Big Game Jackpot in the Massachusetts Lottery in April 1999—the largest-ever win by an individual.

Biggest House in Bingo   The record for the largest-ever house in a bingo session was 15,756 people at the Canadian National Exhibition, Toronto, on August 19, 1983. The competition, which was organized by the Variety Club of Ontario, Canada, offered total prize money of $202,872 and a record one-game payout of $81,084.

Most Bingo Numbers Called in One Hour   The most numbers called in one hour by an individual is 2,668 by Paul Scott at the Riva Bingo Club, Brighton, England, on February 16, 1997.

Biggest Bookmaker   Ladbrokes had a peak turnover of $4,570 million from gambling in 1998 and is the world's largest chain of betting shops, with more than 2,000 outlets in the United Kingdom and the Republic of Ireland at the end of that year and other branches throughout the world.

Biggest Horse Racing Payout   The largest payout for a bet on a horse race was $1,627,084 after tax, paid to Britons Anthony Speelman and Nicholas Cowan on their $64 nine-horse accumulator at Santa Anita Racecourse, California, in 1987.

Largest Racecourse Jackpot in Relation to Stake   On June 15, 1997, the race day Triple Trio (predicting the first, second, and third horses in the second, third, and fifth races on the card) jackpot at Happy Valley Racecourse, run under the auspices of the Hong Kong Jockey Club, stood at $25.9 million for a stake of $1.39.

Biggest Nonprofit Racing Club   All money made by the Hong Kong Jockey Club, after payment of prizes, operating costs, betting tax, and investments to improve racing and betting facilities, is donated to community projects, both social and educational. In 1998, the club donated more than $131.9 million, making it the biggest nonprofit racing club ever.

Highest Annual Betting Turnover for a Racing Club   The total betting turnover of the Hong Kong Jockey Club, China, for the 1997/98 season was $12.1 billion. Approximately one-third of Hong Kong's adult population bets on horse racing during the season. Bets can be placed on the racecourse or at 120 sanctioned betting stations throughout Hong Kong.

Most Accurate Tipsters   The only recorded instance of a horse-racing correspondent forecasting 10 out of 10 winners on a single race card was at Delaware Park, Wilmington, Delaware, on July 28, 1974, by Charles Lamb of the *Baltimore News American*.

In greyhound racing, the best performance is 12 out of 12 by Mark Sullivan of *The Sporting Life* newspaper for a meeting at London, England, on December 21, 1990.

Highest-Ever Odds Secured for an Accumulator   The highest odds for an accumulator bet were 3,072,887 to 1 by an unnamed woman from Nottingham, England, on May 2, 1995. She placed an $0.08 accumulator at Ladbrokes Bookmakers on five horses that won at odds of 66-1, 20-1, 20-1, 12-1, and 7-1 and won $242,496.95 for the accumulator and $328,442.32 in total.

Edward Hodson of Wolverhampton, England, won a 3,956,748 to 1 bet with a $0.73 stake on February 11, 1984, but the bet had a $4,008 payout limit.

Biggest Tote Win   The biggest recorded Totalizator win in the United Kingdom was one of $1,659 from a stake of $0.49, representing odds of 3,410 to 1, by Catharine Unsworth of Liverpool, England, at Haydock Park on a race won by Coole on November 30, 1929.

Biggest Win on Soccer Pools   The world-record individual payout by a soccer pools company is $4,483,153.90 paid by Littlewoods Pools to a syndicate at the Yew Tree Inn, Worsley, England, for games played on November 19, 1994.

FAME

MOVIE STARS

Most Leading Roles   John Wayne acted in 153 films in the course of his career, starting with *The Drop Kick* (1927) and ending with *The Shootist* (1976). He played the lead in all but 11 of them.

Longest Screen Career   Curt Bois made his debut in *Der Fidele Bauer* (Germany, 1908) at the age of eight. His final film appearance was 80 years later in Wim Wenders' *Wings of Desire* (Germany, 1988).

Longest Screen Partnerships   The Indian stars of Malayalam cinema, Prem Nazir and Sheela, starred opposite each other in a total of 130 movies until she retired in 1975.

HIGHEST-EARNING MOVIE STAR   The world's top-earning movie actor is Harrison Ford (above), who earned $58 million in 1998. Ford has appeared in nine of the 45 highest-grossing films of all time. His signature roles include Indiana Jones in the trilogy beginning with *Raiders of the Lost Ark* (1981) and Han Solo in the original *Star Wars* trilogy.

MOST WEIGHT LOST AND GAINED FOR FILM APPEARANCES Many stars go to extremes in their efforts to change size for a role. Jennifer Jason Leigh (pictured) went down to a weight of 86 lb. for her role as an anorexic teenager in the TV movie *The Best Little Girl in the World* (1981). Gary Oldman's efforts to lose 30 lb. to play punk star Sid Vicious in *Sid and Nancy* (UK, 1986) were so successful that the British actor ended up in hospital, where he was treated for malnutrition. However, the record-holder is Robert De Niro, who gained 60 lb. for his role as Jake La Motta in Martin Scorsese's *Raging Bull* (1980), portraying the boxer's decline from world-class athlete to bloated has-been.

The longest Hollywood partnership (excluding performers billed together solely in series films) was 15 films, by Charles Bronson and Jill Ireland from 1968 to 1986.

Longest Comedy Partnerships Americans Stan Laurel and Oliver Hardy acted together in more than 50 comedy films between 1927 and 1940. They first appeared together in *Lucky Dog* (1917) but did not act together again until 1926. *The Music Box* (1932) received an Oscar for Best Short Film.

Myrna Loy and William Powell acted together in 13 films between 1934 and 1947, including the MGM *Thin Man* series, in which they starred as Nick and Nora Charles, a husband-and-wife detective team.

Most Films by a Dancing Partnership Fred Astaire and Ginger Rogers appeared as a dancing partnership in nine movies, starting with *Flying Down to Rio* (1933), in which they had a brief dance number called the Carioca. Their subsequent films included *The Gay Divorcee* (USA, 1934) and *Shall We Dance?* (USA, 1937).

Youngest No.1 Box-Office Star Shirley Temple was seven years old when she became the No. 1 star at the US box office in 1935.

Highest-Paid Child Performer Macaulay Culkin was paid $1 million for *My Girl* (1991) when he was 11 years old. Culkin subsequently earned $5 million plus 5% gross for *Home Alone II: Lost in New York* (1992) and a reputed $8 million for *Richie Rich* (1994).

TOP-GROSSING FEMALE STAR The US gross from the 20 films in which Julia Roberts has appeared to June 20, 1999, is $1.202 billion. They include *Steel Magnolias* (1989), *Pretty Woman* (1990), *My Best Friend's Wedding* (1997), and *Notting Hill* (UK, 1999).

Most Devoted Method Actors Daniel Day Lewis is reputed to have spent many nights without sleep in a mock jail cell in order to prepare for his role in *In the Name of the Father* (Ireland/ GB/US, 1993), while for *Last of the Mohicans* (1992), he went to a survival camp to learn to track and kill animals and make canoes from trees.

Nicolas Cage had two teeth removed without painkillers for his part in *Vampire's Kiss* (1988). He also ate six live cockroaches to make the scene "really shock."

Greatest Age Range Portrayed by an Actor in One Film Dustin Hoffman was 33 when he played the role of Jack Crabb in *Little Big Man* (1970). In the course of the film, his character ages from 17 to 121.

Most Characters Played by an Actor in One Film Alec Guinness played eight members of the ill-fated d'Ascoyne family in *Kind Hearts and Coronets* (UK, 1949).

Fewest Actors in a Narrative Film *Yaadein* (Reminiscences, India, 1964) was written, directed, and produced by Sunil Dutt, who was also its only actor. The two-hour film was shot entirely in one location and featured cartoon characters and balloons to represent other people. The movie's only other living presence is the actress Nargis (Dutt's wife), who is shown in silhouette.

TALLEST FEMALE STARS AND SHORTEST ADULT MALE STAR Actress Sigourney Weaver (pictured left) is 6 ft. tall, the same height as two other leading ladies, Brigitte Nielsen and Geena Davis. Danny DeVito (on the right), who starred opposite Arnold Schwarzenegger in *Twins* (1988), is 5 ft. in height.

Most Appearances as James Bond   Sean Connery and Roger Moore have both starred as British secret agent 007 seven times. Connery appeared in the first Bond movie, *Dr. No*, in 1962 and apparently bowed out after *Diamonds Are Forever* (1971) but made a comeback in *Never Say Never Again* in 1983. Roger Moore made his debut in *Live and Let Die* in 1973 and last played 007 in *A View to a Kill* in 1985.

Tallest Male Star   Christopher Lee, veteran of horror films such as *Dracula* (GB, 1958), is the tallest major movie star, at 6 ft. 5 in. in height.

Shortest Adult Female Star   Linda Hunt, who won an Oscar for her role as a Eurasian cameraman in *The Year of Living Dangerously* (Australia, 1982), is 4 ft. 9 in. tall.

Highest Movie Insurance Quote   The troubled actor Robert Downey Jr. was reputedly working uninsured on *The Gingerbread Man* (1998). The premium for insuring him would have cost a record $1.4 million on a film with a budget of less than $42 million.

POP STARS

Highest-Earning Pop Star   Celine Dion ranked 12th on *Forbes* magazine's list of the 40 richest entertainers, with an income of $55.5 million, making her the world's highest-earning pop star of 1998. She has had many No. 1 hits around the world, and her success has been boosted by movie tie-ins such as "My Heart Will Go On," the love theme from the movie *Titanic* (1997).

Highest-Earning Girl Band   The Spice Girls ranked 20th on *Forbes* magazine's list of the 40 richest entertainers of 1998, with an income of $49 million.

Most Valuable Pop Star on the Stock Market   David Bowie commands an estimated fortune of $250 million. In 1997, Bowie raised $55 million through the issue of bonds, which he then sold to Prudential Insurance. Other pop stars thought to be following Bowie's example include members of the Rolling Stones.

Most Fan Clubs   There are more than 480 active Elvis Presley fan clubs worldwide—more than for any other musical star. This is particularly astonishing in view of the fact that Presley, who died in August 1977, did not record in other languages, except for a few soundtrack songs, and only once performed in concert beyond the borders of the US, in Canada in 1957.

Most Appearances on the Cover of Rolling Stone *Magazine*   Mick Jagger, the singer with the Rolling Stones, has appeared on the cover of *Rolling Stone* magazine a total of 16 times.

Most Grammys Won in a Year   The most Grammy Awards won in a single year is eight, by Michael Jackson in 1984. Jackson began his career

BIGGEST RECORD CONTRACT LAWSUIT George Michael fought a nine-month court battle during 1993 and 1994 in an attempt to end his contract with Sony Music. He eventually lost the case, which cost him an estimated $1.96 million, and his contract was eventually bought out by US company Dreamworks.

as a child star in his brothers' band, the Jackson Five. He launched his solo career in 1972 with the song "Got To Be There," and 10 years later released the album *Thriller*, which sold more than 48 million copies worldwide.

Most Brit Awards Annie Lennox, formerly of the Eurythmics, has won seven Brit awards—more than any other artist or act. Her most recent award was Best British Female Artist in 1996.

British band Blur hold the record for the most wins in a year, with four in 1995.

Piano Played by the Most Pop Stars A Bechstein grand piano was used by a number of influential pop stars during the 1960s and 1970s, including the Beatles on *The White Album*, David Bowie on *The Rise and Fall of Ziggy Stardust and the Spiders from Mars* and *Hunky Dory*, and Elton John on *Goodbye Yellow Brick Road* and *A Single Man*. The instrument, which is now valued at $24,861-$29,833, was rented from the Samuels music shop in London, England, and became the resident piano at Trident Studios, London, England.

Most Valuable Lyrics In February 1998, the autographed lyrics to "Candle in the Wind 1997" sold for $442,500 in Los Angeles, California. The lyrics were rewritten by Bernie Taupin, and the song was performed by Elton John for the funeral of Diana, Princess of Wales, in September

HIGHEST-EARNING POP GROUP The Rolling Stones are the world's wealthiest pop group, with earnings of $94.5 million in 1998 alone. The band was formed in April 1962 in London, England, and has been fronted ever since by Mick Jagger, pictured here with Keith Richards and Ron Wood. By 1964, they were the only serious rivals to the Beatles, and the next few years saw a string of classic singles such as "(I Can't Get No) Satisfaction." In 1970, Austrian financial adviser Prince Rupert Loewenstein took over their affairs, translating their "bad boy" image and live reputation as "The Greatest Rock 'n' Roll Band in the World" into unprecedented earnings.

1997. The three-page manuscript, signed by John and Taupin, was bought by the Lund Foundation for Children, which funds programs for disadvantaged children.

Most Charities Supported by a Pop Star Michael Jackson has supported 39 charity organizations either with monetary donations through sponsorships of their projects or through participating in their silent auctions. The charities involved include AIDS Project L.A., American Cancer Society, BMI Foundation, Inc., Childhelp USA, United Negro College Fund (UNCF), YMCA—28th Street/Crenshaw, The Sickle Cell Research Foundation, and Volunteers of America.

Most Expensive Promotions for an Album by a Pop Star Promotions for Michael Jackson's album *HIStory* (1995) included a 30-ft.-high inflated statue of the pop star on top of Tower Records in Hollywood, California, a huge sign in Times Square, New York City, and another statue floated on a barge down the river Thames in London, England. Jackson's record company, Sony, spent a total of $40 million on promotions for the launch of the album in the US, the United Kingdom, Italy, Australia, Japan, South Africa, and the Netherlands.

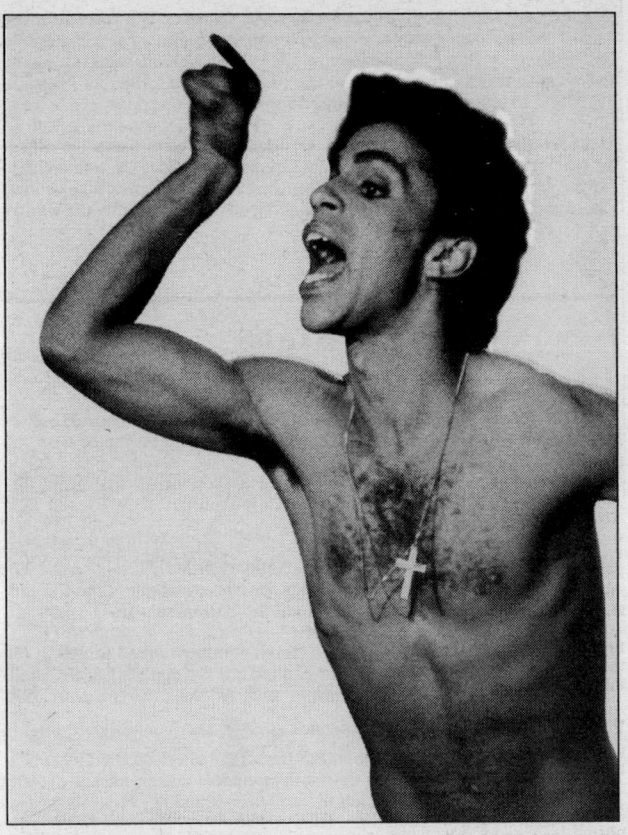

MOST PSEUDONYMS USED BY A POP STAR Prince Rogers Nelson made his first album, *For You*, as Prince in 1978. He has since used the names Tora Tora, Coco, Alexander Nevermind, Victor, Camille, Christopher, Jamie, ♀, The Artist Formerly Known As Prince, and The Artist for his work as performer, producer, and songwriter.

Most Product Endorsements by a Pop Group in a Year The Spice Girls hold the record for the greatest number of promotions by a group in any one year, with 10 different advertisers in 1997, including Sony PlayStation and Mercedes. A $1-million deal with Pepsi involved 40,000 Pepsi drinkers being flown to Istanbul, Turkey, for a Spice Girls concert and after-show party.

Most Paid to a Pop Star for Advertising Rights The software company Microsoft acquired the rights for the Rolling Stones' hit single "Start Me Up" for $8 million and featured it in its *Windows '95* campaign.

Biggest Advertising Deal to be Turned Down   The record for the largest sum of money ever rejected by a pop star for an advertising deal is $12 million, by Bruce Springsteen in 1987. The sum had been offered by car manufacturer Chrysler for the use of Springsteen's 1984 hit "Born in the USA" in one of their car commercials.

Highest-Earning Music Producer   Master P, chief executive officer of No Limit Records, based in New Orleans, Louisiana, is estimated to have a net worth of $56.5 million. Born Percy Miller, Master P has stayed out of the East Coast/West Coast rappers' feud and is currently the world's most successful rap star.

TV STARS

Highest-Paid TV Comedy Actor   Jerry Seinfeld, the former star of *Seinfeld*, tops the 1999 *Forbes* Celebrities 100 List with estimated earnings of $267 million.

Tim Allen was the highest-paid star of a show broadcast during the 1998/99 season, drawing a salary of $1.25 million per show for the final season of *Home Improvement*.

Highest-Paid TV Drama Actor   Anthony Edwards, who plays Dr. Mark Greene on *ER*, earns $400,000 per episode as a result of the $35-million deal that keeps him on the show until the 2001/02 season.

Highest-Paid Talk Show Host   Oprah Winfrey ranked fourth in the 1999 *Forbes* Celebrities 100 List, with an income for that year of $125 million. She has also appeared in movies such as *The Color Purple* (USA, 1985) and *Beloved* (USA, 1999).

Highest-Paid News Broadcaster   Barbara Walters reputedly earns in excess of $13 million a year as news correspondent and co-anchor of *ABC News Magazine*, *20/20*, *The Barbara Walters Specials*, and *The View*. She has interviewed every US president since Richard Nixon, and she made journalistic history when she arranged the first joint interview of President Anwar Sadat of Egypt and Prime Minister Menachem Begin of Israel in November 1977.

Highest-Paid Magician to Appear on TV   The highest-paid magician to appear on TV is David Copperfield, who earned $50 million in 1999 according to the *Forbes* Celebrities 100 List. The fiancé of supermodel Claudia Schiffer, Copperfield's conjuring stunts include making the Statue of Liberty "disappear."

Highest-Paid TV Writer   Larry David, co-writer of the hit comedy *Seinfeld*, was second only to the show's star on the 1999 *Forbes* Celebrities 100 List, despite leaving the show in 1996. He returned to write the finale in 1998. David's earnings for 1999 are estimated at $242 million.

Chris Carter, creator of *The X-Files* and *Millennium*, is the wealthiest active TV writer, earning $52 million in 1999.

Highest-Paid TV Producer Mike Judge, creator of animated series such as *Beavis and Butt-head* and *King of the Hill*, was the leading TV producer in the *Forbes* 1999 rich list, with earnings of $53 million.

Most Watched TV Star David Hasselhoff is the star and producer of *Baywatch*, which has an estimated weekly audience of 1.1 billion in 142 different countries. Hasselhoff, the only actor to have been with the show through its entire run, also starred in the TV show *Knight Rider* (1982-85) and is a major pop star in Germany. He has been named one of TV's 10 most powerful stars by *TV Guide* magazine. Female *Baywatch* stars have included Pamela Anderson, Gena Lee Nolin, and Yasmine Bleeth.

Most Watched TV Star in Japan Akashiya Sanma (real name Sugimoto Takafumi) polled 56.8 points in Video Research (Japan) Ltd.'s twice-yearly survey of television popularity. Japanese television stars flit from show to show as featured or special guests, so, in any given week, a star could be on several different programs across four different networks.

Most Watched TV Star in France Newscaster Patrick Poivre d'Arvor is watched by more viewers than any other French television personality. On December 2, 1997, his news show *TF1 20 hrs* had 15.02 million viewers across the country. The star receives extensive press attention and in April 1996 was the victim of *l'entarteur*—the Belgian anarchist Noel

LONGEST TIME IN THE SAME ROLE William Roache has been playing the character Ken Barlow without a break since the first episode of the British soap opera *Coronation Street* in 1960. The character was first seen as a student, and since then he has had three wives and 23 girlfriends, been a newspaper editor and a teacher, and survived a suicide attempt.

Godin, who pelts his targets with custard pies.

Most Watched TV Star in Germany

Thomas Gottschalk currently hosts Germany's top-ratings show *Wetten Daß* (*I Bet That...*), in which guest celebrities are asked to bet on whether contestants will succeed in record attempts. The program receives 23% of the total audience share. Gottschalk, Germany's most popular TV personality, has appeared in many other TV shows as well as in a great number of national advertising campaigns.

Most Watched TV Star in Russia

Valdis Pelsh, the star of the music show *Uguday Melodiyu* (*Guess the Melody*), is Russia's most popular television personality. The show, which is shown six times a week (three original broadcasts and three morning repeats), receives up to 56% of the total audience share in Russia.

Most Watched Male TV Host in the United Kingdom

Chris Tarrant hosts the quiz show *Who Wants To Be A Millionaire?*, in which contestants have the chance to win £1 million ($1.66 million). The show on March 7, 1999, resulted in BARB ratings of 19.21 million and an audience share

MOST WATCHED TV STAR IN LATIN AMERICA
Brazil's Maria da Graça Meneghel, known as Xuxa, is the most-watched Latin American TV star. A Spanish-language version of the four-and-a-half-hour-long *Xuxa Show* (originally in Portuguese) is shown in 16 countries. The 36-year-old blue-eyed blonde began her TV career as the host of a children's show in 1982 and is renowned for her love of children: in October 1989, she established the Xuxa Meneghel Foundation, which provides food, shelter, and education for Brazilian young people. She has also spearheaded campaigns against AIDS, drug abuse, and polio.

of 67.8%. Tarrant, who first came to national prominence fronting the children's show *TIS-WAS*, is also a successful radio disc jockey.

Most Watched Female TV Host in the United Kingdom Cilla Black, who hosts the popular British dating show *Blind Date*, is currently the most watched TV host in the UK. The show, which has been running since 1984, had an average of 9.1 million viewers per episode in the 1997/98 season. In 1997, Cilla was made an OBE (Officer of the Order of the British Empire) by Queen Elizabeth II for her services to British entertainment.

Longest Career as a TV Host The astronomy program *The Sky At Night*, which airs monthly on British television, has been hosted by Patrick Moore without a break or a missed show since April 24, 1957. By January 1999, a total of 541 episodes had been broadcast.

RICHEST ACTRESS ON TV Helen Hunt, the star of *Mad About You*, is the world's wealthiest TV actress, with a net worth of $31 million. Her TV debut was on *The Mary Tyler Moore Show*, and she has won an Oscar for *As Good As It Gets* (1997).

SPORTS STARS

Highest Earnings in a Year   The greatest earnings by an athlete in a year, excluding monies from sponsorship and endorsements, is $75 million by boxer Mike Tyson in 1996. In 1986, Tyson had become the youngest boxing heavyweight world champion of all time when he beat Trevor Berbick to win the WBC title at the age of 20 years 144 days.

Highest Career Earnings by an Athlete   Retired basketball legend Michael Jordan earned more money during his 13-year basketball career than any other athlete in history, including endorsement deals. Now aged 36, Jordan earned $33 million in salary with the Chicago Bulls for his last season (1998) plus a further $47 million in endorsements, making him *Forbes*'s highest-paid athlete for the fifth time in six years. By 1998 his career earnings had exceeded $300 million.

Highest-Earning Tennis Players   By May 1999, US tennis player Pete Sampras' career earnings from prize money alone totaled $36.1 million. In 1997, he was paid a total of $8 million for his biggest endorsement deals with Nike and Wilson. Sampras also holds the men's record for earnings in a season, at $6.5 million in 1997.

BIGGEST SPORTS CONTRACTS   Kevin Garnett signed a $126 million, 6-year contract extension with the Minnesota Timberwolves on 3 Oct 1997, the biggest contract in the NBA. In 1997 Alonzo Mourning of the Miami Heat (pictured), Shaquille O'Neal (LA Lakers) and Juwan Howard (Washington Wizards) also signed nine-figure deals.

HIGHEST EARNINGS BY A FEMALE ATHLETE Steffi Graf (Germany) had earned a total of $21,512,490 in prize money by June 21, 1999, beating the record set by her fellow tennis star Martina Navrátilová (US, formerly Czechoslovakia). However, Navrátilová still holds the record if endorsements and sponsorship deals are included in the figure.

Andre Agassi (US) made a total of $15.8 million during 1998—the most made by a tennis player in one year. This figure includes his prize money as well as his endorsement deals with companies such as Nike, Canon, and Head.

Highest-Earning Soccer Player Brazilian soccer player Ronaldo Luis Nazario de Lima, known simply as Ronaldo, is the world's highest-earning soccer player. In 1998, the Inter Milan striker earned a total of $8.9 million. This figure results from Ronaldo's monthly wage of $324,000 plus $162,000 in bonuses and an additional $4.8 million from his advertising contracts and other sponsorship deals.

The earnings of Manchester United midfielder David Beckham reached $4.7 million in 1998, making him the highest-earning soccer player in the United Kingdom and the second highest in the world.

Highest-Earning Golfers The highest all-time career earnings on the US PGA Tour is $12.29 million, by Australian golfer Greg Norman between 1976 and May 1999. Norman has had more than 70 victories worldwide in his career.

The season's record on the US PGA Tour is $2.96 million for the US season through June 1999 by David Duvall (US).

Hale Irwin (US) won a record-breaking $2.86 million on the US Seniors PGA Tour in 1997.

The record career earnings for a woman golfer is $6.28 million, by Betsy King (US) from 1977 to 1998.

The record season's earnings by a woman golfer is $1.24 million, by Annika Sorenstam of Sweden in 1997.

Colin Montgomerie (GB) won a season's record of $1.64 million in European Order of Merit tournaments in 1998.

Fastest $1 Million Earned by a Golfer from Turning Pro In 1996 US golfer Tiger Woods broke South African Ernie Els' record for the fewest events played since turning professional to earn $1 million. Woods needed only nine pro starts. By the end of his debut season, he had won five tournaments and earned more than $2 million. Woods was the highest-earning golfer of 1997 and the second-highest-paid endorser in sports, collecting $2.1 million in salary and winnings and $24 million in

MOST PRIZE MONEY WON IN A SEASON Marion Jones (US) notched up one of the greatest seasons by any athlete, male or female, in 1998, when she won all but one of the 36 events she contested and remained undefeated at both 100 m and 200 m. Jones took the overall Grand Prix title as well as individual titles at 100 m and long jump, which meant she received one-third of the Golden League Jackpot— giving her $633,333 from the Grand Prix final alone.

endorsements. In September 1996, he signed a $40 million contract with Nike, which brought out a new Woods apparel line in June 1997.

Oldest High-Earning Athlete In 1997, the 68-year-old US golfer Arnold Palmer earned a total of $16.1 million from salary, winnings, and endorsements, making him the 12th-highest earner in sport. Palmer, who was the first golfer to win more than $1 million on the PGA Tour, still plays on the PGA Senior Tour.

Most Successful Musical Career by an Athlete Shaquille O'Neal, center for the Los Angeles Lakers, also has a successful music career. He released his debut album, *Shaq Diesel* (1993), when he was 21, and in 1997, his record label, TWIsM. (The World Is Mine), formed a joint venture with A&M Records to produce a fourth album.

Highest-Earning Cricketer Indian cricketer Sachin Tendulkar earns around $4 million per year. The vast majority of this figure comes from sponsorship deals for companies such as Pepsi, Visa, Cadbury's, and Colgate. He appears in almost a quarter of all Indian TV commercials and is one of the most well known faces on the entire Indian subcontinent.

Highest-Earning Ice Hockey Player The world's highest-earning ice hockey player is Sergei Federov (Russia), who plays for the Detroit Red

HIGHEST-EARNING FORMULA ONE DRIVER In 1996, German Formula One driver Michael Schumacher was paid a record $25 million to drive for Ferrari's Formula One team—the highest salary in the history of Formula One. Schumacher's total earnings in 1997 have been estimated at $35 million, including salary and winnings as well as sponsorships and endorsements.

Wings. Federov earned a record $29.8 million from a combination of wages and endorsements in 1998.

Highest-Earning NFL Player Based on salary and endorsement contracts the highest earning NFL player in 1998 was Green Bay Packers quarterback Brett Favre, who earned a reported $13.1 million. Based on player salaries only, Deion Sanders of the Dallas Cowboys was the highest paid player in 1998, earning $7,579,000.

Highest-Earning Snooker Player The most successful snooker player ever in terms of tournament earnings is Stephen Hendry (GB). Hendry has won a record total of $9.92 million after he won the World Championship for the seventh time in 1999—itself a record for the modern era. At that championship, Hendry won $368,000, which brought his cumulative earnings from World Championship competitions to a total of over $2.4 million.

SUPERMODELS

Tallest Supermodel The tallest supermodel is Australian-born Elle MacPherson, who is 6 ft. 1 in. tall. She is known as "The Body" because her dimensions—36-24-35 in.—are regarded as perfect.

Shortest Supermodel The shortest supermodel is British model Kate Moss, who was discovered by Storm Agency's Sarah Doukas at JFK Airport in New York City in 1990. At just over 5 ft. 6 in. in height, she seemed an unlikely choice but went on to revolutionize modeling, making way for a new type of model and a new trend called "grunge." The first big designer to use Kate Moss was Calvin Klein, with whom she signed a $2-million contract in 1991.

Longest-Legged Supermodel Of all the supermodels, German model Nadja Auermann has the longest legs, at 45 in. She shot to fame in 1993, when the fashion world rejected grunge in favor of glamour. By 1994, she had appeared on the covers of *Harper's Bazaar* and *Vogue*.

Richest Supermodel
Elle MacPherson is said to be worth $38.12 million, making her the richest supermodel in the world. Although she no longer appears regularly on the catwalk, she still commands huge fees and has various business interests. These include a share in the Fashion Café chain and her own line of lingerie, Elle MacPherson Intimates. Elle has also appeared in several films, including *Sirens, Jane Eyre,* and *Batman & Robin*. Cindy Crawford is the world's second-richest supermodel, with an estimated wealth of $34.8 million.

MOST SUCCESSFUL MODELING AGENCY The agency Elite has a record 35 supermodels on its books, including Karen Mulder (pictured), Claudia Schiffer, Cindy Crawford, and Amber Valletta. It currently earns more than $100 million in modeling fees every year. Set up by John Casablanca (US) in Paris, France, in 1971, Elite only represents female models and has approximately 500 women on its books worldwide.

Biggest Supermodel Joint Venture Claudia Schiffer, Elle MacPherson, and Naomi Campbell all own shares in the Fashion Café theme restaurants. The chain, which aims to reflect the glamour and excitement of the fashion world, has seven branches in major cities worldwide, including Barcelona, Spain, and New York City. Two more restaurants are under construction in Dubai and Singapore, and the chain has secured 27 other locations around the world.

Longest Contract Christy Turlington (US) has represented Calvin Klein for over 10 years—an industry record. She gave up catwalk modeling in 1995 and graduated from New York University in May 1999 with a liberal arts degree.

Biggest Cosmetics Contract In 1993, Claudia Schiffer signed the biggest cosmetics contract ever when she was offered the sum of $6 million to become the face of Revlon. Claudia has done campaigns for all the big fashion houses and was a particular favorite of Karl Lagerfeld. She has also made her own fitness video, and she made her movie debut in 1998 with *The Blackout*.

Top-Paying Catwalk Shows
One of the main forces behind the supermodel phenomenon was the late Italian designer Gianni Versace. Versace is reported to have paid top models as much as $50,000 per half-hour show in the late 1980s on the proviso that they would only appear in his show that season. This is said to have created the elite group of models—Christy Turlington, Naomi Campbell, and Linda Evangelista—who dominated fashion magazines in the early 1990s.

Largest International Modeling Agency Elite Model Management is currently based in 22 countries around the world, with 11 offices in Europe and five in the US. The company has bases as far apart as São Paulo, Brazil, and Hong Kong, China.

YOUNGEST SUPERMODEL TO WIN A MAJOR COSMETICS CONTRACT
Niki Taylor was just 13 when she won $500,000 in a "Fresh Faces" contest run by a New York model agency in 1989. This is the largest sum that any girl who has gone on to become a supermodel has won in a contest of this kind. She went on to sign a deal with L'Oréal for Cover Girl, the youngest model ever to win a major cosmetics contract.

LONGEST SUPERMODEL CAREER
Christy Turlington has been modeling for a longer period of time than any other supermodel since being discovered at the age of 13. She began modeling full-time in 1987, when she was 17. By 1988, she was the face of the perfume Eternity and had secured a deal with Maybelline worth $800,000 for 12 days' work.

Most Magazine Covers Claudia Schiffer was spotted in a disco in Germany when she was 17 and has not stopped working since. She has appeared on approximately 550 magazine covers, more than any other supermodel.

Most Vogue Covers Christy Turlington has appeared on the cover of British *Vogue* a record 21 times. Her first appearance was in July 1986, and her most recent appearance was in January 1996.

Longest Catwalk Career Carmen Dell'Orefici was born in 1931 and has been modeling for the Ford Agency since the 1940s. At the age of 68, she is still in demand for contracts and international shows.

Daphne Self is 70 years old but has had a sporadic modeling career. She is signed to Models 1 in London, England, has been photographed for *Vogue* and *Marie Claire*, and features in the 1999 Laura Ashley campaign.

HIGHEST-PAID SUPERMODEL According to *Forbes* magazine, Claudia Schiffer earns $10.5 million a year—more than any other supermodel. Her wealth is currently estimated at $34 million, making her the richest European supermodel.

OSCARS & AWARDS

Most Versatile Award Winner Actress/singer/director Barbra Streisand has won two Oscars, five Emmys, seven Grammys, seven Golden Globes, and a special Tony in 1970 as Broadway Actress of the Decade.

Most Best Director Oscars John Ford won four Oscars as Best Director for *The Informer* (1935), *The Grapes of Wrath* (1940), *How Green Was My Valley* (1941), and *The Quiet Man* (1952).

Most Best Director Nominations William Wyler was Oscar-nominated a record 12 times for his directing between 1936 and 1965 and won the award three times, for *Mrs. Miniver* (1942), *The Best Years of Our Lives* (1946), and *Ben-Hur* (1959).

Most Best Actress Oscars Katharine Hepburn won a record four Best Actress Oscars, for *Morning Glory* (1933), *Guess Who's Coming to Dinner* (1967), *The Lion in Winter* (UK, 1968—award shared), and *On Golden Pond* (1981). Hepburn also had the longest award-winning career, spanning 48 years.

Most Best Actor Oscars Seven people have won the Best Actor Academy Award twice: Spencer Tracy, for *Captains Courageous* (1937) and *Boys Town* (1938); Fredric March, for *Dr. Jekyll and Mr. Hyde* (1932) and *The Best Years of Our Lives* (1946); Gary Cooper, for *Sergeant York* (1941) and *High Noon* (1952); Marlon Brando, for *On the Waterfront* (1954) and *The Godfather* (1972—award declined); Jack Nicholson, for *One Flew Over the Cuckoo's Nest* (1975) and *As Good As It Gets* (1997); Dustin Hoffman, for *Kramer vs. Kramer* (1979) and *Rain Man* (1988); and Tom Hanks, for *Philadelphia* (1993) and *Forrest Gump* (1994).

Most Best Supporting Actor Oscars Walter Brennan won Oscars for Best Supporting Actor in *Come and Get It* (1936), *Kentucky* (1938), and *The Westerner* (1940).

MOST CONSECUTIVE EMMY AWARDS The comedy series *Frasier* has won five consecutive Emmy Awards as Best Comedy Series. Kelsey Grammer (third from right) has also won three Emmys for Best Actor for his role as psychiatrist Dr. Frasier Crane, and David Hyde Pierce (right of picture), who plays Frasier's brother, Niles, has won two Best Supporting Actor awards.

Most Best Supporting Actress Oscars The record is two: Shelley Winters won Oscars for her roles in *The Diary of Anne Frank* (1959) and *A Patch of Blue* (1965); and Dianne Wiest won for *Hannah and Her Sisters* (1986) and *Bullets Over Broadway* (1994). Both of Wiest's roles were in films directed by Woody Allen.

Most Awards for One Role Marlon Brando won (but declined) the Best Actor award for his role as Vito Corleone in *The Godfather* (1972) and Robert De Niro won a Best Supporting Actor award for his performance as the younger Corleone in *The Godfather Part II* (1974).

Barry Fitzgerald was nominated for both Best Actor and Best Supporting Actor for *Going My Way* (1944), winning the latter. This is the only time that one actor has been nominated in two acting categories for the same film.

Youngest Oscar Winners Tatum O'Neal was 10 years old when she was voted Best Supporting Actress for *Paper Moon* (1973).

Shirley Temple was awarded an honorary Oscar at the age of five in 1934.

Oldest Oscar Winner Jessica Tandy won the Best Actress award for *Driving Miss Daisy* (1990) at the age of 80.

MOST GOLDEN RASPBERRIES The Spice Girls (above) made history at the 1999 Golden Raspberries when all five were given the Worst Actress Award for their collective performance in *Spiceworld: The Movie* (UK, 1997); they were the most people ever to share the prize. The Golden Raspberries (or "Razzies") were instituted by author John Wilson in 1980 to complement the Academy Awards by highlighting the worst the film industry had to offer. Other "winners" have included Bruce Willis, Demi Moore, Leonardo DiCaprio, Pamela Anderson, Kevin Costner, and Madonna. The 20th ceremony, in 2000, will name the 100 Worst Films of the 20th Century. Votes are being taken on the Golden Raspberry website: www.razzies.com.

MOST FAMILY MEMBERS TO HAVE WON OSCARS Walter Huston was named Best Supporting Actor for *The Treasure of the Sierra Madre* (1948), his son John won Best Director for the same film, and John's daughter Anjelica won Best Supporting Actress for *Prizzi's Honor* (1985). Francis Ford Coppola took the Best Director award for *The Godfather Part II* (1974), his father, Carmine, won the Best Original Score award for the same film, and Nicolas Cage (Francis' nephew, right) was named Best Actor for *Leaving Las Vegas* (1995).

Most Oscar Nominations Without an Award Both Richard Burton and Peter O'-Toole have been nominated for the Best Actor Award seven times, but neither has won. Burton was nominated for *My Cousin Rachel* (1952), *The Robe* (1953), *Beckett* (UK, 1964), *The Spy Who Came in from the Cold* (UK, 1965), *Who's Afraid of Virginia Woolf?* (1966), *Anne of the Thousand Days* (UK, 1970), and *Equus* (UK, 1977). O'Toole's nominations were for *Lawrence of Arabia* (UK, 1962), *Beckett* (UK, 1964), *The Lion in Winter* (UK, 1968), *Goodbye Mr. Chips* (UK, 1969), *The Ruling Class* (UK, 1969), *The Stunt Man* (1980), and *My Favorite Year* (1982).

Most Oscars for Best Foreign Language Film by One Country Italy has won 13 Oscars for Best Foreign Language Film, the most recent being *Life Is Beautiful* in 1999.

Most Appearances as a Host at the Oscars Bob Hope hosted the Academy Awards a record 13 times: in 1940 (the second half of the show), 1945, 1946, 1953, 1955, 1958, 1959, 1960, 1966, 1967, 1968, 1975, and 1978.

Youngest People to Win Tonys Daisy Eagan was 11 years old when she won the Tony Award for Best Actress in a Featured Role in a Musical (equivalent to a Best Supporting Actress award) for her part in *The Secret Garden* in 1991.

MOST CÉSAR AWARDS   French star Isabelle Adjani is the only person to have won four Césars, awarded by the French Académie des Arts. Her first was in 1982, for her role in Andrzej Zulawski's *Possession*. She went on to win awards for her work in *L'Eté Meurtrier* in 1984, *Camille Claudel* in 1989, and *La Reine Margot* in 1995.

Liza Minnelli, at the age of 19, was the youngest person to win a lead role Tony. She won for her performance in *Flora, The Red Menace* in 1965.

Most Consecutive BAFTA Wins   Robbie Coltrane won three consecutive Best Television Actor awards for his role as forensic psychiatrist Fitz in Granada Television's series *Cracker* from 1994 to 1996.

Most Grammys   The individual who won the most Grammys was the Hungarian-born British composer Sir Georg Solti, who had 31 by the time of his death in 1997.

WORLD LEADERS

Youngest President   The youngest head of state of a republic is Yaya Jammeh, who became president of the provisional council and head of state of Gambia at the age of 29 on July 26, 1994, and was elected president at the age of 31 on September 27, 1996.

Oldest Prime Minister   Sirimavo Bandaranaike became prime minister of Sri Lanka at the record age of 78 in 1994. She had become the first female prime minister anywhere in the world when she first took office in 1960.

Shortest Presidency   Pedro Lascurain was president of Mexico for one hour on February 18, 1913. The legal successor to President Madero, who was murdered on February 13, 1913, Lascurain was sworn in, appointed General Victoriano Huerta as his successor, and resigned.

Most Reelected Presidents   Cambodia, Iraq, and Lebanon have all had presidents who were reelected to office eight times. Prince Norodom Sihanouk was elected prime minister of Cambodia for the first time in March 1945 and last served as prime minister from 1961 to 1962. Iraq's

OLDEST PRESIDENT AND YOUNGEST PREMIER   The oldest republican head of state is 82-year-old Kiro Gligorov, president of the former Yugoslav republic of Macedonia (right). The country also has the youngest prime minister, Ljupco Georgievski of the Internal Macedonian Revolutionary Organization—Democratic Party of Macedonian National Unity (VMRO-DPMNE), who was born on January 17, 1966 (left). He took office on November 30, 1998, when he was 32 years old.

LONGEST TIME IN POWER Fidel Castro became prime minister of Cuba in July 1959 and has been president and head of government since December 3, 1976. He came to power after his third attempt to overthrow the country's dictator Fulgencio Batista. He nationalized all US-owned businesses in Cuba in 1960, which led to numerous CIA-backed actions against him, ranging from the unsuccessful Bay of Pigs invasion of 1961 to an attempt to kill him with an exploding cigar. The continuing US economic blockade, combined with the Soviet Union's cancelation of economic support in 1991, has caused increasing hardship in the country, although Cuba still maintains one of the highest literacy rates in the world.

Nuri as-Said first served as prime minister in 1930 and served intermittently until his last reelection in 1958. Rashid Karami was elected prime minister of Lebanon for the first time in 1955, and his last term ran between 1984 and 1987.

President Suharto won six consecutive elections from 1967, holding the reins of power in Indonesia for 31 years until he was forced out of power in 1998 following violent demonstrations by university students.

Highest Personal Majorities Boris Yeltsin, the president of the Russian Federation, had a personal majority of 4.73 million votes in the elections in the Soviet Union in March 1989. He received 5.12 million votes out of the 5.72 million cast in his Moscow constituency.

Benazir Bhutto achieved 98.48% of the poll in the Larkana-III constituency at the 1990 general election in Pakistan, with 94,462 votes. The next highest candidate obtained 718 votes.

Most Women Leaders Serving Simultaneously Fourteen women served as prime minister, president, or co-captain regent between January 1 and December 31, 1993, in Dominica, Norway, Pakistan, Bangladesh, Poland, Canada, Turkey, Burundi, Rwanda, Iceland, Nicaragua, Ireland, and San Marino.

Biggest Presidential Staff The republican head of state with the biggest staff is President Bill Clinton. There are more than 1,000 employees at the White House, including domestic staff, caterers, groundskeepers, security personnel, and interns. Some of this number also work for Hillary Rodham Clinton, the First Lady.

Most Expensive Presidential Inauguration The inauguration of the president in Washington, DC, which takes place every fourth year, is the most expensive in the world. The most expensive presidential inauguration ever was that of George Bush in 1989, which cost a total of $30 million.

President with Most Family Members in Power Until 1995, Barzan Ibrahim, a half brother of Iraqi president Saddam Hussein, was ambassador to the UN and controlled much of the family fortune. Another of Saddam's half brothers, Watban Ibrahim, was minister of the interior, and a third half brother, Sabaoni Ibrahim, was chief of general security. Saddam's son-in-law, Saddam Kamal Hussein, was commander of the presidential guard until he fled to Jordan in 1995, and his sons, Udday and Qusay, hold various state and other offices. The latter was head of security services but was replaced by one of Saddam's in-laws.

Most Descendants to Become Prime Minister Pandit Jawaharlal Nehru became India's first prime minister when the country attained independence on August 15, 1947, and remained in power until his death in 1964. His daughter Indira Gandhi served as prime minister from 1966 to 1977 and from 1980 until she was assassinated by her own bodyguards in 1984. Rajiv Gandhi, Indira's eldest son, became prime minister following his mother's death and won the 1984 elections by a landslide. He served until 1989 and was assassinated while campaigning for the premiership in 1991.

MOST MARRIED PRIME MINISTER Currently, the most married prime minister in a monogamous society is Gerhard Schroeder, who has been married four times. The German chancellor is pictured here on the far right with (right to left) his fourth wife, Doris, French prime minister Lionel Jospin, and Jospin's wife, Sylviane.

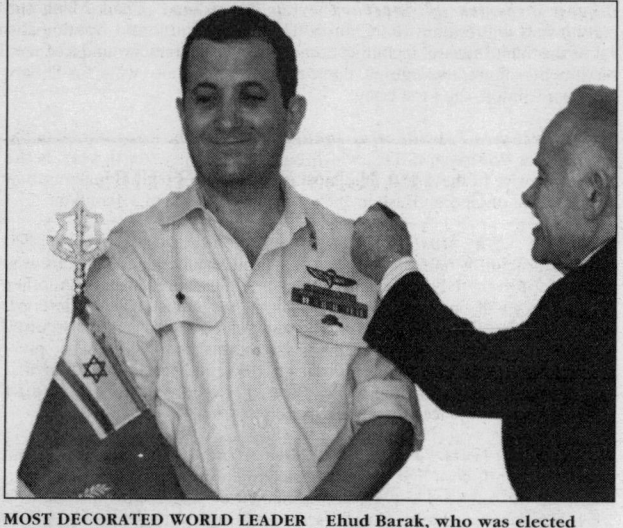

MOST DECORATED WORLD LEADER Ehud Barak, who was elected prime minister of Israel on May 17, 1999, has won more military decorations while on military service than any other current premier. He was awarded four citations for conspicuous gallantry, more than any other soldier in the history of the Israeli Army. He is pictured on the occasion of his promotion to Chief of Staff in May 1991.

Longest 20th-Century House Arrest   Nobel Peace Prize winner Aung San Suu Kyi, leader of the National League for Democracy, was placed under house arrest on July 20, 1989, by Burma's military government and held until July 10, 1995. The daughter of assassinated Burmese leader General Aung San, she was held under martial law that allows detention for up to three years without charge or trial. It was extended to six years in 1994.

President to Have Spent the Least Time in His Country   Valdus Adamkus, who became president of Lithuania in 1998, returned to the republic in 1997 after living in Chicago, Illinois, for more than 50 years.

Most Accessible Prime Minister   With the exception of the leaders of some "microstates," the most accessible head of government is the Danish premier Poul Nyrup Rasmussen, whose home phone number is in the public domain. Rasmussen often personally answers telephone queries from Danish citizens. Openness in government in Denmark extends to the sovereign—any citizen may request an audience with Queen Margrethe II.

Most Hospitalized President   Boris Yeltsin has had 13 known hospital stays between his election as president of the Russian Federation in 1991 and May 1999. He has still managed to surpass the average age attained by Russian males—58—by more than nine years.

Longest Series of Speeches by a Politician   Chief Mangosuthu Buthelezi, the leader of the Inkatha Freedom Party and South African home affairs minister, spoke for an average of 2½ hours on 11 of the 18 days of the KwaZulu legislative assembly in 1993.

CAMPAIGNS & CHARITIES

Biggest Telethons   The Jerry Lewis "Stars Across America" Muscular Dystrophy Association Labor Day Telethon has raised $954 million since it was first broadcast in 1966. The debut show was the first televised fund-raising event of its kind to raise more than $1 million. In 1998, it raised a total of $51.58 million in pledges and contributions.

The Comic Relief program broadcast on BBC television on March 12, 1999, raised $53.04 million. Comic Relief was launched in the UK in 1985 and has since raised over $283.4 million, all of which goes to help some of the poorest and most vulnerable people in the UK and Africa. Apart from UK comedians such as French & Saunders and Rowan Atkinson, movie

MOST MONEY RAISED BY AN INDIVIDUAL IN A MARATHON   Retired advertising executive John Spurling (pictured above) raised $1.87 million for charity by running the London Marathon on April 18, 1999. This more than doubled the previous record of $769,560 set by Sir Roger Gibbs in the 1982 race. The money Spurling raised was divided between the Lord's Taverners—a group of ex-test-match cricketers and celebrities who take part in regular charity cricket matches—and the Animal Health Trust.

BIGGEST SINGLE DONATION TO AIDS RESEARCH In May 1999, the world's richest man, Bill Gates, and his wife, Melinda, donated a record $25 million to research into AIDS and HIV. Other recent donations by the couple have included $1.5 million for Kosovo refugees and a $3.3 billion grant to the William H. Gates Foundation believed to be the largest donation made by a living person to charity. The Foundation supports initiatives in education, global health, and community giving in the Pacific Northwest.

stars such as Johnny Depp and Hugh Grant have performed in the programs, which are broadcast every two years.

Biggest Environmental Fund-Raising Event The Rainforest Foundation International, established by the musician Sting and his wife, Trudi Styler, in 1989, has raised more than $9 million net to support indigenous people and the rain forest. A celebrity benefit concert held in Carnegie Hall in New York City in April 1998 raised a record $2 million gross. It included singers such as Madonna, Elton John, and Billy Joel. The street sign outside Carnegie Hall was renamed "Rainforest Way" during Rainforest Awareness Week, and the Empire State Building was lit up in green.

Most Money Raised for Charity by a Single Sporting Event The London Marathon, run through the streets of London, England, since 1981, raises more money for charity than any other single sporting event in the world. In the 1998 race, a record $26 million was raised.

Longest-Running Charity Soccer Game The Football Association Charity Shield soccer game was inaugurated in 1908 and has been played annually at Wembley Stadium in London, England, since 1924. Money raised from ticket sales is distributed to an average of 90 establishments and causes, including sports charities, hospitals, drug rehabilitation centers, and inner-city development programs. The 1998 charity match between Arsenal and Manchester United raised almost $828,700.

Biggest Rock Benefit Live Aid, the first simultaneous rock concert ever with satellite links between two countries, took place at Wembley Stadium in London, England, and JFK Stadium in Philadelphia, Pennsylvania, on July 13, 1985. The 17-hour concert was attended by 150,000 people (80,000 in Philadelphia and 70,000 in London), and more than 1.6 billion people around the world watched it on television. The concert, which included Queen, Madonna, Tina Turner, and Paul McCartney on the bill, raised $80 million for the Ethiopian Famine Relief Fund, and the charity has raised more than $60 million since then.

MOST OSCAR DRESSES SOLD AT A CHARITY AUCTION   On March 18, 1999, a record 56 dresses and evening gowns that had been worn to the Oscars by actresses such as Julia Roberts, Sharon Stone, and Uma Thurman were auctioned at "Unforgettable: Fashion of the Oscars" at Christie's in New York City. A total of $786,120 was donated to the American Foundation for AIDS Research (AmFAR). The most valuable item was the blue and violet faille-crepe dress worn by Elizabeth Taylor to the 1969 Academy Awards. It sold for $167,500.

Biggest Musical Benefit for AIDS A concert held in memory of rock star Freddie Mercury, who died of AIDS in November 1991, was held at Wembley Stadium in London, England, on April 20, 1992. It was attended by about 75,000 people and is estimated to have been seen by almost 1 billion people in more than 70 countries. The concert raised $35 million for AIDS charities and featured artists such as U2, David Bowie, and Liza Minnelli.

Most Money Raised by a War Relief Benefit Opera star Luciano Pavarotti's War Child charity concert *Pavarotti and Friends* staged on June 1, 1999 raised a record $3.4 million. Held annually in Modena, Italy, since 1995, the concerts have included performances by artists such as Eric Clapton, Mariah Carey, Gloria Estefan and Sheryl Crow. Bono of U2 wrote the hit song "Miss Sarajevo" for the 1995 event.

Most Money Raised in a Secondhand Clothes Sale Elton John's wardrobe has had to be cleared many times due to its size. The star's last two sales made a total of $875,000 for the Elton John AIDS Foundation. The Stage Costume and Memorabilia section of his 1988 sale at Sotheby's in London, England, which included personal possessions as well as clothes, raised $758,133.

Best-Selling Magazine for the Homeless *The Big Issue* was established in London, England, by John Bird with the assistance of Gordon Roddick in September 1991. Between 8,000 and 10,000 homeless and vulnerably housed people sell over 1.1 million copies a month in Los Angeles, California; Cape Town, South Africa; Melbourne, Sydney, and Brisbane, Australia; and throughout the UK.

MEMORABILIA

Most Valuable Dress A blue silk-and-velvet gown worn by Diana, Princess of Wales, when she danced with John Travolta at a White House dinner in 1985 sold for $200,000 at Christie's in New York City on June 26, 1997.

Most Valuable Film Costume The costume for the Cowardly Lion (played by Bert Lahr) in *The Wizard of Oz* (1939) fetched a record $250,000 at auction in Beverly Hills, California, on December 12, 1998.

Most Valuable Film Shoes The red slippers worn by Judy Garland in *The Wizard of Oz* (1939) fetched $165,000 at Christie's in New York City on June 2, 1988.

Most Valuable Film Prop The eponymous statuette from *The Maltese Falcon* (1941) sold for $398,500 at Christie's in New York City in 1994.

Most Valuable Cartoon Poster A poster for Disney's *Alice's Day at Sea* (1924) sold for $34,273 at Christie's in London, England, in April 1994.

MOST VALUABLE STAR DOLL   Elizabeth Taylor and Jamie Lee Curtis are seen here with a one-of-a-kind Elizabeth Taylor doll featuring 27 diamonds set in platinum. It sold for $25,000 at an auction held on October 24, 1998, to raise money for the Children Affected By AIDS Foundation.

Most Valuable Piece of James Bond Clothing   On September 17, 1998, the steel-rimmed bowler hat used as a weapon by Oddjob in *Goldfinger* (UK, 1964) sold for $98,800 at an auction at Christie's in London, England.

Most Valuable Guitar   A Fender Stratocaster that once be-

MOST VALUABLE BASEBALL   The highest price paid for a baseball is $3.054 million, including sales commission, at auction in New York City on January 12, 1999. The ball, which was bought by Todd McFarlane, had been hit by Mark McGwire in September 1998 for a major-league record of 70 home runs in a season. It was retrieved at the game by a fan.

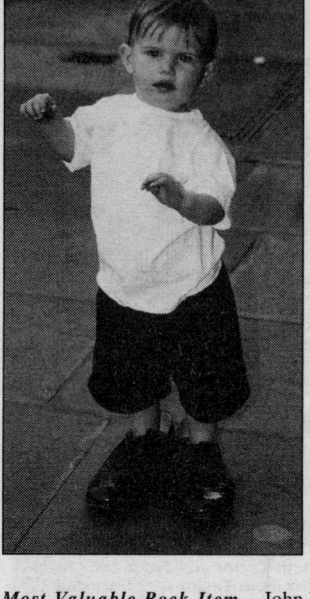

MOST VALUABLE POLITICIAN'S SHOES A young boy is seen here wearing the ostrich-skin shoes that Nelson Mandela wore in 1990, when he walked free after 27 years in a South African prison. They were sold at Christie's in London, England, in May 1995 for $7,100 to Sterling and Hunt, the company that originally made them. Half the proceeds went to help needy children in South Africa, the other half to fund research into premature births in the United Kingdom. The company made a replica of the shoes and presented them to Mandela.

longed to Jimi Hendrix was sold by his former drummer "Mitch" Mitchell for $353,628 at Sotheby's in London, England, on April 25, 1990.

Most Valuable Jazz Instrument A saxophone once owned by jazz legend Charlie Parker sold for $146,328 at Christie's in London, England, in September 1994.

Most Valuable Rock Item John Lennon's 1965 Rolls-Royce Phantom V touring limousine sold for $2.229 million at Sotheby's in New York City on June 29, 1985. It was bought by Jim Pattison, Chairman of the Expo '86 World Fair in Vancouver, British Columbia, Canada, and at the time was the greatest price ever paid for a used car.

Biggest Rock Collection The Hard Rock Café in Philadelphia, Pennsylvania, has 45,000 pieces of rock memorabilia on display, including Madonna's black bustier and vinyl pants that belonged to Sid Vicious, bass player for the Sex Pistols.

Most Valuable Pieces of Rock Star Clothing In 1997, an afghan coat worn by John Lennon on the cover of the Beatles' *Magical Mystery Tour* album (1967) was bought for $57,750 on behalf of his eldest son, Julian.

A complete stage costume worn by ♀ (The Artist Formerly Known as Prince) sold for $20,570 at Christie's in London, England, in December 1991.

A white rhinestone glove owned by Michael Jackson sold for $28,050 in December 1991.

Most Valuable Rock Star Glasses A pair of glasses worn by Buddy Holly sold for $45,000 at auction in New York City in 1990.

Most Valuable Top Hat Sold at Auction On July 15, 1998, a top hat worn on formal occasions by former British prime minister Sir Winston

MOST VALUABLE PIECE OF MADONNA CLOTHING A model is pictured wearing one of Madonna's distinctive studded bras, which sold for $6,400 at Christie's in London, England, in 1997. The biggest sum ever paid for an item of clothing belonging to Madonna is $19,360, for a corset designed by Jean-Paul Gaultier and sold at Christie's in London, England, in May 1994.

Churchill sold for a record $40,480 at Sotheby's in London, England. The hat was sold to an anonymous buyer after a fierce bidding battle.

Most Valuable Tooth In 1816, a tooth belonging to British scientist Sir Isaac Newton sold for $3,785—equivalent to $38,535 today—in London, England.

Most Valuable Hair   In 1988, a lock of hair from the British naval hero Horatio Nelson, who was killed at the Battle of Trafalgar in 1805, sold for $9,475 to a bookseller from Cirencester, England.

Most Valuable Skull   The skull of Emmanuel Swedenborg, the Swedish philosopher and author of *Divine Love and Wisdom*, was bought by the Royal Swedish Academy of Sciences for $10,560 in London, England, on March 6, 1978.

Most Valuable Birth Certificate   Sir Paul McCartney's original birth certificate sold for $84,146 at Bonhams in London, England, in March 1997. The presale estimate was $13,000. The certificate was put on the market by an American collector, and the purchaser remained anonymous.

Most Valuable Formula One Memorabilia   A pair of overalls worn by Brazilian driver Ayrton Senna, who was killed in a high-speed crash at the 1994 San Marino Grand Prix, was bought by an anonymous bidder at Sotheby's in London, England, in December 1996 for $42,140. Senna had worn the overalls in his first Formula One race for the Toleman team in Monaco in 1984. A pair of gloves worn by Senna during the 1987 season went for $4,048 to an anonymous bidder, and a race helmet he wore in 1982 fetched $46,000. It was bought by British racing fan Peter Radcliffe.

Most Valuable Piece of Boxing Memorabilia   A calf-length white robe that once belonged to boxing legend Muhammad Ali sold for $140,000 at Christie's in Los Angeles in October 1997. The buyer chose to remain anonymous. Ali had worn the robe when he defeated George Foreman to regain the world heavyweight championship in the legendary "Rumble in the Jungle" match in Zaïre (now Congo) in 1974.

FANS & FOLLOWERS

Most-Visited Grave Site   Graceland, the former home and final resting place of Elvis Presley, receives more than 700,000 visitors annually from all over the world—more than any other grave site. The record for the greatest number of visitors to Graceland in one year is 753,962 in 1995. On August 17, 1977, the day after his death, Elvis sold in excess of 20 million albums—more than any other artist in a single day.

Biggest Floral Tribute   Between September 1 and 8, 1997, an estimated 9,000–13,000 tons of flowers were laid in memory of Diana, Princess of Wales, at Kensington Palace, St. James's Palace, and Buckingham Palace, London, England. This figure was given by the authorities who removed the flowers at the end of the mourning period; newspapers estimated that there was a total of 5 million bouquets.

Most Impersonated Icon   There are estimated to be more than 48,000 Elvis Presley impersonators around the world, including "the Chinese Elvis" (Paul Chan) and "the Sikh Elvis" (Elvis Singh). One recent addition

MOST WIDELY-SUPPORTED SOCCER TEAM The Supporters Club of Manchester United FC (English Premier Division) has approximately 138,000 members. There is a total of 276 branches in the British Isles and a further 24 branches in countries as diverse as Malaysia and Iceland. The Scandinavian branch is the largest overseas group with around 30,000 members. Accurate figures for unaffiliated supporters are impossible to calculate, but it has been estimated that there are about 20 million Manchester United fans in China alone—enough to fill the team's Old Trafford stadium more than 350 times.

was James Brown from Belfast, Northern Ireland, who performs as "The King." He specializes in performing songs that were written after Presley's death; favorites include Nirvana's "Come As You Are," The Sex Pistols' "Anarchy in the UK" and "Whole Lotta Rosie" by AC/DC.

Biggest Total Audience for a Rock Tour U2 played to 3,940,010 people during their Pop Mart tour, which began in Las Vegas, Nevada, in April 1997 and ended in Johannesburg, South Africa, in March 1998 after 93 concerts.

Biggest TV Audience More people watched the funeral of Diana, Princess of Wales, on September 6, 1998, than any other TV broadcast ever. The global audience was estimated at 2.5 billion people.

Most Ardent Movie Watcher Gwilym Hughes of Gwynedd, Wales, has seen and logged 22,990 films since he saw his first film while in the hospital in 1953. He keeps a diary that contains details of all the movies he has seen. He now watches them on video.

Most Ardent Theatergoers Dr. H. Howard Hughes, Professor Emeritus at Texas Wesleyan College, Fort Worth, attended a record 6,136 shows from 1956 to 1987.

Edward Sutro saw a record 3,000 first-night theatrical productions in the United Kingdom from 1916 to 1956 and possibly more than 5,000 shows in his 60 years of theatergoing.

Nigel Tantrum of East Kilbride, England, attended a record 169 sepa-

rate performances at the 1994 Edinburgh Festival between August 13 and September 4.

Most Pubs Visited

Bruce Masters of Flitwick, England, has visited a total of 31,241 pubs and 1,568 other drinking establishments since 1960, drinking locally brewed beer wherever it is available.

Most Season Tickets Held

Spanish soccer team Barcelona FC sells around 98,000 season tickets (the stadium's capacity) to games at its home field Camp Nou, making it the soccer stadium with the greatest number of season-ticket holders.

MOST POPULAR CULT FILM Sal Piro, the president of the US *Rocky Horror Show* fan club, has seen *The Rocky Horror Picture Show* (UK, 1975) about 1,000 times. *The Rocky Horror Show*, the stage show on which the film is based, was written by Richard O'Brien and opened at the Royal Court Theatre, London, England, in 1973. It rapidly crossed from cult status to the mainstream, and today it has played in all major European countries as well as Australia and the Far East. The film, featuring Tim Curry, Susan Sarandon, and Meat Loaf, is still showing in more than 100 movie theaters in the US and many more across the world, to the delight of fans, who dress as their favorite characters (such as Frank N. Furter and Magenta, above), throw rice, water, and toast at appropriate moments, and chant responses along to the film's soundtrack.

Youngest Fan to Tour Every Soccer League Field

Oliver Newton, from Wakefield, England, had visited every one of the 92 Premiership and Football League fields in England and Wales by the age of five months in 1998. He first visited Nottingham Forest's City Ground when he was just four weeks old and ended his tour at the home of Lincoln City, Sincil Bank. He was accompanied on his travels by his soccer-crazy parents, who have photographed their son next to all of the playing fields.

Most Ardent Train Spotter Bill Curtis from Clacton-on-Sea, England, is the official world-champion train spotter, or "gricer" (a nickname coined in honor of Richard Grice, the first-ever champion, who held the title from 1896 to 1931). Bill Curtis' recorded sightings include approximately 60,000 locomotives, 11,200 electric units, and 8,300 diesel units over 40 years in a number of different countries.

BIGGEST SCI-FI FOLLOWING   The TV series *Star Trek* was first shown in 1966, and there are now more than 350 *Star Trek* web sites and 500 fan publications. After more than 400,000 requests from fans (known as "Trekkies"), NASA named one of its space shuttles *Enterprise*, after the ship in the series.

Most Ardent Bird-Watchers   Phoebe Snetsinger from Webster Groves, Missouri, has spotted 8,040 (82.9%) of the 9,700 known bird species since 1965. She has now seen members of all of the families on the official list and more than 90% of the genera.

The record for the greatest number of bird species to have been spotted in a 24-hour period is 342 by Terry Stevenson, John Fanshawe, and Andy Roberts (all from Kenya) on November 30, 1986, the second day of Birdwatch Kenya '86.

PET SUPERSTARS

Highest-Earning Animal Artist   Ruby the elephant started painting when her keepers at Phoenix Zoo in Arizona saw her making patterns in the dirt with a stick clutched in her trunk and gave her paints, brushes and an easel to work with. Ruby's canvases sell for up to $3,500.

Highest-Earning Literary Dog   In 1991 springer spaniel Mildred Kerr, known as Millie, brought in a salary more than four times that of her

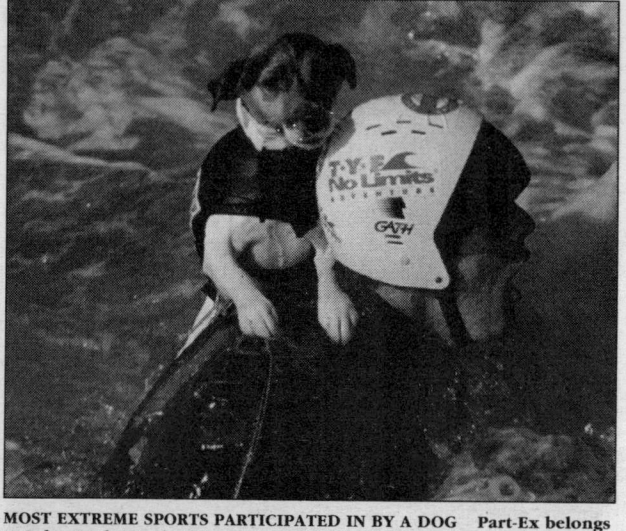

MOST EXTREME SPORTS PARTICIPATED IN BY A DOG Part-Ex belongs to John-Paul Eatock, the manager of Tyf No Limits Adventure Centre, south Wales, UK. The three-year-old Jack Russell terrier joins his owner in a wide range of extreme sports activities including kayaking, abseiling, surfing, windsurfing, and climbing.

master, the then US president George Bush, when her "autobiography" sold 400,000 copies. "Dictated" to First Lady Barbara Bush, *Millie's Book* was described as "an under-the-table look at life in the Bush family." It made a total of $900,000.

Most Tricks Performed by a Dog Chanda-Leah, a champagne-colored toy poodle from Hamilton, Ontario, Canada, performs more than 500 tricks. Chanda-Leah's owner Sharon Robinson has taught the six-year-old to play the piano, count and spell. The dog has appeared on numerous US television shows, including *Regis and Kathie Lee* and *The Maury Povich Show*, and now has her own publicist.

Most Skilled Talking Parrot Alex, an African Grey parrot, has learned words for more than 35 objects and seven colours and can make a distinction between three-, four-, five- and six-sided shapes. His accuracy averages 80%.

Most Patsys Won by an Animal Francis the mule was the first animal to be awarded first place at the PATSY awards, which were held annually from 1951 to 1987 to honor the Picture/Performing Animal Top Stars of the Year and promote the health and safety of showbiz animals. The star of *Francis the Talking Mule* (1949) received his award from actor James Stewart. He went on to win a further six PATSYs—more than any other animal.

Most Successful Drug-Sniffer   Iowa, a black Labrador retriever used by the Port of Miami, made 155 drug seizures worth a record $2.4 billion. Iowa was trained by Armando Johnson and handled by Chuck Meanders, Chief of Canine Operations for the Port of Miami.

The greatest number of seizures by dogs is 969 (worth $182 million) in one year by Rocky and Barco, a pair of malinoises patrolling the Rio Grande Valley along the Texas border. The pair were so proficient that Mexican smugglers put a $30,000 price on their heads.

Most Successful Mouser Towser, a tortoiseshell cat owned by Glenturret Distillery Ltd. near Crieff, Perth and Kinross, Scotland, caught 28,899 mice (an average of three a day) before her death in 1987.

Most People at a Pet's Funeral   In 1920 the funeral of Jimmy the canary from New Jersey was attended by 10,000 mourners. Jimmy's owner, cobbler Edidio Rusomanno, had the bird's body placed in a white casket. The procession was followed by two buses and a 15-piece band.

Richest Cat   Blackie, the last in a household of 15 cats, was left $24 million in the will of his owner, Ben Rea.

Richest Dogs   The biggest legacy ever left to a dog was $15 million, bequeathed by Ella Wendel of New York to her standard poodle Toby in 1931. All of Wendel's dogs were served prime lamb chops by personal butlers and slept in their own bedrooms in hand-carved miniature four-poster beds with silk sheets.

Bathroom fixture magnate Sidney Altman of Beverly Hills, California, left $6 million to his pure-

BIGGEST DOGS   The tallest breeds of dog are the Irish Wolfhound (above) and the Great Dane. The tallest dog on record was Shangret Damzas, a Great Dane owned by Wendy and Keith Comley of Milton Keynes, England. He was 3 ft. 5.5 in. tall at the shoulder and weighed up to 238 pounds. The heaviest dog on record was Aicama Zorba of La Susa, an Old English mastiff owned by Chris Eraclides of London, England. He weighed in at 343 pounds at his heaviest in November 1989.

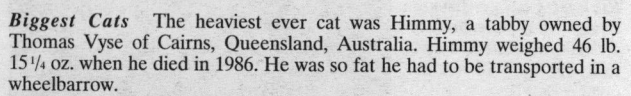

BIGGEST AND SMALLEST RABBITS
The largest breed of rabbit is the Flemish Giant (left of picture), which weighs an average of 22 lb., and the smallest are the Netherland Dwarf and the Polish—a hybrid of which weighed 14 oz. in 1975. The biggest rabbit of all time was a French lop weighing 26 lb. 7 oz., exhibited in Spain in April 1980.

bred cocker spaniel, Samantha, when he died aged 60 in 1996. His widow Marie Dana Altman, who was given a $60,000 annual stipend providing she took care of Samantha, is currently sueing the dog for a greater share of her late husband's fortune.

Smallest Dogs The smallest dog ever was a matchbox-sized Yorkshire terrier owned by Arthur Marples of Blackburn, England, a former editor of *Our Dogs* magazine. He was $2^1/_2$ in. tall and $3^3/_4$ in. long, and weighed 4 oz. He died in 1945, aged nearly two.

The smallest authenticated living dog is Big Boss, a Yorkshire terrier owned by Dr Chai Khanachanakom of Bangkok, Thailand. In December, 1995 he was $4^7/_{10}$ in. tall and $5^1/_{10}$ in. long, and weighed 1 lb. 1 oz.

Smallest Cat Tinker Toy, a male blue point Himalayan-Persian cat owned by Katrina and Scott Forbes of Taylorville, Illinois, is $2^3/_4$ in. tall and $7^1/_2$ in. long.

Biggest Cats The heaviest ever cat was Himmy, a tabby owned by Thomas Vyse of Cairns, Queensland, Australia. Himmy weighed 46 lb. $15^1/_4$ oz. when he died in 1986. He was so fat he had to be transported in a wheelbarrow.

Orange Thing of Minnetonka, Minnesota, is believed to be the heaviest living cat. The tabby, owned by John Posthumus, weighed 40 lb. 13 oz. on October 30, 1998.

The longest domestic cat is four-year-old Snowbie, who measured 3 ft. $4^1/_2$ in. from his nose to the tip of his tail on November 21, 1997. He weighs 21 lb., is 13 in. tall and has a 12-in.-long tail. Owned by Lorna Sutherland of Ellon, Scotland, he thrives on a diet of turkey, tuna, rice pudding and coffee.

Biggest Single-Sex Dog Litters Llana, a four-year-old greyhound/saluki owned by Nigel Wood of Bolsover, England, gave birth to 16 female puppies (three stillborn) on June 27, 1998.

Alpenblick's Great Lady (Cleo) gave birth by Caesarian section to 14 male puppies, the largest ever single-sex male litter on February 19, 1998 in Ladysmith, British Columbia, Canada.

Most-Traveled Cat Hamlet the cat escaped from his cage during a flight from Toronto, Canada, and traveled more than 600,000 miles in just over seven weeks. He was caught in February 1984.

MOST EXPENSIVE CAT The Californian Spangled cat (pictured right) was originally bred by Hollywood scriptwriter Paul Casey, who crossed various types to develop a new breed of domestic cat intended to resemble the spotted wildcat. There are fewer than 200 specimens of the breed in the world. In 1987, a California Spangled sold for $24,000 to an anonymous movie star.

Slowest-Traveled Pet   Chester the tortoise, who was painted with a white streak for identification, escaped from his home in Lyde, England, in 1960 and was found by a neighbor in 1995. He had traveled 2,250 yd. in 35 years.

Most-Petted Dog   Josh the Wonder Dog, owned by Richard Stack of Glen Burnie, Maryland, was petted by 478,802 people between 1989 and his death on July 23, 1997.

Ugliest Dog   Chi Chi, a rare African sand dog, has won the World Championship Ugly Dog Contest at Petaluma, California, five times and took first place in the contest's "Ring of Champions," which pitted the winners from the previous 25 years against one another. Chi Chi has made several TV appearances and is the star of a comic strip called *The Ugliest Dog*.

Biggest Dog Walk On February 20, 1999, 2,114 dogs (accompanied by their walkers) participated in the Mighty Texas Dog Walk in Austin, Texas. The three-mile dog walk was in aid of Texas Hearing & Service Dogs, an organization that adopts dogs from animal shelters and trains them as working partners for disabled people.

RELIGIONS, RITES & CULTS

Biggest Religion Christianity is the world's predominant religion, with some 1.94 billion adherents in 1998, or 32.8% of the world's population. However, religious statistics are necessarily only tentative, because the test of adherence to religion varies widely in rigor, while many individuals, particularly in the East, belong to two or more religions.

Biggest Christian Denomination The largest Christian denomination in the world is the Roman Catholic, which in 1998 had 1.03 billion members, or 17.3% of the total world population.

Biggest Non-Christian Religion The world's largest non-Christian religion is Islam, which has over 1.16 billion followers.

Largest Religion without Rites The Baha'i faith, which is practiced worldwide by about 6 million people, has no ceremonies, no sacraments, and no clergy. Bahaism emphasizes the importance of all religions and the spiritual unity of humanity. It emerged through the teaching of two 19th-century Iranian visionaries and is now adhered to in over 70 countries.

Fastest-Growing Modern Church The Kimbanguist Church was founded in Congo (now Democratic Republic of Congo) in 1959 by Simon

BIGGEST RADIO AUDIENCE FOR A REGULAR RELIGIOUS BROADCAST
Decision Hour, a religious radio show that has been broadcast regularly since 1957 by the Baptist evangelist Billy Graham (pictured above), attracts an average audience of 20 million people.

MOST VISITED SIKH TEMPLE The Golden Temple in Amritsar, India, is the largest and most important Sikh shrine, attracting up to 20,000 visitors per day. This figure rises to 200,000 on special occasions such as Guru Purab (the birthday of one of the 10 Sikh gurus) and Baisakhi (the festival marking the day Sikhism was established). The second story of the temple is covered by an estimated 881 lb. of gold leaf and hundreds of precious stones. The temple's architecture is influenced by both Hindu and Muslim styles. Its sanctuary contains *Adi Grantha*, the sacred scripture of the Sikhs.

Kimbangui, a Baptist student. By 1996, the church, which is a member of the World Council of Churches, had over 6.5 million members.

Biggest Religious Crowd The greatest number of human beings known to have assembled with a common purpose is the estimated 20 million Hindu pilgrims who gathered at a "half" Kumbh Mela held in Prayag (Allahabad), Uttar Pradesh, India, on January 30, 1995. An estimated 200,000 people entered Prayag every hour on the day before the festival. By 10 am, an estimated 15 million people had been in the water, and another 5 million were waiting their turn.

Biggest Temple The largest religious structure is Angkor Wat in Cambodia, which covers 402 acres. It was built to the Hindu god Vishnu by Suryavarman II between A.D. 1113 and 1150.

Biggest Cathedral The largest cathedral in the world is St. John the Divine, cathedral church of the Diocese of New York, with a floor area of 121,000 ft.[2]. The cornerstone was laid on December 27, 1892, but work on the building was stopped in 1941 and only restarted in earnest in July 1979.

SMALLEST CHRISTIAN SECT The Sabbathday Lake community of Shakers in Maine currently has seven members, making it the smallest surviving Christian sect. Sister Frances Carr and Brother Arnold Hadd are pictured rehearsing songs for their 1995 album, *Simple Songs*, the first recording ever made by Shakers of their own music.

The cathedral nave is the longest in the world, at 601 ft. in length, and has a vaulted ceiling 124 ft. high.

Biggest Mosque   The Shah Faisal Mosque in Islamabad, Pakistan, can accommodate 100,000 worshipers in the prayer hall and the courtyard and 200,000 more people in the adjacent grounds, giving a total capacity of 300,000. The complex area is 46.87 acres, and the covered area of the prayer hall takes up 1.19 acres.

Biggest Buddhist Temple   Borobudar, built in the eighth century near Yogyakarta, Indonesia, is 103 ft. tall and has an area of 403 ft.².

Biggest Synagogue   Temple Emanu-El on Fifth Avenue at 65th Street in New York City has an area of 37,928 ft.². When the adjoining Beth-El Chapel and the Temple's other three sanctuaries are in use, a total of 5,500 people can be seated in the synagogue.

Most Visited Hindu Temple   Tirupati Temple in Andhra Pradesh, India, attracts 30,000 to 40,000 visitors per day and an estimated 75,000 on New Year's Day. The temple is also the richest Hindu temple in the world, with an annual budget of $57.02 million. Collection boxes alone raise more than $22.67 million every year, and a similar sum is raised through the auction of hair donated by devotees visiting the temple. It also earns rent from cottages housing devotees and special services. The temple has 13,000 full-time employees and an additional 2,000 contract staff.

Longest Religious Circuit   The longest circuit around a religious site as part of a pilgrimage is 52 miles 1,440 yd., walked by Hindu worshipers around Lake Mansarovar in Tibet.

Biggest Funerals In February 1969, the funeral of C.N. Annadurai, the charismatic chief minister of Madras, India, was attended by 15 million people, according to a police estimate.

The line at the grave of the 42-year-old singer and folk hero Vladimir Visotsky at the Vagankovsyoye Cemetery in Moscow, USSR (now Russia), after his death in 1980 was 6 miles long.

Biggest Percentage of a Population to Attend a Funeral About 10.2 million people—16.6% of the population of Iran—lined the 20-mile route to Tehran's Behesht-e Zahra cemetery for the funeral of Ayatollah Khomeini, the creator of the Islamic state, on June 11, 1989, according to official Iranian estimates. It is believed that 2 million people paid their respects as the body lay in state. In the crush, eight people were killed and

MOST SAINTS CREATED BY A POPE Pope John Paul II has created more saints than any other pope. By January 1999, he had canonized 283 people and beatified 805 (given the title "Blessed" by the Roman Catholic Church)—10 times as many as all his 20th-century predecessors put together and more than any pontiff. Born in Wadowice, Poland, on May 18, 1920, as Karol Wojtyla, he ascended the papal throne in 1978, becoming the first non-Italian to be elected pope in 456 years and the youngest pope this century.

500 injured. At the funeral, people shredded the white shroud, partly exposing the body of the Ayatollah in his casket.

Most Human Sacrifices in a Religious Ceremony   The most human sacrifices made at a single ceremony is believed to have been the 20,000 people killed by Aztec priests at the dedication ceremony for the Great Temple (Teocalli) at Tenochtitlán (now Mexico City) to the war god Huitzilpochtli in 1486.

Most Female-Dominated Religious Sect   Dianic Wicca, a neo-pagan movement, worships a goddess and has female-only covens. The feminist witchcraft sect was founded in California in the 1920s.

Most Male-Dominated Society   Mount Athos, a 129-square-mile autonomous monastic republic within Greece, prohibits all females, including domestic animals and birds, and women are not even allowed to approach its shores by boat. The republic has a population of 1,400 men occupying its 20 Orthodox monasteries and their dependencies.

Most Prolific Crying Statue   A 15-in.-high statue of the Virgin Mary brought from Medjurorje, Bosnia, by a curate from Civitavecchia, Italy, in 1994 appeared to cry tears of blood on 14 days between February 2 and March 17, 1995. One manifestation was witnessed by the diocesan bishop.

Longest Period of Stigmata   Padre Pio (Francesco Forguione), a devout Italian Capuchin friar, bore the stigmata (the wounds received by Christ on the Cross) from 1918 until his death in 1968. They were seen by thousands of pilgrims. He was beatified by Pope John Paul II in May 1999.

CRIMINALS

Most Prolific Murderers   Behram, a member of the Thuggee cult, strangled at least 931 victims with his *ruhmal* (yellow-and-white cloth strip) in Oudh, India, between 1790 and 1840.

The most prolific murderer in the Western world and the most prolific female murderer ever was Elizabeth Bathori of Transylvania (now in Romania). She is alleged to have killed more than 600 girls and young women in order to drink and bathe in their blood, ostensibly to preserve her youth. When the crimes were discovered, the countess was walled up in her home from 1610 until her death in 1614.

The most prolific murderer of the 20th century was the bandit leader Teófilo "Sparks" Rojas, who is said to have killed between 592 and 3,500 people from 1945 until his death in an ambush in Colombia on January 22, 1963.

The world's biggest mass killing ever carried out by one person took place in April 1982, when policeman Wou Bom-kon went on a drunken eight-hour rampage in Kyong Sang-namdo Province of South Korea. He killed 57 people and wounded 35 with 176 rounds of rifle ammunition and hand grenades before blowing himself up.

The most prolific known serial killer of recent times was Pedro Lopez, who

MOST DANGEROUS CAR SECURITY DEVICE The Blaster was invented by Charl Fourie (South Africa) to deter car thieves. A switch controls the flow of gas from a canister in the trunk. The gas exits over a spark via nozzles beneath the doors, and 6-ft.-6-in. fireballs shoot out from both sides of the car.

killed 300 girls in Colombia, Peru, and Ecuador. Known as the "Monster of the Andes," Lopez was sentenced to life imprisonment in Ecuador in 1980.

The Mexican sisters Delfina and Maria de Jesus Gonzales, who abducted girls to work in brothels, formed the world's most prolific murder partnership ever. Known to have murdered at least 90 of their victims but suspected to have killed many more, Delfina and Maria were sentenced to 40 years' imprisonment in 1964.

The world's most prolific murderer by poison was nurse Jane Toppan of Massachusetts, who killed between 30 and 100 patients with morphine or atropine over 20 years. In 1902, Toppan confessed to 30 murders but claimed that they had been acts of mercy. She was subsequently committed to a mental institution.

Biggest Criminal Organization The Six Great Triads of China form the largest organized-crime association in the world today, with an estimated 100,000-plus members worldwide.

Biggest Drug Haul On September 28, 1989, a record 18 tons of cocaine, with an estimated street value of $6–7 billion, was seized in a raid on a warehouse in Los Angeles, California.

Biggest Robberies The plundering of the Reichsbank following the collapse of Germany during April and May 1945 was the world's biggest bank robbery. The book *Nazi Gold* estimated that the total haul would have been worth $3.34 billion at 1984 values.

BIGGEST RANSOM Two Hong Kong businessmen, Walter Kwok and Victor Li, paid gangster Cheung Tze-keung, also known as "Big Spender," a record total of $127 million for their freedom after he kidnapped them in 1996 and 1997, respectively. The case created more notoriety when the businessmen reported the abductions to the authorities in mainland China (where the death penalty is in force) rather than to those in Hong Kong (which, because of its status, does not have the death penalty). Cheung, who was also involved in smuggling and armed robbery, was arrested and charged in Canton, on the Chinese mainland, and executed by firing squad in November 1998. Four of his accomplices were also shot, and 31 of his gang members received long jail sentences.

During the civil disorder that took place in Beirut, Lebanon, in 1976, a guerrilla force blasted its way into the vaults of the British Bank of the Middle East in Bab Idriss and cleared out safe-deposit boxes. The contents were estimated to be worth $50 million by the former finance minister Lucien Dahdah or at least an "absolute minimum" of $20 million by another source.

The biggest jewel robbery ever on record took place in August 1994, when gems with an estimated value of $46 million were stolen from the jewelry shop at the Carlton Hotel in Cannes, France, by a three-man gang.

Biggest Bank Fraud In 1989, Banca Nazionale del Lavoro in Italy admitted that it had been defrauded of a huge amount of money when its branch in Atlanta, Georgia, made unauthorized loan commitments to Iraq. The total loss was subsequently estimated to be about $5 billion.

Biggest White-Collar Crime In February 1997, Japanese copper trader Yasuo Hamanaka pleaded guilty to fraud and forgery in connection with illicit trading that had cost his employer, Sumitomo, Japan's largest trading company, an estimated $2.6 billion over 10 years of unauthorized transactions.

Most Prisoners on Death Row In 1998, there were more than 3,549 prisoners on death row in the 38 US states in which the death penalty was in effect.

Longest Time on Death Row Sadamichi Hirasawa of Japan was convicted of poisoning bank employees with potassium cyanide in order to steal $370 in 1948. He died in Sendai Prison in Japan at the age of 94, after 39 years on death row.

Longest Sentences Chamoy Thipyaso and seven of her associates were each jailed for 141,078 years by the Bangkok Criminal Court in Thailand on July 27, 1989. They had been found guilty of swindling the public.

The longest sentence ever imposed on a mass murderer was 21 consecutive life sentences and 12 death sentences, on John Wayne Gacy, who killed 33 boys and young men between 1972 and 1978. He was sentenced by a jury in Chicago, Illinois, in March 1980 and executed in May 1994.

Longest Time Served Paul Geidel was convicted of second-degree murder at the age of 17 in September 1911 and released from the Fishkill Correctional Facility in Beacon, New York, at the age of 85 in 1980. Geidel, who was refused parole in 1974, served 68 years 245 days.

MOST MAFIA CONVICTIONS Salvatore "Toto" Riina (above), the head of the Sicilian Mafia and the most wanted man in Italy, was tried with 38 other alleged mob bosses at Caltanissetta, Italy. Riina, along with 23 others, was given a life sentence, six were given more lenient terms, and nine were acquitted on September 26, 1997.

MEDIA &
POP CULTURE

HOLLYWOOD

Most Expensive Movies Twentieth Century Fox's epic *Titanic* (1997), starring Leonardo DiCaprio and Kate Winslet and directed by James Cameron, was due to be released in July 1997 but was delayed until December 1997 due to postproduction problems. This delay added at least $20 million to the budget, making *Titanic* the most expensive movie ever made, at almost $250 million.

The most expensive film ever made in terms of real costs adjusted for inflation was Joseph L. Mankiewicz's *Cleopatra* (1963), which starred Elizabeth Taylor and Richard Burton. The $44-million budget would equal more than $260 million in 1999.

Most Expensive Sci-Fi Movie *Waterworld* (1995), starring Kevin Costner, suffered a series of setbacks when the set broke free from its moorings in the Pacific Ocean on several occasions. This problem and additional technical failures made it the most expensive sci-fi movie ever made, at an estimated $160 million.

MOST PROFITABLE FILM SERIES Pierce Brosnan is pictured above as British secret agent James Bond in a scene from *The World Is Not Enough* (1999). The 20 Bond movies, based on novels by Ian Fleming and largely produced by Cubby Broccoli, have grossed more than $1 billion worldwide—more than any other film series. It is estimated that over 50% of the world's population has seen at least one Bond film.

HIGHEST-GROSSING HORROR FILM   Miramax's *Scream* (1996), directed by Wes Craven and starring Drew Barrymore and Neve Campbell, cost about $15 million to make and had grossed $161.6 million by July 1997. *Scream 2* (1997), which starred David Arquette and Courteney Cox (pictured above), grossed $33 million on its opening weekend and took in $160.5 million from December 1997 to August 1998. A second sequel, *Scream 3*, is due for release in 1999. If inflation and the increased price of movie tickets are taken into account, *The Exorcist* (1973), directed by William Friedkin, is the highest-grossing horror movie ever made. The film has grossed more than $381 million in today's terms.

Highest-Grossing Movies   *Titanic* (1997) was released on December 19, 1997, and had made a gross of $1.835 billion worldwide by May 1999. MGM's *Gone With the Wind* (1939) took $193.6 million from 197.55 million admissions in North America alone. Taking into account inflation and the increased price of movie tickets, this is equivalent to $885.3 million today. In an inflation-adjusted list of the highest-grossing movies in the US, *Gone With the Wind* would be first, while *Titanic* would be fifth, with a figure of $600.8 million.

Highest-Grossing Sci-Fi Movies   The original and remastered versions of George Lucas' *Star Wars* (1977 and 1997) have grossed a record total of $1.19 billion, taking into account inflation and the rise in the price of movie tickets.

Fox's *Independence Day* (1996) has grossed $811 million worldwide—the highest box-office gross of any science-fiction film on its first release.

Highest-Grossing Comedy   *Austin Powers: The Spy Who Shagged Me* (1999) grossed a record $54.92 million during its first weekend of release (June 11 through 13, 1999). In two days, it earned more than the entire run of its predecessor, *Austin Powers: International Man Of Mystery (1997)*.

Biggest Loss
MGM's *Cutthroat Island* (1995), starring Geena Davis and directed by her then husband Renny Harlin, cost more than $100 million to produce, promote, and distribute. By May 1996, it had reportedly earned back just $11 million.

Most Expensive Movie Rights The highest price ever paid for film rights was $9.5 million, for the Broadway musical *Annie*. The deal was announced by Columbia in 1978, and the film was released in 1982. It was directed by John Huston and starred Albert Finney.

Most Filmed Author
A total of 350 films based on plays by William Shakespeare have been made to date. Of these, 309 are straight or relatively straight versions of the original text, while 41 are modern versions, such as *10 Things I Hate About You* (1999), which was based on *The Taming Of The Shrew*. There have also been innumerable parodies. *Hamlet* is the most popular choice of play for filmmakers, with 75 versions made, followed by *Romeo And Juliet* with 51. The most recent of these was *William Shakespeare's Romeo And Juliet* (1996), which starred Leonardo DiCaprio and Claire Danes.

FASTEST BOX-OFFICE GROSS *Star Wars: The Phantom Menace* opened in the US on May 19, 1999, and took in $28.54 million in its first 24 hours; $100 million in five days; $200 million in 13 days; and $300 million in four weeks. *The Phantom Menace*, which stars Ewan McGregor (pictured above), Liam Neeson, Samuel L. Jackson, and Natalie Portman, is the prequel to the original *Star Wars* trilogy, released between 1977 and 1983.

Most Filmed Horror Author   More than 20 of Stephen King's novels and short stories have been made into movies, including *Carrie* (1976), *The Shining* (UK, 1980), and *Misery* (1990).

Most Filmed Story   There have been a record 95 films based on the classic fairy tale *Cinderella*, including cartoon, modern ballet, operatic, all-male, and parody versions. The first version was *Fairy Godmother* (UK, 1898), while the most recent was *Ever After* (1998).

Most Frequently Portrayed Characters   The French emperor Napoleon Bonaparte has been the subject of 177 films since 1897—a record for any historical figure.

The fictional character most frequently portrayed on the big screen is Sherlock Holmes, the detective created by Sir Arthur Conan Doyle. He has been portrayed by 75 actors in more than 211 films since 1900.

Longest Movie   The 85-hour *Cure For Insomnia* (1987), which was directed by John Henry Timmis IV, premiered in its entirety at the Art Institute of Chicago from January 31 to February 3, 1987. Much of the film consists of L.D. Groban reading his 4,080-page poem, interspersed with scenes of a rock band and some X-rated footage.

Most Costumes in One Movie   A record 32,000 costumes were worn in *Quo Vadis* (1951).

Most Costume Changes in One Movie   Madonna changed costume a record 85 times in *Evita* (1996) and wore a total of 39 hats, 45 pairs of shoes, and 56 pairs of earrings. The costumes were based on Eva Perón's own clothes, many of which are kept in an Argentinian bank vault.

Oldest Hollywood Director   Hollywood's oldest director was George Cukor (1899–1983), who made his 50th and final film, MGM's *Rich And Famous*, in 1981 at the age of 81.

Youngest Hollywood Producer   Steven Paul was 20 years old when he produced and directed *Falling In Love Again* (1980), which starred Elliott Gould and Susannah York.

Largest Movie-Studio Complex   Universal City in Los Angeles, California, covers 420 acres and has 561 buildings and 34 soundstages.

BOLLYWOOD

Biggest Film Output   In 1990, a record 948 films in 21 languages (including Hindi, Tamil, Telegu, Bengali, and Gujarati) were produced in India.

Highest-Grossing Bollywood Film   *Hum Aapke Hain Kaun* (1994), starring Madhuri Dixit and Salman Khan, is the highest-grossing Bolly-

MOST GENERATIONS OF ACTRESSES IN ONE FAMILY Kajol, who
has starred in a string of recent box-office successes, is one of three
generations of Bollywood actresses. Her mother Tanuja and
aunt Nutan were both leading actresses in the 1960s, while her
grandmother Shobhana Samarth starred in numerous 1940s hits.

wood film of all time. It earned more than $63.8 million in its first year,
breaking the record set by the "curry western" *Sholay* in 1975.

Longest Bollywood Careers P. Jairaj, who made his debut in 1929,
has had an acting career spanning 70 years. Although he has acted in more
than 300 films, he is better known for character roles than as a lead.

Since making his debut in *Jeevan Naiya* in 1936, Ashok Kumar, affec-
tionately known as Dadamoni, has been acting continually for 63 years. A
three-time winner of the *Filmfare* Best Actor Award, his most famous role
was in *Kismet* (1943), which in real terms is the highest-grossing Indian film
of all time. Although no longer a lead actor, Ashok continues to play character roles and to make appearances on TV.

The Bollywood actress with the longest film career was Lalita Pawar,
who acted continually for 70 years. She made her debut at the age of 12
and appeared in more than 700 films. Her best-known role was as the
scheming mother in *Ramshastri* (1944). Lalita's last film, *Bhai*, was completed two months before her death in 1998.

Most Appearances in International Films Saeed Jaffrey has appeared in 18 international films, including *Gandhi* (UK, 1982), *A Passage
to India* (UK, 1984), *Masala* (Canada, 1991), and *My Beautiful Laundrette*
(UK, 1985). He made his film debut in the 1977 Indian film *The Chess
Players* (*Shatranj Ke Khiladi*) and has appeared in almost 100 Hindi films
and one Punjabi film. In 1998, Jaffrey opted out of Indian commercial

HIGHEST-EARNING MALE STAR   The highest-earning male star in Bollywood is Shah Rukh Khan (pictured above), who is reported to earn $599,460 per film. It is said he plans to increase this to $717,986 in the year 2000. Khan, whose most successful movies include *Dilwale Dulhaniya Le Jayenge* (1995), *Dil to Pagal Hai* (1997), and *Kuch Kuch Hota Hai* (1998), made his debut in 1991 and has since won a total of seven *Filmfare* Awards. He is well known for playing unconventional or controversial roles and portrayed psychopaths in both *Baazigar* (1993) and *Darr* (1994). Amitabh Bachchan, the star of most of Bollywood's hits in the 1970s and 1980s, is said currently to command $717,986 per film. However, a string of recent box-office failures seems likely to push his earnings down.

cinema in favor of acting in international films and on British television. He recently became part of the first Indian family to feature regularly in the United Kingdom's longest-running soap opera, *Coronation Street*.

Shabana Azmi has acted in nine international films—more than any other Indian actress. These include *Madame Souzatska* (1988), *City Of Joy* (UK/France, 1992), and *Fire* (Canada, 1995). She has won four National Awards and three *Filmfare* Awards.

Most International Film Awards   Satyajit Ray, nicknamed "God" in Bombay film circles, was India's most celebrated movie director. Prior to his death in 1992, he received a total of 34 international film awards, including an Oscar for Lifetime Achievement. He was also awarded the *Bharat Ratna* and the *Padmashree*, India's highest civilian and arts awards, respectively.

Most Best Actor Awards   Dilip Kumar has won eight *Filmfare* Awards for Best Actor and one award for Lifetime Achievement in a career spanning more than 50 years.

Most Best Actress Awards   Nutan (1936–91) won five *Filmfare* Awards for Best Actress and one for Best Supporting Actress during a career that spanned 47 years. Widely considered the most versatile actress of her generation, she came from a family of top Hindi performers.

Most Best Singer Awards Kishore Kumar, who died in 1987, won eight *Filmfare* Awards for Best Male Playback Singer. He appeared in several comedies in the 1940s before becoming a full-time singer. Although best known for his yodeling and jazz-scat rhythms with nonsense lyrics, it was his melancholic songs that won him the most awards.

Most Prolific Bollywood Recording Artist Since 1948, Lata Mangeshkar is reported to have recorded more than 5,000 songs in Hindi and thousands in 14 other Indian languages. Lata is the older sister of singer Asha Bhosle, celebrated by the UK band Cornershop in their hit single "Brimful of Asha."

Most Roles Played in One Film Sivaji Ganesan played all nine roles in the Tamil film *Navarathri* (1964), which was directed by A.P. Na-garajan. It was remade in

BIGGEST BOLLYWOOD SCREEN FAMILY
Twenty-four members of the Kapoor extended family have acted in films since Prithviraj Kapoor first took to the screen in 1929. He was followed into acting by his three sons, Raj, Shammi, and Shashi. Other famous relatives through marriage include top star Amitabh Bachchan, directors Ramesh Sippy and Manmohan Desai, and Shashi's sister-in-law, British actress Felicity Kendall. One of Bollywood's current leading ladies, Karishma Kapoor (above), is Prithviraj's great-granddaughter.

Hindi in 1974 as *Naya Din Nayi Raat,* with Sanjeev Kumar taking all the parts.

Most Prolific Bollywood Stuntwoman Mary Evans, known as Fearless Nadia, starred in many action movies from 1934 until her retirement in 1961. Her most famous films include *Hunterwali* (1935), *Jungle Princess* (1942), *Stunt Queen* (1947), and *Tigress* (1948). Born in 1909 to an English father and a Greek mother, Mary first went to Bombay at the age of five. She returned in the mid-1920s to work in a touring theater company and got her first big break in Indian films in 1934, in *Desh Deepak* and *Noor-e-Yaman.* She changed her name to Nadia on the advice of a fortune-teller

and later married the filmmaker Homi Wadia.

Longest Production of a Bollywood Film
Love and God (*Qais aur Laila*) (1986) took more than 20 years to make after running into a series of difficulties, including the deaths of lead actor Guru Dutt in 1964 and director K. Asif in 1971. The incomplete film was finally released in 1986, with Sanjeev Kumar taking over the lead role. Asif was also the director of *Mughal-e-Azam* (1960), which took more than 14 years to complete following the death of the lead actor Chandramohan. He was replaced by Dilip Kumar.

Longest Interval Between Screen Kisses
The earliest kiss in Indian cinema took place in 1929, in *Prapancha Pash*. Kissing was subsequently prohibited in Indian films and was not seen again until 1983, in *Betaab*.

Highest-Grossing Bollywood Films at the UK Box Office
In 1998, *Dil Se* and *Kuch Kuch Hota Hai* became the first two Indian films to reach the UK box office Top 10. *Kuch Kuch Hota Hai* earned $284,108 in its first three days of release in the UK alone.

HIGHEST-EARNING FEMALE STAR Bollywood's highest-earning actress is Madhuri Dixit (above), who reportedly has an asking price of $599,460 per film. The star of India's highest-grossing movie ever, *Hum Aapke Hain Kaun* (1994), she made her debut in *Abodb* in 1984 and went on to act in over 60 hit films throughout the late 1980s and the 1990s.

TV & VIDEO

Biggest TV Contract   On September 24, 1998, it was announced that King World Productions Inc. would pay Harpo Productions Inc., Oprah Winfrey's company, a $75 million advance against minimum payments for both the 2000/01 and 2001/02 seasons of Winfrey's top-rated talk show, which she hosts and produces.

Most Expensive TV Deal   In January 1998, the National Football League (NFL) signed contracts with CBS, ABC, Fox, and ESPN totaling $17.6 billion. The contracts give each network rights to NFL games for eight years starting with the 1998/99 season. ESPN will pay the NFL $600 million per year, ABC and Fox will each pay an annual fee of $550 million, and CBS will pay $500 million per year.

Most Expensive TV Show   In January 1998, NBC agreed to pay $13 million for each hourly episode of the medical drama *ER*. It had previously paid $1.6 million per episode. The program is the top US primetime show, with a weekly audience of 32 million people. The three-year deal with *ER* creators Warner Bros. will work out to $873.68 million for 66 episodes.

MOST SUCCESSFUL SOAP OPERA   *Dallas*, starring Larry Hagman (left of picture) and Patrick Duffy (right of picture), began in 1978 and by 1980 had an estimated 83 million US viewers every week (a record 76% share of the TV audience). It ran for 356 episodes from April 1978 to May 1991 and has been aired in 130 countries.

Most Watched TV Network   The government-owned network China Central Television (CCTV) is transmitted to 84% of all Chinese viewers in China. It is estimated that more than 900 million people tune in. The total broadcasting time of its nine channels each day is 162 hours, broadcasting in Mandarin, Cantonese, English, and French. The single most-watched show is the daily *Xin Wen Lian Bo* (*News Hookup*), which attracts 315 million viewers.

Biggest Global TV Network   CNN International can be seen in over 149 million households in 212 countries and territories through a network of 23 satellites.

Biggest TV Audiences   The lifeguard drama *Baywatch*, whose stars have included David Hasselhoff and Pamela Anderson, is the world's most widely viewed TV series, with an estimated weekly audience of more than 1.1 billion people in 142 countries.

"Goodbye, Farewell, and Amen," the final episode of the Korean War black comedy *M*A*S*H*, was transmitted to 77% of all US viewers on February 28, 1983. It was estimated that about 125 million people tuned in.

Most Viewed Trial   From January to October 1995, a record daily average of 5.5 million US viewers watched the trial of O.J. Simpson, the football player and actor charged with the murder of his ex-wife, Nicole, and her friend Ronald Goldman.

MOST PROLIFIC TV PRODUCER Aaron Spelling has produced more than 3,842 episodes of TV shows since 1956. If they were all shown end to end, they would take 128 days to screen. His output has included *Charlie's Angels*, starring Farrah Fawcett-Majors, Kate Jackson, and Jaclyn Smith (pictured left), *Starsky and Hutch*, *Dynasty,* and *Beverly Hills 90210*, which featured his daughter Tori. Spelling's awards include two Golden Globes—for *Burke's Law* in 1964 and *Dynasty* in 1983—two Emmys, the Writers Guild of America Award, and the NAACP Image Award a record six times.

MOST EXPENSIVE STRAIGHT-TO-TV MOVIE Dominique Swain (right) played the lead in Adrian Lyne's adaptation of *Lolita* (1997). With a budget of $58 million, it was the most expensive film to debut on US cable TV. US rights were bought by cable company Showtime Networks after the movie controversially failed to gain an initial US theatrical release. It was first shown on US TV on August 2, 1998, and was released in US movie theaters a month later.

Biggest Soap Opera Producer The Brazilian network Rede Globo is the largest and most profitable producer of *telenovelas* (soap operas) in Latin America, which run on average for more than 100 episodes. It shows soaps from 6 pm each night.

In the 1960s, the *telenovela Simply Mary* was sold to every Spanish-speaking country and once attracted more viewers than the soccer World Cup.

Escrava Isaura (*Isaura The Slave*) has been dubbed and exported to all Spanish-speaking countries, dubbed into Mandarin, and shown in Asia.

Longest-Running Soap Opera The British soap opera *Coronation Street*, about the inhabitants of the fictional district of Weatherfield, Manchester, England, was first shown on

BEST-SELLING VIDEO Walt Disney's *The Lion King* (1994) had sold 55.7 million copies worldwide by May 1999. The 32nd Disney animated feature, it was the first without human characters and the first based on an original story. It featured the voices of Whoopi Goldberg, Jeremy Irons, and Rowan Atkinson.

December 9, 1960, and at least two episodes per week have been broadcast ever since. The show was devised by Tony Warren and is made by Granada TV.

Longest-Running Religious Soap Opera *Mahabharat*, the most popular soap opera in India, was shown every Sunday morning for two years from 1994 to 1996.

Most Expensive Soap Opera The Brazilian soap opera *Torre de Babel* (*Tower of Babel*) cost $17 million to make, with each individual episode costing $100,000. The story was written by Silvio de Abreu.

Most Expensive Chinese Soap Opera *The Romance of Three Kingdoms* cost $12.96 million to make. There were 300,000 people involved in the 44-episode production, which was made in 1996.

Most Actors in a Soap Opera *Torre de Babel* set the record for the soap opera with the most actors—300 were under permanent contract, although the show could not use more than 180 at one time.

Most Expensive Game Show Production costs for NTV's *Trans-America Ultra Quiz* (Japan) rose to over $657,030 per episode in 1990, more than three times that of conventional quiz shows. The show featured ever-changing foreign stopovers, including Hawaii, Europe, and South America.

Most Game Show Contestants A record 28,523 contestants entered the Japanese quiz show *Trans-America Ultra Quiz*. The show featured a total of 213,430 contestants throughout its 16-year run from 1977 to 1993, only 31 of whom ever made it to the final stage at the foot of the Statue of Liberty in New York City.

Most Prolific Game Show Producer   The most prolific game show producer is Mark Goodson (US). He has produced more than 39,000 episodes of game shows, taking up a total of 21,240 hours of airtime.

Highest Price Paid for TV Rights to a Film   The Fox network paid $82 million for the TV rights to Steven Spielberg's *Jurassic Park: The Lost World* in June 1997, before its international release.

Highest Price Paid for TV Rights to a Mini Series   In 1991, a group of US and European investors, led by CBS, paid $8 million for the TV rights to Alexandra Ripley's *Scarlett*, the sequel to Margaret Mitchell's 1936 novel *Gone With the Wind*.

Most Rented Video   George Lucas' *Star Wars* (1977) has made $270.9 million through video rentals in North America alone. Revenues include the proceeds from the original video release and the 1997 digitally remastered version. The rental revenue of the first *Star Wars* trilogy (original and remastered) as a whole, including *The Empire Strikes Back* (1980) and *Return of the Jedi* (1983), totals $636.4 million.

Fastest Video Production   Tapes of the royal wedding of Prince Andrew and Sarah Ferguson on July 23, 1986, were produced by Thames Video Collection. Live filming ended at 4:42 pm, and the first VHS tapes were purchased in London, England, at 10:23 pm, just 5 hr. 41 min. later.

Most Spent on TV and Video Products   The leading consumer market for video and TV products is Japan, with an average expenditure of $43.66 per person a year.

Country with Most TV Sets   There are a record 227.5 million households with TV sets in China.

Country with Most VCRS   A record 81% of US households (78.125 million) own at least one video recorder.

City with Most Video Libraries   Bombay (Mumbai), India, has a total of 15,000 video libraries and 500 video stores—more than any other city in the world.

MUSIC VIDEO

Most Expensive Video   The video for Michael and Janet Jackson's hit single "Scream" (1995) cost a record $7 million to make and was directed by Mark Romanek (US). Shot on seven different sound stages, it features flying electric guitars and complex morphing effects. "Scream" won the

COSTLIEST SPECIAL EFFECTS IN A VIDEO   The video for "What's It Gonna Be?" by Busta Rhymes and Janet Jackson, directed by Hype Williams, cost $2.4 million to produce. Computer-morphing effects accounted for much of this expenditure. The track was taken from Rhymes' millennium-themed album *E.L.E.—The Final World Front.*

MTV Music Video Award for Dance in 1995 and the Grammy for Music Video, Short Form, in 1996.

Longest Videos   Michael Jackson's part feature film, part music video "Ghosts" (1996) is 35 minutes long and was based on an original concept by best-selling author Stephen King. Jackson plays five different roles in the video, which was directed by Stan Winston.

Michael Jackson's legendary "Thriller" (1983) video and Snoop Doggy Dogg's "Murder Was The Case" (1994) both run for 18 minutes. Snoop's video was directed by fellow rap artist Dr. Dre, and the star-studded lineup also included Dr. Dre, Ice Cube, Jewell, and Jodeci.

Shortest Videos   German TV station VIVA-TV made a video to accompany UK grindcore band Napalm Death's single "The Kill" (1992), which is 10 seconds long.

The shortest video made by a record company is German artist Klaus Beyer's "Die Glatze," a super-8 movie transferred to videotape, which has a total running time of 1 min. 23 sec.

Most Videos Made for One Song   There are five different videos for the track "Timber" (1998) by UK dance act Coldcut: the original mix, the EBN remix (New York), the LPC remix (Sweden), the Clifford Gilberto remix (Germany), and the Gnomadic remix (UK). Coldcut offered the "Timber" track to videomakers to encourage them to remix videos in the same way that DJs and producers remix records. Coldcut has been regarded as a pioneer of the remixing concept since their radical reworking of rappers Eric B and Rakim's "Paid In Full" (1987) turned the track into a worldwide hit.

The Swedish group the Cardigans produced three different videos for "Lovefool" (1996): one European version and two US versions, one of which featured scenes from the film *William Shakespeare's Romeo And Juliet* (1996).

Most Played Song on MTV Europe   Grunge band Nirvana's "Smells Like Teen Spirit" (1991) is the most played music video on MTV Europe.

MOST MTV VIDEO AWARDS WON BY A FEMALE ARTIST   Madonna won six MTV Music Video awards in 1998 out of nine nominations—eight for "Ray Of Light" and one for "Frozen." The "Ray Of Light" video, directed by Jonas Okerlund, won for Video of the Year, Best Direction, Best Female Video, Best Editing, and Best Choreography. "Frozen," directed by Chris Cunningham, picked up the Best Special Effects award. Both tracks were taken from her album *Ray Of Light*, which went triple-platinum in the US. Madonna performed "Ray Of Light" at the ceremony, in which her new video for "Power Of Goodbye" received its world premiere. Madonna is shown here performing "Nothing Really Matters" at the 41st Grammy Awards on February 24, 1999.

It ranked first in the Top 10 Singles of the 1990s poll held by the music station in 1996.

Biggest Music TV Channel MTV is beamed into 281.7 million households in 79 countries around the globe, which means it can be seen by one in four of the world's total TV audience. MTV began broadcasting in 1981 and added three new channels to its existing range in July 1999, thus doubling its output. The three new channels are MTV Base (featuring R&B, rap, and dance), MTV Extra (featuring items from MTV UK and Ireland to complement the main MTV channel), and VH1 Classic (focusing on classic hits by artists such as Abba and Eric Clapton).

Most Played Music Videos on the Box
The Box is a music video channel available worldwide. Viewers phone a video "jukebox" line to request the video and artist they want to see. Between its release in January 1998 and July 1999, the love theme from the movie *Titanic* (1997), Celine Dion's

MOST BRIT AWARDS FOR BEST VIDEO
Robbie Williams has won two Brit Awards for Best Video. In 1994, he and the other four members of boy band Take That won with their video for "Pray" (1993). In 1999, Robbie, now a solo artist, won again with his James Bond-inspired pastiche for his single "Millennium." The video featured Robbie wearing a jetpack identical to the one used in the Bond movie *Thunderball* (UK, 1965), and the song featured a sample from the soundtrack of *You Only Live Twice* (UK, 1967).

"My Heart Will Go On" (1997), received an unprecedented 60,474 requests.

The Box's most popular video by a dead artist is by rapper Tupac Shakur, who was killed in September 1996. His single "Changes," which has a sample from Bruce Hornsby and the Range's "The Way It Is" (1986), received 21,380 requests in the 18 weeks after its first showing on The Box in February 1999.

Most Stars from Different Music Genres on One Video A charity recording of the Lou Reed song "Perfect Day," commissioned to show the diversity of music played on BBC Television and Radio, features 27 artists from 18 genres, including jazz (Courtney Pine), reggae (Burning Spear), country (Tammy Wynette and Emmylou Harris), blues (Dr. John), pop (Boyzone), rap (Huey from Fun Lovin' Criminals), and classical music (Lesley Garrett). Reed himself also makes an appearance in the video.

Biggest Advance Paid to a Poet for Music Videos   In June 1997, Murray Lachlan Young, then a 26-year-old unpublished poet, signed a contract worth $416,500 to make approximately 100 90-second poetry videos. He also signed a $1.83-million deal with record company EMI to record two albums. Young's work is often provocative and includes performance pieces such as "Casual Sex," "MTV Party," and "The Closet Heterosexual."

Longest Midair Music Video   The video for Danish group Laidback's single "Bakerman" (1990) featured the whole band in free-fall for the entire video—a total of 4 min. 42 sec.

Most Custard Pies Thrown   British band Electrasy, along with the official Laurel and Hardy Fan Club, threw 4,400 custard pies in three minutes for the video of their single "Best Friend's Girl" (1998). They had special protective Day-Glo outfits made for the video, directed by James Brown.

POP

Most Successful Artist   Elvis Presley was the world's most successful solo artist of the rock era, with 18 No. 1 singles and nine No. 1 albums in the US and 17 No. 1 singles and six No. 1 albums in the UK. He had 94 chart entries in the US and 98 in the UK.

Most Successful Group   The Beatles have sold about 1 billion records and had a record 20 No. 1 singles and 18 No. 1 albums in the US and 17 No. 1 singles and 14 No. 1 albums in the UK.

Most Successful Female Artist   No female artist has sold more records around the world than Madonna, with total sales of more than 100 million. She is the most successful female artist in both the US and the UK, with a US total of 32 Top 10 singles and 11 Top 10 albums and a UK total of 44 separate Top 10 singles and 13 Top 10 albums (including six that reached No. 1—a UK record for any female artist).

Most Successful Family Group   Between 1968 and 1999, the Bee Gees had 24 Top 20 singles in the US and the UK. They have also had 13 Top 20 albums in the US and 12 in the UK.

Most Successful Producer   The producer with the most No. 1 singles in the UK and the US is George Martin, who saw 28 of his productions head the British charts and 23 reach No. 1 in the US. He also holds the record for longest span of UK- and US-produced hits. In the UK, there was an interval of 36 years 4 months between "You're Driving Me Crazy" by the Temperance Seven in April 1961 and "Candle in the Wind 97" by Elton John in September 1997. In the US, the gap between "I Want to Hold Your Hand" by the Beatles and "Candle in the Wind 97/Something About the Way You Look Tonight" by Elton John was 33 years 8 months.

Biggest-Selling Albums   Michael Jackson's *Thriller* (1982) has sold more than 45 million copies globally, including 25 million in the US—an unsurpassed total in that country.

The biggest-selling album in the UK is *Sgt. Pepper's Lonely Hearts Club Band* by the Beatles, with reported sales of 4.5 million since its release in 1967.

Biggest-Selling Single   In the UK, "Candle in the Wind 97/ Something About the Way You Look Tonight" by Elton John sold 658,000 copies on its first day, 1.5 million in one week, 2 million in eight days, and 3 million in 15 days and had passed 5.4 million sales by the sixth week. In the US, there were advance orders of 8.7 million and a first week distribution of 3.4 million. In total, 11 million sales were certified in the US alone. Elton John performed the song at the funeral of Diana, Princess of Wales, and proceeds went to her charitable trust. The single also spent 45 weeks at the top of the Canadian charts. It went in at No. 1 on September 22, 1997, and had earned 19 Canadian platinum discs by Christmas. It remained in the Top 3 until March 1999, 18 months later.

FIRST FEMALE GROUP DEBUT AT NO. 1   On June 6, 1998, Irish pop group B*Witched became the first female group to enter the UK charts at No. 1, with their debut single "C'est La Vie." The group followed through with two more No. 1 hits—"Rollercoaster" on October 3, 1998, and "To You I Belong" on December 19, 1998. The only other act to have entered at No. 1 with its first three singles was duo Robson Green and Jerome Flynn.

Most Played Songs

Only two songs have played more than 7 million times on US radio—"Yesterday," written by John Lennon and Paul McCartney, and "You've Lost That Lovin' Feelin'," written by Phil Spector, Barry Mann, and Cynthia Weill.

Most Hit Singles

Elvis Presley holds the record for the most hit singles in the US, with 151 entries on the *Billboard* Top 100 chart since 1956.

Cliff Richard has had a record 120 UK chart entries since September 1958.

Most Consecutive No. 1 Singles

The record for most consecutive No. 1 singles in the UK is 11, set by the Beatles between 1963 and 1966. The run started with "From Me to You" and ended with "Yellow Submarine."

Elvis Presley holds the US record for most consecutive No. 1 singles, with 10. The run started with "Heartbreak Hotel" in 1956 and ended with "Don't" in 1958.

Most Successful UK Debut

Irish boy band Boyzone's first 15 UK singles all reached the Top 5, beating a record held by Kylie Minogue (Australia). The group is also the only Irish act to have six UK No. 1 singles, up to May 1999.

MOST NO. 1 ENTRIES ON UK CHART The act with the most entries at No. 1 in the UK is Take That, with eight. The female act with the most No. 1 entries is the Spice Girls, with seven, and the solo male act with the most is George Michael, with four. Robbie Williams (pictured), former member of Take That, holds the record for the most Brit Award nominations, receiving six in 1999.

OLDEST FEMALE VOCALIST TO REACH NO. 1 The lead singer of Blondie, Deborah Harry, became the oldest female vocalist to top the UK charts when she went to No. 1 with "Maria" on February 13, 1999, at the age of 53 years 8 months. She broke the record held by Cher, who reached No. 1 in October 1998 with "Believe" at the age of 52 years 6 months. Blondie is also the only US act to have had UK hits in the 1970s, the 1980s, and the 1990s (excluding collaborations) and has the longest gap between newly recorded UK No. 1 hits, from "The Tide Is High" in November 1980 to "Maria" in February 1999. Furthermore, Blondie is the only US act to have had three successive UK No. 1s in the 1980s—"Atomic," "Call Me," and "The Tide Is High."

Youngest Chart Toppers The youngest solo artist to have topped the UK charts was Little Jimmy Osmond, who was at No. 1 for five weeks in 1972 with "Long Haired Lover From Liverpool," at 9 years 8 months. In second place is fellow American Frankie Lymon, who was 13 years 9 months old when he reached No. 1 with "Why Do Fools Fall In Love?" in 1956, followed by Jimmy's older brother Donny, who was 14 years 6 months when "Puppy Love" reached the No. 1 spot in 1972.

Finest Female Year In 1998, female artists or female-fronted acts headed the UK singles charts for 26 weeks of the year, and in the last week of the year, they were featured on nine of the Top 10 singles on the chart. On December 19, 1998, for the first time, the Top 5 artists on the UK charts were all female: B*Witched, Cher, Billie, Mariah Carey and Whitney Houston, and The Honeyz.

Most Successful UK Solo Artist Elton John, who was knighted in 1998, is the most successful UK solo artist in both the US and the UK, with sales of more than 150 million records in the world. In the US, he had at least one Top 40 entry every year from 1970 to 1999, a record run of 30 consecutive years. Elton John holds the records for the biggest-selling album by a British male soloist in both the US and the UK. In the US, *Elton John's Greatest Hits* (1974) has sold 15 million, while in the UK, *The Very Best of Elton John* (1990) has certified sales of 2.7 million.

Longest Span of US/UK Top 20 Albums

Frank Sinatra holds the record for the longest span of Top 20 albums in the US and the UK. His first US chart entry in the rock era was *In The Wee Small Hours*, which entered on May 28, 1955, and his most recent was *Duets II*, which exited the Top 20 on December 31, 1994, 39 years 7 months later. In the UK, he first entered on November 8, 1958, with *Come Fly With Me*, and his most recent Top 20 album, *My Way— The Best of Frank Sinatra*, exited 39 years 7 months later in June 1998, two months after his death. He also had several top-selling albums before the UK album charts started in 1958.

Best-Selling Latin Artist

Spanish vocalist Julio Iglesias is the most successful Latin music artist in the world, with reported global sales of more than 200 million albums. Iglesias' album *Julio* (1994) is also the only foreign-language album to have gone double platinum (2 million copies) in the US.

MOST SUCCESSIVE NO. 1s BY A NEW ACT The record for the most successive UK No. 1 singles by a new act is held by the Spice Girls (the lead singer of which, Mel G., is pictured), who reached No. 1 with their first six singles in the UK. They also topped the charts with two of their next three hits.

Most Successful Latin Record

"Macarena" by Spanish duo Los Del Rio is the most successful Latin recording, selling more than 10 million around the world. It topped the US charts for 14 weeks in 1996 and spent 60 weeks on the Top 100.

Most Successful Record Label Since the US Top 100 was launched in August 1958, the record label with the most No. 1 hits is Columbia, with 83 up to May 1999. It has almost twice as many chart toppers as its closest rivals, Capitol Records, with 46, and RCA Records, with 42.

ROCK

Biggest-Selling Album The Eagles' *Greatest Hits 1971-75* is the biggest-selling rock album in the US, with sales of 25 million.

Biggest-Selling Hard Rock Album *Led Zeppelin IV (Four Symbols)* by British band Led Zeppelin has sold over 21 million copies in the US since 1971.

BIGGEST-SELLING HARD ROCK ALBUM IN THE UK *Bat Out Of Hell* by Meat Loaf has sold more than 2.1 million copies in the UK since 1978. The first collaboration between Meat Loaf (real name Marvin Lee Aday) and writer/producer Jim Steinman, it had spent 472 weeks on the UK album charts by April 1999. Later successes included *Dead Ringer* (1981) and *Bat Out Of Hell II: Back Into Hell* (1993), which spawned the single "I'd Do Anything For Love (But I Won't Do That)," the best-selling single in the UK that year.

Biggest-Selling Solo Rock Album Bruce Springsteen's *Born In The USA* (1984) is the top-selling album by a US solo rock act in the US, with sales of over 15 million.

Biggest-Selling Rock Concept Album The Wall by British band Pink Floyd has sold 23 million copies in the US.

Most Weeks on the US Album Chart Dark Side Of The Moon by Pink Floyd entered the US charts on March 17, 1973, and is still there. It had spent 741 weeks in the Top 200 and 411 weeks on the Pop Catalog chart by May 1999, topping the latter in its 1,154th chart week.

Most Platinum Albums in the US Led Zeppelin holds the record for the most US platinum albums by a rock act, having amassed 94 by June 1999.

Fastest-Selling Album in the UK Be Here Now (1997) by Oasis sold a record 345,000 copies in the UK on the day it was released. By its third day, it had sold 700,000 copies, and within 17 days, sales had passed the 1 million mark. Like Oasis' first two albums, *Be Here Now* entered the chart at No. 1, giving the band the record for the most consecutive releases to enter in this position.

Biggest-Selling Rock Album in Japan Japan's top-selling rock

LONGEST UK NO. 1 TITLE The longest title (without brackets) of a UK No. 1 single is "If You Tolerate This Your Children Will Be Next" by the Manic Street Preachers, which reached No. 1 in September 1998. The band, comprising Nicky Wire (pictured), Richey Edwards, James Dean Bradfield, and Sean Moore, released their first single in 1989. They attracted critical acclaim and a devoted cult following, but when Edwards disappeared in February 1995, a split looked inevitable. However, they returned in 1996 to achieve a new level of commercial success. In 1999, they won Brit Awards for Best British Band and Best Album (*This Is My Truth, Tell Me Yours*). Richey Edwards' whereabouts remain a mystery.

album is *Review* by the Japanese band Glay, which has sold more than 4.7 million copies in its native country alone.

Most Successful Posthumous Albums in the US Nirvana topped the US charts with *MTV Unplugged In New York* in November 1994 and *From The Muddy Banks Of The Wishkah* in October 1996. The band's lead singer, Kurt Cobain, committed suicide in April 1994.

Longest Time Between a Hit Album and Single The first UK hit single by Led Zeppelin, "Whole Lotta Love," entered the charts on September 13, 1997. This was a record-breaking 28 years 5 months after the group's debut album, *Led Zeppelin,* had first charted.

Most Successful Rock Single In 1991, "Everything I Do (I Do It For You)" by Bryan Adams spent a record 16 consecutive weeks at No. 1 in the UK and seven weeks at No. 1 in the US. It also reached No. 1 in 16

HIGHEST US CHART ENTRY BY A ROCK ACT Aerosmith (whose singer Steven Tyler is pictured) is the only rock group to have entered the US singles charts at No. 1. They achieved this with "I Don't Want To Miss A Thing" in September 1998.

other countries, including France, Germany, Australia, Canada, and Belgium.

Most Modern Rock No. 1 Singles in the US The act to have had the most No. 1 singles on the *Billboard* Modern Rock chart is R.E.M., with six. The British acts to have had the highest number are the Cure and Depeche Mode, with four each.

Most Mainstream Rock No. 1 Singles in the US The act to have had the most No. 1 singles on the *Billboard* Mainstream Rock Tracks chart is Van Halen, with 11.

The solo artist to have had the highest number is John Mellencamp, with eight.

Longest US Hit Single "November Rain" by Guns 'N' Roses is the longest single to have reached the US Top 20, with a playing time of 8 min. 40 sec. It reached No. 3 in August 1992.

Most Simultaneous UK Indie Hits The Smiths had the top three hits on the UK indie chart on January 28, 1984.

On July 1, 1995, Oasis had six singles in the top seven of the UK indie chart.

Most Valuable US Rock Record There are only two known copies of *The Freewheelin' Bob Dylan* (Columbia CS-8796, in stereo) as the album was later re-pressed with four songs removed. Copies in near-mint condition would be worth between $20,000 and $30,000 today.

Most Continents Played in a Day On October 24, 1995, UK heavy metal band Def Leppard staged shows on three different continents. They played in Tangiers, Morocco, London, England, and Vancouver, Canada.

Most Deaths at a Rock Concert Eleven fans were trampled to death at a gig by the Who in Cincinnati, Ohio, in 1979.

BIGGEST SCREEN AT A CONCERT
The set for U2's 1997 PopMart tour featured the world's largest LED (light-emitting diode) screen. Measuring 54.8 x 170 ft., the screen showed animation and pop-art masterpieces. U2 (whose singer Bono is pictured) was originally identified with guitar-based anthems, but by the 1990s, they were experimenting with samplers, dance rhythms, and visual effects.

DANCE, R&B & HIP HOP

Biggest-Selling Dance Album in the US   The soundtrack to *Purple Rain* by Prince (now ♀) and the Revolution topped the US charts for a record 24 weeks and has sold more than 13 million copies there since its release in 1985. The film, which starred Prince, was an apparently autobiographical story set in the club scene of Minneapolis, Minnesota. The album yielded the hits. "When Doves Cry" and "Let's Go Crazy."

MOST NO. 1 US RAP SINGLES   The artist who has had the greatest number of No. 1 singles on the *Billboard* Rap Chart is L L Cool J, with a total of eight. These include "I'm That Type Of Guy," "Around The Way Girl," "Loungin'," and "Father." L L Cool J is on the Def Jam label, which holds the record for the greatest number of US No. 1 rap singles, with 15. Other artists on the label include Public Enemy, MC Serch, and Boss.

Biggest-Selling Dance Album in the UK   *Bizarre Fruit* (1994) by the British group M People has sold more than 1.5 million copies in the United Kingdom—more than any other dance album. The album features the hits "Sight for Sore Eyes," "Open Your Heart," and "Search for the Hero."

Most Simultaneous Hits by a Dance Act   On April 20, 1996, all of Prodigy's 10 hit singles were in the UK Top 100. The group's previous nine singles, all of which had originally made the UK Top 15, had been reissued after "Firestarter," released in March 1996, gave them their first-ever No. 1 single.

Fastest-Selling Dance Album in the UK *The Fat Of The Land* (1997) by Prodigy sold a record 317,000 copies in its first week. In the US, it sold more than 200,000 copies in its first week. The album entered the charts at No. 1 in a total of 20 countries.

Most Successful Chart Debuts The only act to enter the US pop charts at No. 1 with its first three albums is rapper Snoop Dogg (aka Snoop Doggy Dogg) with *Doggy Style* (1993), *Tha Dogfather* (1996), and *Da Game Is To Be Sold, Not To Be Told* (1998).

The only act to enter at No. 1 with its first two albums within a year is rapper DMX, with *It's Dark And Hell Is Hot* (June 1998) and *Flesh of My Flesh Blood Of My Blood* (January 1999).

Most Consecutive US No. 1 Singles The record for the most consecutive No. 1 pop singles by an artist is seven, by R&B vocalist Whitney Houston between 1985 and 1988. These included "Saving All My Love For You" (1985), "I Wanna Dance With Somebody (Who Loves Me)," and "So Emotional" (both 1987).

MOST GRAMMY NOMINATIONS In 1999, Lauryn Hill received 10 Grammy nominations—a record for a female recording artist. Most were for her chart-topping album *The Miseducation Of Lauryn Hill*. She won five awards (another female record): Album of the Year, Best New Artist, Best R&B Album, Best Female R&B Vocal Performance and Best R&B Song.

Shortest US Top 10 Title The shortest-titled record to reach the US pop Top 10 is ☥ by Prince (now ⚥) in 1992.

Most US Top 40 Hits without Reaching No. 1 The artist to have had the most US Top 40 pop hits without hitting No. 1 is James Brown, with 44. The next four acts are also R&B artists: Brook Benton (24), Sam Cooke (24), Jackie Wilson (23), and Fats Domino (22).

Longest US Charts Span The act with the longest charts span on the US pop Top 100 is R&B group the Isley Brothers. They first entered the

MOST SUCCESSFUL RAP PRODUCER IN THE US Sean "Puff Daddy" Coombs is the most successful US rap producer, having been responsible for four singles that consecutively headed the US rap charts for a total of 36 weeks in 1997. These included "Hypnotize" and "Mo Money, Mo Problems" by The Notorious B.I.G. Puff Daddy's tribute to The Notorious B.I.G. (aka Christopher Wallace)—"I'll Be Missing You," made with Faith Evans and featuring 112—headed the US charts for 11 weeks and was No. 1 on the UK charts for six weeks in 1997, making it the most successful R&B tribute song in the US and UK. Puff Daddy recorded the single after B.I.G. was gunned down as he left a party in Los Angeles, California, on March 4, 1997.

charts with their much-covered song "Shout" in September 1959 and last charted 37 years 4 months later with "Tears" in January 1997.

Longest US Span of No. 1 Hits The R&B artist with the longest span of US No. 1 hits is Michael Jackson. His first solo No. 1 was "Ben" in October 1972, and he last topped the chart almost 23 years later with "You Are Not Alone" in September 1995. The latter was also the first single ever to enter the US charts at No. 1. He had also topped the charts as lead singer of the Jackson 5 on four occasions before his first solo No. 1.

Most Successful Benelux Single in the UK "No Limits" by Belgian dance music duo 2 Unlimited is the most successful single ever from the Benelux countries on the UK charts. It was No. 1 for five weeks in 1993.

Most Successful Non-English-Language Rap Records In 1993, "Dur Dur d'Etre Bébé (It's Tough To Be A Baby)" by the then four-year-old French rapper Jordy (Lemoine) sold more than 1 million copies in France and was also a minor hit on the Billboard chart in the US. In February 1994, France's main TV channel, TF1, banned Jordy, saying his parents were exploiting him.

"Da Ya Ne" by the Japanese rap trio East End X Yuri sold 1 million copies in Japan in 1995.

Most Successful Female Rap Album in the US   *Chyna Doll* by New York rapper Foxy Brown is the only all-rap album by a female artist to top the US charts. It reached No. 1 in February 1999.

Most Charted Female Singer   No female singer has had more US Top 100 pop chart entries than R&B star Aretha Franklin, who had 76 chart entries between 1961 and 1998.

Most Successful Hit by a Female Duo   The most successful single by a female duo on the US pop charts is "The Boy Is Mine" by Brandy & Monica, which was No. 1 for 13 weeks from June 1998.

Longest-Running Group   The Four Tops were the longest-running successful group with the same members from the start. Levi Stubbs, Renaldo "Obie" Benson, Abdul Fakir, and Lawrence Payton formed the group in 1953 and sang together until Payton's death in 1997.

Longest-Running US R&B No. 1   The longest-running R&B No. 1 hit is "Nobody's Supposed To Be Here" by Canadian vocalist Deborah Cox, which headed the charts for 14 weeks from October 24, 1998, to February 6, 1999.

Most Successful Reggae Single in the UK   The double-sided hit "Rivers Of Babylon/Brown Girl In The Ring" by Germany-based band Boney M is the most successful reggae recording ever in the United Kingdom. It headed the charts for five weeks in 1978 and sold more than 2 million copies.

Biggest-Selling Hip Hop/Rap Album in the US   *Please Hammer Don't Hurt 'Em* (1990) by M.C. Hammer and *Crazysexycool* (1994) by TLC share the record for the biggest-selling hip hop/rap album in the US, with certified sales of 10 million.

COUNTRY MUSIC

Most Successful Country Artist in the US   Garth Brooks is the most successful country recording artist of all time, with album sales expected to equal the Beatles' record-breaking total of 100 million by the end of 1999. Despite his enormous success on the US album charts, Brooks did not have a US Top 100 single until December 1998 with "It's Your Song."

Reba McEntire is the biggest-selling female country vocalist in the US, with 13 platinum and six gold albums to her name by January 1999. These include *Sweet Sixteen* (1989), *Read My Mind* (1994), and *If You See Him* (1998).

Most Successful Country Duo   Kix Brooks and Ronnie Dunn are the most successful country duo of all time. Six of their albums have sold over

HIGHEST-PAID COUNTRY ARTIST In 1998, Garth Brooks earned $35 million—more than any other country music star. On December 6, 1997, Brooks had a record 12 separate tracks on the *Billboard* Top 75 country chart. The highest-paid female country artist of 1998 was Canadian Shania Twain, who grossed over $33.5 million that year.

1 million copies, and 12 of their singles have reached No. 1, including "Boot Scootin' Boogie" (1992), "Little Miss Honky Tonk" (1995), and "Husbands & Wives" (1998).

Most Successful Country Group Alabama holds the records for the most No. 1 singles, albums, and total sales by a country group. They have had 32 No. 1 singles and 10 No. 1 albums and have sold over 57 million records.

Most Played Country Songs in the US Dolly Parton's composition "I Will Always Love You," Jim Webb's song "By The Time I Get To Phoenix," and "Gentle On My Mind" by John Hartford have each been played on the air a certified 4 million times in the US. This figure includes versions by non-country performers.

Most Popular US Jukebox Track The most played record of all time on American jukeboxes is Patsy Cline's recording of "Crazy" (1961). The song was one of the first hits to be composed by Willie Nelson.

Biggest-Selling Country Albums in the US Garth Brooks' 1990 album *No Fences* sold a record total of more than 16 million copies.
The biggest-selling country album ever by a group in the US *Greatest Hits* (1986) by Alabama, which has sold more than 5 million copies.

Most Weeks at No. 1 by a US Album No record has topped any US album chart for longer than *12 Greatest Hits* (1967) by Patsy Cline, which headed the country catalog chart in *Billboard* for 251 weeks.

Most Simultaneous Album Hits in the US On October 10, 1992, four of the Top 5 albums on the US country charts were by Garth Brooks. The albums— *The Chase, Beyond Season, No Fences,* and *Ropin' The Wind* —all featured on the US Top 20 pop album charts too.

Most No. 1 Country Albums in the US "Outlaw" stars Willie Nelson and Merle Haggard have both had a record 15 US No. 1 country albums.

Loretta Lynn has had 10 No. 1 country albums in the US— more than any other female artist.

The most US No. 1 country albums by a group is 10, by Alabama.

Most Entries at No. 1 in the US The country artist with the most albums entering the US pop charts at No. 1 is Garth Brooks, with six.

Most Simultaneous Album Hits in the UK On September 24, 1964, the late Jim Reeves had a record eight entries in the UK Top 20 pop album charts.

TOP-SELLING FEMALE COUNTRY ALBUM The top-selling country album by a female artist in the US is *The Woman In Me* (1996) by Shania Twain, which has sold 11 million copies. It is also the third-biggest-selling album of all time by any female artist. Her 9-million-selling album *Come On Over* is the second-biggest-selling country album by a female artist.

Irish singer Daniel O'Donnell occupied a record six of the top seven places on the UK country album charts on November 16, 1991.

MOST DUETS RECORDED Willie Nelson (above) has recorded duets with about 100 recording artists, including Bob Dylan, Julio Iglesias, Frank Sinatra, Ray Charles, Sinead O'Connor, Neil Young, Joni Mitchell, Bonnie Raitt, and fellow country music legends Merle Haggard, Jim Reeves, Johnny Cash, Brenda Lee, and Dolly Parton. Nelson's first break in country music came when he financed and recorded "No Place For Me" in 1957. Shortly afterward, he sold his first song, "Family Bible," for $50. Nelson went on to write hits for many top country artists in the 1960s, including "Crazy" for Patsy Cline. However, it was his first album for Columbia Records, *Red Headed Stranger,* that established him as one of country music's most popular artists.

Best-Selling Double LP The US sales record for a double album was broken by Garth Brooks' *Double Live* in December 1998. The album, which narrowly missed selling 1 million copies on its first day, had initial orders of a record 7 million copies. It sold 1,085,373 copies in its first week, 1.7 million copies in two weeks, and 2.158 million copies in three. *Double Live* was Brooks' third No. 1 pop album that year—a total only equaled in record history by Elvis Presley, the Beatles, and the Monkees.

Most Country Radio Stations In the US, there are over 2,350 specialist radio stations that play predominantly country music—this far exceeds the number playing other musical formats. Sales of country music records in the US in 1998 went up to 62.1 million from 59 million the previous year.

Biggest Boxed Set to Top the US Charts The six-CD set *The Limited Series* by Garth Brooks is the biggest boxed set to have topped the US pop charts. It reached No. 1 in May 1998.

Biggest-Selling Country Single in the US The only country single with sales of 3 million in the US is "How Do I Live" by LeAnn Rimes, which reached No. 2 on the pop charts in 1998.

Most No. 1 Country Singles in the US   The most No. 1 hits on the *Billboard* country charts by one act is 40, by Conway Twitty between 1968 and 1986.

Most Consecutive No. 1 US Country Singles   The group Alabama notched up a record-breaking 21 consecutive country No. 1 singles between 1980 and 1987.

Most No. 1 Singles by a Woman   The record for the most No. 1 hits on the *Billboard* country charts by a female artist is 24, by Dolly Parton, from "Joshua" (1970) to "The Rockin' Years" (1991), a duet with Ricky Van Shelton. Parton has also had 56 Top 10 singles and 41 weeks in total at No. 1. In 1986, her company, Parton Enterprises, opened Dollywood, an 87-acre theme park near her birthplace in Sevier County, Tennessee.

Most Weeks on Singles Chart in the US   "How Do I Live" by LeAnn Rimes spent a record 69 weeks on the US Top 100 from June 21, 1997, to October 10, 1998. It also broke the record for the most weeks in the Top 40, with 61, and the record (set 55 years earlier) for the most weeks in the Top 10, with 32.

CLASSICAL MUSIC, OPERA & JAZZ

Best-Selling Classical Album   *The Three Tenors In Concert*, recorded by José Carreras, Placido Domingo (both of Spain), and Luciano Pavarotti (Italy) for the 1990 soccer World Cup Finals, has sold an estimated 13 million copies.

Biggest Classical Audience   An estimated 800,000 people attended a free open-air concert by the New York Philharmonic Orchestra on the Great Lawn of Central Park in New York City on July 5, 1986.

Biggest Orchestra   On November 23, 1998, Music For Youth organized the world's largest orchestra, consisting of 3,503 musicians at the National Indoor Arena, Birmingham, England. Conducted by Sir Simon Rattle, they played Malcolm Arnold's *Little Suite No. 2*, lasting 7 min. 40 sec.

Most Prolific Conductor   Herbert von Karajan (Austria), who died in 1989, made more than 800 classical recordings. He conducted the London Philharmonic Orchestra, the Vienna State Opera, La Scala Opera of Milan, and the Berlin Philharmonic Orchestra and founded the Salzburg Festival in 1967.

Longest Symphony   The symphony *Victory at Sea*, written by the American composer Richard Rodgers for the documentary film of the same name and arranged by Robert Russell Bennett for NBC TV in 1952, lasts 13 hours.

BEST-SELLING JAZZ ARTIST
Saxophonist Kenny G has sold an estimated 50 million albums, including the best-selling jazz album of all time, *Breathless* (of which an estimated 13 million copies have been sold). He also holds the record for the longest sustained musical note, an E flat that he held for 45min 47sec at J&R Music World, New York City, on December 1, 1997.

Longest Operas   The Life and Times of Joseph Stalin by Robert Wilson, performed from December 14 to 15, 1973, at the Brooklyn Academy of Music in New York City, lasted almost 13 hr. 25 min.

The longest frequently performed opera is Wagner's *Die Meistersinger von Nürnberg* (1868). An uncut version performed by the Sadler's Wells company in London, England, in 1968 lasted a total of 5 hr. 15 min.

Shortest Opera   The shortest published opera is *The Sands of Time* by Simon Rees and Peter Reynolds, which lasted 4 min. 9 sec. when first per-

formed by Rhian Owen and Dominic Burns at The Hayes in Cardiff, Wales, in March 1993. A 3-min. 34-sec. version was performed under the direction of Peter Reynolds in London, England, in September 1993.

Lowest Note   The lowest vocal note in the classical repertoire is in Osmin's aria in *Die Entführung*

MOST SUCCESSFUL PRETEEN CLASSICAL FEMALE PERFORMER   Charlotte Church was just 12 years old when she earned a double-platinum album for the 300,000 sales of her 1998 album *Voice Of An Angel*. The record also earned the young Welsh soprano gold discs in Australia and New Zealand. Signed to Sony Music UK, she has played sell-out concerts at the Royal Albert Hall and the London Palladium.

aus dem Serail by Wolfgang Amadeus Mozart. It calls for a low D (73.4 Hz).

Highest Note   The highest vocal note in the classical repertoire is G^3, which occurs in Mozart's *Papolo di Tessaglia*.

Longest Operatic Applause   Placido Domingo (Spain) was applauded for 1 hr. 20 min. through 101 curtain calls after a performance of *Otello* at the Vienna State Opera House in Austria in July 1991.

Longest Operatic Career   Danshi Toyotake of Hyogo, Japan, sang *Musume Gidayu* (a traditional Japanese narrative) for 91 years from the age of seven, from 1898 to 1989.

Biggest Opera House   The Metropolitan Opera House at Lincoln Center in New York City was completed in September 1966 at a cost of $45.7 million. It has a capacity of 4,065 people, and the auditorium alone seats 3,800.

Oldest Opera House   In 1737, King Carlo VI commissioned Giovanni Medrano to build the Teatro S. Carlo in Naples, Italy. It was rebuilt under the direction of architect A. Niccolini after a fire in 1816 and has remained essentially the same building ever since. Containing 184 boxes in six tiers,

BEST-SELLING OPERA SINGER   Italian tenor Luciano Pavarotti made his professional debut in 1961 and has sold about 60 million albums worldwide. His entire stage repertoire has reached disc, and every recording is a best-seller. He also holds the record for the most curtain calls in an opera, receiving 165 after singing the part of Nemorino in Donizetti's *L'Elisir d'Amore* at the Deutsche Oper in Berlin, Germany, on February 24, 1988. The applause lasted 1 hr. 7 min. Pavarotti reached a huge worldwide audience in the early 1990s when he began performing with Placido Domingo and José Carreras as "The Three Tenors," under the baton of Zubin Mehta. The partnership was originally formed to celebrate the 1990 World Cup Finals held in Italy.

the theater can seat 1,500 people.

Oldest Classical Music The earliest classical music in written records is classical Chinese music, a musical theory that can be traced back 3,000 years when the philosopher Confucius advocated the practice of music.

Oldest Musical Instrument An ancient bone flute, estimated to be about 43,000 to 82,000 years old, was found by Dr. Ivan Turk, a paleontologist at the Slovenian Academy of Science at a Neanderthal campsite in Ljubljana, Slovenia, in 1998. The oldest known musical instrument, it is made of an old cave-bear femur segment with four holes (two complete and two partial).

Earliest Jazz Record The first jazz record made was "Indiana/The Dark Town Strutters Ball," recorded for the Columbia label in New York City on or around January 30, 1917, by the Original Dixieland Jazz Band. It was released on May 31, 1917.

Biggest Jazz Festival The Festival International de Jazz de Montréal in Québec, Canada, is the world's largest jazz festival. Lasting 11 days, it attracts 1.5 million people to watch 400 concerts by 2,000 musicians from 20 countries.

Longest Jazz Career Saxophonist and pianist Benny Waters (b. 1902) from Maryland has been performing since his mid-teens and is still recording at the age of 97.

Oldest Jazz Club The Village Vanguard cellar jazz club opened in New York City in the 1930s and has hosted mainstream jazz ever since.

CARTOONS

Highest-Grossing First Run Walt Disney's *The Lion King* (1994) grossed a record $766.9 million on its first run, when it was screened in over 60 countries. The film took a 600-animators crew three years to make. In 1995, its hit theme song, "Can You Feel The Love Tonight," was awarded an Oscar for Best Original Song.

Highest-Grossing Animated Film Walt Disney's *The Jungle Book* (1967) is the highest-grossing animated film ever made, with $205.8 million.

Disney's *Snow White* (1937), which has taken $175.3 million, would almost certainly top the list if inflation were taken into account.

MOST EXPENSIVE ANIMATED FILM   DreamWorks' *The Prince of Egypt* **(1998) cost $60 million to make. It was in production for four years and was worked on by 350 artists and animators. The four-minute Red Sea sequence alone took 350,000 working hours to complete.**

Highest-Grossing Japanese Animated Film Series *Princess Mononoke* (Japan, 1997) is Japan's highest-grossing animated film, making $156.6 million in Japan alone. When the film was shown on the Nippon Television Network (NTV) on January 22, 1999, it attracted the biggest audience for a movie in 15 years.

Longest-Running Animated Film Series Harry "Bud" Fisher's animated series *Mutt and Jeff* began as a supplement to the *Pathé's Weekly* movie newsreel on February 10, 1913, and continued as separate weekly reels from April 1, 1916, to December 1, 1926. At least 323 *Mutt and Jeff* films are known to have been made.

MOST CONSECUTIVE OSCAR NOMINATIONS Between 1991 and 1997, Aardman Animation of Bristol, England, received six consecutive Oscar nominations for Best Short Animated Film, a record for any Oscar category. Three of the nominations, *Creature Comforts*, *The Wrong Trousers*, and *A Close Shave*, all directed by Aardman's founder, Nick Park, went on to win Oscars. The last two of these featured the cheese-loving inventor Wallace and his long-suffering canine companion Gromit (pictured). The animation technique for Park's films requires thousands of minute adjustments to clay figures, so each scene can take weeks to complete.

Longest-Serving Actor in an Animated Series Actor Jack Mercer (US) provided the voice of Popeye in the *Popeye The Sailor Man* series for a record-breaking 45 years. The series was produced for the cinema between 1933 and 1957 and was then made for television during the 1970s.

Most Celebrities Featured in an Animated Series *The Simpsons* has featured the voices of 228 celebrities, including Magic Johnson, Elizabeth Taylor, and Paul and Linda McCartney.

Most Valuable Cartoon Cels A black-and-white drawing from Walt Disney's *Orphan's Benefit* (1934) raised a record $280,000 when it was sold at Christie's in London, England, in 1989.

One of the 150,000 color cels from Walt Disney's animated film *Snow White* (1937) was sold in 1991 for $203,000.

Most Fits Caused by a TV Show In December 1997, more than 700 children in Japan were rushed to the hospital when an episode of an animated series based on the Nintendo game *Pocket Monsters* caused them to have convulsions. A total of 208 children aged three and above were detained in the hospital after the broadcast. According to experts, the fits were caused by a sequence in which red lights flashed from the eyes of the character Pikachu.

Biggest Cartoon Museum   The International Museum of Cartoon Art in Boca Raton, Florida, has a collection of over 160,000 original animated drawings from 50 different countries. The collection also includes 10,000 books on animation and 1,000 hours of cartoons, interviews, and documentaries on film and tape.

Longest-Running Comic   *The Dandy*, which was first published by D.C. Thomson on December 4, 1937, brought out its 3,007th edition on July 10, 1999. Featuring Desperate Dan, the creation of cartoonist Dudley Watkins, the comic currently has a fan club of over 350,000 members.

Most Syndicated Comic Strip   *Peanuts* by Charles Schulz was first published in October 1950 in the US. The comic strip, which features the

LONGEST-RUNNING PRIMETIME SERIES   *The Simpsons*, which has been a regularly scheduled TV series since January 14, 1990, broadcast its 225th episode on May 16, 1999. Originally developed as a set of inserts for *The Tracey Ullman Show*, Lisa, Homer, Bart, Marge, and Maggie (pictured left to right) and their fellow inhabitants of Springfield have made their creator Matt Groening a multimillionaire.

characters Charlie Brown and Snoopy, currently appears in 2,620 different newspapers in 75 countries.

Longest-Running Newspaper Comic Strip   The world's longest-running newspaper comic strip is *The Katzenjammer Kids*, which was first published in the *New York Journal* in December 1897 and is still running. Created by Rudolph Dirks, *The Katzenjammer Kids* is now drawn by cartoonist Hy Eisman and is syndicated to 50 newspapers by King Features Syndicate.

Most Valuable Comic   The most valuable comic book is a first-issue copy of *Action Comics* from June 1938, in which Superman made his first appearance. It was sold for $100,000 in 1997, and, according to the *Overstreet Comic Book Price Guide*, it is now valued at $185,000.

Most Prolific Comics Writer   Paul S. Newman (US) had more than 4,000 stories published in 360 different comic books, including *Superman, Mighty Mouse, Prince Valiant, Fat Albert, Tweety and Sylvester,* and *The Lone Ranger*.

Most Filmed Comic Character   Zorro has been portrayed in 69 films to date. Invented by Johnston McCulley, he was also the first comic strip character to be the subject of a major feature film, *The Mark Of Zorro* (1920), starring Douglas Fairbanks. The movie appeared just one year after the comic strip was printed, giving Zorro the record for the fastest transition from comic strip to silver screen. The most recent version was *The Mask Of Zorro* (1998), in which the identity of the masked avenger was passed from Anthony Hopkins to Antonio Banderas.

THEME PARKS & RIDES

Most Expensive Theme Park   Disney is reported to have spent about $1 billion on the design, development, and realization of its Animal Kingdom in Florida.

LARGEST ALL-WEATHER INDOOR WATER PARK   The Ocean Dome is part of a vacation resort at Miyazaki on the island of Kyushi, Japan. The park is 984 ft. 1 in. long, 328 ft. 1 in. wide, and 124 ft. 8 in. tall and has a 459-ft.-3-in.-long beach made up of polished crushed marble from China. The Ocean Dome is a popular destination for honeymoon couples and can accommodate a maximum of 10,000 people at one time with a constant air temperature within the complex of 86°F and a water temperature of 82.4°F. It also contains the world's largest wave-making machine, capable of producing waves up to 8 ft. 2 in. high.

BIGGEST FERRIS WHEEL   The British Airways London Eye, designed by London architects David Marks and Julia Barfield, is scheduled to be unveiled at Jubilee Gardens, London, England, in January 2000. When completed, it will be 446 ft. 7 in. tall with a diameter of 443 ft. Each of the 32 capsules will be able to carry up to 25 passengers, giving views across a 30-mile radius. The wheel will be the fourth-biggest structure in London.

Biggest Theme Park   Disney World, near Orlando, Florida, covers 30,000 acres, making it the largest theme park in the world today. Opened on October 1, 1971, this colossal park cost approximately $400 million to develop.

Most-Visited Theme Park   In 1997, Tokyo Disneyland in Japan attracted a total of 17.83 million visitors. Opened on April 15, 1983, the 114.2-acre park includes areas dedicated to the Wild West, tropical exploration, fairy tales, space travel, and the future and can accommodate up to 85,000 visitors at once.

Most Rides at a Theme Park   Cedar Point in Ohio has a total of 67 different rides—the most of any theme park in the world today. They include classic wooden roller coasters such as *Blue Streak*, which was built in 1964, hair-raising state-of-the-art rides such as *Mantis* (1996), and children's rides such as *Jr. Gemini* (1978).

Most Roller Coasters at a Theme Park   A record-breaking 13 roller coasters dominate the skyline at Cedar Point, Ohio, which has been nicknamed "America's Roller Coast" as a result. At its opening in 1892, the theme park had just one roller coaster, which shuttled riders around at a sedate 10 mph. Today, it has some of the tallest, fastest, and most technically advanced coasters in the world.

Fastest Roller Coaster   *Superman the Escape* at Six Flags Magic Mountain in California is the fastest roller coaster in the world. Riders are shot from 0 to 100 mph in seven seconds and taken up to a height of 415 ft. in 15-seater gondolas before they reach the record-breaking speed once more on the backward descent.

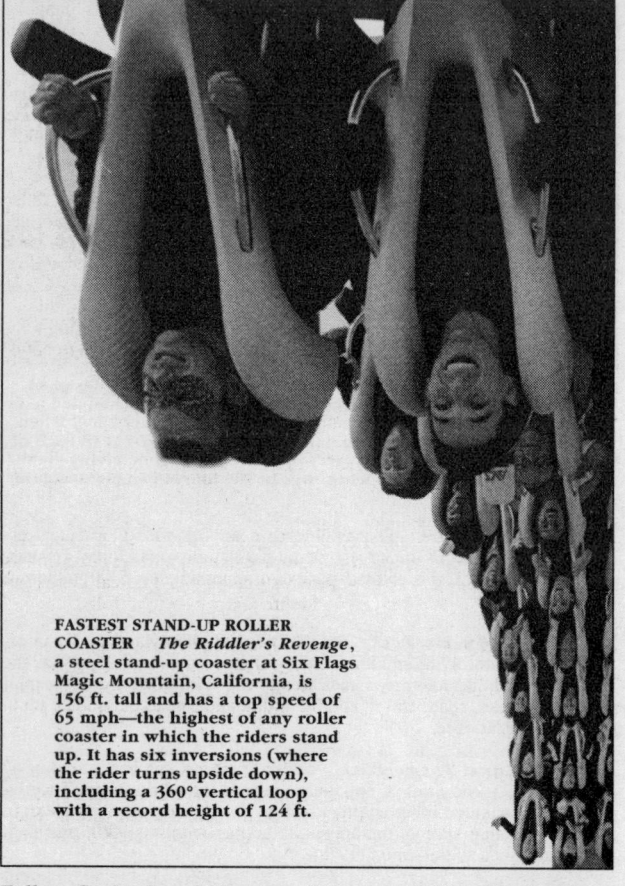

FASTEST STAND-UP ROLLER COASTER *The Riddler's Revenge*, a steel stand-up coaster at Six Flags Magic Mountain, California, is 156 ft. tall and has a top speed of 65 mph—the highest of any roller coaster in which the riders stand up. It has six inversions (where the rider turns upside down), including a 360° vertical loop with a record height of 124 ft.

Tallest Graity-Based Coaster *Fujiyama* at Fujikyu Highland Park, Japan, reaches a height of 259 ft. with a first drop of 239 ft. The ride was built with a design speed of 81 mph, though it does not actually reach it during the ride.

Tallest Free-Fall Coaster *The Drop Zone* at King's Island Theme Park, Ohio, has a 262-ft. drop from its 317-ft. vertical lift tower in an 88-second ride. Up to 40 riders free-fall 141 ft. at zero G, reaching a speed of 67 mph.

Tallest Thrill Ride *The Giant Drop* at Dreamworld in Australia is the tallest free-fall ride in the world at a record 390 ft. or 39 stories. Passengers on the open-air gondolas are hoisted skyward with their legs dangling freely. The ride, which lasts 1 min. 46 sec., reaches speeds of up to 99 mph before free-falling from 0 to 84 mph within five seconds.

Biggest Looping Roller Coaster *The Viper* roller coaster at Six Flags Magic Mountain in California has a 188-ft. drop. The ride turns upside down seven times at a speed of 70 mph. It has three loops and a 40-ft. corkscrew.

Fastest Launched Coaster *Superman the Escape,* a steel roller coaster installed at Six Flags Magic Mountain, Valencia, California, launches its 15-seater gondolas to a height of 415 ft. before they fall back along the tracks at 100 mph. Riders experience a record 6.5 seconds of "airtime" or negative G-force. The coaster was designed by Intamin AG of Switzerland.

Longest Roller Coaster *The Ultimate* roller coaster at Lightwater Valley, England, is 1 mile 753 yd. long, and the ride lasts for 5 min. 50 sec. Built in 1991, *The Ultimate* has steel tracks supported in places by a wooden superstructure.

Roller Coasters with Most Inversions The twisting steel coaster *Dragon Khan* takes riders upside down eight times. The sit-down ride is the main attraction at Port Aventura, Salou, Spain. Built in 1995, the year the park opened, the track is 4,166 ft. 1 in. long.

The *Monte Makaya* at Terra Encantada, Rio de Janeiro, Brazil, also turns riders upside down eight times during each complete circuit of its 2,793-ft. 4-in. steel track. Track elements include one Vertical Loop, two Cobra Rolls, a Double Corkscrew, and three Zero-G-Heart Rolls.

Biggest Portable Thrill Ride *Taz's Texas Tornado* has been in service at Six Flags Astroworld, Texas, since March 14, 1998, but was originally assembled in Germany in 1986. The twisting steel coaster is 112 ft. in total height and has a maximum speed of 60 mph. Its steepest turn is at an angle of 80°.

Oldest Continually Operating Roller Coaster Tivoli Gardens, Copenhagen, Denmark, was founded in 1843 and is one of the oldest amusement parks in the world. It is home to *Rutschebanen* (Scenic Railway) *Mk II*, which was built in 1913 and is the world's oldest operational roller coaster.

Biggest Theme Park Wedding On May 2, 1997, at the opening of *Giant Drop* —a 227-ft.-high free-fall tower at the Six Flags Great America theme park—a record 144 couples were married seconds before a three-second plummet toward the ground at a speed of 62 mph. Most of the wedding ceremony took place in the park's 3,200-seat stunt-show arena. The couples then ascended to the 22-story Giant Drop, where the Reverend Herring completed the ceremony. The couples, who came from all over the United States, had been selected by radio stations to participate in the mass wedding.

ADVERTISING

Biggest Advertising Agency   Japanese advertising agency Dentsu Inc. had sales of $11.8 billion by the end of March 1998 and 5,683 employees worldwide.

Most Expensive TV Ad   A commercial for Apple Computers Inc. cost a total of $600,000 to produce and $1 million to show. Directed by Ridley Scott, who also made *Blade Runner* (1982), and aired only once (in 1984), the ad registered such high viewer recall that it is believed to be one of the most cost-effective commercials ever made.

Biggest Revenue by a TV Network in One Day   Fox TV is reputed to have earned a record $150 million on Super Bowl Sunday (January 31, 1999), making it the most successful day in terms of advertising revenue for any network in television history. About $45 million was made from pre-game advertising revenue.

MOST POPULAR FILM TRAILER   When a 2-min. 10-sec. trailer for *Star Wars: The Phantom Menace* (1999) was first shown in cinemas in 1998, many *Star Wars* fans all over the world paid the full price for a cinema ticket to watch the trailer and then walked out before the feature presentation. Many came back to see the trailer time after time. When LucasFilms, the film's production company, made the trailer available to download on its official website, it is reported to have received 3.5 million visits in five days.

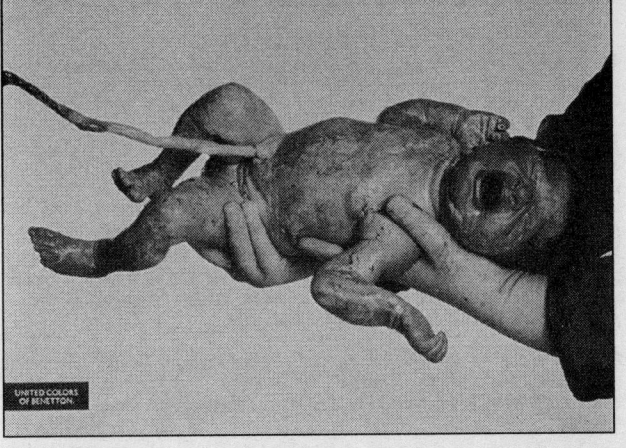

UNITED COLORS
OF BENETTON

MOST CONTROVERSIAL CAMPAIGN The Italian fashion company Benetton is unusual in that it creates all its advertising in-house, rather than using an outside agency. Over the years, its campaigns have consistently caused outrage among many people. Typical images have included a picture of a person with AIDS at the point of death and a child with hair shaped into devil's horns. The advertisement featuring a newborn baby, pictured here, prompted more than 800 complaints to the British Advertising Standards Authority during 1991, when it ran as part of a press and billboard campaign. Benetton's images have won many awards, however, including Best Campaign of 1991 by the European Art Directors Club and the Infinity Award of the International Center of Photography in Houston, Texas.

Most Expensive Commercial Break The TV network Fox earned $2 million for a 30-second advertisement during the transmission peak of the 1999 Super Bowl. The average cost of a 30-second spot during the day was $1.6 million.

Biggest Single Territory Ad Campaign The 1996 advertising campaign for AT&T telephone services cost parent company AT&T Corporation a record $474 million.

Most Ads for a Product in One Evening All 17 versions of a Castlemaine XXXX ad were shown on Granada Sky Broadcasting, UK, on October 1, 1996.

Most Awards Won by an International Commercial The Levi 501 jeans *Drugstore* TV ad won 33 awards in 1995.

Fastest Production of an Ad A television ad for Reebok's InstaPUMP shoes was created, filmed, and aired during Super Bowl XXVII at the Atlanta Georgia Dome on January 31, 1993. Filming took place up to the beginning of the fourth quarter of play, editing began in the middle of the third quarter, and the ad was aired during the break at the two-minute warning of the fourth quarter. The commercial lasted for 30 seconds.

Most Advertising Pages The most pages of advertisements sold in a single issue of a periodical is 938.79 out of a total of 1,162 pages, in the February/March 1998 American edition of *Brides Magazine*.

Shortest Ad An ad lasting four frames (equivalent to 0.133 seconds) was aired on KING-TV's *Evening Magazine* on November 29, 1993. The ad, for Bon Marché's Frango sweets, cost $3,780.

Biggest Cast in an Ad Saatchi and Saatchi's commercial *Face*, for British Airways, was filmed in Utah in October 1989 and starred 6,300 people wearing colored jogging suits. Shot from the air, the ad showed the cast assembled in different configurations to create images of an ear, an eye, a pair of lips, and, finally, a whole face and a globe.

Biggest Cast of Babies in an Ad *As of Right*, a British television commercial made for the Vauxhall Astra car by Tony Kaye in 1996, featured 2,000 babies and no adults. The most babies on set at any one time was 984.

Biggest Billboard On February 2, 1999, a 55-ft.-5-in.-high, 414-ft.-11-in.-long billboard was installed on the facade of the Ukraina Department Store in Kiev, Ukraine. Advertising Organics shampoo, the billboard remained in place for three months.

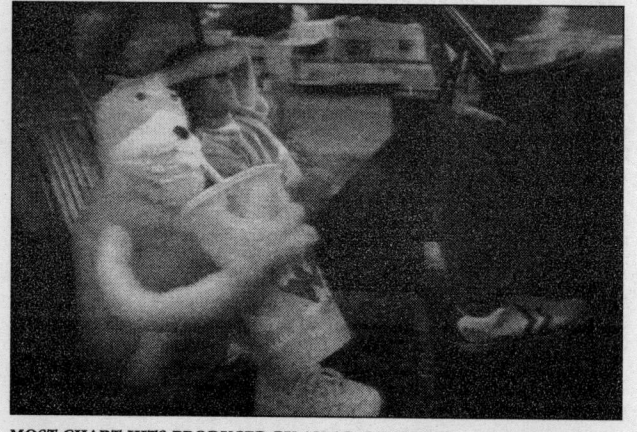

MOST CHART HITS PRODUCED BY AN AD CAMPAIGN Levi Strauss' ads have resulted in chart success for more of the records they have featured than any other ad campaign. Eight songs from the company's ads have reached the No. 1 position in the United Kingdom, including two that went straight to No. 1—"Spaceman" by Babylon Zoo on January 6, 1996, and "Flat Beat" by Mr. Oizo (pictured) on April 3, 1999.

MOST MARKETABLE ATHLETE *Fortune* magazine has estimated Michael Jordan's worth at over $10 billion, including revenue created through endorsements, television, ticket sales and merchandising, including Nike goods. When Jerry Reinsdorf bought 56% of the Chicago Bulls the year after Jordan arrived, his investment grew more than 1,000%. When Jordan announced his retirement in 1999, shares in Nike are reported to have fallen by 5.4%.

Longest Fixed Billboard The Bassat Ogilvy promotional billboard for Ford España is 475 ft. 9 in. in length and 49 ft. 3 in. in height. It is located at Plaza de Toros Monumental de Barcelona in Barcelona, Spain, and was installed on April 27, 1989.

Biggest Moving Billboard An 880-ft.-1-in.-long billboard covering an area of 11,541 ft.^{2} was placed on a train traveling through Gauteng Province, South Africa, on May 11, 1998.

Biggest Neon Advertising Sign The largest neon advertising sign in the world is 298 ft. 6 in. wide and 150 ft. 11 in. high and covers 45,041 ft.^{2} on a wall at Tai Sing Container and Godown Center in Hong Kong, China. Depicting eight horses, it was constructed in December 1997 and contains more than 5,000 lightbulbs.

Longest Advertising Poster A poster produced by Saatchi and Saatchi for the Rome Opera House and set up at the Piazza del Popolo in Rome, Italy, on July 27, 1998, was 898 ft. 11 in. long and 6 ft. 6 in. high.

PUBLISHING

Best-Selling Author   The top-selling fiction writer of all time is Agatha Christie, creator of Hercule Poirot and Miss Marple. Her 78 crime novels have sold an estimated 2 billion copies in 44 different languages.

Best-Selling Books   The world's best-selling and most widely distributed book is the Bible, with an estimated 3.88 billion copies sold between 1815 and 1999.

Excluding non-copyright works, the all-time best-selling book is *The Guinness Book of Records*, first published by Guinness Superlatives in October 1955. Global sales in 37 languages had surpassed 85 million by July 1999.

Best-Selling Novels   Three novels have been credited with sales of over 30 million, all of them by American female authors. They are *Gone With the Wind* (1936) by Margaret Mitchell, *To Kill a Mockingbird* (1960) by Harper Lee, and *Valley of the Dolls* (1966) by Jacqueline Susann, which sold 6.8 million copies in the six months following its publication.

Scottish author Alistair Maclean wrote a total of 30 novels, 28 of which have sold more than 1 million copies in the United Kingdom alone. It has been estimated that a novel by Maclean is purchased somewhere in the world every 18 seconds.

Best-Selling Diary   *The Diary of Anne Frank*, the young author's account of events that took place when her family and their friends were hiding from the Nazis in Amsterdam, Netherlands, during World War II, has been translated into 55 languages and has sold more than 25 million copies.

TOP-SELLING NEWS MAGAZINE *Time*, which was launched in 1923, had a circulation of 4.06 million for the six months ending December 1998 in the US alone. Time Inc. has built up a large news-gathering organization and owns other best-selling magazines, including *Fortune*, *Life*, and *People*.

BEST-SELLING CHILDREN'S BOOK SERIES The 110 titles in the *Goosebumps* series by R.L. Stine have sold 220 million copies worldwide since the first book, *Welcome to Dead House*, was published by Scholastic, Inc. in 1992.

Longest Stay on a Best-Seller List *The Road Less Traveled* by M. Scott Peck spent a record-breaking 694 weeks on the *New York Times* paperback best-seller list before dropping out on April 6, 1997. The book has sold more than 5 million copies.

Most Prolific Novelist The Brazilian novelist José Carlos Ryoki de Alpoim Inoue had a total of 1,046 sci-fi novels, westerns, and thrillers published from June 1986 to August 1996—more than any other writer.

Oldest Authors Sisters Sarah and Elizabeth Delany published *The Delany Sisters' Book of Everyday Wisdom* in October 1994, when they were 105 and 103 years old, respectively. In 1997, Sarah wrote the sequel *On My Own at 107.*

Longest Biography The longest biography in publishing history is the life story of British wartime leader Sir Winston Churchill. Coauthored by his son Randolph and Martin Gilbert, who has been the sole author since Randolph's death in 1968, the book currently comprises a record 22 volumes, both writing and research is still ongoing.

Biggest Bookstore The biggest bookstore in the world is a Barnes & Noble Bookstore in New York City. It covers an area of 154,250 ft.^{2} and has 12 miles 4,594 ft. of shelving.

Oldest Sex Manual Vatsyayana's *Kama Sutra* is believed to be the oldest sex manual in existence. Generally considered the standard work on love in Sanskrit literature, the book is thought to have been written between the 1st and 6th centuries A.D. Today, the *Kama Sutra* is widely available and has been translated into a number of languages.

Top-Selling Newspapers The newspaper with the highest circulation in the world is Tokyo's *Yomiuri Shimbun*, established in 1874. By March 1999, its circulation was 14.42 million—10.18 million for the morning edition and 4.24 million for the evening edition.

Komsomolskaya Pravda, the youth paper of the former Soviet Communist Party, reached a peak daily circulation of 21.9 million copies in May 1990.

More newspapers are sold in the United Kingdom than in any other

RICHEST HORROR AUTHOR
Novelist Stephen King (pictured playing in the celebrity band The Rock Bottom Remainders with writer Amy Tan) is the richest horror author in the world, with an estimated fortune of $84 million. His novels include *Carrie* (1974), *The Shining* (1978), *Pet Sematary* (1983), and *Misery* (1987), all of which have been made into successful films.

country in the European Union. News International's *The Sun* has the highest circulation of any British daily newspaper, with 3.7 million copies sold, while *The Sun's* sister paper, *News of the World*, has a record Sunday circulation of 4.2 million.

Most Newspaper Published in One Country   In 1995, India had more than 4,235 different newspapers, most of them regional and published in different languages, including Hindi, Urdu, Punjabi, Gujarati, and English.

Heaviest Newspaper
The heaviest single issue of a newspaper was the September 14, 1987, edition of the Sunday *New York Times*, which weighed more than 12 lb. and contained 1,612 pages.

Top-Selling Magazines   *Reader's Digest*, which was established in February 1922, has a monthly circulation of more than 27 million copies in 18 different

BEST-SELLING LIVING AUTHOR   The top-selling living author is British romantic novelist Dame Barbara Cartland. Her 635 titles have sold more than 650 million copies worldwide.

languages. Its US edition alone sells more than 15 million copies each month, while its UK edition has a monthly readership of about 1.63 million.

In 1974, *TV Guide* became the first weekly periodical to sell a billion copies in a single year. It currently has a weekly circulation of 11 million copies.

Top-Selling Society Magazine   Spain's *¡Hola!* sells 627,514 copies a week—116,962 more copies than its British sister publication, *Hello!*

Top-Selling Gay Magazine   Los Angeles based *Advocate* magazine sells more than 2 million copies a year in the US.

PERFORMANCE

Longest Continuous Theatrical Run   *The Mousetrap*, a thriller written by Agatha Christie, opened at the Ambassadors Theater, London, England, on November 25, 1952. On March 25, 1974, after a total of 8,862 performances, it moved to St. Martin's Theater next door. On April 14, 1999, the 19,301st performance took place. The box office has grossed $33.3 million from more than 9 million theatergoers.

Longest-Running Musicals   The off-Broadway musical *The Fantasticks* by Tom Jones and Harvey Schmidt opened on May 3, 1960. By March 8, 1999, the show had been performed a record 16,127 times at the Sullivan Street Playhouse, Greenwich Village, New York.

Cats is the longest-running musical in the history of the West End and Broadway, with the 7,675th and 6,896th show performed, respectively, on April 14, 1999. It opened on May 11, 1981, at the New London Theater in England and has since been seen by an estimated 48 million people in approximately 250 cities around the world. Based on the poems in *Old Possum's Book Of Practical Cats* by T.S. Eliot with music by Andrew Lloyd Webber, it has grossed more than $2 billion worldwide.

Longest-Running Comedy   *No Sex Please, We're British*, which was written by Anthony Marriott and Alistair Foot and presented by John Gale, opened at the Strand Theater, London, England, on June 3, 1971, transferred to the Duchess Theater, London, on August 2, 1986, and finally ended on September 5, 1987, after 16 years 3 months—a total of 6,761 performances. The play was directed by Allan Davis throughout its run.

Highest Advance Sales   The musical *Miss Saigon*, written by Alain Boublil and Claude-Michel Schönberg, produced by Cameron Mackintosh, and starring Jonathan Pryce and Lea Salonga, opened on Broadway in April 1991 after generating record advance sales of $36 million.

Highest-Insured Show   The producers of *Barnum*, which opened at the London Palladium, England, on June 11, 1981, insured the musical for the record sum of $10 million. The individual insurance for its star Michael

HIGHEST-PAID DANCER Michael Flatley (US), the star of *Lord Of The Dance*, earned $1.6 million per week for his Irish-style dancing at the peak of the show's success. This included profits from ticket, video, and merchandise sales. The Chicago-born star first found international fame when he performed at the 1994 Eurovision Song Contest in Dublin, Ireland. He is seen here with members of the *Lord Of The Dance* troupe at the 1997 Academy Awards ceremony.

Crawford, who, during the performance, had to walk a high wire and slide down a rope from the highest box to the stage, accounted for $6 million of the total.

Greatest Theatrical Loss The largest-ever loss sustained by a theatrical show was borne by the American producers of the Royal Shakespeare Company's musical *Carrie*, which was based on the novel by Stephen King. The production closed after five performances on Broadway on May 17, 1988, at a total cost of $7 million.

Most Performances in One Production Steven Wayne (UK), the longest-serving cast member of a musical, has been with the West End production of *Cats* since rehearsals began for the opening on May 11, 1981. During that time, he has played and understudied most of the male roles in the show.

Longest Play The longest play on record is *The Non-Stop Connolly Show* by John Arden (UK), which took 26 hr. 30 min. to perform in Dublin, Republic of Ireland, in 1975.

Shortest Play The world's shortest play ever is the 30-second *Breath*, written by the Irish-born playwright and novelist Samuel Beckett in 1969. The play consists of the sound of a single human breath. Beckett, who won the Nobel Prize for Literature in 1969 and died in 1992, was a pivotal figure in the Theater of the Absurd.

Biggest Dance Festival The Festival de Dança de Joinville in Santa Catarina, Brazil, is the largest dance festival in the world, both in terms of the number of dancers and the number of performance categories. About 3,000 dancers from all over the world gather to participate.

Most Curtain Calls for a Ballet The record for the greatest number of curtain calls received at any ballet is 89 by Dame Margot Fonteyn (UK) and Rudolf Nureyev (USSR) after their performance of Tchaikovsky's *Swan Lake* at the Vienna Staatsoper, Austria, in October 1964.

LARGEST AUDIENCE FOR A COMEDIAN On August 24, 1996 Danish-born US satirist Victor Borge performed before a paying audience of 12,989 people at The Hollywood Bowl, Los Angeles, California, a record for a comedian. Borge is renowned for his send-ups of classical music and his "audible punctuation" routine. The UK record is 11,230, by Eddie Izzard (pictured) on February 24, 1999 at Wembley Arena, London, England, during his *Dressed To Kill* world tour. The event raised $240,675 for the Prince's Trust, a charity that provides young people with training and support for new businesses. Izzard, whose surreal routines range in subject matter from accountants on *Star Trek* to cats armed with pneumatic drills, has been known to perform in a mini-skirt and full make-up. His movie appearances have included *Velvet Goldmine* (1998) and *The Avengers* (1998).

BIGGEST ARTS FESTIVAL The annual Edinburgh Fringe Festival in Scotland began in 1947 and saw its busiest year in 1993, when 582 groups gave a total of 14,108 performances of 1,643 shows between August 15 and September 4. Although all kinds of performance arts are on the program, the Fringe has become particularly popular recently for its comedy and cabaret acts, such as the Kamikaze Freak Show (above). The Fringe runs alongside the "official" Festival, which concentrates on international theater and classical music.

Longest Chorus Lines

The longest chorus lines in performing history contained up to 120 dancers as part of some of the early *Ziegfeld's Follies*, which were created in 1907 by Florenz Ziegfeld, the greatest exponent of the American revue. Over the years, the Ziegfeld Girls included future Hollywood stars such as Barbara Stanwyck, Paulette Goddard, and Irene Dunne.

When the show *A Chorus Line* by Nicholas Dante and Marvin Hamlisch broke the then record as the longest-running Broadway show on September 29, 1983, the finale featured a onetime total of 332 top-hatted "strutters."

Fastest Tap Dancer

The fastest rate ever measured for tap dancing is 38 taps per second, achieved by James Devine in Sydney, NSW, Australia, on May 25, 1998.

Fastest Flamenco Dancer

Solero de Jérez attained a rate of 16 heel taps per second in a flamenco routine in Brisbane, Australia, in September 1967.

ART & INSTALLATIONS

Highest Insurance Premium Quoted for a Painting The *Mona Lisa* (*La Gioconda*) by Leonardo da Vinci was valued at $100 million by insurers for a move from the Louvre in Paris, France, to the US for an exhibition in 1962. The painting was not insured, as the premiums would have cost more than the tightest security precautions.

Most Valuable 20th-Century Painting Les Noces de Pierette by Pablo Picasso (Spain) sold for a record $80.44 million in Paris, France, in 1986.

Most Valuable Painting by a Female Artist In the Box by the US Impressionist Mary Cassatt, who died in 1926, sold at Christie's in New York City for $3.67 million on May 23, 1996. Seven of the 10 highest prices paid for works by female artists have been for paintings by Cassatt.

Most Valuable Painting by an Anonymous Artist Departure of the Argonauts (1487) sold at Sotheby's in London, England, for $6.7 million on December 9, 1989.

Most Valuable Photograph Hand With Thimble (1920), Alfred Stieglitz's photograph of one of the hands of his wife, artist Georgia O'Keeffe, raised $398,500 at an auction at Christie's in New York City on October 8, 1993.

Most Valuable Poster A poster by Scottish designer, architect, and painter Charles Rennie Mackintosh for an 1895 art show at the Glasgow Institute of Fine Arts in Scotland sold for $105,028 at Christie's in London, England, in February 1993.

Most Auction Sales by an Artist By May 1999, works by Pablo Picasso, the Spanish pioneer of Cubism, had been sold at auction 3,595 times. The total value of these sales is $1.23 billion.

Most Valuable Sculpture The Three Graces

BIGGEST FLOWER SCULPTURE In 1992, US artist Jeff Koons created *Puppy*, a 40-ft. x 18-ft. x 19-ft.-6-in. flower sculpture at the *Documenta* exhibition in Kassel, Germany. The plants chosen vary according to the climate in which the piece is exhibited. The work has an internal sprinkler system and 5-ft. steel rods attached to a frame to create the coat. Koons is renowned for controversial pieces in media including sculpture, ceramics, and photography.

MOST EXPENSIVE PAINTING *Portrait of Dr. Gachet* by Vincent van Gogh was bought by the Japanese businessman and collector Ryoei Saito at Christie's in New York City for $82.5 million in May 1990. It depicts the doctor into whose care the unbalanced artist was placed and was completed only weeks before van Gogh's suicide in 1890. Ironically, in view of the huge sums his works command today, he sold only one painting in his lifetime.

by Antonio Canova was jointly purchased by the Victoria & Albert Museum in London, England, and the National Gallery of Scotland in Edinburgh, Scotland, for $11.5 million in 1994. The statue, which is scheduled to make the 400-mile journey between London and Edinburgh every seven years, has been permanently disfigured by a hairline fracture sustained during its travels.

Biggest Sculpture   The figures of Jefferson Davis, Robert Edward Lee, and Thomas "Stonewall" Jackson are 90 ft. high and cover 1.33 acres on Stone Mountain in Atlanta, Georgia. Sculptor Walker Kirtland Hancock worked with Roy Faulkner and other helpers to create the sculpture from September 12, 1963, to March 3, 1972.

Biggest Outdoor Installation   *Desert Breath* covers 25 acres and is made up of 178 cones, 89 sand cones, and 89 conical depressions cut into the floor of the desert near the town of Hurghada in Egypt. It took a team of three Greek artists nine months to create, and will have been eroded within a few years.

Biggest Land Portrait   US crop artist Stan Herd uses his tractor to carve enormous pictures into the landscape. His largest work to date is a 160-acre portrait of the 1930s Hollywood star Will Rogers on the plains of southwest Kansas.

MOST EXPENSIVE LANDSCAPE ARTWORK   The $23-million work *The Umbrellas* (1991) by Christo (US) involved opening 1,340 huge yellow umbrellas on farmland in California and an additional 1,760 blue umbrellas in Japan. Christo, who has also wrapped the Reichstag in Berlin, Germany, in silver fabric, is pictured with his wife and collaborator, Jeanne-Claude, in front of another project, constructed from 13,000 oil drums.

Biggest Architectural Installation   *Tight Roaring Circle*, a 39-ft.-tall, 62-ft.-wide bouncy castle made of 29,333 ft.^{2} of white PVC-coated polyester, was designed by Dana Caspersen and William Forsythe. It was constructed inside the Roundhouse, a converted railway turntable shed in London, England, in 1997. Visitors were invited to interact with the structure, spurred on by low lighting, an ambient soundtrack by Joel Ryan, and text by the Japanese writer Yukio Mishima printed on the courtyard walls.

Longest Sketch Project Alan Whitworth (UK) has been sketching Hadrian's Wall, the second-century Roman fortification marking England's northern boundary, for more than 13 years. His sketch will be 73 miles long when it is finished in 2007.

Biggest Gallery Endowment The J. Paul Getty Trust was set up in January 1974 with $1.64 billion and has an annual budget of more than $100 million. It runs the Getty Center in Los Angeles, California, which opened on December 15, 1997, as well as the smaller J. Paul Getty Museum, Malibu, California.

Most Visitors to an Art Gallery in One Year In 1995, the Centre Pompidou in Paris, France, had a record 6.3 million visitors.

Biggest Around-the-Clock Art Exhibition *Buenos Aires No Duerme* (Buenos Aires Doesn't Sleep) is a multidisciplinary art exhibition that runs for 10 days and 10 nights nonstop every year. A total of 1.2 million people visited the exhibition, held at the Centro Municipal de Exposiciones in Buenos Aires, Argentina, in 1998.

Least Valuable Art Collection in a Public Museum The MOBA (Museum of Bad Art) in Garden Grove, California, is the only museum in the world dedicated to the worst excesses of creative endeavor. The maximum sum paid for a work of art is $6.50, and the average is $1.80. Most works are either pulled from trash heaps or donated. MOBA's collection has the lowest value of any public museum's art collection: its 314 works are worth a total of just $587.18. In 1998, the museum held the world's first drive-through car wash and art exhibition, "Awash With Bad Art," a charity event for the Salvation Army.

Most Coats of Paint on a Work of Art In June 1998, US duo the Art Guys (Michael Galbreth and Jack Massing) were commissioned to produce a billboard titled *ABSOLUTly A Thousand Coats Of Paint* to advertise the Absolut brand of vodka. The billboard, in Houston, Texas, features a 14-ft.-tall picture of an Absolut vodka bottle and was covered with 1,000 coats of paint of various colors over a seven-month period. The painting itself was done by Bernard Brunon.

Most Stolen Artwork It is believed that more works of art by Pablo Picasso have been stolen than works by any other artist—about 350 of his pieces are missing worldwide. Also missing are nearly 270 Mirós and 250 Chagalls.

HIGH FASHION

Oldest Designer Label   Charles Edward Worth, who died in 1895, was the first designer to sign his work with a label and to show garments on live models. Born in Lincolnshire, England, Worth moved to Paris, France, in 1845, where his talent for design was soon discovered by the ladies of the court of Napoleon III. He then started his own business and by 1871 had 1,200 people in his employment and was making $80,000 a year. His business was inherited by his son after his death and continues today through the perfumes of the House of Worth, such as Worth Pour Homme and Je Reviens.

Biggest-Selling Designer Clothing Label   The biggest-selling designer clothing brand in the world is Ralph Lauren, which had annual global sales of $1.5 billion in 1998. This represents an increase of 24.6% over the previous year's figure. Boasting labels such as Polo Ralph Lauren, Polo Sport, and the Ralph Lauren Collection, Ralph Lauren has nearly 200

YOUNGEST INTERNATIONALLY ESTABLISHED DESIGNER
British designer Julien MacDonald (pictured), who was born in 1973, was spotted by Karl Lagerfeld during his graduation show at the Royal College Of Art in London, England, when he was 24, and was asked to design a knitwear range for Chanel. After success in Paris, France, MacDonald went on to present his own collection, "Mermaids," in 1997. The youngest established designer of all time is Frenchman Yves Saint-Laurent (b.1936), who became Christian Dior's assistant at the age of 17 and was named head of the House of Dior in 1957.

FASTEST RISE TO HEAD OF A DESIGN HOUSE Stella McCartney, the daughter of Paul and Linda McCartney, was appointed the new designer at Parisian fashion house Chloé in April 1997, just 18 months after graduating from Central Saint Martins College of Art and Design in London, England. McCartney, who replaced Karl Lagerfeld, currently commands a six-figure salary. She famously dedicated her 1999 spring collection to the memory of her mother.

Polo shops and outlet stores world-wide and also sells its designs through approximately 1,600 department stores and specialty stores.

Richest Luxury Goods Maker Bernard Arnault (France), who heads the luxury goods empire LVMH (Moet Hennessy Louis Vuitton), is worth an estimated $6 million. The company sells Christian Lacroix, Givenchy, and Kenzo Mode fashions, the Louis Vuitton bags to carry them in, and Christian Dior, Guerlain, and Givenchy perfumes, as well as top drinks brands such as Dom Perignon and Hennessy. In 1998, the company had sales of $7.5 billion, 57% of which came from their fragrance, cosmetics, fashion, and leather goods lines.

Biggest-Selling Designer Perfume The world's biggest-selling designer perfume is Chanel No. 5, which sells more than 10 million bottles a year. Developed in 1925, Chanel No. 5 has more than 80 ingredients. Its creator, Gabrielle "Coco" Chanel, was the first couturier ever to attach her name to a perfume.

Biggest Stock of Designer Clothing The department store Saks Fifth Avenue currently stocks a total of 1,252 designer brands—more than any other store in the world. Saks, which was founded in 1924, has a total of 59 stores throughout the US and employs approximately 1,200 people.

Oldest Designer British designer Sir Hardy Amies, who was born in 1909, is still actively involved in the fashion industry. Sir Hardy joined the fashion house Lachasse on Farm Street in London, England, in 1934 and founded his own dressmaking business on nearby Savile Row in 1946. He is currently dressmaker by appointment to Queen Elizabeth II.

Most Expensive Designer Hat

In 1977, UK designer David Shilling created a straw-colored hat valued at $34,833. The hat was decorated with a selection of diamond-encrusted jewelry, all of which could be worn separately. A chain of diamonds covering the crown of the hat could be worn as a necklace, a rose decoration as a brooch, and a dewdrop design as a pair of earrings. The hat would be worth $109,776 in today's terms.

Most Expensive Tiaras

The world's most expensive tiara was designed by Gianni Versace and had an estimated retail value of $5 million in 1996. Set in yellow gold and decorated with 100-karat diamonds, the tiara weighed approximately $10\frac{1}{2}$ oz.

An 18-karat-gold crown set with cut diamonds and surmounted by a 6.9-karat yellow diamond retailed for $414,000 at Harrods in London, England, in 1998. The tiara was designed by Slim Barrett, whose headwear is worn by celebrities such as Madonna and Sinead O'Connor.

Most Expensive Jacket

In 1998, Naomi Campbell modeled the world's most expensive jacket as part of Gai Mattioli's 1998 collection. Worth $1 million, it has 100-karat Burmese rubies—the biggest on the market—and 250-year-old 36-karat emeralds as buttons.

Most Expensive Metallic Shoes

Manolo Blahnik made six pairs of gold shoes with heels covered in 18-karat gold and 18-karat-gold front bands for Antonio Berardi's 1999 spring/summer catwalk show. The shoes were priced from $9,944, depending on their size. During the show, the shoes were protected by bodyguards.

Most Expensive Bra

The Dream Angels Bra was designed by Janis Savitt for M+J Savitt. Costing $5 million, it is embellished with 77 carats of rubies and has straps stud-

MOST SPENT ON A DESIGNER STORE Helena Christiansen is seen modeling an outfit by Gianni Versace. Versace's store on Bond Street in London, England, opened in 1992 and, at $21.2 million, is said to have cost more to set up than any other designer store. Versace is one of the most commercially successful fashion houses in the world, grossing $50.8 million in 1978 and $533.8 million in 1997.

RICHEST DESIGNER Ralph Lauren, pictured above with President Bill Clinton, has a personal fortune estimated at $1.7 billion—the highest of any designer. Described by *New York* magazine as "the first image-maker," Lauren was born Ralph Lipschitz in New York in 1939. He began his career as a sales assistant and changed his name before opening his first store—which sold ties—in the 1960s. The Ralph Lauren empire is currently valued at about $3 billion.

ded with 330 carats of diamonds set in platinum. It was available exclusively through Victoria's Secret Christmas Dreams and Fantasy Catalog 1998.

Most Expensive Jeans Gucci "genius jeans"—original Guccis decorated with African beading, tribal feather trims, and silver metal buttons and rivets—went on sale in Gucci stores worldwide after being launched in Milan, Italy, in October 1998. Although they cost $3,050 a pair, they were quickly snapped up by buyers, many of whom had put their names down on a waiting list after seeing the jeans on the catwalk. After being manufactured, "genius jeans" spend two weeks at a distressing plant, where they are faded and ripped before having their decorations sewn on by hand.

Most Expensive Canceled Catwalk Show Giorgio Armani's Emporio show during Paris fashion week in March 1998 was canceled by French police concerned about safety at the venue. By that time, Armani had spent $300,000 on the show and $1 million more on the after-show party, making it the most expensive fashion show never to have happened.

STREET FASHION

Biggest Sportswear Company The sportswear giant Nike was founded in Oregon by Bill Bowerman, one of the US's top athletics coaches, and his former student Phil Knight. The company had revenues of $9.55 billion in 1998, making it the 166th largest company on the *Fortune* 500 list. Nike controls more than 40% of the US sportswear market.

Best-Selling Brand of Clothing Levi Strauss and Co. is the biggest brand-name clothing manufacturer. Its clothes, sold under the Levis, Dockers, and Slates brands, are sold in more than 30,000 retail outlets in 60 countries. In 1998, the company's sales totaled $6 billion.

Dockers, a brand of casualwear created by Levi Strauss and Co., was launched in the US in 1986 and by the early 1990s had become the fastest-growing sub-brand in US history, with the highest level of brand awareness of any casual pants. After a $10-million promotion campaign, Dockers was the best-selling brand in the casualwear market.

Biggest Fashion Store On October 3, 1998, the street-fashion chain Top Shop unveiled its new three-level store at Oxford Circus in London, England, covering an area of 85,000 ft.²—25% bigger than the previous

BIGGEST SURFWEAR MANUFACTURER Quiksilver had a revenue in the fiscal year 1998 of approximately $316 million, making it the largest manufacturer of surfwear in the world to date. The company sells to more than 130 countries and sponsors hundreds of athletes, including surf champions Robbie Naish, Kelly Slater, and Lisa Andersen.

Oxford Circus store. The menswear shop Top Man is located in the same building and covers 11,000 ft.^{2} of floor space. In total, the building, which already attracted 7 million customers per year, now has six sections on its upper floors and three sections belowground. The 18-month refurbishment included checks on 98 columns, 3,300 girders, and 12 million rivets and repairs to 3 miles of concrete beams. A total of 96,875.1 ft.^{2} of rubble and debris was removed.

Biggest Fashion Franchise The Benetton Group dresses customers in more than 120 countries through its 7,000 franchised stores and company-owned megastores. The Italian company's clothing consists primarily of knitwear and sportswear, and it is the world's largest consumer of wool in the garment sector. Today, it has nine factories in different parts of the world. Its sales totaled $2.3 billion in 1998.

Biggest Charity-Store Chain Oxfam opened its first charity store in 1948 and now has 836 stores in the United Kingdom and Ireland, making it the biggest charity store chain in the world. In 1998, the company—which fights hunger, disease, exploitation, and poverty worldwide regardless of race or religion—had an income of $26.52 million from its stores. This is almost one-third of its annual income from voluntary work.

Biggest Secondhand-Clothes Store Domsey's Warehouse and Annex in Brooklyn, New York, is the largest secondhand-

FASTEST-GROWING DESIGNER LABEL Tommy Hilfiger clothes are sold in more than 2,000 department and specialty stores and in about 55 specialized retail outlets all over the world. In 1998, the company had sales of $847.1 million—an increase of 28% on the previous year. In 1995, Hilfiger won the "From Catwalk to Sidewalk" Award, which honors the designer whose clothing is most easily worn unaltered by the man or woman on the street. The company is also the official clothing supplier to the Ferrari Formula 1 car-racing team.

clothes store, with an area of 250,000 ft.^{2}, of which 40,000 ft.^{2} is the sales floor. The family business has been handed down through three generations and has been based in Brooklyn for 18 years. It stocks about 350,000 garments at any one time.

Biggest Footwear Retailer and Manufacturer The Bata Shoe Organization was founded in Zlin, Bohemia (now Czech Republic), in 1894 and now has 4,458 company-run stores worldwide, as well as more than 100,000 independent retailers and franchisees. It has more than 62 manufacturing units, which together produce about 170 million pairs of shoes. Bata sells its shoes through companies in more than 60 countries.

Biggest-Selling Skate Shoes Vans is the ninth largest footwear manufacturer in the US and, according to *Sporting Goods Intelligence,* leads the market in alternative footwear. The company, which is known mainly for its skateboarding shoes, had worldwide sales of $187 million in 1998, $143 million of which were in the US.

BIGGEST-SELLING UNDERWEAR British retail chain Marks & Spencer sells 50 million pairs (counting multi-packs as a pair) of its own brand of women's underwear globally each year—nearly 137,000 pairs a day. The company operates about 700 stores in some 30 countries and sells mid-price clothing, food, and household items under its St. Michael brand. It also owns more than 190 Brooks Brothers clothing stores in the US and Asia.

Oldest Athletic Shoe Endorsement Converse's basketball shoes, cross-training casual shoes, and children's shoes are sold under the Chuck Taylor Converse All-Star brands, named after Chuck Taylor, who became the very first athletic shoe endorser in 1923. Taylor's name was added to the ankle patch to honor his contribution to basketball.

Biggest-Selling Brand of Designer Underwear   The world's most popular designer underwear brand is Calvin Klein. In the 1980s, Klein identified the trend among women of buying men's underwear for themselves and launched boxers for women. In 1998, the company sold 30 million pairs of briefs and panties, with a total retail value of $425 million.

Best-Selling Bra   Sara Lee controls 32% of the US bra market. The company, which had total sales of $20 billion in 1998, owns the Wonderbra and the best-selling Playtex brand, which includes the 18-hour Cross-Your-Heart and Playtex Secrets lines.

Biggest Hose Manufacturer   One in every five pairs of pantyhose in the world is made by Sara Lee, making it the largest hose manufacturer, with 51% of the US market in 1998. Its hosiery brands include L'Eggs, Hanes, and Pretty Polly.

Biggest Designer Hat Company   Kangol was founded in northern England in 1938. The company's hats have been long worn by golfers and members of the British armed forces (who wore Kangol berets) but have recently been adopted by young people because of the hats' connection with hip-hop stars. Sales are reported to have increased by 50% in the wake of Quentin Tarantino's film *Jackie Brown* (1998), in which Samuel L. Jackson wore a Kangol hat.

Fastest-Selling Watch   The Swatch watch, which was invented by the Swiss watchmaker Dr. Ernest Thomke and Nicholas Hayek in 1981, had sold more than 100 million units within 10 years, making it the fastest-selling brand of watch in history. In 1989, the company asked Italian artist Mimmo Paladino to design a watch, which was produced in limited editions of 120. Two years later, a Paladino Swatch sold at an auction in Europe for $24,000.

Most Popular Sunglasses   Ray-Ban sunglasses sold 10 million units worldwide in 1998. Ray-Ban's best known model, the Wayfarer, has been available since 1953 and is reported to be the best-selling style in history.

Biggest Clothing Industries   The largest clothing industry in the world in terms of the value of the goods produced is that of the US, which manufactured approximately $39.5 billion worth of clothing, excluding footwear, in 1996. It had about 800,000 employees in 1997.

The biggest clothing industry in terms of the number of employees is China's. Its total clothing production, excluding footwear, was worth $17.9 billion in 1996.

THE BODY

BODY TRANSFORMATION

Most Artists Tattooing Simultaneously Enigma, an American circus star, was tattooed by 22 artists simultaneously during the Amsterdam Tattoo Convention in the Netherlands on May 9, 1996. A member of Jim Rose's Circus, Enigma has had his body covered in jigsaw-puzzle tattoos. He also has horns, a tail, and porcupine quills, which were implanted into his body using coral. Bone is growing around the implants, and the horns on his head grow at a rate of 1½ in. a year.

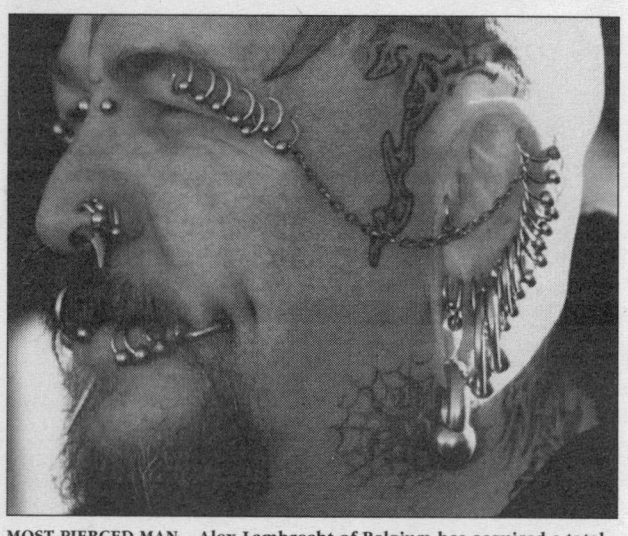

MOST PIERCED MAN Alex Lambrecht of Belgium has acquired a total of 137 piercings, with a combined weight of approximately 1 lb. 1 oz., over a period of 40 years, making him the most pierced man in the world. At an average of $83 a time, Lambrecht's piercings would have cost him $11,400 had he not done them himself.

Longest Tattoo Session The longest tattoo session lasted 25 hours, when Chris Masterson had his legs and arms tattooed for charity by Ian Barfoot in Reading, England, in 1992.

Greatest Coverage by Tattoos Tom Leppard, a retired soldier who lives on the Isle of Skye, UK, has had 99.9% of his body tattooed with a leopard-skin design. His body is now covered with dark spots, and the skin between them is tattooed saffron yellow. The only parts of his body that remain free of tattoos are the insides of his ears and the skin between his toes.

The record for tattoo coverage of a woman is 95%, held by Julia Gnuse of Foothill Ranch, California, who appeared on the TV show *Guinness®*

THICKEST MAKEUP The thickest three-dimensional makeup is "Chutti," unique to the South Indian Kathakali dance-theater tradition. The makeup takes hours to apply and the colors used, together with the styles of the costumes, denote the different nature of each of the characters. Green, for example, represents a heroic, divine character, while a white beard represents piousness. The villainous Redbeard characters have masklike attachments, built up using rice paste and paper, that extend 6 in. from the face.

World Records: Primetime on October 6, 1998, and "Krystyne Kolorful" from Alberta, Canada.

Most Individual Tattoos Bernie Moeller of Pennsylvania had had his body covered by a total of 14,006 individual tattoos by April 3, 1997. His tattoos have made him a popular guest at various outdoor events, and he has made several television appearances.

Biggest Tattoo Archive The Tattoo Archive is run by the Paul Rodgers Foundation in Berkeley, California, and has tens of thousands of items relating to the history of tattooing and to modern tattoos. It is the world's first tattoo research resource center. Lyle Tuttle of the Tattoo Archive has a private collection of American tattoo memorabilia, including tens of thousands of business cards and machines.

Biggest Tattoo Museum The Tattoo Museum, opened in 1995 in Amsterdam, Netherlands, is the world's largest collection of tattoos on view to the public. It puts on demonstrations and has a library and permanent exhibition of memorabilia and ethnographic tattoo history. It attracts up to 23,000 visitors a year.

Oldest Tattoos Ötzi, the world's oldest preserved human body, has 15 tattoos. Found in a glacier near the Ötz Valley on the Italy-Austria border in 1991, Ötzi is believed to be 5,300 years old and to have died at the age of 40. He has a series of blue parallel lines covering his lower spine, as well as stripes across his right ankle and a tattoo of a cross behind his right knee.

Two Egyptian mummies dating back to 2160-1994 B.C. have abstract patterns of dots and dashes on their bodies. The tattoos were probably believed to offer protection from evil spirits.

Most Common Form of Cosmetic Surgery Liposuction is the most common form of cosmetic surgery in the US. The American Society of Plastic and Reconstructive Surgeons estimates that 149,042 liposuction procedures were performed in 1997, the latest year for which figures are available.

FASTEST HENNA ARTIST Jyoti Taglani completed 64 henna armband tattoos in one hour (each measuring a minimum of 4 in. x 1 in., per *Guinness® Book Of Records* guidelines) at the *Cosmopolitan* show, held at Earl's Court, London, England, on April 30, 1999. One of her designs is pictured.

Most Expensive Form of Cosmetic Surgery Face-lifts are the most expensive form of cosmetic surgery: the minimum cost is around $6,000 to tighten and pull the skin behind the ears. The removal of eye bags and laser resurfacing of the skin starts at $10,000, while a full face-lift costs about $20,000.

Most Plastic Surgery Undergone by a Criminal Drug baron Richie Ramos of Philadelphia had an extra 16 months of freedom from the FBI after plastic surgery. He had five bullet scars removed and the skin on his fingertips changed, in addition to work on his "bull-like chest, flabby waist, and fleshy face." The operations cost a total of $74,900.

Most Doubles Created by Plastic Surgery The dictator Stalin, who controlled the USSR between 1924 and 1953, was reportedly so paranoid that he employed several doubles to lessen the likelihood of his being assassinated. The look-alikes, who had plastic surgery to make them resemble him, are said to have attended most state funerals, and even Stalin's own guards often failed to tell the difference.

Most Plastic Surgery for Art Since May 1990, Orlan, a French performance artist whose most recent work has been herself, has undergone a series of plastic-surgery operations to transform herself into a new being, the Reincarnation of Saint Orlan, modeled on Venus, Diana, Europa, Psyche, and Mona Lisa. Orlan has been exhibited worldwide and is supported by the French Ministry of Culture. Her video *New York Omnipresence* shows implants being sewn into her temples.

Most Sex Changes It is estimated that there are about 12,000 surgeons in the US who carry out sex-change operations, making it the sex-change capital of the world. (It has been suggested that Thailand leads the field, and there is great demand for operations in Asia, but no figures are available.)

Oldest Sex Change The greatest age at which a person is known to have had sex-change surgery is 74. According to the US Educational Gender Information Service, retirement age is a common time for individuals to change their gender roles.

Most Weight Gained Doris James from San Francisco, California, is alleged to have gained 325 lb. in the 12 months before her death at the age of 38 in August 1965, when she weighed 675 lb. She was 5 ft. 2 in. tall.

MOST PLASTIC SURGERY Cindy Jackson has spent $99,600 on 27 operations over a period of nine years. Born on a pig farm in Ohio, 43-year-old Jackson has had three full face-lifts, two nose operations, knee, abdomen, and jawline surgery, thigh liposuction, breast reduction and augmentation, and semipermanent makeup. Her look is based on Leonardo da Vinci's theory of a classically proportioned face. Dubbed the "human Barbie doll," Jackson is now the director of the London-based Cosmetic Surgery Network.

BIG & SMALL

Heaviest People   The heaviest person in medical history was Jon Minnoch from Bainbridge Island, Washington, who was 6 ft. 1 in. in height and weighed more than 1,400 lb. when he was rushed to the hospital suffering from heart and respiratory failure in 1978, although much of that was due to fluid retention. It took 12 firemen and an improvised stretcher to move him from his house to the ferry that was needed to take him to the hospital, where he was put into two beds lashed together. After two years on a 1,200-calorie-per-day diet, he had dropped down to a weight of 476 lb., but when he died on September 10, 1983, his weight had gone back up to 798 lb.

The heaviest woman ever is Rosalie Bradford (US), who registered a peak weight of 1,200 lb. in January 1987, before she developed heart failure and began a rigorous diet in order to save her life. By February 1994, her weight had reduced to 283 lb. She appeared on the TV show *Guinness® World Records: Primetime* on August 4, 1998.

Heaviest Single Birth   Anna Bates (Canada) gave birth to a boy weighing a record 24 pounds in Seville, Ohio, in 1879.

Heaviest Twins   The world's heaviest twins were Billy and Benny McCrary of Hendersonville, North Carolina. Normal in size until they were six years old, Billy and Benny weighed in at 743 lb. and 723 lb., respectively, in November 1978, when each had a waist measurement of 7 ft.

SMALLEST LIVING WOMAN   Madge Bester (third from left) of Johannesburg, South Africa, is the shortest woman alive, measuring just 2 ft. 1½ in. in height, with a weight of 66 lb. She suffers from *Osteogenesis imperfecta*, a hereditary condition that results in brittle bones and other deformities of the skeleton. She is pictured at a news conference in Taipei, Taiwan, with the country's shortest man and shortest women.

They were billed at weights of up to 770 lb. when they took part in wrestling matches.

Largest Waist Walter Hudson (US) had a waist measurement of a record 9 ft. 11 in. in 1987, at which time he weighed 1,197lb.

Lightest Person Lucia Xarate, a 26½-in. dwarf from San Carlos, Mexico, weighed just 4 lb. 11oz. at the age of 17. She had increased to 13 lb. at the time of her 20th birthday.

Lightest Single Births A premature baby girl weighing only 9⁹/₁₀ oz. is reported to have been born at the Loyola University Medical Center, Illinois, on June 27, 1989.

The lowest definite birth weight ever recorded for a surviving infant is 10 oz. for Marian Taggart (née Chapman), who was born six weeks premature in Tyne & Wear, England, in 1938. The 12-in.-long child was nursed by Dr. D. A. Shearer, who fed her hourly for the first 30 hours with brandy, glucose and water through a fountain-pen filler.

Smallest Waists
The smallest waist of a person of normal height was 1 ft. 1 in. for Ethel Granger of Peterborough, England. She reduced from a natural 1 ft. 10 in. between 1929 and 1939.

The 19th-century French actress Mlle Polaire (Emile Marie Bouchand) also claimed to have a waist measurement of 1 ft. 1 in.

Tallest People The tallest person ever for whom there is irrefutable

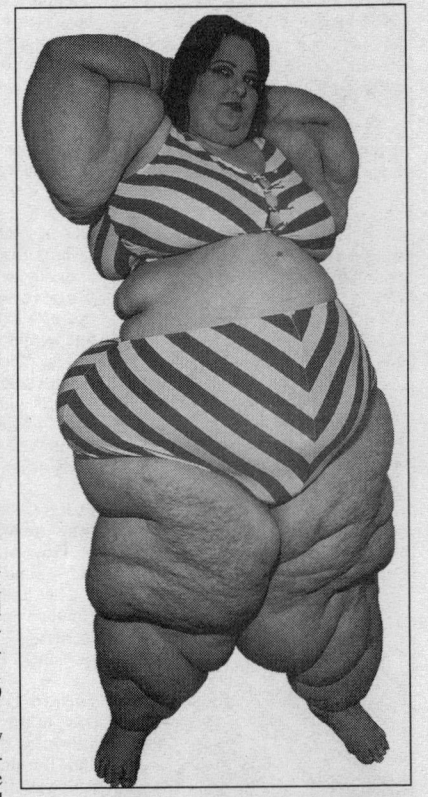

HEAVIEST MODEL US model Teighlor reached a maximum weight of 719 lb. in the early 1990s and has forged a successful modeling career, appearing in movies and on greeting cards and advertising posters. However, she has now lost 180 lb. after her weight started to adversely affect her health.

Big & Small ● 255

evidence was Robert Wadlow (US), who was 8 ft. 11^{1}/$_{10}$ in. tall in 1940, shortly before his death. He would probably have exceeded 9 ft. in height had he survived for another year.

The world's tallest "true" (non-pathological) giant was Angus McCaskill, who stood 7 ft. 9 in. when he died in Canada in 1863.

The tallest living man in the US is Manute Bol, who is 7 ft. 6^{3}/$_{4}$ in. tall and was born in 1962 in Sudan. He is now a US citizen and has played for the Philadelphia 76ers and other basketball teams.

The tallest living man in the United Kingdom is Christopher Greener, who is 7 ft. 6^{1}/$_{4}$ in. tall.

The tallest woman ever was Zeng Jinlian of Yujiang village in the Bright Moon Commune, Hunan Province, China. She was 8 ft. 1^{3}/$_{4}$ in. when she died in 1982 (taking into account her severe curvature of the spine).

Sandy Allen (US) is the tallest living woman at 7 ft. 7^{1}/$_{4}$ in. By the age of 10, she stood 6 ft. 3 in. tall. She weighs 462 pounds.

The tallest married couple were Anna Hanen Swan of Nova Scotia, Canada, and Martin van Buren Bates of Kentucky, who stood 7 ft. 5^{1}/$_{2}$ in. and 7 ft. 2^{1}/$_{2}$ in. tall, respectively, when they married in 1871.

Tallest Twins The tallest living twins are Michael and James Lanier of Troy, Michigan, who were born in 1969 and are both 7 ft. 4 in. tall.

The tallest female twins are Heather and Heidi Burge of Palos Verdes, California. Born in 1971, they are both 6 ft. 4^{3}/$_{4}$ in. tall.

Tallest Tribe The tallest major tribe in the world is the Tutsi (also known as the Watussi) of Rwanda and Burundi, central Africa. The young adult males of the Tutsi average 6 ft.

Shortest People The shortest-ever mature human of whom there is independent evidence was Gul Mohammed of New Delhi, India. In 1990, he was 1 ft. 10^{1}/$_{2}$ in. in

TALLEST PERSON   The tallest living person is Radhouane Charbib of Tunisia. When he was measured under controlled conditions on April 22-23, 1999, in Tunisia, he was 7 ft. 8^{9}/$_{10}$ in. tall.

height and weighed 37½ lb. He died at age 36 in 1997 of a heart attack after fighting a long battle with asthma and bronchitis.

The shortest female was Pauline Musters, who measured 1 ft. at birth in Ossendrecht, Netherlands, in 1876 and at the age of nine was 1 ft. 9¾ in. tall. An examination after her death from pneumonia with meningitis at the age of 19 in New York City showed her to be exactly 2 ft. in height (there was some evidence of elongation of the body after death).

The shortest twins ever were Matyus and Béla Matina of Budapest, Hungary (later the US), who were both only 2 ft. 6 in. tall.

Smallest Tribe   The smallest tribe is the Mbutsi pygmies of Congo (formerly Zaïre), with an average height of 4 ft. 6 in. for men and 4 ft. 5 in. for women. Pygmy children are not significantly shorter than other children, but they do not grow in adolescence because they produce too little IGF (insulin-like growth factor).

Most Variable Stature   Adam Rainer (Austria) was only 3 ft. 10½ in. tall at the age of 21, but then started growing at a rapid rate until, at the age of 32, he was 7 ft. 1¾ in. tall. He became so weak as a result of this unprecedented growth spurt that he remained bedridden for the rest of his life. At the time of his death in 1950 at the age of 51, he had managed to grow another 6¼ in., reaching a height of 7 ft. 8 in.

SMALLEST TWINS   John and Greg Rice of West Palm Beach, Florida, are both 2 ft. 10 in. tall, making them the world's smallest living twins. Their size has not prevented them from becoming highly successful businessmen. Having made their fortunes as real-estate speculators in the 1970s, they now own and run a multimillion-dollar motivational-speaking company called Think Big, which organizes seminars on creative problem solving.

Most Dissimilar Couple   When 3-ft.-1-in. Natalie Lucius married 6-ft.-2-in. Fabien Pretou at Seyssinet-Pariset, France, in 1990, there was a height difference of 3 ft. 1 in. between bride and groom, the greatest ever on record.

BODILY PHENOMENA

Most Fingers and Toes   A baby boy was found to have 14 fingers and 15 toes at an inquest in London, England, in September 1921.

Fewest Toes   Some members of the Wadomo tribe of Zimbabwe and the Kalanga of Botswana have two toes on each foot.

Most Arms and Legs on One Person   Rudy Santos of Bacolad City, Philippines, has four arms and three legs. The extra limbs belong to a dead twin lodged in his abdomen.

Longest Time a Twin Has Remained Undiscovered   In July 1997, a fetus was discovered in the abdomen of 16-year-old Hisham Ragab of Egypt, who had been complaining of stomach pains. A swollen sac found pressing against his kidneys turned out to be his 7-in.-long, 4-lb.-6-oz. identical twin.

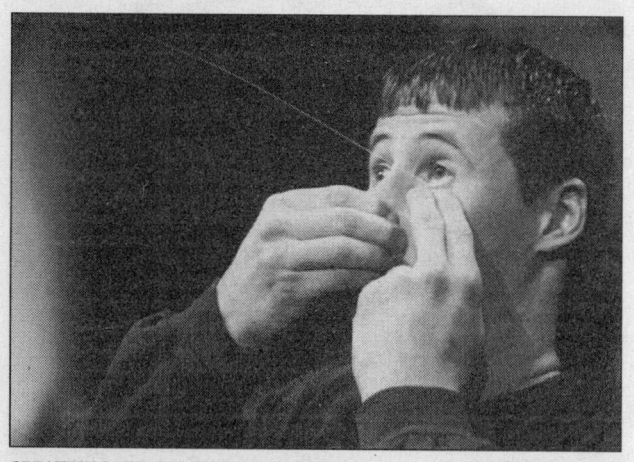

GREATEST DISTANCE MILK SHOT FROM EYE   Jim Chichon from Milford, Pennsylvania, squirted milk from his eye a distance of 6 ft. 7½ in. on *Guinness® World Records: Primetime* on November 20, 1998, beating the old record of 5 ft. set by Mike Moraal (Canada). Chichon can squirt liquid from his eye because his tear ducts work in two directions rather than one. He realized he had this ability when, as a child, he held his nose underwater and bubbles emerged from his eyes.

GREATEST EYEBALL PROTRUSION Kimberley Goodman, a former medical courier from Chicago, Illinois, can protrude her eyeballs a distance of ⅔ in. She was examined on *Guinness® World Records: Primetime* on June 17, 1998, by Dr. Martin Greenspoon, an optical special-effects designer. Kimberley gained the ability to "pop" her eyes after being hit on the head with a hockey mask, but medical experts do not know how she and a few others in the world are able to perform this feat. She is pictured here alongside Keith Smith from Columbus, Ohio, who was one of two others participating in the "pop-off" challenge.

The fetus, which had been growing inside him, had lived until 32 or 33 weeks after conception.

Longest-Lived Conjoined Twins   Chang and Eng Bunker, the conjoined twins from Siam (now Thailand), were born on May 11, 1811, married sisters Sarah and Adelaide Yates of Wilkes County, North Carolina, and fathered 22 children between them. They died within three hours of each other at the age of 63, on January 17, 1874. The pair, who were never separated as it was thought that to do so would endanger both their lives, earned their living in the US as an attraction in the Barnum & Bailey Circus.

Ronnie and Donnie Galyon are the oldest living conjoined male twins. They are 47 years old and live in Ohio. For 36 years, they traveled in sideshows, carnivals, and circuses, before retiring in 1991.

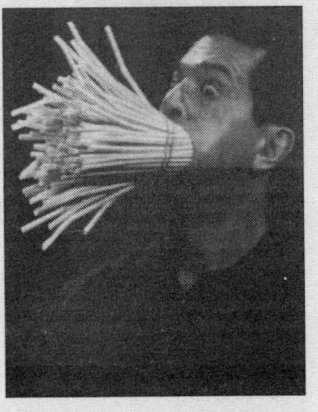

MOST STRAWS STUFFED IN MOUTH   Jim Purol of Whitter, California, stuffed 151 regular drinking straws in his mouth on *Guinness® World Records: Primetime* on August 11, 1998.

The Two-Headed Boy of Bengal was born in 1783 and died from a cobra bite at the age of four. His two heads, each of which had its own brain, were the same size and were covered with black hair at their junction. When the boy cried or smiled, the features of the upper head were not always affected, and its movements were thought to be a reflex.

Longest Survival with Heart Outside Body

Christopher Wall of Philadelphia, Pennsylvania, was born on August 19, 1975, with his heart outside his body, a condition known as "ectoipia cordis." No other person with this condition has been known to survive for more than 48 hours. Wall is now 23 years old, and works for a construction tubing company in Philadelphia.

Longest Human Tail

In 1889, *Scientific American* described a 12-year-old Moi boy from Thailand who had a soft tail almost 1 ft. in length. In ancient literature, there are many reports of adult men and women with 6- to 7-in.-long tails. Today, tails are removed at birth.

LONGEST FINGERNAILS The world's longest fingernails are those of Shridhar Chillal (pictured above) of Pune, India, whose nails on his left hand were measured on *Guinness® World Records: Primetime* on July 10, 1998, as having a total length of 20 ft. 2¼ in. His nails are 4 ft. 8 in. long on his thumb, 3 ft. 7 in. long on his index finger, 3 ft. 10¼ in. long on his middle finger, 4 ft. 1½ in. long on his ring finger, and 3 ft. 11½ in. long on his little finger.

Longest Beards Hans Langseth had a record-breaking 17½-ft.-long beard at the time of his death in Kensett, Iowa, in 1927. It was presented to the Smithsonian Institute in Washington, DC, in 1967.

Janice Deveree from Bracken County, Kentucky, had a 14-in. beard in 1884—the longest of any "bearded lady."

Longest Mustache   Kalyan Ramji Sain of India began growing a mustache in 1976. In July 1993, it had a total span of 11 ft. 11 in.

Biggest Feet   If cases of elephantiasis are excluded, the biggest feet of a living person are those of Matthew McGrory of Los Angeles, California, who wears size 29½ shoes.

Longest Nose   Thomas Wedders (UK) had a record 7½-in.-long nose. He was exhibited as a freak in a circus.

Oldest Baby Tooth   A maxillary right cuspid (baby tooth) was extracted from the mouth of Mary H. Norman of North Carolina on December 15, 1998. She was born on December 16, 1915, so the tooth was 82 years 364 days old.

MEDICAL EXTREMES

Heaviest Brain   The heaviest brain ever recorded weighed 5 lb. 1 oz. and belonged to a 30-year-old male. It was reported by Dr. T. Mandybur of the Department of Pathology and Laboratory Medicine at the University of Cincinnati in Ohio in December 1992.

Lightest Brain   The lightest "normal" or nonatrophied brain on record weighed 1 lb. 8 oz. It belonged to Daniel Lyon, who died at age 46 in New York, in 1907. He was just over 5 ft. in height and weighed 145 lb.

Largest Gallbladder   On March 15, 1989, at the National Naval Medical Center in Bethesda, Maryland, Professor Bimal C. Ghosh removed a gallbladder weighing 23 lb. from a 69-year-old woman. The patient had been complaining of increasing swelling around the abdomen. After the gallbladder—which was more than three times the weight of an average newborn baby—was removed, the patient made a full recovery.

Biggest Tumor   In 1905, Dr. Arthur Spohn reported operating on an ovarian cyst estimated to weigh 328 lb. in Texas. It was drained during the week prior to surgical removal of the shell, and the patient made a full recovery.

Biggest Tumor to Have Been Removed Intact   The largest tumor ever removed intact by a surgeon was a multi-cystic mass of the right ovary weighing 303 lb. The operation, which took more than six hours, was performed by Professor Katherine O'Hanlan of Stanford University Medical Center in California. The growth had a diameter of 3 ft. and was removed in its entirety from the abdomen of an unnamed 34-year-old woman in October 1991. The patient, who weighed 210 lb. after the operation and made a full recovery, left the operating room on a stretcher. The cyst left on another.

Most Pills Taken   The record for the greatest number of pills known to have been taken by one patient is 565,939, by C.H.A. Kilner of Bindura, Zimbabwe, between June 9, 1967, and June 19, 1988. This works out to an average of 73 tablets per day. It is estimated that, if all the pills he took were laid out end to end, they would form an unbroken line 2 miles 186 yd. long.

Longest Coma Elaine Esposito from Tarpon Springs, Florida, fell into a coma at the age of six, after undergoing an appendectomy on August 6, 1941. She died at the age of 43 years 357 days on November 25, 1978, having remained unconscious for a record period of 37 years 111 days.

Most Injections Received Samuel Davidson from Glasgow, Scotland, has had at least 78,900 insulin shots since he was 11, in 1923.

Longest Time Spent in an Iron Lung James Farwell from Chichester, England, has been using a negative-pressure respirator since May 1946.

John Prestwich from Kings Langley, England, has been dependent on a respirator since November 24, 1955.

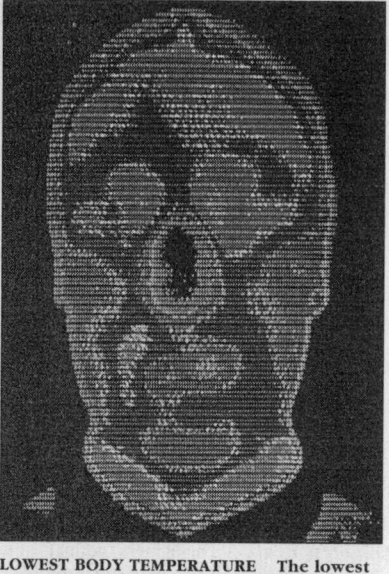

LOWEST BODY TEMPERATURE The lowest authenticated body temperature was 57.5°F, by two-year-old Karlee Kosolofski (Canada) on February 23, 1994. She had been locked outside for six hours in a temperature of 8°F and had to have her frostbitten left leg amputated but otherwise made a full recovery. Pictured above is a thermograph showing relative temperatures inside a human head.

Longest-Lasting Tracheotomy Winifred Campbell from Wanstead, London, England, breathed through a silver tube in her throat for a record-breaking 86 years. She died in 1992.

Oldest Mother Arceli Keh (US) is said to have been 63 years old when she gave birth at the University of Southern California in 1996. Menopause occurs in the majority of women between 45 and 55 years but recent hormonal techniques have led to post-menopausal women becoming fertile. It is now theoretically feasible for women of any age to become pregnant.

Largest Multiple Births In 1971, Dr. Gennaro Montanino from Rome, Italy, claimed to have removed 15 fetuses from the uterus of a 35-year-old woman after four months of pregnancy. A fertility drug was responsible for this unique instance of quindecaplets.

The most surviving births is seven (septuplets), born to Bobbie McCaughey in Iowa on November 19, 1997, and to Hasna Mohammed Humair in Aseer, Saudi Arabia, on January 14, 1998. Geraldine Broderick gave birth to nine babies in Sydney, Australia, on June 13, 1971, but two were stillborn. Nkem Chukwu gave birth to octuplets (eight babies) at the Texas Children's Hospital in Houston, Texas—one born naturally on December 8, 1998, the others delivered by cesarean section on December 20, 1998. Seven babies survived.

Longest Gestation Interval of a Postmortem Birth On July 5, 1983, a baby girl was delivered from a woman who had been classified as brain-dead for 84 days in Roanoke, Virginia.

Longest Cardiac Arrest On December 7, 1987, fisherman Jan Egil Refsdahl suffered a cardiac arrest lasting a record four hours after falling overboard in the freezing waters off Bergen, Norway. He was rushed to the hospital when his body temperature fell to 75°F and his heart stopped beating, but he went on to make a full recovery after being hooked up to a heart-lung machine.

MOST ORGANS TRANSPLANTED Daniel Canal, aged 13, of Miami, Florida, received his third set of four new organs in June 1998. Daniel was given a new stomach, liver, pancreas, and small intestine at Jackson Children's Hospital in Miami three times in a little over a month, having waited five years for his first transplant. His first multi-organ transplant was in early May, but his body rejected it. The second, on June 2, was unsuccessful when the liver failed. After the third, he remained critical. However, he went on to make a full recovery. All three procedures were performed by Dr. Andreas Tzakis, who gave Daniel a total of 12 organs.

Biggest Blood Transfusion Warren Jyrich, a 50-year-old hemophiliac, required a record 2,400 donor units of blood—the equivalent of 237 gallons—during open-heart surgery at the Michael Reese Hospital in Chicago, Illinois, in December 1970.

Highest Body Tempature On July 10, 1980—a day when the temperature reached 90°F—52-year-old Willie Jones was admitted to Grady Memorial Hospital in Atlanta, Georgia, with heatstroke and a body temperature of 115.7°F—the highest on record. He was discharged after 24 days.

Loudest Snorer Snores by Kåre Walkert of Kumla, Sweden, who suffers from the breathing disorder apnea, were recorded at 93 dBA at the Örebro regional hospital on May 24, 1993.

Longest Dream The longest recorded period of REM sleep (the rapid eye movements that characterize dreaming) lasted 3 hr. 8 min. It was

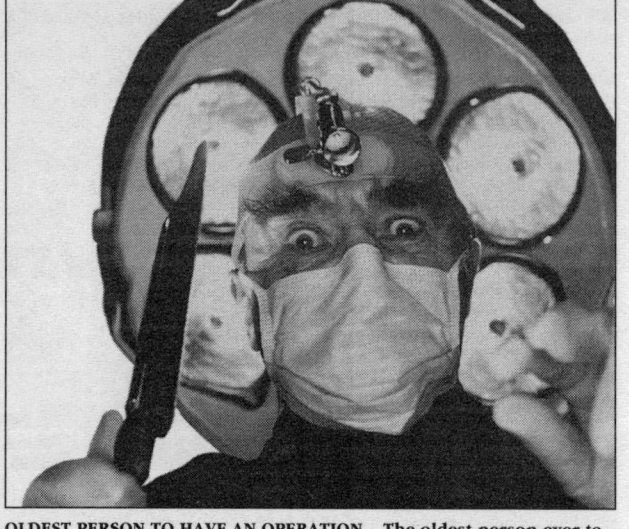

OLDEST PERSON TO HAVE AN OPERATION The oldest person ever to have an operation was James Henry Brett Jr., whose hip was operated on in Houston, Texas, on November 7, 1960, when he was 111 years 105 days old.

recorded in David Powell at the Puget Sound Sleep Disorder Center in Seattle, Washington, on April 29, 1994.

Longest Hiccuping Fit Charles Osborne from Anthon, Iowa, began hiccuping in 1922 and continued until February 1990. He was unable to find a cure but led a normal life, marrying twice and fathering eight children.

BODYBUILDING

Greatest Strong Men Magnus Ver Magnusson (Iceland) won the World's Strongest Man contest four times, in 1991, 1994, 1995, and 1996, becoming only the second man (after Bill Kazmaier of the US) to win three years in a row. He began power lifting in 1984 and won senior titles in Europe in 1989 and 1990. He also won the World Muscle Power Championship in 1995. Born in 1963, he is 6 ft. 2 in. tall, weighs 287 lb., and has a chest measurement of 4 ft. 3 in. He now owns Magnus' Gym in Reykjavik, Iceland.

Jon Pall Sigmarsson (Iceland) also won the World's Strongest Man contest four times, in 1984, 1986, 1988, and 1990. Sigmarsson, who weighed 294 lb. and had a 4-ft.-9-in. chest, dominated the WSM competition in the mid- and late 1980s and won five World Muscle Power titles. He died of a heart attack while weight lifting in 1993.

Biggest Biceps   The biceps of Denis Sester of Bloomington, Minnesota, each measure 2 ft. 6⅝ in. when cold. He began building his biceps as a teenager, when he wrestled pigs on his parents' farm.

Biggest Muscular Chest Measurement   Isaac "Dr. Size" Nesser of Greensburg, Pennsylvania, has a record muscular chest measurement of 6 ft. 3 in. Now 37 years old, he has been lifting weights since he was eight years old.

Most Prize Money   The 1998 Mr. Olympia pageant, held by the International Federation of Body Builders (IFBB), had a total prize pot of $310,000, with $110,000 going to the champion.

Biggest Attendance at a Bodybuilding Show   Although Mr. Olympia is more prestigious, the Arnold Schwarzenegger Classic weekend show ("Arnold Classic") draws about 50,000 people every year.

Most Arnold Classics Titles   Ken "Flex" Wheeler, nicknamed the "Sultan of Symmetry," won the "triple crown" (the Ironman, the Arnold Classic, and the San Jose Classic) in 1997 and the Arnold Classic in 1993, 1997, and 1998. He has been training since the age of 15.

Most Mr. Olympia Contestants   In 1989, at the Mr. Olympia event held in Rimini, Italy, a record 26 contestants vied for the title, which was won by Lee Haney (US). He equaled Arnold Schwarzenegger's then record of six consecutive titles.

Fewest Mr. Olympia Contestants   In 1968, Sergio Oliva (US), known as "The Myth," defended his Mr. Olympia title unopposed at the Brooklyn Academy of Music in New York City. In Paris, France, Arnold Schwarzenegger (Austria) was also unopposed in 1971. Oliva and Schwarzenegger had a series of epic battles for the title between 1969 and 1972. Oliva won three times, from 1967 to 1969, but the 1969 title was a close run. Schwarzenegger won the 1970 and 1972 titles, edging Oliva into second place both times.

Heaviest Mr. Olympia Champion   In 1993, Dorian Yates (UK) weighed 257 lb. when he was crowned Mr. Olympia for the second year in succession in Atlanta, Georgia. Yates went on to win the Mr. Olympia title six times in a row, from 1992 to 1997.

Tallest Mr. Olympia Contestant   Lou Ferrigno (US) was 6 ft. 5 in. tall when he competed in the 1974 Mr. Olympia contest held at the Felt Forum in Madison Square Garden in New York City.

Shortest Mr. Olympia Contestant   Flavio Baccanini from San Francisco, California, competed in the 1993 Mr. Olympia contest held in Atlanta, Georgia. Baccanini, originally from Italy, was 4 ft. 10 in. tall and weighed 160 lb. He failed to win a medal.

Biggest Time Gap Between Mr. Olympia Wins   Arnold Schwarzenegger won the contest for the sixth time in 1975 and announced his retirement immediately afterward. In 1980, he was seen training, but it was assumed that he was preparing for a new film. When he boarded a flight to Australia (where Mr. Olympia was held that year) with the other competitors, they thought he was making a TV documentary. That year, he won the Mr. Olympia title for the seventh time.

Most Consecutive Mr. Universe Titles   Lou Ferrigno of California is the only man in history to have won the Mr. Universe title two years in succession, in 1973 and 1974. He starred in the TV show *The Incredible Hulk* and has appeared in a series of films, including *Hercules* (1983) and *The Adventures Of Hercules* (1985). He is 6 ft. 5 in. tall and weighs 300 lb.

Most IFBB Pro Wins   Vince Taylor of Pembroke Pines, Florida, has had a record 19 wins from competitions all over the world recognized by the International Federation of Body Builders (IFBB). He won the Masters Olympia for those aged 40 and over in 1996 and 1997.

Biggest Ms. Olympia Contest   In 1990, a total of 30 women competed in the Ms. Olympia contest, which has been held annually since 1980.

Smallest Ms. Olympia Contest   In 1996, just 12 competitors participated in the contest.

MOST FILMS MADE BY A BODYBUILDER   Arnold Schwarzenegger has appeared in 25 feature films, including *The Terminator* (1984), *Terminator 2: Judgment Day* (1991), *Total Recall* (1990), *True Lies* (1994), and *Batman And Robin* (1997). He has won 13 world titles (seven Mr. Olympia titles, five Mr. Universe titles, and one Mr. World title) and has been producing bodybuilding contests for 20 years.

MOST MR. OLYMPIA TITLES Lee Haney of South Carolina won the Mr. Olympia contest eight times, from 1984 to 1991. After winning his final title in Orlando, Florida, Haney announced his retirement from the sport. Haney, who has been bodybuilding for 28 years, holds seminars at correctional institutions, motivating inmates to maximize their physical and spiritual potential.

Heaviest Ms. Olympia Contestant Nicole Bass (US) weighed 204 lb. when she participated in 1997. She was also the tallest-ever contestant, at 6 ft. 2 in.

Shortest Ms. Olympia Contestant Michele Ralabate (US), who competed in 1995, is 4 ft. 11 in. tall.

Lightest Ms. Olympia Contestant Erika Mes (Netherlands) weighed 100 lb. when she competed in 1984.

Youngest Ms. Olympia Contestant Lorie Johnson from the US was 17 years old when she took part in the first Ms. Olympia competition in 1980.

Oldest Ms. Olympia Contestant Christa Bauch (Germany) was 47 years old when she competed in the 1994 competition.

Most Consecutive Ms. Universe Contests Entered   Laura Creavalle, a Guyanese national resident in the US, participated in 10 contests from 1988 to 1997.

Biggest Chain of Gyms   Gold's Gym opened in Venice, California, in 1965 and became internationally famous when it featured in *Pumping Iron* (1975), which featured up-and-coming stars Arnold Schwarzenegger and Lou Ferrigno. It is now the world's biggest international gym chain, with more than 500 centers. Its many star clients include Janet Jackson, Charlie Sheen, Jodie Foster, and Hollywood Hogan, and it boasts its own motion picture and TV divisions.

Most Successful Trainers   Jake Steinfeld has trained film director Steven Spielberg and actors Harrison Ford and Priscilla Presley and heads a multimillion-dollar fitness empire that includes a cable television network, FiT TV—the world's only 24-hour fitness channel—a national magazine, home videos, and branded equipment and merchandise. In three years, his Body By Jake Enterprises sold more than $250 million in licensed products through infomercials.

Radu Teodorescu, known as the "Grand Master" of exercise, has been a personal trainer for more than 20 years. Voted "Toughest Trainer In Town" by *New York* magazine, Radu has been featured in more than 400 magazine articles and created Cindy Crawford's multimillion-selling fitness video *Shape Your Body Workout*.

LONGEST-RUNNING BODYBUILDING TV SHOW Jack LaLanne, who is now 84, opened the first health club in the US in 1936, as well as hosted the longest-running exercise TV show, in which he encouraged housewives to use broomsticks and chairs to get fit. *The Jack LaLanne Show* was first transmitted in San Francisco, California, in 1951, went coast-to-coast in 1959, and ran until 1984.

TECHNOLOGY

THE INTERNET 1

Most Internet Users   At the end of 1998, there were about 150 million Internet users—an increase of 246% over two years. The global figure is expected to increase to 327 million by the end of 2000. There may be more computers hidden behind corporate "firewalls" designed to exclude electronic visitors, including hackers.

Most Wired Country   The United States had over 76 million Internet users in December 1998—nearly 51% of the worldwide total. Japan is second, with 9.75 million users, and the UK is third, with 8.1 million.

Most Internet Users Per Capita   Of every 1,000 people in Finland, 244.5 are Internet users, according to the 1998 *Computer Industry Almanac*.

Biggest Internet Domain Ownership   According to NetNames Ltd., the US has a total of 1.35 million domains, which represents 50.9% of the overall domain ownership in the world. The United Kingdom is the second largest, with 160,004, or 6%.

Biggest Free E-Mail Provider   Hotmail is the world's largest free Web-based E-mail service provider, with more than 35 million subscribers.

Greatest Number of Active On-Line New Accounts   Charles Schwab & Co., the US stockbroker, has more than 900,000 on-line accounts holding in excess of $66.6 billion in assets and constituting more than one-third of its 99,000 daily trading operations.

Biggest Internet Crash   At approximately 11:30 am Eastern Standard Time on April 25, 1997, the global computer network ran into major problems, and

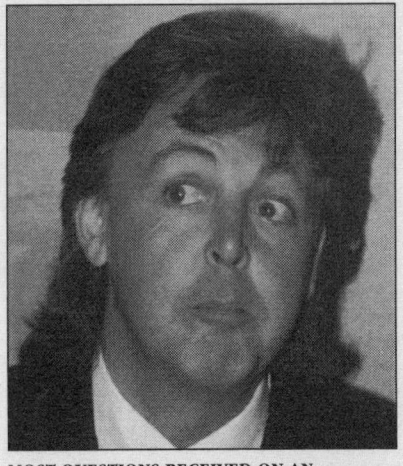

MOST QUESTIONS RECEIVED ON AN INTERNET SITE IN 30 MINUTES   On May 17, 1997, former Beatle Sir Paul McCartney received more than 3 million questions from fans in 30 minutes during a Web event to promote his album *Flaming Pie*. On November 19, 1997, McCartney also set a record for the first debut performance of a classical work live on the Internet, when he performed his new work, the 75-minute symphonic poem *Standing Stones*, live at Carnegie Hall in New York City.

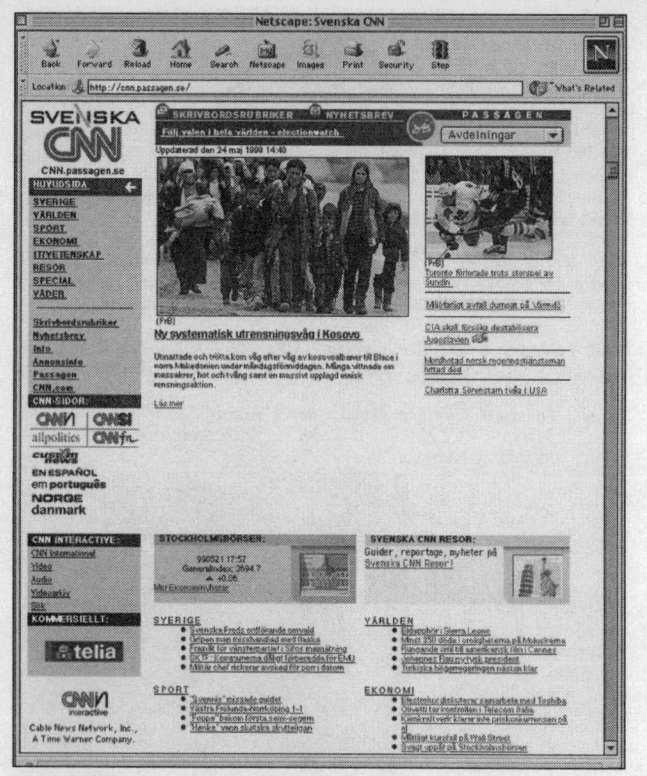

MOST POPULAR INTERNET NEWS SERVICE   The seven sites of the international news service CNN, based in Atlanta, Georgia, have a combined average of 55 million page views per week. The sites also receive more than 3,000 user comments per day via CNN message boards. The sites currently contain more than 210,000 pages but grow by 90 to 150 pages daily. The 24-hour television news channel, which began broadcasting on June 1, 1980, is part of Turner Broadcasting, owned by Time Warner Inc. A total of 1 billion people worldwide have access to a CNN service.

much of the system became unusable. Human error and equipment failure had led a network in Florida to claim ownership of 30,000 of the Internet's 45,000 routes. Data packets were routed incorrectly, and connections across the Internet failed. Some service providers took action within 15 minutes, but the problem persisted until 7 pm.

Smallest Web Server   The Web page of the Wearables Laboratory at Stanford University in Palo Alto, California, is supported by Jumptec's DIMM-PC, a single-board AMD 486-SX computer with a 66MHz CPU, 16

MB RAM, and 16 MB flash ROM. The setup is big enough to hold a useful amount of RedHat 5.2 Linux, including the HTTP demon that runs the Web server. At relatively low usage levels, it consumes 800 milliwatts from a 5V power supply, rising to 2 watts at 100% CPU usage. By January 1999, it was averaging 40 hits a minute. The "matchbox" server is only slightly higher and wider than a box of matches but is one-third the thickness, measuring $2^7/_{10}$ x $1^7/_{10}$ x $^1/_4$ in. It has a volume of about 1 in.^{3}—less than a tenth the size of the previous record holder.

Biggest Multilingual Web Broadcast The opening and closing ceremonies of the Third Conference of the Parties of the United Nations Framework Convention on Climate Change in Kyoto, Japan, in December 1997 were broadcast simultaneously via the Internet in seven languages—Arabic, Chinese, English, French, Japanese, Russian, and Spanish.

MOST DOWNLOADED WOMAN Images of Cindy Margolis (US) have been downloaded an estimated 7 million times. In 1995, Margolis was filmed by a television crew modeling a swimsuit. A picture of her was then posted on the Internet, and 70,000 people downloaded her image in the first 24 hours. She subsequently featured in a TV program, which resulted in her image being downloaded once every ten seconds for 48 hours. In 1998, a poll in the magazine *Internet Life* recognized Margolis as the most downloaded woman of the year for the third year running. She has also appeared in several advertising campaigns, in TV shows, including *Baywatch* and *Married... With Children,* and in the movie *Austin Powers: International Man Of Mystery* (1997), in which she played one of the deadly, seductive Fembots.

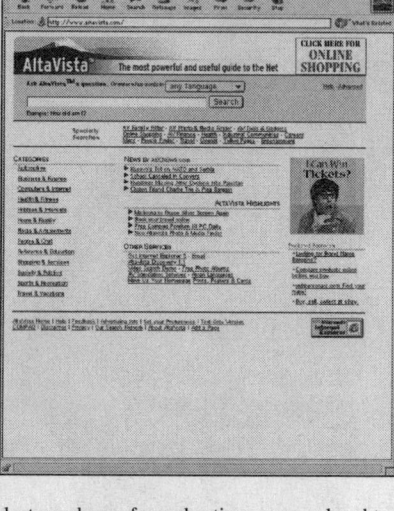

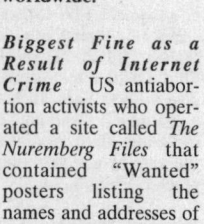

The biggest search engine is AltaVista, with 150 million indexed pages. Its closest rival is Northern Light, which has 125 million pages. AltaVista is also the most popular search engine, with more than 21 million users and in excess of 1 billion page views every month worldwide.

Biggest Fine as a Result of Internet Crime US antiabortion activists who operated a site called *The Nuremberg Files* that contained "Wanted" posters listing the names and addresses of doctors who perform abortions were ordered to pay more then $107.7 million in damages on February 3, 1999. Four doctors and two clinic workers who had been killed by activists since 1993 had their names crossed off on the site, and the wounded were highlighted in gray. The defendants were 12 individuals and organizations known collectively as the American Coalition of Life Activists and Advocates for Life Ministries. The case is currently under appeal.

Biggest Saving of Paper Through Using the Internet The delivery firm Federal Express has announced that it saves approximately 2 billion sheets of paper a year in the US by tracking packages on-line.

Biggest Voluntary Internet Safety Organization Formed in June 1995 by Colin Gabriel Hatcher (US), the Cyber Angels (the cyberbranch of the Guardian Angels) have dealt with more than 200 cases of cyberstalking. The Cyber Angels have recently been commissioned by the United Nations Educational Scientific and Cultural Organization (UNESCO) to monitor the Internet.

THE INTERNET 2

Biggest Cyberstar Merchandise Sales During 1998, Dancing Baby T-shirt sales in the US totaled more than $2.8 million wholesale. Music CD sales exceeded $425,000 wholesale, while international and US sales of the electronic Dancing Baby doll topped $550,000 wholesale. Other Dancing Baby merchandise across the US, Australia, and Europe grossed over $900,000.

Most Commerce Conducted on the Internet   Businesses in the US will exchange an estimated $17 billion in goods and services in 1999—more than any other country.

Biggest Internet Shopping Mall   The Internet Mall has a record 27,000 on-screen virtual stores and more than 1 million subscribers in the UK alone. It uses 65,000 stores around the globe to create the service, which is available in more than 150 countries. Products ranging from pop-corn to car insurance are delivered within 48 hours.

Biggest Cyberstore   Amazon.com was founded in 1994 by Jeff Bezos (US) and has now sold products to more than 5 million people in more than 160 countries. Its catalog of 4.7 million books, CDs, and audiobooks makes it the largest on-line store in the world.

Biggest Internet Auction   In October 1996, Nick Nuttall displayed 1,400 items of oriental art in the biggest collection of items for auction shown on the Internet at the same time. The items ranged from Japanese wooden carvings to bronzes and antique furniture. Prospective buyers can E-mail questions about the items, order the catalog, and E-mail bids.

Biggest Internet Music Database   ProMusicFind.Com, a site for buying and selling new and used musical instruments and audio and elec-

MOST DOWNLOADED CYBERPET   More than 10 million people worldwide have downloaded MOPy, a lifelike pet fish screensaver, since its release on the Web in October 1997. MOPy was designed for Hewlett Packard by Global Beach, a digital communications agency. It will respond to care and attention from its owner and thrive on regular feeding but will grow sulky, ill, and may even "die" if neglected. Global Beach has also designed three more pets: two cybertarantulas and a cyberscorpion.

tronic music equipment, as well as new, used, and rare records, CDs, videos, music, and books, has more than 1 million items on its database.

Biggest Internet Album Release In March 1998, British band Massive Attack launched the whole of its third album, *Mezzanine,* on-line, together with a preview of the video for the first single from the album, three weeks before it was available in stores. The site received 1,313,644 hits, and the songs were downloaded a total of 101,673 times before the album went on sale on April 20. A month after the store release, 1,602,658 hits were recorded. Despite its availability on the Internet, *Mezzanine* went straight to No. 1 on the British album charts.

Biggest On-Line Video Cyberstore With over 100,000 titles, Reel.com is the largest on-line video cyberstore in the world. Offering films for sale or rent across the Net, it can supply movies in a variety of formats, including VHS, laser disc, and DVD. In addition to new releases, the virtual store holds the world's largest stock of secondhand videos and employs 30 reviewers to supply written evaluations of every film in stock.

Highest Internet Advertising Revenue Internet advertising revenues totaled $1.3 billion in the nine months to September 1998. Quarterly revenues peaked at $491 million for the third quarter of 1998—an increase of 116% over the third quarter of 1997, according to a report by PricewaterhouseCoopers.

Biggest Internet Advertisers Microsoft Corporation spent $30.9 million on Internet advertising in 1997. The IBM Corporation is the second-biggest Internet advertiser, having spent $20.1 million in the same year.

Biggest Cyber Dating Agency Match.com, which is based in the US, charges its 1 million members $12.95 a month for introductions and has been attracting 20,000 new members every week. During 1998,

BIGGEST NETWORKED ROLE-PLAYING GAME With each of its 10 servers able to hold 2,500 players at the same time, Origin's *Ultima Online* is the largest multiplayer networked role-playing game in the world. At present, up to 14,000 players take part each day, many of them staying on-line for up to four hours at a time. In its first three months on the market, it sold 100,000 copies. With 32,000 interacting "inhabitants," 15 major cities, nine sites of religious significance, and at least seven dungeons, Britannia (the setting for *Ultima Online*) is the largest parallel universe on the Internet. With more inhabitants joining daily and with enormous regions of this parallel universe left to explore, Britannia seems likely to grow even larger.

it saw its business grow by 250%, and it looks set to grow even more since the release of the Internet dating film *You've Got Mail* (1998), starring Tom Hanks and Meg Ryan.

Most Popular Search Words The most frequently used search word on the Yahoo engine is "sex," with an average of 1.55 million searches a month. In second place is "chat," with 414,320 searches. Other popular choices are words relating to Netscape software, games, celebrities, and weather.

Most Mentioned People The Internet search engine AltaVista links President Bill Clinton to 1.84 million sites, making him the most mentioned man on the Internet. "Clinton" and "Bill Clinton" have a combined monthly average of 89,160 hits on the Yahoo browser. The most mentioned woman is former *Baywatch* actress and model Pamela Anderson, who is linked to over 1.54 million sites. She inspires an average of 172,760 hits a month on the Yahoo browser.

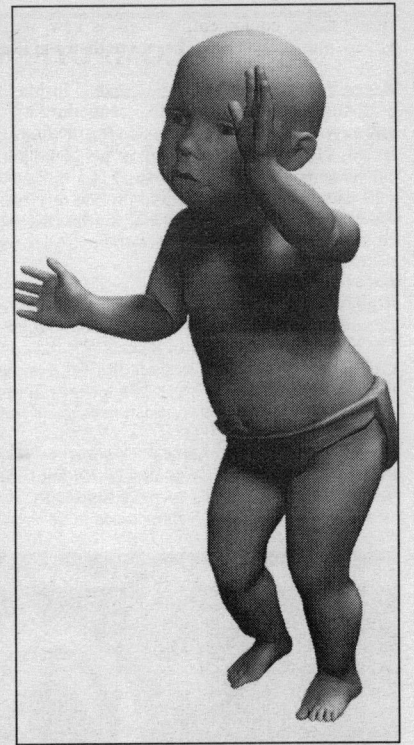

MOST CYBERSTAR VARIATIONS There are an estimated 2,000 variations of the Dancing Baby, a cyberstar originally created as an animated 3-D graphics model in October 1996 by Kinetix, a subsidiary of Autodesk Inc. Dancing Baby is the only character originated on the Internet to have achieved a popular following prior to its appearance in mainstream media. The Internet spurred the creation of new variations of Dancing Baby by amateur animation artists on hundreds of Web sites; these included July 4 Baby, Kickboxing Baby, Rasta Baby, and Clinton Baby. The official Dancing Baby Web site has an average monthly page view rate of 55,000. After Dancing Baby's appearance in an episode of the television show *Ally McBeal* in January 1998, the page view rate increased to 35,000 per day, with the Unofficial Dancing Baby Page recording 51,000 hits a day.

COMPUTERS

Highest Market Valuation of a Computer Company   The Microsoft Corporation was valued at $418.6 billion at the end of the 1998 fiscal year. Its annual revenue was $14.5 billion. The corporation develops, sells, and licenses software and on-line services to computer users around the world. Its chairman, Bill Gates, who currently owns about 30% of Microsoft, founded the company with Paul Allen in 1975, and it has made him the richest man in the world.

Biggest PC Manufacturer   Compaq—the name is derived from "compatibility" and "quality"—was founded in Houston, Texas, by Rod Canion, Jim Harris, and Bill Murto. Since 1995, the company has held the largest slice of the worldwide PC market. In 1998, Compaq sold a total of 13,275,204 PCs—equivalent to one every 2.38 seconds. It provides the systems for 75% of the world's cash-point transactions and 60% of all lotteries.

Biggest Direct Marketing Computer Sales Company   The Dell Computer Corporation, founded by Michael Dell in 1984, employs 17,800 people worldwide. Dell's revenue figures for the year ending January 29, 1999, were $18.2 billion—an increase of 48% on the previous year. For the

DENSEST HARD DRIVE   The IBM microdisk can fit 2.5 gigabytes of data into 1 in.^{2} of disk space. The disk was unveiled in March 1999 by a team at IBM's Storage System's Division in San Jose, California. High-density drives that are light in weight consume less energy, which is particularly important for designers of portable computers.

One Every 15 Seconds

SHORTEST INSTRUCTION MANUAL FOR A HOME COMPUTER The Apple iMac personal computer was released in the US in August 1997 and in the UK the following month. The distinctive one-piece machine with translucent casing comes with an instruction manual that consists of just six pictures and 36 words, allowing the computer to live up to the sales pitch stating that a user can just take it out of the box and plug it in. Worldwide iMac sales were approaching 2 million units by April 1999, and the success of the iMac has helped boost Apple's profits, which had been flagging for a number of years. After having lost nearly $2 billion between 1995 and 1997, the company has turned in six consecutive quarters of profit.

fourth quarter, Dell averaged customer sales of $14 million a day via its Web site.

Best-Selling Software Since its release on August 24, 1995, approximately 193 million copies of the Microsoft operating system *Windows '95* have been sold. The update *Windows '98* is now packaged with 90% of the desktop computers that are sold around the world, and 22.3 million copies have been sold since it became available in June 1998. Only sales of MS-DOS, the basic operating system that is preinstalled on almost all desktop PCs, have outstripped sales of this software.

Fastest Computers The fastest general-purpose vector-parallel computer is the Cray Y-MP C90 supercomputer, which has two gigabytes of central memory and 16 CPUs (central processing units), giving a combined peak performance of 16 gigaflops.

The fastest supercomputer was installed by Intel at Sandia National Laboratories in Texas in 1996. Using 9,072 Intel Pentium Pro processors, each running at about 200 MHz, and 608 gigabytes of memory, it has a peak performance of about 1.8 tetraflops (1.8 trillion conversions per second).

"Massively parallel" computers have a theoretical aggregate performance exceeding that of a C-90. Performances on real-life applications are often less impressive, perhaps because it is harder to harness the power of many small processors than a few large ones.

In September 1997, the US Defense Projects Research Agency (DARPA) commissioned researcher John McDonald to build the world's first PetOps supercomputer—a machine that can perform 1,000 trillion operations per second. DARPA gave $1 million to finance this three-year project, which will result in the fastest computer ever to have been commissioned. They want to use the system to simulate battles and natural disasters for training purposes.

SMALLEST COMPUTER WITH "FULL SCREEN" CAPABILITY The main unit of the Wearable PC, developed by IBM in Japan, is roughly the same size as a personal portable stereo. The "screen" is a $1/4$-in.^{2} viewer worn $1^1/5$ in. from the eye. The screen gives the illusion of a full-size display without impairing depth perception or lateral vision. Technicians who need to refer to complex manuals as they work can look at the documentation without taking their attention away from the job at hand.

The world supercomputing speed record was set in December 1994 by a team of scientists from Sandia National Laboratories and Intel Corporation, who linked together two of the largest Intel Paragon parallel-processing machines. The system achieved a performance of 281 gigaflops on the Linpack benchmark. The massively parallel supercomputer also achieved 328 gigaflops running a program used for radar signature calculations. The two-Paragon system used 6,768 processors working in parallel.

Fastest-Spreading Computer Virus *Melissa*, a macro virus operating in the Microsoft *Outlook* package through Microsoft *Word* documents, was discovered on March 26, 1999. The virus mails itself to the first 50 addresses in the affected computer's mailbox. One large organization reported that up to 500,000 E-mail messages were generated by the virus in less than three hours—enough to swamp a company's communications system and shut it down. Experts calculate that within five generations *Melissa* has the capacity to infect more than 312 million PCs.

Most Physically Damaging Virus The *CIH* virus has affected 1 million PCs since it was first triggered on April 26, 1998, the 12th anniversary of the nuclear reactor disaster in Chernobyl, USSR (now Ukraine). *CIH* irreversibly alters a computer's BIOS chip, which is soldered onto the motherboard. The damage can make a computer totally useless.

Biggest Number Crunched In April 1997, it was announced that computer scientists at Purdue University in Indiana had coordinated researchers around the world to find the two largest numbers that, multiplied together, equal a known 167-digit number, $(3^{349}-1) \div 2$. The breakthrough came after about 100,000 hours of computing time. The two factors had 80 digits and 87 digits. The previous factorization record was 162 digits.

Biggest Prime Number Found Using a Computer On January 27, 1998, 19-year-old student Roland Clarkson discovered the prime number $23,021^{377}-1$. This number, which is 909,526 digits long when written out in full, was traced using software written by George Woltman and Scott Kurowski. It is the 37th known "Mersenne prime." Clarkson, one of several thousand volunteers contributing to the Great Internet Mersenne Prime Search (GIMPS), found the number on his ordinary 200 MHz Pentium desktop computer.

"Most Human" Computer System A computer running the program *Albert* was awarded the 1999 Loebner Prize for the "most human" computer system, winning $2,000 for its author, Robby Garner from Georgia. *Albert* is a program that a user can communicate with using human speech. The 11 judges of the annual Loebner Prize put systems through a restricted version of the Turing test, the classic test of machine intelligence. *Albert One* won the 1997 Loebner Prize, and Mr. Garner won the 1998 award with another program called *Sid*.

COMPUTER GAMES

Most Games Sales In 1998, worldwide retail sales of video games were worth $15 billion. The games industry has grown dramatically since the 1970s, when the majority of consoles were produced by Atari. Today, the leading players in the market are Nintendo, SEGA, and Sony.

Most Popluar Hand-Held Game System The world's most popular video game system is the Nintendo Game Boy, which sold more than 80 million units between 1989 and 1999. The company currently occupies more than 99% of the US hand-held games market through its Game Boy, Game Boy Pocket and Game Boy Color units. Game Boy Color features an eight-bit processor and a high-quality LCD screen with the ability to display up to 56 different colors simultaneously from a palette of 32,000. More than 1,000 Game Boy titles are available worldwide.

Best-Selling Games Console The Sony PlayStation console had sold approximately 54.42 million units worldwide by March 1999, making it the best-selling computer games console in the world. Sony Computer Entertainment Inc. has spent more than $300 million developing the PlayStation, which runs hit games such as *Tomb Raider* and *Final Fantasy VII*, and about 430 million units of PlayStation software have been produced.

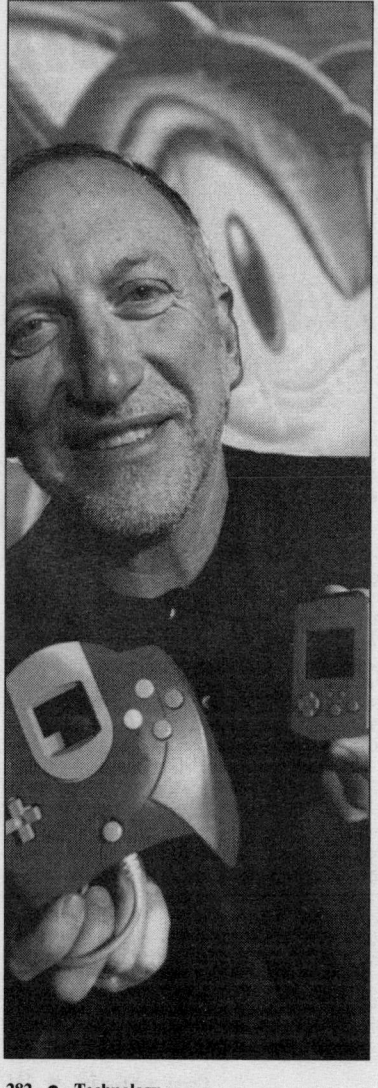

Biggest Chain of Video Game Arcades SEGA Gameworks, a partnership between games company SEGA, movie studio DreamWorks, and music/entertainment company MCA, has 11 video entertainment supercenters in the US and Guam. The largest of the centers, in Las Vegas, Nevada, has a floor area of 45,000 ft.^{2} and 300 game units.

Most Successful Games Manufacturer In the financial year ending March 1999, the games manufacturer Electronic Arts of California reported sales of $1.22 billion and profits of $73 million. The company develops, publishes, and distributes software for PCs and entertainment systems, including Sony PlayStation and Nintendo 64.

MOST ADVANCED GAME CONSOLE Bernard Stolar, the president and chief operating officer of the US arm of SEGA, is pictured displaying SEGA's new Dreamcast video game console. The SEGA Dreamcast, which was released in Tokyo, Japan, on November 20, 1998, is a 128-bit 200MHz games console with a 33.6-Kbps onboard modem. Its graphic engine is capable of drawing more than 3 million polygons a second, and its maximum simultaneous-color capacity is 16.77 million colors.

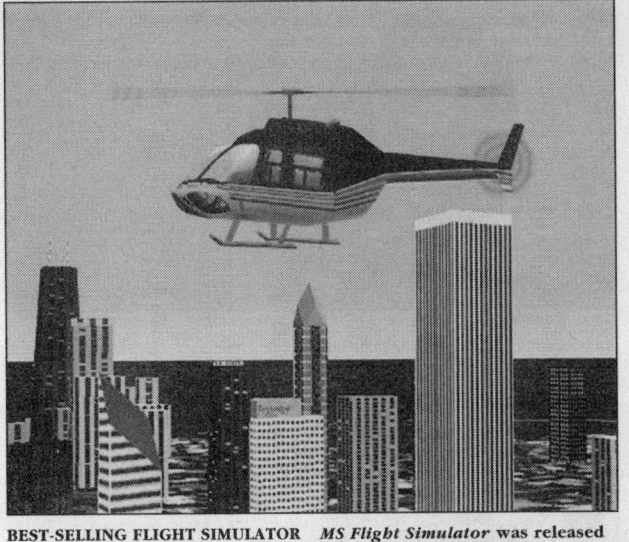

BEST-SELLING FLIGHT SIMULATOR *MS Flight Simulator* was released by Microsoft in April 1992 and had sold a total of 21 million units by June 1999. Aircraft featured in *Flight Simulator 2000* include the Concorde, the Learjet 45, the Bell 206B JetRanger helicopter, and the Sopwith Camel.

Best-Selling Games The Nintendo game *Super Mario Brothers* is the best-selling computer game ever, with a total sale of 40.23 million copies worldwide. The 26 games featuring Mario, the character who first appeared in the arcade game *Donkey Kong* in 1982, have sold more than 152 million copies in total since 1983.

Most Advance Orders for a Game More than 325,000 US consumers put down deposits for copies of *The Legend of Zelda: Ocarina of Time,* a Nintendo 64 game, to ensure that they received their copy as soon as it went on sale on November 23, 1998.

Fastest-Selling Game *Resident Evil 2* by Capcom Entertainment of Sunnyvale, California, was released on January 21, 1998, and sold more than 380,000 units in its first weekend, making more than $19 million. The game, developed for the Sony PlayStation platform, broke records set by some of the industry's most popular video games, including *Final Fantasy VII* and *Super Mario 64*. It was supported by a $5-million advertising campaign. Over 5 million units had been sold to June 1999.

Fastest-Selling PC Game *Myst*, which was developed by Cyan and released by Broderbrund in 1993, sold 500,000 copies in its first year. Sales of the game have now topped 4 million, and it has made total profits of over $100 million. *Myst* was the first CD-ROM entertainment to sell more than 2 million copies. *Riven*, the sequel to *Myst*, was developed by Cyan and re-

MOST POPULAR GAME CHARACTERS
Lara Croft, the heroine of the *Tomb Raider* series, was created by Core Design, and the games featuring her have sold a total of 15 million copies. She has also featured in advertisements for SEAT cars and Lucozade, and in November 1998, she was appointed the UK's Ambassador for Scientific Excellence by the British Department of Trade and Industry. The most popular male character is Mario the plumber, the star of Nintendo's *Super Mario Brothers* (see "Best-Selling Computer Games"). Mario, with his brother Luigi, has also featured in three cartoon series and the film *Super Mario Brothers* (1993), in which he was played by Bob Hoskins.

leased by Broderbrund in December 1997. By May 1998, it had sold over 1 million units and made $43.7 million. *Riven* comprises five CD-ROMS and has three times more animation than *Myst*.

Most Complex Game
Jane's Combat Simulations' game *688(I) Hunter/Killer* is reportedly the most realistic submarine simulation developed for PCs. The game was developed by defense contractors who design submarine simulators for the US Navy. A knowledge of flight dynamics is an advantage for players, who have to master sonar and weapons systems, develop real target solutions, and outfit a boat with the latest weaponry.

Best-Selling Fitness Game Released in March 1998, *Pocket Pikachu* by Nintendo sold 1.5 million units in its first three months. Pikachu is a yellow squirrel-like character based on the popular Japanese cartoon *Pocket Monsters*. The aim of the game is to keep Pikachu's cheeks rosy by taking it for regular walks. Pikachu is kept in its owner's pocket and "complains" when it is not being exercised enough.

Best-Selling Strategy War Games The *Command & Conquer* line of war games, developed by Westwood Studios (US), sold more than 10 million units between its release in 1995 and December 1998. The line includes the original *Command & Conquer* for MS-DOS, Windows,

BEST-SELLING SOCCER GAME The *FIFA* series of games, developed by EA Sports, has sold more than 16 million units. *FIFA 99* provides more teams and methods of play than any other game currently on the market. Launched in PC format on November 27, 1998, the game features a full pop soundtrack, including *"Rockafeller Skank"* by Fatboy Slim.

Macintosh, Sony PlayStation, and Sega Saturn; *The Covert Operations*; and *Command & Conquer Red Alert*, the prequel to *Command & Conquer*.

Most Popular DJ-Simulation Arcade Game By May 1999, Japanese company Konami had released 6,700 copies of the arcade game *Beatmania* (known as *Hiphopmania* outside Japan), a DJ-simulation game in which the player has to handle two turntables and an "effects" button. They are rated on their competence at mixing and timing sound effects.

Most Rigorous Software Regulations Germany has regulations stipulating that blood shown on computer games be green and that "victims" likely to end up getting killed be portrayed as "zombies," or as far from human as possible.

ROBOTS & ARTIFICIAL INTELLIGENCE

Biggest Robot In 1993, US company Amblin Entertainment, which is owned by Steven Spielberg, created an 18-ft.-tall, 46-ft.-long, 9,000-lb. robotic *Tyrannosaurus rex* for the film *Jurassic Park*. Made of latex, foam

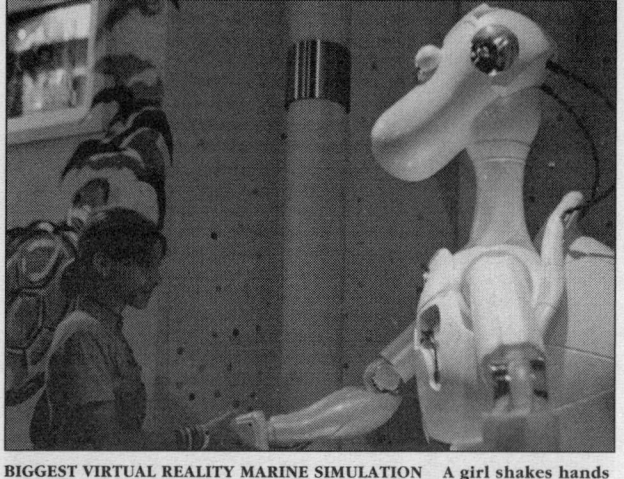

BIGGEST VIRTUAL REALITY MARINE SIMULATION A girl shakes hands with a turtle-shaped robot at Expo 98, held in Lisbon, Portugal. The exhibition was the setting for the world's biggest virtual reality marine simulation ever. Visiting "divers" could explore the Atlantic, Pacific, Indian, and Antarctic Oceans by means of a VR headset and an Onyx 2 supercomputer.

rubber, and urethane, it was the same size as the original dinosaur and the biggest robot ever made for a motion picture.

Smallest Robot The light-sensitive Monsieur microbot, developed by the Seiko Epson Corporation in Japan in 1992, measures less than $3/50$ in.^{3} and weighs $5/20$ oz. Made from 97 separate watch parts, it can move at a speed of $2/5$ in. per sec. for about five minutes when charged.

Toughest Robot A robot named Commander Manipulator has been developed by British Nuclear Fuels Ltd. to help with the cleanup of contamination at Windscale Pile 1 (now called Sellafield) in Cumbria, England — the scene of one of the world's worst nuclear accidents. The technology available at the time of the accident in 1957 was unable to cope with the extreme conditions in the plant's defective reactor, so the 14 tons of uranium fuel inside it were simply buried under several yards of concrete. The robot is largely resistant to the effects of radiation, and its hydraulically powered five-jointed arm can shift weights of up to 280 lb.

Cheapest Robot Walkman, a 5-in.-tall robot, was built from the remains of a Sony Walkman for $1.75 at the Los Alamos National Laboratory in New Mexico in 1996. In tests, it struggled to get free when its legs were held without being programmed to do so and without making the same movement twice.

Most Used Industrial Robot Puma (Programmable Universal Machine for Assembly), designed by Vic Schienman in the 1970s and manufactured by Swiss company Staubli Unimation, is the most commonly used robot both on assembly lines and in university laboratories.

Fastest Industrial Robot   In July 1997, Japanese company Fanuc developed the LR Mate 100I high-speed conveyance robot, the axis speed of which is estimated to be 79% faster than previous models. The robot can carry objects for up to 1 mile 1,513 yd. and can move up and down 1 in. and back and forth 12 in. in a time of 0.58 seconds—60% faster than previous models and an industry record.

Most Humanoid Robot   In 1997, Japanese company Honda launched the 5-ft.-3-in.-tall P3 robot. The robot, which has three-dimensional sight, can turn its head, step over obstacles, change direction, and correct its balance if pushed. Developed by 150 engineers over 11 years at a total cost of $80 million, it is intended for use in nursing and for tasks that are too dangerous or strenuous for humans.

Most Advanced Robot Toy   In January 1998, the Danish toy company Lego unveiled MindStorms, "intelligent" plastic building blocks that can be made into "thinking" robots and brought to life through a home computer. Developed over more than 10 years by Professor Papert of Massachusetts

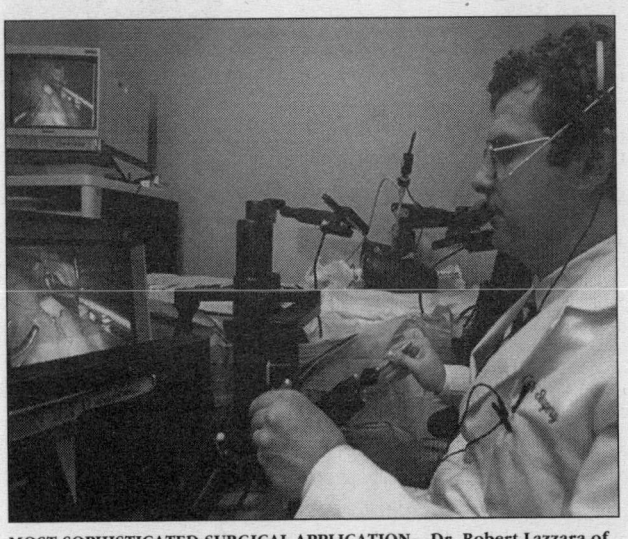

MOST SOPHISTICATED SURGICAL APPLICATION   Dr. Robert Lazzara of Seattle, Washington, is seen practicing a coronary artery bypass on a model thorax using Computer Motion Inc.'s Zeus robot. Zeus, which was released in February 1998, allows surgeons to perform heart bypasses through three incisions the width of pencils, using thin instruments that fit inside tubes in the patient's body. Computer Motion Inc. is currently planning to produce a new version of the robot that allows surgeons to operate over a high-speed telephone line.

MOST INTELLIGENT ROBOT Based at the Massachusetts Institute of Technology (MIT) in Cambridge, Massachusetts, the Cog Project is an attempt to bring together the many different fields of artificial intelligence and robotics. When completed, Cog (pictured right), the robot under construction, will represent the ultimate in AI robotics—it will be an intelligent humanoid that can think, hear, feel, touch, and speak.

Institute of Technology (MIT) in Cambridge, Massachusetts, the bricks contain a microchip and sensors.

Fastest-Selling Robot Pet   Aibo (Japanese for "partner") is Sony's robot dog, which retails for $2,066. When Aibo made its first appearance on Sony's Web site on May 31, 1999, 3,000 were sold within 20 minutes. The 11-in.-tall Aibo can recognize its surroundings with a built-in sensor. It can play independently or be programmed to do tricks. When another 2,000

Aibos went on sale on the Internet in the US on June 1, 1999, the initial rush to buy the pet caused Web servers to crash.

Most Advanced Robotic Arm   In 1997, the US company Barret Technology developed a $250,000 robotic arm that has cables that act like tendons and that can hold weights of 11 lb. in any position. The arm has a total of seven gearless joints, driven by brushless motors. It can throw a ball and could also be developed for cleaning, assisting people in and out of the bathtub, opening doors, and preparing meals.

Most Advanced Form of Artificial Intelligence   *Deep Blue*, IBM's RS/6000 SP chess-playing parallel supercomputer, beat world chess champion Garry Kasparov by $3\frac{1}{2}$ games to $2\frac{1}{2}$ in 1997. Equipped with chess-specific coprocessors, Deep Blue can examine 200 million moves a second, which translates into 50 billion possible moves in three minutes (the time normally allowed for a single move in chess competitions). This astonishing amount of processing power allows Deep Blue to be, in Kasparov's words, "brilliantly subtle."

Biggest Robotic Telescope   The world's largest robotic telescope, situated at La Palma in the Canary Islands, has been built as a joint project between the Royal Observatory in Greenwich, London, and the astrophysics department at Liverpool's John Moores University, both in England. Controlled remotely from an office at the university's astronomy department, the telescope has a 6-ft.-7-in. aperture that will allow researchers to study black holes, red giants, and distant galaxies.

Biggest Producer of Commercial Robots   Formed in 1982, Japanese robot manufacturer Fanuc is the largest producer of commercial robots.

Fanuc Robotics in the US has more than 1,100 employees and 21,000 robots in service.

Country with the Most Industrial Robots   Since 1991, approximately 325,000 robots have been installed in Japan—more than half of the 580,000 installed worldwide. For every 10,000 people that are employed in the Japanese manufacturing industry, there are now 265 robots in use.

Most Automated Facility   In March 1997, the Fanuc assembly plant in Yamanashi, Japan, became the most automated facility in the world when a number of two-armed intelligent robots began to assemble mini-robots, resulting in a completely automated manufacturing system.

Longest Journey by a Robot   On July 4, 1997, NASA's Sojourner robot rover completed its 80-million-mile journey to Mars, landing on its surface within sight of the earlier Pathfinder lander. Weighing just 38 lb. 10 oz., the robot was controlled remotely from Earth and roamed the surface of Mars conducting scientific experiments. Because it was so far away from its Earth-based controller, maneuvering instructions took almost 20 minutes to reach it.

SATELLITES & COMMUNICATIONS

Brightest Artificial Satellite Visible from Earth   The *Mir* space station is the brightest artificial object that can be seen from Earth. In astronomers' terms, it is about zeroth magnitude, which sets it at a similar brightness in the night sky as the nearest star to Earth, Alpha Centauri.

Most Distant Artificial Object Visible from Earth   In 1998, NASA's *Near Earth Asteroid Rendezvous* (*NEAR*) spacecraft made a slingshot around Earth to propel itself out to the giant asteroid Eros.

It swung by closest to Earth in January—making it the first interplanetary craft to be visible to the naked eye—and on April 1, it was photographed by astronomer Gordon Garradd of Loomberah, Australia. At 20.90 million miles from Earth—100 times the distance to the moon—it became the most distant artificial object ever to be seen from Earth.

Closest Approach to the Moon by a Commercial Orbiter   The communications satellite *HGS-1* was left in an unusable elliptical orbit when its rocket malfunctioned shortly after launch in 1998. To correct the spacecraft's orbit, mission controllers slingshot the satellite around the moon. During the maneuver, it passed within 3,858 miles of the lunar surface—the closest any commercial communications satellite has ever gotten to the moon.

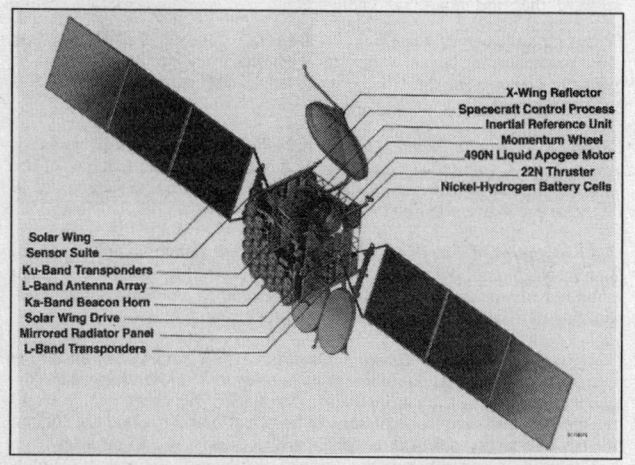

X-Wing Reflector
Spacecraft Control Process
Inertial Reference Unit
Momentum Wheel
490N Liquid Apogee Motor
22N Thruster
Nickel-Hydrogen Battery Cells

Solar Wing
Sensor Suite
Ku-Band Transponders
L-Band Antenna Array
Ka-Band Beacon Horn
Solar Wing Drive
Mirrored Radiator Panel
L-Band Transponders

MOST POPULAR COMMUNICATIONS SATELLITE MODEL   The bestselling model of commercial communications satellite in the world, with 73 orders placed by the end of 1998, is the Hughes Space and Communications HS601. The list of customers using HS601s includes the US Navy and NASA. ICO Global Communication of London, England, has a fleet of 12 satellites, making the company the largest single user of HS601s.

Most Powerful Communications Satellite   The Hughes Space and Communications *HS702* satellite is capable of emitting a 15kW signal, making it the most powerful commercial communications satellite in the world. To achieve such a high output, the satellite draws on twin high-efficiency solar cells.

Oldest Man-Made Satellite Still Orbiting   On March 17, 1958, a US satellite called *Vanguard 1* was boosted into orbit around Earth. It is now the world's oldest orbiting satellite.

Heaviest Satellite Launched by a Space Shuttle   The heaviest spacecraft ever carried into orbit and deployed by a US space shuttle is the Compton Gamma Ray Observatory (CGRO), which weighs 15.66 tons. CGRO is an astronomy satellite that has spent its eight-year orbital lifetime studying high-energy cosmic rays.

Most Prolific Satellite Launcher   Russia and the other former states of the USSR have launched a total of 1,337 satellites into orbit, making it the world's most prolific satellite-launching nation.

Most Prolific Communications Satellite Manufacturer
Hughes Space and Communications Company, based in Los Angeles, California, has supplied 137 communications satellites to the commercial sector—nearly 40% of those currently in operation.

Biggest Commercial Satellite Factory   With 602,799 ft.^{2} of floor space dedicated to satellite manufacturing, the Hughes Integrated Satellite Factory in El Segundo, California, is the world's largest commercial communications satellite factory. The factory is

WIDEST MOBILE PHONE COVERAGE   In May 1998, the Iridium mobile phone network launched its final five communications satellites, bringing the size of its fleet up to 66 spacecraft—the largest number of networked communications satellites in existence. The system, which is to be operated and maintained on behalf of Iridium by Motorola, provides the world's widest mobile phone coverage. The phones are a little larger than normal mobiles, and the Iridium network allows users to make calls from anywhere on the surface of the planet. Pictured is a refugee from Kosovo at a camp in Macedonia using an Iridium satellite phone to contact relatives.

BIGGEST STRUCTURE IN SPACE The International Space Station is the largest structure in space. When completed in 2004, it will be 290 ft. long, have a wingspan of 356 ft. 4½ in., and weigh 414 tons. It will take 44 launches to complete and is the largest international space project ever undertaken, involving teams from the US, Russia, Canada, Japan, Brazil, and 11 European countries.

now the central location for the construction of Hughes Space and Communications satellites.

Most Expensive Satellite Failure The world's most costly satellite accident happened on August 12, 1998, when a US Air Force *Titan 4* rocket exploded 41 seconds after liftoff from Cape Canaveral, Florida, destroying the $1.035-billion spy satellite it was carrying. The rocket's guidance system is believed to have been responsible for the failure.

Biggest Telecommunications Failure The most disruptive failure of a telecommunications system happened in May 1998, when *Galaxy 4*, a $265-million Hughes Space and Communications satellite operated by PanAmSat, developed a fault. An estimated 41 million people in the US temporarily lost the use of their pagers as a result of the failure.

Biggest Orbital Litterbug Space debris, which includes rocket stages left behind in orbit by space missions, is an ongoing problem for mission planners. Having left a total of 3,173 pieces of space debris in orbit around Earth, the US scoops the title of biggest orbital litterbug.

Biggest Radio Telescope   Our largest radio ear on the universe is the Arecibo Radio Observatory in Puerto Rico. The telescope's mammoth dish is 1,000 ft. in diameter. Currently used by scientists scouring the skies for elusive signals from intelligent extraterrestrial life-forms, the Arecibo Observatory has also been featured in the films *GoldenEye* (UK/US, 1995) and *Contact* (1997).

Most Efficient Solar Panels   Whereas most terrestial solar panels are made from silicon, satellite solar panels are constructed from gallium arsenide, a compound that is lighter than silicon and more resistant to radiation. They are also the most efficient solar panels in the world, converting 27% of the light energy falling on them into electricity—almost double the percentage of previous designs.

Narrowest Optical Fibers   Physicists at the University of Bath in England have produced the world's narrowest optical fibers for communications. Stretching 6 miles 376 yd. and with cores just $^1/_{400,000,000}$ in. thick, the length-to-width ratio of each fiber is equivalent to the Channel Tunnel extended all the way from Earth to Jupiter.

GADGETS

Smallest Cellular Phone   The PHS (Personal Handyphone System), made by the Nippon Telegraph and Telephone Corp., is a wristwatch-style phone that dispenses with the conventional keypad. Numbers are selected by voice-recognition circuitry. The unit weighs $2^2/_5$ oz. and measures 2 x $1^1/_2$ x $^3/_5$ in.

Smallest Solid-State Storage Device   The SanDisk Multimedia Card, which was developed by SanDisk and Siemens for use in portable equipment such as mobile phones and digital voice recorders, is $1^1/_4$ x $^9/_{10}$ x $^1/_{20}$ in. thick and can store up to 10 megabytes of data.

SMALLEST CAMCORDER
The Sony CCD-CR1 Ruvi measures 5 x $2^1/_2$ x $1^3/_4$ in. and can store 30 minutes of moving images. The camera has a $2^1/_2$-in. LCD screen and an optical zoom, and the tape is enclosed in a plastic cartridge along with the record and playback heads, which plug in and out with every new cartridge inserted.

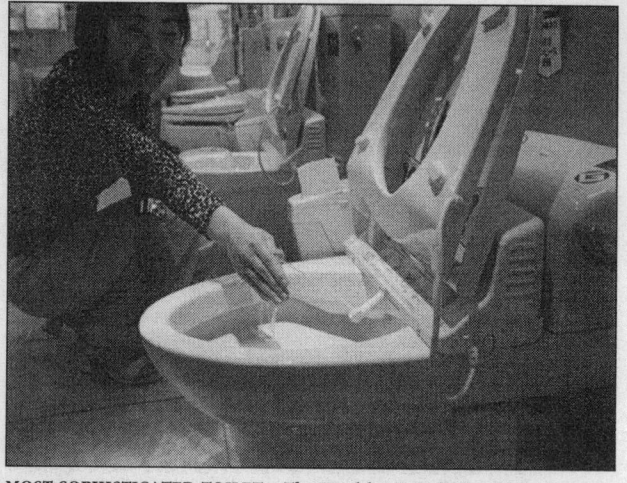

MOST SOPHISTICATED TOILET The Washlet Zoë, first sold in May 1997 by Toto of Japan, has a seat and lid that lift automatically and a flush "simulator"—a sound effect that serves to cover any embarrassing noises. The seat is heated, and the toilet can wash and dry the user. The entire unit can be controlled remotely, and it automatically freshens the air after every use. The Zoë retails for $699. Toto is also developing a toilet that can analyze your urine and take your blood pressure, then transmit these statistics to a doctor via a built-in modem.

Smallest Video Recorder The smallest video recorder is Sony's EVO 220 Micro 8 mm, which weighs 1 lb. 8 oz. and measures $2^{3}/_{10}$ x $8^{1}/_{2}$ x $5^{7}/_{10}$ in.

It can record up to five hours of video onto $^{3}/_{10}$-in. tape.

Smallest Video Transmitter The VID1 from AE Inc. allows the wireless transmission of a picture to a base station 2,000 ft. away. Measuring $^{3}/_{5}$ x $^{9}/_{10}$ x $^{3}/_{10}$ in.,

THINNEST MINIDISC RECORDER Sony's MZ-R55 is $^{3}/_{4}$ in. thick and weighs 6 oz. with its lithium ion battery and alkaline AA cells. It can play for up to 16 hours.

it transmits either PAL- or NTSC-encoded video at 900 MHz, reducing the need for powerful output and allowing use for up to 11 hours.

Smallest Video-CD Player   The smallest video-CD player with its own screen is Panasonic's SL-DP70, which measures 5 x 1²/₅ x 5³/₅ in. It can function for up to two hours with six AA batteries and costs about $528.

Smallest DVD Player Monitor   The Panasonic Palm Theater has an area of 6¹/₃ in.², is 1³/₅ in. thick, and weighs 2 lb. without the battery. Its 5⁴/₅-in. LCD screen has 280,000 pixels and can handle 16:9 and 4:3 aspect ratio films. The unit also boasts stereo speakers and virtual surround sound.

Most Shockproof CD Player   The PCD-7900, manufactured by Sanyo-Fisher, is the first personal CD player to incorporate a 40-second antishock memory, which compensates for errors in the disc tracking caused by external shock. The shock-guard capability is so extensive that the user can listen to music from the original disc while changing discs.

Most Expensive Power Amplifier   The AudioNote Ongaku costs $93,200, making it the world's most expensive power amplifier. The Ongaku is a valve amplifier with a Class A output configuration, giving purity of sound at the expense of electrical efficiency. The main reason for its high cost is the solid-silver windings for the output transformers.

Most Expensive Production 35mm SLR Camera   The Canon Eos 1N-RS costs $3,840, making it the most expensive production 35 mm SLR camera in the world to date. The 1N-RS has a shutter speed from ¹/₈,₀₀₀ of a second up to 30 seconds, accepts film speeds from 25 to 5,000 ASA, and can shoot up to three frames every second. Its Pentaprism viewfinder offers 100% of the view that is relayed to the film, and the main body can accept any Canon EF mount lenses.

BEST-SELLING MP3 PLAYER   The Diamond Rio PMP300 MP3 player sold 400,000 units between its release in November 1998 and May 1999. The MP3 format, available on the Internet, is a digital method of storing and retrieving audio files. The PMP300, measuring 3¹/₂ x 2¹/₂ x ³/₅ in., stores up to 60 minutes of digital-quality sound. MP3 players are smaller than an audio cassette and have no moving parts, so they never skip.

Smallest Computer　The smallest handheld computer is the Psion Series 5, which weighs 12 oz. including batteries. It has a touch-type keyboard and a touch-sensitive screen.

Smallest Calculator　Scientists at IBM's Research Laboratory in Zurich, Switzerland, have designed a calculating device with a diameter of less than $^{39}/_{100,000,000}$ in.

Most Intelligent Pen　The SmartQuill, developed by British Telecom, can function as a diary, calendar, contacts database, alarm, note taker, calculator, pager, E-mail receiver, and pen. It can store the equivalent of 10 pages before information is downloaded to the "inkwell." Silicon strips measure the gravity against the fingers, so no matter how bad your handwriting is, the pen will recognize it. The SmartQuill is expected to be in stores by 2001, priced at about $330.

Smallest Sheet-Feed Scanner　The smallest sheet-feed scanner is the CanoScan 300S, which uses Canon's LED InDirect Exposure (LIDE) technology and weighs just 3 lb. 4 oz.

Smallest Document Shredder　Piranha's PRO26 measures $6^{1}/_{2}$ x $2^{1}/_{3}$ x $1^{1}/_{2}$ in. and deals with any kind of document by nibbling off slices and shredding them into slivers.

Smallest Fax Machine　Philips' smart phone add-on connects to the Philips PCS 1900 Digital Phone to send faxes and E-mails, access the Internet, and provide other communications services. At $6^{7}/_{10}$ in. in length and $5^{3}/_{5}$ oz. in weight, the PCS 1900 is the smallest and lightest mobile fax.

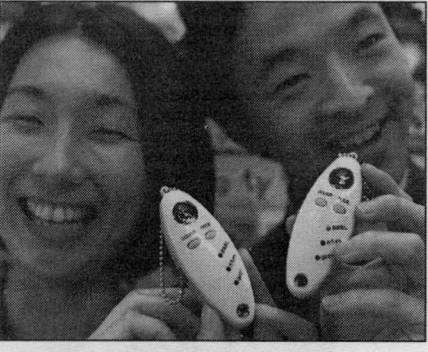

Smallest Binoculars　The U-C 8×18 series binoculars, with 8× magnification and optics that allow focusing down to 6 ft. 7 in., weighs 5 oz. and measures 3 x $2^{7}/_{10}$ x $^{7}/_{10}$ in.

Cheapest GPS Receiver　The cheapest portable Global Positioning by Satellite receiver in the world today is the GPS Pioneer, which is manufactured by Magellan Systems Corporation in the US. The Pioneer is the first GPS receiver to cost less than $100

BEST-SELLING MATCHMAKER　The Lovegety, manufactured by Erfolg in Japan, has sold more than 1.3 million units since its release in February 1998. The palm-sized beeper, which retails for $22, recognizes signals sent from a Lovegety held by someone of the opposite sex within a range of 15 ft. It was invented by Takeya Takafuji, who wanted to create "a machine that can recognize the other's mind."

and allows users to find their location on the planet through its ability to decode information from the Nav-Star network of 24 orbiting geostationary satellites.

CARS

Fastest Road Car   The highest speed ever reached by a standard-production car is 240.1 mph, by a McLaren F1 driven by Andy Wallace at the Volkswagen Proving Ground in Wolfsburg, Germany, on March 31, 1998.

Fastest Diesel-Engined Car   The diesel-engined prototype 3-liter Mercedes C 111/3 attained 203.3 mph in tests on the Nardo Circuit in southern Italy on October 5 to 15, 1978. In April 1978, the car maintained an average speed of 195.4 mph over a period of 12 hours, covering a record distance of 2,344 miles 1,232 yd.

Fastest Electric Car   The highest speed achieved for an electric vehicle is 183.822 mph over a two-way flying kilometer (1,094 yd.), by General Motors' Impact, driven by Clive Roberts (UK) at Fort Stockton Test Center in Texas on March 11, 1994.

Fastest Acceleration   The fastest road-tested acceleration on record is 0–60 mph in 3.07 seconds, by a Ford RS200 Evolution driven by Graham Hathaway at Millbrook Proving Ground in England in May 1994.

Lowest Gas Consumptions   In 1989, Stuart Bladon drove a Citroën AX 14DTR 112 miles 18 yd. on one gallon of fuel on the M11 superhighway in the United Kingdom.
    A vehicle designed by Team 1200 from Honda in Suzuka City, Japan, achieved 9,426 mpg in the Pisaralla Pisimmälle mileage marathon at Nokia, Finland, on September 1, 1996.

MOST POWERFUL CAR   **The most powerful production car currently on the market is the McLaren F1 6.1, which develops in excess of 627 bhp. The vehicle can accelerate to 60 mph in 3.2 seconds.**

LONGEST CAR A 100-ft.-long, 26-wheel limo (pictured above) designed by Jay Ohrberg of Burbank, California, includes a swimming pool with a diving board and a king-size waterbed among its many features. It can be driven as a rigid vehicle or altered to bend in the middle. Designers of these super-stretched cars try to outdo each other not just with the length of their creations but with the additional features—for example, the 68-ft., 22-wheel Cadillac *Hollywood Dream* has six telephones, a satellite dish, a putting green, and a helicopter landing pad.

Longest Fuel Range The greatest distance ever traveled by a vehicle on the contents of a standard fuel tank is 1,338 miles 18 yd., by an Audi 100 TDI diesel car. The car's fuel-tank capacity was $17\frac{1}{2}$ gal. The car was driven by Stuart Bladon from John O'Groat's, Scotland, to Land's End, Cornwall, England, and back again between July 26 and 28, 1992.

SMALLEST CAR IN PRODUCTION The Smart car made by Daimler-Benz is the smallest car currently in production. With an exterior length of just under 8 ft. 4 in., it beats its nearest rival, the Rover Mini, by 1 ft. 8 in. The two-seater car has removable body panels made out of thermoplastic, allowing owners to change the color of their vehicles.

Greatest Distance Covered on a Single Charge by a Production Vehicle   A Solectria force NiMH electric sedan established a new distance record by completing 249 miles on a single charge in the 1997 North East Sustainable Energy Association (NESEA) American Tour de Sol, using state-of-the-art nickel-metal hydride batteries produced by the Ovonic Battery Company. Solectria broke its existing record of 244 miles, set at the 1996 Tour de Sol.

Highest Car Mileage   The highest recorded mileage for a car is 1,690,000 miles, by a 1966 Volvo P-1800S owned by Irvine Gordon of East Patchogue, New York, as of February 1999.

Biggest Car   The biggest car ever to have been produced for private use was the Bugatti "Royale" type 41, assembled at Molsheim, France, by the Italian designer Ettore Bugatti. First built in 1927, the car has an eight-cylinder engine with a capacity of $2^3/4$ gallons and is more than 22 ft. long. The hood alone is 7 ft. in length.

Widest Cars   The Koenig Competition:2417, built in 1989, and the Koenig Competition Evolution:2418, built in 1990, both from Germany, are the widest cars on record, at 7 ft. $2^2/5$ in. in width.

Smallest Car   The smallest car ever was the Peel P50, which was constructed by the Peel Engineering Company on the Isle of Man in 1962. It was 4 ft. 5 in. in length, 3 ft. 3 in. in width, and 4 ft. 5 in. in height and weighed 132 lb.

Lightest Car   The world's lightest car ever was built and driven by Louis Borsi of London, England, and weighs 21 lb. It has a 2.5 cc engine and can reach a maximum speed of 15 mph.

Heaviest Car   The heaviest car in recent production is the Soviet-built Zil-41047 limousine, which has a 12-ft.-9-in. wheelbase weighing 3.025 tons. A "stretched" Zil, of which only two to three were made annually, was used by former Soviet president Mikhail Gorbachev until December 1991. It

MOST EXPENSIVE PRODUCTION CAR   The most expensive production car is the Mercedes Benz CLK/LM, which costs $1,547,620. It has a top speed of 200 mph and can travel from 0 to 62 mph in 3.8 seconds.

weighed 6 tons and used 3-in. armor-plated steel for protection in key areas. The eight-cylinder, seven-liter engine guzzled fuel at the rate of 6 mpg.

Cheapest Car The 1922 Red Bug Buckboard, built by the Briggs & Stratton Company in Milwaukee, Wisconsin, was on the market for $125 to $150. This would be equivalent to $1,130 to $1,870 in 1999 terms. It had a 62-in. wheelbase and weighed 245 lb. Early models of the King Midget cars, which were made in the US in kit form for self-assembly, sold for as little as $100 in 1948, the equivalent of $842 in 1999 terms.

Longest Production Run The Morgan 4/4, built by the Morgan Motor Car Company of Malvern, England, celebrated its 63rd birthday in December 1998. There is currently a waiting list of between six and eight years for the car.

Best-Selling Sports Car Mazda manufactured 492,645 MX5 sports cars between 1989 and 1998. The car, which is called a Miata in the US and a Roadster in Japan, became so successful that the market was subsequently flooded with two-seater sports cars.

Most Cars Produced in a Year In 1997, a record 57.84 million vehicles were constructed worldwide. Of this total, more than 41 million were cars, making 1997 a record-breaking year for car production.

BIKES

Biggest Bicycle The largest bicycle in the world, as measured by wheel diameter, is *Frankencycle*, which was built by Dave Moore of Rosemead, California, and first ridden by Steve Gordon of Moorpark, California, on June 4, 1989. The wheel diameter is 10 ft., and the bicycle itself is 11 ft. 2 in. tall.

Longest Bicycle The longest true bicycle (defined as a two-wheeled cycle without a third stabilizing wheel) was designed and built by Terry Thessman of Pahiatua, New Zealand. It measures 72.96 ft. in length and weighs 750 lb. It was ridden a distance of 807 ft. by a team of four people on February 27, 1988. It performs well when ridden in a straight line, but cornering remains a problem.

Smallest Bicycle The world's smallest-wheeled rideable bicycle has wheels of ³/₄ in. in diameter. It was ridden by its constructor, Neville Patten of Gladstone, Queensland, Australia, for a distance of 13 ft. 5 in. on March 25, 1988.

Tallest Unicycle Steve McPeak (US) rode a 101-ft.-9-in.-tall unicycle, with a safety wire suspended from an overhead crane, a distance of 376 ft. in Las Vegas, Nevada, in October 1980.

Biggest Tricycle The world's biggest tricycle was designed and constructed by 16 students at Bay de Noc Community College in Escabana, Michigan, in July 1998. It has a front wheel diameter of 15 ft. 3 in., the

MOST EXPENSIVE MOTORCYCLE The world's most expensive production motorcycle is the Morbidelli 850 V8, which retails for $102,872.

back wheels have a diameter of 7 ft. 3 in., and the overall height of the tricycle is 23 ft. 4³/₄ in.

Smallest Tandem Jacques Puyoou of Pau, Pyrénées-Atlantiques, France, has built a tandem that is 14 in. in length. It has been ridden by himself and his wife.

Most Expensive Mountain Bike "The Flipper," the most expensive retail mountain bike in the world, costs $12,025. Made by Stif (UK), it weighs just 20 lb. and is designed for off-road racing circuits. It includes some of the world's most expensive bicycle components—the brakes, gears, and pedals are made in Japan, the frame is from the US, the forks and handlebars are British, and the saddle is Italian.

Biggest Producer of Folding Biycycles Dahon California Inc. (US) is the world's largest producer of folding bicycles. Since 1982, Dahon has produced over 1.2 million bicycles, their best-selling model being the Classic, with over 400,000 units sold worldwide.

Longest Motorcycle Douglas and Roger Bell of Perth, Western Australia, designed and built a 24-ft.-11-in.-long motorcycle weighing nearly 2 tons.

Smallest Motorcycle Simon Timperley and Clive Williams of Progressive Engineering Ltd. in Ashton-under-Lyne, England, designed and constructed a motorcycle with a wheelbase of $4\frac{1}{4}$ in., a seat height of $3\frac{3}{4}$ in., and a wheel diameter of $\frac{3}{4}$ in. at the front and $\frac{9}{10}$ in. at the back. The bike was ridden a distance of 3 ft. 3 in.

Biggest Motorcycle Manufacturer The Honda Motor Company of Japan is the largest manufacturer of motorcycles in the world. The company has 95 production facilities in 34 countries for motorcycles and automobiles. In 1998, Honda sold a total of 5.1 million units to retailers worldwide.

Earliest Motorcycle The first internal-combustion-engine motorized bicycle was *Einspur*, a wooden-framed machine built by Gottlieb Daimler in Bad Cannstatt, Germany, in 1885 and first ridden by Wilhelm Maybach. It had a top speed of 12 mph and developed $\frac{1}{2}$ hp from its single-cylinder 264 cc four-stroke engine at 700 rpm.

Largest-Capacity Scooter The Suzuki Bergman 400 cc has the largest capacity of any scooter currently in production. It has a power output of 31.5 bhp at 8,000 rpm, together with a torque output of 14.46 lb ft.[2] at 6,000 rpm.

SMALLEST UNICYCLE The smallest ridden unicycle is 8 in. high with a wheel diameter of $\frac{7}{10}$ in., and it has no attachments or extensions fitted. It was made by Signar Berglund of Sweden. It has been ridden on a number of occasions by Peter Rosendahl (Sweden), the greatest distance being 24 ft. $10\frac{1}{4}$ in. on the TV show *Guinness World Records: Primetime*, shown on May 14, 1999.

LIGHTEST FOLDABLE BICYCLE
The Triancle 6500 B-PEHT23, developed in Japan by the National Bicycle Industrial Co., Matsushita Electric Industrial Co., and the East Japan Railway Co., weighs 14 lb. 5 oz. The frame and front fork are made of titanium. The bicycle is small enough to be carried easily onto a train or to fit into a locker at a station.

Most Expensive Production Scooter   The Suzuki AN 400 is the most expensive scooter currently in production, costing $6,628, with an on-road charge of $456.

Longest-Running Scooter Manufacturer   Vespa of Italy is the oldest company manufacturing scooters. The prototype of the first Vespa scooter was tested and approved in December 1945, with production beginning in April 1946. In 1949, the company was awarded a royal warrant to supply the Duke of Edinburgh with scooters.

FASTEST PRODUCTION BIKE   The Suzuki Hayabusa Gsx1300R is reported to reach speeds of 194 mph, making it the fastest production bike in the world. The motorcycle is a 1298 cc DOHC with four valves per cylinder, a narrow 14° valve angle, and electronic fuel injection with ram air. The result is a powerful bike with 173 bhp at 9,800 rpm but an overall weight of 474 lb. "Hayabusa" is Japanese for peregrine falcon.

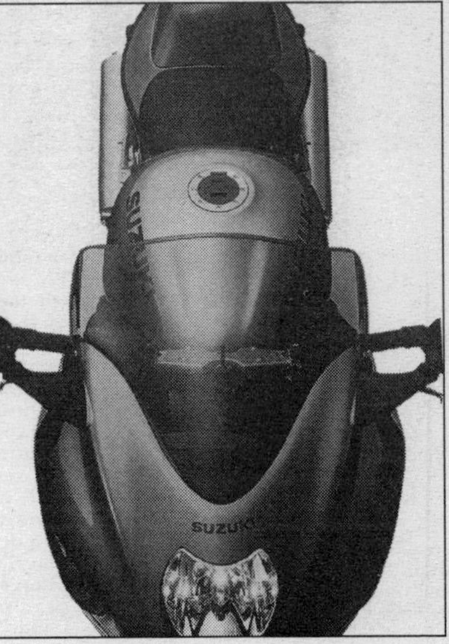

PLANES & BOATS

Fastest Airliners   The Tupolev Tu-144, first flown in 1968, was reported to have achieved Mach 2.4 (1,600 mph), although its normal cruising speed was Mach 2.2. In May 1970, it became the first commercial transport ever to exceed Mach 2.

The BAC/Aérospatiale Concorde was first flown in 1969. It cruises at speeds of up to Mach 2.2 (1,450 mph) and is the fastest supersonic airplane.

Fastest Aircraft   The USAF Lockheed SR-71, a reconnaissance aircraft, was the fastest jet ever, reaching a speed of 2,193.22 mph. First flown in its definitive form in 1964, the Lockheed was reportedly capable of attaining an altitude of 98,000 ft. It was 107 ft. 5 in. long, had a wingspan of 55 ft. 7 in., and weighed 69.9 tons at takeoff. Its reported range at Mach 3 was 3,000 miles at 79,000 ft.

The fastest propeller-driven aircraft was the Soviet Tu-95/142, which had four 14,795-hp engines driving eight-blade contrarotating propellers and a maximum level speed of Mach 0.82, or 575 mph.

The highest speed achieved by a piston-engine aircraft is 528.33 mph over a 1-mile-1,584-yd. course, by *Rare Bear*, a modified Grumman F8F Bearcat piloted by Lyle Shelton, in Las Vegas, Nevada, in August 1989.

The fastest biplane was the one-of-a-kind Italian Fiat CR42B, which had a 1,010-hp Daimler-Benz DB601A engine. It reached a speed of 323 mph in 1941.

FASTEST SAILING VESSEL   On October 26, 1993, the trifoiler *Yellow Pages Endeavour* (pictured left) reached a speed of 46.52 knots (53.57 mph) while on a timed run of 547 yd. at Sandy Point near Melbourne, Victoria, Australia. This is the highest speed ever reached by any craft under sail on water. The trifoiler, which has a 40-ft.-high sail and three short planing hulls, was designed by Lindsay Cunningham (Australia), who also designed Australia's Little America's Cup catamarans. It was piloted on its record-breaking run by Simon McKeon and Tim Daddo, both of Australia.

Fastest Flying Boat   The Martin XP6M-1 SeaMaster, a four-jet-engine US Navy minelayer flown from 1955 to 1959, had a top speed of 646 mph.

Biggest Aircraft   The jet airliner with the highest capacity is the Boeing 747-400, which first entered service in 1989. It has a wingspan of 213 ft. and a range of 8,290 miles and can carry up to 566 passengers. The airliner that holds the record for the greatest volume is the Airbus Super Transporter A300-600 ST Beluga, which has a 49,440-ft.^{3} main cargo compartment, a maximum takeoff weight of 165 tons, a 147-ft.-1-in. wingspan, and an overall length of 184 ft. 2 in. The usable length of its cargo compartment is 123 ft. 8 in.

Biggest Wingspans   The $40-million Hughes H4 Hercules flying boat, also known as *Spruce Goose*, had the biggest wingspan of any aircraft ever, at 320 ft. The 213-ton, 218-ft.-8-in.-long, eight-engine aircraft reached a height of 70 ft. in a 1,000-yd. test run piloted by US tycoon Howard Hughes off Long Beach Harbor, California, in 1947 but never flew again.
   The biggest wingspan of a current aircraft is 240 ft. 6 in., on the Ukrainian Antonov An-124 Ruslan.

Smallest Monoplane   The smallest monoplane ever flown is *Baby Bird*, which was designed and built by Donald Stits. It is 11 ft. long, has a wingspan of 6 ft. 4 in., and weighs just 252 lb. when empty. First flown in 1984, the plane has a maximum speed of 110 mph.

SMALLEST BIPLANE   The smallest biplane ever flown was *Bumble Bee Two* (pictured above), which was designed and constructed by Robert Starr of Tempe, Arizona. Capable of carrying just one person, *Bumble Bee Two* was 8 ft. 10 in. in overall length and had a wingspan of 5 ft. 6 in. It weighed 396 lb. when empty. In 1988, it crashed and was totally destroyed after attaining an altitude of 394 ft.

BIGGEST PRODUCTION AIRCRAFT   The production airliner with the greatest volume is the Ukrainian Antonov An-124 Ruslan (pictured above), the cargo hold of which has a usable volume of 35,800 ft.^{3} and a maximum takeoff weight of 447 tons. The heavy-lift version of the An-124, the An-225 Mriya, has a stretched fuselage providing as much as 42,000 ft.^{3} of usable volume. Its cargo compartment includes an unobstructed 141-ft.-long hold and has a maximum width of 21 ft. and height of 14 ft. 5 in.

Smallest Twin-Engine Aircraft   The world's smallest twin-engine aircraft ever is believed to be the Colombian MGI5 Cricri, which was first flown in 1973. The Cricri has a wingspan of 16 ft. and an overall length of 12 ft. 10 in. It is powered by two 15-hp JPX PUL engines.

Biggest Sailing Vessel   The biggest sailing vessel currently in service is the 358-ft.-long *Sedov*, built in 1921 in Kiel, Germany, and now used by the Russian navy. It has a beam of 48 ft., a displacement of 6,946 tons, and a sail area of 45,124 ft.^{2}. *Sedov* can reach speeds of up to 17 knots (19 mph) and has a crew of 65 cadets and 120 officer trainees.

Longest Sailing Vessel   The longest sailing vessel is the 614-ft. French-built *Club Med 1*, which has five aluminum masts and 30,100 ft.^{2} of computer-controlled polyester sails. It operates as a Caribbean cruise ship for the Club Med vacation company and can carry 425 passengers.

Biggest Aircraft Carriers   The Nimitz class US Navy aircraft carriers USS *Nimitz, Dwight D. Eisenhower, Carl Vinson, Theodore Roosevelt, Abraham Lincoln, George Washington,* and *John C. Stennis* (the last three of which displace 114,263 tons) have the biggest full-load displacement of any warships. They are 1,092 ft. in length with 4^1/$_2$ acres of flight deck. Driven by four nuclear-powered 260,000-shp geared steam turbines, they can reach speeds of more than 30 knots (35 mph). The *Nimitz* has four C-13 Mod 1 catapults, or "cats," that propel aircraft off the flight deck. These can accelerate even the heaviest carrier-based aircraft to speeds of 170 mph from a standing start.

Biggest Cargo Vessel   The oil tanker *Jahre Viking* (formerly known as *Happy Giant* and *Seawise Giant*) is 1,504 ft. long and weighs 564,763 dwt. It has a beam of 226 ft. and a draft of 80 ft. 8 in. The tanker was almost totally destroyed during the Iran-Iraq war but underwent a $60-million renovation in Singapore and the United Arab Emirates. It was relaunched under its new name in November 1991.

Biggest Container Ship The biggest container vessel currently in service is *Regina Maersk*, which was built in Odense, Denmark, in 1996. It has a gross tonnage of 89,843 and a capacity of 6,000 TEU.

Biggest Hydrofoil The 212-ft.-long *Plainview* naval hydrofoil, which weighs 285 tons with a full load, was launched by the Lockheed Shipbuilding and Construction Co. in Seattle, Washington, on June 28, 1965. It has a service speed of 57.2 mph.

Biggest Yachts The Saudi Arabian royal yacht *Abdul Aziz*, built in Denmark and completed at Vospers Yard in Southampton, England, in June 1984, is 482 ft. long.

The biggest nonroyal yacht in the world is the 407-ft.-long *Savarona*, which was built for Turkish president Mustafa Kemal Atatürk in 1931.

Biggest Junk The seagoing *Zheng He* had a displacement of 3,473 tons and an estimated length of 538 ft. The flagship of Admiral Zheng He's 62 treasure ships c. 1420, it is believed to have had nine masts.

Fastest Hovercraft
On January 25, 1980, a 79-ft.-long, 121-ton US Navy test hovercraft reached a speed of 65.7 mph in the Chesapeake Bay Test Range in Virginia.

Oldest Commissioned Warship Ordered in 1758, HMS *Victory* took a total of six years to build. It has 27 miles of rigging and 4 acres of sails. Now being restored to its original condition, the ship is the only remaining specimen of its kind anywhere in the world. It is currently docked at Portsmouth, England.

Oldest Iron Steamship SS *Great Britain* was launched in Bristol, England, in 1843 and was the first propeller-driven iron

SMALLEST JET The smallest jet in the world is *Silver Bullet* (pictured above), which was built by Bob and Mary Ellen Bishop of Aguila, Arizona, in 1976. It is 12 ft. long, has a wingspan of 17 ft., and weighs approximately 437 lb. *Silver Bullet* can fly straight and level at a speed of 300 mph.

vessel to cross the Atlantic. It was also used on the UK–Australia route and from 1855 to 1856 carried troops to the Crimean War. After running into trouble off Cape Horn in 1884, the ship sailed for shelter to Port Stanley in the Falkland Islands, where it was subsequently used as a storage vessel. It was salvaged from the Falklands in 1970 and brought back to Bristol, where it was restored to its original appearance.

ROCKETS

Biggest Rocket   The US craft *Saturn V* was the biggest rocket ever, at a record 363 ft. in height with the *Apollo* spacecraft on top. It weighed 2,633 tons on the launchpad.

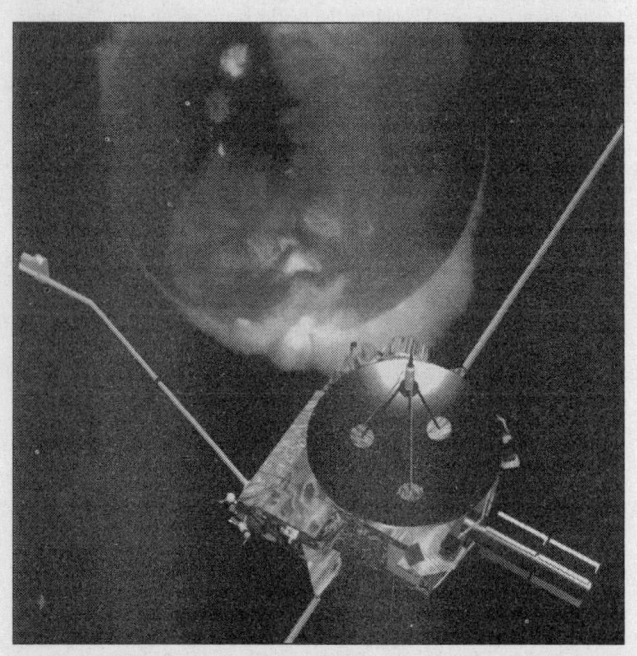

FASTEST ESCAPE VELOCITY FROM EARTH   The ESA *Ulysses* spacecraft is seen passing over one of the sun's poles. The craft, which is powered by an IUS-PAM upper stage, achieved a record escape velocity of 33,936 mph from Earth after deployment from the space shuttle *Discovery* on October 7, 1990. The information it is relaying back to Earth has allowed scientists to build up a new three-dimensional picture of the sun.

Smallest Rocket   The smallest satellite launch vehicle in the world was *Pegasus*, a 49-ft.-3-in.-long three-stage booster. The original *Pegasus*, which has since been succeeded by an operational *Pegasus XL* version, was air-launched from an aircraft in 1990.

Most Expensive Rockets

The *Saturn V* rocket was constructed for the *Apollo* moon-landing program, which had cost approximately $25 billion by the time of the first flight to the moon in July 1969.

Commercial customers have been charged more than $120 million in total for launches to orbit communications satellites aboard the US commercial rocket *Titan*, which is no longer on the market.

Cheapest Satellite Launcher

The least expensive US satellite launcher was *Pegasus*, which was developed with a budget of $45 million and cost approximately $10 million per launch.

Most Intelligent Rockets

The launch and flight of the space shuttles are computer controlled and guided from nine minutes before liftoff to the crafts' arrival in orbit eight minutes after launch.

Most Advanced Rocket Engine

The revolutionary Aerospike engine, which will be used to power the next generation of shuttle craft, has no nozzle, unlike conventional rocket engines. Instead, exhaust

MOST SATELLITES DESTROYED AT A LAUNCH   This artist's impression shows the *Ariane 5* launcher lifting off from the launchpad at Kourou, French Guiana. The launcher, an upgrade of the *Ariane 4* rocket, is capable of delivering a 16-ton satellite into a low earth orbit and a 5.4-ton payload into geostationary orbit. On June 6, 1996, *Ariane 5*'s first flight ended in disaster when its onboard computer malfunctioned 40 seconds after launch, causing it to veer wildly off course. An automatic self-destruct mechanism then blew it into pieces. The rocket was carrying four identical Cluster satellites. *Ariane 5* has since made two successful launches, in October 1997 and October 1998.

MOST RELIABLE LAUNCH SYSTEMS Mission STS-78 of the US space shuttle *Columbia* is seen lifting off from Cape Canaveral, Florida, on June 20, 1996. Between April 1981 and January 1998, the space shuttle completed a total of 89 launches with only one failure—a 98% success rate. The Russian *Soyuz U* series has flown a total of 781 times with 766 successes since 1973, twice recording 100 consecutive successful launches.

gas flows over a centrally positioned ramp that changes position in flight to give better efficiency and more power. Prototypes of the Aerospike are already flying on converted SR-71 spy planes.

Most Powerful Rocket Engine Built in the former USSR by the Scientific Industrial Corporation of Power Engineering in 1980, the RD-170 has a thrust of 731 tons in open space and 639 tons at Earth's surface. It also has a turbo pump rated at 190MW and burns liquid oxygen and kerosene. The RD-170 powered the four strap-on boosters of the *Energiya* booster, launched in 1987 but now grounded by budget cuts.

Most Complex Heat Shield The heat shield fitted to the space shuttle on its early missions, to protect it from the heat of reentry, consisted of 32,000 silica tiles that had to be individually glued into position and tested for strength—a difficult, expensive, and time-consuming job. Improvements to the shuttle's heat protection system have slightly reduced the number of tiles needed today. The shuttle's replacement, the Reusable Launch Vehicle, will not use tiles—its body will be made from advanced graphite compounds instead.

Most Spectacular Launch Failure Designed as a key part of the Soviet program to land a human on the moon, the giant *N1* rocket was abandoned after its third failure to launch on July 3, 1969, less than two weeks before the start of the US's successful *Apollo 11* mission. The last failure of *N1* resulted in a huge explosion that killed many people at the launch site.

Least Reliable Launch System The Russian-Ukrainian *Zenit* launcher has had 21 successful and seven failed missions since 1985—a success rate of 72%.

Longest-Serving Launch Vehicle The *A2* rocket, now used to launch *Soyuz* ferry craft to the *Mir* space station, is a more advanced version of the one used to launch *Sputnik* in 1957. Beginning life in the mid-1950s as the

SS-6, it was the first Soviet inter-continental ballistic missile (ICBM). Over the years, it has achieved many important milestones—including launching the first animal and the first human into space in 1961. In its sixth decade, it will play an important part in the servicing of the new International Space Station.

Smallest Manned Spacecraft The Manned Maneuvering Unit (MMU), used by astronauts working outside the space shuttle, is 4 ft. tall, 2 ft. 8 in. wide, and 3 ft. 8 in. deep and weighs just 240 lb. Powered by nitrogen thrusters, it was first used on shuttle mission STS-41-B when astronaut Bruce McCandless maneuvered up to 328 ft. away from *Challenger*.

Closest Approach to the Sun by a Rocket On April 16, 1976, the research spacecraft *Helios B* approached within 27 million miles of the Sun, carrying both US and West German instrumentation.

Most Successful Amateur Rockets The *Halo* rocket, built by a US group called HAL5, reached an altitude of 36 miles on May 11, 1998. *Halo* was carried to a height of 11 miles 654 yd. by a helium-filled balloon before being launched. The height it achieved is just 14 miles short of NASA's official definition of the beginning of space.

The highest altitude reached by a ground-launched amateur-built rocket is 22 miles 634 yd. The *Hyperion I*

LOUDEST LAUNCH The noise created by the launch of the unmanned *Apollo 4* (pictured above) on November 9, 1967, was so great that the resulting air-pressure wave was detected at the Lamont-Doherty Geological Observatory 1,100 miles away. The reverberations from the launch also caused the roof to be torn from the press site 3 miles away. Subsequent *Saturn V* launches were muffled in order to reduce noise levels.

rocket, built by Korey Kline, was launched from NASA's Wallops Island facility in Virginia on January 7, 1997. The 106-lb. rocket accelerated to three times the speed of sound using a mixture of solid and liquid fuel.

LETHAL WEAPONS

Most People Killed by a Bomb   The atomic bomb dropped on Hiroshima, Japan, by the US on August 6, 1945, killed more than 100,000 people instantly. An additional 55,000 people died from radiation sickness within a year.

Most Powerful Nuclear Weapon   The most powerful ICBM (intercontinental ballistic missile) is the former USSR's SS-18 (Model 5), which is thought to be armed with 10,750-kiloton MIRVs (multiple independently targetable reentry vehicles). By the end of April 1995, all SS-18 ICBMs had been returned to Russia, where 150 are still operational. If the START 2 (Strategic Arms Reduction Talks 2) agreement is fully implemented, the remaining SS-18s and all other ICBMs with more than one warhead will be destroyed.

Most Powerful Thermonuclear Device   A thermonuclear device with power equivalent to about 52 megatons of TNT was detonated by the former USSR in the Novaya Zemlya area in October 1961. The shock wave circled Earth three times, with the first circuit taking 36 hr. 27 min. Estimates put the power of the device at between 62 and 90 megatons.

Longest-Range Attacks   In January 1991, seven B-52G bombers took off from Barksdale Air Force Base in Louisiana to deliver cruise missiles against Iraq just after the start of the Gulf War. Each flew 14,000 miles, refueling four times in the 35-hour round trip.

In September 1996, B-52s flew nonstop from Guam in the western Pacific to launch cruise missiles around Baghdad, Iraq—a distance of 12,604 miles.

MOST EXPENSIVE MILITARY AIRCRAFT The world's most expensive military aircraft is the US B2 Spirit (pictured left), which is priced at $1.3 billion. A long-range multi-role bomber, it is capable of delivering both conventional and nuclear munitions and has a number of stealth characteristics that enable it to penetrate an enemy's defenses without being observed: these include its special coatings and flying-wing design. The B2 has an unfueled range of 5,965 miles and can carry a payload of 20.004 tons. It made its first flight on July 17, 1989.

BIGGEST SUBMARINE The Russian Akula submarine (pictured right), which has the NATO code name "Typhoon," is believed to have an overall length of 562 ft. 8 in. and a displacement of 29,217 tons. The launch of the first "Typhoon" is reported by NATO to have taken place at the secret covered shipyard at Severodvinsk on the White Sea on September 23, 1980. At present, six Akula submarines are said to be in service, each of them armed with 20 multiple-warhead SS-N-20 missiles with a range of 5,158 miles.

Longest-Range Missiles The US Atlas missile entered service in 1959 and had a range of 10,360 miles—about 3,000 miles more than was necessary to hit any point in Soviet territory from launch sites in the West.

The longest-range Russian missile is the SS-18, code-named "Satan," which entered service in the early 1980s and has a range of 7,500 miles.

Most Advanced Fighter Plane The US F22 Raptor was developed by Lockheed Martin Aeronautical Systems, Lockheed Martin Fort Worth, and Boeing in the late 1990s. It cost about $13.3 billion—twice as much as its European counterpart, the Eurofighter. The F22 is capable of carrying a number of different air-to-air weapons in its internal bays: these include radar-guided AIM-120C medium-range air-to-air missiles (AMRAAMs), longer-finned AIM-120A AMRAAMs, and heat-seeking short-range AIM-9M sidewinders.

It will also carry an internal M61A2 20-mm cannon, an advanced version of the M61 Gatling-type gun. The F22 is 62 ft. long with a wingspan of 43 ft. 11 in.

Fastest Combat Jet The world's fastest combat jet is the Mikoyan MiG-25 fighter—the NATO code name for which is "Foxbat"—developed by the former USSR. The single-seat "Foxbat-A" has a wingspan of 45 ft. 9 in., is 78 ft. 2 in. long, and has an estimated maximum takeoff weight of 41.2 tons. The reconnaissance "Foxbat-B" has been tracked by radar at speeds of about Mach 3.2.

Fastest Bombers The US variable-geometry, or "swing-wing," General Dynamics FB-111A has a maximum speed of Mach 2.5.

The Russian swing-wing TupolevTu-22M, which is known to NATO as "Backfire," has an estimated over-target speed of Mach 2 but could be as fast as Mach 2.5.

Fastest Destroyer The highest speed ever attained by a destroyer is 45.25 knots (52 mph), by the 3,576-ton French ship *Le Terrible* in 1935. Built in Blainville, France, and powered by four Yarrow small tube boilers

and two Rateau geared turbines, giving 100,000 shaft horsepower, the destroyer was decommissioned at the end of 1957.

Fastest Military Hovercraft On January 25, 1980, the 78-ft.-long, 110-ton test vehicle SES-100B, a US Navy hovercraft, achieved a speed of 91.9 knots (106 mph).

Most Advanced Combat Ship In July 1998, the UK Defence Evaluation Research Agency (DERA) commissioned Vosper Thornycroft of Southampton, England, to build the world's biggest steel oceangoing trimaran, which could shape the future of naval ship development in the next century. The diesel-electric-driven vessel, *Triton*, will be 318 ft. long, displace 998 tons, and have a maximum speed of 20 knots (23 mph). Its advanced design offers 20% less

MOST ACCURATE HUMAN-PORTABLE ANTIAIRCRAFT MISSILE US Marines are seen with a Stinger missile launcher during exercises. The Stinger missile, which was introduced in the early 1980s, is 5 ft. long, weighs 22 lb., and has a range of about 3 miles and a speed of about 1,300 mph. The Stinger's cryogenically cooled infrared seeker distinguishes between an aircraft's infrared signature and countermeasures such as flares. In the early 1990s, the US Army took delivery of the Stinger POST (passive optical seeker technology), which is flown to target by a programmable microprocessor. The missile can "think," and once it is locked on, there is little the pilot of the target aircraft can do other than outfly the missile or eject.

drag than a conventional monohull and the stability to mount detection systems higher up on the ship. The *Triton*'s planned launch date is April 2000, followed by 18 months of sea trials.

Biggest Unmanned Air Vehicle The biggest unmanned air vehicle in development is *Global Hawk*, which was unveiled at Teledyne Ryan Aeronautical in San Diego, California, on February 20, 1997. Its first flight was at Edwards Air Force Base in California on February 28, 1998. The aircraft, which has a 116-ft. wingspan and a 14,000-mile range, will be used by the USAF for aerial reconnaissance.

Most Powerful Torpedo The Russian Type 65, a 26-in. torpedo, carries a warhead of nearly one ton of conventional explosive or a 15-kiloton nuclear warhead—giving it slightly less explosive power than the bombs that destroyed Hiroshima and Nagasaki in 1945. It can home in acoustically on the turbulence left in the wake of a ship more than 50 miles away

FASTEST-FIRING MACHINE GUN Designed for use in helicopters and armored vehicles in the late 1960s, the ³/₁₆-in. M 134 Minigun (pictured above, mounted in the nose turret of a Cobra gunship) is the world's fastest-firing machine gun. Based on the multiple-barreled Gatling design, it has six barrels that are revolved by an electric motor and fed by a 4,000-round link belt. This allows for a firing rate of 6,000 rounds per minute—about 10 times that of an ordinary machine gun.

and can close at more than 43½ knots (50 mph)—far in excess of the speed of the fastest surface ships.

Most Advanced Helicopter The Russian Ka-52 Alligator is the world's most advanced helicopter. A two-seat derivative of the Ka-50 Black Shark, it is intended primarily as a gunship and is equipped with a wide range of weapons as well as devices that allow it to fly missions in extreme weather conditions.

DANGER
& DISASTER

DANGER ZONES

Highest Murder Rate The country with the highest murder rate in proportion to its population varies from year to year, but the rate for Colombia was consistently high throughout the 1990s, with an average of 77.5 murders per 100,000 people. This is nine times higher than the US rate. More than 27,000 murders a year currently take place in Colombia.

The city with the highest murder rate in proportion to its population is Bogotá, Colombia's capital. More than 8,600 murders take place there every year (an average of nearly one an hour), and violence is the leading cause of death for males aged 11 to 59.

Highest Rape Rate The country with the highest rape rate in the world is South Africa. Official figures released by the South African Police Service, based on estimates calculated from the 1996 census results, indicate a rape rate of 116 per 100,000 people in 1998.

MOST CONTAMINATED AGRICULTURAL LAND Members of a delegation to the Chernobyl nuclear power plant view the "sarcophagus" built over the destroyed fourth reactor after it exploded in April 1986. The former Soviet republic of Belarus suffered more damage than anywhere else in the region from the disaster—almost 99% of the land there has been contaminated to degrees above internationally accepted levels. Despite the fact that a third of the total fallout fell on land used for agriculture, food produced in the country continues to be consumed. An estimated 1.5 million people have suffered adverse physical effects as a result of the disaster.

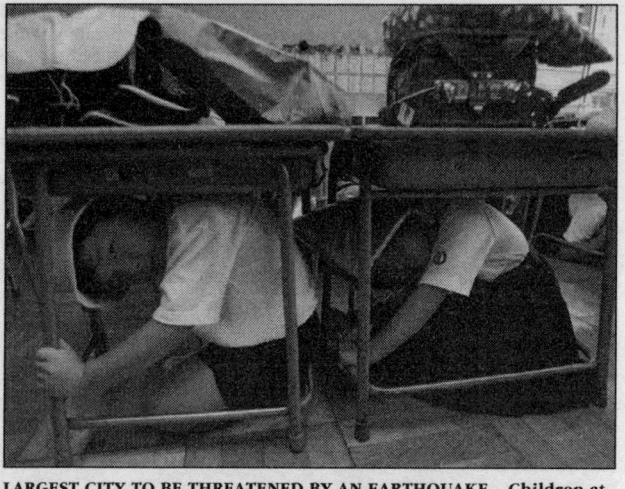

LARGEST CITY TO BE THREATENED BY AN EARTHQUAKE Children at a Tokyo primary school are seen taking part in an earthquake drill. Since being struck by an earthquake with a magnitude of 8.4 on the Richter scale in December 1854, the Tokyo region has been subjected to thousands of small tremors every year. The area is now an urban sprawl housing almost 30 million people, with skyscrapers, overpass highways, and millions of tons of fuel oil and poisonous chemicals stored in tanks around Tokyo Bay. Scientists predict that, at some point in the future, another earthquake will occur in the Tokai region, and it will be much larger than the quake which wrecked the western Japanese city of Kobe in 1995.

Most Road Fatalities India's roads are rated the most dangerous in the world. The country contains only 1% of the world's road vehicles but accounts for 6% of its road accidents. Of 9.34 million deaths in India in 1998, 217,000—or 1 in 43—were the result of road accidents.

Portugal had a rate of 28.9 deaths per 1,000 people in 1996, giving it the worst record in Europe. Greece has the second-highest number of road deaths in Europe, with an average of 22.5 deaths for every 1,000 people.

Most Air Crashes The number of people killed in air crashes on scheduled flights has decreased sharply since 1988, when there was an average of 175 fatalities per million departures. By 1998, the figure had fallen to 75 fatalities per million departures.

The chances of being killed in an air accident are highest in the skies over Africa, where there was an average of 190 fatalities per million departures in 1998. The second most dangerous continent is Asia, with 160 fatalities per million departures.

Most Fatal Shootings There are currently more than 200 million guns in the US, where one in four adults owns a firearm and about 40,000 fatalities are caused by guns each year. In the last 10 years, gun-related homicides in the US have risen by 18%.

Highest Incidence of Piracy   In the last 10 years, about 1,500 acts of piracy have been reported in southeast Asia. Most pirates operating in the region are armed with submachine guns and use small speedboats to "jump" targeted vessels. Financial losses from piracy in the Pacific area alone are estimated to exceed $100 million a year.

Worst Place to Be a Journalist   The most dangerous place in the world to be a journalist is Algeria, where over 70 journalists were murdered between May 23, 1993 and 1998. On arriving in the country, journalists are now met by a government protection team.

A total of 190 journalists and media workers were killed worldwide between 1995 and 1998: 46 in Europe and the republics of the former Soviet Union, 44 in the Americas, 62 in Africa, and 38 in Asia. Between 1990 and 1994, 370 journalists were murdered worldwide.

Largest City Threatened by a Volcanic Eruption   Mt. Vesuvius near Naples, Italy, is regarded as one of the most dangerous volcanoes in the world. More than 700,000 people live within a 6-mile-376-yard radius of its summit crater, and the outskirts of Naples are within 9 miles 564 yd. of the vent. If enough warning of an eruption can be given, the Italian government envisages an evacuation of at least 600,000 people. This would take a week, during which time Naples' outer suburbs could suffer the same fate as Pompeii.

WORST PLACE FOR KIDNAPPINGS   Families of kidnapping victims and supporters from various non-governmental organizations parade through the streets of Medellin, Colombia, to call for an end to kidnappings. Of the 8,000 kidnap cases reported worldwide in 1996, 6,500 took place in Latin America, and more than 4,000 occurred in Colombia, where an average of 10 people are kidnapped every day. The crime is alleged to be worth $200 million a year in the country. Only 3% of Colombia's kidnappers are convicted, compared to 95% in the US.

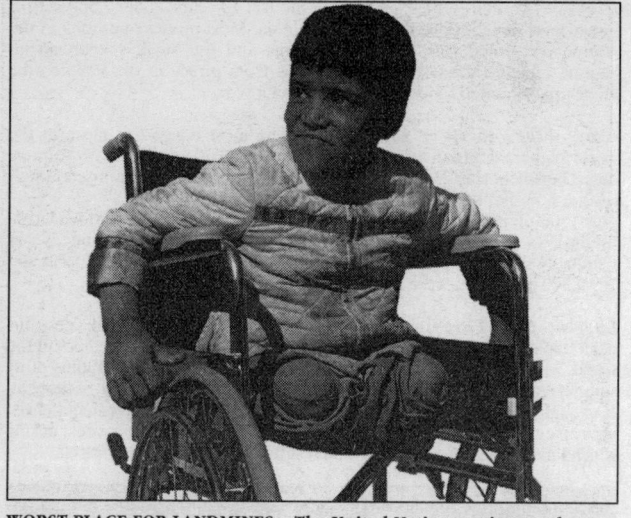

WORST PLACE FOR LANDMINES The United Nations estimates that more than 110 million active landmines are currently buried in 70 countries, with an equal number stockpiled in readiness for use. However, the International Campaign To Ban Landmines puts the stockpile figure at 250 million. The country with the most landmines is Egypt, with approximately 13 million, left after the Battles of El Alamein in 1942 and the Arab/Israeli conflicts between 1948 and 1973. Pictured above is Mohammed Saber, an Afghani boy who lost both his legs when he stepped on a landmine while out collecting firewood.

Most "Unintentional" Deaths The World Health Organization defines "unintentional" deaths as traffic accidents, poisonings, falls, fires, drownings, and other accidental injuries (not counting homicide, violence, and war). Of a total of 9.34 million deaths in India in 1998, 723,000—or 1 in 13—were defined as "unintentional." They included 32,000 poisonings, 50,000 falls, 135,000 fires, and 92,000 drownings.

Most Likely Place to Be Killed by a Snake Humans are most likely to die from a snakebite in Sri Lanka, where an average of 800 people a year are killed by snakes.

WAR & TERRORISM

Most Expensive War The material cost of World War II (1939–45) has been estimated at $1.5 trillion—more than the cost of all other wars put together.

BIGGEST WARTIME ASSAULT ON THE ENVIRONMENT In January 1991, Iraqi president Saddam Hussein gave the order for an estimated 740,000 tons of crude Gulf oil to be pumped from Kuwait's Sea Island terminal and from seven large oil tankers. During the same campaign, Iraqi forces set fire to 600 oil wells, creating clouds of black smoke up to 1 mile 569 yd. high, enveloping warships 50 miles offshore and depositing soot as far away as the Himalayas. The last blazing well was extinguished on November 6, 1991.

Most Televised Wars In terms of transmission hours, the Vietnam War is likely to remain the most televised war in history for many decades to come. In 1965, NBC screened *Actions of a Vietnamese Marine Battalion*, showing shocking action sequences, and as its ratings rocketed, CBS, ABC, and foreign broadcasters rushed to put camera teams into Vietnam as well. It is estimated that the three major US networks and their subsidiaries devoted about 10,000 hours of prime viewing time to coverage of the war between 1965 and 1975.

The collapse of the former Yugoslavia and associated conflicts between 1991 and 1996 eclipsed Vietnam in density of TV coverage, because by then it was much easier for freelance journalists to travel with their own equipment and satellite dishes. During the five years of conflict, journalists shot and recorded millions of hours of footage, of which only a tiny percentage was broadcast.

Bloodiest Wars The costliest war in terms of human life was World War II, in which the total number of military and civilian fatalities was an estimated 56.4 million. In Poland, 6.028 million people were killed—17.2% of the prewar population.

In Paraguay's war against Brazil, Argentina, and Uruguay from 1864 to 1870, Paraguay's population was reduced from 525,000 to 221,000. Fewer than 28,000 survivors were adult males.

Highest Battlefield Since 1984, the Indian and Pakistani armies have faced each other on the Siachen Glacier, Kashmir, at a height of up to

BIGGEST REWARD FOR COUNTERTERRORISM The US State Department offers a maximum reward of $5 million for information that leads to the prevention of terrorist acts or the capture of international terrorists. The most recent maximum reward was offered at the time of the bombing of the US embassies in Kenya and Tanzania in August 1998. A total of 243 people were killed in the attack in Nairobi, Kenya (pictured)—the highest death toll from terrorist action against an embassy. The State Department appealed for information on Osama bin Laden, believed to have been behind the bombing. Since the counterterrorism reward was established, a total of $7 million has been awarded for information.

22,000 ft. in temperatures as low as -76°F. Reports suggest that Pakistan spends as much as $588,000 a month and India about $1 million a month maintaining troops on the glacier.

Most Deaths Caused by Chemical Weapons in One War Exact figures for those wounded and killed by chemical weapons between January 1915 and November 1918, during World War I, are unreliable, but at least 100,000 people died, and 900,000 were injured. The Russian army, which was equipped with inadequate respirators, alone sustained some 56,000 fatalities and 475,000 injuries.

Biggest Single Chemical Warfare Attack The greatest number of people killed in a single chemical warfare attack is an estimated 4,000, at Halabja, Iraq, in March 1988. President Saddam Hussein used chemical weapons against his country's Kurdish minority for the support it had given to Iran in the Iran–Iraq war.

Bloodiest UN Peacekeeping Operation The ongoing conflict in the Balkans has led to more fatalities than any other UN peacekeeping mission. The total number of fatalities for all missions in the region is 268, including 210 fatalities in UNPROFOR (United Nations Protection Force) alone.

Longest-Running UN Peacekeeping Operation The longest-running UN peacekeeping mission is UNTSO (United Nations Truce Supervi-

MOST EXPENSIVE PEACEKEEPING OPERATION The most expensive
United Nations peacekeeping mission to date is UNPROFOR (United
Nations Protection Force), which cost $4.6 billion from January 12,
1992, to March 31, 1996, and included all the missions deployed in the
former Yugoslavia during this period.

sion Organization), which has been in place since June 1948. UNTSO's
headquarters are in Jerusalem, but it maintains military observation posts
throughout the Middle East.

Most Time Elapsed Between War Crimes and Trial In 1997,
Maurice Papon was indicted for "crimes against humanity" committed 56
years earlier during World War II. In 1942, Papon was responsible for the
deportation of Jews from unoccupied Vichy France to the German-occu-
pied zone in the north of the country, from where they were taken to
Auschwitz death camp. He was sentenced to 10 years of imprisonment in
1998.

Most People Killed in a Terrorist Attack The highest death toll
ever from a single terrorist attack was 329 people when a bomb exploded
aboard the Air India Boeing 747 "Kanishka" above the Atlantic Ocean in
June 1985.

Longest Embassy Siege In response to the exiled Shah of Iran's ad-
mission to the US for medical treatment in September 1979, a crowd of
about 500 people seized the US embassy in Tehran, Iran. Of the approximately 90 people inside the embassy, 52 remained in captivity until the end
of the crisis 444 days later, on January 20, 1981. This was the day of President Reagan's inauguration, when the US released almost $8 billion in
Iranian assets.

Most Hostages Held The greatest number of hostages to have been
held by a terrorist organization was over 500 people captured by Tupac

LONGEST TIME HELD HOSTAGE   Terry Anderson (US) was held in Beirut, Lebanon, for 2,454 days (6 years 264 days) by Hezbollah terrorists. After his release on December 4, 1991, he saw his six-year-old daughter for the first time—she was born shortly after he was kidnapped.

Amaru terrorists at the Japanese embassy in Lima, Peru, on December 17, 1996. The group gradually released the majority of the hostages, and the final 72 were rescued when Peruvian commandos stormed the embassy on April 22, 1997, killing all 14 rebels, including their leader, Nestor Cerpa.

During the Palestinian Liberation Front's hijacking of the Italian cruise liner *Achille Lauro* in October 1985, 413 people were held hostage for two days until the terrorists surrendered to the Egyptian authorities. The US passengers are considered to have been at the greatest risk, because they were separated from the other passengers as key targets by the hijackers. One US passenger, 69-year-old Leon Klinghoffer, was shot as he sat in his wheelchair and then thrown overboard.

Most Fatalities from an Attack on a Subway   Members of the Aum Shinrikyo cult released poisonous sarin gas on train lines of the Tokyo subway during the morning rush hour on March 20, 1995. Twelve commuters died as a result of the attack, and over 5,000 required treatment due to inhalation of noxious fumes.

DISASTERS: AIR, LAND & SEA

Worst Air Accidents   The world's worst air disaster ever took place on March 27, 1977, when two Boeing 747s, operated by Pan Am and KLM, collided on the runway at Los Rodeos Airport, Tenerife, Canary Islands, killing 583 people. Amazingly, 63 people on the Pan Am flight survived the disaster.

The worst air accident involving a single aircraft occurred on August 12,

WORST UNDERGROUND TRAIN DISASTER On October 28, 1995, approximately 300 people were killed in a fire that broke out in an underground train at Baku, Azerbaijan. Apart from those who were burned to death, many people died from smoke inhalation, being crushed, or electrocution on the live rails. The Azerbaijan Interior Ministry blamed the disaster on a technical fault. The picture (left) shows the funeral of one of the victims.

1985, when a JAL Boeing 747, flight 123, crashed between Tokyo and Osaka, Japan, killing 520 passengers and crew on board.

Worst Midair Collision On November 12, 1996, a total of 351 passengers and crew were killed in a collision between a Saudi Boeing 747 scheduled flight and a Kazakh Illushin 76 charter flight just 50 miles southwest of New Delhi, India. Only the tail section of the Saudi aircraft remained intact after the planes plunged to the ground.

Worst Ballooning Disaster The greatest loss of life to have resulted from a hot-air balloon accident occurred on August 13, 1989, when two passenger balloons that were launched a few minutes apart for a sight-seeing flight over Alice Springs, Australia, collided at a height of 2,000 ft. The basket of one of the balloons tore a hole in the fabric of the other, which then collapsed, sending the pilot and 12 passengers to their deaths.

Worst Disaster in Space The worst disaster ever during actual space flight took place on June 29, 1971, when astronauts Georgi Dobrovolsky, Viktor Patsayev, and Vladislav Volkov (all USSR), who were not wearing space suits, died when their *Soyuz 11* spacecraft depressurized during reentry.

The worst space disaster on the ground took place when a rocket exploded during fueling at the Baikonur Cosmodrome, USSR (now Kazakhstan), on October 24, 1960, killing 91 people.

Worst Maritime Collision On December 15, 1977, the tanker *Venoil* (300,175 deadweight tons) struck her sister ship *Venpet* (300,098 dwt) off the coast of southern Africa, causing the worst collision ever at sea.

Worst Shipwreck The 291,396-deadweight-ton VLCC (very large crude carrier) *Energy Determination* blew up and broke in two in the Strait

WORST SKI LIFT DISASTER The world's worst ski lift accident ever occurred at the resort of Cavalese, Italy, on March 9, 1976, when a ruptured cable caused the deaths of 42 people. Italy was also the scene of a recent disaster when an EA-6B Prowler Jet piloted by Capt. Richard Ashby of the US Marine Corps severed the cables of a car on Mt. Cermis (pictured above) on February 3, 1998. Twenty passengers plunged to their deaths. Ashby was acquitted of manslaughter but found guilty of obstructing justice for destroying a video of the incident. The US government paid compensation of $51,172 to the family of each victim, plus $20 million to the village to replace the lift.

of Hormuz, Persian Gulf, on December 12, 1979, causing the world's biggest shipwreck ever.

Worst Ferry Disaster In the early hours of December 21, 1987, the ferry *Dona Paz* collided with the tanker *Victor* while it was sailing from Tacloban to Manila, Philippines. After being engulfed by flames, both vessels sank within minutes. The *Dona Paz* officially had 1,550 passengers, but overcrowding is common in the region so it may actually have held 4,000.

Worst Submarine Disaster During Peacetime On April 10, 1963, the 3,409-ton US nuclear submarine *Thresher* failed to surface while carrying out deep-diving tests in the Atlantic, off Cape Cod, Massachusetts. It had 112 officers and 17 civilian technicians on board. The following year, the Navy announced that large sections of the vessel's hull had been discovered at a depth of 6,400 ft. by the bathyscaphe *Trieste II*, but the cause of the tragedy has never been properly explained.

Worst Train Disaster On June 6, 1981, more than 800 passengers died when their train plunged off a bridge into the river Bagmati in Bihar, India.

WORST AIR SHOW DISASTER At Ramstein Air Base, Germany, on August 28, 1988, three Italian jets collided in midair during an air show. One of the jets exploded and plowed into the crowd below, killing 70 people and injuring more than 400.

Worst Train Tunnel Disaster On March 2, 1944, 521 passengers and crew suffocated when their train stalled in a tunnel near Salerno, Italy.

Worst Elevator Accident An elevator operating at the Vaal Reefs gold mine in South Africa fell 1,600 ft. on May 11, 1995, killing 105 workers.

Worst Mass Panic In 1991, 1,426 Muslim pilgrims were trampled to death in a stampede along a tunnel between Mecca and Medina, Saudi Arabia.

Worst Soccer Riots In May 1964, 318 fans were killed and 500 injured in a riot at an Olympic qualifying match between Argentina and Peru in Lima, Peru. The riot was sparked when a last-minute Peruvian goal was disallowed by the referee. Had the goal stood, it would have sent Peru to the Olympics that year.

WORST SPACE MISSION DISASTER The greatest number of people to have perished in a manned spaceflight is seven (five men and two women)—the crew of *Challenger 51L*, which exploded 73 seconds after liftoff from the Kennedy Space Center in Florida, on January 28, 1986.

On October 21, 1982, a large number of supporters of Spartak Moscow were crushed to death in an icy corridor at the end of a UEFA Cup game against Haarlem (Netherlands) at the Luzhniki stadium in Moscow, USSR. Following the relaxation of reporting restrictions under *glasnost*, estimates of up to 340 fatalities were given to the world's media.

Worst Bullfight Disaster   On January 20, 1980, in Sincelejo, Colombia, a stand at a bullring collapsed, leaving 222 people dead.

NATURAL DISASTERS

Costliest Year for Natural Disasters   The year ending December 31, 1995, was the costliest ever in terms of natural disasters, with a total bill amounting to $180 billion, much of which was accounted for by the Kobe earthquake in Japan. The figures are collated every year by Munich Re, the world's largest reinsurers.

Biggest Power Failure Caused by a Natural Disaster   During Hurricane George in September 1998, winds of 110 mph hit the Domini-

MOST PEOPLE KILLED BY AN AVALANCHE   During World War I, between 40,000 and 80,000 men are believed to have been killed by avalanches triggered by the sound of gunfire in part of the southern Tirolean Alps, Austria (now in Italy). The Tirol was also the scene of a disaster (above) on February 23, 1999, when 31 people in Galtuer in the Paznaun Valley, Austria, were killed in one of a series of avalanches that swept through villages and ski resorts in the area. Seven more people died in avalanches in the Tirol that month, bringing the death toll to 38.

MOST DEVASTATING ICE STORM   In January 1998, an ice storm
wrought havoc across eastern Canada and parts of the northeastern
US, shutting down airports and train stations, blocking roads, and
cutting off power to 3 million people. After two weeks, 1 million
people were still without power, and some areas remained without
power for three weeks. The total cost of the damage was estimated at
$650 million.

can Republic, leaving 100,000 people homeless and almost the entire population (8 million) without power.

Most People Killed by Earthquakes   In July 1201, approximately 1.1
million people are believed to have been killed by an earthquake in the
eastern Mediterranean. Most of the casualties were in Egypt and Syria.

The earthquake that struck the Shaanxi, Shanxi, and Henan provinces of
China on February 2, 1556, is believed to have been responsible for the
death of 830,000 people.

The highest death toll in modern times was caused by the quake in
Tangshan in eastern China on July 28, 1976. According to the first official
figure, 655,237 people were killed. This was subsequently adjusted to
750,000 and then to 242,000.

Most People Made Homeless by an Earthquake   More than 1 million Guatemalans in a 3,400-mile^2 area were made homeless on February
4, 1976, when an earthquake ripped along the Montagua Fault between the
Caribbean and North American plates. The material damage was estimated at $1.4 billion, and the quake is widely cited as the worst natural dis-

MOST MADE HOMELESS BY A HURRICANE   Hurricane Mitch, which
struck Central America in late 1998, caused 9,745 deaths and destroyed
93,690 dwellings. Approximately 2.5 million people were left
dependent on international aid efforts.

aster in Central American history. This disaster was almost matched by the
1972 Nicaraguan earthquake, which devastated the people of Managua
and caused $1.3 billion worth of material damage.

An earthquake on Japan's Kanto plain on September 1, 1923, destroyed
575,000 homes in Tokyo and Yokohama. The official figure for the number of people killed and missing due to the quake is 142,807.

Most People Trapped by Avalanches   A total of 240 people died and
more than 45,000 were trapped when a series of avalanches thundered
through the Swiss, Austrian, and Italian Alps on January 20, 1951. The
avalanches were caused by a combination of hurricane-force winds and wet
snow overlaying powder snow.

Most People Killed by Landslides   On May 31, 1970, about 18,000
people were killed by a landslide on the slopes of Huascaran in the Yungay
region of Peru, making it the most devastating single landslide in history.
Ten villages and most of the town of Yungay were buried by the landslide,
which was caused by an earthquake. It was one of the worst disasters of the
20th century in terms of the number of fatalities.

On December 16, 1920, a series of landslides triggered by a single earthquake that hit Gansu Province, China, killed about 180,000 people.

Most People Killed by a Volcanic Eruption   When the Tambora
volcano in Sumbawa, Indonesia (then the Dutch East Indies), erupted in
April 1815, 92,000 people were killed either directly or as a result of the
subsequent famine.

Most People Killed by a Flood   In October 1887, the Huang He (Yellow River) in Huayan Kou, China, flooded its banks, killing about 900,000 people. Despite causing devastating seasonal floods, the Huang He suffers from water shortages and is the biggest river to dry up. The river's dry periods are getting longer, jeopardizing 17.3 million acres of crops and the livelihoods of 52 million people.

Most Devastating Monsoons   Monsoons in Thailand in 1983 killed about 10,000 people and caused more than $396 million worth of damage. Up to 100,000 people are estimated to have contracted diseases, and about 15,000 people had to be evacuated from their homes.

Most Devastating Cyclone   Between 300,000 and 500,000 people are estimated to have died in the worst known cyclone, which hit East Pakistan (now Bangladesh) on November 12, 1970. Winds of up to 150 mph and a 50-ft.-high tidal wave lashed the coast, the Ganges Delta, and the offshore islands of Bhola, Hatia, Kukri Mukri, Manpura, and Rangabali.

Most People Killed by a Tornado   On April 26, 1989, approximately 1,300 people lost their lives, and as many as 50,000 people were made homeless when a tornado hit the town of Shaturia in Bangladesh.

Most People Killed by a Typhoon   Approximately 10,000 people died when a violent typhoon with winds of up to 100 mph struck Hong Kong on September 18, 1906.

Most People Killed by a Drought   A drought in China between 1876 and 1879 led to the deaths of between 9 million and 13 million people.

Most People Killed by a Geyser   In August 1903, four people were killed when Waimangu geyser in New Zealand erupted. The victims had been standing 90 ft. away

COSTLIEST NATURAL DISASTER   The Kobe earthquake of January 1995 resulted in overall losses of $100 billion, making it the costliest natural disaster to befall any one country. Japan, with its large fiscal resources and modern construction techniques, is relatively well prepared for the inevitable tremors that occur there due to its geographic location on the Pacific "Rim of Fire."

from it, but their bodies were found up to 875 yd. away. One was jammed between rocks, and another was suspended from a tree.

Most People Killed by a Lightning Strike   On December 8, 1963, a Boeing 707 jet airliner was struck by lightning near Elkton, Maryland, causing it to crash. A total of 81 passengers were killed.

ENVIRONMENTAL DISASTERS

Most Endangered Ecosystem   Western Asia's coastal zone is the most fragile ecosystem in the world, due to the decline of its coral reefs and forests. The region lost 11% of its natural forest in the 1980s, and many countries suffer from water scarcity. In addition, about 42 million gallons of oil are spilled into the Persian Gulf annually.

Most Contaminated Spot   Chelabinsk, Russia, is the most radioactive point on the planet and has probably been so since 1940, when the Mayak weapons complex was built. Since then, there have been three nuclear disasters in the area, affecting up to 500,000 people with levels of radiation similar to those in Chernobyl. Scientists designated it the most contaminated spot on Earth in 1992.

Biggest Toxic Dump   In February 1990, 2,721 tons of waste were found dumped near the seaport of Sihanoukville, Cambodia. The waste, which came from Taiwanese company Formosa Plastics Corp., contains unsafe levels of mercury. Several villagers who rummaged through the waste have complained of nausea, exhaustion, and stomach pains.

Biggest Toxic Cloud   In September 1990, a fire at a factory handling beryllium in Ust Kamenogorsk, USSR (now Kazakhstan), released a toxic cloud that extended at least as far as the Chinese border more than 190 miles away.

Worst Nuclear Accidents   The worst nuclear-reactor disaster ever took place at Chernobyl No. 4 in the USSR (now Ukraine), in 1986. Contamination was experienced over 10,900 miles^2, and about 1.7 million people were exposed to varying amounts of radiation. A total of 850,000 people are still living in contaminated areas.

The worst nuclear-waste accident occurred at Kyshtym, USSR (now Russia), in 1957, when an overheated waste container exploded, releasing radioactive compounds that dispersed over 8,900 miles^2. Within three years, more than 30 small communities within a 460-mile^2 radius were eliminated from maps of the USSR, and about 17,000 people were evacuated. Also, a total of 8,015 people died over 32 years of observation as a direct result of the nuclear accident.

Greatest Ozone Depletion   The largest "hole" in the ozone layer is above the Antarctic region. Each austral spring, a 14-mile-high area of ozone $1\frac{1}{4}$ times the size of the US disappears. Above this height, the

MOST POLLUTED MAJOR CITY Levels of sulfur dioxide, carbon monoxide, and suspended atmospheric particulate matter in Mexico City, the capital of Mexico, are more than double those deemed acceptable by the World Health Organization (WHO).

ozone is unaffected, so the gap is perhaps better described as a "thinning" than as a "hole."

Biggest Emissions of "Greenhouse Gases" The US is home to 4% of the world's population but produces 25% of the world's annual emissions of carbon dioxide and other greenhouse gases.

The biggest emitter of carbon dioxide in relation to its population is Luxembourg, which produces 18% more per head than the US.

Most Acidic Acid Rain A pH reading of 2.83 was recorded over the Great Lakes in the US and Canada in 1982.

Greatest Sulfur Dioxide Pollution The Maritsa power complex in Bulgaria releases a record 317,000 tons of the acidic gas sulfur dioxide into the River Maritsa every year. Sulfur dioxide is a major cause of acid rain.

Most Devastating Air Pollution More than 6,300 people have died from the effects of a poisonous cloud of methyl isocyanate that escaped from Union Carbide's pesticide plant near Bhopal, India, on December 3, 1984. The company made a settlement of $380.1 million to compensate victims and their relatives.

Biggest Threat to Ancient Forests About 80% of the world's large areas of ancient forest have been destroyed, mainly by big logging compa-

MOST DESTRUCTIVE FIRES   The worst year in recorded history for the destruction of the natural environment was 1997, mainly because of fires that were deliberately lit to clear forest areas but also because of fires resulting from the droughts caused by the El Niño effect in the Pacific. The largest and most numerous fires occurred in Brazil, where they raged on a 1,000-mile front. People from the Xingu Reservation, Mato Grosso, Brazil, are pictured surveying the damage caused by fires that burned more than 579 miles² of the state. About 11,600 miles² of Brazilian rain forest is also deliberately felled and burned by subsistence farmers and big business every year.

nies. The ancient forests contain 90% of the world's land-based species, and millions of flora and fauna species have been rendered extinct by their loss. In total, 76 countries have lost all of their ancient forest areas.

Worst Land Pollution   From February to October 1994, thousands of tons of crude oil flowed across the Arctic tundra of the Komi Republic, Russia. An estimated 91,000 tons of oil were lost in a slick up to 11 miles 325 yd. long.

Most Oil Spilled in a Year   The largest quantity of oil spilled into the sea in one year is 551,000 tons in 1979. The *Atlantic Empress* produced the biggest offshore oil spill that year when it collided with the *Aegean Captain* off the coast of Tobago in the Caribbean. It was responsible for 260,000 tons of the spillage.

Worst Coastal Oil Damage   The *Exxon Valdez* oil tanker ran aground in Prince William Sound, Alaska, in March 1989, spilling more than 27,000 tons of oil and polluting a 1,500-mile-long stretch of coast. The ship's owner, Exxon, was fined $5 billion and was ordered to pay a bill of $3 billion to clean up the damage and pollution.

Worst River Pollution   In November 1986, firefighters attending a blaze at the Sandoz chemical works in Basel, Switzerland, flushed 30 tons of agricultural chemicals into the Rhine, killing about 500,000 fish.

MOST CHEMICALLY POLLUTED TOWN The Russian town of Dzerzhinsk, which has a population of 287,000, is home to dozens of factories producing chlorine and pesticides. The Kaprolaktam plant in particular emits 544 tons of vinyl chlorine, a carcinogenic gas, every year. Greenpeace has named Dzerzhinsk the site of the worst chemical pollution in Russia and its lake—the source of the fish pictured here—the most poisonous in the world. Average life expectancy in the town is only 42 years for men and 47 for women.

Between 1953 and 1967, a plastics factory in Minimata Bay, Kyushu, Japan, deposited mercury waste into the sea. Up to 20,000 people were affected, and 4,500 were seriously harmed. Between 43 and 800 people died.

Worst Marine Pollution   Between 1953 and 1967, a plastics factory in Minimata Bay, Kyushu, Japan, deposited mercury waste into the sea. Up to 20,000 people were affected, and 4,500 were seriously harmed. Between 43 and 800 people died.

DISEASE, PLAGUES & EPIDEMICS

Deadliest Diseases   The deadliest disease is rabies encephalitis. The only known survivor of rabies was Matthew Winkler (US), who was bitten by a rabid animal in 1970.

The most widespread fatal disease of our era is Acquired Immune Deficiency Syndrome (AIDS), believed to result from the Human Immunodeficiency Virus (HIV). The virus has now caused more cases in heterosexuals than homosexuals. Recent research shows that some African victims apparently remain healthy after seemingly repeated exposure to the virus, offering hope that the epidemic may be conquered.

Yellow fever is a mosquito-borne infection prevalent in the Caribbean and Brazil and on the west coast of Africa. Some reports suggest it kills as many as 90% of those infected.

Oldest Diseases Cases of leprosy were described in ancient Egypt as early as 1350.

Tuberculosis schistosomiasi, an infectious disease of the liver and kidneys, has been discovered in Egyptian mummies from the 20th dynasty (1250 to 1000 B.C.).

Newest Germ The most recently discovered disease that infects humans is the prion, a malformed nerve protein that spreads through the brain cells. It produces a human spongiform encephalopathy known as new variant Creutzfeldt-Jakob Disease (*nv* CJD). In 1999, there were 40 cases, all of which were fatal.

Most Urgent Health Problem The World Health Organization (WHO) estimates that by 2020 tobacco-related illness will be the leading killer, responsible for more deaths than AIDS, tuberculosis, road accidents, murder, and suicide put together. Populations in developing countries face the greatest risk, as 85% of all smokers will come from the world's poorer countries by the mid-2020s. The WHO estimates that tobacco-related illness will be killing 7 million people per year in these countries by 2030.

Biggest Killer of Women Tuberculosis (TB) has now become the single biggest killer of women globally. It has been estimated that one-third of all women in Asia are infected with it. Some recently discovered strains are resistant to all conventional antibiotics.

FASTEST-GROWING DISEASE According to the UN AIDS report of December 1998, 5.8 million people were infected with HIV in that year. The number of people living with the virus had risen by 10% since 1997 to 33.4 million worldwide. India has the largest infected population— an estimated 4 million people. In the picture (left), protesters march through the Indian capital, New Delhi, demanding jobs and medical facilities for HIV and AIDS sufferers.

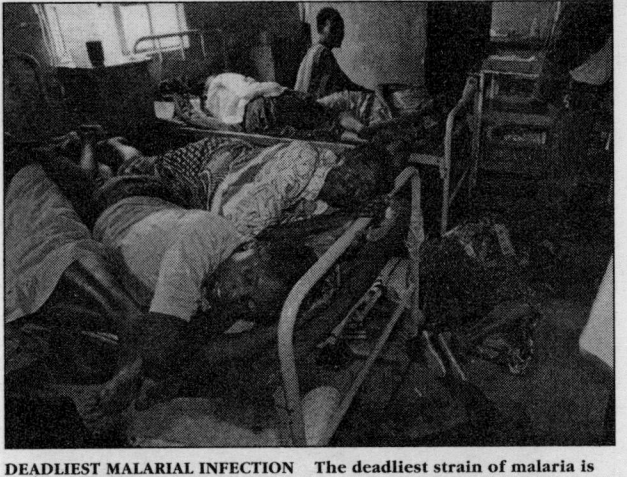

DEADLIEST MALARIAL INFECTION The deadliest strain of malaria is *Plasmodium falciparum*, which causes malignant tertian malaria. It can affect the brain, causing fits, coma or even sudden death. The women shown here, in Kisii, Kenya, were among thousands hospitalized in a malaria outbreak after four months of unseasonal rain—possibly due to the El Niño weather phenomenon—caused extensive flooding in the northeast and west of the country. Over 14,000 Kenyans were diagnosed as having contracted the infection, and, according to United Nations and Oxfam reports, 1,500 people died of the disease between December 1997 and February 1998. The problem was exacerbated by the fact that Kenya has more drug-resistant mosquitoes than any other country on the African continent.

Most Successful Immunization Campaign The WHO declared the world free of smallpox on January 1, 1980. Formerly one of the world's deadliest plagues (it caused an estimated 2 million deaths per year in the mid-1960s), smallpox was eradicated by the availability of one type of vaccine that was effective against all forms of the disease. The last known death from smallpox was in August 1978, when a medical photographer at Birmingham University, England, was infected with a sample kept for research purposes.

Most Resurgent Disease The deterioration in health services following the collapse of the Soviet Union in 1991 has been a major factor in the spread of diphtheria in the area. The International Red Cross estimates that there were between 150,000 and 200,000 cases in the countries of the former USSR in 1997. This compares with 2,000 cases in the Soviet Union in 1991. Cases of tuberculosis and cholera are also increasing rapidly there.

Deadliest Flu Outbreak A record 21.64 million people died of influenza in 1918 and 1919.

Deadliest Avian Flu Outbreak Avian flu, a strain of influenza previously only known to affect birds, was found to have infected 16 people in

DEADLIEST PANDEMIC A rat catcher in Dan Phuong, Vietnam, holds specimens he has caught. Migrating Asian black rats, infested with fleas carrying the *Yersinia pestis* bacterium, caused the Black Death that killed up to half the population of Europe in the 14th century.

Hong Kong, China in 1997. Four people died from the virus, which is the first to have been passed directly from birds to humans.

Deadliest E. Coli Outbreak Twenty people died, and 500 became ill after consuming contaminated meat from a butcher's shop in Wishaw, Scotland, in 1998. It was infected with *Escherichia coli* O157-H7, a dangerous strain of a normally harmless bacterium, which is believed to be transmitted by food.

More than 9,500 cases of *E. coli* food poisoning were reported in Japan during an outbreak in the summer of 1996. Eleven people died as a result of becoming infected by O157-H7.

Deadliest Ebola Outbreak The highest known toll in an Ebola fever outbreak is 232 fatalities out of 296 possible cases in the Democratic Republic of Congo (ex-Zaïre) in 1995. The disease causes massive bleeding and throws the body into shock.

Greatest Incidence of Leprosy The country with the most cases of leprosy is Brazil, with 160,000 cases per annum; that is 10.2 people per 100,000 of the population. Leprosy causes damage to the skin and nerves.

Most People Killed by Infection The West African island-republic of Sao Tome and Principe has a record 241 deaths per annum through infectious diseases for every 100,000 people.

Leading Cause of Death   Diseases of the heart and blood account for more than 50% of all deaths in industrialized nations. The most prevalent direct causes of death are heart attacks and strokes.

ANIMAL ATTACK

Most Dangerous Animal   Malarial parasites of the genus *Plasmodium* carried by mosquitoes of the genus *Anopheles* have probably been responsible for half of all human deaths since the Stone Age, excluding those caused by wars and accidents. According to 1997 World Health Organization estimates, malaria is still causing 1.5 million deaths every year.

Most Poisonous Animal   Poison arrow frogs (*Dendrobates* and *Phyllobates*) from South and Central America secrete some of the deadliest biological toxins in the world. The skin secretion of the golden poison arrow frog (*Phyllobates terribilis*) is the most poisonous of all. Scientists have to wear thick gloves when handling specimens.

Most Venomous Snake   The most venomous snake in the world is Belcher's sea snake (*Hydrophis belcheri*) from the region around Ashmore

BIGGEST PREDATORY FISH   The largest predatory fish is the rare Great White shark (*Carcharodon carcharias*). Adult specimens average 14 ft. 9 in. in length and generally weigh about 1,433 lb. There is evidence to suggest that some Great Whites grow to more than 20 ft. in length.

Reef off northwestern Australia. Its myotoxic venom is many times more potent than the venom of any land snake.

The most venomous land snake is the 5-ft.-7-in.-long small-scaled snake (*Oxyuranus microlepidotus*) of western Australia, which is closely related to the taipan. One specimen can yield enough venom to kill 250,000 mice.

Most Venomous Spider   The Brazilian huntsman (*Phoneutria fera*) has the most active neurotoxic venom of any spider. Large and aggressive, huntsmen hide in clothing or shoes and bite furiously several times if disturbed. Hundreds of accidents involving the Brazilian huntsman are reported annually, but an antivenin is now available. Most of the deaths that do occur are of children under the age of seven.

Most Poisonous Fish   The death puffer fish or maki-maki (*Arothron hispidus*) of the Red Sea and Indo-Pacific region contains a deadly toxin called tetrodotoxin, one of the most powerful nonproteinous poisons. Less than 0.004 oz. of this poison—which is contained in the fish's ovaries, eggs, blood, liver, intestines, and skin—is enough to kill an adult human in as little as 20 minutes.

The stonefish (*Synanceia horrida*), found in the tropical waters of the Indo-Pacific, has the largest venom glands of any known fish. Contact with the spines of its fins, which contain neurotoxic poison, can be fatal for humans.

Most Ferocious Fish   Razor-toothed piranhas of the genera *Serrasalmus* and *Pygocentrus* will attack any creature that is injured or makes a commotion in the water, regardless of its size. In 1981, more than 300 people are reported to have been eaten by piranhas when an overloaded boat capsized and sank while docking at Obidos, Brazil.

Most Shocking Fish   The electric eel or paroque (*Electrophorus electricus*) lives in freshwater in Brazil and the Guiana. Live from head to tail, it has two pairs of longitudinal organs that can release an electric shock of up to 650 volts. This force is strong enough to light an electric bulb or incapacitate an adult human.

Most Venomous Jellyfish   The cardiotoxic venom of the Flecker's sea wasp or box jellyfish (*Chironex fleckeri*) has killed at least 70 people off the coast of Australia in the last hundred years. If medical aid is unavailable, some victims have been known to die within four minutes. One effective defense is women's hosiery—the jellyfish's stinging cells cannot penetrate the material.

Most Dangerous Sea Urchin   Toxin from the spines and pedicels (small pincerlike organs) of the flower sea urchin (*Toxopneustes pileolus*) causes severe pain, respiratory problems, and paralysis in humans.

Most Dangerous Bee   The venom of the hybrid Africanized honeybee (*Apis mellifera scutellata*) is no more potent than that of other bees, but the number of stings that the species inflicts when in swarms is sometimes sufficient to kill humans.

Most Venomous Centipede   In the Solomon Islands, there is a peculiarly dangerous form of centipede called *Scolopendra subspinipes*. So potent is its venom, injected into its victim by a modified pair of front limbs

MOST DANGEROUS CROCODILIAN The saltwater crocodile (*Crocodylus porosus*) kills an estimated 2,000 people every year, although most of these deaths go unrecorded. The largest reputed death toll in a crocodile attack occurred toward the end of World War II on the night of February 19, 1945. Allied troops invaded Ramree Island off the coast of Burma (now Myanmar), trapping between 800 and 1,000 Japanese infantrymen in a coastal mangrove swamp. By the following morning, only 20 of the Japanese soldiers were still alive: most of the rest are believed to have been eaten alive by crocodiles.

rather than by its jaws, that human victims have been known to plunge their bitten hands into boiling water in order to mask the pain.

Most Dangerous Ant Native to South America, the fire ant (*Solenopsis invicta*) first reached the US in the 1930s in ships carrying soil. In May 1998, an estimated 23,000 rainbow trout were killed after ingesting fire ants in a 15-mile stretch of the Guadalupe River in central Texas. The fire ant is attracted to electrical sources and often bites through insulation, causing electricity blackouts and fires.

Most Venomous Lizards Unusually for lizards, both the Gila monster (*Heloderma suspectum*) of Mexico and the southwestern US and its close relative the Mexican beaded lizard (*H. horridum*) from western coastal Mexico have a venomous bite. The venom contained in their glands is powerful enough to kill two adult humans.

Most Dangerous Small Mammals The small mammals that pose the most danger to humans are rats. More than 20 pathogens are carried by them, including the bacterium that causes the bubonic plague, or "Black Death." They also carry leptospirosis (Weil's disease), Lassa fever, rat-bite fever, and murine typhus, all of which can be fatal.

Most Dangerous Bear The only species of bear that actively preys on humans is the polar bear (*Ursus maritimus*). Most attacks occur during the

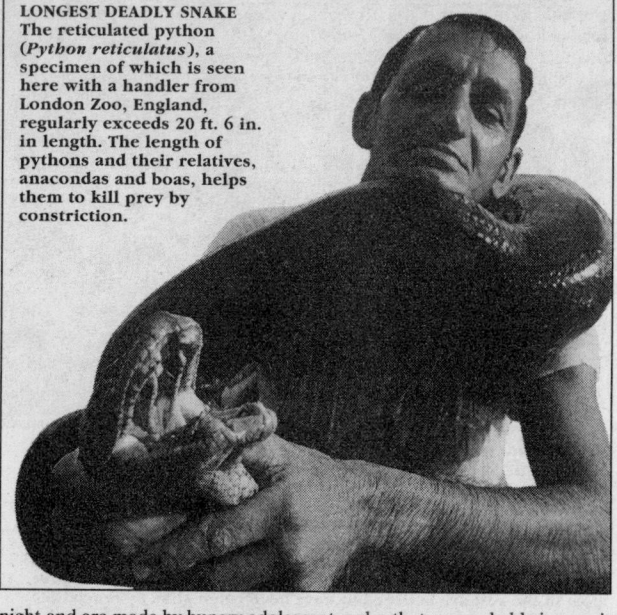

LONGEST DEADLY SNAKE
The reticulated python (*Python reticulatus*), a specimen of which is seen here with a handler from London Zoo, England, regularly exceeds 20 ft. 6 in. in length. The length of pythons and their relatives, anacondas and boas, helps them to kill prey by constriction.

night and are made by hungry adolescent males that are probably inexperienced hunters and are likely to have been driven from their usual prey by larger bears.

Most Dangerous Big Cat Tigers attack humans more frequently than other cats do, probably because humans fall within the natural size range of a tiger's prey and are fairly easy to catch, even for old or injured tigers.

Strongest Animal Bite Experiments carried out with a "Snodgrass gnathodynamometer" (shark-bite meter) at the Lerner Marine Laboratory in Bimini, Bahamas, revealed that a dusky shark (*Carcharhinus obscurus*) 6 ft. 6 in. long could exert a force of 132 lb. between its jaws. This is equivalent to a pressure of 19.6 tons/in.^{2} at the tips of the teeth. The bites of larger sharks, such as the Great White (*Carcharodon carcharias*), must be considerably stronger but have never been measured.

PARASITES

Longest Tapeworm The broad or fish tapeworm, *Diphyllobothrium latum*, which lives in the small intestine of fish and sometimes humans, can reach 40 ft. in length. Over 10 years, it would shed bodily segments 5 miles long and release about 2 billion eggs.

Taeniarhynchus saginatus, the beef tapeworm, usually grows to about 16 ft. However, the largest known specimen was 75 ft. long—three times longer than a human intestine.

Biggest Tick   Ticks are parasitic arachnids that prey on mammals and birds. They swell up as they suck blood through the skin. The largest belong to the suborder Ixodida and can measure 1²/₅ in. in length when fully bloated.

Biggest Fluke   A didymozoid digenean species *Nematobibothriodes histoidii* found in the body wall tissues of the sunfish *Mola mola* can grow to 40 ft. long.

Biggest Roundworm   The world's largest parasitic species of nematode or roundworm is *Placentonema gigantissimus*, which can reach a length of 25 ft. It inhabits the placenta of sperm whales.

Biggest Flea   The giant flea *Hystrichopsylla schefferi*, dubbed "super flea," can measure ½ in. in length. Its only known host is the North American mountain beaver *Aplodontia rufa*.

Biggest Leech   *Haementeria ghilianii*, an Amazonian leech, grows up to 1 ft. in length.

Biggest Parasitic Protozoans in Humans *Balantidium coli*, which sometimes lives in the large intestine of humans, is only ⁴/₁₂₅ in. x ³/₁₂₅ in length.

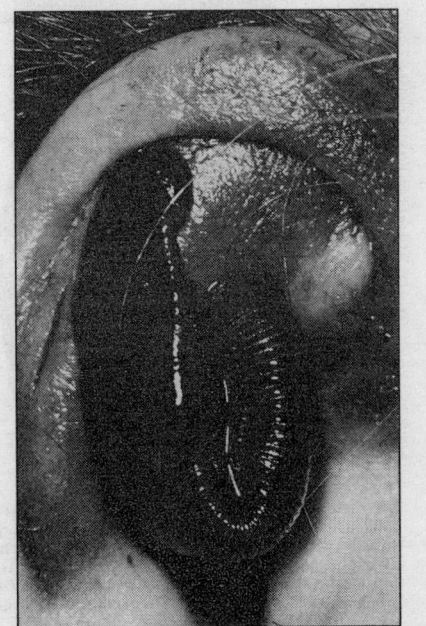

MOST USEFUL PARASITE   The medicinal leech *Hirudo medicinalis*, traditionally used by doctors for bloodletting, has made a comeback. In 1991, a team of Canadian surgeons led by Dr. Dean Vistnes took advantage of the anticoagulants in leeches' saliva to drain away blood and prevent it from clotting during an operation to reattach a patient's scalp. The animals used in these procedures have been specially cultured in sterile conditions.

Longest Thorny-Headed Worm Acanthocephalan (or thorny-headed) worms are usually no more than 1 in. long, but at over 3 ft. in length, female specimens of *Nephridiacanthus longissimus* are the world's longest acanthocephalan worms. Each species of thorny-headed worm inhabits different species—*Nephridiacanthus longissimus* inhabits the intestines of aardvarks.

Most Bloodthirsty Parasites The indistinguishable eggs of the hookworms *Ancylostoma duodenale* and *Necator americanus* are found in the feces of 1.3 billion people worldwide. In cases of heavy infestation, the lining of the gut is so thickly covered with worms that they look like the pile of a carpet. The bleeding that results from their feeding adds up to a total of 10 million liters of blood worldwide every day.

Longest-Living Parasite A life span of 27 years has been reliably recorded for the medicinal leech *Hirudo medicinalis*.

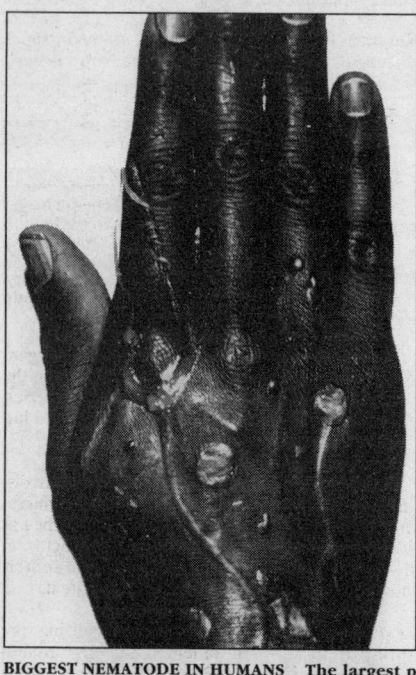

Longest Parasitic Fasts The common bedbug *Cimex lectularius*, which feeds on human blood, is famously able to survive without feeding for more than a year. However, the soft tick *Ornithodoros turicata* (which spreads the spirochete that causes relapsing fever) can survive periods of up to five years without food.

Most Parasitized Host Species *Stagnicola emarginata*, a type of freshwater snail from the Great Lakes in the US and Canada, transmits parasites that cause swimmer's itch. This snail is a host for the larvae of at least 35 species of parasitic fluke.

BIGGEST NEMATODE IN HUMANS The largest parasitic nematode found in humans is the Guinea worm *Dracunculus medinensis*, a subcutaneous species whose females can reach 3 ft. 11 in. in length. The elongated adult worms spend their lives traveling through the human body and eventually emerge through blisters in the skin to shed eggs. As seen here, the worms can then gradually be wound out of the body on a stick.

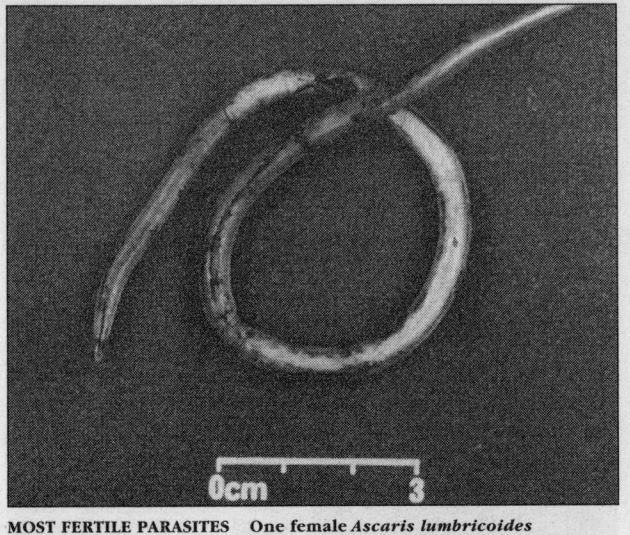

0cm   **3**

MOST FERTILE PARASITES One female *Ascaris lumbricoides*
roundworm (above) can produce up to 200,000 eggs every day of her
adult life and has a total productive capacity of 26 million eggs. The
body of the beef tapeworm *Taeniarhynchus saginatus,* meanwhile,
can consist of more than 1,000 segments, each of which contains
approximately 80,000 eggs. A human host infected with a single
specimen (which can live for up to 25 years) is liable to excrete about
nine of the constantly renewed segments, and therefore approximately
720,000 eggs, each day.

Most Adaptable Fluke Most flukes infect very few different organ-
isms, but the liver fluke *Fasciola hepatica* has been found as an adult in the
liver, gall bladder, and associated ducts in a range of mammalian species,
including sheep, cattle, goats, pigs, horses, rabbits, squirrels, dogs, and humans.

Most Significant New Parasite Many new species of parasites are discovered every year, but none more zoologically significant than a microscopic ectoparasite known as *Symbion pandora.* Discovered living on the lips
of the scampi lobster *Nephrops norvegicus,* it is fundamentally distinct from
all other groups of animals—so much so that, in December 1995, an entirely
new phylum, the Cycliophora, was created in order to accommodate it.

Most Successful Parasitic Worm in Humans Parasitizing the
small intestine and measuring up to 1 ft. 6 in. in length, the large roundworm *Ascaris lumbricoides* infects approximately 25% of the world's human
population. Victims are usually infected with an average of 10–20 specimens, though much higher numbers have been recorded. The simultaneous migration of large quantities of *Ascaris* larvae through the lungs can
cause severe hemorrhagic pneumonia.

DANGEROUS & STRANGE PLANTS

Most Poisonous Plant The castor-oil plant (*Ricinus communis*), which is cultivated worldwide to make castor oil, contains ricin, the most lethal plant poison. A single seed weighing $^9/_{1,000}$ oz. (0.25 g.) is enough to kill a human being. If the poison is injected, $^1/_{10,000,000}$ oz. per 14 lb. of body weight is fatal.

Most Dangerous Trees The manchineel tree (*Hippomane mancinella*) of the Caribbean coast and the Florida Everglades has had an evil reputation since Spanish explorers learned to fear it in the 16th century. The whole tree exudes a highly poisonous and caustic sap, once used as an arrow poison. One drop in the eye can blind a person, and one bite of the fruit causes blistering and severe pain. The slightest contact causes the skin to erupt in blisters.

For sheer numbers of victims, nothing rivals *Toxicodendron*, the genus that includes poison oak and poison ivy. Both produce the poison urushiol, which causes severe skin reactions in millions of Americans every year and is a major cause of disability in people who work outdoors.

Most Poisonous Flower All parts of the attractive oleander (*Nerium oleander*), a plant common throughout the world, are extremely dangerous. Bees that gather too much nectar from its flowers make poisonous honey,

BIGGEST CACTUS The largest cactus is the saguaro (*Cereus giganteus* or *Carnegiea gigantea*) found in the southwestern US. The green fluted column is surmounted by candelabra-like branches rising to a height of 57 ft. 11 in. in a specimen discovered in the Maricopa Mountains, near Gila Bend, Arizona, on January 17, 1988. The characteristic spines that protect many species of cactus from animal attack are actually reduced leaves.

ITCHIEST CACTUS *Opuntia robusta*, native to Mexico and more commonly known as the prickly pear, has bristles barbed like bee stingers. They are used to make the world's itchiest itching powder.

and people have died after eating meat cooked on skewers made from oleander wood.

Most Carcinogenic Plant The microscopic fungus *Aspergillus flavus* produces aflatoxin B1, one of the most powerful carcinogens known. As little as $^1/_{3,333,333}$ oz. triggers liver cancer in rats. *A. flavus* contaminates certain foodstuffs, most notoriously peanuts.

Most Fatal Fungi The toadstool *Galerina sulcipes* is the world's most lethal fungus, with a fatality rate of 72% in humans who eat it.

The yellowish-olive death cap (*Amanita phalloides*), which can be found worldwide, is responsible for 90% of the fatal poisonings caused by fungi. Its total toxin content is 0.105–0.135 grains dry weight. The estimated lethal amount of amanitins for humans, depending on body weight, is 0.075–0.105 grains, which is equivalent to less than 1¾ oz. of a fresh fungus. The death cap belongs to a group that contains both edible and poisonous fungi. The effects of eating it are vomiting, delirium, collapse, and ultimately death after 6–15 hours.

Nastiest Stingers New Zealand's tree nettle (*Urtica ferox*) can kill a horse. Its stinging hairs inject a mixture of potent poisons. In 1961, a man in New Zealand's hill country stumbled into the plant and, by the time he got to the hospital, was blind, paralyzed and had severe breathing problems. He died within five hours.

Australia's stinging trees, armed with large hollow hairs on their leaves and twigs, are as feared as New Zealand's tree nettle. The worst, the gympie bush (*Dendrocnide moroides*), causes intense stabbing pains that can recur months later.

Nastiest Underwater Stinger   Toxins produced by *Lyngbya majuscula*, a fine, hairlike blue-green alga found worldwide, cause a burn-like rash known as sea bather's dermatitis. In severe cases, the skin blisters and peels, and the victim suffers irritation of the eyes, nose, and throat, skin sores, headache, and tiredness. Sores can last two weeks. However, its toxins are being investigated as a cure for cancer.

Most Damaging Weed   The weed that attacks the largest number of crops in the most countries is the purple nut grass or nutsedge (*Cyperus rotundus*). The land weed is native to India but attacks 52 crops in 92 countries.

Earliest Botanical Weapon   The Christmas rose (*Helleborus niger*) is said to have played a part in breaking the siege of Kirra in central Greece in 600 B.C. The attackers added poisonous hellebore roots to the town's water supply, triggering an outbreak of severe diarrhea in the defending troops, who gave up the fight.

Fastest-Acting Plant Trap   The *Utricularia* genus of plants has the fastest-acting trap of any plant. The underwater plant acts by sucking its prey into its bladders in 0.03 seconds.

Smallest Plant Prey   The underground leaves of *Genlisea* have recently been discovered to capture and digest soil-dwelling protozoa. Attracted by a chemical lure, thousands of microorganisms a day squeeze through microscopic slits to the interior of the leaf, where the plant produces digestive juices. This is the only known example of a plant feeding on microscopic animals.

Best Animal Mimic   Some orchids famously imitate the bees and wasps that pollinate them. The best mimic is *Drakaea glyptodon*, a hammer orchid from western Australia, which has flowers that look like wingless female thynnid wasps and produce an identical pheromone to the insect's. When a male wasp finds a mate, he grabs her around the waist and carries her off. If he grabs a dragon orchid by mistake, the hinged lip of the flower hurls him against the pollen-bearing sex organs so that sacs of pollen stick to him. If the wasp then approaches another orchid, he delivers the sacs and pollinates the flower.

Most Unusual Pollination   Flowers of *Microloma sagittatum*, a South African milkweed, clip packages of pollen to the tip of a sunbird's tongue with a snap-lock device. The bird carries this pollen to the next flower inside its beak. All other identical milkweeds are pollinated by insects.

Hardiest Plant   *Buellia frigida*, a lichen that lives in the Antarctic, can survive the temperature of liquid nitrogen (−321°F). Along with the world's most southerly plant, *Lecidea cancriformis* (found at latitude 86°S), it endures natural temperatures as low as –94°F in winter and 86°F in summer, a range of 180°F. These hardy lichens can carry out photosynthesis between –4°F and 68°F.

Biggest Carnivorous Plants Plants of the *Nepenthes* genus have vines that reach a length of up to 33 ft., making them the largest species of carnivorous plant. They capture some of the biggest prey of any plants, including creatures as large as frogs.

MOST DEVIOUS PLANT *Sarracenia leucophylla* **uses a series of lures to trap and digest insects. Around the mouth of each tube is an array of glands producing sweet-smelling nectar surrounding patterns of glistening tissue that attract flies. The tube is lined with downward-pointing hairs so that, once the flies have alighted, they find it impossible to escape. Their struggle weakens them to the point of exhaustion, and they drop into a pool of powerful enzymes that digests them alive.**

SPORTS

EXTREME SPORTS: AIR

Biggest Bungee Jump   On September 19, 1997, Jochen Schweizer (Germany) made a bungee jump from a height of 1 mile 974 yd. above the town of Reichelsheim, near Frankfurt, Germany. Making the jump from an SA 365 Dauphine helicopter, Schweizer used a 931-ft.-9-in.-long bungee cord. The first free-fall phase, using the cord, covered 1,246 ft. 8 in.—the cord had a natural expansion length of more than 311 ft. 6 in., allowing Schweizer to jump a total distance of 3,320 ft. 3 in. The jump out of the helicopter to the lower turning point took 17 seconds. Schweizer detached at 1 mile and then free-fell for 16 seconds, opening his parachute at an altitude of 2,952 ft.

Highest Land-Based Bungee Jump   David Kirke, a member of the Oxford University Dangerous Sports Club in England, leaped from the Royal Gorge Bridge, Colorado, in 1980. The distance from the jump point to the ground was 1,050 ft. Kirke used 420 ft. of unstretched bungee rope in the attempt.

Highest Toy Balloon Flight   In September 1987, Ian Ashpole (UK) set a world altitude record for toy balloon flight when he reached a height of 1 mile 1,575 yd. over Ross-on-Wye, England. Ashpole was lifted to the target altitude by the hot-air balloon *Mercier*. When he

BIGGEST MASS BUNGEE JUMP
On September 6, 1998, 25 people jumped from a 170-ft. platform suspended in front of the twin towers of the Deutsche Bank headquarters in Frankfurt, Germany. The event, organized by the Frankfurt City Council, was part of a "skyscraper festival" held to draw public attention to the city's modern architecture and burgeoning business district. The people involved in the jump were volunteers who had been attending the festival.

BIGGEST MASS FREE-FALL FORMATION On July 26, 1998, a record 246 sky divers came together for 7.3 seconds in the sky above Ottawa, Illinois, to set a new world record for the world's largest free-fall formation.

reached the desired height, he cut himself free from the balloon, then one by one from the 400 helium-filled toy balloons that suspended him in midair. Once freed from all the balloons, he free-fell at a speed of approximately 90 mph before parachuting to a safe landing on the ground.

Highest Balloon Sky Walk Mike Howard (UK) walked on an aluminum bar between two hot-air balloons at a height of 3 miles 986 yd. over Marshall, Michigan, on May 4, 1998. He used only a pole for balance and no safety ropes. The feat was later shown on the TV show *Guinness® World Records: Primetime*.

Longest Formation Skydiving Sequence (Four-Way) Thierry Boiteux, Marin Ferre, Marial Ferre, and David Moy (France) arranged themselves into 36 different formations while free-falling over Pujaut, France, on June 27, 1997.

Most Jumps by a Sky Surfer Eric Fradet from Le Tignet, France, has logged 17,200 jumps, including 4,700 sky-surfing jumps and 500 team jumps, since 1976.

Most Parachuting Descents Cheryl Stearns (US) holds the record for the most descents undertaken by a woman, with 12,800, mainly over the US, up to the end of 1998.

Longest Delayed Drops by Parachute Joseph Kittinger made the longest delayed parachute drop ever, falling 16 miles from a balloon at an altitude of 19 miles 872 yd. over Tularosa, New Mexico, on August 16, 1960.
   Elvira Fomitcheva (USSR) made the longest delayed parachute drop ever by a woman, falling 9 miles 352 yd. in the skies over Odessa, USSR (now Ukraine), on October 26, 1977.

Longest Parachute Fall   William Rankin fell for a record 40 minutes over North Carolina on July 26, 1956. The great length of the fall was due to thermals.

Highest Parachute Base Jump   Glenn Singleman and Nicholas Feteris jumped from a 3-mile-1,102-yd. ledge on the Great Trango Tower, Kashmir, on August 26, 1992.

Biggest Parachute Canopy Stack   The world's largest canopy stack ever involved a total of 53 people from a number of countries over Kassel, Germany, in September 1996. They held the stack for six seconds.

Longest Upside-Down Flight   The longest period spent flying in an inverted position was 4 hr. 38 min. 10 sec. The record was set by Joann Osterud, who flew between Vancouver and Vanderhoof, British Columbia, Canada, in July 1991.

Most Inside Loops During Flight   David Childs (US) achieved a record 2,368 inside loops in a Bellanca Decathalon. He performed the feat over Alaska on August 9, 1986.

Most Outside Loops   Joann Osterud made a total of 208 outside loops in a "Supernova" Hyperbipe over North Bend, Oregon, on July 13, 1989.

Longest Microlight Distance   The greatest distance ever covered in a straight line by a microlight was 1,011 miles 845 yd. The record was set by Wilhelm Lischak (Austria), flying from Volsau, Austria, to Brest, France, on June 8, 1988.

Greatest Microlight Altitude   The record for the greatest altitude ever reached in a microlight is 6 miles 70 yd. by Serge Zin (France). He achieved this over Saint Auban, France, in 1994.

HIGHEST BUNGEE JUMP FROM A BUILDING
In October 1998, A.J. Hackett made a 590-ft.-11-in. jump from the Sky Tower, the highest building in Auckland, New Zealand. He attached himself to two steel cables to avoid hitting the tower. Hackett was also the first man to bungee jump from the Eiffel Tower and from a helicopter.

MOST PARACHUTE DESCENTS Don Kellner (US) holds the record for the most parachuting descents. By 1998, he had completed 26,000. It is estimated that the human body reaches 99% of its low-level terminal velocity after falling 1,880 ft.

Longest Paragliding Flights The men's paragliding distance world record is 179 miles 1,703 yd., achieved by Will Gadd (US) on May 30, 1998.

The greatest distance flown by a female paraglider is 177 miles 169 yd., by Kat Thurston (UK) at Kuruman, South Africa, on December 25, 1995.

The greatest distance flown on a tandem paraglider is 124 miles 493 yd., by Richard and Guy Westgate (UK) at Kuruman, South Africa, on December 23, 1995.

Greatest Paraglider Height Gains The height-gain record is 2 miles 1,429 yd., by British paraglider Robby Whittal at Brandvlei, South Africa, on January 6, 1993.

The greatest height gained by a woman is 2 miles 1,209 yd., by Kat Thurston (UK) at Kuruman, South Africa, on January 1, 1996.

The record for the greatest height gained with a tandem paraglider is 2 miles 1,271 yd., set by Richard and Guy Westgate (UK) at Kuruman, South Africa, on January 1, 1996.

Longest Hang Glides The record for the greatest straight-line distance is 307 miles 1,165 yd., by Larry Tudor (US) from Rock Springs, Wyoming, on July 1, 1994.

The greatest distance by a woman is 219 miles 715 yd., by Tiki Mashy (US) on June 19, 1998.

Greatest Height by a Hang Glider Larry Tudor (US) gained 2 miles 1,232 yd. over Owens Valley, California, in 1985.

EXTREME SPORTS: LAND

Fastest Skateboarders Gary Hardwick from Carlsbad, California, set a skateboard record of 62.55 mph at Fountain Hills, Arizona, on September 26, 1998. The event was sanctioned by Alternative International Sports, based in Phoenix, Arizona.

Eleftherios Argiropoulos covered 271 miles 510 yd. in 36 hr. 33 min. 17 sec. at Ekali, Greece, from November 4 to 5, 1993.

Highest Skateboard Jump The skateboarding high-jump record is 5 ft. 5¾ in. by Trevor Baxter (UK) on September 14, 1982, at Grenoble, France.

LONGEST SKATEBOARD JUMP Tony Alva set a long-jump record of 17 ft., clearing 17 barrels at the World Professional Skateboard Championships held at Long Beach, California, on September 25, 1977.

FASTEST STREET LUGER On May 29, 1998, Tom Mason (left) from Van Nuys, California, set an official world record for street luge when he achieved a speed of 81.28 mph at Mount Whitney, California. Mason, who took up street luge in 1995, set the record on a 23-lb. board and was timed by Bob Pererya from the street luge sanctioning body RAIL (Road Racing Association for International Luge). RAIL was formed in 1990 and is based in Los Angeles, California. The association currently has over 100 members, both racing and non-racing.

Biggest Mountain-Board Spin While doing a 360° aerial spin during competition in Big Bear, California, Mike Reinoehl (US) reached a height of about 7 ft. and covered a distance of about 20 ft.

Fastest Butt Boarder Darren Lott of Tustin, California, achieved a record speed of 65.24 mph on a butt board in Fountain Hills, Arizona, on September 26, 1998.

Highest Jump on In-Line Skates The record for the highest jump ever on in-line skates is 8 ft. 11 in., by Randolph Sandoz (Switzerland) at Amsterdam, Netherlands, on December 15, 1996.

Fastest Backwards Roller Skater Jay Edington achieved a record speed of 46.69 mph while roller skating backwards in his home town of Fountain Hills, Arizona, on September 26, 1998.

Fastest In-Line Skating Road Times Eddy Matzger (US) skated 21 miles 1,126 yd. and set the one-hour record at Long Beach, California, in February 1991.

Jonathan Seutter (US) holds the 12-hour road record, having covered a distance of 177 miles 1,109 yd. at Long Beach, California, on February 2, 1991.

Kimberly Ames (US) set the 24-hour road record when she skated 283 miles 123 yd. in Portland, Oregon, on October 2, 1994.

Highest In-Line Skating Speed Graham Wilkie and Jeff Hamilton (both US) both achieved a speed of 64.02 mph in Arizona on September 26, 1998, in an official attempt sanctioned by Alternative International Sports.

Fastest Street Skier The highest speed achieved downhill on a public road on an in-line wheeled frame not exceeding 42 in. in length and attached to the feet by ski bindings and boots is 63 mph, by Douglas Lucht (US) on Golden Eagle Boulevard, Fountain Hills, Arizona, on March 7, 1998.

Fastest Roller-Skiing Relay The greatest distance achieved by a team of four roller skiers in 24 hours is 303 miles 1,223 yd., by a team of four at RAF Alconbury, England, from May 23 to 24, 1998.

Fastest Sand Boarders Nancy Sutton (US) was clocked at 44.7 mph at Sand Mountain, Nevada, on September 19, 1998.

Marco Malaga (Peru) attained a speed of 44.2 mph—the highest speed by a man—at Dumont Dunes, California, on November 26, 1998.

Most Sand-Boarding World Championships Marco Malaga (Peru) holds the world record for the most sand-boarding World Championships won by a man, with three wins (1996, 1997, and 1998) in championships sanctioned by Dune Riders International, the world governing body for sand boarders.

Julie Pilcic (US) is the female record holder, having won three World Championships (1996, 1997, and 1998).

MOUNTAIN-BIKING WORLD CUP WINS The most cross-country World Cup wins by a man is 15, by Thomas Frischknecht (Switzerland, above) from 1991 to 1998.

Fastest Sand Yachters The official top speed reached in a sand yacht is 66.48 mph, by Christian-Yves Nau (France) in *Mobil* at Le Touquet,

MOST MOUNTAIN-BOARDING TITLES Jason T. Lee (US) won the overall titles at Dirt Duel '97 and Dirt Duel '98, the mountain-boarding World Championship. Lee had the fastest qualifying times at both events and has had the fastest times at all but one event in the past four years of local and national races.

France, on March 22, 1981.

Most Mountain-Biking World Championships The record for the most downhill World Championship wins by a man is seven, by Nicolas Vouilloz (France): three in the junior championship from 1992 to 1994 and four in the senior class from 1995 to 1998.

The most downhill wins by a woman is five, by Anne-Caroline Chausson (France)—two in the junior championship in 1994 and 1995 and three in the senior class from 1996 to 1998.

The most cross-country wins is three, by Henrik Djernis (Denmark) from 1992 to 1994 and by Alison Sydor (Canada) from 1994 to 1996.

Most Mountain-Bike World Cup Wins The most mountain-biking cross-country World Cup wins by a woman is 28, by Juli Furtado (US) from 1991 to 1996.

The most downhill World Cup wins by a woman is 13, by Anne-Caroline Chausson (France) from 1993 to 1998.

The most downhill World Cup wins by a man is seven, by Nicolas Vouilloz (France) from 1992 to 1998.

Highest Bunny Hop The highest bunny hop achieved on a mountain bike was 45 in., by Steve Geall (UK) on April 18, 1998.

Most Dirt-Jumping Titles Ryan Nyquist from Los Gatos, California, has won the National Bicycle League's Dirt Circuit, the Pioneer King of Dirt, and the K2 Pro Dirt Jump Series and has been crowned the ABA King of Dirt.

EXTREME SPORTS: WATER

Biggest Surfing Competition   The G-Shock US Open of Surfing, which takes place at Huntington Beach, California, is generally regarded as the biggest surfing competition in the world today. The competition, which forms part of the world qualifying series, has attracted an average of 200,000 spectators every year since it started in 1994 and has about 700 competitors. The total prize money is $155,000. Of this, $100,000 goes to the winner of the men's surfing contest, and $15,000 goes to the winner of the women's contest.

Most World Professional Series Surfing Titles   The men's title has been won six times by Kelly Slater (US) in 1992 and from 1994 to 1998.

The women's professional title has been won a record four times by Frieda Zamba (US), 1984–86 and 1988; Wendy Botha (Australia, formerly of South Africa), 1987, 1989, 1991, and 1992; and Lisa Anderson (Australia), 1993–96.

Most World Amateur Championship Surfing Titles   The most titles is three, by Michael Novakov (Australia) in the Kneeboard event in 1982, 1984, and 1986.

The most world amateur championship surfing titles won by a woman is two, by Joyce Hoffman (US) in 1965 and 1966 and Sharon Weber (US) in 1970 and 1972.

MOST SUCCESSFUL WAKE BOARDERS   Tara Hamilton (US, above) became women's wake-board World Champion in 1998. Shaun Murray (US) became men's World Champion in the same year. The World Champion is the wake boarder who has won the most prestigious wake-board contests in one season. Wake boarding is a combination of surfing, skateboarding, snowboarding, and water-skiing. The board resembles a fat snowboard with a pair of bindings attached to it.

BAREFOOT WATER-SKIING The greatest number of men's World Barefoot Championship Overall titles is three, by Brett Wing (Australia, above) in 1978, 1980, and 1982 and Ron Scarpa (US) in 1992, 1996, and 1998. The most World Barefoot Championship Overall titles is four, by Kim Lampard (Australia) in 1980, 1982, 1985, and 1986 and Jennifer Calleri (US) in 1990, 1992, 1994, and 1996. The World Barefoot Championship team title has been won by the US a record six times between 1988 and 1998. Barefoot skiers perform without water skis, boards, or shoes.

Most Body-Surfing Championships Mike Stewart has won nine World Championships, eight national tour titles, and 11 pipeline championships. He has won every body-surfing competition he has entered in the last seven years as well as every *BodyBoarding Magazine* Readers' Poll.

Longest Swell Ridden by a Bodysurfer Mike Stewart (US) surfed a swell in Tahiti on July 19, 1996, then flew to Hawaii to meet it again. He surfed it a third time in California and finally in Alaska on July 27.

Highest Wave Ridden by a Bodysurfer In January 1996, Mike Stewart (US) rode a 60-ft. wave off the coast of Jaws, Maui, Hawaii. He was towed in by a Wave Runner. He also holds the record for the highest wave ever paddled into—50 ft.

Most Knee-Boarding World Championships Mario Fossa (Venezuela), known to his fans as the "King Of Dizzy," won five consecutive Pro Tour Titles from 1987 to 1991. Knee boarders perform their tricks while kneeling on a short, squat board.

Top Windsurfing Speed The fastest overall speed by a windsurfer is 45.34 knots (52.21mph), by Thierry Bielak (France) at Camargue, France, in 1993.

The women's record for top windsurfing speed is 40.36 knots (46.44 mph), by Elisabeth Coquelle of France at Tarifa, Spain, on July 7, 1995.

Most Water-Skiing Titles The record for the greatest number of individual category titles won is eight by Liz Allan-Shetter (US). She is also the only person to have won all four titles—slalom, jumping, tricks, and overall—in one year, at Copenhagen, Denmark, in 1969.

The US won the team championship on 17 successive occasions from 1957 to 1989.

The World Overall Championships have been won five times by Patrice Martin (France) in 1989, 1991, 1993, 1995, and 1997.

The record for the most women's titles in the World Overall Championships is three, by Willa McGuire (US) in 1949, 1950, and 1955 and Liz Allan-Shetter (US) in 1965, 1969, and 1975.

Highest Water-Skiing Speed   The highest speed known to have been attained by any water-skier in the world is 143.08 mph, by Christopher Massey (Australia) on the Hawkesbury River, Windsor, Australia, on March 6,1983.

Donna Patterson Brice (US) set a women's water-skiing record of 111.11 mph at Long Beach, California, on August 21, 1977.

Most Water-Skiers Towed by One Boat   On October 18, 1986, a record-breaking 100 skiers were towed on double skis over a nautical mile by the cruiser *Reef Cat* at Cairns, Queensland, Australia. This event was organized by the Cairns and District Powerboating and Ski Club.

Most World And Olympic Canoeing Titles   A record 34 world titles (including Olympic titles) were won by Birgit Schmidt from 1979 to 1998.

The men's record is 13, jointly held by Gert Fredriksson from 1948 to 1960, Rüdiger Helm (GDR, now Germany) from 1976 to 1983, and Ivan Patzaichin (Romania) from 1968 to 1984.

Highest Canoeing Speeds   At the 1995 World Canoeing Championships, the Hungarian four-man team won the 200-m title in 31.155 seconds at an average speed of 14.36 mph.

On August 3, 1996, at the Olympic Games in Atlanta, Georgia, the four-man kayak team from Germany covered 1,000 m in 2 min. 51.52 sec.—an average speed of 13.04 mph.

Fastest Cross-Channel Paddleboarders   In July 1996, seven members of the Southern California Paddleboard Club—Derek and Mark Levy,

MOST SUCCESSFUL AQUA BIKER   Since 1997, the Union Internationale Monoautique, based in Monaco, has staged World Championships in three aqua-bike categories. Marco Sickerling of Germany, competing in the freestyle category, was crowned UIM European and World Champion in 1997 and European Champion in 1998.

HIGHEST-EARNING SURFERS
Kelly Slater (US), pictured right,
had earned a record $708,230 by
April 1999. In 1991, he was the
subject of a bidding war between
the major surfwear companies, that
was eventually won by Quiksilver.
The women's career record is
$270,275 by Pam Burridge
(Australia) up to April 1999.

Craig Welday, Tim Ritter, Michael Lee, Charlie Didinger, and John Matesich—completed a crossing of the English Channel from Dover, England, to Cap Griz-Nez, France, in 6 hr. 52 min.

Most Successful Nation in White-Water Freestyle Kayaking The most successful nation to date in white-water freestyle kayaking is Germany. They won the inaugural World Championships in St. David's, Dyfed, Wales, in 1991 and then in front of their home crowd at Augsburg in 1995.

EXTREME SPORTS: SNOW

Most X Games Snowboarding Medals The most X Games snowboarding medals won by a woman is six, by Barrett Christy (US). Christy took the gold medal in the Big Air event and the silver medal in the Slopestyle category at the 1999 Winter X Games. She also won both events in the inaugural X Games and silver for both in 1998. The Winter X

SNOWBOARDING CHAMPIONS The record for the most World Cup titles is 11 by Karine Ruby (France; pictured above). She won the overall from 1996 to 1998, the slalom from 1996 to 1998, the giant slalom from 1995 to 1998, and the snowboard cross in 1997. Mike Jacoby (US) has won a record three men's World Cup titles: the overall in 1996 and the giant slalom in 1995 and 1996.

Games were launched by ESPN in 1997 and feature ice climbing, snow mountain biking, free skiing, ski boarding, snowboarding, and snow cross.

Most World Championship Snowboarding Titles Karine Ruby (France) holds the record for the most World Championship titles (including Olympics titles) with three. She won the giant slalom in 1996 and 1998 and the snowboard cross in 1997. No man has ever won more than one World Championship title.

Fastest Snowboarder The highest officially recorded speed attained by a snowboarder is 125.463 mph by Daren Powell (Australia) at Les Arcs, France, on May 1, 1999.

Most "Vertical Miles" Snowboarded in a Day Over 15 hours on April 20, 1998, Tammy McMinn snowboarded down a slope in Atlin,

MOST X GAMES MEDALS WON BY A MALE SNOWBOARDER Shaun Palmer (US; above left) battles for position with Norway's Tor Bruserud during the 1999 ISF Boardercross World Championships at Passo del Tonale, Italy. Palmer has claimed a record three gold medals at the Winter ESPN X Games for the Boarder X category, winning every year since the inaugural X Games in 1997. This is in addition to a 1997 X Games gold in the Snow Mountain Biking Dual Downhill event.

Canada, 101 times, making a total vertical descent of 57 miles 1,524 yd. She was lifted back to the top each time by helicopter. She performed her feat alongside skier Jennifer Hughes (see below).

Most "Vertical Miles" Skied in a Day Edi Podivinsky, Luke Sauder, Chris Kent (all Canada), and Dominique Perret (Switzerland) hold the record for the most "vertical miles" skied in a day. On April 29, 1998, they skied a total of 66 miles 1,709 yd. in 14 hr. 30 min. on a slope at Blue River, British Columbia, Canada, 73 times and were lifted back to the summit each time by helicopter.

The women's record is 57 miles 1,524 yd., set by Jennifer Hughes (US) at Atlin, Canada, on April 20, 1998, alongside snowboarder Tammy McMinn (see above).

Most Ski-Boarding Medals Mike Nick (US) won a gold medal in the 1998 ESPN Winter X Games Skiboarding Slopestyle and a silver in the Triple Air category at the 1999 Games. The 1998 Winter X Games gave ski boarders their first opportunity to take part in a full international ski-boarding competition.

Most Snow Mountain Biking Medals   The most medals won for snow mountain biking is three, by Cheri Elliott (US)—the 1997 gold speed medal, the 1998 silver speed medal, and the silver difficulty medal.

Most Two-Seater Luging Titles   Stefan Krauße and Jan Behrendt (both GDR, now Germany) have won a record six two-seater titles (1989, 1991–93, 1995, and 1998).

Fastest Luger   The highest photo-timed speed was 85.1 mph by Asle Strand (Norway) at Tandådalens Linbana, Sälen, Sweden, on May 1, 1982.

Closest Olympic Luge Race   The final of the women's luge event at the 1998 Winter Olympic Games in Nagano, Japan, on February 11, 1998, was decided by 0.002 seconds. Germany's Silke Kraushaar edged out teammate Barbara Niedernhueber to take the gold with a combined time of 3 min. 23.779 sec. over four runs on the championship course.

Most World Skibob Titles   The most World Championship skibob titles ever won by a man is three, by Walter Kronseil (Austria) from 1988 to 1990.

The record for the most individual World Championship combined skibob titles is four, by Petra Tschach-Wlezcek (Austria) from 1988 to 1991.

Fastest Skibobber   The record for the highest speed reached in a skibob is 105 mph, by Romuald Bonvin (Switzerland) at Les Arcs, France, on May 1, 1999.

Highest Ice-Yachting Speed   The highest officially recorded speed ever reached by an ice yacht is 143 mph, by John Buckstaff (US) on Lake Winnebago, Wisconsin, in 1938.

MOST SINGLE-SEATER LUGE TITLES   The record for the most World Championship luge titles won (including Olympic titles) is six, by Georg Hackl (GDR, now Germany), who won the single-seater in 1989, 1990, 1992, 1994, 1997, and 1998. Steffi Walter (GDR) won a record two Olympic single-seater titles at the women's event in 1984 and 1988. Margit Schumann (GDR) won the most women's titles overall, with five between 1973 and 1977.

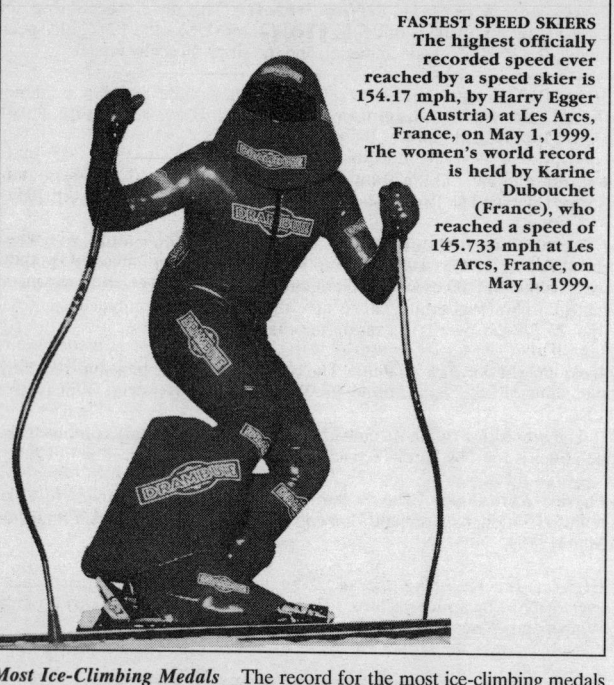

FASTEST SPEED SKIERS The highest officially recorded speed ever reached by a speed skier is 154.17 mph, by Harry Egger (Austria) at Les Arcs, France, on May 1, 1999. The women's world record is held by Karine Dubouchet (France), who reached a speed of 145.733 mph at Les Arcs, France, on May 1, 1999.

Most Ice-Climbing Medals The record for the most ice-climbing medals ever won at the X Games is three, by Will Gadd (US). He took the gold speed and difficulty medals in 1998 and the gold difficulty medal in 1999.

Fastest Olympic Speed Skiers The highest skiing speed ever reached in an Olympic event is 142.47 mph, by Michel Pruefer (France) at the 1992 Winter Olympic Games in Albertville, France, when the sport was introduced as a demonstration event.

The youngest speed skier to reach 100 mph is Tatiana Fields (US). She was 12 years old when she achieved this record at the 1999 Red Bull US Speed-Skiing Championships in Snowmass, Colorado.

Most World Ski-Orienteering Titles The most individual titles is four, by Ragnhild Bratberg (Norway). She won the classic in 1986 and 1990 and the sprint in 1988 and 1990.

The men's record is three, by Anssi Juutilainen of Finland (classic 1984 and 1988, sprint 1992) and Nicolo Corradini of Italy (classic 1994 and 1996, sprint 1994).

Fastest Monoskier David Arnaud (France) reached a speed of 122.107 mph at Les Arcs, France, on May 1, 1999.

SKIING

Most World Alpine Championship Titles   The record for the most titles in the World Alpine Championships is 12, by Christl Cranz (Germany), who won seven individual (four slalom, 1934 and 1937–39, and three downhill, 1935, 1937, and 1939) and five combined (1934–35 and 1937–39). Cranz also won the gold medal for the combined in the 1936 Olympics.

The most titles won by a man is seven, by Toni Sailer (Austria), who won all four Alpine events (giant slalom, slalom, downhill, and the non-Olympic Alpine combination) in 1956 and the downhill, giant slalom, and combined in 1958.

Most World Nordic Championship Medals   The most medals won by a woman in the World Nordic Championships is 23, by Raisa Petrovna Smetanina (USSR, later CIS), including a total of seven golds (1974–92).

Most Alpine World Cup Wins   The record for the greatest number of individual-event wins in the Alpine category is 86 (46 giant slalom and 40 slalom) in a total of 287 races by Ingemar Stenmark (Sweden), from 1974 to 1989. This included a men's record of 13 wins in one season (1978/79). Of these, 10 were part of a record 14 successive giant slalom wins from March 1978 to January 1980.

MOST OLYMPIC TITLES   Katja Seizinger of Germany (pictured above) is one of two women to have won a record three Olympic Alpine titles and five Olympic Alpine medals. The other is Vreni Schneider of Switzerland. Seizinger won the downhill in 1994 and 1998 and the combined in 1998 and took bronze in the supergiant slalom in 1992 and 1998. She has also won a record five supergiant slalom World Cup titles (1993–96, 1998).

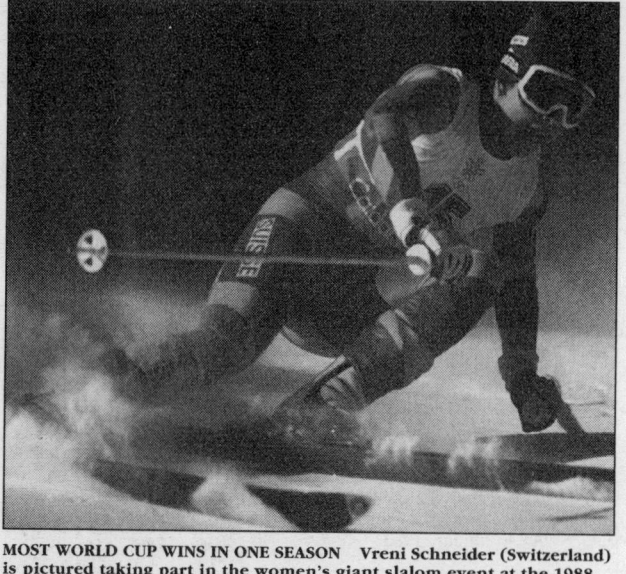

MOST WORLD CUP WINS IN ONE SEASON Vreni Schneider (Switzerland) is pictured taking part in the women's giant slalom event at the 1988 Winter Olympics. Schneider holds the record for the most World Cup wins in a single season: in 1988/89, she won a record total of 13 individual events and one combined event, including all seven slalom events.

Franz Klammer (Austria) won 25 downhill races from 1974 to 1984.

Annemarie Moser (Austria) won a women's record of 62 individual events from 1970 to 1979. She also had a record 11 consecutive downhill wins from 1972 to 1974.

Most Nordic World Cup Wins Bjørn Dæhlie of Norway holds the record for the most World Cup titles won in the cross-country category with six (1992–93, 1995–97, and 1999).

Yelena Välbe (USSR, now Russia) has won a women's record of four cross-country titles (1989, 1991–92, 1995).

Most Ski-Jumping World Cup Wins The most titles won by a ski jumper in the World Cup is four, by Matti Nykänen of Finland (1983, 1985–86, 1988).

Most Freestyle Titles Edgar Grospiron (France) has won a record three World Championship titles (moguls in 1989 and 1991 and aerials in 1995). He also won an Olympic title in 1992.

The record for the most men's overall titles in the World Cup is five, by Eric Laboureix (France) from 1986 to 1988 and in 1990 and 1991.

The most women's overall titles in the World Cup is 10, by Connie Kissling (Switzerland) from 1983 to 1992.

LONGEST SKI JUMPS The longest ski jump ever officially recorded in the finals stage of a World Cup event is 704 ft., by Martin Schmitt (Germany; pictured above) at Planica, Slovenia, on March 19, 1999. This distance was achieved in the second of his two jumps in the competition. His first jump had been measured at 718 ft., but he fell, so the distance was not officially recorded. On the following day, Tommy Ingebrigsten (Norway) completed a jump of 720 ft. in the qualifying round.

Highest Speeds The highest speed reached in a World Cup downhill is 69.84 mph, by Armin Assinger (Austria) at Sierra Nevada, Spain, on March 15, 1993.

The highest average speed ever reached in an Olympic downhill is 66.64 mph, by Jean-Luc Cretier (France) at Nagano, Japan, on February 13, 1998.

MOST WORLD TITLES

The most titles won by a skier (including Olympic titles) is 18, by Bjørn Dæhlie (Norway; pictured left), who won 12 individual and six relay titles in the Nordic category from 1991 to 1998. Dæhlie won a record 29 medals between 1991 and 1999. The most titles won by a woman is 17, by Yelena Välbe (Russia), with 10 individual and seven relay titles from 1989 to 1998. The most titles by a jumper is five, by Birger Ruud (Norway) in 1931 and 1932 and from 1935 to 1937. Ruud is the only person to have won Olympic events in both the Alpine and Nordic categories: the ski jumping and the Alpine downhill in 1936.

The record time for a 31-mile race in a major championship is 1 hr. 54 min. 46 sec., by Aleksey Prokurorov (Russia) at Thunder Bay, Canada, in 1994. His average speed was 16.24 mph.

The highest speed ever attained by a person skiing on one leg is 115.309 mph, by Patrick Knaff (France) in 1988.

The highest speed reached by a grass skier is 57.21 mph, by Klaus Spinka (Austria) in Waldsassen, Germany, on September 24, 1989.

Longest Races   The longest Nordic ski race is the 55-mile 528-yd. annual Vasaloppet in Sweden. There were a record 10,934 starters in 1977.

The longest downhill race is the 9-mile 1,439-yd. Inferno, starting from the top of the Schilthorn to Lauterbrunnen, Switzerland. The fastest recorded time for the race is 13 min. 53.4 sec., set by Urs von Allmen of Switzerland in 1991.

Longest All-Downhill Ski Run   The Weissfluhjoch-Küblis Parsenn downhill skiing course near Davos, Switzerland, is a record 7 miles 1,038 yd. in length.

Biggest Race The Finlandia Ski Race is 46 miles 1.056 yd. long and runs from Hämeenlinna to Lahti, Finland. In February 1984, it had a record 13,226 starters and 12,909 finishers.

Greatest Distance Covered Seppo-Juhani Savolainen (Finland) covered 258 miles 352 yd. in 24 hours at Saariselkä, Finland, from April 8 to 9, 1988.

The women's 24-hour record is 205 miles by Sisko Kainulaisen (Finland) at Jyväskylä, Finland, from March 23 to 24, 1985.

Most World Grass-Skiing Championship Titles The World Grass-Skiing Championships have been held biennially since 1979. The most titles won is 14, by Ingrid Hirschhofer (Austria) between 1979 and 1993.

The most titles won by a man is seven, by Erwin Gansner of Switzerland (1981–87) and Rainer Grossman of Germany (1985–93).

Only two people have ever won all four titles (Super-G, giant slalom, slalom, and combined) in one year: Rainer Grossman (Germany) in 1991 and Ingrid Hirschhofer (Austria) in 1993.

ICE SPORTS

Fastest Skaters Jeremy Wotherspoon (Canada) set a new 500-m speed-skating record with a time of 34.76 seconds in Calgary, Canada, on February 20, 1999.

The women's 500-m record is 37.55 seconds set by Catriona Le May Doan (Canada) in Calgary, Canada, on December 29, 1997.

Jan Bos (Netherlands) skated 1,000 m in 1 min. 8.55 sec. in Calgary, Canada, on February 21, 1999—a men's record.

The women's 1,000-m record is held by Monique Garbrecht (Germany), who skated in 1 min. 15.61 sec. at Calgary, Canada, on February 21, 1999.

Most Men's World Speed-Skating Titles The greatest number of world overall titles won by a male skater is five, by Oscar Mathisen (Norway), 1908–09 and 1912–14, and by Clas Thunberg (Finland), 1923, 1925, 1928–29, and 1931.

Most Olympic Speed-Skating Titles The most Olympic gold medals won is six, by Lidiya Pavlovna Skoblikova (USSR) in 1960 (two) and 1964 (four).

The most Olympic gold medals won by a man is five, by Clas Thunberg (Finland) in 1924 and 1928 and Eric Arthur Heiden (US) at one Games at Lake Placid, New York, in 1980.

Most World Figure-Skating Titles The greatest number of men's individual world figure-skating titles is 10, by Ulrich Salchow (Sweden) in 1901–05 and 1907–11.

The women's individual record is also 10, by Sonja Henie between 1927 and 1936.

The most world pair titles is 10, by Irina Rodnina—four with Aleksey Nikolayevich Ulanov from 1969 to 1972 and six with her husband, Aleksandr Gennadyevich Zaitsev, from 1973 to 1978.

MOST WOMEN'S SPEED-SKATING TITLES Gunda Neimann-Stirnemann (Germany) holds the record for most world titles won in women's speed-skating events. In total, she took seven titles from 1991 to 1993 and 1995 to 1998. After a disastrous fall in the 1994 Olympics, she returned to form in the 1998 Olympics in Calgary, Canada, when she set a new record (4:01.67) in the women's 3,000 m. She is seen here setting a new world record in the women's 5,000-m event during the World All-Round Speed-Skating Championships in Hamar, Norway, on February 7, 1999. She recorded a time of 6:57.24, scoring an all-time low of 161.479 points overall.

Highest Figure-Skating Marks The highest tally of maximum six marks awarded in an international championship is 29, to Jayne Torvill and Christopher Dean (GB) at the World Ice Dance Championships in Ottawa, Canada, in March 1984. It comprised seven in the compulsory dances, a perfect set of nine for presentation in the set-pattern dance, and 13 in the free dance.

MOST FIGURE-SKATING GRAND SLAMS Katarina Witt (GDR, now Germany) achieved a double "Grand Slam" when she won the World, Olympic, and European titles in both 1984 and 1988. The only other figure skaters to have matched this feat were Austria's Karl Schäfer and Norway's Sonja Henie, both in 1932 and 1936.

The most sixes by a soloist is seven, by Donald Jackson (Canada) in the World Men's Championships at Prague, Czechoslovakia (now Czech Republic), in 1962 and by Midori Ito (Japan) in the World Women's Championships in Paris, France, in 1989.

Fastest Cresta Run Times The Cresta Run course at St. Moritz, Switzerland, is 3,977-ft. long with a drop of 514 ft. The fastest time

MOST WORLD FOUR-MAN BOBSLED TITLES Switzerland has won the four-man bobsled world title a record 20 times (1924, 1936, 1939, 1947, 1954–57, 1971–73, 1975, 1982–83, 1986–90, and 1993). This total includes a record five Olympic victories (1924, 1936, 1956, 1972, and 1988). The Swiss team—Marcel Rohner (driver), Silvio Schaufelberger, Markus Nuessli, and Beat Hefti of Swiss 1—is seen here on the way to second place in the World Championships in Cortina d'Ampezzo, Italy, in February 1999.

recorded there is 50.09 seconds by James Sunley (GB) on February 13, 1999. His average speed was 54.13 mph.

Most Cresta Run Wins The most wins in the Cresta Run Grand National is eight, by the 1948 Olympic champion Nino Bibbia (Italy) from 1960 to 1964 and in 1966, 1968, and 1973 and by Franco Gansser (Switzerland) in 1981, from 1983 to 1986, from 1988 to 1989, and in 1991.

Most World Two-Man Bobsled Titles Switzerland has won the two-man world title a record 17 times (1935, 1947–50, 1953, 1955, 1977–80, 1982–83, 1987, 1990, 1992, and 1994). This total includes a record four Olympic successes (in 1948, 1980, 1992, and 1994).

Eugenio Monti (Italy) won 11 titles—eight two-man from 1957 to 1961 (a record five consecutive titles) and in 1963, 1966, 1968 and three four-man in 1960, 1961, and 1968.

Most Individual Four-Man Bobsled Titles Bernhard Germeshausen (GDR, later Germany) won four titles (1976, 1977, 1980, 1981), as did Wolfgang Hoppe (GDR, later Germany; 1984, 1991, 1995, 1997).

Most Olympic Bobsled Medals   The most Olympic gold medals won by an individual is three, by Meinhard Nehmer and Bernhard Germeshausen (both GDR, later Germany) in the 1976 two-man and the 1976 and 1980 four-man events.

The most medals won is seven (one gold, five silver, one bronze), by Bogdan Musiol (GDR, later Germany) from 1980 to 1992.

Oldest Olympic Bobsled Champion   Jay O'Brien (US) was 48 years 357 days old when he was a member of the four-man bobsled team that won a gold medal at the Winter Olympics in Lake Placid, New York, in 1932.

Youngest Olympic Bobsled Champion   William Guy Fiske was on the US team that won the five-man bobsled event at the Winter Olympics in St. Moritz, Switzerland, in 1928, when he was 16 years 260 days old.

Most World Curling Championship Titles   The most men's World Championship titles are held by Canada, which has won 25 times (1959–64, 1966, 1968–72, 1980, 1982–83, 1985–87, 1989–90, 1993–96, 1998).

The most women's titles held is 10, by Canada (1980, 1984–87, 1989, 1993–94, 1996–97).

Longest Curling Throw   A curling stone was thrown a record distance of 576 ft. 4 in. by Eddie Kulbacki (Canada) at Park Lake, Manitoba, Canada, on January 29, 1989. The attempt took place on a specially prepared sheet of curling ice.

Fastest Curling Game   Eight curlers from the Burlington Golf and Country Club curled an eight-end game in a record time of 47 min. 24 sec. with time penalties of 5 min. 30 sec. at Burlington, Ontario, Canada, on April 4, 1986.

ICE HOCKEY

Most Games Played   Gordie Howe (Canada) played in a record 1,767 regular-season games (and 157 play-off games) over a record 26 seasons in the National Hockey League (NHL), from 1946 to 1971 (for the Detroit Red Wings) and then in the 1979/80 season (for the Hartford Whalers). He also played 419 regular-season games (and 78 games in the play-offs) for the Houston Aeros and for the New England Whalers in the World Hockey Association (WHA) between 1973 and 1979, giving him a career total of 2,421 major-league games.

Most Goals Scored   The most goals scored in professional hockey is 1,072, by Wayne Gretzky (Edmonton Oilers, Los Angeles Kings, St. Louis Blues, and New York Rangers). In the NHL, he scored 894 goals in the regular season and 122 in Stanley Cup games, between 1979 and 1999. He scored 56 goals in the WHA in 1978/79. He broke Gordie Howe's record of 1,071 goals on March 29, 1999, for the New York Rangers against the New York Islanders.

MOST WORLD AND OLYMPIC TITLES   The USSR won 22 world titles (including the Olympic titles in 1956, 1964, and 1968) from 1954 to 1990, as well as one title playing as Russia in 1993. They won a further five Olympic titles in 1972, 1976, 1984, 1988, and 1992 (as the CIS, with an all-Russian team) for an Olympic record of eight. The USSR also holds the record of a 47-game unbeaten streak in the World Championships. Canada has secured 21 world titles and holds the record for the most medals (gold, silver, and bronze) won in both the World Championships and the Olympics, with 42 and 12, respectively. The US women's ice hockey team won the first Olympic title at Nagano in 1998, beating arch rivals Canada 3–1.

By the time he had played his last professional game, against the Pittsburgh Penguins on April 18, 1999, Gretzky had amassed 61 NHL records.

Most Goals and Points in a Season   Wayne Gretzky holds the record for the most goals scored in one season—92 for the Edmonton Oilers in 1981/82. He also scored a record 215 points, including a record 163 assists in 1985/86. In all his games in 1984/85, including Stanley Cup playoffs, he scored a record 255 points (90 goals, 165 assists).

Most Goals in a Game   The most goals in a game is seven, by Joe Malone for the Québec Bulldogs against Toronto St. Patricks in Québec City on January 31, 1920.

Most Assists in a Game   The most assists in a game is seven, achieved once by Billy Taylor for Detroit against Chicago on March 16, 1947, and three times by Wayne Gretzky for Edmonton against Washington on February 15, 1980, against Chicago on December 11, 1985, and against Québec on February 14, 1986.

Most Points in a Game   The most points scored by one player in a North American major-league game is 10, by Jim Harrison (three goals,

MOST SUCCESSFUL GOALTENDERS   Three-time Stanley Cup winner Patrick Roy (pictured) of the Colorado Avalanche has won 110 play-off games, more than any other goaltender. Terry Sawchuk played a record 971 NHL regular-season games as goaltender for five teams from 1949 to 1970. He had a record 447 wins and a record 103 shutouts. Jacques Plante holds the record for the most regular-season wins by a goalie in a professional career, with 449 victories (434 in the NHL and 15 in the WHA).

seven assists) for Alberta, later Edmonton Oilers, in a WHA game at Edmonton on January 30, 1973, and by Darryl Sittler (six goals, four assists) for Toronto Maple Leafs against Boston Bruins in an NHL game in Toronto on February 7, 1976.

Most Team Goals   The most goals by a team in a World Championship game is 58, a record set by Australia against New Zealand (who failed to score) at Perth, Australia, on March 15, 1987.

The most team goals scored in an NHL season is 446, by the Edmonton Oilers in the 1983/84 season, when they also achieved a record 1,182 scoring points.

Most Team Points   The Montréal Canadiens scored a record 132 team points (60 wins, 12 ties) from 80 games played in 1976/77. Their tally of eight losses was also the lowest ever in a season of 70 or more games.

Most Successful Teams   The Detroit Red Wings won a record 62 games in 1995/96.

The highest percentage of wins in a season was 0.875, by the Boston Bruins, with 38 wins in 44 games in the 1929/30 season.

Longest Undefeated Run   The longest unbeaten run in a season is 35 games (25 wins, 10 ties), by the Philadelphia Flyers from October 14, 1979, to January 6, 1980.

Fastest Goal   The shortest time taken to score from the opening whistle is five seconds, by Doug Smail for the Winnipeg Jets on December 20, 1981, by Bryan Trottier for the New York Islanders on March 22, 1984, and by Alexander Mogilny for the Buffalo Sabres on December 21, 1991.

Most Stanley Cup Points   Wayne Gretzky scored 382 points, 122 goals, and 260 assists (all records) in Stanley Cup games.

The most points scored in a single game is eight, by Mario Lemieux, with five goals and three assists for Pittsburgh against Philadelphia on April 25, 1989, and by Patrik Sundström, with three goals and five assists for New Jersey against Washington on April 22, 1988.

Most Stanley Cup Goals   The most goals in a game is five, by Newsy Lalonde for Montréal against Ottawa on March 1, 1919, Maurice Richard for Montréal against Toronto on March 23, 1944, Darryl Sittler for Toronto against Philadelphia on April 22, 1976, Reggie Leach for Philadelphia against Boston on May 6, 1976, and Mario Lemieux for Pittsburgh against Philadelphia on April 25, 1989.

The record for the most goals in a season is 19, set by Reggie Leach for Philadelphia in 1976 and by Jari Kurri for Edmonton in 1985.

Most Stanley Cup Assists   The most assists in a game is six, by Mikko Leinonen for the New York Rangers against Philadelphia on April 8, 1982, and by Wayne Gretzky for Edmonton against Los Angeles on April 9, 1987.

Most Olympic Gold Medals   The most Olympic gold medals is three, by Vitaliy Davydov, Anatoliy Firsov, Viktor Kuzkin, and Aleksandr Ragulin (USSR: 1964, 1968, 1972), Vladislav Tretyak (USSR: 1972, 1976, 1984), and Andrey Khomutov (USSR: 1984, 1988; CIS: 1992).

Most NCAA Wins   Michigan has won the NCAA Championships a record nine times, in 1948, 1951–53, 1955–56, 1964, 1996, and 1998.

Most Women's World Championships   Canada won the first five women's World Championships (1990, 1992, 1994, 1997, and 1999) without losing a single game.

MOST STANLEY CUP WINS The Montréal Canadiens have had a record 24 wins (1916, 1924, 1930–31, 1944, 1946, 1953, 1956–60, 1965–66, 1968–69, 1971, 1973, 1976–79, 1986, and 1993) from a record 32 finals. Henri Richard of the Canadiens played on a record 11 cup-winning teams from 1956 to 1973. Stephane Quintal of the Canadiens is shown here upending Trevor Linden of the New York Islanders.

TRACK & FIELD

Most Olympic Titles The most gold medals won is 10 (an absolute Olympic record), by Raymond Ewry (US): standing high, long, and triple jumps in 1900, 1904, 1906, and 1908.

The most gold medals won by a woman is four, by Fanny Blankers-Koen (Netherlands) in the 100 m, 200 m, 80-m hurdles, and 4 x 100-m relay, 1948; Betty Cuthbert (Australia) in the 100 m, 200 m, and 4 x 100-m relay, 1956, and the 400 m, 1964; Bärbel Wöckel (GDR) in the 200 m and 4 x 100-m relay, 1976 and 1980; and Evelyn Ashford (US) in the 100 m, 1984, and 4 x 100-m relay, 1984, 1988, and 1992.

Most Olympic Medals The most medals is 12 (nine gold, three silver), by distance runner Paavo Nurmi (Finland) in 1920, 1924, and 1928.

The most medals by a female athlete is seven, by Shirley de la Hunty (Australia), with three gold, one silver, and three bronze in 1948, 1952, and 1956. A reread of the photo finish indicated that she was third, not fourth, in the 1948 200-m event, which unofficially makes her medal count eight.

MOST WORLD CHAMPIONSHIP MEDALS Merlene Ottey (Jamaica) has won a record 14 medals in the World Track and Field Championships, with three gold, four silver, and seven bronze from 1983 to 1997. The most medals won by a man is 10, by Carl Lewis (US): a record eight gold (100 m, long jump, and 4 x 100-m relay, 1983; 100 m, long jump, and 4 x 100-m relay, 1987; and 100 m and 4 x 100-m relay, 1991), a silver at long jump in 1991, and a bronze at 200 m in 1993.

Irena Szewinska (Poland), the only female athlete to win a medal in four successive Games, also won seven medals (three gold, two silver, and two bronze in 1964, 1968, 1972, and 1976), as did Merlene Ottey (Jamaica) with two silver and five bronze in 1980, 1984, 1992, and 1996.

Most Wins at One Games The most gold medals at one Games is five, by Paavo Nurmi (Finland) in 1924 (1,500 m, 5,000 m, 10,000-m cross-country, 3,000-m team and cross-country team).

The most medals at individual events is four, by Alvin Kraenzlein (US) in 1900 (60 m, 110-m hurdles, 200-m hurdles, and long jump).

Oldest Olympic Champions The oldest winner of an Olympic event was Patrick "Babe" McDonald (US), who was 42 years 26 days old when he won the 56-lb. weight throw in Belgium in August 1920.

The oldest female champion was Lia Manoliu (Romania), who was 36 years 176 days old when she won the gold medal for the discus in Mexico in 1968.

Youngest Olympic Champions The youngest gold medalist was Barbara Jones (US), who was a member of the winning 4 x 100-m relay team at Helsinki, Finland, when she was 15 years 123 days in July 1952.

The youngest male champion was Bob Mathias (US), who won the decathlon aged 17 years 263 days in London, England, in 1948.

Most World Championship Gold Medals (One Event) Sergey Bubka (Ukraine, formerly USSR) won the pole vault at a record six consecutive championships from 1983 to 1997.

Most World Championship Golds by a Woman   The most gold medals won by a woman is four, by Jackie Joyner-Kersee (US): in the long jump in 1987 and 1991 and the heptathlon in 1987 and 1993.

Oldest and Youngest Record Breakers   Marina Styepanova (USSR) set a 400-m-hurdle record (52.94 sec.) at Tashkent, USSR (now Uzbekistan), in 1986 at the age of 36 years 139 days.

Wang Yan (China) set an individual women's 5,000-m walk record of 21 min. 33.8 sec. aged 14 years 334 days in China on March 9, 1986.

The youngest male record breaker was Thomas Ray (GB), who pole-vaulted 3.42 m (11 ft. 2 ¼ in.) aged 17 years 198 days on September 19, 1879.

Most Records Set in a Day   Jesse Owens (US) set six world records in 45 min. at Ann Arbor, Michigan, on May 25, 1935. He ran 100 yd. in 9.4 sec. at 3:15 pm, made an 8.13-m (26-ft.-8¼-in.) long jump at 3:25 pm, ran 220 yd. (and 200 m) in 20.3 sec. at 3:45 pm, and covered the 220-yd. (and 200-m) low hurdles in 22.6 sec. at 4 pm.

FASTEST 100 M   Maurice Greene (USA) is pictured setting a new world record of 9.79 sec. in the men's 100 m on 16 June 1999 in Athens, Greece. Greene took 0.05 sec. off the previous record, set by Canada's Donovan Bailey at the 1996 Olympics in Atlanta, Georgia, USA. This was the biggest margin taken off the 100-m record since electronic timing was introduced in the 1960s. Greene also equalled the time set by Ben Johnson (Canada) in 1988. Johnson's time was subsequently invalidated after a positive drugs test.

FASTEST FEMALE SPRINTER Florence Griffith Joyner, known to her fans as Flo-Jo, caused a sensation when she smashed two world records—the women's 100 m and 200 m—at the US Olympic trials in July 1988. Her 100 m time of 10.49 sec. still stands, but she went on to break her 200-m record twice at the Olympic Games in Seoul, South Korea, setting a time of 21.56 in the semifinal and achieving 21.34 sec. in the final on September 29, 1988. Flo-Jo died on September 21, 1998.

FASTEST 1,500 M Hicham el-Guerrouj (Morocco) broke the 1,500-m world record in Rome, Italy, on July 14, 1998. His time of 3:26.00 improved the previous record set by Noureddine Morceli (Algeria) by more than a second.

Longest Winning Sequences The record winning sequence at a track event is 122, by Ed Moses (US) at the 400-m hurdles between August 1977 and June 1987.

Iolanda Balas (Romania) won a 150 consecutive high-jump competitions between 1956 and 1967.

Highest Jump Above Own Head The greatest height cleared by an athlete above his own head was 1 ft. 11¼ in., by 5-ft.-8-in.-tall Franklin Jacobs (US), who jumped 7 ft. 7¼ in. in New York City on January 27, 1978.

The greatest height cleared by a female athlete above her own head was 1 ft. ¾ in., by 5-ft.-6-in.-tall Yolanda Henry (US), who jumped 6 ft. 6¼ in. in Seville, Spain, on May 30, 1990.

Best Standing Jumps   The best high jump from a standing position was 6 ft. 2¾ in., by Rune Almen (Sweden) at Karlstad, Sweden, on May 3, 1980.

The women's best is 4 ft. 11¾ in., by Grete Bjørdalsbakka (Norway) in 1984.

Fastest Mass Relays   The fastest 100 x 100-m was 19 min. 14.19 sec., by a team from Antwerp in Belgium on September 23, 1989.

The fastest time over 100 miles by 100 runners was 7 hr. 35 min. 55.4 sec., by the Canadian Milers Athletic Club at York University, Toronto, Canada, on December 20, 1998.

The greatest distance covered by 10 runners in 24 hours is 302 miles 494 yd., by Puma Tyneside Running Club in Jarrow, England, in September 1994.

GOLF

Best Scores in the British Open   The best score in a round is 63, by Mark Hayes (US) at Turnberry, England, in 1977; Isao Aoki (Japan) at Muirfield, Scotland, in 1980; Greg Norman (Australia) at Turnberry in 1986; Paul Broadhurst (GB) at St. Andrews, Scotland, in 1990; Jodie Mudd (US) at Royal Birkdale, England, in 1991; Nick Faldo (GB) at Royal St. George's, England, in 1993; and Payne Stewart (US) in 1993, also at Royal St. George's.

Nick Faldo completed the first 36 holes at Muirfield, Scotland, in a record 130 strokes (66, 64) from July 16 to 17, 1992.

Best US Open Scores   The best score in a round in the US Open is 63, by Johnny Miller (US) on the 6,920-yd., par-71 Oakmont Country Club course in Pennsylvania in June 1973 and by Jack Nicklaus and Tom Weiskopf (both US) at Baltusrol Country Club (7,014 yd.) in Springfield, New Jersey, on June 12, 1980.

The best score over two rounds is 134, by Jack Nicklaus of the United States (63, 71) at Baltusrol in 1980; Chen Tze-chung of Taiwan (65, 69) at Oakland Hills, Michigan, in 1985; and Lee Janzen of the US (67, 67) at Baltusrol in June 1993.

The best score over four rounds is 272, by Jack Nicklaus (63, 71, 70, 68) at Baltusrol Country Club, Springfield, New Jersey, in June 1980 and his fellow US player Lee Janzen (67, 67, 69, 69) at Baltusrol in June 1993.

Oldest US Open Champion   Hale Irwin (US) won the US Open at the age of 45 years 15 days on June 18, 1990. Irwin won the tournament in 1974 and 1979 but had not been a contender for several years and was only eligible via a special exemption given to him by the USGA. Although he has never been the top player in the world, he has been in the US top-10 money winners eight times, from 1973 to 1978, in 1981, and in 1990.

Best Masters Scores   The top score in a round is 63, by Nick Price (Zimbabwe) in 1986 and Greg Norman (Australia) in 1996.

MOST WORLD CUP WINS US golfers Arnold Palmer (left of picture) and Jack Nicklaus (right of picture), seen here with Tom Watson, have been on a record six winning teams in the World Cup: Palmer in 1960, 1962–64, and 1966–67 and Nicklaus in 1963–64, 1966–67, 1971, and 1973. Nicklaus has also taken the most individual titles, winning three times (1963–64 and 1971).

The best score over two rounds is 131 (65, 66), by Raymond Floyd (US) in 1976.

Best PGA Scores The best-ever score in any round in the PGA is 63, by Bruce Crampton (Australia) at Firestone, Akron, Ohio, in 1975; Raymond Floyd (US) at Southern Hills, Tulsa, Oklahoma, in 1982; Gary Player (South Africa) at Shoal Creek, Birmingham, Alabama, in 1984; Vijay Singh (Fiji) at Inverness Club, Toledo, Ohio, in 1993; and Michael Bradley and Brad Faxon (both US) at the Riviera Golf Club, Pacific Palisades, California, in 1995.

The record aggregate is 267, by Steve Elkington (Australia), with 68, 67, 68, 64, and Colin Montgomerie (GB), with 68, 67, 67, 65, both at Riviera Golf Club, Pacific Palisades, California, in 1995.

Most Tournament Wins In 1945, Byron Nelson (US) won 18 PGA Tour events and an unofficial tournament; his 11 consecutive PGA Tour wins was also a record.

Sam Snead (US) turned professional in 1934 and by 1965 had won 81 official PGA Tour events.

The womens' record on the LPGA Tour is 88, by Kathy Whitworth (US) between 1959 and 1991.

The most career victories in European Order of Merit tournaments is 55, by Spaniard Severiano Ballesteros from 1974 to 1995.

Biggest Winning Margin The record for the greatest margin of victory in a professional tournament is 21 strokes, by Jerry Pate (US), who won the 1981 Colombian Open with a score of 262.

Youngest and Oldest National Champions   Thuashni Selvaratnam won the Sri Lankan Ladies' Amateur Open Golf Championship when she was aged 12 years 324 days in 1989.

Pamela Fernando was a record 54 years 282 days old when she won the Sri Lankan Women's Championship on July 17, 1981.

Most Holes Played   Eric Freeman (US) played 467 holes, using a cart, at the Glen Head Country Club, New York, in 12 hours in 1997. The nine-hole course is 3,272 yd. long.

Ian Colston played a record 401 PGA holes on foot in 24 hours at Bendigo Golf Club, Victoria, Australia (par 6,061 yd.), in 1971.

Using a motorized golf cart, Joe Crowley (US) completed a record 1,702 holes at Green Valley Country Club, Clermont, Florida, from June 23 to 29, 1996.

Longest Putt   The longest holed putt in a major tournament was 110 ft., achieved by Jack Nicklaus in the 1964 Tournament of Champions and Nick Price in the 1992 PGA.

Most Balls Hit in One Hour   The record for the most balls driven in one hour over 100 yards and into a target area is 2,146, by Sean Murphy of Canada at Swifts Practice Range, Carlisle, England, on June 30, 1995.

BEST FOUR ROUNDS IN THE MASTERS   Tiger Woods holds the record for the best four rounds in the US Masters, with 270 (70, 66, 65, 69) in 1997. At the same time, he broke the record for shots below par in the championship with -18 and became the youngest person ever to win the tournament at 21 years 104 days. He also equaled Raymond Floyd's 54-hole record of 201 set in 1976. Born on December 30, 1975, Woods became the youngest golfer ever to reach number one in the Official World Golf Ranking at the age of 21 years 167 days on June 15, 1997, getting to the top after only his 42nd week as a professional.

BEST FOUR ROUNDS IN THE BRITISH OPEN Greg Norman (Australia) holds the record for the best score in four rounds at the Open, with 267 (66, 68, 69, 64). He set the record at Royal St. George's, Sandwich, England, from July 15 to 18, 1993.

Longest Straight Hole in One Shot The longest straight hole ever achieved in one shot was the 10th, covering 446 yards, at the Miracle Hills Golf Club, Nebraska, by Robert Mitera on October 7, 1965. He was a two-handicap player who normally drove about 245 yards. A 50-mph gust of wind helped carry Mitera's shot over a 290-yard drop-off to the hole.

The women's record is 393 yd., by Marie Robie on the first hole of the Furnace Brook Golf Club, Wollaston, Massachusetts, on September 4, 1949.

Longest "Dogleg" Hole The longest "dogleg" hole achieved in one stroke is 496 yd., on the 17th, by Shaun Lynch at Teign Valley Golf Club, Christow, England, on July 24, 1995.

BEST WORLD CUP SCORE Fred Couples holds the record for the lowest-ever individual score in the World Cup. He achieved a score of 265 from November 10 to 13, 1994, when he and Davis Love III represented the US at the championships in Dorado, Puerto Rico. Couples and Love also broke the record for the lowest aggregate score for 144 holes, with 536. The US has won the World Cup a record 21 times.

Most Consecutive Aces There are at least 20 cases of holes in one being achieved at two consecutive holes. Perhaps the greatest was Norman Manley's unique "double double eagle" on the par-4 330-yd. seventh and par-4 290-yd. eighth holes on the Del Valle Country Club course in Saugus, California, on September 2, 1964.

TENNIS

Most Grand-Slam Wins The most singles championships won in grand-slam tournaments is 24, by Margaret Court (Australia): 11 Australian, five US, five French, and three Wimbledon, 1960–73.

The record for the most men's singles championships is 12, won by Roy Emerson (Australia): six Australian and two each French, US, and Wimbledon, from 1961 to 1967.

The most grand-slam tournament wins by a doubles partnership is 20, by Althea Brough and Margaret Du Pont (US): 12 US, five Wimbledon, and three French from 1942 to 1957; and Martina Navrátilová and Pam Shriver (US): seven Australian, five Wimbledon, four French, and four US, 1981–89.

YOUNGEST TENNIS MILLIONAIRE In 1997, at 16 years of age, Martina Hingis (Switzerland) became the youngest sportswoman to earn $1 million. When she won her quarterfinal at the 1998 Italian Open, she became the youngest tennis player to earn $6 million at the age of 17 years, seven months and eight days.

Most Wimbledon Wins Billie-Jean King (US) won a record 20 women's titles between 1961 and 1979: six singles, 10 women's doubles, and four mixed doubles.

Martina Navrátilová (US) won nine women's singles titles: 1978–79, 1982–87, and 1990.

Elizabeth Ryan (US) won 19 women's doubles titles (12 women's, seven mixed) from 1914 to 1934.

The most titles won in the men's championships is 13, by Hugh Doherty (GB) with five singles titles (1902–06) and a record eight men's doubles (1897–1901 and 1903–05). He was partnered with his brother Reginald in all tournaments.

The most men's singles wins since the abolition of the Challenge Round in 1922 is five, a record jointly held by Björn Borg (Sweden), 1976–80, and Pete Sampras (US), 1993–95 and 1997–98. Sampras is still competing at top level.

Youngest and Oldest Wimbledon Champions Lottie Dod (GB) was 15 years 285 days old when she won the women's singles title in 1887.

Margaret Du Pont (US) was 44 years 125 days old when she won the mixed doubles in 1962.

Most US Open Wins Margaret Du Pont (US) won 25 titles from 1941 to 1960: a record 13 women's doubles (12 with Althea Brough, US), nine mixed doubles, and three singles.

The most women's singles titles is eight, by Molla Mallory (US), 1915–18, 1920–22, and 1926.

The record for the most men's US Open titles is 16, by Bill Tilden (US);

this includes a total of seven singles (1920–25, 1929). Seven singles titles were also won by Richard Sears (US), 1881–87, and William Larned (US), 1901–02, 1907–11.

Youngest and Oldest US Open Winners Vincent Richards (US) was 15 years 139 days old when he won the men's doubles in 1918.

The oldest champion was Margaret Du Pont (US), who won the mixed doubles at the age of 42 years 166 days in 1960.

Most Wins in the Australian Open Margaret Court (Australia) won a record total of 21 titles: 11 women's singles (1960–66, 1969–71, and 1973), eight women's doubles, and two mixed doubles.

Roy Emerson (Australia) won a record six men's singles (1961, 1963–67).

Adrian Quist (Australia) won 10 men's doubles and three men's singles titles between 1936 and 1950.

Most French Open Wins Margaret Court (Australia) won a record 13 titles from 1962 to 1973: five singles, four women's doubles, and four mixed doubles.

The men's record is nine, by Henri Cochet (France), with four singles, three men's doubles, and two mixed doubles from 1926 to 1930.

The singles record is seven, by Chris Evert (US): 1974–75, 1979–80, 1983, and 1985–86.

Björn Borg (Sweden) won six men's singles titles: 1974–75 and 1978–81.

Most Davis Cup Wins The US has won the Davis Cup 31 times since 1900.

Most Wins in the ATP Tour Championship Ivan Lendl (US, formerly Czechoslovakia) won a total of five titles: 1982, 1983, 1986 (two), and 1987.

Seven doubles titles were won by the legendary pairing of John McEnroe and Peter Fleming (both US) from 1978 to 1984.

BIGGEST ATP TOUR EARNERS Stefan Edberg (Sweden) is one of only three players to have won more than $20 million on the ATP (Association of Tennis Professionals) Tour, the others being Boris Becker (Germany) and Pete Sampras (US). The ATP Tour was launched in 1990 as a partnership of players and tournaments and replaced the Men's Tennis Council as the governing body for the men's professional tennis circuit. Edberg first captured the imagination of the tennis world in 1983, when he won the junior singles titles at all four Grand-Slam tournaments in one year. He went on to win full singles titles at all the Grand-Slam tournaments with the exception of the French Open.

FASTEST SERVES   The record for the fastest-timed women's service ever was set by Venus Williams (US) during the European Indoor Championships at Zürich, Switzerland, on October 16, 1998, and stands at 127.4 mph. The record for the fastest service timed with modern equipment is 149 mph, achieved by Greg Rusedski (GB) during the ATP Champions' Cup at Indian Wells, California, on March 14, 1998.

YOUNGEST WINNER IN THE FEDERATION CUP Anna Kournikova (Russia) came to attention in 1996, when she became the youngest player to compete and win in the Federation Cup competition at the age of 14, helping Russia to defeat Sweden 3–0. She turned professional in 1995, reached the singles semifinals at Wimbledon in 1997, and won the Princess Cup doubles in 1998 with Monica Seles.

Longest Grand-Slam Match   A 5-hr.-31-min. match between Alex Corretja (Spain) and Hernan Gumy (Argentina) took place in the third round of the French Open on May 31, 1998. Corretja eventually won 6–1, 5–7, 6–7, 7–5, 9–7.

SOCCER 1

Most Expensive Player   The highest transfer fee ever for a soccer player is $46.4 million, paid by Internazionale to Lazio (both of Italy) for Christian Vieri. It was the Italian striker's ninth transfer in 10 seasons and took his salary from $3.31 million to $5.14 million.

Most Expensive Defender   In May 1998, Dutch defender Jaap Stam struck a deal to go to Manchester United for a record transfer fee of $18 million. The 26-year-old PSV Eindhoven star accepted a seven-year deal that is worth $18.3 million, including bonuses. He began his professional career at 19 and made his international debut in 1996 for the Netherlands.

Most Appearances   British goalkeeper Peter Shilton made a record 1,390 senior appearances, including a record 1,005 national league matches: 286 for Leicester City (1966–74), 110 for Stoke City (1974–77), 202 for Nottingham Forest (1977–82), 188 for Southampton (1982–87), 175 for Derby County (1987–92), 34 for Plymouth Argyle (1992–94), one for Bolton Wanderers (1995), nine for Leyton Orient (1996–97); one League play-off, 86 FA Cup matches, 102 League Cup matches, 125 internationals for England, 13 Under-23 matches, four Football League XI matches, and 53 European and other team competitions.

MOST EUROPEAN CUP WINS   The European Cup, contested since 1956 by the champion teams of the various national leagues in Europe, has been won a record seven times by Real Madrid of Spain (1956–60, 1966, and 1998). Clarence Seedorf (left of picture) is seen fending off Edgar Davids of Juventus (Italy) in the 1998 final, which Real won 1-0.

MOST CUP-WINNERS CUP WINS The Cup-Winners Cup, contested between 1960 and 1999 by the winners of the major national cup competitions in Europe, was won a record four times by the Spanish team Barcelona (1979, 1982, 1989, and 1997). The team has been home to many international greats, including Johan Cruyff (Netherlands), Gary Lineker (England), and Brazilian stars Rivaldo (back row, second from right) and Ronaldo.

Most Career Goals The greatest number of goals scored by a player in a specified period is 1,281, by Pelé (Edson Arantes do Nascimento) for Santos, the New York Cosmos, and Brazil between September 7, 1956, and October 1, 1977.

Artur Friedenreich of Brazil scored an undocumented 1,329 goals in a 26-year professional career from 1909 to 1935.

Franz "Bimbo" Binder scored 1,006 goals in 756 games in Austria and Germany between 1930 and 1950.

Most Goals in a Match The most goals scored by one player in a professional match is 16, by Stephan Stanis for Racing Club de Lens v. Aubry-Asturies in a wartime French Cup game in Lens, France, on December 13, 1942.

Most Consecutive Hat Tricks The record for the most consecutive league games in a top division in which one player has scored a hat trick is four: Masahi Nakayama of Jubilo Iwata scored five, four, four, and three goals in successive matches in the Japanese League in April 1998.

Fastest Goals In professional soccer, the record for the fastest goal is six seconds, by Albert Mundy for Aldershot v. Hartlepool United in a British Fourth Division match at Victoria Ground in Hartlepool, England, in October 1958; by Barrie Jones for Notts County v. Torquay United in a British Third Division match in March 1962; and by Keith Smith for Crystal Palace v. Derby County in a British Second Division match at the Baseball Ground in Derby, England, on December 12, 1964.

MOST GOALS SCORED BY A GOALKEEPER José Luis Chilavert, who plays for Paraguay and for Vélez Sarsfeld of Argentina, scored 44 official league and international goals between July 1992 and May 1999. A penalty and free-kick specialist, he is also the only goalkeeper to have scored in a World Cup qualifying match and the only goalie to have scored twice in one game.

Fastest Hat Trick   The fastest confirmed time in which three goals have been scored is 2 min. 13 sec., by Jimmy O'Connor for Shelbourne against Bohemians at Dallymount Park in Dublin, Republic of Ireland, on November 19, 1967.

Maglioni is said to have scored a hat trick in 1 min. 50 sec. when playing for Independiente against Gimnasia y Escrima de la Plata in Argentina on March 18, 1973.

Highest Score   The highest score recorded in a professional match was 36, in the Scottish Cup match between Arbroath and Bon Accord on September 5, 1885. Arbroath won 36–0 at their home field.

Biggest Victory Margins in National Cup Finals In 1935, Lausanne-Sports beat Nordstern Basel 10–0 in the Swiss Cup Final. Lausanne were defeated by the same margin by Grasshopper Club (Zürich) in the 1937 Swiss Cup Final.

Most National League Championships CSKA Sofia of Bulgaria hold a European postwar record of 27 league titles, including two under the name CFKA Sredets (renamed CSKA).

Dynamo Berlin (German Democratic Republic) won 10 successive national championships from 1979 to 1988.

Longest-Held National Soccer League Title The Cairo club Al Ahly maintained the Egyptian national soccer title from the 1948/49 season until the 1959/60 season. However, the 1952 championship was abandoned because of the Egyptian revolution, and the 1955 league program was not completed.

Most Copa Libertadores Wins Independiente (Argentina) has won the Copa Libertadores, contested since 1960 by the champions of the South American leagues, a record seven times (1964–65, 1972–75, and 1984).

Most World Club Championships The record for wins in the World Club Championship, contested since 1960 between the winners of the European Cup and the Copa Libertadores, is three, held by Peñarol of Uruguay (1961, 1966, and 1982); Nacional of Uruguay (1971, 1980, and 1988); and AC Milan of Italy (1969, 1989, and 1990).

Most Cup of Champion Clubs Wins The Cup of Champion Clubs, contested since 1964 by the winners of the African national leagues, has been won a record four times by Zamalek of Egypt (1984, 1986, 1993, and 1996).

Most African Cup-Winners Cup Wins Al Ahly (Egypt) have won the African Cup-Winners Cup a record four times (1984–86 and 1993).

Most Successful Goalkeeper The longest period that a goalkeeper has prevented goals being scored past him in professional competition is 1,275 minutes, by Abel Resino of Athletico Madrid, Spain, in 1991.

Biggest Crowd The biggest crowd at a European Cup match is 136,505, at the semifinal between Celtic and Leeds United at Hampden Park, Glasgow, Scotland, on April 15, 1970.

Farthest Distance Traveled for a League Game The farthest distance traveled between two teams in the top division of a national soccer league is 2,979 miles, between the fields of LA Galaxy, California, and New England Revolution, Massachusetts, in the US Major League.

Most Undisciplined Match On June 1, 1993, it was reported that referee William Weiler dismissed 20 players in a league match between Sportivo Ameliano and General Caballero in Paraguay. Trouble flared up after two Sportivo players were sent off. A 10–minute fight ensued, and Weiler sent off 18 more players, including the rest of the Sportivo team. The match was then abandoned.

SOCCER 2

Biggest Soccer Stadium   The Maracaña Stadium in Rio de Janeiro, Brazil, has a normal capacity of 205,000, with seats for 155,000.

Biggest Crowd   The largest crowd ever at a soccer game consisted of 199,854 people for the World Cup deciding match between Brazil and Uruguay at the Maracaña Stadium, Rio de Janeiro, Brazil, on July 16, 1950.

The record for the greatest number of spectators at a tournament is 3,587,538 for the 52 matches in the 1994 World Cup in the US.

Most International Appearances   The record for the greatest number of games played for a national team is 147, by Majed Abdullah Mohammed of Saudi Arabia from 1978 to 1994.

Most International Goals   The most goals by a player in an international match is 10, by Sofus Nielsen for Denmark v. France (17–1) in the 1908 Olympics and by Gottfried Fuchs for Germany v. Russia (16–0) in the 1912 Olympic tournament (consolation event) in Sweden.

Most Successful International Goalkeeper   The longest period that a goalie has prevented goals in international games is 1,142 minutes, by Dino Zoff (Italy) from September 1972 to June 1974.

Highest International Margin   The highest winning margin is 17, by England in their 17–0 win vs. Australia at Sydney, Australia, on June 30, 1951 (not listed by England as a full international), and by Iran in their 17–0 win vs. the Maldives at Damascus, Syria, in June 1997.

Fastest International Hat Trick   The fastest time in which three goals have been scored in an international is $3^{1}/_{2}$ minutes, by George Hall of Tottenham Hotspur for England against Ireland at Old Trafford, Manchester, England, on November 16, 1938.

Most Individual World Cup Wins   Pelé (Brazil) is the only player to have been on three World Cup-winning teams, in 1958, 1962, and 1970.

Most World Cup Goals   Gerd Müller (West Germany) scored a record 14 goals in the World Cup, 10 in 1970 and four in 1974.

Just Fontaine (France) has scored the most goals in one tournament, with a total of 13 in six games in 1958.

Alcides Ghiggia (Uruguay, 1950) and Jairzinho (Brazil, 1970) are the only players to have scored in every match in every round of a final series.

Brazil holds the team record, having scored 173 goals in a total of 80 games since 1930.

Most Goals in a World Cup Game   The record for the most goals in a game in the finals stage of the World Cup is 11. This has been achieved three times: when Brazil beat Poland 6–5 in Italy on June 5, 1938, in Hun-

MOST WORLD CUP HAT TRICKS Four players have scored two hat tricks in World Cup tournaments: Sandor Kocsis (Hungary) at the 1954 tournament in Switzerland, Just Fontaine (France) in Sweden in 1958, Gerd Müller (West Germany) at the 1970 tournament in Mexico, and Gabriele Batistuta (Argentina, pictured) in his World Cup debut against Greece in the US in 1994 and against Jamaica in France in 1998.

gary's 8–3 victory over Germany in Switzerland on June 20, 1954, and when Hungary beat El Salvador 10–1 in Spain on June 15, 1982.

Oleg Salenko scored five goals in Russia's 6–1 win over Cameroon on June 28, 1994—a record for a player in one game.

Most Goals in a World Cup Final The record for the most goals in a World Cup final is seven, when Brazil beat Sweden 5–2 in Stockholm, Sweden, on June 29, 1958.

Geoff Hurst scored three goals—the only hat trick in a final—when England beat West Germany 4–2 at Wembley, London, England, on June 30, 1966.

Fastest World Cup Goals Bryan Robson (England) scored 27 seconds into a match against France at Bilbao, Spain, on June 16, 1982.

Based on timing from film, Vaclav Masek of Czechoslovakia scored against Mexico in 15 seconds at Viña del Mar, Chile, in 1962.

Most World Cup Appearances The record number of World Cup tournaments participated in by a player is five, by Antonio Carbajal of Mexico (1950, 1954, 1958, 1962, and 1966) and Lothar Matthäus of (West) Germany (1982, 1986, 1990, 1994, and 1998). Matthäus also holds the record for matches played, with 25.

Youngest World Cup Player Norman Whiteside was 17 years 41 days old when he played for Northern Ireland against Yugoslavia in June 1982.

Oldest World Cup Player Roger Milla was 42 years 39 days old when he played for Cameroon against Russia on June 28, 1994.

Most Olympic Wins   The Olympic soccer championship has been won three times by Great Britain (1900, 1908, and 1912) and Hungary (1952, 1964, and 1968).

Most Copa America Wins   The record for wins in the Copa America (the South American Championships until 1974) is 14, by Uruguay (1916–17, 1920, 1923–24, 1926, 1935, 1942, 1956, 1959, 1967, 1983, 1987, and 1995) and Argentina (1921, 1925, 1927, 1929, 1937, 1941, 1945–47, 1955, 1957, 1959, 1991, and 1993).

Most CONCACAF Gold Cup Wins   The CONCACAF Gold Cup (the CONCACAF Championships until 1990) has been won 10 times by Costa Rica (1941, 1946, 1948, 1953, 1955, 1960, 1961, 1963, 1969, and 1989).

Most Asian Cup Wins   The Asian Cup, held every four years since 1956, has been won three times by Iran (1968, 1972, and 1976) and Saudi Arabia (1984, 1988, and 1996).

Most African Cup Of Nations Wins   The African Cup Of Nations was first held in 1957. Two countries have each won four times: Ghana in 1963, 1965, 1978, and 1982 and Egypt in 1957, 1959, 1986, and 1998.

MOST EUROPEAN CHAMPIONSHIPS WINS   Germany has won the European Championships a record three times, in 1972 and 1980 (as West Germany) and in 1996. Jürgen Klinsmann is pictured (center) after the 1996 final at Wembley Stadium, London, England. Germany beat the Czech Republic 2-1 in the first final of any senior championship to be decided by a "golden goal."

MOST WORLD CUP WINS Brazil has won the World Cup a record four times (1958, 1962, 1970, and 1994). Romario is pictured holding the trophy after their most recent win. Brazil is the only team to have taken part in all 16 finals tournaments and has won a record 53 matches out of 80 in the finals stage.

Most Women's World Cup Wins The women's cup was initiated in 1991 and is held every four years. It was won by the US in 1991 and by Norway in 1995.

Highest Score in a Women's International The record score in a women's international game is 21–0, by China against the Philippines at the 1995 Asian Women's Championship in Malaysia; by Canada against

Puerto Rico at Centennial Park, Toronto, Canada, on August 28, 1998; by Australia against American Samoa at Mt. Smart Stadium, Auckland, New Zealand, on October 9, 1998; and by New Zealand, against Samoa on the same date and at the same place.

The highest score ever during the women's World Cup Finals, 8–0, was by Sweden against Japan in Foshan, China, on November 19, 1991, and by Norway against Nigeria on June 6, 1995, in Karlstad, Sweden.

FOOTBALL

Most Super Bowl Wins   The greatest number of team wins is five, by the San Francisco 49ers (1982, 1985, 1989–90, and 1995) and by the Dallas Cowboys (1972, 1978, 1993–94, and 1996).

The individual player to have been on the most winning teams is Charles Hayley, who won five Super Bowls, two with the San Francisco 49ers (1989–90) and three with the Dallas Cowboys (1993–94 and 1996).

Chuck Noll holds the record for the most wins by a coach. He led the Pittsburgh Steelers to four Super Bowl titles between 1975 and 1980: IX, X, XIII, and XIV.

Highest Super Bowl Scores   The highest team score was set by the San Francisco 49ers when they beat the Denver Broncos 55–10 at New Orleans, Louisiana, on January 28, 1990. As well as being the highest victory margin, San Francisco's eight touchdowns are a Super Bowl record.

In 1995, the San Francisco 49ers also set the record for the highest aggregate score when they beat the San Diego Chargers 49–26.

Highest NFL Attendance   The record for the greatest number of spectators at a regular season game is 102,368 on November 10, 1957. The game was between the LA Rams and the San Francisco 49ers and was played at the Los Angeles Coliseum, California.

Most NFL Titles   The Green Bay Packers have won a record 13 NFL/NFC titles: 1929–31, 1936, 1939, 1944, 1961–62, 1965–67, 1996, and 1997.

Most AFL Titles   The record for the most AFL/AFC titles is held by the Buffalo Bills, who won six titles in 1964 and 1965 and from 1990 to 1993. The last four titles led to Super Bowl finals, but the Bills lost on each occasion—another record.

Most Consecutive NFL Wins   The Chicago Bears hold the record for the most consecutive NFL regular-season victories, winning 17 games in succession in 1933 and 1934.

The Miami Dolphins set a record for the most consecutive games won in a single season with 14 in 1972.

Longest Unbeaten NFL Streak   The most consecutive games played without defeat in the NFL is 25 by the Canton Bulldogs, with a total of 22 wins and three ties between 1921 and 1923.

MOST YARDS GAINED RUSHING   On November 26, 1998, Barry Sanders of the Detroit Lions became only the second back to rush for more than 15,000 yards, with a career total at the end of the 1998 season of 15,269 yards. The record is held by Walter Payton of the Chicago Bears, who rushed for 16,726 yards between 1975 and 1987.

Most NFL Wins in a Season   The record for the most wins in a season is 15, by the San Francisco 49ers in 1984, the Chicago Bears in 1985, and the Minnesota Vikings in 1998.

The Miami Dolphins won all their games in the 1972 season (14 regular-season games and three playoff games, including the Super Bowl).

Highest NFL Scores   The highest individual team score in a regular-season game is 72, by the Washington Redskins against the New York Giants (who scored 41) on November 27, 1966. This game also holds the record for the highest aggregate score for an NFL game.

The Chicago Bears beat the Washington Redskins 73–0 in the NFL Championship on December 8, 1940.

Most NFL Games Played   George Blanda played in 340 games in a record 26 seasons in the NFL (Chicago Bears 1949–58, Baltimore Colts 1950, Houston Oilers 1960–66, and Oakland Raiders 1967–75).

Most Successful NFL Coach   The record for the greatest number of games won as coach is 347, by Don Shula for the Baltimore Colts (1963–69) and the Miami Dolphins (1970–95).

Most NFL Games Lost   The Tampa Bay Buccaneers lost a record 26 consecutive games in 1976 and 1977.

Longest NFL Pass Completion   A pass completion of 99 yards has been achieved on eight occasions and has always resulted in a touchdown. The most recent 99-yard pass was from Brett Favre to Robert Brooks of the Green Bay Packers against the Chicago Bears on September 11, 1995.

Longest NFL Punt   Steve O'Neal kicked a punt of 98 yards for the New York Jets against the Denver Broncos on September 21, 1969.

Longest NFL Punt Return   The longest return is 103 yards by Robert Bailey for the Los Angeles Rams against the New Orleans Saints on October 23, 1994.

Longest Interception Returns in an NFL Game   The longest recorded return for a touchdown is 104 yards. It was achieved by James Willis and Troy Vincent for the Philadelphia Eagles in a game against the Dallas Cowboys on November 3, 1996. Willis returned the ball 14 yards

LONGEST FIELD GOAL (NFL)   The longest field goal kicked is 63 yards by Tom Dempsey of the New Orleans Saints and Jason Elam (pictured) of the Denver Broncos. Dempsey's record was set on November 8, 1970, while playing against the Detroit Lions; with two seconds remaining and with the Saints trailing 17–16, Dempsey stepped up and made his historic kick. The record was equaled on October 25, 1998, when Elam's kick for the Broncos at the end of the first half against the Jacksonville Jaguars sailed between the posts. Dempsey was watching the game on TV and said he cheered when the record was equaled. Elam also holds the record for being the most accurate point-after-touchdown maker in NFL history, having converted 259 out of 260 during his six-year career with the Broncos.

MOST PASSES COMPLETED Dan Marino of the Miami Dolphins has completed more passes than any other NFL football player, with 4,763 between 1983 and 1998. Marino also holds records for the most passing attempts (7,989), the most yards gained passing in a career (58,913) and in a season (5,084 in 1984), and the most touchdown passes in a career (408) and in a season (48 in 1984).

and lateraled it to Vincent, who returned it for the remaining 90 yards.

The longest interception return for a touchdown by one player is 103 yards. This was set by Vencie Glenn for the San Diego Chargers in a game against the Denver Broncos on November 29, 1987. This was equaled by Louis Oliver for the Miami Dolphins against the Buffalo Bills on October 4, 1992.

Longest NFL Kickoff Return   The record for the longest-ever NFL kickoff return for a touchdown is 106 yards, by three players: Al Carmichael for the Green Bay Packers against the Chicago Bears on October 7, 1956; Noland Smith for the Kansas City Chiefs against the Denver Broncos on December 17, 1967; and Roy Green for the St. Louis Cardinals against the Dallas Cowboys on October 21, 1979.

Most NFL Kickoff Returns   The New York Giants hold the record for the most kickoff returns in one game, making 12 against the Washington Redskins on November 27, 1966. Washington themselves had seven returns, so there was a record number of kickoff returns in one game.

Longest Runs from Scrimmage (NCAA)   The record for the longest run from scrimmage is 99 yards by Gale Sayers (Kansas v. Nebraska), 1963; Max Anderson (Arizona State v. Wyoming), 1967; Ralph Thompson (West Texas State v. Wichita State), 1970; and Kelsey Finch (Tennessee v. Florida), 1977.

Largest Crowd (NCAA Bowl Games)   A record 106,869 people were at the 1973 Rose Bowl when Southern California beat Ohio State 42–17.

MOST PASS ATTEMPTS IN A GAME Drew Brees (above) of Purdue University set an NCAA record, with 83 pass attempts against Wisconsin in October 1998. He also made 55 pass completions, equaling the record set by Rusty LaRue of Wake Forest. The NFL record for pass attempts is 70 (45 completions), by Drew Bledsoe for the New England Patriots against the Minnesota Vikings on November 13, 1994.

CRICKET

Highest Team Innings Victoria scored 1,107 runs in 10 hr. 30 min. v. New South Wales in an Australian Sheffield Shield match at Melbourne in December 1926.

The test-match record is 952 for six by Sri Lanka v. India at Colombo, Sri Lanka, from August 4 to 6, 1997.

Lowest Team Innings The traditional first-class record is 12, shared by two teams: Oxford University (a man short) v. Marylebone Cricket Club at Cowley Marsh, Oxford, England, in 1877 and Northamptonshire v. Gloucestershire at Gloucester, England, in June 1907.

A team called "The Bs" scored six in their second innings against England at Lord's, London, England, in 1810.

The test-match record is 26, by New Zealand v. England at Auckland, New Zealand, in 1955.

Most Sixes in an Innings   Andrew Symonds hit 16 sixes in an innings of 254 not out for Gloucestershire v. Glamorgan in a County Championship match at Abergavenny, Wales, in August 1995. He added four in his second innings of 76 for a record match total of 20.

Chris Cairns hit a record 14 sixes in a limited-overs international in his 157 (from 89 deliveries) for New Zealand against Kenya at Nairobi, Kenya, on September 7, 1997.

Most Sixes in a Test Innings   Wasim Akram hit a record 12 sixes in his 257 not out for Pakistan against Zimbabwe at Sheikhupura, Pakistan,

FASTEST BOWLERS   Allan Donald of South Africa is one of the fastest bowlers playing today, with deliveries that are regularly recorded at speeds of up to 93 mph. Nicknamed "White Lightning," Donald gives the batsman only about 4/10 of a second to react from the moment a ball leaves his hand to the moment it arrives at the wicket. This devastating speed contributed to his 107 international wickets in test matches and one-day internationals in 1998, which made him the world's leading wicket taker. The highest electronically measured speed for a bowled ball is 99.7 mph, bowled by Jeff Thomson of Australia against the West Indies in December 1975.

from October 18 to 20, 1996. Akram also holds the record for the greatest number of wickets taken in a one-day international career, with a total of 371 in 265 matches—an average of 23.49—between 1985 and 1999.

Most Wickets in a Match   Jim Laker took 19 wickets for 90 runs (9–37 and 10–53) for England v. Australia at Old Trafford, England, in July 1956.

Most Wickets in an Innings   Alfred Freeman of Kent, England, took all 10 wickets in an innings on three occasions against Lancashire in 1929 and 1931 and against Essex in 1930.

The fewest runs to have been scored off a bowler taking all 10 wickets is 10, off Hedley Verity for Yorkshire v. Nottinghamshire at Leeds, England, in 1932 (the full analyses for earlier performances of the feat are unknown).

Most Catches (Fielder)   The greatest number in an innings is seven, by Michael Stewart for Surrey v. Northamptonshire at Northampton, England, on June 7, 1957, and by Anthony Brown for Gloucestershire v. Nottinghamshire at Nottingham, England, on July 26, 1966.

Most Catches in a Match (Fielder)   Walter Hammond held a total of 10 catches for Gloucestershire in a game against Surrey at Cheltenham, England, from August 16 to 17, 1928.

Most Catches in a Test Match (Fielder)   Seven catches were made by Greg Chappell for Australia v. England at Perth, Australia, in 1974; Yajurvindra Singh for India v. England at Bangalore, India, in 1977; and Hashan Prasantha Tillekeratne for Sri Lanka v. New Zealand at Colombo, Sri Lanka, in 1992.

HIGHEST INDIVIDUAL INNINGS   Brian Lara scored 501 not out in 7 hr. 54 min. for Warwickshire against Durham at Edgbaston, UK, in June 1994. His innings included the most runs in a day (390) and the most runs from strokes worth four or more (308: 62 fours and 10 sixes). Lara also holds the test-match record, with a score of 375 in 12 hr. 48 min. for the West Indies against England at Recreation Ground, St. John's, Antigua, in April 1994.

MOST WICKETS IN A TEST-MATCH INNINGS   India's Anil Kumble took all 10 wickets in his country's defeat of Pakistan at Delhi, India, in February 1999, which tied the two-match test series. He equaled the record held by Jim Laker, who took 10 wickets for England against Australia at Old Trafford, England, in July 1956. While Laker conceded fewer runs than Kumble—53 compared to 74—Kumble took fewer deliveries, ending his feat in 26.3 overs to Laker's 51.2 overs.

Most Dismissals (Wicket Keeper)   The record for the most ever dismissals in an innings is nine, by Tahir Rashid (eight catches and a stumping) for Habib Bank against Pakistan Automobile Corporation at Gujranwala, Pakistan, in November 1992 and by Wayne James (seven catches and two stumpings) for Matabeleland against Mashonaland Country Districts at Bulawayo, Zimbabwe, on April 19, 1996.

The most stumpings in an innings is six, by Hugo Yarnold for Worcestershire against Scotland at Broughty Ferry, Dundee, Scotland, on July 2, 1951.

The most dismissals in a match is 13, by Wayne James (11 catches, two stumpings) for Matabeleland v. Mashonaland Country Districts at Bulawayo, Zimbabwe, from April 19 to 21, 1996.

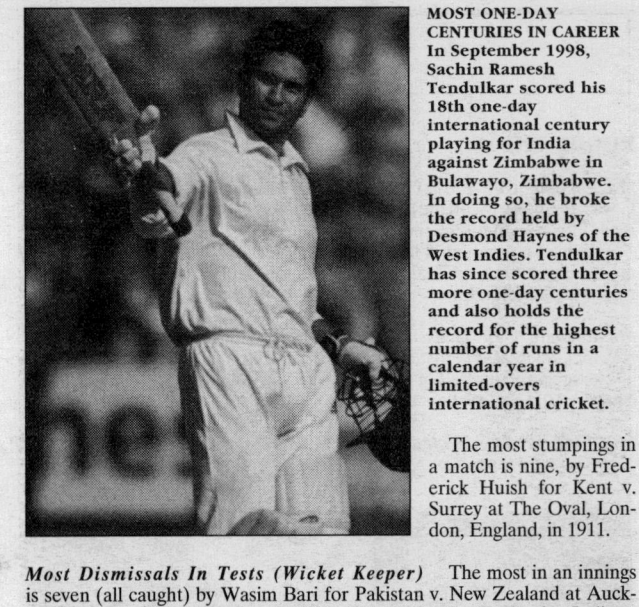

MOST ONE-DAY CENTURIES IN CAREER In September 1998, Sachin Ramesh Tendulkar scored his 18th one-day international century playing for India against Zimbabwe in Bulawayo, Zimbabwe. In doing so, he broke the record held by Desmond Haynes of the West Indies. Tendulkar has since scored three more one-day centuries and also holds the record for the highest number of runs in a calendar year in limited-overs international cricket.

The most stumpings in a match is nine, by Frederick Huish for Kent v. Surrey at The Oval, London, England, in 1911.

Most Dismissals In Tests (Wicket Keeper) The most in an innings is seven (all caught) by Wasim Bari for Pakistan v. New Zealand at Auckland, New Zealand, in February 1979; Bob Taylor for England v. India at Bombay, India, in February 1980; and Ian Smith for New Zealand v. Sri Lanka at Hamilton, New Zealand, in February 1991.

The most in a match is 11, all caught by Jack Russell for England v. South Africa at Johannesburg, South Africa, from November 30 to December 3, 1995.

Most Test-Match Appearances Allan Border of Australia played 156 test matches between 1979 and 1994.

Most Career Matches Played in One-Day Internationals Mohammad Azharuddin of India played 315 international games from the start of his career in 1985 to 1999. He has also made a record 148 career catches by a fielder.

Most Career Runs Scored in One-Day Internationals Desmond Haynes of the West Indies scored a total of 8,648 runs in 238 matches (an average of 41.37 a match) from 1977 to 1994.

Most Career Dismissals in One-Day Internationals Ian Healy of Australia made 234 (195 caught, 39 stumped) in 168 matches from 1988 to 1997.

RUGBY

RUGBY UNION

Most World Cup Points   The leading scorer in World Cup matches is Gavin Hastings (Scotland), with 227 points. Hastings holds the overall record for penalties (36) and conversions (39).

The most points scored in a World Cup match by one player is 45, by Simon Culhane for New Zealand against Japan in 1995. This total included a record 20 conversions.

Most World Cup Tries   The leading try scorer in World Cup matches is Rory Underwood (England), with a total of 11.

The most tries scored in a match by an individual is six, by Marc Ellis of New Zealand against Japan in 1995.

Most World Cup Appearances   The most individual appearances is 17, by Sean Fitzpatrick of New Zealand.

MOST POINTS IN A RUGBY LEAGUE MATCH   Dean Marwood (center of picture) scored 42 points in two separate games when Workington beat Highfield 78–0 on November 1, 1992, and when they beat Leigh 94–4 on February 26, 1995. This is a record for a League match. The most points scored in any game was 53, by George "Tich" West for Hull Kingston Rovers in their 73–5 defeat of Brookland Rovers in the Challenge Cup on March 4, 1905.

Most Points Scored in an International   The record for the highest score in any full international was set when Hong Kong beat Singapore 164–13 in a World Cup qualifying match at Kuala Lumpur, Malaysia, on October 27, 1994.

The highest aggregate score between two of the eight major nations under the modern points system is 109. This occurred when South Africa beat Wales 96–13 at Pretoria, South Africa, on June 27, 1998.

The most points scored by one player in an international match is 50 (10 tries), by Hong Kong's Ashley Billington in the World Cup qualifying match between Hong Kong and Singapore at Kuala Lumpur, Malaysia, on October 27, 1994.

The highest individual points scored in a match between the major nations is 27, by Rob Andrew (one try, two conversions, five penalty goals, and a drop goal) for England against South Africa at Pretoria, South Africa, on June 4, 1994.

The record number of tries scored by one participant in a match between the major nations is five, by George Lindsay for Scotland v. Wales

MOST POINTS SCORED IN A RUGBY LEAGUE INTERNATIONAL   A record 32 points were scored by Bobby Goulding (above; three tries, 10 goals) for England v. Fiji at Nadi, Fiji, on October 5, 1996, and by Andrew Johns (two tries, 12 goals) for Australia v. Fiji at Newcastle, Australia, on July 12, 1996.

on February 26, 1887, and by Douglas "Daniel" Lambert for England v. France on January 5, 1907.

Most Goals Kicked in an International The most penalty goals kicked in a match is eight, by Mark Wyatt (Canada) against Scotland at St. John, New Brunswick, Canada, on May 25, 1991; Neil Jenkins (Wales) against Canada at Cardiff, Wales, on November 10, 1993; Santiago Meson (Argentina) against Canada at Buenos Aires, Argentina, on March 12, 1995; Gavin Hastings (Scotland) against Tonga at Pretoria, South Africa, on May 30, 1995; Thierry Lacroix (France) against Ireland at Durban, South Africa, on June 10, 1995; and Paul Burke (Ireland) against Italy at Dublin, Republic of Ireland, on January 4, 1997.

Fastest Tries The fastest try in an international game was when Herbert "Bart" Price scored less than 10 seconds after kickoff for England v. Wales at Twickenham, England, on January 20, 1923.

The fastest known try in any game was scored eight seconds after kickoff by Andrew Brown for Widden Old Boys against Old Ashtonians at Gloucester, England, on November 22, 1990.

Most Points Scored in International Careers Michael Lynagh scored a record 911 points in 72 international matches for Australia between 1984 and 1995.

The most tries is 64, by David Campese in 101 internationals for Australia between 1982 and 1996.

Most International Appearances Philippe Sella (France) played 111 times for France between 1982 and 1995.

The most consecutive appearances is 63, by Sean Fitzpatrick (New Zealand) between 1986 and 1995.

Most Hong Kong Sevens Wins Fiji has won the Hong Kong Sevens nine times (1977–78, 1980, 1984, 1990–92,

MOST WORLD CUP MATCH WINS
Since the Rugby Union World Cup was first held in 1987, the competition has been won by New Zealand (1987), Australia (1991), and South Africa (1995). New Zealand holds the record for the most matches won in the championships, with 16 (six in 1987, five in 1991, and five in 1995). The All Blacks, as they are known to their fans, also set the World Cup record for the highest score when they beat Japan 145–17 at Bloemfontein, South Africa, on June 4, 1995. During the match, New Zealand scored 21 tries—another World Cup record. Wing three-quarter Jonah Lomu (left) shared the tournament record for the most tries (seven) with teammate Marc Ellis.

and 1998–99). The 1997 event was replaced by the World Cup Sevens, which was also won by Fiji.

Biggest Crowd   The biggest ever paying attendance was 104,000 people for Scotland's 12–10 win over Wales at Murrayfield, Edinburgh, Scotland, on March 1, 1975.

RUGBY LEAGUE

Most World Cup Wins   Australia has won the World Cup seven times, in 1957, 1968, 1970, 1977, 1988, 1992, and 1995. They also won the International Championship of 1975.

Highest Score in an International   Australia defeated South Africa with a record-high 86–6 at Gateshead, England, on October 10, 1995.

Most Career Points   Neil Fox scored 6,220 points (2,575 goals, including four drop goals, and 358 tries) in a senior Rugby League career that lasted from April 10, 1956, to August 19, 1979. Of those, 4,488 were for Wakefield Trinity, 1,089 were for five other teams, 228 were for Great Britain, and 147 were for Yorkshire; the remaining 268 were scored in other representative games.

Most Career Tries
Brian Bevan (Australia) scored a total of

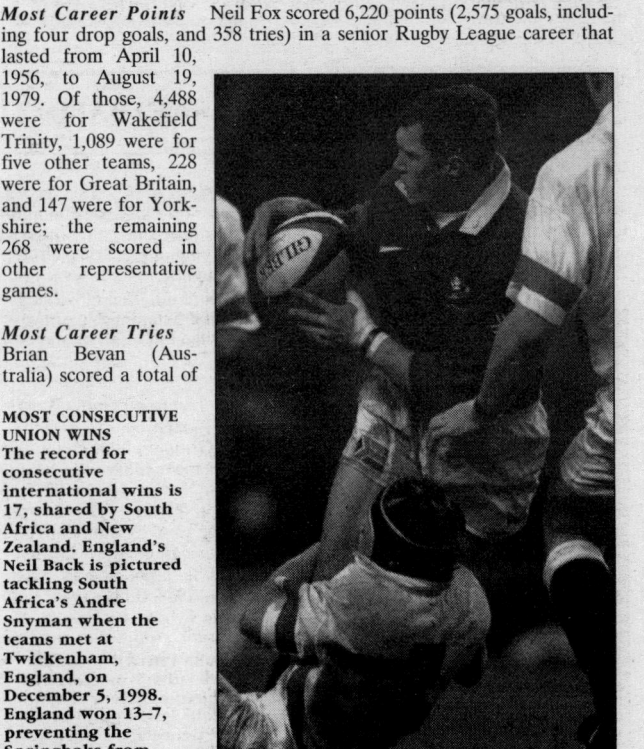

MOST CONSECUTIVE UNION WINS
The record for consecutive international wins is 17, shared by South Africa and New Zealand. England's Neil Back is pictured tackling South Africa's Andre Snyman when the teams met at Twickenham, England, on December 5, 1998. England won 13–7, preventing the Springboks from taking the record outright.

796 tries in 18 seasons from 1945 to 1964. He scored 740 tries for Warrington, 17 for Blackpool, and 39 in representative matches.

Most Career Goals Jim Sullivan (Wigan) kicked 2,867 goals in his team and representative career from 1921 to 1946.

Most International Matches Jim Sullivan played 60 internationals for Wales and Great Britain from 1921 to 1939, kicked the most goals (160), and scored the most points (329).

Most International Tries Michael Sullivan (Huddersfield, Wigan, St. Helens, York, and Dewsbury) scored a record 45 tries in 51 matches for England and Great Britain from 1954 to 1963.

Biggest Crowd The highest attendance was 104,583 people for a doubleheader (Newcastle Knights v. Manly Sea Eagles and Parramatta Eels v. St. George Illawarra Dragons) in Sydney, Australia, on March 7, 1999.

BASKETBALL

Most World Titles The record for the most men's World Championship (instituted in 1950) titles is four, by Yugoslavia (1970, 1978, 1990, and 1998).

The record for the most women's World Championship titles is six, jointly held by the US and the USSR.

Highest International Score Iraq beat Yemen by 251 to 33, at the Asian Games in New Delhi, India, in November 1982.

Most NBA Titles The Boston Celtics have won 16 National Basketball Association titles: in 1957, from 1959 to 1966, and in 1968, 1969, 1974, 1976, 1981, 1984, and 1986.

BIGGEST NBA CROWD Atlanta Hawks forward Tyrone Corbin (right of picture) drives past Chicago Bulls guard Ron Harper in Atlanta, Georgia, on March 27, 1998. The Bulls defeated the Hawks 89–74 before an NBA record crowd of 62,046 people.

Highest NBA Scores

The highest aggregate score in a game was 370, when the Detroit Pistons beat the Denver Nuggets 186–184 at Denver, Colorado, on December 13, 1983. Three overtimes were played after a 145–145 tie in regulation time.

The highest aggregate score ever in regulation time was 320, when the Golden State Warriors beat the Denver Nuggets 162–158 at Denver, Colorado, on November 2, 1990.

The highest-scoring individual in an NBA game was Wilt Chamberlain, who scored a record 100 points for the Philadelphia Warriors against the New York Knicks at Hershey, Pennsylvania, on March 2, 1962. This included a record 36 field goals and 28 free throws from 32 attempts, as well as a record 59 points in one half.

Chamberlain's free-throw record was equaled by Adrian Dantley for Utah against Houston at Las Vegas, Nevada, in January 1984.

Greatest NBA Winning Margin

The Cleveland Cavaliers beat the Miami Heat 148–80 on December 17, 1991—a record margin of 68 points.

HIGHEST AVERAGE POINTS (NBA) Michael Jordan, who retired from the game on January 13, 1999, set 21 NBA records while playing for the Chicago Bulls, including the highest average number of points per game (31.5), the most seasons as the league's leading scorer (10), the most seasons as the league's leading scorer of field goals (10), and the most seasons as the league player with the highest number of field-goal attempts (10). On April 20, 1986, he scored 63 points in a play-off game against the Boston Celtics—a record number of points by an individual player in an NBA play-off game. He also played on the gold-medal-winning US Olympic teams of 1984 and 1992. Off the court, Jordan owns a restaurant, has hosted the TV show *Saturday Night Live* and starred in *Space Jam*, a film in which he plays basketball with cartoon characters. He has earned more from endorsement deals than any other player.

Most NBA Season Wins

The Chicago Bulls had 72 NBA wins in the 1995/96 season—a record number within a single season.

Longest NBA Winning Streak

The Los Angeles Lakers won a record 33 games in succession from November 5, 1971, to January 7, 1972.

MOST NBA DEFENSIVE PLAYER AWARDS Dikembe Mutombo (number 55, bottom of picture) of the Atlanta Hawks secured a record-breaking third NBA Defensive Player of the Year award in May 1998. He first won the title in the 1994/95 season with the Denver Nuggets and then won it again in the 1996/97 season with Atlanta. Here, he is seen preparing to rebound in a game against the LA Lakers.

Most NBA Games

Robert Parish played 1,611 regular-season games over 21 seasons for the Golden State Warriors (1976–80), the Boston Celtics (1980–94), the Charlotte Hornets (1994–96), and the Chicago Bulls (1996–97).

The record for the greatest number of complete games played in a single season is 79, by Wilt Chamberlain for Philadelphia in 1961/62. During this period, he was on court for a record total of 3,882 minutes.

The record for most consecutive games is 1,028, by A.C. Green for the LA Lakers, Phoenix Suns, and Dallas Mavericks from November 19, 1986 to May 4, 1999.

Most NBA Points Kareem Abdul-Jabbar scored a record 38,387 points during his NBA career—an average of 24.6 points per game. This included a record 15,837 field goals in regular-season games and 5,762 points and a record 2,356 field goals in NBA play-off games.

Most Points in NBA Season In 1961/62, Wilt Chamberlain set season records for Philadelphia for points and scoring average, with 4,029 at 50.4 per game, and for field goals (1,597).

Youngest NBA Player Jermaine O'Neal was 18 years 53 days old when he made his debut for the Portland Trail Blazers against the Denver Nuggets on December 5, 1996.

Oldest Regular NBA Player   Robert Parish of the Chicago Bulls was still playing at the age of 43 years 231 days on April 19, 1997.

Highest Game Attendance   The biggest crowd ever at a basketball game was 80,000 people, for the final of the European Cup Winners' Cup between AEK Athens and Slavia Prague at the Olympic Stadium, Athens, Greece, on April 4, 1968.

Highest Vertical Dunk   Sean Williams and Michael Wilson, both of the Harlem Globetrotters, dunked a basketball at a record rim height of 11 ft. 8 in. at Disney-MGM Studios in Orlando, Florida, on September 16, 1996.

Longest Field Goal in a Game   Christopher Eddy scored a 90-ft.-$2^{1}/_{4}$-in. field goal for Fairview High School against Iroquois High School at Erie, Pennsylvania, on February 25, 1989. The record-breaking shot was made in overtime and won the game 51–50 for Fairview.

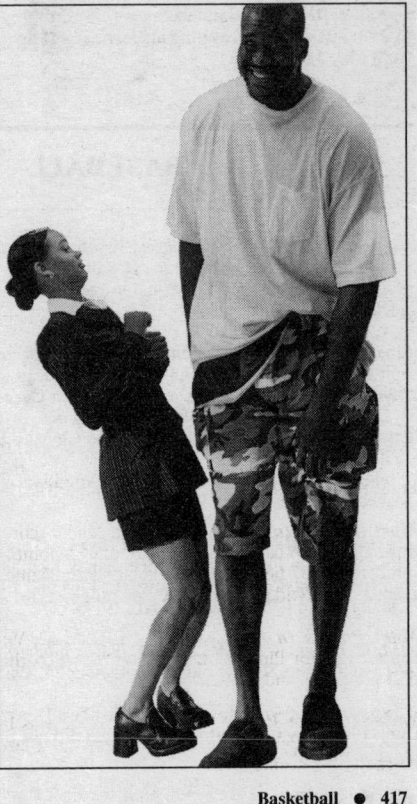

Top Shooting Speeds   John Connolly scored 280 out of 326 attempts in 10 minutes using one

MOST OLYMPIC TITLES   The US has won 11 men's Olympic titles, winning 100 games and losing just two since 1936. When the rules on amateurism were relaxed, star NBA players such as Shaquille O'Neal (pictured with actress Meagan Good), Michael Jordan, Magic Johnson, and Charles Barkley made the "Dream Teams" of 1992 and 1996 even stronger. The women's title has been won a record three times, by the USSR in 1976, 1980, and 1992 (the last as the Unified team from the ex-USSR) and by the US in 1984, 1988, and 1996.

basketball and one rebounder at St. Peter's School, Pacifica, California, on October 12, 1998.

Jeff Liles scored 53 points in one minute, shooting from seven positions as stated by Guinness World Records rules, at the YMCA in Carthage, Missouri, on May 8, 1997.

In 24 hours on September 29 and 30, 1990, Fred Newman scored 20,371 free throws from a total of 22,049 taken (a success rate of 92.39%) at Caltech in Pasadena, California.

Ted St. Martin scored a record 5,221 consecutive free throws at Jacksonville, Florida, on April 28, 1996.

Most Balls Spun   On May 26, 1999, Michael Kettman (US) spun 28 basketballs across his chest on the *Guinness® World Records* show.

Most Balls Dribbled   Joseph Odhiambo of Arizona has demonstrated the unique ability to dribble five basketballs—two with each hand, the fifth between his feet.

Longest Dribble   Jamie Borges (US) dribbled a basketball 96.89 miles in 24 hours without traveling at Barrington High School in Rhode Island, from May 3 to 4, 1998.

BASEBALL

Biggest Contract   The biggest baseball contract is an average of $15 million per year for seven years. It was signed by Kevin Brown of the LA Dodgers on December 12, 1998. On completion, Brown's contract will be worth a total of $105 million.

Most Spectators   An estimated 114,000 spectators watched an exhibition game between Australia and an American services team during the Olympic Games in Melbourne, Australia, on December 1, 1956.

The record attendance for a single game in the US is 92,706, for a game between the LA Dodgers and the Chicago White Sox on October 6, 1959.

The record for the highest season's attendance ever in all major-league baseball games is 70,372,221 in 1998.

Most Valuable World Series Player   Three players have won the Most Valuable Player award twice: Sandy Koufax (Los Angeles NL; 1963 and 1965); Bob Gibson (St. Louis NL; 1964 and 1967); and Reggie Jackson (Oakland AL, 1973; New York AL, 1977).

Oldest Player   Leroy "Satchel" Paige pitched for the Kansas City A's (AL) at 59 years 80 days old on September 25, 1965.

Youngest Player   Joseph Nuxhall played one game for Cincinnati in June 1944, at age 15 years 314 days, and did not play again in the National League until 1952.

MOST WORLD SERIES WINS The New York Yankees (AL) hold the record for the most World Series wins, achieving their 24th in 1998, the year they set an American League record for the most wins in a regular season, with 114, and a total season record of 125. Here, Scott Brosius, the Series' Most Valuable Player, celebrates the Yankees' triumph.

Most Consecutive Hits Pinky Higgins had 12 consecutive hits for Boston (AL) from June 19 to 21, 1938. This record was equaled by Moose Droppo for Detroit (AL) from July 14 to 15, 1952.

Joe DiMaggio hit in 56 consecutive games for the New York Yankees in 1941, earning him the nickname "Joltin' Joe." In 223 times at bat, he had 91 hits—56 singles, 16 doubles, four triples, and 15 home runs.

Most Home Runs Hank Aaron scored 755 career home runs: 733 for the Milwaukee Braves (NL; 1954–65) and the Atlanta Braves (NL; 1966–74) and 22 for the Milwaukee Brewers (AL) from 1975 to 1976.

The record for the most home runs in a major-league game is four. This was first achieved by Bobby Lowe for Boston against Cincinnati on May 30, 1894, and has been repeated 11 times since.

The most consecutive games hitting home runs is eight, achieved by Dale Long for Pittsburgh (NL) in May 1956, Don Mattingly for New York (AL) in July 1987, and Ken Griffey Jr. for Seattle (AL) in July 1993.

Longest Home Run The record for the longest measured home run in a major-league game is 634 ft., by Mickey Mantle for the New York Yankees against the Detroit Tigers at Briggs Stadium in Detroit, Michigan, in September 1960.

Longest Game The Brooklyn Dodgers (NL) and the Boston Braves played to a 1–1 tie after 26 innings on May 1, 1920. The Chicago White Sox (AL) played the longest game in elapsed time—8 hr. 6 min.—before beating the Milwaukee Brewers 7–6 in the 25th inning on May 9, 1984.

Most Games Played Pete Rose played in 3,562 games and was at bat a record 14,053 times for Cincinnati (NL; 1963–78, 1984–86), Philadelphia (NL; 1979–83), and Montreal (NL; 1984).

Cal Ripken played a total of 2,632 consecutive games for the Baltimore Orioles between May 30, 1982, and September 19, 1998.

HIGHEST-PAID CATCHER Mike Piazza (above) of the NY Mets has the most lucrative contract ever signed by a catcher. Over seven years, he stands to earn a total of $91 million. He also gets the use of a luxury box for family and friends at all home games and a hotel suite when the team is on the road.

Most Games Pitched The record for the most games pitched in a single career is 1,071, by Dennis Eckersly. He played for five different teams between 1975 and 1998.

Most Games Won by a Pitcher The most games won by a pitcher is 511, by Cy Young, who also played a record 749 complete games in his career for Cleveland (NL; 1890 to 1898), St. Louis (NL; 1899 to 1900), Boston (AL; 1901 to 1908), Cleveland (AL; 1909 to 1911), and Boston (NL; 1911). Young also pitched a record total of 7,356 innings.

Most Consecutive Games Won by a Pitcher The most consecutive games won by a pitcher is 24 by Carl Hubbell of the New York Giants (NL)—16 in 1936 and eight in 1937.

Most Consecutive Scoreless Innings Orel Hershiser IV of the LA Dodgers pitched a record 59 consecutive scoreless innings from August 30 to September 28, 1988.

Most Stolen Bases The career record for stolen bases is 1,299 (to April 22, 1999) by Rickey Henderson, Oakland Athletics (AL), 1979–84, 1989–93, 1994–95, 1998; New York Yankees (AL), 1985–89; Toronto Blue Jays (AL), 1993; San Diego Padres (NL), 1996–97; Anaheim Angels (AL),

MOST HOME RUNS Mark McGwire hit 70 home runs in 162 games for the St. Louis Cardinals (NL) in the 1998 season. He broke Roger Maris's record of 61 home runs in 162 games for the New York Yankees (AL), which had stood since 1961. McGwire was chased most of the way to the record by Sammy Sosa of the Chicago Cubs (NL), who finished the season with 66 home runs.

1997; and New York Mets (NL) 1999. Henderson also holds the single season record with 130 stolen bases in 1982.

Most Cy Young Awards Five Cy Young Awards have been won by Roger Clemens (Boston AL, in 1986, 1987, 1991, and Toronto AL, in 1997 and 1998).

The most Cy Young Awards won by a National League pitcher is four, by Steve Carlton (Philadelphia; 1972, 1977, 1980, and 1982) and Greg Maddux (Chicago, 1992, and Atlanta, from 1993 to 1995).

Fastest Pitcher The greatest reliably recorded speed at which a baseball has been pitched is 100.9 mph by Lynn Nolan Ryan (California Angels) at Anaheim Stadium in California on August 20, 1974.

Longest Throw Glen Gorbous (Canada) threw a baseball 445 ft. 10 in. on August 1, 1957.

Longest Throw by a Woman Mildred "Babe" Didrikson threw a baseball 296 ft. on July 25, 1931.

Fastest Base Runner The record for the fastest time for circling bases is 13.3 seconds, set by Ernest Swanson at Columbus, Ohio, in 1932. His average speed around the bases was 18.45 mph.

Shortest and Tallest Players The shortest major league player was 3-ft. 7-in. Eddie Gaedel, who pinch-hit for the St Louis Browns (AL) vs. the Detroit Tigers on August 19, 1951. The batter with the smallest-ever

MOST STRIKEOUTS Kerry Wood (left) of the Chicago Cubs (NL) threw 20 strikeouts in a nine-inning game on May 6, 1998, equaling the major-league record. Here, he is shown pitching in the fifth inning of the game against the Houston Astros in Chicago. Wood matched the record of five-time Cy Young Award winner Roger Clemens, who struck out 20 batters on two occasions when playing for the Boston Red Sox (AL).

major league strike zone walked on all four pitches. Following the game, major league rules were hastily rewritten to prevent any recurrence.

The tallest major leaguers of all time are two 6-ft. 10-in. pitchers: Randy Johnson, who played in his first game for the Montréal Expos (NL) on September 15, 1988; and Eric Hillman, who debuted for the New York Mets (NL) on May 18, 1992.

Biggest Replica Bat The world's biggest-ever replica baseball bat is 120 ft. high and weighs 30.85 tons. Modeled on the "R43" bat made for Babe Ruth, who is credited with inventing the modern baseball bat, the replica stands in front of bat maker Hillerich & Bradsby's headquarters in Louisville, Kentucky.

AUTO SPORTS

Most Successful Grand Prix Drivers The World Drivers' Championship was won five times by Juan-Manuel Fangio (Argentina) in 1951 and from 1954 to 1957. When Fangio retired in 1958, he had won 24 Grand Prix races (two shared) from a total of 51 starts.

Alain Prost (France) had 51 wins from a total of 199 races between 1980 and 1993. During his career, he gained a record 798.5 Grand Prix points.

The most pole positions is 65, by the late Ayrton Senna (Brazil) from 161 races (41 wins) between 1985 and 1994.

The most Grand Prix starts is 256, by Ricardo Patrese (Italy) from 1977 to 1993.

The most Grand Prix wins in a year is nine, by Nigel Mansell (GB) in 1992 and by Michael Schumacher (Germany) in 1995.

Most Successful Grand Prix Manufacturers The greatest number of Grand Prix race victories by a manufacturer is 119, a record held by Ferrari at the end of the 1998 Grand Prix season. Excluding the Indianapolis

MOST SUCCESSFUL FIA GT CHAMPIONSHIP CAR The Mercedes-Benz CLK-LM won all 10 races (winning the first two meets as the CLK-GT) of the 1998 FIA GT Championships. The two competing CLK-LM cars took double pole (places one and two on the grid) in all 10 races that make up the Championship season.

500, which in the 1950s was still part of the World Drivers' Championship, Ferrari won all seven races in 1952 and the first eight (of nine) in 1953.

Williams has won a record nine Grand Prix championships (1980–81, 1986–87, 1992–94, and 1996–97).

The McLaren team won 15 of the 16 Grand Prix races in the 1988 season: Ayrton Senna had eight wins and Alain Prost had seven.

Closest Grand Prix Finish Peter Gethin (GB) beat Ronnie Peterson (Sweden) by 0.01 seconds in the 1971 Italian Grand Prix.

Fastest Grand Prix Race Peter Gethin (GB) drove at an average speed of 150.759 mph in a BRM during the 1971 Italian Grand Prix at Monza.

Fastest Qualifying Lap in a Grand Prix Keke Rosberg (Finland) set a record lap time of 1 min. 5.59 sec. in a Williams-Honda at the 1985 British Grand Prix at the Silverstone track. His average speed for the circuit was 160.817 mph.

Oldest and Youngest Grand Prix Drivers The oldest Grand Prix driver was Louis Alexandre Chiron (Monaco), who finished sixth in the Monaco Grand Prix on May 22, 1955, at the age of 55 years 292 days.

The youngest driver was Michael Thackwell (NZ), who drove in the Canadian Grand Prix on September 28, 1980, at age 19 years 182 days.

The oldest winner of a Grand Prix race was Tazio Nuvolari (Italy) at Albi, France, on July 14, 1946, at age 53 years 240 days.

The youngest winner was Bruce McLaren (NZ), who won the US Grand Prix at Sebring, Florida, at age 22 years 104 days.

Troy Ruttman (US) was just 22 years 80 days old when he won the Indianapolis 500 on May 30, 1952. It was part of the World Drivers' Championship at the time.

MOST CONSECUTIVE WORLD RALLY TITLES Tommi Makinen and his co-driver Risto Mannisenmaki (Finland) won a third consecutive World Rally Championship title in November 1998. They are seen (above left) in the first leg of the 18th Argentine Rally on May 21, 1998, in Cordoba and (above right) celebrating their win in the 67th Monte Carlo Rally on January 20, 1999, which improves their chances of taking a fourth title. They are posing on the hood of the Mitsubishi Lancer that took them to their record.

Most Successful Indianapolis 500 Drivers Three drivers have each won the Indianapolis 500 race four times: A.J. Foyt Jr. (US) in 1961, 1964, 1967, and 1977; Al Unser Sr. (US) in 1970, 1971, 1978, and 1987; and Rick Mears (US) in 1979, 1984, 1988, and 1991.

Best Indianapolis 500 Starting Statistics A.J. Foyt Jr. started a record 35 consecutive Indianapolis 500 races from 1958 to 1992.

Rick Mears has started the race in pole position a record six times (1979, 1982, 1986, 1988, 1989, and 1991).

Fastest Indianapolis 500 Race Arie Luyendyk (Netherlands) won in 2 hr. 41 min. 18.404 sec. on May 27, 1990. His average speed was 185.986 mph.

Fastest Qualifying Laps in the Indianapolis 500 The highest average speed over the four qualifying laps is 236.992 mph, by Arie Luyendyk (Netherlands) in a Reynard-Ford Cosworth on May 12, 1996. Luyendyk's time included a world record speed for a single lap of 237.498 mph. Also that week, on May 10, 1996, Luyendyk had set the unofficial track record of 239.260 mph.

Biggest Indianapolis 500 Prizes The record for the largest prize fund ever is $9,047,150, in 1999.

The biggest individual prize awarded was $1,568,150, to Arie Luyendyk (Netherlands) in 1997.

Most Le Mans Wins The most wins by one driver is six, by Jacky Ickx (Belgium): 1969, 1975–77, and 1981–82.

The record for the most Le Mans wins by a manufacturer is 16, by Porsche (1970–71, 1976–77, 1979, 1981–87, 1993, 1996–98).

Fastest Laps at Le Mans   The fastest lap ever in the Le Mans 24-hour race is 3 min. 21.27 sec., by Alain Ferté (France) in a Jaguar XJR-9 on June 10, 1989. His average speed over the 8-mile-728-yd. lap was 150.429 mph.

Hans Stück (West Germany) set the fastest practice lap speed on June 14, 1985, attaining a speed of 156.381 mph.

Greatest Distance Covered in a Le Mans Race   Dr. Helmut Marko (Austria) and Gijs van Lennep (Netherlands) covered 3,315 miles 363 yd. in their 4,907 cc Flat-12 Porsche 917K Group 5 sports car from June 12 to 13, 1971.

The greatest distance covered on the current Le Mans circuit was 3,313 miles 264 yd., by Jan Lammers (Netherlands), Johnny Dumfries (GB), and

MOST SUCCESSFUL GRAND PRIX FAMILY Graham Hill (GB) was World Drivers' Champion in 1962 and 1968 and runner-up three times. His son Damon (right) became World Drivers' Champion on October 13, 1996.

Andy Wallace (GB) in a Jaguar XJR-9 from June 11 to 12, 1988. Their average speed was 138.047 mph.

Longest Rally   The Singapore Airlines London-Sydney Rally covered 19,330 miles from Covent Garden, London, England, to Sydney Opera House, Australia, in 1977. It was won by Andrew Cowan, Colin Malkin, and Michael Broad (GB), racing in a Mercedes 280E.

Most Monte Carlo Rally Wins   The Monte Carlo Rally has been won four times by Sandro Munari (Italy) in 1972 and from 1975 to 1977 and by Walter Röhrl (West Germany), with co-driver Christian Geistdorfer, in 1980 and from 1982 to 1984.

Most World Rally Championship Wins   Juha Kankkunen (Finland) won four times, in 1986, 1987, 1991, and 1993.

Carlos Sainz (Spain) has won a record 22 World Championship races in his career.

Most Rac Rally Wins   Hannu Mikkola (Finland), with co-driver Arne Hertz (Sweden), has had four wins, in a Ford Escort in 1978 and 1979 and in an Audi Quattro in 1981 and 1982.

Fastest Race   The Busch Clash race, over a distance of 50 miles on a 2-mile-880-yard, 31° banked track at Daytona, Florida, is the world's fastest race. In 1987, Bill Elliott (US) averaged a record speed of 197.802 mph in a Ford Thunderbird during the race.

BIKE SPORTS

Most World Championship Cycling Titles   Koichi Nakano of Japan won 10 professional sprint titles in a row from 1977 to 1986.

The most wins at a men's amateur event is seven, by Daniel Morelon (France) in the sprint (1966, 1967, 1969–71, 1973, and 1975) and Leon Meredith (GB) in the 100-km motor paced (1904–05, 1907–09, 1911, and 1913).

Most Olympic Cycling Titles   The most gold medals won in cycling events at the Olympic Games is three, by Paul Masson (France) in 1896, Francisco Verri (Italy) in 1906, Robert Charpentier (France) in 1936, and Daniel Morelon (France) in 1968 (two) and 1972. Morelon also won a silver medal at the 1976 Olympic Games and a bronze medal at the 1964 Games.

Most Tour de France Wins   The greatest number ever of wins in the annual Tour de France race is five, a record held by four men: Jacques Anquetil (France) in 1957 and from 1961 to 1964; Eddy Merckx (Belgium) from 1969 to 1972 and in 1974; Bernard Hinault (France) in 1978, 1979, 1981, 1982, and 1985; and Miguel Induráin (Spain) from 1991 to 1995.

BIGGEST BEACH RACE More than 250,000 spectators turned out for Le Touquet Beach Race in France on February 22, 1998. This annual event features 800 riders pitting themselves against Le Touquet beachfront. In the 1997 race, only 100 riders completed the course. Beach racing is an offshoot of motocross, a popular off-road motorcycle sport. The most prestigious international motocross competition in the world is the Motocross des Nations, where the world's best riders represent their countries in a two-day contest. This annual "World Cup" is held in a different country each year and regularly includes riders representing more than 30 countries. Each country enters three riders, one in each class—a 125 cc, a 250 cc, and an open-class racer.

Fastest Tour de France Speed The fastest average speed in the Tour de France was 24.547 mph by Miguel Induráin (Spain) in 1992. Induráin won five consecutive Tour de France races and won both the Giro d'Italia and the Tour de France in 1992 and 1993. He retired from cycling at the end of 1996, having never won the Vuelta a España, the major tour of his native country.

Longest One-Day Cycling Race The longest single-day "massed start" road race is the 342- to 385-mile event from Bordeaux to Paris, France. The highest average speed was 29.32 mph, by Herman van Springel (Belgium) in 1981. He covered 363 miles 176 yd. in 13 hr. 35 min. 18 sec.

Most Successful Motorcyclist The most World Championship titles won is 15, by Giacomo Agostini (Italy): seven at 350 cc from 1968 to 1974 and eight at 500 cc from 1966 to 1972 and in 1975. Agostini is also the only man to have won two World Championships in five consecutive years (350 cc and 500 cc titles from 1968 to 1972). He won 122 races (68 at 500 cc and 54 at 350 cc) in the World Championship series between April 24, 1965, and September 25, 1977, including 19 in 1970. That season's total equaled the record set before by Mike Hailwood (GB) in 1966.

PURSUIT RECORDS   Since its introduction at the 1974 Commonwealth Games, the 4,000-m team pursuit has been won by the Australian team five times. They also hold the Games record of 4 min. 3.84 sec. set in Victoria, British Columbia, Canada, in 1994. The world record is currently held by Italy, who were timed at 4 min. 00.94 sec. at the Manchester Velodrome in England in 1996.

Most Supercross Wins   The record for the most Supercross wins is six, by Jeremy McGrath (US), who won the AMA (American Motorcycle Association) Supercross Champion 250 cc title from 1993 to 1996 and in 1998 and 1999. McGrath also won the World Supercross title in 1994 and 1995.

MOST WINS IN ONE SEASON Australian Michael Doohan's 12 wins in the 500 cc class during 1997 gave him the record for the most wins in a single class in one season. Doohan's victory on October 4, 1998, at the Australian Grand Prix gave him a fifth consecutive World 500 cc Motorcycle Championship, the most achieved by a currently competitive motorcyclist.

Most Tourist Trophy Wins   The record for the greatest number of victories in the Isle of Man TT races is 23, by Joey Dunlop (Ireland) between 1977 and 1998.

The most events won in the Isle of Man TT races in one year is four (Formula One, Junior, Senior, and Production), by Phillip McCallen (Ireland) in 1996.

Highest Tourist Trophy Speeds   The Isle of Man TT circuit record is 123.61 mph, set by Carl Fogarty on June 12, 1992.

MOST WOMEN'S ROAD CHAMPIONSHIPS The record for the most women's World Cycling Championship titles is 11, by Jeannie Longo-Ciprelli (France). She won titles for pursuit (1986 and 1988–89), road (1985–87, 1989, and 1995), points (1989), and time trial (1995 and 1996). She also holds the world one-hour record, covering 29 miles 1,629 yd. in Mexico City, Mexico, on October 26, 1996—the same year she won an Olympic gold medal.

On June 12, 1992, Steve Hislop set the race speed record of 1 hr. 51 min. 59.6 sec.—an average speed of 121.28 mph—when he won the Senior TT on a Norton.

The record for the fastest average speed around the "Mountain" circuit by a woman is 112.65 mph, by Sandra Barnett (GB) in the Junior TT on June 4, 1997.

Most Trials Wins Jordi Tarrès (Spain) won seven World Trials Championships: in 1987, from 1989 to 1991, and from 1993 to 1995. He secured his first World Championship at the age of 20 and has also been runner-up twice.

Youngest World Cup Winner The youngest rider to win an event at the World Cup is Marco Melandri (Italy), who won the Dutch TT Grand Prix at Assen in June 1997 at age 15 years 10 months, riding for the Benetton team on a 125 cc Matteoni.

Longest Motorcycle Circuit   The 37-mile 284-yd. "Mountain" circuit on the Isle of Man has hosted the principal TT races since 1911 (with minor amendments in 1920). The circuit has 264 curves and corners and is the longest used for any motorcycle race.

Fastest Motorcycle Circuit   The highest average lap speed attained on any closed circuit on a motorcycle is 160.288 mph by Yvon du Hamel (Canada) on a modified 903 cc four-cylinder Kawasaki Z1 at the 31° banked 2¼-mile Daytona International Speedway in Florida in March 1973. His lap time was 56.149 seconds.

SWIMMING & DIVING

Most Olympic Medals   The most individual Olympic gold medals is five, by Krisztina Egerszegi (Hungary)—the 100-m backstroke in 1992, the 200-m backstroke in 1988, 1992, and 1996, and the 400-m medley in 1992.

The most individual gold medals won by a man is four, by Charles Daniels (US) in the 220-yd freestyle in 1904, the 440-yd freestyle in 1904,

FASTEST BUTTERFLY SWIMMER   James Hickman (GB) currently holds two world records for the butterfly stroke—he took the world short-course record for 200 m in Paris, France, on March 28, 1998, in a time of 1 min. 51.76 sec. and then on December 13 of the same year went on to beat Michael Klim's world 100-m short-course record with a time of 51.02 seconds, shaving 0.02 seconds off the previous time. Hickman was in top form at the European short-course championships in Sheffield, England, winning both the 200-m butterfly and the 200-m individual medley, as well as gaining a bronze in the 100-m individual medley. The butterfly stroke developed from a loophole in the rules governing the breaststroke and was officially recognized as a distinct stroke in 1952.

and the 100-m freestyle in 1906 and 1908; Roland Matthes (GDR) in the 100-m and 200-m backstroke in 1968 and 1972; Tamás Daryni (Hungary) in the 200-m and 400-m medley in 1988 and 1992; Aleksandr Popov (Russia) in the 50-m and 100-m freestyle in 1992 and 1996; and Mark Spitz (see below).

The most golds won by a swimmer is nine, by Mark Spitz (US) in the 4 x 100-m and 4 x 200-m freestyle in 1968, the 100-m and 200-m freestyle, the 4 x 100-m and 4 x 200-m freestyle, the 100-m and 200-m butterfly, and the 4 x 100-m medley in 1972. He set a world-record time in all but one (the 1968 4 x 200-m freestyle).

The most golds won by a woman is six, by Kristin Otto (GDR) in 1988: the 100-m freestyle, backstroke, and butterfly, the 50-m freestyle, the 4 x 100-m freestyle, and the 4 x 100-m medley.

Mark Spitz has won the most medals, 11: a silver (100-m butterfly) and a bronze (100-m freestyle) in 1968, as well as his nine golds. This record was equaled by Matt Biondi (US), with a gold in 1984, five golds, one silver, and one bronze in 1988, and two golds and a silver in 1992. Spitz's record of seven medals at a single Games (1972) was also equaled by Biondi in 1988.

The most medals won by a woman is eight, by Dawn Fraser (Australia), with four gold and four silver from 1956 to 1964; Kornelia Ender (GDR), with four gold and four silver from 1972 to 1976; and Shirley Babashoff (US), with two gold and six silver from 1972 to 1976.

Most Wins in One Event   Two swimmers have won the same event at three Olympic Games: Dawn Fraser (Australia) in the 100-m freestyle (1956, 1960, 1964) and Krisztina Egerszegi (Hungary) in the 200-m backstroke (1988, 1992, 1996).

Most Medals in the World Championships   Michael Gross (West Germany) won 13 World Championship medals (five gold, five silver, and three bronze) from 1982 to 1990.

The most medals won by a woman is 10, by Kornelia Ender (GDR)—eight gold and two silver in 1973 and 1975.

The most golds won by a man is six (two individual and four relay) by James Montgomery (US) in 1973 and 1975.

The most medals at a single championship is seven, by Matt Biondi (US), with three gold, one silver, and three bronze in 1986.

Most World Records   The most world records set by a man is 32, by Arne Borg (Sweden) between 1921 and 1929.

The most world records set by a woman is 42, by Ragnhild Hveger (Denmark) from 1936 to 1942.

The most world records set by a man in currently recognized events (metric distances in 50-m pools) is 26, by Mark Spitz (US) from 1967 to 1972.

The most world records set by a woman in currently recognized events is 23 by Kornelia Ender (GDR, now Germany) from 1973 to 1976.

The most world records set in one pool is 86 in the North Sydney pool in Australia between 1955 and 1978. This includes 48 imperial distance records.

Longest Swims   The greatest distance known to have been swum in the ocean measured 128 miles 1,432 yd., by Walter Poenisch Sr. (US) from Havana, Cuba, to Little Duck Key, Florida, in 34 hr. 15 min. from July 11 to 13, 1978.

Fred Newton swam 1,826 miles down the Mississippi River between

DEEPEST CONSTANT-BALLAST DIVE On November 30, 1998, Tanya Streeter (Cayman Islands) broke the world record for constant-ballast free diving in freshwater, reaching a depth of 185 ft. at a sinkhole in Florida. In a constant-ballast dive, weights are worn for the ascent as well as the descent. Streeter also holds the record for the assisted free dive using a balloon, attaining a depth of 370 ft. on May 9, 1998. She made this free dive with a single breath and used a weighted sled. The Caymans have produced some of the world's best divers because of their excellent diving infrastructure and superb water conditions.

Ford Dam and Carrollton Ave., New Orleans, Louisiana, from July 6 to December 29, 1930. He was in the water for a total of 742 hours.

The greatest distance swum in 24 hours is 63 miles 559 yd., by Anders Forvass (Sweden) at the 25-m Linköping public swimming pool in Sweden from October 28 to 29, 1989.

The greatest distance swum by a woman in 24 hours is 59 miles 771 yd., by Kelly Driffield at the Mingara Leisure Center Pool, Tumbi Umbi, Australia, in June 1997.

The greatest distance ever swum underwater is 49 miles 68 yd. in 24 hours by Paul Cryne (GB) and Samir Sawan al Awami (Qatar) from Doha to Umm Said, Qatar, and back again in 1985.

YOUNGEST DIVING CHAMPIONS Canadian Alexandre Despatie (seen here left of picture with British diver Tony Ali) won gold in the 1998 Commonwealth Games platform-diving final in Kuala Lumpur, Malaysia, at the age of 13 years 104 days, making him the youngest-ever male winner of an international diving event. The youngest female winner was Fu Mingxia (China), who took the women's world platform title in Australia in 1991 at age 12 years 141 days.

The greatest distance ever to have been swum underwater by a relay team is 94 miles 774 yd., by six people who set the record in a swimming pool in Czechoslovakia (now Czech Republic) from October 17 to 18, 1987.

Longest Relays The 20-strong New Zealand national relay team swam a record 113 miles 1,040 yd. in Lower Hutt, New Zealand, in a time of 24 hours from December 9 to 10, 1983.

Biggest Relays   The most participants in a one-day swim relay was 2,454, each of whom swam one length at the Karosa swimming club, Vysoké Myto, Czech Republic, on April 1, 1998.

Most Olympic Diving Medals   The greatest number of Olympic medals ever won by a diver is five, by Klaus Dibiasi (Italy), with three gold and two silver from 1964 to 1976, and by Greg Louganis (US), with four gold and one silver in 1976, 1984, and 1988. Dibiasi is also the only diver to ever have won the same event (high board) at three successive Olympic Games (1968, 1972, and 1976).

Most World Diving Titles   Greg Louganis has won a record five world titles—high board in 1978 and both high board and springboard in 1982 and 1986, in addition to his four Olympic gold medals in 1984 and 1988.

The record for the greatest number of gold medals ever to have been won in a single event since the inaugural World Championship in 1973 is three, by Philip Boggs (US) in the springboard in 1973, 1975, and 1978 and Greg Louganis (see above). Boggs also won the 1976 Olympic springboard title.

COMBAT SPORTS

Most Successful Sumo Wrestlers   *Yokozuna* (grand champion) Sadaji Akiyoshi, alias Futabayama, holds the all-time record of 69 consecutive match wins (1937–39).

Yokozuna Koki Naya, alias Taiho ("Great Bird"), had won the Emperor's Cup a record 32 times by the time he retired in 1971.

The *ozeki* (second-highest rank) Tameemon Torokichi, alias Raiden, won 254 matches and lost only 10 in 21 years, giving him the highest-ever winning rate of 96.2%.

Most Successful Sumo Brothers   *Ozeki* Wakanohana was promoted to the rank of *yokozuna*, a rank held by his younger brother Takanohana since 1994, after winning the *Natsu* (summer) *Basho* in 1998. This is the first time in the 1,500-year history of the sport that two brothers have attained the rank of *yokozuna*.

Most Sumo Tournament Wins   *Yokozuna* Mitsugu Akimoto, alias Chiyonofuji, won the *Kyushu Basho* (one of the six annual tournaments) for a record eight successive years (1981–88). He also holds the record for the most career wins (1,045) and the most *Makunouchi* (top-division) wins (807).

Most Top-Division Sumo Bouts   Jesse Kuhaulua (US) fought 1,231 consecutive matches (1981). He was the first non-Japanese wrestler to win a top-division sumo tournament in 1972.

The most matches in all divisions is 1,631, by Yukio Shoji from 1964 to 1986.

The most matches contested in a career is 1,891, by Kenji Hatano (Oshio) from 1962 to 1988.

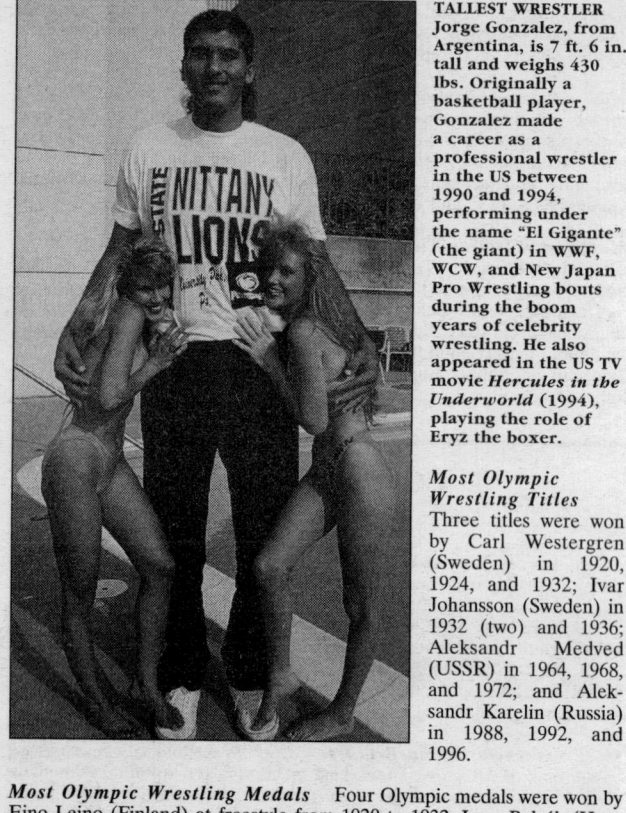

TALLEST WRESTLER
Jorge Gonzalez, from Argentina, is 7 ft. 6 in. tall and weighs 430 lbs. Originally a basketball player, Gonzalez made a career as a professional wrestler in the US between 1990 and 1994, performing under the name "El Gigante" (the giant) in WWF, WCW, and New Japan Pro Wrestling bouts during the boom years of celebrity wrestling. He also appeared in the US TV movie *Hercules in the Underworld* (1994), playing the role of Eryz the boxer.

Most Olympic Wrestling Titles

Three titles were won by Carl Westergren (Sweden) in 1920, 1924, and 1932; Ivar Johansson (Sweden) in 1932 (two) and 1936; Aleksandr Medved (USSR) in 1964, 1968, and 1972; and Aleksandr Karelin (Russia) in 1988, 1992, and 1996.

Most Olympic Wrestling Medals   Four Olympic medals were won by Eino Leino (Finland) at freestyle from 1920 to 1932; Imre Polyák (Hungary) at Greco-Roman from 1952 to 1964; and Bruce Baumgartner (US) at freestyle from 1984 to 1996.

Most Greco-Roman World Wrestling Titles   Aleksandr Karelin (Russia) won 11 titles in the 30 kg. class between 1988 and 1998.

Longest Wrestling Match   The longest recorded match lasted 11 hr. 40 min., when Martin Klein (Estonia representing Russia) beat Alfred Asikáinen (Finland) in the Greco-Roman 75 kg. "A" event in the 1912 Olympics.

Longest Reigns as Boxing Champion   Joe Louis (US) was world heavyweight champion for 11 years 252 days from 1937 to his retirement in 1949.

Heavyweight Rocky Marciano (US) is the only world champion at any weight to have won every fight of his entire professional career (49 fights from 1947 to 1955).

Longest Boxing Match The longest world-title fight under Queensberry Rules was between lightweights Joe Gans and Oscar Nelson (both US) at Goldfield, Nevada, on September 3, 1906. Gans won in the 42nd round on a foul.

Shortest Boxing Match The shortest world-title fight lasted 20 seconds, when Gerald McClellan (US) beat Jay Bell in a WBC middleweight bout in Puerto Rico on August 7, 1993.

Longest Boxing Career Without A Defeat On November 13, 1998, Ricardo Lopez (Mexico) outpointed Rosendo Alvarez in Las Vegas to retain his WBA Strawweight title. Lopez has remained unbeaten throughout his professional career, which has lasted 48 fights over 13 years 11 months.

Most Judo Titles Yasuhiro Yamashita (Japan) won one Olympic and four world titles: the Over 95 kg. in 1979, 1981, and 1983, the Open in 1981, and the Olympic Open in 1984. He retired undefeated after a total of 203 successive wins (1977–85).

Four world titles were also won by Shozo Fujii (Japan) at Under 80 kg. in 1971, 1973, and 1975, and the Under 78 kg. in 1979, and by Naoya Ogawa (Japan) in the Open in 1987, 1989, and 1991 and the Over 95 kg. in 1989.

Ingrid Berghmans (Belgium) won six women's world titles: the Open in 1980, 1982, 1984, and 1986 and the Under 72 kg. in 1984 and 1989. She

LONGEST-RUNNING KUNG FU TV SERIES The Warner Bros. series *Kung Fu* ran for 62 episodes from 1972 to 1975, starring David Carradine as Kwai Chang Caine. A new series was produced between 1992 and 1996, with Carradine as the grandson of the original Caine. It ran for four series and 88 episodes.

HEAVIEST SUMO WRESTLER Hawaiian-born Salevaa Atisance, known as Konishiki, tipped the scales at 605 lb. in his prime. He retired in May 1998 and now works as an *oyakata* (stable master) under the name Sanoyama.

won the Olympic 72 kg. title in 1988, when women's judo was introduced as a demonstration sport.

Most Successful Tae Kwon Do Practitioners Juan Moreno (US) won a silver medal in the finweight (lightest) class at the Olympics in Seoul, South Korea, in 1988 and took the silver again in Barcelona, Spain, in 1992, making him the most successful male tae kwon do contestant. Tae kwon do was a demonstration sport during these two Olympics but will be an official event at the 2000 Olympics in Sydney, Australia.

Chen Yi-an (Taiwan) is the most successful female tae kwon do contestant, having won gold in the 51 kg. class at Seoul in 1988 and the 60 kg. class in Barcelona in 1992.

Most World Karate Titles Great Britain has won a record six world titles at the Kumite team event (1975, 1982, 1984, 1986, 1988, and 1990).

The record for the most men's individual Kumite titles is two, shared by four competitors: Pat McKay (GB) at the Under 80 kg. in 1982 and 1984; Emmanuel Pinda (France) at the Open in 1984 and the Over 80 kg. in 1988; Thierry Masci (France) at the Under 70 kg. in 1986 and 1988; and José Manuel Egea (Spain) at the Under 80 kg. in 1990 and 1992.

Most Successful Arm Wrestler John Brzenk (US), a middleweight, has dominated many weight classes in arm wrestling over the past 17 years. During the 1998 World Championships in Petaluma, California, Brzenk won championships at five different weights, three with his right arm, two with his left. In the same year, he was named the greatest arm wrestler in the history of the sport during the World Wristwrestling Championship.

TAMASHIWARI CHAMPION Bruce Haynes broke 15 cement slabs with a combined weight of 683 lb. on March 22, 1998, in Sydney, Australia. Haynes, the undisputed *tamashiwari* (breaking objects with a blow from a bare hand) champion of the world, is a seventh-dan karate black belt and has been International Sports Karate Association World Champion eight times.

MARATHONS & ENDURANCE

Longest Running Race   The world's longest race ever covered a distance of 3,665 miles from New York City to Los Angeles in 1929. Finnish-born Johnny Salo won in 79 days and an elapsed time of 525 hr. 57 min. 20 sec., averaging 6.97 mph.

Most Marathon Finishers   The record number of confirmed finishers in a marathon is 38,706 at the centennial race in Boston, Massachusetts, on April 15, 1996.

Highest-Altitude Marathon   The biennial Everest Marathon, first run on November 27, 1987, is the highest-altitude marathon. It begins at 17,100 ft. at Gorak Shep and ends at Namche Bazar at an altitude of 11,300 ft.

Most Marathons Run   Horst Preisler (Germany) ran 631 races of 26 miles 385 yd. or longer from 1974 to May 29, 1996.

Henri Girault (France) ran a total of 330 100-km races from 1979 to June 1996 and has completed a run on every continent except Antarctica.

Fastest Three Marathons in Three Days   The fastest combined time for three marathons in three days is 8 hr. 22 min. 31 sec., by Raymond Hubbard (Belfast 2 hr. 45 min. 55 sec., London 2 hr. 48 min. 45 sec., and Boston 2 hr. 47 min. 51 sec.) from April 16 to 18, 1988.

Fastest Backward Marathon   Timothy "Bud" Badyna (US) ran a marathon backward in 3 hr. 53 min. 17 sec. on April 24, 1994 in Toledo, Ohio.

Fastest Three-Legged Marathon   Identical twins Nick and Alastair Benbow (UK) set a three-legged running record of 3 hr. 40 min. 16 sec. in the London Marathon in England on April 26, 1998. They were tied together at the wrist and shared a three-legged pair of running pants.

Oldest Marathon Finishers   Dimitrion Yordanidis (Greece) was 98 years old when he raced in Athens, Greece, in October 1976. His time was 7 hr. 33 min.

The oldest woman to complete a marathon was Thelma Pitt-Turner (New Zealand), who was 82 when she raced in New Zealand in August 1985. Her time was 7 hr. 58 min.

Most Modern Pentathlon World Titles   András Balczó (Hungary) won six individual and seven team titles in the modern pentathlon World Championships from 1960 to 1972.

The USSR holds the record for team titles with 18.

The most women's titles is four, by Eva Fjellerup (Denmark), who won the individual World Championship titles in 1990, 1991, 1993, and 1994.

Poland has won a record eight women's world team titles (1985, 1988–92, 1995, and 1998).

FASTEST HALF MARATHONS The world best time for a half marathon course is 59 min. 17 sec., by Paul Tergat (above) of Kenya at Milan, Italy, on April 4, 1998. The official women's record is 66 min. 43 sec., set by Masako Chika (Japan) at Tokyo, Japan, on April 19, 1997. Ingrid Kristiansen (Norway) ran a half marathon in 66 min. 40 sec. at Sandnes, Norway, on April 5, 1987, but the course measurement was not confirmed.

Most Pentathlon Olympic Titles   The record for the most Olympic gold medals won is three, by András Balczó of Hungary, who took the team title in 1960 and 1968 and the individual title in 1972.

The record for individual Olympic titles is two, by Lars Hall (Sweden) in 1952 and 1956.

Pavel Lednev (USSR) won a record seven medals (two team gold, one team silver, one individual silver, and three individual bronze) from 1968 to 1980.

Most World Biathlon Titles   Frank Ullrich (GDR) won six individual titles: four at 10 km from 1978 to 1981 and two at 20 km in 1982 and 1983.

Aleksandr Tikhonov was a member of a record 10 winning Soviet relay teams from 1968 to 1980 and won four individual titles.

The women's record is four, set by Petra Schaaf (Germany): 5 km in 1988 and 15 km in 1989, 1991, and 1993.

Longest Triathlon   David Holleran (Australia) completed a 2,542-km (1,578-mile) triathlon, consisting of a 42-km (26-mile) swim, 2,000-km

(1,242-mile) cycle ride, and 500-km (310-mile) run, in 17 days 22 hr. 50 min. from March 21 to April 8, 1998.

Best World Triathlon Championship Times   The best time in the men's championship is 1 hr. 48 min. 20 sec., set by Miles Stewart (Australia) in 1991.

The best women's time in a triathlon is 1 hr. 59 min. 22 sec., set by Emma Carney (Australia) in 1997.

Most World Triathlon Championship Wins   The World Championship consists of a 1.5-km (4,921-ft.-3-in.) swim, a 40-km (24-mile-1,496-yd.) cycle ride, and a 10-km (6-mile-370-yd.) run. Simon Lessing (GB) has won a record four times (1992, 1995, 1996, and 1998).

The most wins in the women's event is two, by Michelle Jones (Australia) in 1992 and 1993 and Karen Smyers (US) in 1990 and 1995.

FASTEST MARATHONS   The fastest marathon ever by a man was 2 hr. 6 min. 5 sec., run by Ronaldo da Costa of Brazil (pictured above) at Berlin, Germany, on September 20, 1998. The women's record was set by Tegla Loroupe (Kenya) at Rotterdam, Netherlands, on April 19, 1998, with a time of 2 hr. 20 min. 7 sec. The marathon is supposedly based on the legendary run by the Greek messenger Pheidippides, bringing news of a Persian attack in 490 BC. The race was run at the first modern Olympic Games in Athens, Greece, in 1896, but the distance of the race varied until 1924, when it was set at 26 miles 385 yd. It is widely expected that a marathon time of under 2 hr. 5 min. will be set in the next decade. Because of problems in measuring the road courses precisely, the fastest times for marathons are officially referred to as world bests rather than records.

FASTEST IRON MAN TIMES   The fastest time ever in an iron man race—a 3.8-km (2-mile-634-yd.) swim, a 180-km (112-mile) cycle ride, and a full marathon of 42.195 km (26 miles 385 yd.)—is 7 hr. 50 min. 27 sec., by Luc van Lierde of Belgium (above) at Roth, Germany, on July 13, 1997.

Prior to 1989, a race held annually in Nice, France, was regarded as the unofficial World Championship. Mark Allen (US) won 10 titles from 1982 to 1986 and from 1989 to 1993.

Greatest Distance Run in 24 Hours   Yiannis Kouros (Australia) ran a record 188 miles 1031 yd. in 24 hours at Adelaide, South Australia, from October 4 to 5, 1997.

The women's record for a 24-hour period is 154 miles 1161 yd., by Yelena Siderenkova (Russia) in February 1996 on an indoor track.

MOST PENTATHLON WINS   Sweden has won a record nine gold medals at the modern pentathlon. Swedish athletes have also won seven silvers and five bronzes. Aleksandr Parygin of Kazakhstan (above) is the current Olympic champion.

GYMNASTICS & WEIGHT LIFTING

Most Men's World Gymnastics Titles   The most individual men's titles won is 13, by Vitaliy Scherbo (Belarus) between 1992 and 1995. Scherbo also won a team gold medal in 1992.

The USSR won a record 13 team titles (eight World Championships and five Olympics) between 1952 and 1992.

Most Women's World Gymnastics Titles   The most women's titles won is 18 (12 individual and six team), by Larisa Semyonovna Latynina (USSR) between 1954 and 1964.

The USSR won the women's team title on a record 21 occasions (11 World Championships and 10 Olympics).

Youngest World Gymnastics Titles Winners   Aurelia Dobre (Romania) won the women's overall world title at the age of 14 years 352 days at Rotterdam, Netherlands, on October 23, 1987.

In 1990, Daniela Silivas (Romania) revealed that she was born a year later than she had previously claimed and had in fact been 14 years 185 days old when she won the gold medal for balance beam in 1985.

The youngest male was Dmitriy Bilozerchev (USSR), who was 16 years

315 days old when he won the men's overall world title in Budapest, Hungary, on October 28, 1983.

Most Men's Olympic Gymnastics Titles The most men's individual gold medals won is six, by Boris Shakhlin (USSR)—one in 1956, four (two shared) in 1960, and one in 1964—and by Nikolay Andrianov (USSR)—one in 1972, four in 1976, and one in 1980.

The men's team title has been won five times by Japan (1960, 1964, 1968, 1972, and 1976) and the USSR (1952, 1956, 1980, 1988, and 1992—the last as the Unified team).

Most Men's Olympic Gymnastics Medals Nikolay Andrianov (USSR) won a record 15 Olympic medals (seven gold, five silver, and three bronze) from 1972 to 1980.

Aleksandr Dityatin (USSR) won a record eight medals (three gold, four silver, and one bronze) at one Games, in Moscow, Russia (then USSR), in 1980.

MOST WOMEN'S TEAM OLYMPIC GYMNASTICS TITLES The USSR has won the Olympic women's title a record 10 times (from 1952 to 1980 and in 1988 and 1992). The last title was won by the Unified team from the republics of the former USSR. Pictured is Svetlana Khorkina, a member of the Russian team that took the gold medal at the 1998 World Cup in Sabae, Japan.

MOST WORLD RHYTHMIC GYMNASTICS TITLES The most overall individual world titles won in rhythmic gymnastics is three, by two Bulgarian gymnasts: Maria Gigova in 1969, 1971, and 1973 and Maria Petrova (pictured above) in 1993, 1994, and 1995.

Most Women's Olympic Gymnastics Titles Vera Caslavska-Odlozil (Czechoslovakia) holds the record for the most individual women's titles, with seven: three in 1964 and four (one shared) in 1968.

Most Women's Olympic Gymnastics Medals Larisa Latynina (USSR) won six individual gold medals and three team golds from 1956 to 1964. She also won five silver and four bronze medals, making an Olympic record total of 18.

Most World Cup Gymnastics Titles Li Ning (China) and Nikolay Andrianov, Aleksandr Dityatin, and Maria Yevgenyevna Filatova (all USSR) have each won two World Cup overall titles.

Most World Team Rhythmic Gymnastics Titles Bulgaria has won a record nine team titles: 1969, 1971, 1981, 1983, 1985, 1987, 1989 (shared), 1993, and 1995.

Most Rhythmic Disciplines in Which Perfect Scores Achieved At the 1988 Olympics in Seoul, South Korea, Marina Lobach (USSR) won the rhythmic gymnastics title with perfect scores in all six disciplines.

Youngest International Gymnast Pasakevi "Voula" Kouna (Greece) was just 9 years 299 days old at the start of the Balkan Games held at Serres, Greece, in 1981.

MOST MEN'S WEIGHT LIFTING TITLES   Naim Suleymanoglü (Turkey; pictured above) won 10 world titles (including Olympic titles): in 1985, 1986, 1988, 1989, and from 1991 to 1996. He was just 16 years 62 days old when he set world records for clean and jerk (160 kg, or 352 lb. 8 oz.) and total (285 kg, or 628 lb. 8 oz.) in the 56-kg class at Allentown, New Jersey, on March 26, 1983. Born to a Turkish family in Bulgaria, Suleymanoglü was forced to take a Bulgarian version of his surname and competed as Suleimanov until he defected to Turkey in 1986. Suleymanoglü was banned from international competitions for a year after his defection but subsequently competed for Turkey before retiring in 1997.

Most Trampolining Titles   The most men's trampolining titles won is five, by Aleksandr Moskalenko of Russia (three individual from 1990 to 1994 and pairs in 1992 and 1994), and by Brett Austine of Australia (five individual from 1982 to 1986).

Judy Wills (US) has won a record nine women's titles: five individual from 1964 to 1968, two pairs in 1966 and 1967, and two tumbling in 1965 and 1966.

Fastest Somersaults   On April 30, 1986, Ashrita Furman (US) performed 8,341 forward rolls in 10 hr. 30 min. over 12 miles 390 yd. from Lexington to Charleston, Massachusetts.

On July 21, 1996, Ashrita Furman somersaulted 1 mile in 19 min. 38 sec. at Edgewater Park in Cleveland, Ohio.

On August 31, 1995, Vitaliy Scherbo (Belarus) somersaulted 54 yd. backward in 10.22 seconds in Chiba, Japan.

Most Men's Weight Lifting Medals   Norbert Schemansky (US) has won a record four Olympic medals: gold in the middle-heavyweight class in 1952, silver heavyweight in 1948, and bronze heavyweight in 1960 and 1964.

Most Women's Weight Lifting Medals   Li Hongyun (China) won 13 medals in the 60/64-kg class from 1992 to 1996.

Oldest Weight Lifting World Record Breaker   Norbert Schemansky (US) was 37 years 333 days old when he snatched a record 164.2 kg (362 lb.) in the then unlimited heavyweight class in Detroit, Michigan, in 1962.

Most World Power Lifting Titles   The most men's world titles won is 17, by Hideaki Inaba (Japan) in the 52-kg class from 1974 to 1983 and 1985 to 1991.

The most women's power lifting titles is six, by Beverley Francis of Australia (in the 75-kg class in 1980 and 1982 and the 82.5-kg class in 1981 and from 1983 to 1985); Sisi Dolman of the Netherlands (in the 52-kg class in 1985 and 1986 and from 1988 to 1991); and Natalia Rumyantseva of Russia (in the 82.5-kg class from 1993 to 1998).

Best Timed Lifts   A world 24-hour dead lifting record of 3,137,904 kg (6,917,886 lb.) was set by a team of 10 people at the Pontefract Sports and Leisure Centre in England from May 3 to 4, 1997.

The individual 24-hour deadlift record is held by Steph Smit (South Africa), who lifted 456,677.5 kg (1,004,595 lb.) at Warren's Health Club in Pietermaritzburg, South Africa, from September 13 to 14, 1997.

A 24-hour bench press record of 4,748,283 kg (10,468,160 lb.) was set by a team of nine men at the Pontefract Sports and Leisure Centre in England from April 11 to 12, 1998.

An individual bench press record of 815,434 kg (1,797,724 lb.) was set by Glen Tenove (US) in 12 hours at Irvine, California, on December 17, 1994.

SPORTS REFERENCE

Football

NFL RECORDS

MOST POINTS
Career: 2,002
George Blanda, Chicago Bears, Baltimore Colts, Houston Oilers, Oakland Raiders, 1949–75
Season: 176
Paul Hornung, Green Bay Packers, 1960
Game: 40
Ernie Nevers, Chicago Cardinals v. Chicago Bears, November 28, 1929

MOST TOUCHDOWNS
Career: 175
Jerry Rice, San Francisco 49ers, 1985–98
Season: 25
Emmitt Smith, Dallas Cowboys, 1995
Game: 6
Ernie Nevers, Chicago Cardinals v. Chicago Bears, November 28, 1929
Dub Jones, Cleveland Browns v. Chicago Bears, November 25, 1951
Gale Sayers, Chicago Bears v. San Francisco 49ers, December 12, 1965

MOST YARDS GAINED RUSHING
Career: 16,726
Walter Payton, Chicago Bears, 1975–87
Season: 2,105
Eric Dickerson, Los Angeles Rams, 1984
Game: 275
Walter Payton, Chicago Bears v. Minnesota Vikings, November 20, 1977

MOST YARDS GAINED RECEIVING
Career: 17,612
Jerry Rice, San Francisco 49ers, 1985–98
Season: 1,848
Jerry Rice, San Francisco 49ers, 1995
Game: 336
Willie Anderson, Los Angeles Rams v. New Orleans Saints, Nov. 26, 1989

MOST COMBINED NET YARDS GAINED
Career: 21,803
Walter Payton, Chicago Bears, 1975–87
Season: 2,535
Lionel James, San Diego Chargers, 1985
Game: 404
Glyn Milburn, Denver Broncos v. Seattle Seahawks, December 10, 1995

MOST YARDS GAINED PASSING
Career: 58,913
Dan Marino, Miami Dolphins, 1983–98
Season: 5,084
Dan Marino, Miami Dolphins, 1984
Game: 554
Norm Van Brocklin, Los Angeles Rams v. New York Yanks, September 28, 1951

MOST PASSES COMPLETED
Career: 4,763
Dan Marino, Miami Dolphins, 1983–98
Season: 404
Warren Moon, Houston Oilers, 1991

Field goal kicker Gary Anderson scores for the Minnesota Vikings against the Tennessee Oilers.

Game: 45
Drew Bledsoe, New England Patriots v. Minnesota Vikings, November 13, 1994

PASS RECEPTIONS
Career: 1,139
Jerry Rice, San Francisco 49ers, 1985–98
Season: 123
Herman Moore, Detroit Lions, 1995
Game: 18
Tom Fears, Los Angeles Rams v. Green Bay Packers, December 3, 1950

MOST TOUCHDOWN PASSES
Career: 408
Dan Marino, Miami Dolphins, 1983–98
Season: 48
Dan Marino, Miami Dolphins, 1984
Game: 7
Sid Luckman, Chicago Bears v.

New York Giants, November 14, 1943
Adrian Burk, Philadelphia Eagles v. Washington Redskins, Oct. 14, 1954
George Blanda, Houston Oilers v. New York Titans, November 19, 1961
Y.A. Tittle, New York Giants v. Washington Redskins, Oct. 28, 1962
Joe Kapp, Minnesota Vikings v. Baltimore Colts, September 28, 1969

FIELD GOALS
Career: 420
Gary Anderson, Pittsburgh Steelers, Philadelphia Eagles, San Francisco 49ers, Minnesota Vikings, 1982–98
Season: 37
John Kasay, Carolina Panthers, 1996
Game: 7
Jim Bakken, St. Louis

Cardinals v. Pittsburgh Steelers,
Sept. 24, 1967
Rich Karlis, Minnesota Vikings v.
Los Angeles Rams, November 5,
1989
Chris Boniol, Dallas Cowboys v.
Green Bay Packers, November
18, 1996

SUPER BOWL GAME & CAREER RECORDS

POINTS
Game: 18
Roger Craig, San Francisco
49ers, 1985
Jerry Rice, San Francisco 49ers,
1990 and 1995
Ricky Watters, San Francisco
49ers, 1995
Terrell Davis, Denver Broncos,
1998
Career: 42
Jerry Rice, 1989–90, 1995

TOUCHDOWNS
Game: 3
Roger Craig, 1985
Jerry Rice, 1990 and 1995
Ricky Watters, 1990
Terrell Davis, 1998
Career: 7
Jerry Rice, 1989–90, 1995

TOUCHDOWN PASSES
Game: 6
Steve Young, San Francisco
49ers, 1995
Career: 11
Joe Montana, San Francisco
49ers, 1982, 1985, 1989–90

YARDS GAINED PASSING
Game: 357
Joe Montana, 1989
Career: 1,142
Joe Montana, 1982, 1985,
1989–90

YARDS GAINED RECEIVING
Game: 215
Jerry Rice, 1989
Career: 512
Jerry Rice, 1989–90, 1995

YARDS GAINED RUSHING
Game: 204
Timmy Smith, Washington
Redskins, 1988
Career: 354
Franco Harris, Pittsburgh
Steelers, 1975–76, 1979–80

PASSES COMPLETED
Game: 31
Jim Kelly, Buffalo Bills, 1994
Career: 83
Joe Montana, 1982, 1985,
1989–90

PASS RECEPTIONS
Game: 11
Dan Ross, Cincinnati Bengals,
1982
Jerry Rice, 1989
Career: 28
Jerry Rice, 1989–90, 1995

FIELD GOALS
Game: 4
Don Chandler, Green Bay
Packers, 1968
Ray Wersching, San Francisco
49ers, 1982
Career: 5
Ray Wersching, 1982, 1985

MOST VALUABLE PLAYER
Joe Montana, 1982, 1985, 1990

Fishing

FRESHWATER AND SALTWATER
A selection of all-tackle angling
records ratified by the
International Game Fish
Association by January 1999.
Barracuda, Great: 85 lb.
John W. Helfrich
Christmas Island, Kiribati, April
11, 1992
Bass, Striped: 78 lb. 8 oz.
Albert R. McReynolds
Atlantic City, New Jersey
September 21, 1982
Catfish, Flathead: 123 lb. 9 oz.
Ken Paulie

Alfred C. Glassell Jr. with his 707.61-kg (1,560-lb.) black marlin.

Elk City Reservoir, Independence, Kansas, May 14, 1998
Cod, Atlantic: 98 lb. 2 oz.
Alphonse J. Bielevich
Isle of Shoals, New Hampshire
June 8, 1969
Conger: 133 lb. 6 oz.
Vic Evans
Berry Head, Devon, England
June 5, 1995
Halibut, Pacific: 459 lb.
Jack Tragis
Dutch Harbor, Alaska
June 11, 1996
Mackerel, King: 90 lb.
Norton I. Thomton
Key West, Florida, February 16, 1976
Marlin, Black: 1,560 lb.
Alfred C. Glassell Jr.
Cabo Blanco, Peru, August 4, 1953

Pike, Northern: 55 lb. 1 oz.
Lothar Louis
Grefeern Lake, Germany
October 16, 1986
Sailfish, Pacific: 221 lb.
C.W. Stewart
Santa Cruz, Ecuador, Feb. 12, 1947
Salmon, Atlantic: 79 lb. 3 oz.
Henrik Henriksen
Tana River, Norway, 1928
Shark, Hammerhead: 991 lb.
Allen Ogle
Sarasota, Florida, May 30, 1982
Shark, Porbeagle: 507 lb.
Christopher Bennett
Pentland Firth, Caithness, Scotland, March 9, 1993
Shark, Thresher: 802 lb.
Dianne North
Tutukaka, New Zealand, Feb. 8, 1981

Shark, White: 2,664 lb.
Alfred Dean
Ceduna, Australia, April 21, 1959
Sturgeon, White: 468 lb.
Joey Pallotta III
Benicia, California, July 9, 1983
Swordfish: 1,182 lb.
L. Marrón, Iquique, Chile,
May 7, 1953
Trout, Brook: 14 lb. 8 oz.
Dr. W.J. Cook
Nipigon River, Ontario, Canada
July 1916
Trout, Brown: 40 lb. 4 oz.
Howard L. Collins
Heber Springs, Arkansas
May 9, 1992
Trout, Lake: 66 lb. 8 oz.
Rodney Harback
Great Bear Lake, NWT, Canada
July 19, 1991
Trout, Rainbow: 42 lb. 3 oz.
David Robert White
Bell Island, Alaska, June 22, 1970
Tuna, Bluefin: 1,496 lb.
Ken Fraser
Aulds Cove, Nova Scotia, Canada
October 26, 1979
Tuna, Yellowfin: 388 lb. 2 oz.
Curt Wiesenhutter
San Benedicto Island, Mexico
April 1, 1977
Wahoo: 158 lb. 8 oz.
Keith Winter
Loreto, Baja California, Mexico
June 10, 1996

Archery

MEN (SINGLE FITA ROUNDS)
FITA: Oh Kyo-moon (South
Korea) scored 1,368 points from a
possible 1,440 in 1995.
90 m: Jang Yong-ho (South
Korea) scored 331 points from a
possible 360 in 1999.
70 m: Jackson Fear (Australia)
scored 345 points from a possible
360 in 1997.
50 m: Kim Kyung-ho (South
Korea) scored 351 points from a
possible 360 in 1997.
30 m: Han Seuong-hoon (South

Korea) scored 360 points from a
possible 360 in 1994.
Team: South Korea (Oh Kyo-
moon, Lee Kyung-chul, Kim Jae-
pak) scored 4,053 points from a
possible 4,320 in 1995.

**WOMEN (SINGLE FITA
ROUNDS)**
FITA: Kim Jung-rye (South
Korea) scored 1,377 points from
a possible 1,440 in 1995.
70 m: Chung Chang-sook (South
Korea) scored 341 points from a
possible 360 in 1997.
60 m: Kim Jo-sun (South Korea)
scored 350 points from a possible
360 in 1998.
50 m: Kim Moon-sun (South
Korea) scored 345 points from a
possible 360 in 1996.
30 m: Ha Na-young (South
Korea) scored 360 points from a
possible 360 in 1998.
Team: South Korea (Kim Soo-
nyung, Lee Eun-kyung, Cho
Yuon-jeong) scored 4,094 points
from a possible 4,320 in 1992.

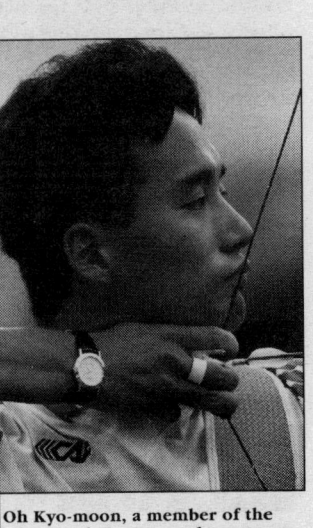

**Oh Kyo-moon, a member of the
1995 South Korean archery team.**

INDOOR (18 M)
Men
Magnus Pettersson (Sweden) scored 596 points from a possible 600 in 1995.
Women
Lina Herasymenko (Ukraine) scored 591 points from a possible 600 in 1996.

INDOOR (25 M)
Men
Magnus Pettersson (Sweden) scored 593 points from a possible 600 in 1993.
Women
Petra Ericsson (Sweden) scored 592 points from a possible 600 in 1991.

Track & Field

MEN'S OUTDOOR RECORDS
World outdoor records for the men's events scheduled by the International Amateur Athletic Federation. Fully automatic electric timing is mandatory for events up to 400 m.

Running
100 m: 9.79
Maurice Greene (US)
Athens, Greece, June 16, 1999
200 m: 19.32
Michael Johnson (US)
Atlanta, August 1, 1996
400 m: 43.29
Harry Lee "Butch" Reynolds Jr.

Mike Powell (US) has held the world long-jump record since 1991.

(US) Zürich, Switzerland, August 17, 1988
800 m: 1:41.11
Wilson Kipketer (Denmark)
Cologne, Germany, August 24, 1997
1,000 m: 2:12.18
Sebastian Coe (GB)
Oslo, Norway, July 11, 1981
1,500 m: 3:26.00
Hicham El Guerrouj (Morocco)
Rome, Italy, July 14, 1998
1 mile: 3:44.39
Noureddine Morceli (Algeria)
Rieti, Italy, September 5, 1993
2,000 m: 4:47.88
Noureddine Morceli (Algeria)
Paris, France, July 3, 1995
3,000 m: 7:20.67
Daniel Komen (Kenya)
Rieti, Italy, September 1, 1996
5,000 m: 12:39.36
Haile Gebreselassie (Ethiopia)
Helsinki, Finland, June 13, 1998
10,000 m: 26:22.75
Haile Gebreselassie (Ethiopia)
Hengelo, Netherlands, June 1, 1998
20,000 m: 56:55.6
Arturo Barrios (Mexico, now US)
La Flèche, France, March 30, 1991
25,000 m: 1:13:55.8
Toshihiko Seko (Japan)
Christchurch, New Zealand
March 22, 1981
30,000 m: 1:29:18.8
Toshihiko Seko (Japan)
Christchurch, New Zealand
March 22, 1981
1 hour: 21,101 m
Arturo Barrios (Mexico, now US)
La Flèche, France, March 30, 1991
110-m hurdles: 12.91
Colin Jackson (GB)
Stuttgart, Germany, August 20, 1993
400-m hurdles: 46.78
Kevin Young (US)
Barcelona, Spain, August 6, 1992
3,000-m steeplechase: 7:55.72
Bernard Barmasai (Kenya)
Cologne, Germany, August 24, 1997

4 x 100-m: 37.40
US (Michael Marsh, Leroy Burrell, Dennis A. Mitchell, Carl Lewis)
Barcelona, Spain, August 8, 1992
and US (John A. Drummond Jr., André Cason, Dennis A. Mitchell, Leroy Burrell)
Stuttgart, Germany, August 21, 1993
4 x 200-m: 1:18.68
Santa Monica Track Club (US)
(Michael Marsh, Leroy Burrell, Floyd Wayne Heard, Carl Lewis)
Walnut, California, April 17, 1994
4 x 400-m: 2:54.20
US (Jerome Young, Antonio Pettigrew, Tyree Washington, Michael Johnson)
New York, July 22, 1998
4 x 800-m: 7:03.89
Great Britain (Peter Elliott, Garry Cook, Steve Cram, Sebastian Coe)
London, England, August 30, 1982
4 x 1,500-m: 14:38.8
West Germany (Thomas Wessinghage, Harald Hudak, Michael Lederer, Karl Fleschen)
Cologne, Germany, August 17, 1977
Field Events
High Jump: 2.45 m (8 ft. ¹/₂ in.)
Javier Sotomayor (Cuba)
Salamanca, Spain, July 27, 1993
Pole Vault: 6.14 m (20 ft. 1 in.)
Sergey Nazarovich Bubka (Ukraine) Sestriere, Italy, July 1, 1994
Long Jump: 8.95 m (29 ft. 4¹/₂ in.)
Mike Powell (US)
Tokyo, Japan, August 30, 1991
Triple Jump: 18.29 m (60 ft. ¹/₄ in.)
Jonathan Edwards (GB)
Gothenburg, Sweden, August 7, 1995
Shot: 23.12 m (75 ft. 10¹/₄ in.)
Randy Barnes (US)
Los Angeles, California
May 20, 1990
Discus: 74.08 m (243 ft.)
Jürgen Schult (GDR)

Gabriela Szabo (Romania) is pictured after setting a new indoor 5,000-m record.

Neubrandenburg, Germany, June 6, 1986
Hammer: 86.74 m (284 ft. 7 in.)
Yuriy Georgiyevich Sedykh (USSR, now Russia), Stuttgart, Germany, August 30, 1986
Javelin: 98.48 m (323 ft. 1 in.)
Jan Zelezny (Czech Republic) Jena, Germany, May 25, 1996
Decathlon: 8,891 points
Dan Dion O'Brien (US)
Talence, France, September 4-5, 1992
Day 1: 100 m: 10.43 sec.; long jump: 8.08 m (26 ft. 6 1/4 in.); shot: 16.69 m (54 ft. 9 1/4 in.); high jump: 2.07 m (6 ft. 9 1/2 in.); 400 m: 48.51 sec.
Day 2: 110-m hurdles: 13.98 sec.; discus: 48.56 m (159 ft. 4 in.); pole vault: 5.00 m (16 ft. 4 1/4 in.); javelin 62.58 m (205 ft. 4 in.); 1,500 m: 4:42.10

WOMEN'S OUTDOOR RECORDS

World outdoor records for the women's events scheduled by the International Amateur Athletic Federation. Fully automatic electric timing is mandatory for all events up to 400 m.

Running
100 m: 10.49
Florence Griffith Joyner (US)
Indianapolis, Indiana, July 16, 1988
200 m: 21.34
Florence Griffith Joyner (US)
Seoul, South Korea, Sept. 29, 1988
400 m: 47.60
Marita Koch (GDR)
Canberra, Australia, October 6, 1985
800 m: 1:53.28
Jarmila Kratochvílová
(Czechoslovakia) Munich, Germany, July 26, 1983

1,000 m: 2:28.98
Svetlana Masterkova (Russia)
Brussels, Belgium, August 23,
1996
1,500 m: 3:50.46
Qu Yunxia (China)
Beijing, China, September 11,
1993
1 mile: 4:12.56
Svetlana Masterkova (Russia)
Zürich, Switzerland, August 14,
1996
2,000 m: 5:25.36
Sonia O'Sullivan (Ireland)
Edinburgh, Scotland, July 8, 1994
3,000 m: 8:06.11
Wang Junxia (China)
Beijing, China, September 13, 1993
5,000 m: 14:28.09
Jiang Bo (China)
Beijing, China, October 23, 1997
10,000 m: 29:31.78
Wang Junxia (China)
Beijing, China, September 8,
1993
20,000 m: 1:06:48.8
Isumi Maki (Japan)
Amagasaki, Japan, Sept. 20, 1993
25,000 m: 1:29:29.2
Karolina Szabo (Hungary)
Budapest, Hungary, April 23,
1988
30,000 m: 1:47:05.6
Karolina Szabo (Hungary)
Budapest, Hungary, April 23,
1988
1 hour: 18,340 m
Tegla Loroupe (Kenya)
Borgholzhausen, Germany, Aug.
7, 1998
100-m hurdles: 12.21
Yordanka Donkova (Bulgaria)
Stara Zagora, Bulgaria, Aug. 20,
1988
400-m hurdles: 52.61
Kim Batten (US)
Gothenburg, Sweden, August 11,
1995
4 x 100-m: 41.37
GDR (Silke Gladisch, Sabine
Rieger, Ingrid Auerswald,
Marlies Göhr)
Canberra, Australia, October 6,
1985

4 x 200-m: 1:28.15
GDR (Marlies Göhr, Romy
Müller, Bärbel Wöckel, Marita
Koch)
Jena, Germany, August 9, 1980
4 x 400-m: 3:15.17
USSR (Tatyana Ledovskaya, Olga
Nazarova, Maria Pinigina, Olga
Bryzgina)
Seoul, South Korea, October 1,
1988
4 x 800-m: 7:50.17
USSR (Nadezhda Olizarenko,
Gurina Lyubova, Lyudmila
Borisova, Irina Podyalovskaya)
Moscow, USSR, August 5, 1984
Field Events
High Jump: 2.09 m (6 ft. 10 $^1/_4$ in.)
Stefka Kostadinova (Bulgaria)
Rome, Italy, August 30, 1987
Pole Vault: 4.60 m (15 ft. 1 in.)
Emma George (Australia)
Sydney, Australia, February
20, 1999
Long Jump: 7.52 m (24 ft. 8 in.)
Galina Chistyakova (USSR)
Leningrad, USSR, June 11, 1988
Triple Jump: 15.50 m (50 ft.
10 in.)
Inessa Kravets (Ukraine)
Gothenburg, Sweden, August
10, 1995
Shot: 22.63 m (74 ft. 3 in.)
Natalya Venedictovna Lisovskaya
(USSR) Moscow, USSR, June
7, 1987
Discus: 76.80 m (252 ft.)
Gabriele Reinsch (GDR)
Neubrandenburg, Germany,
July 9, 1988
Hammer: 73.14 m (239 ft. 11 in.)
Mihaela Melinte (Romania)
Poiana Brasov, Romania, July
16, 1998
Javelin: 80.00 m (262 ft. 5 in.)
Petra Felke (GDR)
Potsdam, Germany, September
9, 1988
Heptathlon: 7,291 points
Jackie Joyner–Kersee (US)
Seoul, South Korea, Sept. 23–24,
1988: 100-m hurdles: 12.69; high
jump: 1.86 m (6 ft. 1$^1/_4$ in.); shot:
15.80 m (51 ft. 10 in.); 200 m:

22.56; long jump: 7.27 m (23 ft. 10¼ in.); javelin: 45.66 m (149 ft. 10 in.); 800 m: 2:08.51

MEN'S INDOOR RECORDS
Running
Track performances around a turn must be made on a track of circumference no longer than 200 m.
50 m: 5.56*
Donovan Bailey (Canada)
Reno, Nevada, February 9, 1996
and: Maurice Greene (US)
Los Angeles, February 13, 1999
60 m: 6.39
Maurice Greene (US)
Madrid, Spain, February 3, 1998
200 m: 19.92
Frankie Fredericks (Namibia)
Liévin, France, February 18, 1996
400 m: 44.63
Michael Johnson (US)
Atlanta, Georgia, March 4, 1995
800 m: 1:42.67
Wilson Kipketer (Denmark)
Paris, France, March 9, 1997
1,000 m: 2:15.26
Noureddine Morceli (Algeria)
Birmingham, England, Feb. 22, 1992
1,500 m: 3:31.18
Hicham El Gerrouj (Morocco)
Stuttgart, Germany, Feb. 2, 1997
1 mile: 3:48.45
Hicham El Gerrouj (Morocco)
Ghent, Belgium, February 12, 1997
3,000 m: 7:24.90
Daniel Komen (Kenya)
Budapest, Hungary, February 6, 1998
5,000 m: 12:50.38
Haile Gebreselassie (Ethiopia)
Birmingham, England, Feb. 14, 1999
50-m hurdles: 6.25
Mark McKoy (Canada)
Kobe, Japan, March 5, 1986
60-m hurdles: 7.30
Colin Jackson (GB)
Sindelfingen, Germany, March 6, 1994
4 x 200-m: 1:22.11
Great Britain (Linford Christie,

Darren Braithwaite, Ade Mafe, John Regis)
Glasgow, Scotland, March 3, 1991
4 x 400-m: 3:03.05
Germany (Rico Lieder, Jens Carlowitz, Karsten Just, Thomas Schönlebe)
Seville, Spain, March 10, 1991
5,000-m walk: 18:07.08
Mikhail Shchennikov (Russia)
Moscow, Russia, Feb. 14, 1995
Ben Johnson (Canada) ran 50 m in 5.55 seconds at Ottawa, Canada, on January 31, 1987, but this was invalidated after he admitted taking drugs, following his disqualification at the 1988 Olympics.

Field Events
High Jump: 2.43 m (7 ft. 11½ in.)
Javier Sotomayor (Cuba)
Budapest, Hungary, March 4, 1989
Pole Vault: 6.15 m (20 ft. 2¼ in.)
Sergey Nazarovich Bubka (Ukraine)
Donetsk, Ukraine, February 21, 1993
Long Jump: 8.79 m (28 ft. 10¼ in.)
Carl Lewis (US)
New York, January 27, 1984
Triple Jump: 17.83 m (58 ft. 6 in.)
Alliacer Urrutia (Cuba)
Sindelfingen, Germany, March 1, 1997
Shot: 22.66 m (74 ft .4 in.)
Randy Barnes (US)
Los Angeles, California, January 20, 1989
Heptathlon: 6,476 points
Dan Dion O'Brien (US)
Toronto, Canada, March 13 to 14, 1993
60 m: 6.67; long jump: 7.84 m (25 ft. 8½ in.); shot: 16.02 m (52 ft. 6¾ in.); high jump: 2.13 m (6 ft. 11¾ in.); 60-m hurdles: 7.85; pole vault 5.20 m (17 ft. ¾ in.); 1,000 m: 2:57.96

WOMEN'S INDOOR RECORDS
Running
50 m: 5.96
Irina Privalova (Russia)

Australia's Emma George was a circus performer before she became a pole vaulter.

Madrid, Spain, February 9, 1995
60 m: 6.92
Irina Privalova (Russia)
Madrid, Spain, February 11, 1993
200 m: 21.87
Merlene Ottey (Jamaica) Liévin,
France, February 13, 1993
400 m: 49.59
Jarmila Kratochvílová
(Czechoslovakia) Milan, Italy,
March 7, 1982
800 m: 1:56.36
Maria Lurdes Mutola
(Mozambique)
Liévin, France, February 22, 1998
1,000 m: 2:30.94
Maria Lurdes Mutola
(Mozambique)
Stockholm, Sweden, February 25,
1999
1,500 m: 4:00.27
Doina Melinte (Romania)
East Rutherford, NJ, February 9,
1990
1 mile: 4:17.14

Doina Melinte (Romania)
East Rutherford, New Jersey,
February 9, 1990
3,000 m: 8:33.82
Elly van Hulst (Netherlands)
Budapest, Hungary, March 4,
1989
5,000 m: 14:47.35
Gabriela Szabo (Romania)
Dortmund, Germany, Feb. 13,
1999
50-m hurdles: 6.58
Cornelia Oschkenat (GDR)
Berlin, Germany, Feb. 20, 1988
60-m hurdles: 7.69*
Lyudmila Narozhilenko
(Russia)
Chelyabinsk, Russia, February 4,
1993
4 x 200-m: 1:32.55
S.C. Eintracht Hamm (West
Germany)
(Helga Arendt, Silke-Beate
Knoll, Mechthild Kluth, Gisela
Kinzel)

Dortmund, Germany, Feb. 19, 1988
1:32.55
LG Olympic Dortmund (Germany)
(Esther Moller, Gabi Rockmeier, Birgit Rockmeier, Andrea Phillip)
Karlsruhe, Germany, February 21, 1999
4 x 400-m: 3:26.84
Russia (Tatyana Chebykina, Olga Goncharenko, Olga Kotlyarova, Tatyana Alekseyeva)
Paris, France, March 9, 1997
3,000-m walk: 11:40.33
Claudia Iovan (Romania)
Bucharest, Romania, January 30, 1999
Field Events
High Jump: 2.07 m (6 ft. 9 $\frac{1}{2}$ in.)
Heike Henkel (Germany)
Karlsruhe, Germany, Feb. 9, 1992
Pole vault: 4.55 m (14 ft. 11 in.)
Emma George (Australia)
Adelaide, Australia, March 26, 1998
Long Jump: 7.37 m (24 ft. 2$\frac{1}{2}$ in.)
Heike Drechsler (GDR)
Vienna, Austria, February 13, 1988
Triple jump: 15.16 m (49 ft. 8$\frac{3}{4}$ in.)
Ashia Hansen (GB)
Valencia, Spain, February 28, 1998
Shot: 22.5 m (73 ft. 10 in.)
Helena Fibingerová (Czechoslovakia) Jablonec, Czechoslovakia, Feb. 19, 1977
Pentathlon: 4,991 points
Irina Belova (Russia)
Berlin, Germany, February 14–15, 1992
60-m hurdles: 8.22 sec; high jump: 1.93 m (6 ft. 4 in.); shot: 13.25 m
(43 ft. 5$\frac{3}{4}$ in.); long jump: 6.67 m (21 ft. 10 in.); 800 m: 2:10.26
* Narozhilenko recorded a time of 7.63 seconds at Seville, Spain, on November 4, 1993, but was disqualified after a positive drugs test.

Badminton

Most World Championships
The most wins at the men's World Team Badminton Championships for the Thomas Cup (instituted in 1948) is 11, by Indonesia (1958, 61, 64, 70, 73, 76, 79, 84, 94, 96, and 98).

The most wins at the women's World Team Badminton Championships for the Uber Cup (instituted in 1956) is six, by China (1984, 86, 88, 90, 92, and 98).

Baseball

AL = American League
NL = National League

MAJOR LEAGUE
Batting records
Average
Career: .367
Ty Cobb (Detroit AL, Philadelphia AL), 1905–28
Season: .438
Hugh Duffy (Boston NL), 1894
Runs
Career: 2,245
Ty Cobb, 1905–28
Season: 196
Billy Hamilton (Philadelphia NL), 1894
Home runs
Career: 755
Hank Aaron (Milwaukee NL, Atlanta NL, Milwaukee AL), 1954–76
Season: 70
Mark McGwire (St. Louis NL), 1998
Runs batted in
Career: 2,297
Hank Aaron, 1954–76
Season: 191
Hack Wilson (Chicago NL), 1930
Game: 12
Jim Bottomley (St. Louis NL), Sept. 16, 1924; Mark Whiten (St. Louis NL), September 7, 1993

Innings: 7
Edward Cartwright (St. Louis AL), September 23, 1890
Base hits
Career: 4,256
Pete Rose (Cincinnati NL, Philadelphia NL, Montreal NL, Cincinnati NL), 1963–86
Season: 257
George Sisler (St. Louis AL), 1920
Total bases
Career: 6,856
Hank Aaron, 1954–76
Season: 457
Babe Ruth (New York AL), 1921
Consecutive hits: 12
"Pinky" Higgins (Boston AL), June 19–21, 1938; Moose Dropo (Detroit AL), July 14–15, 1952
Consecutive games batted safely: 56
Joe DiMaggio (New York AL), May 15–July 16, 1941
Stolen bases
Career: 1,315
Rickey Henderson (Oakland AL, New York AL, Oakland AL, Toronto AL, Oakland AL, San Diego NL, Anaheim AL, Oakland AL, New York NL), 1979–99
Season: 130
Rickey Henderson (Oakland AL), 1982
Consecutive games played: 2,632
Cal Ripken Jr. (Baltimore AL), May 30, 1982–September 19, 1998
Pitching records
Games won
Career: 511
Cy Young (Cleveland NL, St. Louis NL, Boston AL, Cleveland AL, Boston NL), 1890–1911
Season: 60
"Hoss" Radbourn (Providence NL), 1884
Consecutive games won: 24
Carl Hubbell (New York NL), 1936–37
Shutouts
Career: 110
Walter Johnson (Washington AL), 1907–27
Season: 16

Cal Ripken played 2,632 consecutive games over 17 seasons.

Rickey Henderson, currently of the New York Mets, holds career and season records for stolen bases.

George Bradley (St. Louis NL), 1876; Grover Alexander (Philadelphia NL), 1916
Strikeouts
Career: 5,714
Nolan Ryan (New York NL, California AL, Houston NL, Texas AL), 1966–93
Season: 383
Nolan Ryan (California AL), 1973
Game (nine innings): 20
Roger Clemens (Boston AL) v. Seattle, April 29, 1986, and v. Detroit, Sept. 18, 1996; Kerry Wood (Chicago NL) v. Houston, May 6, 1998
No-hit games
Career: 7
Nolan Ryan, 1973–91
Earned run average
Season: .90 Ferdinand Schupp (140 inns) (New York NL), 1916; .96 Dutch Leonard (222 inns) (Boston AL), 1914; 1.12 Bob Gibson (305 inns) (St. Louis NL), 1968

WORLD SERIES RECORDS
Most series played: 14
Yogi Berra (New York AL), 1947–63
Most series played by pitcher: 11
"Whitey" Ford (New York AL), 1950–64
Most home runs in a game: 3
Babe Ruth (New York AL), October 6, 1926, and October 9, 1928; and Reggie Jackson (New York AL), October 18, 1977
Runs batted in: 6
Bobby Richardson (New York AL), October 8, 1960
Strikeouts: 17
Bob Gibson (St. Louis NL), October 2, 1968
Perfect game: (9 innings)
Don Larsen (New York AL) v. Brooklyn, October 8, 1956

Cricket

FIRST-CLASS (FC) AND TEST CAREER
Batting
Most runs: FC: 61,237
Sir Jack Hobbs (1882–1963) (av. 50.65), Surrey/England, 1905–34
Test: 11,174 Allan Border (av. 50.56), Australia (156 tests), 1978–94

Most centuries: FC: 197
Sir Jack Hobbs (in 1,315 innings), Surrey/England, 1905–34
Test: 34 Sunil Gavaskar (in 214 innings), India, 1971–87
Highest average: FC: 95.14
Don Bradman, NSW/South Australia/Australia, 1927–49 (28,067 runs in 338 innings, including 43 not outs)
Test: 99.94
Don Bradman (6,996 runs in 80 innings), Australia (52 tests), 1928–48
Bowling
Most wickets: FC: 4,187
Wilfred Rhodes (av. 16.71), Yorkshire/England, 1898–1930
Test: 434

Kapil Dev (av. 29.62), India (131 tests), 1978–94
Lowest average: Test 10.75
George Lohmann (112 wkts), England (18 tests), 1886–96 (min 25 wkts)
Wicket keeping
Most dismissals: FC: 1,649
Bob Taylor, Derbys/England, 1960–88
Test: 389
Ian Healy, Australia (115 tests), 1988–99
Most catches: FC: 1,473
Bob Taylor, Derbys/England, 1960–88
Test: 360
Ian Healy, Australia (115 tests), 1988–99
Most stumpings: FC: 418
Leslie Ames, Kent/England, 1926–51

Test: 52
William Oldfield, Australia, 1920–37
Fielding
Most catches: FC: 1,018
Frank Woolley, Kent/England, 1906–38
Test: 157
Mark Taylor, Australia (104 tests), 1989–99

TEST SERIES
Batting
Most runs: 974
Don Bradman (av. 139.14), Australia v. England (5), 1930
Most centuries: 5
Clyde Walcott, West Indies v. Australia (5), 1954/55
Highest average: 563.00
Walter Hammond, England v.

Mark Taylor made 157 catches in his test career.

Ian Healy's 389 test victims have included England's Mark Ramprakash, in 1997.

New Zealand (2), 1932/33 (563 runs, 2 innings, 1 not out)
Bowling
Most wickets: 49
Sydney Barnes (av. 10.93), England v. South Africa (4), 1913/14
Lowest average: 5.80
George Lohmann (35 wkts), England v. South Africa (3), 1895/96
(min 20 wkts)
Wicket-keeping
Most dismissals: 28
Rodney Marsh (all caught), Australia v. England (5), 1982/83
Most stumpings: 9
Percy Sherwell, South Africa v. Australia (5), 1910/11

Fielding
Most catches: 15
Jack Gregory, Australia v. England (5), 1920/21
All-around
400 runs/30 wkts. 475/34, George Giffen (1859–1927), Australia v. England (5), 1894/95

Cycling

These records are recognized by the Union Cycliste Internationale (UCI). Since January 1, 1993, their list no longer distinguishes between those set by professionals and amateurs, indoor and outdoor records, or records set at altitude and sea level.

Men
Unpaced standing start
1 km: 1:00.613
Shane Kelly (Australia)
Bogotá, Colombia, September
26, 1995
4 km: 4:11.114
Chris Boardman (GB)
Manchester, England, August 29,
1996
4 km team: 4:00.958
Italy
Manchester, England, August 31,
1996
1 hour :56.3759 km
Chris Boardman (GB)
Manchester, England, Sept. 6,
1996
Unpaced flying start
200 m: 9.865
Curtis Harnett (Canada)
Bogotá, Colombia, Sept.
28, 1995
500 m: 26.649
Aleksandr Kiritchenko
(USSR)
Moscow, USSR, Oct. 29, 1988

Women
Unpaced standing start
500 m: 34.017
Felicia Ballanger (France)
Bogotá, Colombia, September
29, 1995
3 km: 3:30.974
Marion Clignet (France)
Manchester, Eng., Aug. 31, 1996
1 hour: 48.159 km
Jeanie Longo–Ciprelli (France)
Mexico City, Mexico, Oct. 26,
1996
Unpaced flying start
200 m: 10.831
Olga Slyusareva (Russia)
Moscow, Russia, April 25, 1993
500 m: 29.655
Erika Salumäe (USSR)
Moscow, USSR, August 6, 1987

Darts

24–HOUR
Men (8 players): 1,722,249, by
Broken Hill Darts Club at

Chris Boardman, 4-km record holder

Felicia Ballanger

Broken Hill, Australia, September 28–29, 1985
Women (8 players): 830,737, by a team at Cornwall Inn, Killurin, Ireland, August 1–2, 1997
Individual: 567,145, by Kenny Fellowes at The Prince of Wales, Cashes Green, England, Sept. 28–29, 1996
Bulls and 25s: (8 players) 526,750, by a team at George Inn, Morden, England, July 1–2, 1994

10-HOUR
Most trebles: 3,056 (from 7,992 darts) by Paul Taylor at Woodhouse Tavern, London, Oct. 19, 1985
Most doubles: 3,265 (from 8,451 darts), by Paul Taylor at Lord Brooke, London, September 5, 1987

Highest score: 465,919 (retrieving own darts), by Jon Archer and Neil Rankin at Royal Oak, Cossington, England, November 17, 1990
Bulls (individual): 1,321, by Jim Damore (US) at Parkside Pub, Chicago, Illinois, June 29, 1996
6-Hour
Men: 210,172, by Russell Locke at Hugglescote Working Men's Club, Coalville, England, September 10, 1989
Women: 99,725, by Karen Knightly at the Lord Clyde, London, England, March 17, 1991
Million and One Up
Men: (8 players) 36,583, by a team at Buzzy's Pub and Grub, Lynn, Massachusetts, October 19–20, 1991

Women: (8 players) 70,019 darts, by the "Delinquents" team at Top George, Combe Martin, Devon, England, September 11–13, 1987

Soaring

World Soaring Single-Seater Records
Straight Distance: 1,460.8 km (907 miles 1,232 yd.)
Hans-Werner Grosse (West Germany), Lübeck, Germany, to Biarritz, France, April 25, 1972
Declared Goal Distance: 1,383 km (859 miles 704 yd.)
Jean Nöel Herbaud (France), Vinon, France, to Fes, Morocco, April 14, 1992
Gérard Herbaud (France), Vinon, France, to Fes, Morocco, April 17, 1992
Goal and Return: 1,646.68 km (1,023 miles 352 yd.)
Thomas L. Knauff (US) Gliderport to Williamsport, Pennsylvania, April 25, 1983
Absolute Altitude: 14,938 m (49,009 ft)
Robert R. Harris (US) California, February 17, 1986
Height Gain: 12,894 m (42,303 ft.)
Paul F. Bikle (US) Mojave, Lancaster, California, February 25, 1961

SPEED OVER TRIANGULAR COURSE
100 km: 217.41 kmh (135.09 mph)
James Payne (US) California, March 4, 1997
300 km: 176.99 kmh (109.97 mph)
Beat Bünzli (Switzerland) Bitterwasser, Namibia, Nov. 14, 1985
500 km: 171.7 kmh (106.7 mph)
Hans-Werner Grosse (West Germany)
Mount Newman, Australia, December 31, 1990

750 km: 161.33 kmh (100.24 mph)
Hans-Werner Grosse (West Germany)
Alice Springs, Australia, January 10, 1988
1,250 km: 143.46 kmh (89.14 mph)
Hans-Werner Grosse (West Germany)
Alice Springs, Australia, Jan. 10, 1987

Golf

Most Major Golf Titles
British Open: 6
Harry Vardon 1896, 1898–99, 1903, 11, 14
British Amateur: 8
John Ball 1888, 90, 92, 94, 99, 1907, 10, 12
US Open: 4
Willie Anderson 1901, 03–05
Bobby Jones Jr. 1923, 26, 29–30
Ben Hogan 1948, 50–51, 53
Jack Nicklaus 1962, 67, 72, 80
US Amateur: 5
Robert Jones Jr.
1924–25, 27–28, 30
PGA Championship: 5
Walter Hagen 1921, 24–27
Jack Nicklaus 1963, 71, 73, 75, 80
The Masters: 6
Jack Nicklaus 1963, 65–66, 72, 75, 86
US Women's Open: 4
Betsy Earle-Rawls 1951, 53, 57, 60
Mickey Wright 1958–59, 61, 64
US Women's Amateur: 6
Glenna Collett Vare 1922, 25, 28–30, 35
British Women's Amateur: 4
Charlotte Pitcairn Leitch 1914, 20–21, 26
Joyce Wethered 1922, 24–25, 29
Jack Nicklaus is the only golfer to have won five different major titles (The Open, US Open, Masters, PGA, and US Amateur) twice and a record 20 all told (1959–86). In 1930, Bobby Jones achieved a unique

The legendary Jack Nicklaus has won a record 20 major titles.

"Grand Slam" of the US and British Open and Amateur titles.

Field Hockey

WORLD CUP
Women's wins: 5
Netherlands: 1974, 1978, 1983, 1986, and 1990
Men's wins: 4
Pakistan: 1971, 1978, 1982, and 1994

OLYMPIC GAMES
India was Olympic champion from the reintroduction of Olympic field hockey in 1928 until 1960. They had their eighth win in 1980. Of the six Indians who have won three Olympic team gold medals, two have also won a silver medal—Leslie Walter Claudius, in 1948, 1952, 1956, and 1960 (silver), and Udham Singh, in 1952, 1956, 1964, and 1960 (silver).

A women's tournament was added in 1980, and Australia has won twice—in 1988 and 1996.

CHAMPIONS' TROPHY
The most wins is seven, by Germany, 1986–87 (as West Germany), 1991–92, 1995, and 1997.

The first women's Champions' Trophy was held in 1987. Australia has won four times: 1991, 1993, 1995, and 1997.

Horse Racing

MAJOR RACE RECORDS

1000 GUINEAS (UK)
Record time: 1 min. 36.71 sec.
Las Meninas 1994
Most wins (jockey): 7
George Fordham 1859, 61, 65, 68, 69, 81, 83
Most wins (trainer): 9
Robert Robson 1818, 19, 20, 21, 22, 23, 25, 26, 27
Most wins (owner): 8
Duke of Grafton 1819, 20, 21, 22, 23, 25, 26, 27

2000 GUINEAS (UK)
Record time: 1 min. 35.08 sec.
Mister Baileys 1994
Most wins (jockey): 9
Jem Robinson 1825, 28, 31, 33, 34, 35, 36, 47, 48
Most wins (trainer): 7
John Scott 1842, 43, 49, 53, 56, 60, 62

Most wins (owner): 5
Duke of Grafton 1820, 21, 22, 26, 27
Earl of Jersey 1831, 34, 35, 36, 37

CHAMPION HURDLE (UK)
Record time: 3 min. 48.4 sec.
Make A Stand 1997
Most wins (jockey): 4
Tim Molony 1951, 52, 53, 54
Most wins (trainer): 5
Peter Easterby 1967, 76, 77, 80, 81
Most wins (owner): 4
Dorothy Paget 1932, 33, 40, 46

CHELTENHAM GOLD CUP (UK)
Record time: 6 min. 23.4 sec.
Silver Fame 1951
Most wins (jockey): 4
Pat Taaffe 1964, 65, 66, 68
Most wins (trainer): 5
Tom Dreaper 1946, 64, 65, 66, 68

The Netherlands has won more women's field hockey World Cups than any other country.

Most wins (owner): 7
Dorothy Paget 1932, 33, 34, 35, 36, 40, 52

DERBY (UK)
Record time: 2 min. 32.31 sec.
Lammtarra 1995
Most wins (jockey): 9
Lester Piggott 1954, 57, 60, 68, 70, 72, 76, 77, 83
Most wins (trainer): 7
Robert Robson 1793, 1802, 09, 10, 15, 17, 23
John Porter 1868, 82, 83, 86, 90, 91, 99
Fred Darling 1922, 25, 26, 31, 38, 40, 41
Most wins (owner): 5
Earl of Egremont 1782, 34, 1804, 05, 07, 26
Aga Khan III 1930, 35, 36, 48, 52

GRAND NATIONAL (UK)
Record time: 8 min. 47.8 sec.
Mr. Frisk 1990
Most wins (jockey): 5
George Stevens 1856, 63, 64, 69, 70

Most wins (trainer): 4
Fred Rimell 1956, 61, 70, 76
Most wins (owner): 3
James Machell 1873, 74, 76
Sir Charles Assheton–Smith 1893, 1912, 13
Noel Le Mare 1973, 74, 77

IRISH DERBY (REPUBLIC OF IRELAND)
Record time: 2 min. 25.60 sec.
St. Jovite 1992
Most wins (jockey): 6
Morny Wing 1921, 23, 30, 38, 42, 46
Most wins (trainer): 6
Vincent O'Brien 1953, 57, 70, 77, 84, 85
Most wins (owner): 5
Aga Khan III 1925, 32, 40, 48, 49

KENTUCKY DERBY (US)
Record time: 1 min. 59.4 sec.
Secretariat 1973
Most wins (jockey): 5
Eddie Arcaro 1938, 41, 45, 48, 52
Bill Hartack 1957, 60, 62, 64, 69

Bart Cummings (pictured above right) has trained 10 Melbourne Cup winners.

Most wins (trainer): 6
Ben Jones 1938, 41, 44, 48, 49, 52
Most wins (owner): 8
Calumet Farm 1941, 44, 48, 49, 52, 57, 58, 68

KING GEORGE VI AND QUEEN ELIZABETH DIAMOND STAKES (UK)
Record time: 2 min. 26.98 sec. Grundy 1975
Most wins (jockey): 7
Lester Piggott 1965, 66, 69, 70, 74, 77, 84
Most wins (trainer): 5
Dick Hern 1972, 79, 80, 85, 89
Most wins (owner): 3
Sheikh Mohammed 1990, 93, 94

OAKS (UK)
Record time: 2 min. 34.19 sec. Intrepidity 1993
Most wins (jockey): 9
Frank Buckle 1797, 98, 99, 1802, 03, 05, 17, 18, 23
Most wins (trainer): 12
Robert Robson 1802, 04, 05, 07, 08, 09, 13, 15, 18, 22, 23, 25
Most wins (owner): 6
Duke of Grafton 1813, 15, 22, 23, 28, 31

PRIX DE L'ARC DE TRIOMPHE (FRANCE)
Record time: 2 min. 24.6 sec. Peintre Célèbre 1997
Most wins (jockey): 4
Jacques Doyasbère 1942, 44, 50, 51
Frédéric Head 1966, 72, 76, 79
Yves St-Martin 1970, 74, 82, 84
Pat Eddery 1980, 85, 86, 87
Most wins (trainer): 4
Charles Semblat 1942, 44, 46, 49
Alec Head 1952, 59, 76, 81
François Mathet 1950, 51, 70, 82
Most wins (owner): 6
Marcel Boussac 1936, 37, 42, 44, 46, 49

ST. LEGER (UK)
Record time: 3 min. 1.6 sec.
Coronach 1926 and Windsor Lad 1934

Most wins (jockey): 9
Bill Scott 1821, 25, 28, 29, 38, 39, 40, 41, 46
Most wins (trainer): 16
John Scott 1827, 28, 29, 32, 34, 38, 39, 40, 41, 45, 51, 53, 56, 57, 59, 62
Most wins (owner): 7
9th Duke of Hamilton 1786, 87, 88, 92, 1808, 09, 14

VRC MELBOURNE CUP (AUSTRALIA)
Record time: 3 min. 16.3 sec. Kingston Rule 1990
Most wins (jockey): 4
Bobby Lewis 1902, 15, 19, 27
Harry White 1974, 75, 78, 79
Most wins (trainer): 10
Bart Cummings 1965, 66, 67, 74, 75, 77, 79, 90, 91, 96
Most wins (owner): 4
Etienne de Mestre 1861, 62, 67, 78

Hurling

Most Titles
The greatest number of All-Ireland Championships won by one team is 27, by Cork between 1890 and 1990.

Most Appearances
The most appearances in All-Ireland finals is 10, by Christy Ring (Cork and Munster), John Doyle (Tipperary), and Frank Cummings (Kilkenny). Ring and Doyle share the record of All-Ireland medals won, with eight each. Ring's appearances on the winning side were in 1941–44, 46, and 52–54, while Doyle's were in 1949–51, 58, 61–62, and 64–65. Ring also played in a record 22 interprovincial finals (1942–63) and was on the winning side 18 times.

Lacrosse

Men's World Titles
The US has won seven of the eight World Championships, in

1967, 1974, 1982, 1986, 1990, 1994, and 1998. Canada won the other world title in 1978, beating the US 17–16 after extra time—this was the first drawn international match.

Women's World Championships/World Cup
The first World Cup was held in 1982, replacing the World Championships that had been held three times since 1969. The US has won five times, in 1974, 1982, 1989, 1993, and 1997.

Highest Scores (Men)
The highest score in a World Cup match is Scotland's 34–3 win over Germany at Greater Manchester, England, on July 25, 1994.

In the World Cup Premier Division, the record score is the US's 33–2 win over Japan at Greater Manchester, England, on July 21, 1994.

Highest Score (Women)
The highest score by any women's international team was by Great Britain and Ireland with their 40–0 defeat of Long Island during their 1967 tour of the US.

Polo

Most Polo World Championships
Of the five world championships contested, three have been won by Argentina: in 1987 in Argentina, 1992 in Chile, and 1998 in the US. World Championships are held every three years under the auspices of

The US won their fifth women's lacrosse World Cup in 1997.

Argentina has won three of the five World Polo Championships.

the Federation of International Polo (FIP).

Most Goals in World Championships

Argentina has scored 35 goals during the finals of the FIP Polo World Championships. Brazil is second, with 19.

Power Lifting

(All weights in kilograms)

MEN
52 kg
Squat: 277.5
Andrzej Stanaszek (Poland), 1997
Bench press: 177.5
Andrzej Stanaszek (Poland), 1994
Dead lift: 256
E.S. Bhaskaran (India), 1993
Total: 592.5
Andrzej Stanaszek (Poland), 1996
56 kg
Squat: 287.5
Magnus Carlsson (Sweden), 1996
Bench press: 187.5
Magnus Carlsson (Sweden), 1996
Dead lift: 289.5
Lamar Gant (US), 1982
Total: 637.5
Hu Chun-hsing (Taiwan), 1997
60 kg
Squat: 315
Magnus Carlsson (Sweden), 1999
Bench press: 186.5
Magnus Carlsson (Sweden), 1999
Dead lift: 310

Lamar Gant (US), 1988
Total: 707.5
Joe Bradley (US), 1982
67.5 kg
Squat: 305
Wade Hooper (US), 1998
Bench press: 201
Aleksey Sivokon (Kazakhstan), 1998
Dead lift: 316.5
Aleksey Sivokon (Kazakhstan), 1998
Total: 800
Aleksey Sivokon (Kazakhstan), 1998
75 kg
Squat: 328
Ausby Alexander (US), 1989
Bench press: 217.5
James Rouse (US), 1980
Dead lift: 337.5
Daniel Austin (US), 1994
Total: 850
Rick Gaugler (US), 1982
82.5 kg
Squat: 379.5
Mike Bridges
(US), 1982
Bench press: 240
Mike Bridges (US), 1981
Dead lift: 357.5
Veli Kumpuniemi
(Finland), 1980
Total: 952.5
Mike Bridges (US), 1982
90 kg
Squat: 375
Fred Hatfield (US), 1980
Bench press: 255
Mike MacDonald (US), 1980
Dead lift: 372.5
Walter Thomas (US), 1982
Total: 937.5
Mike Bridges (US), 1980
100 kg
Squat: 423
Ed Coan (US), 1994
Bench press: 261.5
Mike MacDonald (US), 1977
Dead lift: 390
Ed Coan (US), 1993
Total: 1035
Ed Coan (US), 1994
110 kg

Squat: 415
Kirk Karwoski (US), 1994
Bench press: 270
Jeffrey Magruder (US), 1982
Dead lift: 395
John Kuc (US), 1980
Total: 1,002.5
Aleksey Gankov (Russia), 1998
125 kg
Squat: 455
Kirk Karwoski (US), 1995
Bench press: 278.5
Tom Hardman (US), 1982
Dead lift: 387.5
Lars Norén (Sweden), 1987
Total: 1,045
Kirk Karwoski (US), 1995
125+ kg
Squat: 447.5
Shane Hamman (US), 1994
Bench press: 322.5
James Henderson (US), 1997
Dead lift: 406
Lars Norén (Sweden), 1988
Total: 1,100
Bill Kazmaier (US), 1981

WOMEN
44 kg
Squat: 167.5
Raija Koskinen (Finland), 1998
Bench press: 87.5
Svetlana Tesleva (Russia), 1998
Dead lift: 166
Raija Koskinen (Finland), 1998
Total: 405
Raija Koskinen (Finland), 1998
48 kg
Squat: 175
Raija Koskinen (Finland), 1999
Bench press: 112.5
Irina Krylova (Russia), 1998
Dead lift: 182.5
Majik Jones (US), 1984
Total: 420
Raija Koskinen (Finland), 1999
52 kg
Squat: 182.5
Oksana Belova (Russia), 1997
Bench press: 107.5
Anna Olsson (Sweden), 1997
Dead lift: 197.5
Diana Rowell (US), 1984
Total: 475

Oksana Belova (Russia), 1997
56 kg
Squat: 191.5
Carrie Boudreau (US), 1995
Bench press: 127.5
Valentina Nelubova (Russia), 1998
Dead lift: 222.5
Carrie Boudreau (US), 1995
Total: 522.5
Carrie Boudreau (US), 1995
60 kg
Squat: 210
Beate Amdahl (Norway), 1994
Bench press: 120
Yelena Fomina (Russia), 1998
Dead lift: 213.5
Ingeborg Marx (Belgium), 1997
Total: 525
Ingeborg Marx (Belgium), 1997
67.5 kg
Squat: 230
Ruthi Shafer (US), 1984
Bench press: 142.5
Svetlana Miklazevich (Russia), 1998
Dead lift: 244
Ruthi Shafer (US), 1984
Total: 572.5
Lisa Sjöstrand (Sweden), 1997
75 kg
Squat: 245.5
Yelena Zhukova (Ukraine), 1998
Bench press: 147.5
Marina Zhguleva (Russia), 1998
Dead lift: 255
Yelena Zhukova (Ukraine), 1998
Total: 617.5
Yelena Zhukova (Ukraine), 1998
82.5 kg
Squat: 242.5
Anne Sigrid Stiklestad (Norway), 1997
Bench press: 151
Natalia Rumyantseva (Russia), 1997
Dead lift: 257.5
Cathy Millen (New Zealand), 1993
Total: 637.5
Cathy Millen (New Zealand), 1993
90 kg
Squat: 260

Cathy Millen (New Zealand), 1994
Bench press: 162.5
Cathy Millen (New Zealand), 1994
Dead lift: 260
Cathy Millen (New Zealand), 1994
Total: 682.5
Cathy Millen (New Zealand), 1994
90+ kg
Squat: 278.5
Chao Chen-yeh (China), 1999
Bench press: 178
Chao Chen-yeh (China), 1999
Dead lift: 263.5
Katrina Robertson (Australia), 1998
Total: 672.5
Chao Chen-yeh (China), 1999

Rowing

Most Olympic Golds
The record for the most Olympic rowing golds is four, by Steven Redgrave (GB): coxed fours (1984) and coxless pairs (1988, 92, and 96).

The women's record is three, by Canadian pair Kathleen Heddle and Marnie McBean: coxless pairs 1992, eights 1992, and double sculls 1996.

World Championships
World rowing championships—distinct from the Olympic Games—were first held in 1962, at first four yearly, but from 1974 annually, except in Olympic years.
The most gold medals won at World Championships and Olympic Games is 12, by Steven Redgrave, who, in addition to his four Olympic successes, won world titles at coxed pairs 1986; coxless pairs 1987, 91, 93–95; and coxless fours 1997–98.
Francesco Esposito (Italy) has won nine titles at lightweight

Marnie McBean (left) and Kathleen Heddle (right) have won three Olympic rowing golds.

events: coxless pairs 1980–84, 88, 94; and coxless fours 1990, 92. At women's events, Yelena Tereshina has won a record seven golds, all in eights for the USSR: 1978–79, 81–83, 85–86.

The most wins at single sculls is five, by: Peter-Michael Kolbe (West Germany), 1975, 78, 81, 83, and 86; Pertti Karppinen, 1976, 79–80, 84–85; and Thomas Lange (East Germany/ Germany), 1987–89, 91–92; and in the women's events by Christine Hahn (East Germany), 1974–78.

Fastest speed
The record time for 2,000 m on nontidal water is 5:23.90 (13.80 mph), by the Dutch National team (eight) at Duisburg, Germany, on May 19, 1996.

Fastest speed
The women's record time for 2,000 m on nontidal water is 5:8.50 (12.48 mph), by Romania at Duisburg, Germany, on May 18, 1996.

Fastest speed
The single sculls record is 6:37.03 (18.13 kmh or 11.26 mph), by Juri Jaanson (Estonia) at Lucerne, Switzerland, on July 9, 1995.

Fastest speed
The single sculls record is 7:17.09 (16.47 kmh or 10.23 mph), by Silken Laumann (Canada) at Lucerne, Switzerland, on July 17, 1994.

Shooting

These records are recognized by the International Shooting Sport Federation (ISSF). The score for the number of shots specified is in parentheses plus the score in the additional final round.

MEN
Free Rifle 50 m 3 x 40 shots
1,287.9 (1,186+101.9)
Rajmond Debevec (Slovenia)
Munich, Germany, August 29, 1992

Free Rifle 50 m 60 Shots Prone
704.8 (600 + 104.8)
Christian Klees (Germany)
Atlanta, Georgia, July 25, 1996
Air Rifle 10 m 60 shots
700.6 (598 + 102.6)
Jason Parker (US)
Munich, Germany, May 23, 1998
Free Pistol 50 m 60 shots
675.3 (580 + 95.3)
Taniu Kiriakov (Bulgaria)
Hiroshima, Japan, April 21, 1995
Rapid-Fire Pistol 25 m 60 shots
699.7 (596 + 107.5)
Ralf Schumann (Germany)
Barcelona, Spain, June 8, 1994
Air Pistol 10 m 60 shots
695.1 (593 + 102.1)
Sergey Pyzhyanov (USSR)
Munich, Germany, October 13,
1989
Running Target 10 m 30/30 shots
687.9 (586 + 101.9)
Ling Yang (China)
Milan, Italy, June 6, 1996
Trap 125 targets
150 (125 + 25)
Marcello Tittarelli (Italy)
Suhl, Germany, June 11, 1996
Skeet 125 targets
150 (125 + 25)
Ennio Falco (Italy)
Lonato, Italy, April 19, 1997
Harald Jensen (Norway)
Kumamoto City, Japan, June 1,
1999
Jan Henrik Heinrich (Germany)
Lonato, Italy, June 5, 1996
Andrea Benelli (Italy)
Suhl, Germany, June 11, 1996
Double trap 150 targets
193 (145 + 48)
Richard Faulds (GB)
Atlanta, Georgia, May 15, 1998

WOMEN
Standard Rifle
50 m 3 x 20 shots
689.7 (591 + 98.7)
Wang Xian (China)
Milan, Italy, May 29, 1998
Air Rifle 10 m 40 shots
503.5 (398 + 105.5)
Gaby Bühlmann (Switzerland)

Munich, Germany, May 24, 1998
Sport Pistol 25 m 60 shots
696.2 (594 + 102.2)
Diana Jorgova (Bulgaria)
Milan, Italy, May 31, 1994
Air Pistol 10 m 40 shots
493.5 (390 + 103.5)
Ren Jie (China)
Munich, Germany, May 22, 1999
Skeet 100 targets
99 (75 + 24)
Svetlana Demina (Russia)
Kumamoto City, Japan, June 1,
1999
Trap 100 targets
95 (71 + 24)
Satu Pusila (Finland)
Nicosia, Cyprus, June 13, 1998
Double Trap 120 targets
149 (111 + 38)
Deborah Gelisio (Italy)
Munich, Germany, September 3,
1995

Speed Skating

WORLD SPEED SKATING RECORDS

MEN
500 m: 34.76
Jeremy Wotherspoon (Canada)
Calgary, Canada, February 20,
1999
1,000 m: 1:08.55
Jan Bos (Netherlands)
Calgary, Canada, February 21,
1999
1,500 m: 1:46.43
Ådne Søndrål (Norway)
Calgary, Canada, March 28, 1998
3,000 m: 3:45.23
Steven Elm (Canada)
Calgary, Canada, March 19, 1999
5,000 m: 6:21.49
Gianni Romme (Netherlands)
Calgary, Canada, March 27,
1998
10,000 m: 13:08.71
Gianni Romme (Netherlands)
Calgary, Canada, March 29, 1998

WOMEN
500 m: 37.55
Catriona Le May Doan (Canada)

Norway's Ådne Søndrål holds the world 1,500-m speed skating record.

Calgary, Canada, December 29, 1997
1,000 m: 1:14.61
Monique Gabrecht (Germany)
Calgary, Canada, February 21, 1999
1,500 m: 1:55.50
Annamarie Thomas (Netherlands)
Calgary, Canada, March 20, 1999
3,000 m: 4:01.67
Gunda Niemann-Stirnemann (Germany)
Calgary, Canada, March 27, 1998
5,000 m: 6:57.24
Gunda Niemann-Stirnemann (Germany)
Hamar, Norway, February 7, 1999

WORLD RECORDS— SHORT TRACK

MEN
500 m: 41.938
Nicola Franceschina (Italy)
Bormio, Italy, March 29, 1998
1,000 m: 1:28.23
Marc Gagnon (Canada)
Seoul, South Korea, April 4, 1997
1,500 m: 2:15.50
Kai Feng (China)
Habin, China, November 11, 1997
3,000 m: 4:53.23
Kim Dong-sung (South Korea)
Szekesfehervar, Hungary, Nov. 8, 1998
5,000 m relay: 7:00.042
South Korea
Nagano, Japan, March 30, 1997

WOMEN
500 m: 44.690
Yevgenia Radanova (Bulgaria)
Szekesfehervar, Hungary, Nov. 7,
1998
1,000 m: 1:31.991
Yang Yang (China)
Nagano, Japan, February 21, 1998
1,500 m: 2:25.146
Yevgenia Radanova (Bulgaria)
Szekesfehervar, Hungary, Nov. 6,
1998
3,000 m relay: 4:16.26
South Korea
Nagano, Japan, February 17,
1998

Skiing

MOST OLYMPIC SKIING TITLES

MEN
Alpine: 3
Toni Sailer (Austria)
Downhill, slalom, giant slalom
1956
Jean-Claude Killy (France)
Downhill, slalom, giant slalom
1968
Alberto Tomba (Italy)
Slalom, giant slalom 1988; giant
slalom 1992
Nordic: 8
Bjørn Dæhlie (Norway)
15 km, 50 km, 4 x 10 km 1992;
10 km, 15 km 1994;
10 km, 50 km, 4 x 10 km 1998
Jumping: 4
Matti Nykänen (Finland) 70 m
hill 1988; 90 m hill 1984, 88;
Team 1988

WOMEN
Alpine: 3
Vreni Schneider (Switzerland)
Giant slalom, slalom 1988; slalom
1994
Katja Seizinger (Germany)
Downhill 1994; combined,
downhill 1998
Deborah Campagnoni (Italy)
Supergiant slalom 1992; giant
slalom 1994; giant slalom 1998

Nordic: 6
Lyubov Yegorova (Russia)
10 km, 15 km, 4 x 5 km 1992; 5
km, 10 km, 4 x 5 km 1994

Most Medals
12 (men): Bjørn Dæhlie
(Norway) won eight gold and
four silver in Nordic events,
1992–98.
10 (women): Raisa Smetanina
(USSR/CIS), four gold, five
silver, and one bronze in Nordic
events, 1976–92.
In Alpine skiing, the record is
five: Alberto Tomba won three
golds, plus silver in the 1992 and
94 slalom; Vreni Schneider won
three golds, silver in the
combined and bronze in the giant
slalom in 1994; Katja Seizinger
won three golds, bronze in the
1992 and 98 supergiant slalom;
and Kjetil André Aamodt
(Norway) won one gold
(supergiant slalom 1992), two
silver (downhill, combined 1994),
and two bronze (giant slalom
1992, supergiant slalom 1994).

MOST WORLD CUP TITLES

MEN
Alpine
Overall: 5
Marc Girardelli (Luxembourg),
1985–86, 89, 91, 93
Downhill: 5
Franz Klammer (Austria),
1975–78, 83
Slalom: 8
Ingemar Stenmark (Sweden),
1975–81, 83
Giant Slalom: 7
Ingemar Stenmark (Sweden),
1975–76, 78–81, 84
Supergiant Slalom: 4
Pirmin Zurbriggen (Switzerland)
1987–90
Two men have won four titles in
one year: Jean-Claude Killy
(France) won all four possible
events (downhill, slalom, giant
slalom, and overall) in 1967; and

Deborah Campagnoni has won three Olympic Alpine titles—a record she shares with two other women.

Pirmin Zurbriggen (Switzerland) won four of the five possible events (downhill, giant slalom, supergiant slalom [added 1986], and overall) in 1987.

Nordic Cross Country: 6
Bjørn Dæhlie (Norway), 1992–93, 95–97, 99

Jumping: 4
Matti Nykänen (Finland), 1983, 85–86, 88

WOMEN
Overall: 6
Annemarie Moser-Pröll (Austria), 1971–75, 79
Downhill: 7
Annemarie Moser-Pröll, (Austria), 1971–75, 78–79
Slalom: 6
Vreni Schneider (Switzerland), 1989–90, 92–5
Giant Slalom: 5
Vreni Schneider (Switzerland), 1986–87, 89, 91, 95

Supergiant Slalom: 5
Katja Seizinger (Germany), 1993–96, 98
Nordic Cross Country: 4
Yelena Välbe (USSR/Russia), 1989, 91–92, 95

Squash

WORLD CHAMPIONSHIPS
The most men's world team titles is six, by: Australia 1967, 69, 71, 73, 89, and 91; and Pakistan 1977, 81, 83, 85, 87, and 93.

The women's title has been won six times, by Australia, 1981, 83, 92, 94, 96, and 98.

Jansher Khan (Pakistan) has won eight World Open (instituted 1976) titles, 1987, 89–90, 92–96.

Jahangir Khan (Pakistan) won six World Open titles, 1981–85 and 88, and the International Squash

Rackets Federation world individual title (formerly World Amateur, instituted in 1967) in 1979, 83, and 85.

Geoffrey B. Hunt (Australia) won four World Open titles, 1976–77 and 79–80, and three World Amateur, 1967, 69, and 71.

The most women's World Open titles is four, by Susan Devoy (New Zealand), 1985, 87, 90, and 92.

Swimming

WORLD RECORDS (50-M POOLS)

MEN
Freestyle
50 m: 21.81
Tom Jager (US)
Nashville, Tennessee
March 24, 1990
100 m: 48.21

Aleksandr Popov (Russia)
Monte Carlo, Monaco, June 18, 1994
200 m: 1:46.67
Grant Hackett (Australia)
Brisbane, Australia, March 23, 1999
400 m: 3:43.80
Kieren John Perkins (Australia)
Rome, Italy, September 9, 1994
800 m: 7:46.00
Kieren John Perkins (Australia)
Victoria, Canada, August 24, 1994
1,500 m: 14:41.66
Kieren John Perkins (Australia)
Victoria, Canada, August 24, 1994
4 x 100 m: 3:15.11
US (David Fox, Joe Hudepohl, Jon Olsen, Gary Hall)
Atlanta, Georgia, August 12, 1995
4 x 200 m: 7:11.86
Australia (Ian Thorpe, Daniel Kowlaski, Matthew Dunn, Michael Klim)

Frédéric Deburghgraeve won the 100-m breaststroke at the 1996 Olympics and set a new world record as well.

Kuala Lumpur, Malaysia, Sept. 13, 1998

Breaststroke
100 m: 1:00.60
Frédéric Deburghgraeve (Belgium)
Atlanta, Georgia, July 20, 1996
200 m: 2:10.16
Michael Ray Barrowman (US)
Barcelona, Spain, July 29, 1992

Butterfly
100 m: 52.15
Michael Klim (Australia)
Brisbane, Australia, October 9, 1997
200 m: 1:55.22
Denis Pankratov (Russia)
Paris, France, June 14, 1995

Backstroke
100 m: 53.86
Jeff Rouse (US)
Barcelona, Spain, July 31, 1992
200 m: 1:56.57
Martin López-Zubero (Spain)
Tuscaloosa, Alabama, Nov. 23, 1991

Medley
200 m: 1:58.16
Jani Nikanor Sievinen (Finland)
Rome, Italy, September 11, 1994
400 m: 4:12.30
Tom Dolan (US), Rome, Italy, Sept. 6, 1994
4 x 100 m: 3:34.84
US (Gary Hall Jr., Mark Henderson, Jeremy Linn, Jeff Rouse)
Atlanta, Georgia, July 26, 1996

WOMEN
Freestyle
50 m: 24.51
Le Jingyi (China)
Rome, Italy, September 11, 1994
100 m: 54.01
Le Jingyi (China)
Rome, Italy, September 5, 1994
200 m: 1:56.78
Franziska van Almsick (Germany)
Rome, Italy, September 6, 1994

Krisztina Egerszegi holds the women's 200-m backstroke record.

Jenny Thompson holds the 100-m individual medley short-course record.

400 m: 4:03.8
Janet Evans (US)
Seoul, South Korea, Sept. 22, 1988
800 m: 8:16.22
Janet Evans (US)
Tokyo, Japan, August 20, 1989
1,500 m: 15:52.10
Janet Evans (US)
Orlando, Florida, March 26, 1988
4 x 100 m: 3:37.91
China (Le Jingyi, Shan Ying, Le Ying, Lu Bin)
Rome, Italy, September 7, 1994
4 x 200 m: 7:55.47
GDR (Manuela Stellmach, Astrid Strauss, Anke Möhring, Heike Friedrich)
Strasbourg, France, August 18, 1987
Breaststroke
100 m: 1:07.02
Penelope Heyns (South Africa)
Atlanta, Georgia, July 21, 1996
200 m: 2:24.76
Rebecca Brown (Australia)
Brisbane, Australia, March 16, 1994
Butterfly
100 m: 57.93

Mary Terstegge Meagher (US)
Brown Deer, Wisconsin, August 16, 1981
200 m: 2:05.96
Mary Terstegge Meagher (US)
Brown Deer, Wisconsin, August 13, 1981
Backstroke
100 m: 1:00.16
He Cihong (China)
Rome, Italy, September 10, 1994
200 m: 2:06.62
Krisztina Egerszegi (Hungary)
Athens, Greece, August 25, 1991
Medley
200 m: 2:09.72
Wu Yanyan (China)
Shanghai, China, October 17, 1997
400 m: 4:34.79
Chen Yan (China)
Shanghai, China, October 17, 1997
4 x 100 m: 4:01.67
China (He Cihong, Dai Guohong, Liu Limin, Le Jingyi)
Rome, Italy, September 10, 1994

SHORT-COURSE RECORDS (25-M POOLS)

MEN
Freestyle
50 m: 21.31
Mark Foster (GB)
Sheffield, England, December 13, 1998
100 m: 46.74
Aleksandr Popov (Russia)
Gelsenkirchen, Germany
March 19, 1994
200 m: 1:43.28
Ian Thorpe (Australia)
Hong Kong, China, April 1, 1999
400 m: 3:35.01
Grant Hackett (Australia)
Hong Kong, China, April 2, 1999
800 m: 7:34.90
Kieren Perkins (Australia)
Sydney, NSW, Australia, July 25, 1993
1,500 m: 14:19.55
Grant Hackett (Australia)
Perth, Australia, September 27, 1998
4 x 50 m: 1:26.99

Netherlands
Sheffield, England, December 13, 1998
4 x 100 m: 3:10.45
Brazil
Rio de Janeiro, Brazil, Dec. 20, 1998
4 x 200 m: 7:02.74
Australia
Gothenburg, Sweden, April 18, 1997
Backstroke
50 m: 24.13
Thomas Rupprath (Germany)
Sheffield, England, December 11, 1998
100 m: 51.43
Jeff Rouse (US)
Sheffield, England, April 12, 1993
200 m: 1:52.51
Martin Lopez-Zubero (Spain)
Gainesville, Florida, April 10, 1991
Breaststroke
50 m: 26.70
Mark Warnecke (Germany)

Grant Hackett holds three individual world swimming records.

Sheffield, England, December 11, 1998
100 m: 58.79
Frédéric Deburghgraeve (Belgium)
College Station, Texas, Dec. 3, 1998
200 m: 2:07.79
Andrey Korneev (Russia)
Paris, France, March 28, 1998
Butterfly
50 m: 23.35
Denis Pankratov (Russia)
Paris, France, February 8, 1997
100 m: 51.02
James Hickman (GB)
Sheffield, England, December 13, 1998
200 m: 1:51.76
James Hickman (GB)
Paris, France, March 28, 1998
Medley
100 m: 53.10
Jani Nikanor Sievinen (Finland)
Malmö, Sweden, January 30, 1996
200 m: 1:54.65
Jani Sievinen (Finland)
Kuopio, Finland, January 21, 1994
400 m: 4:05.41
Marcel Wouda (Netherlands)
Paris, France, February 8, 1997
4 x 50 m: 1:35.51
Germany
Sheffield, England, December 13, 1998
4 x 100 m: 3:28.88
Australia, Hong Kong, China, April 4, 1999

WOMEN
Freestyle
50 m: 24.23
Le Jingyi (China)
Palma de Mallorca, Spain, Dec. 3, 1993
100 m: 53.01
Le Jingyi (China)
Palma de Mallorca, Spain, Dec. 2, 1993
200 m: 1:54.17
Claudia Poll (Costa Rica)

Gothenburg, Sweden, April 18, 1997
400 m: 4:00.03
Claudia Poll (Costa Rica)
Gothenburg, Sweden, April 19, 1997
800 m: 8:15.34
Astrid Strauss (GDR)
Bonn, Germany, February 6, 1987
1,500 m: 15:43.31
Petra Schneider (GDR)
Gainesville, Florida, January 10, 1982
4 x 50 m: 1:39.56
Germany
Sheffield, England, Dec. 13, 1998
4 x 100 m: 3:34.55
China
Gothenburg, Sweden, April 19, 1997
4 x 200 m: 7:51.70
Sweden
Hong Kong, China, April 1, 1999
Backstroke
50 m: 27.27
Sandra Volker (Germany)
Sheffield, England, December 13, 1998
100 m: 58.50
Angel Martino (US)
Palma de Mallorca, Spain, Dec. 3, 1993
200 m: 2:06.09
He Cihong (China)
Palma de Mallorca, Spain December 5, 1993
Breaststroke 50 m: 30.77
Han Xue (China)
Gelsenkirchen, Germany February 2, 1997
100 m: 1:05.70
Samantha Riley (Australia)
Rio de Janeiro, Brazil, Dec. 2, 1995
200 m: 2:20.22
Masami Tanaka (Japan)
Hong Kong, China, April 3, 1999
Butterfly
50 m: 26.05
Jenny Thompson (US)
College Station, Texas, Dec. 2, 1998
100 m: 56.90
Jenny Thompson (US)

Andy Mapple, slalom joint record holder

College Station, Texas
December 1, 1998
200 m: 2:05.65
Susan O'Neill (Australia)
Malmö, Sweden, February 17,
1999
Medley
100 m: 59.30
Jenny Thompson (US)
Hong Kong, China, April 2,
1999
200 m: 2:07.79
Allison Wagner (US)
Palma de Mallorca, Spain, Dec.
5, 1993
400 m: 4:29.00
Dai Guohong (China)
Palma de Mallorca, Spain
Dec. 2, 1993
4 x 50 m: 1:52.13
Germany
Sheffield, England
December 13, 1998
4 x 100 m: 3:57.62
Japan
Hong Kong, China
April 3, 1999

Waterskiing

SLALOM
Men: 1 buoy on 32-ft. line
Jeff Rogers (US)
Charleston, South Carolina,
August 31, 1997
Andy Mapple (GB)
Miami, Florida,
October 4, 1998
Women: 1 buoy on 34-ft. line
Kristi Overton Johnson (US)
West Palm Beach, Florida,
September 14, 1996

TRICKS
Men: 11,680 points
Cory Pickos (US)
Zachary, Louisiana, May 10, 1997
Women: 8,580 points
Tawn Larsen (US)
Groveland, Florida, July 4, 1992

JUMPING
Men: 222 ft.
Bruce Neville (Australia)
Orangeville, Canada, July 27,
1997

John Swanson (US)
Bow Hill, Washington,
September 13, 1997
Women: 165 ft.
Brenda Nichols Baldwin (US)
Okahumpka, Florida, April 27,
1997

Weightlifting

*On January 1, 1998, the
International Weightlifting
Federation (IWF) introduced
modified body-weight categories,
thereby making the then-world
records redundant. This is the
current list, with world standards
where no record has yet been set.
Records achieved at IWF-approved
events exceeding the world
standard/record by 0.5 kg for snatch
or clean and jerk, or by 2.5 kg for
the total, are acceptable as records.*

MEN
Body weight 56 kg
Snatch: 135.5 kg
Halil Mutulu (Turkey), La
Coruna, Spain, April 14, 1999
Jerk: 165.5 kg
Lan Shizang (China)
Szekszárd, Hungary, May 9, 1998
Total: 300 kg
World standard

Body weight 62 kg
Snatch: 147.5 kg
Leonidas Sabanis (Greece)

Ronny Weller holds two weightlifting world records in the body
weight +105 kg class.

Lahti, Finland, November 11, 1998
Jerk: 180 kg
World standard
Total: 325 kg
World standard
Body weight 69 kg
Snatch: 160 kg
Plamen Jeliazkov (Bulgaria)
Lahti, Finland, November 12, 1998
Jerk: 187.5 kg
Zhang Guozheng (China)
Chiba, Japan, May 1999
Total: 352.5 kg
Galabin Boevski (Bulgaria)
La Coruna, Spain, April 16, 1999
Body weight 77 kg
Snatch: 168 kg
Georgi Asanidze (Georgia)
Lahti, Finland, November 12, 1998
Jerk: 205 kg
World standard
Total: 372.5 kg
World standard
Body weight 85 kg
Snatch: 180 kg
Georgi Gardev (Bulgaria)

La Coruna, Spain
April 17, 1999
Jerk: 218 kg
Zhang Yong (China)
Tel Aviv, Israel, April 24, 1998
Total: 395 kg
World standard
Body weight 94 kg
Snatch: 187.5 kg
World standard
Jerk: 230 kg
World standard
Total: 417.5 kg
World standard
Body weight 105 kg
Snatch: 197.5 kg
World standard
Jerk: 242.5 kg
World standard
Total: 440 kg
World standard
Body weight +105 kg
Snatch: 205.5 kg
Ronny Weller (Germany)
Riesa, Germany, May 3, 1998
Jerk: 262.5 kg
World standard

Poland's Agata Wrobel is one of the few female world weightlifting record holders from outside China.

Total: 465 kg
Ronny Weller (Germany)
Riesa, Germany, May 3, 1998

WOMEN
Body weight 48 kg
Snatch: 83.5 kg
Liu Xiuhua (China)
Bangkok, Thailand, December 7, 1998
Jerk: 112.5 kg
Li Xuezhao (China)
Tel Aviv, Israel, April 24, 1998
Total: 192.5 kg
Li Xuezhao (China)
Tel Aviv, Israel, April 24, 1998
Body weight 53 kg
Snatch: 97.5 kg
Meng Xianjuan (China)
Chiba, Japan, May 1, 1999
Jerk: 120 kg
Yang Xia (China)
Bangkok, Thailand, December 8, 1998
Meng Xianjuan (China)
Chiba, Japan, May 1, 1999
Total: 217.5 kg
Meng Xianjuan (China)
Chiba, Japan, May 1, 1999
Body weight 58 kg
Snatch: 97.5 kg
Zhijuan Song (China)
Chiba, Japan, May 1, 1999
Jerk: 125 kg
Ri Song-hui (North Korea)
Bangkok, Thailand, December 9, 1998
Zhijuan Song (China)
Chiba, Japan, May 1, 1999
Total: 222.5 kg
Zhijuan Song (China)
Chiba, Japan, May 1, 1999
Body weight 63 kg
Snatch: 110 kg
Lei Li (China)
Chiba, Japan, May 2, 1999
Jerk: 128.5 kg
Hou Kang-feng (China)
Sofia, Bulgaria, May 21, 1998
Total: 237.5 kg
Lei Li (China)
Chiba, Japan, May 2, 1999
Body weight 69 kg
Snatch: 111 kg

Sun Tianni (China)
Bangkok, Thailand, Dec. 11, 1998
Jerk: 135.5 kg
Milena Trendafilova (Bulgaria)
La Coruna, Spain, April 16, 1999
Total: 245 kg
Sun Tianni (China)
Bangkok, Thailand, December 11, 1998

Body weight 75 kg
Snatch: 115 kg
Wai Xiangying (China)
Bangkok, Thailand, Dec. 12, 1998
Jerk: 140 kg
Tang Weifang (China)
Chiba, Japan, May 3, 1999
Total: 250 kg
World standard
Body weight +75 kg
Snatch: 120.5 kg
Agata Wrobel (Poland)
La Coruna, Spain
April 18, 1999
Jerk: 155.5 kg
Tang Gonghong (China)
Tel Aviv, Israel
April 24, 1998
Total: 275 kg
Ding Meiyuan (China)
Chiba, Japan, May 1999

Yachting

Olympic titles
The first sportsman ever to win individual gold medals in four successive Olympic Games was Paul Elvstrøm (Denmark), in the firefly class in 1948 and the Finn class in 1952, 1956, and 1960.

Paul Elvstrøm also won eight other world titles in a total of six classes.

America's Cup
There have been 29 challenges since 1870, with the US winning on every occasion except 1983 (to Australia) and 1995 (to New Zealand). In individual races sailed, US boats have won 81 races, and challengers have won 13.

Dennis Conner, America's Cup veteran

Most appearances in the America's Cup
Dennis Conner (US) has made six appearances since 1974.

Admiral's Cup
The ocean racing team series to have had the most participating nations (three boats allowed to each nation) is the Admiral's Cup, organized by the Royal Ocean Racing Club.

A record 19 nations competed in 1975, 1977, and 1979.

Britain has had a record nine wins.

Highest speeds
MEN
The highest speed reached under sail on water by any craft over a 500-m (547-yd.) timed run is 46.52 knots (86.21 kmh, or 53.57 mph), by trifoiler *Yellow Pages Endeavour* piloted by Simon McKeon and Tim Daddo, both of Australia, at Sandy Point near Melbourne, Australia, on October 26, 1993.

WOMEN
The highest speed reached under sail on water by any craft over a 500-m (547-yd.) timed run is by Elisabeth Coquelle (France), with 40.38 knots (74.83 kmh, or 46.5 mph) at Tarifa, Spain, on July 7, 1995.

BECOMING A
RECORD BREAKER

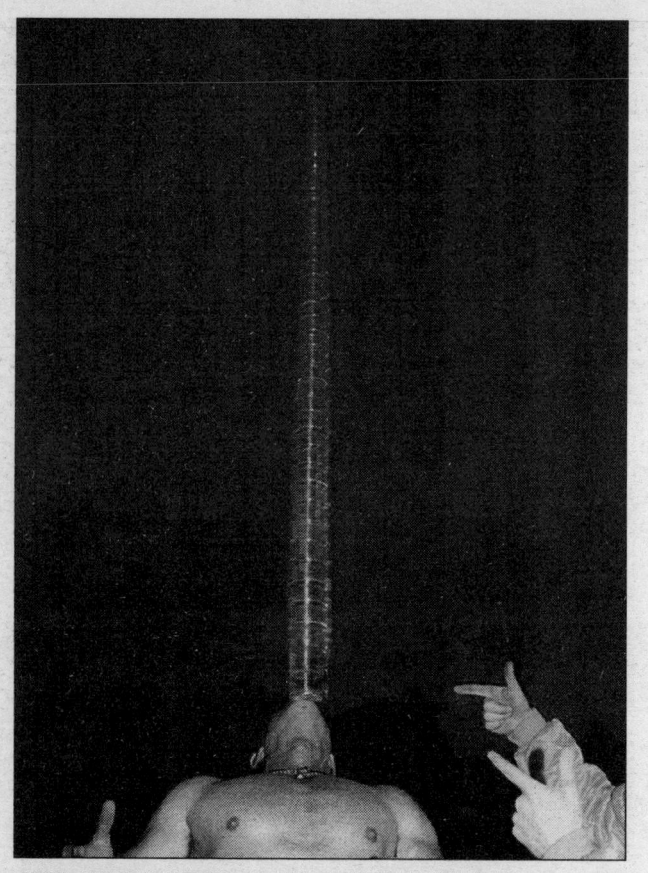

MOST GLASSES BALANCED ON THE CHIN Terry Cole is pictured balancing 80 pint glasses on his chin at London, England. Before embarking on a record attempt, you must get in touch with us to find out what the relevant *Guinness Book of Records* guidelines are.

The Guinness Book of Records features many people who have accomplished extraordinary feats. Do you think you have what it takes to become one of those extraordinary people? If you think you would like to break or establish a record, you are on the way to getting into the book.

"I Can Do That!" Not everyone can break the 100-m track record, walk the high wire at a record altitude, or become the world's youngest supermodel. But everyone can break or set a record, as an individual or as part of a team.

MOST DOMINOES STACKED Edwin Sirko (US) stacked 545 dominoes on top of a single vertical domino on April 11, 1998, in Irvine, California. The stack remained standing for 1 hour. Could you do better?

One option might be to start a large and unusual collection. This does not need to entail great expense: among current record-breaking collections are four-leaf clovers and lightbulbs. You do not have to be a professional dancer to take part in an attempt at the world line-dance record.

Even the most sedentary could participate in a record-breaking event—by joining in the biggest gathering of couples kissing simultaneously, for instance. Another way of getting into the book could be to devise your own record category.

Every day brings innovative suggestions for new record categories, and we try to find ways of accepting as many of these ideas as possible. What we are looking for in a new category is a challenge that is interesting, requires skill, is safe, and—most importantly—is likely to attract subsequent challenges from other people.

One recent expansion of record categories has been the reintroduction of marathons, from DJ broadcasts and quizzes to musical and sports feats. These were temporarily rested in 1990–91 owing to increasing concerns about safety. We have found ways to reintroduce marathons in a new form, with strict guidelines emphasizing the safety of the competitor. A line has been drawn under the marathon records of the past—those records will never be broken.

All record breakers receive a certificate recognizing that they have become members of an exclusive body—official *Guinness Book of Records*

BIGGEST SWATCH WATCH COLLECTION Fiorenzo Barindelli is pictured with his record-breaking collection of 3,524 Swatch watches—the biggest in the world. Interest in collections is evident from the many requests from collectors received by *The Guinness Book of Records*. To be considered for inclusion, collections should be clearly themed or contain broadly similar, but different, items. Duplicates do not count.

LONGEST CHEWING GUM WRAPPER CHAIN Gary Duschl (Canada) began making a chain of chewing gum wrappers in 1965. By March 1999, it was 5 miles 1,458 yd. long. He provided full documentation to support his claim, including articles from local newspapers and signed witness statements.

record holders. To receive that sought-after certificate, you have not only to break a record, either as an individual or as part of a team, but also to prove that you have done so.

Documentation Dozens of people have attempted to break records in the most public way possible—in front of millions of viewers on the *Guinness® World Records: Primetime* TV show. But any potential record breaker must allow his or her attempt to be scrutinized.

A requirement for all record challenges is a clearly labeled VHS videotape (with the official clock in view when appropriate to the record category). Reproducible color photographs or transparencies should also be submitted with the record claim. Newspaper clippings, usually local, are useful additional evidence. It is a good idea to get your local newspaper interested in your record challenge and persuade a reporter to be present.

Each and every record claim must be accompanied by detailed documentation. Two independent witness statements are the minimum requirement, and your witnesses should be people of some standing in the local community: a doctor, lawyer, council member, or police officer or an official of a professional or sports organization, for example. Certain records may also require the judgment of an expert, such as a surveyor or a public-health official. Neither witness can be related to you. Witnesses should be able to confirm not only that they have seen the successful progress and completion of the record attempt but also that the guidelines have been followed. *The Guinness Book of Records* is unable to supply personnel to monitor attempts but reserves the right to do so.

Many record attempts also require a logbook or some form of similar documentation. These requirements are specified in the guidelines.

Apply Early   Whatever record category you decide to attempt, it is important to contact us early. If your proposal is accepted as a new category, we may have to draw up new guidelines with the assistance of experts. So please allow both us and you plenty of time for preparation. You should also check with us just before the attempt to make sure that the record has not recently been broken.

Getting in Touch   To contact *The Guinness Book of Records*, write to us at:

GUINNESS MEDIA, INC.
6 Landmark Square
Stamford, CT 06901
Alternatively, you can E-mail us at:
infousa@guinnessrecords.com

Will It Be in the Book?   Not all new records appear in the book. With tens of thousands of records in the *Guinness Book of Records* database, the book is a selection of the subjects and categories that we believe are of the most interest to our readers.

Taking Care   Safety precautions are an important factor in record guidelines. All record attempts are undertaken at the sole risk of the competitor. Guinness World Records Ltd. cannot be held responsible for any (potential) liability whatsoever arising out of any such attempt, whether to the claimant or to any third party.

Guidelines   For most human-endeavor categories, *The Guinness Book of Records* has specific guidelines to ensure that all contestants are attempting a record under exactly the same conditions as previous and subsequent challengers. Only in this way will we be able to compare achievements.

Guinness® World Records Primetime was first shown on July 28, 1998. Hosted by former Cincinnati Bengals wide receiver Cris Collingsworth and Mark Thompson, it was produced by LMNO Productions and broadcast on the Fox television network. Here's a reminder of some of the amazing people featured on the program.

Highest Balloon Skywalk   Mike Howard, Manchester, UK, 18,000 ft.

Most Glasses Balanced on Chin   Ashrita Furman, Jamaica, NY, 62 glasses for 10 seconds.

Farthest Protrusion of Eyeballs   Kim Goodman, Chicago, IL, $^2/_5$ in.

Sword Swallowing   Brad Byers, Moscow, ID, swallowed nine 27-in. swords and then rotated them 180°, beating his own record of eight set earlier in the series.

World's Largest Feet   Matthew McGrory, Ventura, CA, 19-in. long (size $26^1/_2$).

Longest Free-Fall Sky Glide   Adrian Nicholas, Enfield, England (4 miles 1,232 yd.).

Most Bubbles Blown with a Tarantula in Mouth   Ray Macareg, San Jose, CA, 99.

Body Squeezed Through Smallest Tennis-Racket Head   Jeff Brennan, LaCrescent, MN, 163 in.^{2} in area (strings removed).

Triple-Decker Bed of Nails Lee Graber, Tallmadge, OH, supported two people and four beds of nails, while lying on a bed of nails himself. Three 10-lb. concrete blocks lying across the person at the top of the sandwich were smashed. The total weight was 590 lbs.

World's Largest Free-Fall Formation 246 sky divers held formation for 7.3 seconds.

Fastest Rocket-Powered Street Luge Billy Copeland, Ashland City, TN, 70 mph.

Most Hamburgers in Mouth Johnny Reitz, Nashville, TN, three burgers.

Most Ear Flips and Catches Mark Needle, Marietta, GA, flipped 16 M&Ms using only his ear into his brother Ben's mouth in 60 seconds.

Longest "No Hands" Motorcycle Jump Robbie Knievel, 17 semi-trucks.

Mark Thompson, who has brought dozens of amazing record breakers to millions of viewers on *Guinness*® *World Records* Primetime

Biggest Mantle of Bees Mark Biancaniello, Los Olivos, CA, about 353,150 bees (87 lb. 8 oz.).

Heaviest Weight of Kegs on Head John Evans, Derbyshire, UK, 11 kegs (339 lb.) for 10 seconds.

Longest-Lived Survivor of Ectopia Cordis (Heart Outside Body) Christopher Wall, Philadephia, PA, b. August 10, 1975.

Most Rattlesnakes in Bathtub Jackie Bibby, Fort Worth, TX, 35 western diamondback rattlesnakes.

Tightest Squeeze Yogi Coudoux squeezed his body into a $15^7/_{10}$ x $16^9/_{10}$ x $20^9/_{10}$-in. box that was submerged in icy water for 4 min. 49 sec.

Farthest Human Cannonball David Smith Sr., Halfway, MO—185 ft. 10 in.

Fastest Rapper Rebel XD, Chicago, IL, 683 syllables in 54.5 seconds.

Longest Building-to-Building Motorcycle Jump Joe Reed, Van Nuys, CA, 14 stories.

Most Tattooed Woman Julia Gnuse, Foothill Ranch, CA, 95% (record shared with Krystyne Kolorful).

World's Most Extensive Cranial Reconstruction Ahad Israfil, Dayton, OH, skull rebuilt using silicon mold after 12 operations.

Most Boards Broken on Head Jonathan Marden, Waterville, ME, 29 in 30 seconds.

Most Bees in Mouth Dr. Norman Gary, Fair Oaks, CA, 109 venomous bees held in mouth for 10 seconds.

Highest Free-Fall Jump into an Air Bag Stig Günther, Denmark, dove 343 ft. into a 39-ft. $4^1/_2$-in. x 49-ft. $2^1/_2$-in. x 14-ft. 9-in. air bag, traveling at a speed of 90 mph.

Most Weight Lifted Using Multiple Body Parts Joe Herman (Mr. Lifto) lifted 29 lb. 2 oz. for 10 seconds with his ears, tongue, and nipples.

Fastest Upside-Down Stair Walker Mark Kenny, Norwood, MA, 77 stairs of the Philadelphia Art Museum on his hands in 39.4 seconds.

Most Straws Stuffed in Mouth Jim Purol, Whittier, CA, 151.

Most Beads Used in a Work of Art Liza Lou, Topanga, CA, created a kitchen and backyard from 40 million glass beads.

Most Yo-Yo Tricks in One Minute Chris Ciosek, MA, 30 tricks.

Blown Up the Most Times Allison Bly, Waterbury, CT, has blown herself up inside a box more than 1,100 times.

Most Organs Transplanted into a Person in a Single Operation
Eugenia Borgos, Italy, received seven organs in one operation.

Archery (Distance and Accuracy) Justin Huish, CA, hit a bull's-eye on an Olympic-sized target at a distance of 101 yd.

World's Longest Toenails Louise Hollis, Compton, CA, 7 ft. 3 in.

Longest Foot-Juggling of a Table Chester Cable, Riverside, CA, juggled a table for 17 consecutive rotations. The table weighed 103 lb. 11 oz., and was 35 in. wide and 27¹/₄ in. high.

Highest and Longest Skywalk Blindfolded Jay Cochrane, Atlantic City, NJ, walked blindfolded 600 ft. at night along a tightrope between the towers of the Flamingo Hilton, Las Vegas, NV, which is 30 stories high.

Most Buildings Destroyed The Loizeaux family building implosion firm of Phoenix, MD, has destroyed approximately 7,000 buildings.

Fastest Board Breaker Billy Muzzy, West Warwick, RI, broke 206 1 x 9 x 11-in. boards stacked three high in one minute using only his hands.

Most Steps on a Knife Stairway Lou Guozhu climbed up 20 upside-down meat cleavers.

Longest Trapeze Throw and Catch Surgei Tur, 43 ft. after eight attempts.

Most Watches Eaten Seung Do Kim, South Korea, ate five stainless steel watches measuring 1 in. in diameter, including the glass faces but not the straps.

Longest Fingernails Shridar Chillal, Pune, India, has the world's longest fingernails, measuring 20 ft. 2¹/₄ in. in total.

World's Farthest Cliff-Rope Free Fall Dan Osman, CA, 1,000 ft.

Most Consecutive Head Spins Jason "EZ Rock" Geoffrey, CA, 28 spins.

Most Concentric Bubbles Fan-Yang, Missisauga, Ontario, Canada, nine concentric bubbles blown.

Most Night Crawlers Eaten Mark Hogg, Louisville, KY, 62 night crawlers in 30 seconds, breaking his own record of 57 set previously in the series.

Most Inverted Flat Spins Wayne Handley, Greenfield, CA, used a super-light stunt plane to do 78 spins.

Biggest Bagel Lender's Bagels, Mattoon, IL, 1998, 714 lb.

Trolley Pulled Farthest with One Ear Li Jian Hua, Tanshan, China, pulled a 4.2-ton trolley 67 ft.

Plane Pulled Farthest   David Huxley, Sydney, Australia, pulled a 206.1-ton jumbo jet 298 ft. 6 in.

Most Knives Thrown at a Revolving Door   Larry Cisewski, La Mesa, CA, eight in 30 seconds.

Crossbow Bolt Relay   Ross and Elisa Hartzells, Las Vegas, NV, shot one bolt that set off eight more deflecting bolts, with the final two hitting apples on the Hartzells' heads.

Fastest Speed on Two Wheels   Goran Eliasson, Sweden, 112 mph in a Volvo 850 Turbo.

Biggest Candy Cane   Employees at Fabiano's Candy, 36 ft. 7 in. long

Heaviest Woman/Greatest Weight Loss   Rosalie Bradford, Perkasie, PA, holds two records. She was the heaviest woman in the world when she was weighed at 1,200 lb. in 1987, and she also recorded the greatest weight loss ever, when she dropped 938 lb. by 1994.

Longest Vertical Ski Fall   Bridget Mead, New Zealand, fell more than 1,300 ft. in a plunge during the 1997 World Extreme Skiing Championships in Valdez, AK.

Greatest VW Beetle Stuffing   18 students from Southern Illinois University stuffed into a 1998 Volkswagen Beetle for a period of 49 seconds.

Most Basketballs Spun   Michael Kettman, St. Augustine, FL, spun 25 basketballs simultaneously for five seconds.

World's Shortest Twins   John and Greg Rice, FL, 2 ft. 10 in. tall.

Largest Waist   Walter Hudson, Hempstead, NY, had the world's biggest waist, measured at 9 ft. 11 in. He died on December 24, 1991.

Smartest Parrot   Alex, an African gray parrot, can count, reason, and identify colors, textures, sizes, and shapes. He has a vocabulary of a little over 80 words.

Longest Uncombed Hair   Hoo Sateow, Chiang Mai, Thailand, has hair measuring 16 ft. 11 in.

Biggest Cheese Steak Sandwich   Philadelphia Eagles, 36 ft. 7 in.

Tallest Living Woman   Sandy Allen, Indianapolis, IN, is 7 ft. 7 $\frac{1}{4}$ in. tall.

Biggest Pecan Pie   Pecan Festival, Okmulgee, OK, in 1989, 40 ft. in diameter.

Tallest House of Cards   Bryan Berg, Spirit Lake, LA, built a 111-story house of cards measuring 21 ft. 3 $\frac{1}{2}$ in., using approximately 54,000 cards.

Most Feet Sniffed   Madeline Albrecht worked at Dr. Scholl's Hill Top Research Laboratories as a tester of new products and has sniffed about 5,600 feet.

Greatest Dog Tire Climb   Duke, a Border collie/Australian shepherd cross, jumped up a stack of tires 9 ft. 6 in. high, retrieved a toy from inside, and climbed out.

Farthest Skin Stretch   Gary Turner of Caistor, UK, has a rare skin condition called Ehlers Danlos syndrome, enabling his skin to stretch out 6 in.

Most Elastic Man   Pierre Beauchemin has the uncanny ability to turn his arms and legs around in extreme contorted positions.

Most Trampoline Somersaults   Ken Kovatch, Warwick, NY, made 101 somersaults through a standard 3-ft.-diameter hoop in one minute.

Most Successful Bionic Arm   Campbell Aird, Moffatt, Scotland, has trained his shoulder muscles to activate sensors in his artificial arm.

Biggest Canopy Stack   53 sky divers linked together in a canopy stack for six seconds in the airspace over Kassel, Germany.

Most Tattooed Human   Tom Leppard, Skye, Scotland, has 99.9% of his body covered in a leopard-print tattoo.

Longest Sword-to-Sword Balance   Ali Bandbaz balanced his brother Massoud on two 14½-in. steel swords placed tip to tip in their mouths, joined by a connector smaller than a thimble, for 29 seconds in Las Vegas, NV.

Greatest Teeth Balancer   Frank Simon, Key West, FL, balanced a motorcycle weighing 127.8 lb. on his teeth for 15.25 seconds.

Highest Bungee Jump   A.J. Hackett, New Zealand, jumped from New Zealand's tallest building, the Sky Tower, a record distance of 591 ft.

Greatest Memory Man   Dominic O'Brien, Hertfordshire, England, memorized and then recalled 50 random items in order.

Fastest Speed Climber   Dan Osman climbed the 400-ft. "Lover's Leap" cliff at Lake Tahoe, CA, in 5 min. 52 sec.

Woman with Longest Fingernails   Lee Redmond, Salt Lake City, UT, has fingernails with a combined length of 21 ft. 9 in.

Most People to Do a Wheelie   The most people to ride on a motorcycle while doing a wheelie is nine, set in Lake Whales, FL, by stunt rider Todd Colbert, driving a stock Suzuki GSXR 1100 with the rear tire inflated to twice its normal size.

Smallest Unicycle   Peter Rosendahl, Sweden, rode an 8-in.-high unicycle with a wheel diameter of $^{78}/_{100}$ in. for a distance of 24 ft. 10¼ in.

Oldest Person to Make a Solo Sky Dive   Herb Tanner, Mayfield Heights, OH, was 92 when he made an unassisted sky dive on June 19, 1998.

Oldest Living Conjoined Twins Twins Ronnie and Donnie Galyon, OH, are 45 years old and are joined at the hip. They are the oldest living conjoined twins in the US.

Smallest Horse Tara Stables' Hope for Tomorrow, owned by Kenneth and Elizabeth Garnett, Vinton, VA, measures 1 ft. 9 in. and weighs 60 lb.

Most Premature Baby James Gill, Brockville, Ontario, Canada, was born after only 145 days in the womb.

Longest-Running Primetime Animated Series *The Simpsons*, on Fox TV, is the longest running primetime animated series ever, with over 200 screened episodes.

STOP PRESS

Records are being broken all the time, and our thorough verification process at Guinness World Records means that sometimes we cannot include all of the latest records in the main body of the book. Our Stop Press page allows us to bring you the very latest developments in the world of record breaking that were happening just as we went to press. More details may appear in the 2001 edition.

Most Valuable Oscar Pop star Michael Jackson paid a record $1.54 million at Sotheby's in New York City for the Best Film Oscar won by producer David O. Selznick for *Gone With The Wind* (1939).

Most Valuable Guitar The 1956 Fender Stratocaster "Brownie" used by Eric Clapton (UK) on his classic song "Layla" earned $497,500 at a charity auction at Christie's in New York City. The auction raised over $5 million for the Crossroads Center in Antigua, a drug and alcohol treatment center founded in 1997 by Clapton, a former member of the Yardbirds, Cream, and Blind Faith.

Oldest Ships Dr. Robert Ballard (US), who located *Titanic* in 1985 and *Bismarck* in 1988, discovered two Phoenician vessels that have been sitting half buried in the seabed 1,000 ft. below the water's surface off the coast of Israel for 2,700 years. The two vessels, which measure 58 ft. and 48 ft. in

Babu Chhiri Sherpa, who stayed on Mt. Everest for a record 21 hours

length, appear to have had a crew of six in addition to a team of oarsmen. The Phoenicians, who founded the city of Carthage on the coast of North Africa, were a seagoing people who lived on the eastern Mediterranean coast from 2,300 B.C. to 300 B.C.

Longest Stay on Mt. Everest   Babu Chhiri Sherpa of Nepal completed a stay of 21 hours at the summit of Mt. Everest (29,029 ft.) without the use of bottled oxygen—other climbers who reach the summit usually stay for no longer than an hour. Chhiri climbed Mt. Everest again just weeks later to become the first person to climb the mountain twice in the same season.

Eric Clapton, with the world's most valuable guitar

Biggest Art Competition   The Winsor & Newton Millennium Painting Competition, held from 1997 to 1999, attracted a record total of 22,367 entries from amateur and professional artists in 51 countries.

Longest DJ Marathon   Disc jockey Steve Harris of URN in Nottingham, England, broadcast nonstop for 40 hours. Live coverage of the marathon was also provided on the Internet.

Longest Tap Dance (Woman)   The greatest distance tap-danced by a woman was 20 miles 63 yd., by Angell Husted of Palmyra, Virginia, who tapped for 8 hr. 50 min. on a 304-ft. plywood track at the Fluvanna County High School gym in Palmyra.

Most Valuable Cézanne   *Still Life With a Curtain, Pitcher, and Bowl of Fruit* by Paul Cézanne sold at Sotheby's in New York City for $58.2 million, making it the most valuable picture by the artist and the fourth most expensive painting ever sold at auction.

Strongest Commercially Available Beer   The strongest beer currently available commercially is Samuel Adams Triple Bock. Brewed by the Boston Beer Company in Massachusetts, its alcohol content is 18% by volume and 14.4% by weight.

Longest Lawn Mower Ride   Brad Hauter of Lake in the Hills, Illinois, rode a lawn mower a record 4,039 miles 1,056 yd. from Atlanta, Georgia, to Blanding, Utah.

Most Tennis Grand Slams (Men)   Pete Sampras (US) won his 12th Grand Slam tournament at Wimbledon, equaling the record that had been set by Roy Emerson (Australia) in 1967.

Most Penalties Missed in an International Soccer Game   Martín Palermo (Argentina) missed three penalties during his team's 0–3 defeat by Colombia in the 1999 Copa América, played in Paraguay. His first shot hit the crossbar, his second went into the stands, and his third was saved.

Fastest Mile   Hicham el-Guerrouj (Morocco) set a new record for the mile in Rome, Italy, with a time of 3:43.13.

Men's Decathlon   8,994 points: Tomas Dvorak (Czech Republic). Set at Prague, Czech Republic.
   Day 1: 100 m 10.54 sec.; long jump 7.90 m; shot 16.76 m; high jump 2.04 m; 400 m 48.08 sec.
   Day 2: 110-m hurdles 13.73 sec.; discus 48.33 m; pole vault 4.90 m; javelin 72.32 m; 1,500 m 4:37.20 sec.

Women's 50-m Butterfly   Inge de Bruijn (Netherlands) set a new women's swimming record of 26.54 seconds for the 50-m butterfly at Amersfoort, Netherlands.

Largest Bunny Hop   The largest Bunny Hop took place at Walt Disney World, Orlando, Florida, USA, during the Happy Easter Parade. A record 1,241 participants formed a continuous line and hopped for the required time of five minutes.

Tallest Snowman Residents of Bethel, Maine, took 14 days to build the world's tallest snowman. It was 113 ft. 7$\frac{1}{2}$ in. tall and consisted of approximately 162,000 ft.^{3} of snow.

The world's most valuable Oscar, now owned by pop legend Michael Jackson

INDEX

PHOTO CREDITS

55t Vic Thomasson/Rex Features
56 Daniel Heuclin/Sipa Press/Rex Features
57 Blondin/Sipa Press/Rex Features
58 Incredible Features/Rex Features
61 Dimitry Kinkladze
64 John Pryke/Reuters
63 Jeff Werner/Incredible Features/Rex Features
65 Ron Tom/Fox Television
66 Mike Jones/Fox Television
67 Mike Jones/Fox Television
69b Fox Television
69t Miguel Najdorf
71 Dan White
70 Simon Roberts/BBC Radio 1
72 Bristol Evening Post
73 Totally in Sand
75 David Rozing/CameraPress
76 Remy Bricka
77 Nils Jorgensen/Rex Features
79 Rex Features
82 Chris Drown/Sipa Press/Rex Features
81 Ron Rosenfeld/Rosenfeld Photography
83 Peter Brooker/Rex Features
80 Ian Sumner/Wessex Water
84 Gary Tramontina/AP
85 K.H. Wallis
87 Savita Kirloskar/Reuters
88 Santiago Lyon/AP
89 Joe Viles/Fox Television
91 Paul Chesley/Tony Stone
93 Azadour Guzelian/Rex Features
92 North of England Newspapers/Newsquest Northeast Ltd
95 Jiji Press/AFP/EPA/PA
94 Matija Kokovic/Sipa Press/Rex Features
97 GBR
98 Peter Brooker/Rex Features
99 Ken McKay/GBR
101 Charlotte Observer/AP
102tl Rex Features
103 Clive Limpkin/Rex Features
102cr Richard Young/Rex Features
104 Keystone/AP
105 Alexander Zemlianichenko/AP
106 Fabian Bimmer/AP
109 Eugene Hoshiko/AP
108 Lennox McLendon/AP
110 Kevin Wisniewski/Rex Features
111 Nils Jorgensen/Rex Features
112 Ken McKay/Rex Features
113 Wurlitzer/GBR
114 Mathmos Ltd
116 Diamond Cutters/GBR

172 Yoshikazu Tsuno/EPA/PA
174 Terry Schmitt/AP
175 Krishnan Guruswamy/AP
177 Plinio Lepri/AP
176 Adam Nadel/AP
180 Xinhua/AP
179 Peter Andrews/Reuters
181 Sintesi/Sipa Pess/Rex Features
184 Miramax Films
183 MGM
185 LucasFilm Ltd
187 Gautam Rajadhyaksha/Cine Blitz
188 Gautam Rajadhyaksha/Cine Blitz
189 Gautam Rajadhyaksha/Cine Blitz
190 Gautam Rajadhyaksha/Cine Blitz
191 Rex Features
192 Spelling Entertainment/Columbia Television
193 Chris Pizzello/AP
194 Disney/AP
197 Kevork Djansezian/AP
196 Mychal Watts/East West Records/Warner Music
198 Hamish Brown/Chrysalis Records
200 Warren Johnson/Rex Features
202 Richard Young/Rex Features
203 TKY/Rex Features
201 Richard Young/Rex Features
207 Ian Waldie/Rex Features
205 Scarlet Page/Rex Features
204 John Rogers/Rex Features
206 Rex Features
210 Greg Brennan/Rex Features
208 Rex Features
209 Reed Saxon/AP
212 Dave Lewis/Rex Features
214 Mark Lennihan/AP
213 Dave Hogan/Rex Features
217 Suzanne Plunkett/AP
216t H. Kuehn/Fotex/Rex Features
216b Phil Rees/Rex Features
218 Geoff Wilkinson/Rex Features
219 Dreamworks SKG
220 Aardman Animations Ltd
221 Matt Groening/Fox Television
223 Rex Features
222 Seagaia Group
224 Reuters
226 Lucasfilm Ltd
227 Benetton/Rex Features
229 Fred Prouser/Reuters
228 Levi Strauss Ltd
230 Time/AP
231 Jim Cooper/AP

292 NASA
293 Sony Corporation
294t Koji Sasahara/AP
295 Diamond
296 Koji Sasahara/AP
294b Sony Corporation
297 McLaren Cars
298t GBR
298b Rex Features
299 Mercedes Benz
302 Peter Rosendahl
301 Morbidelli Motorcycles
303t Eriko Sugita/Reuters
303b Suzuki
304 Yellow Pages Endeavour
305 Donald Stits
306 Linda Radin/AP
307 Oxley/Rex Features
308 Jet Propulsion Laboratories/AP
309 ESA/Ducros/AP
310 NASA
311 NASA
312 GBR
313 GBR
315 Tony Larkin/Rex Features
314 U.S. Army
317 Gleb Garanich/Reuters
318 Itsuo Inouye/AP
319 AP
320 Zaheeruddin Abdullah/AP
321 John Gaps III/AP
322 George Mulala/Reuters
324 Al Jawad/Rex Features
323 Reuters
326 Felice Calabro/AP
325 Sergo Edisherashvilli/Reuters
327t Charles Daughty/AP
327b NASA/AP
329 Jacques Boissinot/AP
328 Austrian Defense Ministry/AP
330 Victor R. Caivano/AP
331 Toko Shimbun/AP
334 Humberto Pradera/Agencia Estado/AP
333 Dario Lopex Mills & Joe Cavaretta/AP
335 Sergei Karpukhin/AP
337 Corinne Dufka/Reuters
336 R.J. Kumar/AP
338 Tran Viet Duc/YNS/AP
339 Rex Features
341 Apichart Weerawong/Reuters
342 Peter Frey/Rex Features
343 Wellcome Trust

404 Tony Gutierrez/AP
409 Matthew Ashton/Empics
406 Max Nash/AP
408 Saurabh Das/AP
407 Chris Turvey/Empics
410 Steve Morton/Empics
412 Mark Baker/Reuters
411 Neal Simpson/Empics
413 Paul Hackett/Reuters
416 Kevork Djansezian/AP
414 Alan Mothner/AP
415 Moliere/Rex Features
417 Damian Dovarganes/AP
420 Beth A. Keiser/AP
422 Fred Jewell/AP
419 Eric Draper/AP
421 Gene J. Puskar/AP
423 Wilhelm/Mercedes-Benz/GBR
424tl Eduardo Di Baia/AP
424tr Lionel Cironneau/AP
425 Geoff Wilkinson/Rex Features
428 Tony Marshall/Empics
427 Michel Spingler/AP
430 Eric Gaillard/Reuters
429 Alejandro Pagni/AP
433 John Moran/Rex Features
431 Michel Euler/AP
434 Frank Gunn/Canadian Press/AP
437 Vim Jethwa/Rex Features
436 Jeffrey Werner/Rex Features
439 Steve Christo/Sydney Morning Herald/AP
438 Paul Sakuma/AP
442 Hans Edinger/AP
441 ANSA/Reuters
443 Ronen Zilberman/AP
444 John Bazemore/AP
445 Chiaki Tsukumo/AP
447 Kang Hyungwon/AP
446 Laszlo Balogh/Reuters
450 Wade Payne/AP
452 International Game Fish Association
453 Jeff Yinnick/Reuters
454 Lynne Sladky/AP
456 Ina Fassbender/Reuters
459 Remy Steinegger/Reuters
462 Alan Diaz/AP
461 Nick Wass/AP
464 Adrian Dennis/AP
463 Rick Rycroft/AP
465 Michel Euler/AP
466 Fernando Llano/AP
468 Rusty Kennedy/AP

ACKNOWLEDGEMENTS

Founder editor: Norris McWhirter • Guinness World Records Ltd would like to thank the following organizations and individuals: Eddie Anderson • John Arblaster • Dr Joseph Arditti at Department of Developmental and Cell Biology University of California, USA • Irvine Caroline Ashasian at Fox Television • Simon Baylis • Catherine Bonifassi • Stephen Booth • Richard Braddish • Ben Brandstätter • Nandita Choudhary • Eric Christin • Debra Clapson • Deborah Colin • Mike Davis • Andrew Durham • Nick Edser • Mark Elliott • Richard Fairbairn • Adrian Fisher • Charlotte Freemantle • Mike Flynn • Sean Greer • Simon Gold • Michelle Gupta • Kevin Hardy • Sue Harper • Martin Harvey • Liz Hawley • Tom Hibbert • Ron Hildebrant • Jennifer Jaffrey • Sir Peter Johnson • Bernardo Joselvich • Kathy Kanable • Dr Ludger Kappen at Christian-Albrechts-University, Kiel, Germany • Adam Kesek • Elizabeth Leicester • Claire Lieberman • Dave McAleer • Pamela McCroskery at the Audubon Society, Fort Worth, Texas, USA • Juliet MacDonald • Chris McHugh • Bruce McLaughlin • Alexandra Maier at Autodesk • Nisse Matti • Bill Morris • Liliana Najdorf • Charlene Nikolai • Barry Norman • Karen O'Brien • Stephanie Pain • Joseph J. Pankus • Ulrike Papin • Greg Parkinson • Dr Paul Parsons • Jayne Parsons • Dr Rod Peakall at Australian National University • Matthew Pettit • Roger Pfister • Dr Ronald Pine at Illinois Mathematics and Science Academy, USA • Sir Ghillean Prance at Royal Botanic Gardens, Kew, UK • Mariano Rao • Lois Reamy • Sir Martin Rees, Astronomer Royal, Cambridge University, UK • David Roberts • Dr Larry S. Roberts at Texas Technical University and University of Miami, USA • Adrián Roldán • Jim Schelberg • Henk Schiffmacher • Dr Mark Seaward at University of Bradford, UK • Dr Karl Shukur • Arvind Sikand at CineAsia Publications • Ingrid Sterner • Gary Still • Dan Stopczynski • Jackie Swanson • Paul Tidwell • Sharon Traer at Aardman Animation • Colin Uttley • Juhani Virola • Jonathan Wall • Lt Col Digby Willoughby

HISTORY OF THE BOOK

In 1759, Arthur Guinness founded the Guinness Brewery at St. James' Gate in Dublin, and by 1833, the brewery was the largest in Ireland. Arthur Guinness Son & Co. Ltd. became a limited liability company in London in 1886, and by the 1930s, Guinness had two breweries in Britain producing its special porter stout. The slogans "Guinness is good for you," "Guinness for strength," and "My Goodness, My Guinness" appeared everywhere. Guinness was the only beer on sale in every bar and saloon, yet Guinness did not actually own any of the pubs—except for the Castle Inn on its hop farms in Bodiam, England. Thus the company was always on the lookout for promotional ideas.

While at a shooting party in County Wexford, Ireland, in 1951, Sir Hugh Beaver, the company's managing director, was involved in a dispute as to whether the golden plover was Europe's fastest game bird. In 1954, another argument arose as to whether grouse were faster than golden plovers. Sir Hugh realized that such questions could arise among people in pubs, and a book that provided answers for debates such as these would be of great use to licensees.

Chris Chataway, the record-breaking track star, was then a brewer in training at Guinness' Park Royal Brewery in London. He recommended the ideal people to produce the book—the twins Norris and Ross McWhirter, whom he had met through track and field events. The McWhirters were then running a fact-finding agency in Fleet Street, London. They were commissioned to compile what became *The Guinness Book of Records*, and, after a busy year of research, the first copy of the 198-page

CASTLEBRIDGE HOUSE   Castlebridge House in County Wexford, Ireland, where Sir Hugh Beaver first put forward the idea of a book of records.

If he can say as you can
Guinness is good for you
How grand to be a Toucan
Just think what Toucan do

THE GUINNESS TOUCAN   Pictured above is the first Guinness
advertisement to feature the toucan—arguably Guinness advertising's
most recognizable icon. The poster was produced by the advertising
agency S.H. Benson of London, England, in 1935. Crime writer Dorothy
L. Sayers, then a Benson employee, provided the copy, and the design
was by John Gilroy. The toucan went on to appear in countless
Guinness print advertisements, in animated commercials, on
promotional merchandise, and on posters, often sporting two pints of
Guinness on its beak.

PARK ROYAL BREWERY   A shot of Guinness' Park Royal Brewery in London, England, taken in the 1960s.

book was bound on August 27, 1955. It was an instant success and became Britain's No. 1 best-seller before Christmas.

The Guinness Book of Records English edition is now distributed in 70 different countries, with another 22 editions in foreign languages. Sales of all editions passed 50 million in 1984 and 75 million in 1994 and will reach the 100 million mark early in the next decade.